CAMBRIDGE STUDIES IN
INTERNATIONAL AND COMPARATIVE LAW

General Editors

H. C. GUTTERIDGE, H. LAUTERPACHT, SIR A. D. MCNAIR

III

RECOGNITION IN INTERNATIONAL LAW

RECOGNITION
IN
INTERNATIONAL LAW

BY

H. LAUTERPACHT, M.A., LL.D.
Whewell Professor of International Law in the University of Cambridge;
Fellow of Trinity College, Cambridge;
of Gray's Inn, Barrister-at-Law

CAMBRIDGE
AT THE UNIVERSITY PRESS
1947

CAMBRIDGE UNIVERSITY PRESS
Cambridge, New York, Melbourne, Madrid, Cape Town,
Singapore, São Paulo, Delhi, Mexico City

Cambridge University Press
The Edinburgh Building, Cambridge CB2 8RU, UK

Published in the United States of America by Cambridge University Press, New York

www.cambridge.org
Information on this title: www.cambridge.org/9781107609433

First published 1947
First paperback edition (with new Introduction) 2013

A catalogue record for this publication is available from the British Library

ISBN 978-1-107-60943-3 Paperback

PREFACE

THERE are only very few branches of international law which are of greater, or more persistent, interest and significance for the law of nations than the question of Recognition of States, of Governments and of Belligerency. Yet there is probably no other subject in the field of international relations in which law and politics appear to be more closely interwoven. As the result, there has grown up a tendency to maintain that the crucial question of granting or refusing recognition is not one of international law. This view I believe to be both inaccurate in itself and retrogressive as a matter of the future development of the law of nations. In the present book I have attempted to show that Recognition is essentially a part of international law—as distinguished from international politics—not only in the matter of some of its incidental consequences, such as the legal effects of recognition and non-recognition, but also with regard to the primary aspect of its function.

The practice of States in the sphere of recognition contains more law and more conscious adherence to legal principle than the student has often been led to believe. Indeed, even in the literature of international law, taken as a whole, there is a wider acknowledgment of the legal nature and of the legal content of the practice of Recognition than appears at first sight. It is perhaps not unnatural that some writers have tended to be more impressed by the abuses and aberrations of the function of Recognition rather than by its less conspicuous adherence to legal principle. That tendency must be discouraged. For it not only simplifies the issue at the expense of accuracy; it has also the incidental disadvantage of lending colour to the belief—which, in the main, is not warranted by facts—that international law breaks down with regard to one of the principal—perhaps *the* principal—manifestations of statehood. If it were true that the widely accepted view as to the purely political nature of the act of recognition is supported by the practice of States to any substantial degree, then the problem of recognition would constitute as serious a defect in the structure of international law as did the legal admissibility of war prior to the radical changes introduced by the Covenant of the League of Nations, the Pact of Paris, and the Charter of the United Nations. There is a further advantage in impressing upon the student the fact that the practice of States in the matter of recognition is more permeated with law and principle than is currently assumed. For the realization of that fact necessarily brings to mind that the existing legal position is sufficiently advanced to render possible some much needed improvements in the machinery of recognition.

These are the reasons why what was originally intended as a monograph of modest dimensions has grown into something in the nature of a text-book devoted not only to a discussion of the doctrinal aspects of the subject, but also to an analysis of the relevant diplomatic practice and of judicial decisions. A book which is, in effect, a challenge to a widely accepted view cannot limit itself to generalities. This is also the reason why I have felt justified in including Part IV of the book relating to Problems of Recognition such as Implied Recognition, *De Facto* Recognition, and the Principle of Non-Recognition.

The greater part of this book has grown out of articles and notes which have appeared in various periodicals and publications. These include *The Modern Law Review*, the *British Year Book of International Law*, the *Yale Law Journal*, the *Columbia Law Review*, the *Revue Générale de Droit International Public*, and *Legal Problems in the Far Eastern Conflict* (edited in 1941 by Professor Quincy Wright). I have to thank the Editors and Editorial Boards of these publications for leave to make use of the contributions previously published.

I have thought it useful to include a number of Opinions, hitherto unpublished, of British Law Officers of the Crown. These Opinions cannot, of course, claim an authority higher than that to which they are entitled by virtue of the reputation of their authors or of their intrinsic value. They are, in any case, of considerable interest as an illustration of both actual incidents and of the attitude of governments to questions of Recognition. In this connection I recall with gratitude the kindness which the late Sir Stephen Gaselee, Librarian and Keeper of the Papers at the Foreign Office, showed me in permitting me to share his room at the time when I was engaged in examining the Opinions of the Law Officers and other papers at the Foreign Office. I also wish to thank the staff of the Library of the Foreign Office for their courtesy and assistance.

I am grateful to Judge McNair, who had some share in the decision to write this book, for valuable advice and suggestions. I have also benefited from the criticism of Professor Jessup, of Columbia University.

I am indebted to the Cambridge University Press and their staff for their patient and scholarly collaboration, to Mrs Gladys Lyons, B.Sc. (Econ.), who has given valuable help by her able secretarial assistance and by reading the proof; and to Mr C. J. Staines, Assistant Librarian, Squire Law Library, Cambridge, who has helped by compiling the Table of Cases and in many other ways.

H. LAUTERPACHT

TRINITY COLLEGE
CAMBRIDGE

August 1946

CONTENTS

Chapter IV. The Declaratory and Constitutive Views of Recognition

Chapter V. The Declaratory and Constitutive Views of Recognition (*continued*)

Chapter VI. The Procedure of Recognition

Appendix to Chapters I–VI

PART II. RECOGNITION OF GOVERNMENTS

Chapter VII. INTERNATIONAL LAW AND REVOLUTIONARY CHANGES OF GOVERNMENTS

Chapter VIII. THE TESTS OF RECOGNITION OF GOVERNMENTS

Chapter IX. THE PRINCIPLE OF EFFECTIVENESS AND THE CONSENT OF THE GOVERNED

Chapter X. THE LEGAL EFFECTS OF NON-RECOGNITION OF GOVERNMENTS

Chapter XI. The Legal Nature of Recognition and the Duty of Recognition

PART III. RECOGNITION OF BELLIGERENCY AND OF INSURGENCY

Chapter XII. The Principles of Recognition of Belligerency

Chapter XIII. The Right of the Insurgents and of the Lawful Government to Recognition of Belligerency

Appendix to Chapters XII and XIII

APPENDIX TO CHAPTERS XIV AND XV

Chapter XX. IMPLIED RECOGNITION

Chapter XXI. THE PRINCIPLE OF NON-RECOGNITION

TABLE OF CASES

LIST OF ABBREVIATIONS

A.J.	= *American Journal of International Law.*
Annual Digest	= *Annual Digest and Reports of Public International Law Cases.*
Anzilotti, *Corso*	= Anzilotti, *Corso di diritto internazionale* (3rd ed. 1928).
B.F.S.P.	= *British and Foreign State Papers.*
B.Y.	= *British Year Book of International Law.*
Clunet	= *Journal de droit international* (ed. by Clunet).
Fauchille	= Fauchille, *Traité de droit international public,* vol. I (Part I) (1922).
Hackworth	= Hackworth, *Digest of International Law,* 7 vols. (1940–3).
Hague Recueil	= *Recueil des Cours, Académie de droit international de la Haye.*
Hyde	= Hyde, *International Law,* 2 vols. (1922) (or, when expressly indicated, 2nd ed., 3 vols. (1945)).
Kunz	= Kunz, *Die Anerkennung von Staaten und Regierungen im Völkerrecht* (1928).
Martens	= Martens, *Recueil de Traités.*
Moore	= Moore, *Digest of International Law,* 8 vols. (1906).
Off.J. (or *Official Journal*)	= *Official Journal of the League of Nations.*
Oppenheim	= Oppenheim, *International Law,* vol. I (5th ed., by Lauterpacht, 1937).
R.G.	= *Revue générale de droit international public.*
R.I.	= *Revue de droit international et de la législation comparée.*
R.I. (Paris)	= *Revue de droit international.*
Rivista	= *Rivista di diritto internazionale.*
Scalfati	= Scalfati Fusco, *Il riconoscimento di stati nel diritto internazionale* (1938).
Smith	= Smith, *Great Britain and the Law of Nations. A Selection of Documents,* vol. I (1932); vol. II (1935).
Z.ö.V.	= *Zeitschrift für ausländisches öffentliches Recht und Völkerrecht.*
Z.V.	= *Zeitschrift für Völkerrecht.*

Recognition in International Law: An Introduction to the Paperback Edition 2013

James Crawford[1]

I

Hersch Lauterpacht's *Recognition in International Law*[2] was completed in 1946 and published in 1947. Lauterpacht had produced a trilogy of monographs in the interwar period, each great in its own way – *Private Law Sources and Analogies of International Law*,[3] *The Function of Law in the International Community*,[4] and *The Development of International Law by the Permanent Court of International Justice*.[5] He also delivered the general course at The Hague Academy of International Law in 1938, devoting no less than three chapters of 15 to various aspects of recognition.[6]

The book on that subject, although only published after the War, was already in mind by the late 1930s, and but for the War would undoubtedly have been published earlier.[7]

---

1 SC, FBA, LLD; Whewell Professor of International Law in the University of Cambridge. Many thanks to Cameron Miles, Associate, Lauterpacht Centre for International Law, for his assistance. Thanks also are due to Sir Elihu Lauterpacht QC for permitting me access to Hersch Lauterpacht's correspondence, and to Professor John Dugard for helpful comments.

2 H. Lauterpacht, *Recognition in International Law* (Cambridge University Press, 1947) (hereinafter ***Recognition***).

3 H. Lauterpacht, *Private Law Sources and Analogies of International Law* (Longmans, Green & Co, 1927).

4 H. Lauterpacht, *The Function of Law in the International Community* (Cambridge University Press, 1933; revised edn: Oxford University Press, 2011) (hereinafter ***Function of Law***).

5 H. Lauterpacht, *The Development of International Law by the Permanent Court of International Justice* (Longmans, Green & Co, 1934) reappearing in its revised edition as *The Development of International Law by the International Court* (Stevens & Sons, 1958).

6 H. Lauterpacht, 'Règles générales du droit de la paix' (1937) 62 Hague *Recueil* 99, reprinted in English in E. Lauterpacht (ed), 1 *International Law, being the Collected Papers of Hersch Lauterpacht* (Cambridge University Press, 1970) 316 (hereinafter ***Collected Papers***).

7 The book was the subject of continual revision and expansion throughout the Second World War: E. Lauterpacht, *The Life of Hersch Lauterpacht* (Cambridge University Press, 2010) (hereinafter ***Life of Hersch Lauterpacht***) 98, 221, 236, 239, 242, 244, 267, 299-300.

On 8 March 1937 Arnold McNair wrote to Lauterpacht about a planned 'Series in International Law (Public and Private) and Comparative Law' being proposed to Cambridge University Press. In the context of the proposed series he asked…

> Whether you would be so good as to give [the series editors] a promise of a volume, and in particular whether you would consider sympathetically the suggestion of a volume on 'Recognition in International Law'. It seems to me that such as book would have a very considerable appeal for the following reasons: What before the [First World] war was considered as Recognition, namely, of new States, of new Governments and of belligerents, although the subject of a good deal of periodical literature, has never been comprehensively treated in a monograph in English. Moreover, since the war it has developed enormously in importance, and there have been a considerable number of decisions upon it. In addition, the whole question of Recognition and non-recognition of situations, facts, treaties etc., in the Stimsonian sense of the word is completely new, and practically nothing has been written except Fischer Williams' 'Hague Lectures' and articles in periodicals. What is really wanted now is some new Historicus to enlighten the public as was done in the 1860's…

In a side-note McNair added that he had asked John Fischer Williams, who had declined.[8]

Evidently Lauterpacht's reply was positive, for on 25 March 1937 McNair wrote again: 'With regard to your lectures at Rappard's Institute next year. The fact that you are going to write a book on Recognition for our series constitutes not the least objection to your lecturing on that subject in Geneva, or anywhere else; in fact it seems to me an argument in favour of choosing that subject'. But later in the same letter, in the context of a detailed discussion of proposed changes to the fourth edition of Oppenheim which McNair had edited but which (like so much else) he had passed on to Lauterpacht, McNair let slip his own views on the so-called duty to recognize:

8 Fischer Williams' Hague Lectures of 1933 took a very different position from Lauterpacht. Recognition was declaratory, the acknowledgment of an already existing situation: J Fischer Williams, 'La Doctrine de la Reconnaissance en Droit International et ses developpements recents' (1933) 44 Hague *Recueil* 199, 235-8. But there was no legal duty to recognize: each state is free to decide whether to recognize a new state or not: ibid, 238-9, and likewise for governments, although the possibility for each state to decide whether to recognize a new government or not is an unsatisfactory state of affairs: ibid, 259-60. The recognition of belligerents was not considered an interesting question: ibid, 263-4. As for collective (non-)recognition, Fischer Williams is positive: given the League of Nations, there is at last an international organization that has a potentially universal character and that has as its aim the prohibition of war as a means of resolution of international conflicts; non-recognition plays a completely different and more important role than in the past: ibid, 268-70. Fischer Williams' views on recognition reflected mainstream opinion.

> p. 151, lines 6-10 from bottom. I am not quite clear of the precise passage about which you are in doubt. Is it this: 'A State has no right to demand from other States recognition of a new head which is in every respect a matter for the discretion of other States.' Is it certain that Russia had a right against Great Britain to the recognition of the Soviet Government, and that between December 1917 and March 1921 we were violating that right?

Apparently McNair felt not. In fact the passage in question was deleted from the fifth edition,[9] with the new editor Lauterpacht adding a new section describing a supposed duty to recognize especially in the context of governments.[10] He wrote:

> As in the case of recognition of new States, so also in the matter of recognition of Governments the act of recognition is not a function which International Law can, in principle, leave to be decided by purely political considerations on the part of third States. A State whose government is refused recognition is for most purpose deprived of the benefits of membership of the international community. It is accordingly difficult to admit that the withholding or withdrawal of these benefits is a question entirely outside legal regulation. A Government which enjoys the habitual – though not necessarily willing – obedience of the bulk of the population with a reasonable expectancy of permanence, can be said to represent the state in question and as such to be entitled to recognition.[11]

Apart from shedding light on what became Cambridge Studies in International and Comparative Law,[12] the correspondence is revealing in a number of respects. It shows

---

9 Lauterpacht, 1 *Oppenheim's International Law* (5th edn, Longmans, 1937) 128.

10 Ibid, 129-31.

11 Ibid, 129-30.

12 The series was not inaugurated until 1946 with the publication of Gutteridge's *Comparative Law: An Introduction to the Comparative Method of Legal Study and Research* (Cambridge University Press, 1946). Lauterpacht's *Recognition* was the third in the series. Lauterpacht was by now (with McNair and Gutteridge) a series editor. Of the other books proposed by McNair in his letter of 8 March 1937, only Mervyn Jones' *Full Powers and Ratification of Treaties* (Cambridge University Press, 1946) saw the light of day in the series. McNair's 'three contemplated books on treaties' were actually published by Oxford as *The Law of Treaties: British Practice and Opinions* (Oxford University Press, 1938), later revised as *The Law of Treaties* (Oxford University Press, 1961). The proposed 'disintegration of Dicey; that is to say, the production of half a dozen or more volumes on different branches of Conflict of Laws' never happened: see now A.V. Dicey, J.H.C. Morris, L. Collins and A. Briggs (eds), *Dicey, Morris and Collins on the Conflict of Laws*, 2 vols (14th edn, Sweet and Maxwell, 2006). The first phase of Cambridge Studies in International and Comparative Law (edited after Lauterpacht by R.Y. Jennings) produced some 15 volumes over 40 years, the latest in 1986. It was revived in 1994, and has since produced nearly 100 further volumes, in

that Lauterpacht was not the first choice for a monograph on recognition, that the idea emanated from McNair, not Lauterpacht, that the first choice author (Fischer Williams) held very different views on key points, that the proposed book included from the beginning a study in modern developments, notably the Stimson doctrine of non-recognition, and that its initial proponent, McNair, steeped in the British tradition of thinking about recognition going back to the American Civil War and the Letters of Historicus,[13] likewise did not accept the idea of a duty of non-recognition, at least in the context of recognition of governments. By contrast, Lauterpacht already in 1937 had doubts about 'the widely accepted view as to the purely political nature of the act of recognition'.[14]

He said as much in his Hague General Course in 1938. Writing in that year of imminent breakdown of the international legal system (a breakdown characterised not least by unprincipled and indiscriminate acts of recognition and withdrawal of recognition), he began the three chapters devoted to that subject by stating that

> International law is a weak system of law. This is generally admitted, and nothing but good can come from such an admission so long as it is not maintained that the shortcomings of international law are permanent and inherent in its very nature.[15]

Among these weaknesses, as a matter of positive law, was the 'practically unlimited right to declare war' – at least a practically unlimited right prior to the League Covenant and the Kellogg-Briand Pact[16] – since in the exercise of that right a state could by unilateral act dissolve, *vis-à-vis* its belligerent, the 'minute and exacting duties' of the international law of peace.[17] But he denied that the same was true of the international law of recognition:

> A parallel phenomenon can be witnessed in the matter of recognition of States, Governments, and belligerency – if we assume that the predominant doctrine in the matter gives an accurate statement of the existing practice. The State is bound by minute rules to respect the sovereignty and independence of other States. But just as it is left to its free discretion to terminate the existence of other States as the result of a successful war, so, according to the predominant doctrine, it is free to decide,

the same broad-based spirit as that outlined by McNair in 1937: http://www.cambridge.org/aus/series/sSeries.asp?code=CSIL

13 *Letters by Historicus on Some Questions of International Law* (Macmillan, 1863). 'Historicus' was W.V. Harcourt, who was elected first Whewell Professor at Cambridge in 1868 on the strength of these collected letters to *The Times*, and concurrently held high political office. On Harcourt see A.G. Gardiner, *The Life of Sir William Harcourt*, 2 vols (Constable, 1923).

14 *Recognition*, v.

15 1 *Collected Papers* 308.

16 General Treaty for the Renunciation of War, 27 August 1928, 94 *LNTS* 57.

17 1 *Collected Papers* 308-9.

> according to discretion and by consulting its own interests only, whether a foreign community should begin to enjoy those rights of sovereignty and independence. By the simple device of refusing recognition a State is legally entitled, according to a widely adopted doctrine, to deny the right to live to a political community apparently fulfilling the conditions of statehood….
>
> However, it will be submitted here that while with regard to war the defect in the structure of international law is one of historical fact and positive law, in the matter of recognition it is largely the creation of writers wedded to the doctrine of consent as the only source of obligation in the international sphere. It will be submitted here that as a matter of legal principle and of weight of practice, recognition is not a question of the arbitrary will of States but of international law, of which the States are organs. This applies to all kinds of recognition – of States, Governments, and belligerency. They are all governed by the same principle. With regard to all of them the matter is governed by the same question: Is recognition a matter of law or politics, of rule or arbitrariness.[18]

The problem was obscured by the constitutive/declaratory debate, since recognition was both and neither of these things:

> Although it is a function performed not by courts but the executive department, recognition is an essentially judicial or quasi-judicial function of the administration of the law. This applies to all kinds of recognition – of States, Governments, and belligerency. The true division of opinion is, it will be suggested, not between the constitutive and declaratory, but between the political and legal view of the nature of the function of recognition.[19]

The same considerations applied, in his view, to recognition of governments, even though (he mysteriously added) 'for obvious reasons, the controversy as to the declaratory or constitutive effect of recognition is not relevant to the recognition of Governments'.[20] As to governments:

> Recognition is a branch of international law administered not by the Judiciary but by the Executive. But it is international law that is administered. The difference is only in the nature of the organ applying international law. As in the matter of recognition of Governments there is no evidence to show that Governments deem themselves entitled to proceed regardless of principle, and to grant or refuse recog-

18 1 *Collected Papers* 309.

19 Ibid, 309-10; to similar effect, ibid, 319-320.

20 Ibid, 323.

> nition of foreign Governments as a matter of bargain, grace or expediency.[21]

The criteria for recognition of governments were less well established than for states, but they could be discerned. In particular 'the principle of legitimacy and constitutionality is now being abandoned over the whole of the American continent… As a matter of principle the requirement of both legitimacy and constitutionality is indefensible in the present stage of international organization… [I]nternational law must be satisfied with a quite different function, namely, of ensuring continuity – otherwise radically broken – between the revolutionary and the old order'.[22]

> Likewise with regard to recognition of belligerency…
>
> As in the matter of recognition of States and Governments so also in the matter of recognition of belligerency the accurate view, it is believed, is that its grant is not a matter of political convenience, interest or grace, but a duty following from an impartial consideration of the facts of the situation. Once given the objective conditions of a state of belligerency, as laid down by international law, the contesting parties are legally entitled to be recognized as such and third States are, in normal circumstances, under a duty to grant recognition. This is not a view supported by the majority of writers. But it is a view which, it is submitted, has been repeatedly acted upon by Governments and which is supported by considerations of principle.[23]

A third lecture dealt with 'Recognition of new territorial titles and international situations'. It dealt presciently with the Stimson doctrine, with illegality as a source of rights, and with the problem of reconciling illegality with the need for continuing international relations. But it distinguished that issue from the case of new states and governments:

> Generally speaking, the refusal of recognition referred to in these instruments can have no bearing on the question of recognition of States. A State cannot come into existence contrary to a treaty. A new State is not bound by any international obligation; it is certainly not bound by an international obligation not to secede. If, to give a concrete example, Manchuria had voluntarily seceded from China and formed a new State, there would have been no question of non-recognition as intended by these instruments. The legal basis of non-recognition of Manchuko as a State is apparently that it is not a State inasmuch as, in view of its relations with Japan, it lacks actual independence. In so far as the doctrine of non-recognition applies in this case it is an announcement of the intention of non-recognition of any future situation amounting to formal incorporation of Manchuria as part of Japan.

---

21 Ibid, 324.

22 Ibid, 326-7.

23 Ibid, 329.

> Neither does the rule of non-recognition properly conceived extend to recognition of Governments. A new Government cannot as such be the result of a violation of international law – except perhaps when a State is under an international duty to possess a certain form of government or constitution. Non-recognition as announced in these instruments would therefore appear to refer to international situations other than recognition of States and Governments.[24]

But he returned to that problem in a final footnote:

> In the abnormal event of the invalid situation taking the form of a separate political unit claiming to be an independent State – as in the case of Manchukuo – the consequences of non-recognition are more far-reaching but, as said, such cases must be regarded as exceptional.[25]

This at a time which, apart from Manchukuo, saw the *de facto* disappearance of Ethiopia, Austria, Albania and Czechoslovakia, the temporary emergence of Slovakia and Croatia and within a few years the suppression of Poland and the Baltic states![26]

Thus Lauterpacht had firmly developed views of the role of recognition by 1938, views which are essentially those he would expound nearly a decade later in *Recognition*, views which were uninfluenced (obviously) by the United Nations Charter, or even by the League Covenant or the Pact of Paris, but held as a matter of general international law based on his reading of state practice and on his strong view of the need for coherence, and held against the opinions of almost all writers.

II

During the Second World War, Lauterpacht's focus was on issues of immediate practical concern[27] – the law of qualified neutrality,[28] the need for recognition of universal human

---

24 Ibid, 339.

25 Ibid, 348 fn 2.

26 Lauterpacht's only explicit reference to the poisonous international situation of 1938 was in a long footnote on the Spanish Civil War in which, after noting that Hague Academy lecturers were enjoined to avoid current controversies, he suggested that the Anglo-French policy towards Spain could possibly be excused on the ground that 'the circumstances of the situation were abnormal at a time when the operation of rules of international law were suspended as the result of the conduct of a number of States, and that it would have been neither possible for just rigidly to apply a principle of international law to some aspects of the situation while tolerating its isolation with regard to others': ibid, 335 fn 1.

27 Generally: *Life of Hersch Lauterpacht*, ch 5-7.

28 Ibid, 135-7. Further: 5 *Collected Papers* 635ff.

rights,[29] and the forthcoming war crimes trials.[30] But systematic concerns remained on his agenda and he remained as concerned with the integrity of international law as he had been in 1934. In 1939, E.H. Carr had noted, as if in negative response to the closing pages of *Function of Law:*

> [International law] can have no existence except in so far as there is an international community which, on the basis of a 'minimum common view' recognizes it as binding. International law is a function of the political community of nations. Its defects are due, not to any technical shortcomings, but to the embryonic character of the community in which it functions. Just as international morality is weaker than national morality, so international law is necessarily weaker and poorer in content than the municipal law of a highly organized modern state.[31]

Lauterpacht would not have disagreed – but he might have qualified Carr's statement by observing that 'technical shortcomings' still mattered, especially when they concerned the coherence of international law as a whole. Just such a field was the diplomatic recognition of states and governments:[32]

> It is perhaps not unnatural that some writers have tended to be more impressed by the abuses and aberrations of the function of Recognition than by its less conspicu-

29 *Life of Hersch Lauterpacht*, ch 8. Further: H. Lauterpacht, 'The Law of Nations, the Law of Nature and the Rights of Man' (1943) 29 *GST* 1; H. Lauterpacht, *An International Bill of the Rights of Man* (Columbia University Press, 1945). Also: B. Simpson, 'Hersch Lauterpacht and the Genesis of the Age of Human Rights' (2004) 120 *LQR* 49.

30 *Life of Hersch Lauterpacht*, 198, 203-4, 212-13, 229, 268ff. Lauterpacht was responsible for the first definition of 'crimes against humanity', and prepared a first draft of the closing speech of Sir Hartley Shawcross to the International Military Tribunal at Nuremberg: H. Lauterpacht, 'Draft Nuremberg Speeches' (2012) 1 *Cambridge JICL* 45. Further: H. Lauterpacht, 'The Law of Nations and the Punishment of War Crimes' (1944) 21 *BYIL* 58.

31 E.H. Carr, *The Twenty Years' Crisis, 1919-1939* (Palgrave, 1939; reprinted 2001) 165. Similar doubts in the post-war era led to the development of rule scepticism and the 'realist' school of international relations in the 1950s by scholars such as Hans Morgenthau: see H.J. Morgenthau, *Politics Among Nations* (Knopf, 1948). Further: M. Koskenniemi, *The Gentle Civilizer of Nations: The Rise and Fall of International Law 1870-1960* (Cambridge University Press, 2002) 437-8.

32 Much has been written on both limbs of recognition, but for an overview of the recent practice, see further: I. Brownlie, 'Recognition in Theory and Practice' (1982) 53 *BYIL* 197; J. Dugard, *Recognition and the United Nations* (Grotius, 1987); S. Talmon, *Recognition of Governments in International Law* (Oxford University Press, 1998); T.D. Grant, *The Recognition of States: Law and Practice in Debate and Revolution* (Praeger, 1999); S. Talmon, 'The Constitutive versus the Declarative Theory of Recognition: *Tertium non Datur?*' (2004) 75 *BYIL* 101; J.A. Frowein, 'Recognition' in R. Wolfrum (gen ed), *Max Planck Encyclopedia of International Law* (online edn,

ous adherence to legal principle. That tendency must be discouraged. For it not only simplifies the issue at the expense of accuracy; it has the incidental disadvantage of lending colour to the belief – which, in the main, is not warranted by the facts – that international law breaks down with regard to one of the principal – perhaps *the* principal – manifestations of statehood. If it were true that the widely accepted view as to the purely political nature of the act of recognition is supported by the practice of States to any substantial degree, then the problem of recognition would constitute as serious a defect in the structure of international law as did the legal admissibility of war prior to the radical changes introduced by the Covenant of the League of Nations, the Pact of Paris, and the Charter of the United Nations.[33]

Although both classes of recognition involve a pronouncement by a state, they are not identical or even closely related – it might instead be best to say that they share a common ancestor. Recognition of a state refers to the acknowledgement by an existing state that another entity is considered to have attained statehood with all its legal consequences. Recognition of a government, on the other hand, refers to the recognition of a state's governing entity as lawful or legitimate and thereby entitled to represent that state for all international purposes. The former is a question of international *existence*; the latter, of international *representation*. One may recognize a state without recognizing its government but not the contrary.[34]

To these two forms of recognition is sometimes still added a third category – the recognition of belligerency, i.e. the recognition that two or more entities are engaged in hostilities 'of such character and scope as to entitle the parties to be treated as belligerents engaged in a war in the sense ordinarily attached to that term by international law'.[35]

In 1947, the debate over recognition was principally concerned with statehood. In the *Tinoco* arbitration,[36] Taft C.J. had pronounced authoritatively in favour of the declaratory theory of the acts of *de facto* governments *vis-à-vis* non-recognizing states. Recognition of belligerency was a textbook phenomenon sustained against an erratic practice by the notoriety of the American Civil War.[37] In light of this practice, and the distance between statehood on the one hand, and governments and belligerency on the other with regard to recognition, it is surprising that Lauterpacht dealt with them collectively.

Oxford University Press, 2011); Crawford, *Brownlie's Principles of Public International Law* (8th edn, Oxford University Press, 2012) ch 6. Further: S. Talmon, *Recognition in International Law: A Bibliography* (Martinus Nijhoff Publishers, 2000).

33 *Recognition*, v.

34 1 *Restatement Third: The Foreign Relations Law of the United States* (1987) §203, comment (a).

35 *Recognition*, 175.

36 *Tinoco Concessions* (1923) 1 *RIAA* 369, 381.

37 Generally: W.L. Walker, 'Recognition of Belligerency and Grant of Belligerent Rights' (1937) 23 *GST* 177. Also: L. Moir, *The Law of Internal Armed Conflict* (Cambridge University Press, 2002) 11ff.

In a sense, it is a tribute to the hold that categories such as recognition have on even the best international lawyers.[38] For the purposes of this introduction, the distinction will be maintained; recognition of belligerency will be excluded entirely as a non-functional institution, and recognition of governments dealt with only briefly.

At least with respect to statehood, Lauterpacht was correct in stating that 'there is probably no other subject in the field of international relations in which law and politics appear more closely interwoven'.[39] As noted already, he was concerned with the integrity of international law and its capacity to function – and be seen to function – as a complete system of rules, proposing thereby a position of at least formal coherence in response to the rule scepticism professed by Carr and Morgenthau, amongst others. He was anxious to avoid the conclusion that recognition was entirely inter-subjective, a hole in the heart of international law as a coherent system:

> [N]otwithstanding its obvious significance, recognition, as taught by writers, constitutes one of the weakest links in international law. The science of international law can no longer avoid the task of enquiring whether this state of affairs is due to a clear defect of the law of nations as expressed in the practice of States or whether it is attributable to the failure of lawyers to give an accurate account of the practice of States and to analyse it by reference to a jurisprudential principle of order as distinguished from the amorphous maxims of policy. An inquiry of this nature is of special urgency at a time when the foundations are being laid of an improved international order.[40]

What was the intellectual weakness that Lauterpacht perceived in the debate over the recognition of states as it stood in the 1940s? That debate was polarized. On the one hand were the adherents of the constitutive theory,[41] according to which the political act of recognition is a precondition of the legal rights of a state: at its extreme this implies that the very personality of a state depends on the internal political decisions of other states. As Oppenheim posits, '[a] State is, and becomes, an International Person through recognition only, and exclusively'.[42] That view was implicit in the famous pronounce-

38 McNair himself in his compendium of international law opinions grouped recognition of states and governments (but not belligerency) together, noting that '[the two categories] are different things, but it is convenient to group the Reports': A. McNair, 1 *International Law Opinions* (Cambridge University Press, 1956) 132. For belligerency, see: ibid, 138.

39 *Recognition*, v.

40 Ibid, 3.

41 Further: Grant (1999) 2-4; Talmon (2004) 75 *BYIL* 101, 102-5.

42 L.F.L. Oppenheim, 1 *International Law* (1st edn, Longmans, Green & Co, 1905) 109. Lauterpacht as the fourth editor of Oppenheim modified the latter's firmly constitutive position to comply with his own, more nuanced, view: H. Lauterpacht (ed), 1 *Oppenheim's International Law* (8th edn, Longmans, 1955) 125-8.

ment of Warren R. Austin, the second US Ambassador to the United Nations, on the recognition of Israel:

> I should regard it as highly improper for me to admit that any country on earth can question the sovereignty of the United States of America in the exercise of that high political act of recognition of the *de facto* status of a state. Moreover I would not admit here, by implication or by direct answer, that there exists a tribunal of justice or of any other kind, anywhere, that can pass upon the legality or the validity of that act of my country.[43]

The constitutive view of recognition may be traced back in particular to Hegel, who stressed the absolute sovereignty of the state within international law but managed to reconcile this axiom with a dependence on recognition by other states, for example in the following passage:

> The nation state is mind in its substantive rationality and immediate actuality and is therefore the absolute power on earth. It follows that every state is sovereign and autonomous against its neighbours. It is entitled in the first place and without qualification to be sovereign from their point of view, i.e. to be recognized by them as sovereign. At the same time, however, this title is purely formal, and the demand for this recognition of the state, merely on the ground that it is a state, is abstract. Whether a state is in fact something absolute depends on its content, i.e. on its constitution and general situation; and recognition, implying as it does an identity of both form and content, is conditional on the neighbouring state's judgement and will.[44]

The first modern formulation of the constitutive theory was given by Jellinek, who insisted that in a system such as international law in which there was no identifiable *primus inter pares* and no external sovereign, legal personality and the rights and duties thereby accruing could only be attained through mutual recognition.[45] Jellinek drew a distinction between the *general* community of states – into which *de facto* entry could be obtained – and the *juridical* community of states, entry into which could only be

---

43 Reported in the *New York Times*, 19 May 1949, cited in Brierly, *The Law of Nations* (4th edn, Oxford University Press, 1949) 125 n 1.

44 G.W.F. Hegel, *Elements of the Philosophy of Right* (Nicolaifchen Buchhandlung, 1821; tr T.M. Knox, Oxford University Press, 2000) §331 (but cf §547, implying a duty incumbent on a state to recognize in certain situations: *Recognition*, 38)

45 G. Jellinek, *Die rechtliche Natur der Staatenverträge* (Alfred Hölder, 1880) 91; *De Lehre von den Staatenverbindungen* (Alfred Hölder, 1882) 92-6

obtained through recognition; this distinction (which Lauterpacht considered 'of little worth'[46]) was later adopted by von Liszt[47] and Oppenheim.[48]

Further contributions to the theory were made by Anzilotti, whose work was to prove influential. Anzilotti did away with Jellinek's distinction, arguing instead that as rules of international law are created through the consent of states, application of those rules is also the province of states. Thus, a subject of international law may be deemed to exist at the point at which the first agreement as expressed by the treaty of recognition or its equivalent is entered into:[49] recognition so conceptualized is constitutive of statehood and reciprocal insofar as each party to the treaty recognizes that each counterparty is legally capable of entering into an agreement on the international plane.

The pure form of constitutive theory was the subject of considerable criticism. Brierly stressed that statehood in order to be effective must be considered a binary condition, opposable against all other states or against none. As it stood, the constitutive theory saw recognition as either a monolithic act undertaken by all states simultaneously, which was unrealistic and could only occur in practice at some general conference or congress, or by each state individually, which frustrated any hope of a definitive answer: '[t]he status of a state recognized by state A but not by state B, and therefore apparently both an "international person" and not an "international person" at the same time, would be a legal curiosity'.[50] Other commentators such as Kelsen,[51] Kunz,[52] Diena[53] and Cavaglieri,[54] attacked the position on logical grounds, noting that an entity without juridical existence cannot without paradox conclude a treaty which presupposes its legal personality. As Kelsen wrote:

---

46 *Recognition*, 38.

47 F. Von Liszt, *Das Völkerrecht: systematisch Dargestellt* (12th edn, J. Springer, 1925; ed M. Fleischmann) 91.

48 1 Oppenheim (1905) 108-9. Given Lauterpacht's views on the merits of Jellinek's distinction, it was not surprisingly deleted – or at least heavily diluted – by the 8th edition: 1 Oppenheim (8th edn, 1955) 125.

49 D. Anzilotti, *Cours de droit international*, vol 1 (3rd edn, Atheneum, 1928; tr G. Gidel, Recueil Sirey, 1929) 160ff.

50 Brierly (4th edn, 1949) 123.

51 H. Kelsen, 'Théorie générale du droit international public. Problèmes choisis' (1932) Hague *Recueil* 117, 260-94. Kelsen was overall a constitutivist, though he saw the weaknesses in the theory. Earlier, he had been a declaratist: H. Kelsen, 'La naissance de l'Etat et la formation de sa nationality' (1929) 4 *RDI* 613, 617-8. Further: Kelsen, 'Recognition in International Law: Theoretical Observations' (1941) 35 *AJIL* 605, 608-9; cf P.M. Brown, 'The Effects of Recognition' (1942) 36 *AJIL* 106.

52 J.L. Kunz, *Die Anerkennung von Staaten und Regierungen im Völkerrecht* (W. Kohlhammer, 1928) 90.

53 G. Diena, 24 *Rivista di diritto internazionale* (Giuffrè, 1932) 478-9.

54 Ibid, 338.

> To maintain that the legal personality of a State is the result of an act in which it is created by that very State is to put forward an assertion reminiscent of the attempt by Baron Munchausen to extricate himself with the aid of his pigtail from the morass into which he had fallen.[55]

Lauterpacht acknowledged these criticisms as valid,[56] but noted that they all missed what he considered to be 'the cardinal defect' of the purist position – that it subsumed the legal consequences of recognition wholly within a political conception of the act of recognition itself: 'the constitutive act creative of statehood is an act of unfettered political will divorced from binding considerations of legal principle'.[57]

Constitutivism as a model of recognition of states was opposed by the declaratory theory. This holds that recognition merely establishes, confirms or provides evidence of a legal situation which is already extant.[58] Thus, the legal effect of the act of recognition is limited: in a relatively objective forum such as an international tribunal, a declaratory view of recognition would permit the adjudicator to accept the existence of a state even when the other parties to the dispute, or third states, have failed to recognize it.[59]

Early indications of the declaratory theory emerged with Vattel in the eighteenth century:[60] it developed into a fully-fledged doctrine at approximately the same time as constitutive theory.[61] The *Institut de Droit International* in Article 1 of its Brussels Resolutions Concerning the Recognition of New States and New Governments declared:

> The recognition of a new State is the free act by which one or more States acknowledge the existence on a definite territory of a human society politically organized,

---

55 Kelsen (1932) Hague *Recueil* 117, 269. Kelsen's solution to this was to make statehood in the first instance contingent on the entity's own declaration of independence, which is then constituted in actuality by the recognition of other states: Kelsen (1941) 35 *AJIL* 605, 609.

56 *Recognition*, 39-41.

57 Ibid, 41.

58 As Talmon says, it is status *confirming* rather than status *creating*: Talmon (2004) 75 *BYIL* 101, 101-2.

59 See e.g. *Tinoco Concessions* (1923) 1 *RIAA* 369; *Deutsche Continental Gesellschaft v Polish State* (1929) 5 *ILR* 11.

60 E. de Vattel, *Le Droit des gens* (1758; tr Anon, G.G. & J. Robinson, 1797; reprinted Liberty Fund, 2000) bk I, ch I, §4:

> Every nation that governs itself, under what form soever, without dependence on any foreign power, is a *sovereign state*. Its rights are naturally the same as those of any other state. Such are the moral persons who live together in a natural society, subject to the law of nations. To give a nation a right to make an immediate figure in this grand society, it is sufficient that it be really sovereign and independent, that is, that it govern itself by its own authority and laws.

61 See e.g. J. K. Bluntschli, *Das modern Völkerrecht der civilisierten Staaten* (Nördlingen, 1868) §35; A. Rivier, 1 *Principes du droit des gens* (A. Rousseau, 1896) 57. Also: 1 Lorimer (1883) 104-5.

> independent of any other existing State, and capable of observing the obligations of international law, and by which they manifest therefore their intention to consider it a member of the international Community.

Recognition has a declaratory effect;

> The existence of a new State with all the juridical effects which are attached to that existence, is not affected by the refusal of recognition by one or more States.[62]

Support for the declaratory theory increased in the first part of the twentieth century[63] with the conclusion of the Pan-American Convention on the Rights and Duties of States (the ***Montevideo Convention***).[64] Article 3 of the Convention provided that '[t]he political existence of a state is independent of recognition by other states'. Article 6 specified that 'the recognition of a state merely signifies that the state which recognizes it accepts the personality of the other with all the rights and duties determined by international law'.

According to this view recognition is a response triggered by certain facts and conditioned by law.[65] Unlike the constitutive model, it seems relatively less political: indeed recognition may appear little more than a declaration of intent to establish ordinary diplomatic relations.[66] But the declaratory theory has serious shortcomings. First, it fails to reflect the practice of diplomatic recognition, which is after all not the same as the establishment of diplomatic relations or the exchange of ambassadors (two states can recognize each other without having diplomatic relations or ambassadors), and which is taken much more seriously as an expression of consent and support to the new state than the declaratory theory would seem to allow. Secondly, it is a sorry comforter to the unrecognized state, which will in practice be confined, in the short and even in the long term, to a narrow repertoire of international contacts, as witness the long-standing

---

62 23 April 1936, reproduced in English in (1936) 30 *AJIL Supp* 185.

63 See e.g. J. Westlake, *International Law, Part I: Peace* (Cambridge University Press, 1904) 49-50; Brierly (4th edn, 1949) 124-5; T-C. Chen, *The International Law of Recognition: With Special Reference to Practice in Great Britain and the United States* (Stevens & Sons, 1951) 15. Further: *Recognition*, 41 n 2. Cavaré identified a further group of writers as *mi-constitutive* and *mi-declarative*: L. Cavaré, 'La Reconnaissance de l'Etat et la Mandchoukou' (1935) 42 *RGDIP* 1, 53ff. These writers accepted that recognition was declarative with respect to certain basic rights, but constitutive with respect to certain additional rights. Fundamentally this amounts to a repudiation of the basic constitutive view: see e.g. Kunz (1928) 85-95; Kelsen (prior to his conversion to constitutivism) (1929) 4 *RDI* 613, 617-8.

64 26 December 1933, 165 *LNTS* 20.

65 Grant (1999) 4.

66 *Recognition*, 42.

situation of unrecognised Somaliland.[67] Thirdly, it assumes that the identification of an entity as a state is essentially a question of 'fact' and is relatively unproblematic. Reference is usually made in this context to apparently straightforward definitions such as that in Article 1 of the Montevideo Convention. But, although stable independence in fact is highly relevant to statehood in contested cases, it does not seem to be sufficient, as the examples of Southern Rhodesia and more recently Somaliland show.[68] Quite apart from the principle of territorial integrity (which has not been treated as indefeasible), a difficulty with the declaratory theory is the enduring uncertainty over what exactly constitutes a state. In the first place, the precise factors are indeterminate: Article 1 of the Montevideo Convention is often cited by declarativists as a starting point from which a list of factors which trigger statehood may be drawn, providing that '[t]he State as a person of international law should possess the following qualifications: (a) a permanent population; (b) a defined territory; (c) government; and (d) capacity to enter into relations with other States',[69] though other models existed in 1947.[70] In the second place the evidentiary question of whether an entity has *de facto* attained those benchmarks identified by international law can be hotly contested.[71] This element was identified and developed by Lauterpacht, who argued that the declaratory view of recognition not only reduced the significance of the act to the vanishing point, but was also fundamentally

67 See on Somaliland: Brenthurst Foundation, *The Consequences of Somaliland's International (Non) Recognition*, Discussion Paper 2011/05 (2011). Further, the various pronouncements of the British government in the UK Materials on International Law: (2006) 88 *BYIL* 597, 618-19; (2007) 78 *BYIL* 634, 682; (2008) 79 *BYIL* 565, 596-7; (2009) 80 *BYIL* 661, 709-10, 712-13; (2010) 81 *BYIL* 435, 503-5; and generally J. Crawford, *The Creation of States in International Law* (2nd edn, Oxford University Press, 2006) 412-18.

68 In the period before the completion of *Recognition* there were analogues: e.g. Armenia after 1918, as to which see Crawford (2nd edn, 2006) 510-12.

69 J. Crawford, 'The Criteria for Statehood in International Law' (1976) 48 *BYIL* 93, 111; Dugard (1987) 7 n 1. The provision simplifies what is undoubtedly a complicated question, and the reality of statehood – at least insofar as the doctrine has developed in modern times – is far more complex: Crawford (2nd edn, 2006) 37-95.

70 Such as that developed by Oppenheim, who considered statehood to require: (a) a people; (b) a country; (c) a government; and (d) a sovereign government: 1 Oppenheim (1905) 100-1. Further: Chen (1951) 55. Somewhat heretically, other authors took the view that the elements of statehood could be left up to the individual entity desirous of independence: J. Lorimer, 1 *The Institutes of the Law of Nations* (W. Blackwood and Sons, 1883) 107; Kelsen (1941) 35 *AJIL* 605, 610. Lauterpacht in his 1937 Hague Academy course had earlier identified 'a reasonably well-defined territory, a population, and the existence of an independent Government enjoying a reasonable degree of stability', which he believed to be suitably clear and resistant to arbitrary application: 1 *Collected Papers* 316. Further: *Recognition*, 26-31.

71 Witness most recently the controversy over Kosovo: *Accordance with international law of the unilateral declaration of independence in respect of Kosovo*, Advisory Opinion of 22 July 2010.

naive and at odds with reality, presuming the emergence of political entities within the international community to be a question of fact alone: rather, he thought, the extreme variety of state and government models defied simple clarification, and often required human (i.e. political) interpretation.[72]

> A State may exist as a physical fact. But it is a physical fact which is of no relevance for the commencement of particular international rights and duties until by recognition – and by nothing else – it has been lifted into the sphere of law, until by recognition it has become a juridical fact. Recognition declares the existence of a physical, not of a legal, phenomenon. This explains why, although declaratory of a fact, it is at the same time constitutive of legal consequences. It is, if we desire to put it so, merely evidence of facts to which the law attaches importance. But it is indispensible evidence without which the potential international rights are a mere claim.[73]

Thus, as Lauterpacht saw it, states still conceived of recognition as a political act, and any legal rights which an entity might acquire through statehood were useless unless recognized as such by the international community at large (i.e. by states generally). Furthermore, given the difficulty in ascertaining from a factual point of view whether the declaratory criteria had been met, intervention *by an interpreter* (i.e. by a political actor) was an essential element of the process.

What then, was Lauterpacht's view? Having identified what he saw as substantial deficiencies in both popular models of recognition, his solution was to combine them. On the one hand, he saw that recognition was a subject that ought not to be left to the unfettered and potentially parochial discretion of domestic politicians. But on the other, it was clear that if recognition was to retain any real meaning as a device of international relations, some scope for political agency had to be retained. Thus, Lauterpacht was to conclude that recognition was not constitutive or declarative of statehood: both theories on their own had unsatisfactory implications. Rather, recognition was *both* constitutive *and* declaratory.

III

So lay the academic landscape as it existed in the middle part of the twentieth century and to which Lauterpacht's *Recognition* was to make its distinctive contribution. The principles underpinning *Recognition* had been developing for some time, as we have seen.

72 *Recognition*, 45-51. Further: M. Koskenniemi, 'Hersch Lauterpacht (1897-1960)' in J. Beatson & R. Zimmermann (eds), *Jurists Uprooted: German-Speaking Emigré Lawyers in Twentieth Century Britain* (Oxford University Press, 2004) 601, 636-7.

73 *Recognition*, 75.

Jenks links the development of the book as a whole (including its discussion of governments and belligerency) to a range of articles written by Lauterpacht and inspired by the Manchurian and Ethiopian wars and the Spanish Civil War.[74] From the perspective of statehood, however, he clearly in his Hague Academy lectures of 1937 conceived of recognition as both a constitutive and declaratory process:

> [Recognition] is constitutive in the meaning that it is not a formality: that it requires the active, deliberate and conscientious exercise of discretion in a manner which is frequently of extreme difficulty. It is declaratory in the meaning that, once given the requirements of statehood, the recognizing State is not free in law to refuse recognition for reasons connected with its own policy and convenience.[75]

In *Recognition* these ideas ripened definitively and fixed on the wider horizon of the rule of law as an essential component of the international system. Its central thread is that recognition in all its forms is a legal act with political aspects and that this basal premise is fundamental to the rule of law. Thus 'it is a sustained and powerful plea for collectivizing the procedure of recognition in an appropriate international authority'.[76]

In Lauterpacht's own words, the book aimed to 'introduce an essential element of order into what is a fundamental aspect of international relations [and to] prevent it from being treated as a purely physical phenomenon uncontrolled by legal rule and left entirely within the precarious orbit of politics'.[77] What is more, he saw this project as one of vital importance if international law was to develop as a normative system ensuring the peaceful relations of states. To his mind, the total politicization of recognition as a hallmark of diplomatic practice reflected the essentially decentralized and parochial character of the family of nations.[78] The solution, as posited by Lauterpacht, was to frame recognition as constitutive, but to place on states a legal duty to recognize in the presence of certain facts declaratory of an entity's matriculation to statehood:

---

74 C.W. Jenks, 'Hersch Lauterpacht – The Scholar as Prophet' (1960) 36 *BYIL* 1, 36. Further: H. Lauterpacht, ''Resort to War' and the Interpretation of the Covenant during the Manchurian Dispute' (1934) 28 *AJIL* 43; H. Lauterpacht, 'The Credentials of the Abyssinian Delegation to the Seventeenth Assembly of the League of Nations' (1937) 18 *BYIL* 184; H. Lauterpacht, 'Recognition of Insurgents as a *De Facto* Government' (1939) 3 *Modern LR* 1; H. Lauterpacht, 'Implied Recognition' (1944) 21 *BYIL* 123; H. Lauterpacht, 'Recognition of States in International Law' (1944) 53 *Yale LJ* 385; H. Lauterpacht, '*De facto* Recognition, Withdrawal of Recognition, and Conditional Recognition' (1945) 22 *BYIL* 164; H. Lauterpacht, 'Recognition of Governments, I' (1945) 45 *Columbia LR* 815; H. Lauterpacht, 'Recognition of Governments, II' (1946) 46 *Columbia LR* 37. Also: *Recognition*, vi.

75 1 *Collected Papers* 309

76 Jenks (1960) 36 *BYIL* 1, 36.

77 *Recognition*, 73.

78 Koskenniemi, in Beatson & Zimmerman (2004) 601, 636.

> To recognize a political community as a State is to declare that it fulfils the conditions of statehood as required by international law. If these conditions are present, then existing States are under the duty to grant recognition. In the absence of an international organ competent to ascertain and authoritatively to declare the presence of requirements of full international personality, States already established fulfil that function in their capacity as organs of international law. In thus acting they administer the law of nations. This legal rule signifies that in granting or withholding recognition States do not claim and are not entitled to serve exclusively the interests of their national policy or convenience regardless of the principles of international law in the matter. Although recognition is thus declaratory of an existing fact, such declaration, made in the impartial fulfilment of a legal duty, is constitutive, as between the recognizing State and the community so recognized, of international rights and duties associated with full statehood.[79]

Lauterpacht did not, however, consider his thesis to be a statement *de lege ferenda*, but carefully based his argument on what he saw as the facts. *Recognition* was written against the background of an extensive survey of diplomatically significant state practice, principally that of the United Kingdom[80] and the United States[81] in relation to the recognition of the new states of Latin America.[82] In his (artfully presented) view, these states had continually projected their policies of recognition in terms of a duty, eschewing the terminology of political preference.[83]

In this, Lauterpacht identified two relevant species of government pronouncements: first, pronouncements such as Ambassador Austin's defence of the right to grant recognition; and second, pronouncements making reference to his hypothesized duty to recognize. The first, he conceded, were comparatively frequent, the latter less so, a fact he attributed to the greater diplomatic need to defend the 'free hand' of national interest.[84] Despite this apparent preponderance of contrary state practice, he maintained that recognition as reflected in state practice was nonetheless a legal duty. In the first place, he noted, '[t]here is probably no deliberate pronouncement of a government on the record in which the granting or refusal of recognition of statehood is expressly claimed to be a matter of grace or, exclusively, of political expediency' (this was before Ambassador Aus-

79 *Recognition*, 6.

80 Ibid, 12-18.

81 Ibid, 18-24.

82 Further: M. Fabry, *Recognizing States. International Society and the Establishment of New States since 1776* (Oxford University Press, 2010) ch 2.

83 *Recognition*, 25. Lauterpacht did not suggest that this practice was *uniform* as between states, writing that 'although followed in practice with some regularity, [the duty] cannot be regarded as having been uniformly acted upon or clearly perceived by governments. Neither [has it] secured the assent of the majority of writers on the subject': ibid, 6.

84 Ibid, 13.

tin's outburst).[85] In the second, he drew attention to more principled pronouncements of high ranking officials such as the British Foreign Secretary, George Canning, who, *inter alia* remarked:

> It appears manifest to the British Government that if so large a portion of the globe should remain much longer without any recognized political existence or any definite political connexion with the established Governments of Europe, the consequences of such a state of things must at once be most embarrassing to those Governments, and most injurious to the interests of all European nations. For this reason, and not from the mere views of selfish policy, the British Government is decidedly of the opinion that the recognition of such New States as have established, *de facto*, their separate political existence, cannot be much longer delayed.[86]

Lauterpacht's reliance on such statements may be criticized as credulous. As Koskenniemi remarks, '[a] 'realist' has no difficulty in interpreting Canning's policy as a political manoeuvre to extend British influence in the Western hemisphere'.[87] Lauterpacht anticipates this enfilade, noting that 'any such retort is probably unsound' on the basis that:

> Official pronouncements of governments express what in their view are the correct legal rules and principles capable of general application. It is with these alone that the jurist is concerned. The particular legal rule may suit the political interest and convenience of the State enunciating it. But the lawyer abandons his legitimate province once he begins to probe into the motives which have induced governments to express their obligation to act upon a legal rule. Such realism may be appropriate for the historian and the sociologist. The jurist is concerned with the legal rule upon which governments profess to act. The fact that the particular rule has been

85 Ibid. The sole example Lauterpacht identifies, a dispatch from the British Foreign Secretary of 30 November 1822 to the British Minister in Madrid, stated 'The Recognition [of the new States of Latin America] of any other power [other than Spain] may undoubtedly be given or withholden at its own good pleasure and may be made conditional or contingent' (reproduced in C.K. Webster, 1 *Britain and the Independence of Latin America, 1812-1830* (Oxford University Press, 1838) 400). Lauterpacht recontextualizes this as 'a clear and emphatic reservation of the right to grant or to refuse recognition irrespective of the attitude of Spain': *Recognition*, 13-14.

86 Reproduced in 2 Webster (1938) 414. Cf the letter of 6 July 1950 written by Sir Eric Beckett, the Legal Advisor to the Foreign Office to Lauterpacht, stating that the British government had never considered recognition in terms of legal duties or rights: reproduced in E. Lauterpacht (2010) 337-8. Further: Koskenniemi, in Beatson & Zimmerman (2004) 601, 638. But cf Fitzmaurice & Vallat, 'Sir (William) Eric Beckett, KCMG, QC (1896-1966)' (1968) 17 *ICLQ* 267, 285, stating that Beckett believed in a duty to recognize insofar as the recognition of governments was concerned, and that this was consistent with the traditional practice of the British government.

87 Koskenniemi, in Beatson & Zimmerman (2004) 601, 637.

found to suit the interests of States does not derogate from its legal value; it adds to it. International law is not so rich as to be able to discard, in a spirit of realism of questionable propriety, legal rules acknowledged and acted upon by States.[88]

Having established to his satisfaction the joint constitutive/declaratory view of recognition, and the existence of the duty to recognize as reflected in (his reading of) certain state practice, Lauterpacht moved to give content to the duty. Insofar as the declaratory aspects of the duty are concerned, he identified three factors which he considered to be 'the requirements of statehood as laid down by international law',[89] namely (a) an independent government, (b) exercising effective authority, (c) in a defined territory.[90] These differ slightly from the factors he referred to in his 1937 Hague lectures.[91] An equally significant contribution to his thesis was the identification of those factors which Lauterpacht considered to be irrelevant criteria for statehood. These reflect his desire to excise overt political influence from his ideal of recognition, though political calculation could not be removed entirely without violating the principle of *ex iniuria ius non oritur*.[92] Conspicuous by its absence from Lauterpacht's calculus – as indeed it is from Oppenheim's writings on recognition[93] and from the Montevideo Convention – is any reference to the relevant level of 'civilization' that the prospective state is expected to demonstrate.[94]

Lauterpacht also took steps to further articulate the duty to recognize in international law and to account for those situations in which the duty might not be fulfilled for reasons connected to the national interest of a state, attributing this shortcoming to the character of international law as it then stood (and indeed still stands today in key respects) as a system with no external auditor capable of holding states to account with respect to their legal obligations:

In a properly constituted political society the function ... of ascertaining the presence of the conditions of legal capacity and existence is performed by impartial organs delegated by the law for that purpose. In international society that task is as a rule fulfilled by individual States acting on their own responsibility and endowed with wide discretion in the appreciation of the relevant facts. That discretion is

88 *Recognition*, 25.

89 Ibid, 26.

90 Ibid, 26-30.

91 1 *Collected Papers* 316.

92 Translated, 'law does not arise from injustice': *Recognition*, 420-6.

93 Though Oppenheim was not above such sentiments generally, noting that 'the civilized States are, with only a few exceptions, Christian States': 1 Oppenheim (1905) 10-11.

94 See e.g. 1 Lorimer (1883) 123: '[t]o talk of the recognition of the Mahomedan States as a question of time, is to talk nonsense'. Lauterpacht's view was that 'some aspects of Lorimer's treatment of the subject border on absurdity': *Recognition*, 32.

> unfettered only in the meaning that, at present, the State which takes any decision on the issue of recognition is not accountable for any of its acts to any superior jurisdiction. In essence, it is a discretion determined by international law.[95]

A further concern of Lauterpacht's was the concept of non-recognition.[96] Just as the creation of a state in accordance with international law was to be accompanied by a duty to recognize on the part of states, the creation of a situation illegally was to be accompanied by non-recognition. Lauterpacht remarked:

> It follows from the same principle that facts, however undisputed, which are the result of conduct violative of international law cannot claim the same right to be incorporated automatically as part of the law of nations. They do not impose upon other States the duty of recognition. These may, if they so wish and if, in exceptional circumstances, they deem it compatible with the maintenance of the authority of international law, recognize them as creating internationally valid rights as against themselves. If they do so, it is a concession on their part which they are under no duty to grant. On the other hand, they may announce their intention to treat in the future such unlawful acts as devoid of any validity in international law.[97]

As Lauterpacht saw it, the concept of non-recognition was vital for the integrity of the international system, arising jurisprudentially (again) from the maxim *ex injuria jus non oritur*. Even if recognition is not necessary for the validity of an otherwise legally unimpeachable title, he thought, non-recognition served to prevent the validation by the international community of what as a matter of law amounted to a legal nullity.[98] Although historically left to the discretion of individual states, Lauterpacht saw non-recognition harden into a duty through the practice of the League of Nations, and in particular with the practice of the League in relation to the Japanese invasion of Manchuria, and the 'creation' of the puppet state of Manchukuo in 1932.[99]

Thus Lauterpacht saw recognition as one element in the wider goal of the effective political integration of international society. He considered the subversion of the international interest to further national goals as a problem *of* international law; a source of weakness, no doubt, but not itself system-threatening: as earlier noted 'nothing but good can come from such an admission so long as it is not maintained that the shortcomings of international law are permanent and inherent in its very nature'.[100] His solution to the politicization of recognition – the introduction of a legal duty to recognize – was

95 Ibid.

96 Generally: *Recognition*, ch 21.

97 Ibid, 410.

98 Ibid, 412-13.

99 Ibid, 417-20.

100 1 *Collected Papers* 308.

effectively intended as a transitional measure until such time as the collective efforts of the international community produced an organ capable of deciding questions of statehood on its behalf. Anything short of this legal view of recognition, in his view, would subvert international law's hard fought claim to be called law as such.[101] He remarked, *de lege ferenda*:

> Only [a legal] view of recognition, coupled with a clear realization of its constitutive effect, permits us to introduce a stabilizing principle into what would otherwise have been a pure exhibition of power and negation of order. The grotesque spectacle of a community being a State in relation to some but not to other States is a grave reflection upon international law. It cannot be explained away, amidst some complacency, by questionable analogies to private law or to philosophical relativism. The paradoxical phenomenon, which more than anything else signifies the negation of the unity of international law as a system of law, may be unavoidable pending the collectivization of the process of recognition. In that intermediate period adherence to the legal view of recognition [...] will naturally tend to reduce the occasions for divergency.[102]

IV

Given that *Recognition* rejected both of the pure strains of constitutive and declaratory theory that had hitherto dominated the debate, it is not surprising that Lauterpacht's views were considered to be controversial, even inflammatory.[103] The most excoriating review of *Recognition* came from Josef Kunz,[104] a hard-line declarativist whose own treatise of 1928, *Die Anerkennung von Staaten und Regierungen im Völkerrecht*,[105] was frequently used by Lauterpacht to demonstrate the difficulties with the declaratory position.[106] Kunz clearly admired aspects of *Recognition*, but as far as Lauterpacht's central thesis as to statehood was concerned '[the] assertion of a right to recognition and a duty to recognize, is certainly untenable as not being in accord with positive international law'.[107] Kunz saw *Recognition* as devolving from the constitutive defence mounted by

101 Further: *Brownlie's Principles* (8th edn, 2012) ch 1.

102 *Recognition*, 77-8.

103 Dugard (1987) ch 2; Grant (1999) 126-8.

104 J.L. Kunz, 'Critical Remarks on Lauterpacht's *Recognition in International Law*' (1950) 44 *AJIL* 713. Dugard characterizes the review as 'savage': Dugard (1987) 8.

105 Kunz was quite enamoured with his work, claiming (in the third person) that '[h]is neutral and impartial study led to the adoption of the so-called "declaratory doctrine"': (1950) 44 *AJIL* 713, 713.

106 Generally: *Recognition*, chs 4 & 5.

107 Kunz (1950) 44 *AJIL* 713, 713.

Kelsen following his conversion from declaratory theory,[108] though without the 'logical reasoning and wonderful lucidity'[109] which Kelsen had to Kunz's mind displayed:

> It is from [the] idea of recognition as a legal act of ascertaining the fulfilment of requirements laid down by international law that Lauterpacht's book is written, coupled with the idea of a right to, and a duty of, recognition. This principal thesis the author tries to prove as positive international law from the practice of states. In this endeavour, it must be said in the interest of scientific truth, he has failed completely.[110]

To a certain extent – as demonstrated by his treatment of Kelsen's apostasy – Kunz had accepted the validity, or at least the plausibility, of the constitutive view. Lauterpacht's hybrid model appears to have been intolerable on the basis that whatever the differences in the constitutive and declaratory theories, neither posited a legal duty on a state to grant recognition – a duty for which there was no evidence whatever. Thus Kunz accused Lauterpacht of engaging in 'a falsification of the positive law'[111] in propagating his ideas:

> In teaching these doctrines, in contradiction to positive international law, Lauterpacht forgot that the science of international law cannot by its defect correct the structural defects of the primitive international legal order. He forgot what [Oppenheim], in words which are equally true today, warned against forty-two years ago, what he himself recently emphasized: the scholar of international law is not in the rôle of a legislator, but of a judge; of a judge, and not in the rôle of counsel for plaintiff or defendant. It is the duty of the scholar to state what the law is, whether he likes it or not. It is fundamental to distinguish between *lex lata* and *lex ferenda*. Lauterpacht's dialectic efforts to make the practice of states tell what it does not contain, however talented and powerful, are of no help; neither is the attitude of joining the now fashionable accusations against positivism.[112]

After continuing to attack what he saw as Lauterpacht's selective use of state practice and the manner in which it was couched (which led Kunz to accuse Lauterpacht of 'nourishing non-English assertions against an Anglo-American superiority complex of righteousness'[113]), Kunz also derided Lauterpacht's focus on collective recognition as unrealistic, repeating Jessup's argument that such recognition was impossible 'in the

108 Kelsen (1941) 35 *AJIL* 605.

109 Kunz (1950) 44 *AJIL* 713, 714.

110 Ibid.

111 Ibid, 715.

112 Ibid, 716.

113 Ibid, 717.

absence of organized international machinery to enforce the obligation'[114] and claimed, moreover, that the isolationist tendencies of the United States would prevent any such initiative in the future.[115]

Other contemporary reviews of *Recognition* adopted a similar position to Kunz, albeit in less incendiary language.[116] One of the more observant was Briggs, who identified Lauterpacht's discussion as conceptualist in character[117] – a trait he shared with allied theorists such as Kelsen and Anzilotti. Briggs noted that Lauterpacht's conceptualism enabled him to 'minimize the embarrassment' resulting from the fact that any theory of recognition proceeding from an *a priori* constitutive base (as *Recognition's* views on statehood did) was 'logically forced to regard the new state as without rights or obligations under international law until recognized'.[118]

Ultimately, however, Briggs felt that Lauterpacht's argument – that recognition was in any event constitutive of statehood – was undone by reference to what Briggs referred to as 'unofficial relations' between state and proto-state entities, citing an incident on 9 May 1922, in which the American Commissioner in Albania was instructed to lodge a formal protest with the unrecognized Albanian state over the Albanian practice of requiring American citizens of Albanian origin to surrender their US passports and replace them with Albanian documentation. Despite the fact that the communication was not

---

114 P.C. Jessup, *A Modern Law of Nations* (Macmillan, 1948) 44, cited by Kunz (1950) 44 *AJIL* 713, 718.

115 Kunz (1950) 44 *AJIL* 713, 718.

116 See e.g. E.J. Cohn, 'Review: *Recognition in International Law*' (1948) 64 *LQR* 404, 405: 'It is with great hesitation that the present reviewer admits that in respect of this starting point the learned author has not succeeded in convincing him'. Also: R. Oglesby, 'Review: *Recognition in International Law*' (1948) 42 *AJIL* 245, critiquing Lauterpacht's views on the recognition of belligerency.

117 H.W. Briggs, 'Recognition of States: Some Reflections on Doctrine and Practice' (1949) 43 *AJIL* 113, 114:

> Conceptualists … like Lauterpacht … start from the premise that every juridical order, including international law, must determine who are its subjects and at what point juridical personality must be attributed to them, feel compelled by their own abstractions to regard the act of recognition as constitutive – as creating of legal personality in international law. Because international law possesses no central organ to perform this 'legal' function of the establishment (*la constatation*) of the 'legal fact' that a 'state-in-the-sense-of-international-law' exists, the function of recognition is attributed to each previously existing state as an 'organ' of international law.

118 Briggs (1949) 43 *AJIL* 113, 117. Lauterpacht deflected this by noting that the question 'whether a state exists as a question of fact [is] to predicate that a given legal result is a question of fact', thereby divorcing the legal rights and duties attending statehood from the factual questions leading to recognition. According to Lauterpacht, only the legal and political act of recognition could convert a factual set of attributes into a state: *Recognition*, 24, 45ff.

couched in terms of international law, Briggs noted, 'the evidence suggests that … international law was regarded by both states as regulating their relations and as establishing both the delictual responsibility and the contractual capacity of the unrecognized state'.[119] Briggs identified incidents such as this as not only establishing the declaratory view of recognition, but as removing any suggestion of a duty to recognize from diplomatic practice:

> Since 'unofficial relations' are a convenient, though juridically ambiguous, device for dealing with communities from which, because of their indeterminate status or for political reasons, it is considered desirable to withhold recognition, foreign offices have been reluctant to admit a legal duty to recognize.[120]

Some constitutivists also disagreed, though less markedly. In a lengthy letter to Lauterpacht dated 24 September 1947, Quincy Wright raised questions as to the validity of the duty to recognize, and the characterization of recognition as a legal act.[121] Indeed, he argued that the restriction of the constitutive position via the imposition of a legal duty represented an affirmation of the declaratory position:

> If one regards recognition as a legal obligation under certain circumstances, it would seem to follow that the failure of states to act in accordance with this legal obligation should not operate to the disadvantage of the victim of that dereliction of duty. This would seem to be an application of the principle *jus ex injuria non oritur* […] If this argument is correct, then it would seem that if the community seeking recognition is in such condition that states are under a duty to recognize, the new political entity should be considered a state entitled to rights under international law, even if not recognized. In other words, recognition is merely declaratory.

Wright then posited a different solution to the overtly political nature of recognition:

> I would solve the problem by a somewhat different emphasis, accepting recognition as a political act, but one which states should not exercise arbitrarily but responsibly as members of the international community. I would consider the position analogous to the position of members of Congress of the United States in dealing with the application of a territory for admission as a state of the Union. There is no doubt that a territory cannot become a state without an enabling act properly passed by Congress, and it is also clear that the passage of such an enabling act is a political act in which the members of Congress exercise political judgment, but a political

---

119 Briggs (1949) 43 *AJIL* 113, 118.

120 Ibid.

121 Letter from QW to HL, 24 September 1947, on file with the author.

judgment which ought to be guided by broad considerations of national welfare, not by particular prejudices of the individual.

Not every contemporary reviewer disagreed with Lauterpacht. Writing under the pseudonym 'E'[122] in the *British Yearbook of International Law*, one writer agreed that both a legal conceptualization of recognition and collective recognition were worthy of consideration *de lege ferenda*, and noted that '[i]n the reviewer's opinion Professor Lauterpacht makes a very fair case of showing that the law is in accordance with his thesis. The reviewer also thinks that, taking a broad view, the acceptance of Professor Lauterpacht's thesis relieves governments of far more political embarrassments than it creates'.[123]

V

How then has the law of recognition developed since 1947, and what impact might this have on Lauterpacht's thesis? The prevailing modern view is that recognition is a substantially declaratory phenomenon, and that it is not subject to any legal duty *vis-à-vis* the entity to be recognised,[124] in other words the polar opposite of the view promoted

122 It appears that 'E' was a pseudonym used by Sir Eric Beckett when Legal Adviser: Sir Elihu Lauterpacht QC, pers comm. If this is the case, then it certainly fits within Beckett's wider professional agreement with Lauterpacht's views. This is evidenced in Lauterpacht's publication of a letter in *The Times* on 6 January 1950 at the instigation of Beckett and the Foreign Office regarding the UK government's recognition of the Communist People's Republic of China. The broad thrust of the letter was that British recognition of the Communist regime – at the expense of the Republic of China as led by the remnants of the Kuomintang/Nationalist Party – was not a discretionary act of policy designed to obtain a transitory political advantage, but was driven by a legal duty to recognize a government in effective control of its territory. Lauterpacht's generosity of spirit was further demonstrated by a separate private letter to the Nationalist ambassador explaining that it was his duty to respond to the invitation of the Foreign Office and set forth his view of recognition in the context of governments. His explanation was graciously accepted: *Life of Hersch Lauterpacht*, 332-6.

123 E., 'Review: *Recognition in International Law*' (1947) 24 *BYIL* 507, 508. *Recognition* was also reviewed positively by P.H. Winfield in *The Times Literary Supplement* (30 August 1947) and N. Bentwich in *The Manchester Guardian* (29 July 1947). Further: *Life of Hersch Lauterpacht*, 299-300.

124 Chen (1951) 13-78; H. Waldock, 'General Course on Public International Law' (1962) 106 Hague *Recueil* 1, 147-51; 1 *Restatement Third* §202(1); J. Duursma, *Fragmentation and the International Relations of Micro-States* (Cambridge University Press, 1996) 110-15; C. Tomuschat, 'International Law: Ensuring the Survival of Mankind on the Eve of a New Century. General Course on Public International Law' (1999) 281 Hague *Recueil* 1, 118; Crawford (2nd edn, 2006)

in *Recognition*. T-C. Chen – whose 1951 treatise on recognition sets forth an influential declaratory view – saw certain logical defects within Lauterpacht's view of recognition as both constitutive and declaratory. He noted:

> One question naturally suggests itself: if recognition – in the constitutive sense – is a legal duty, to whom is that duty owed? It cannot be to the new State, since it has not yet begun to exist. To the international community as a whole? The international community cannot be deemed to be *entitled* to the right of having a new member recognized unless each of its members is *entitled to claim* from the recalcitrant State the performance of the duty of recognition. That claim cannot be made unless it can be established, in point of fact and according to the notion prevailing in that society, the conditions of statehood are present. But if this fact can be established, the recognition by any particular State would become tautologous. For, by the very establishment of that fact, the possession of personality by the State would have also been established, and there would consequently be no longer any need for creative recognition by any particular State. In other words, the international community can only claim the duty of recognition of a new State from a member State when, in the mind of the international community, the new State-person is already in existence.[125]

Modern state practice also supports the declaratory view in the form of treaties[126] and direct statements.[127] The perspective appears to have been accepted (at least tacitly) by the International Court of Justice in two cases. In the early Advisory Opinion on *Reparation for Injuries*,[128] the Court was asked whether the personality of the UN would be

26-8; *Brownlie's Principles* (8th edn, 2012) ch 6.

125 Chen (1951) 53 (italics in original).

126 Montevideo Convention, Art 3; Charter of the Organization of American States (as amended), 30 April 1948, 119 UNTS 3, Art 12: 'The political existence of the State is independent of recognition by other States. Even before being recognized, the State has the right to defend its integrity and independence'.

127 See e.g. a letter of the German Foreign Office dated 10 February 1994, which reads '[w]e and our partners in the EU have not recognized the [Federal Republic of Yugoslavia] [...] This is of no relevance for the question of the international legal personality of the Federal Republic of Yugoslavia, as recognition does not have constitutive effect': (1996) 56 *ZaöRV* 1007. Also, the statements by Australia in oral argument during the *East Timor* case (CR 95/10, 52):

> The question whether a particular territorial entity is a State depends on the application of rules of international law to the circumstances of a particular case. Statehood is not a legal status which is 'conferred' by the United Nations. However, United Nations organs may be required to determine for their own purposes whether a particular entity is a State.

128 *Reparation for Injuries suffered in the Service of the United Nations*, ICJ Reports 1949 p 174.

opposable as against a non-member, Israel.[129] The Court said:

> Fifty States, representing the vast majority of the members of the international community, had the power, in conformity with international law, to bring into being an entity possessing objective international personality, and not merely personality recognised by them alone, together with capacity to bring international claims.[130]

As Waldock points out,[131] the Court here speaks in general terms, and asserts that the personality of the UN exists *vis-à-vis* another state independently of recognition by that state. Put another way, if Israel were subsequently to recognize the UN (as it subsequently did), such recognition would be purely declaratory, from a legal point of view.

Nearly half a century later, in the *Bosnian Genocide* case[132] it was argued by Yugoslavia that the allegations of the breach of the Genocide Convention[133] made by Bosnia and Herzegovina were not admissible as the parties to the dispute had not recognized each other at the time of the events in question. The Court dismissed this argument on the basis that, as recognition had been given subsequently in the Dayton Accord,[134] any defect caused by non-recognition was solely procedural in character, and could be cured by re-filing the claim even in relation to alleged events of genocide occurring prior to 1995.

Further support for the declaratory view can be seen in the opinions of the Badinter Commission which considered a range of issues following the dissolution of the Socialist Federal Republic of Yugoslavia *(SFRY)*. In its *Opinion No 10* the Commission declared simply that 'recognition is not a prerequisite for the foundation of a State and is purely declaratory in its impact'.[135] In its *Opinion No 11*, the Commission identified dates of succession for the various successor states of the SFRY: in all cases, the date of emergence

---

129 Israel is also proof of the validity of the declaratory position, as it is often the subject of claims under international humanitarian and human rights law by certain Arab states that persistently deny it recognition: M. Craven, 'Statehood, Self-Determination and Recognition' in M. Evans (ed), *International Law* (3rd edn, Oxford University Press, 2010) 203, 244.

130 ICJ Reports 1949 p 174, 185.

131 Waldock (1962) 106 Hague *Recueil* 1, 150-1.

132 *Application of the Convention on the Prevention and Punishment of the Crime of Genocide (Bosnia and Herzegovina v Yugoslavia)*, Preliminary Objections, ICJ Reports 1996 p 595, 612-13.

133 Convention on the Prevention and Punishment of the Crime of Genocide, 9 December 1948, 78 *UNTS* 277.

134 General Framework for Peace in Bosnia and Herzegovina, 14 December 1995, 35 *ILM* 75.

135 (1992) 92 *ILR* 206, 208. Further: *Opinion No 1* (1991) 92 *ILR* 162, 165 ('the effects of recognition by other States are purely declaratory'); *Opinion No 8* (1992) 92 *ILR* 199, 201 ('[…] while recognition of a State by other States has only declarative value'). Also: *Reference re Secession of Quebec* (1998) 115 *ILR* 536, 589-90.

so identified preceded official recognition by other states by several months or, in some cases, by several years.[136]

Notwithstanding these decisions, however, the recent practice on recognition does not indicate the unqualified acceptance of the declarative position and its central tenet that the recognition of states is fundamentally a political question left to the discretion of the recognizing state. Although the International Court in its advisory opinion on *Kosovo*[137] ultimately considered issues of recognition to be beyond the scope of the question asked of it, those states which sought to advance arguments on recognition went to great lengths to present those submissions in legal terms, even if their overall position was that recognition was fundamentally an act of discretion. They thereby confirmed – at least in part – the view that recognition is governed by law. For its part the Court was markedly evasive, even formalistic – a posture made easier by the curious formulation of the question.[138]

In addition, Lauterpacht's views on non-recognition have stood the test of time, perhaps incongruously, as he saw non-recognition as a counterpart to the duty to recognize (i.e. as part of a system in which acts of recognition and non-recognition were governed by law). The International Court has affirmed on several occasions the existence of an obligation of non-recognition with respect to situations created in serious violation of international law,[139] and confirmed it as custom in the *Wall* advisory opinion.[140] Most significantly in the present context, the International Court has accepted that a state does not come into existence where the Security Council determines the circumstances of its

136 (1993) 32 *ILM* 1587. Further: Talmon (2004) 75 *BYIL* 101, 106-7.

137 *Kosovo*, Advisory Opinion of 22 July 2010, para 51.

138 See *Brownlie's Principles* (8th edn, 2012) 140-1. There is already a substantial body of commentary on the Opinion, mostly critical of it: see, e.g., 'Agora: The ICJ's Kosovo Advisory Opinion' (2011) 105 *AJIL* 50; Panel, (2011) 105 *Proc ASIL* 259; D. Jacobs & Y. Radi, 'Waiting for Godot: An Analysis of the Advisory Opinion on Kosovo' (2011) 24 *LJIL* 311; J. Vidmar, 'The Kosovo Advisory Opinion Scrutinized' (2011) 24 *LJIL* 355; E. Cirkovic, 'An Analysis of the ICJ Advisory Opinion on Kosovo's Unilateral Declaration of Independence' (2010) 11 *German Law Journal* 895.

139 *Brownlie's Principles* (8th edn, 2012) 155-7. With the passage of the International Law Commission's (*ILC*) Articles on the Responsibility of States for Internationally Wrongful Acts (*ARSIWA*), ILC *Ybk* 2001/II(2), it has been clarified that the duty applies with respect to situations created in violation of the peremptory norms of international law: see ARSIWA Art 41(2).

140 *Legal Consequences of the Construction of a Wall in the Occupied Palestinian Territory*, ICJ Reports 2004 p 136, 171; cf ibid, 232 (Judge Kooijmans). The duty is not, however, without limitations in modern international law: *Legal Consequences for States of the Continued Presence of South Africa in Namibia (South West Africa) notwithstanding Security Council Resolution 276 (1970)*, ICJ Reports 1971 p 16, 56. Also: *Loizidou v Turkey (Merits)* (1996) 108 *ILR* 443, 462; *Brownlie's Principles* (8th edn, 2012) 162-5.

creation to be in violation of international law.[141]

But beyond this, the apparent ascendency of declaratory theory should not be seen as a final victory. In the six decades since *Recognition* was published, the number of states has grown more than threefold. The United Nations functions as an international organization, more effectively than the League of Nations. In practical terms – and leaving aside the wider theoretical relevance of the work – *Recognition* promoted the idea of the United Nations as an organ of collective acceptance if not formal 'recognition'.[142] Lauterpacht himself saw this potential, noting:

> The provisions of the Charter of the United Nations in the manner of admission of new members are such as to render feasible the adoption of the rule as here suggested. The concurrence of all the permanent members of the Security Council and of two-thirds of the General Assembly is required for the admission of a new members, it would appear that a majority thus constituted ought to be treated as sufficient proof that the new State or government possesses the necessary qualifications entitling it to recognition.[143]

This ideal was frustrated by the Cold War.[144] Obstruction of new Members of the UN by the permanent members of the Security Council was a common phenomenon. Consequently, the Secretary-General, Trygve Lie, warned in 1950 that:

> [T]he United Nations does not possess any authority to recognize either a new State or a new government of an existing State. To establish the rule of collective recognition by the United Nations, would require either an amendment to the Charter or a treaty to which all members would adhere.[145]

But with the end of major geopolitical conflict between the US and USSR, might it be argued that the UN now functions as an effective organ of collective recognition?

---

141 *Kosovo*, Advisory Opinion of 22 July 2010, para 81. See e.g. SC Res 216 (1965) and SC Res 217 (1965), concerning Southern Rhodesia; SC Res 541 (1983) concerning the Turkish Republic of Northern Cyprus; and SC Res 787 (1992), concerning *Republika Srpska*.

142 See e.g. H. Kelsen, *The Law of the United Nations. A Critical Analysis of its Fundamental Problems* (London Institute of World Affairs, 1951) 947; H. Briggs 'Community Interest in the Emergence of New States: the Problem of Recognition' (1950) 44 *ASIL Proc* 169; Q. Wright, 'Some Thoughts about Recognition' (1950) 44 *AJIL* 548; Dugard (1987) ch 4.

143 *Recognition*, 403.

144 Dugard (1987) 43.

145 S/1466, 9 March 1950. Further: Wright (1950) 44 *AJIL* 548. Additional evidence for this position comes from the fact that an amendment proposed at the San Francisco Conference in 1945 that the UN be given the power to recommend collective recognition was not adopted: Dugard (1987) 44.

There are difficulties with such a presumption, most obviously in the words of the Charter itself. The admissions procedure set down in Article 4(1) states that membership 'is open to all other peace-loving *States* which accept the obligations contained in the present Charter': if statehood is a precondition of membership, admission to the UN cannot have a completely constitutive effect.[146] It may, however, have a qualified role in the process,[147] as 'a step forward towards the principle of collective recognition'.[148]

More positively, the institution of UN membership has eliminated in part what Lauterpacht saw as the greatest deficiency of recognition, the 'grotesque spectacle'[149] of relative statehood: once admitted to the UN, an entity is considered a full member of the community of states, whether or not recognized. Although another UN member would not be forced thereby to extend to another member normal diplomatic or consular relations – Tehran is not forced to place an embassy in Jerusalem – it would be considered a breach of international law for the former to treat the latter as non-existent, as for all purposes lacking international personality. One may see in this a manifestation of Lauterpacht's duty to recognize, promoted not by the fulfilment of his objective criteria of territory, government, etc, but by the single criterion of UN membership.

But the nascent collective recognition of UN membership is not a complete solution to the problems identified in *Recognition*. In particular, it cannot account for the legal position of a state in between its declaration of independence and admission to the UN, which in the case of the two Koreas was to last some 43 years.[150] As a result, the 'collective recognition' promised by UN membership serves as the ultimate, but not sole, confirmation of statehood: a substitute 'to a large extent, but not to all aspects' of the traditional doctrine of recognition.[151] Hard cases remain, and the debate over Belorussia, Ukraine and Israel[152] half a century ago has been replaced with questions about Kosovo, Palestine and Somaliland. Lauterpacht's vision has yet to be completely realized, but it is unlikely that this would have surprised him. Even after *Recognition* was published, he remained aware that the work of law remained unfinished. To this end, he recommended that the ILC consider issues of recognition ('from the practical point of view, one of the most important questions of international law') as part of its programme of work in 1949,[153]

146 Chen (1951) 222.

147 T.D. Grant, *Admission to the United Nations: Charter Article 4 and the Rise of Universal Organization* (Martinus Nijhoff, 2009) 252-7.

148 Waldock (1962) 106 Hague *Recueil* 1, 155. Also: Dugard (1987) 44-5.

149 *Recognition*, 78.

150 Talmon (2004) 75 *BYIL* 101, 105. The Republic of Korea was established on 15 August 1948 and the Democratic People's Republic of Korea on 9 September 1948. Both were admitted to the UN in 1991: SC Res 702 (1991); GA Res 46/1, 17 September 1991.

151 H. Mosler, 'The International Society as a Legal Community' (1974) 140 Hague *Receuil* 1, 60.

152 Dugard (1987) 80.

153 *Survey of International Law in Relation to the Work of Codification of the International Law Commission*, A/CN.4/1/Rev.l, 10 February 1949, paras 40-3.

sounding the call to arms in familiar terms:

> The main reason for the inability – or reluctance – to extend the attempts at codification to what is one of the central and most frequently recurring aspects of international law and relations has been the widely held view that questions of recognition pertain to the province of politics rather than of law. There are many who believe that that view is contrary to the evidence of international practice – governmental and judicial – and that if acted upon it is probably inconsistent with the authority of international law and its effectiveness in one of the most crucial manifestations of the international relations of States. It would seem inconsistent with the authority of international law that the question of the rise of statehood and the capacity of States to participate in international intercourse should be regarded as a matter of arbitrary discretion rather than legal duty.[154]

But despite the utility of such issues being considered systematically by a body such as the ILC, Lauterpacht's suggestion was not taken up.[155]

VI

The point has already been made that the recognition of governments differs from the recognition of states. Over the long run, relative to states, governments represent a temporary phenomenon. Even systems of government referred to in a constitution can change, and change unconstitutionally. The state is our method of projecting the past and present onto the future, thereby seeking to ensure the consistency of international relations: it is the positive mode of human representation across time and for the time being.

Moreover, the institution of recognition of governments has never been as firmly established as the recognition of states. The Estrada Doctrine,[156] first enunciated in 1930, reflected the widespread concern that the recognition of governments could be used as a modality of intervention, adding one source of instability to another. More recently, concern that the recognition of governments could be used precisely as a mode of intervention, as reflecting the favouring of one faction over another has led to the decline in

154 Ibid, para 42.

155 It was briefly revisited by the ILC in 1996 as part of its consideration of possible new topics, and again not taken up: see Crawford (2nd edn, 2006) 757-59, reprinting the internal working paper on the subject.

156 As enunciated by the Mexican Secretary of Foreign Relations at the time: G. Estrada, 'Estrada Doctrine of Recognition' (1931) 25 *AJIL Supp* 203. Also: P. Jessup, 'The Estrada Doctrine' (1931) 25 *AJIL* 719.

the practice of recognition of governments.[157] States have indicated their intention to withhold the recognition of new governments, and instead to deal with regimes on a de facto basis. The change has not been entirely without resistance, with scholars such as Peterson emphasising the positive role played by the recognition of governments in international relations, first in cases of extended civil war, where recognition becomes a tool of coordination and order if used effectively, and second where there is a lack of diplomatic contact between two states, in which case recognition fulfils a valuable function in the regulation of the relationship.[158]

The implications of this change of practice were demonstrated in *Somalia v Woodhouse Drake & Carey (Suisse) SA*,[159] where Hobhouse J. was required to determine for himself which of Somalia's warring factions, if any, could be considered to be its 'government.' He determined, in light of equivocal statements from the UK Foreign Office,[160] and following his own assessment of the situation, that that state in reality possessed no effective government whatsoever.[161] The result was to preserve for the time being assets of the state against partial claimants and their friends in the arms trade.[162]

This trend to abandon recognition of governments has to some extent been cast into doubt by recent practice during the so-called 'Arab Spring'. The uprisings against the regime of Muammar Ghaddafi in Libya led to a cavalcade of states seeking to recognize

157 Talmon (1998) 3-14. The adoption by the UK and other Commonwealth countries of this position in the 1980s resulted in considerable commentary: see e.g. C. Warbrick, 'The New British Policy on Recognition of Governments' (1981) 30 *ICLQ* 568; S. Talmon, 'Recognition of Governments: An Analysis of the New British Policy and Practice' (1992) 63 *BYIL* 231; H. Charlesworth, 'The New Australian Recognition Policy in Comparative Perspective' (1991) 18 *MULR* 1. But the UK was a comparative latecomer to the practice; for example, the Belgian government affirmed in 1965 that the lack of formal recognition of governments was the 'traditional policy of Belgium': (1968) 4 *RBDI* 541.

158 Generally: M.J. Peterson, 'Recognition of Governments Should Not be Abolished' (1983) 77 *AJIL* 31.

159 [1993] QB 54. Noted: C. Warbrick in (1993) 56 *Modern LR* 92; B. Kingsbury in (1993) 109 *LQR* 377; J. Crawford in (1993) 52 *CLJ* 4. Also: *Sierra Leone Telecommunications Co Ltd v Barclays Bank plc* [1998] All ER 821

160 E.g. 'The United Kingdom maintains informal contact with all the factions involved, but there have been no dealings on a Government to Government basis': [1993] QB 54, 65.

161 [1993] QB 54, 65:

> Accordingly, if the question before the court is to be decided on the basis of the attitude adopted by Her Majesty's Government, an order cannot be made in favour of the interim government or Crossman Block. The basis for its attitude is clearly not any disapproval of an established regime but rather that there is no regime which has control, let alone any administrative control which has the requisite element of stable continuity.

162 Crawford (1993) 52 *CLJ* 4, 6.

the 'National Transitional Council' as the legitimate government of Libya.[163] In the UK this recrudescence of recognition produced predictable judicial consequences.[164] In *British Arab Commercial Bank v National Transitional Council of the State of Libya*,[165] Blair J., on receipt of an executive certificate from the Foreign Office confirming the UK government's recognition of the National Transitional Council,[166] stated in effect that he was bound by the recognition so given, and thus had no scope to determine the question for himself,[167] as Hobhouse J. had done in the *Somalia* case. It may be that, having been rejected as potentially interventionist, the recognition of governments is making a comeback on that same ground, supporting or inducing a change of government in cases where the regime in question is perceived as lacking popular support.

VII

Why then, should *Recognition* – a controversial work the predictions of which have not entirely come to pass – be republished? John Dugard, writing four decades after its initial release, said:

> Despite [its shortcomings], Lauterpacht's *Recognition* remains the starting point and the inspiration for any student of the contemporary law of recognition. The very features of the study that were perceived by critics to be weaknesses are today seen to be its strengths. Lauterpacht's refusal to be a mere scribe of State practice ensures that *Recognition* is denied the ephemeral quality that characterizes so many international law treatises. Furthermore, the integration of theory and practice, the failure to distinguish clearly between *lex lata* and *lex ferenda*, the broad historical sweep, the commitment to a consistent jurisprudential creed and the unashamed allegiance to idealism resulted in a study which, like Grotius' *De Jure Belli ac Pacis*, has been able to withstand the fluctuations of international practice and the passage of time.[168]

Dugard's analysis of the resilience and merit of *Recognition* remains sound, not as a sim-

---

163 Generally: C. Warbrick, 'British Policy and the National Transitional Council of Libya' (2012) 61 *ICLQ* 247.

164 Ibid, 259-62.

165 [2011] EWHC 2274 (Comm).

166 On the effect of such certificates, see generally: E. Wilmshurst, 'Executive Certificates in Foreign Affairs: The United Kingdom' (1986) 35 *ICLQ* 157.

167 [2011] EWHC 2274 (Comm), paras 21-5: 'In so far as it goes, the Foreign Secretary's certificate of 24 August 2011 is conclusive [evidence of the Council's legitimacy as government of Libya for the purposes of the Court], because in the field of foreign relations, the Crown in its executive and judicial functions speak with one voice'.

168 Dugard (1987) 9-10.

ple reflection of international law as it is, but how it might be. Martti Koskenniemi, introducing another of Lauterpacht's enduring works, *Function of Law*, observed that it 'could only have been written from within the German tradition, from a vivid sense of the urgency of the question of the legal system's ultimate foundation'.[169] The same may be said of *Recognition*, which by its terms sought to understand, widen and legitimate the underpinnings of international law as a legal system. As such, it serves as a case study for Lauterpacht's model of 'progressive interpretation'.[170]

Progressive interpretation as a methodology acts as a lodestone for the advancement of international law. In essence, it posits that international law 'should be functionally oriented towards both the establishment of peace between nations and the protection of fundamental human rights'.[171] The approach requires that various facts associated with life on the international plane – such as state practice or the behaviour of international organizations – 'be interpreted in line with [the] substantive function and value orientation'[172] of international law. Thus in the present context, if state practice pertaining to recognition can be interpreted so as to support an outcome conducive of the overall aims of international law, it ought to be.

Lauterpacht produced multiple works detailing the rationale and methodology of progressive interpretation, culminating in *Function of Law*. In doing so he drew on and then departed from the ideas of his teacher, Kelsen. One of the pioneers of positivism as it applies to modern international law, Kelsen's analysis of international law as a legal science was notably austere.[173] In contrast, Lauterpacht expressly adopted an empirical

---

169 Koskenniemi, in *Function of Law*, xxxv.

170 See e.g. H. Lauterpacht, 'The Reality of the Law of Nations' (Lecture given at the Royal Institute of International Affairs, Chatham House, London, 27 May 1941), reprinted in 2 *Collected Papers* 22, 47:

> [The] legitimate province [of international lawyers] is and must remain the exposition and *progressive interpretation* of the existing law in terms of the abiding purpose of the Law of Nations.

For a reappraisal along these lines see P. Capps, 'Lauterpacht's Method' (2012) 83 *BYIL* (*forthcoming*).

171 Capps (2012) 83 *BYIL* (*forthcoming*), §I. This was an enduring interest of Lauterpacht's, and his first article in English, on Westlake, highlights the purposive importance of the law of peace: H. Lauterpacht, 'Westlake and Present Day International Law' (1925) 5 *Economica* 307. Lauterpacht would later claim that international law had five social purposes, being (a) the prohibition of the use of force and protection of independence via collective security, (b) the peaceful settlement of disputes and obedience to the dictates of 'a supra-national political authority decreeing changes in the existing law' (i.e. the UN), (c) the promotion of human rights, (d) the development of moral standards applicable to states and individuals alike, and (e) the creation of a 'Commonwealth of States [...] rendered just and secure by the power of the impersonal sovereignty of a *civitas maxima*': 2 *Collected Papers* 22-55.

172 Capps (2012) 83 *BYIL* (*forthcoming*), §III.

173 Generally: H. Kelsen, *The Pure Theory of Law* (2nd edn, Verlag Franz Deuticke, 1960; tr M.

approach which was 'morally substantive and purposively oriented',[174] writing:

> A more satisfactory solution [to Kelsen's form of positivism] can be found in a hypothesis which, by courageously breaking with the traditions of a past period, incorporates the rational and ethical postulate, which is gradually becoming a fact, of an international community of interests and functions.[175]

Sentiments such as these led Koskenniemi, the foremost modern commentator on Lauterpacht, to draw certain conclusions about his position within the broad trajectory of international legal scholarship.[176] Koskenniemi sees Lauterpacht as representing the 'Victorian tradition' in international law, in comparison to Kelsen's modernism:

> Lauterpacht's Victorianism [...] relies on the interlocutor's willingness to take for granted the intrinsic rationality of a morality of sweet reasonableness, the non-metaphysical doctrine of the golden middle. It relies not on general principles or logical deductions as would a Thomistic, religious morality. It is a morality of attitude at least as much as substance, a morality of putting one's foot down when everybody's arguments have been given a hearing [...] It is an individualist morality controlled by the attempt to balance right with duty and freedom with reason. It is the morality of control and self-control for which the greatest desire is the end of desire. Lauterpacht accepts Spinoza's dictum: '[t]he man is free who lives, not according to the right of nature but according to reason. And it is liberty achieved through obedience to reason which is the ultimate object of the state'.[177]

Lauterpacht's so-called 'Victorian' sensibilities reveal his essential, almost unshakable optimism about the capacity of international law to provide a complete and ordered legal system: '[h]is utopianism remained grounded in the idea that a rational man, convinced that peace and social order through law were inescapable rational necessities and political passion an external distortion'.[178] From a theoretical standpoint, this was manifested

---

Knight, University of California Press, 1970). Also: J. Von Bernstorff, *The Public International Law Theory of Hans Kelsen. Believing in Universal Law* (Cambridge University Press, 2010).

174 Capps (2012) 83 *BYIL* (*forthcoming*), §III(1). Further: Koskenniemi (2002) 366; von Bernstorff (2010) 207-12.

175 H. Lauterpacht, 'The Nature of International Law and General Jurisprudence' (1932) 12 *Economica* 301, reprinted in 2 *Collected Papers* 3, 18. On Lauterpacht's rejection of Kelsen, see further: Koskenniemi (2002) 408-9.

176 Generally: M. Koskenniemi, 'Lauterpacht: The Victorian Tradition in International Law' (1997) 8 *EJIL* 215, essentially reprinted in Koskenniemi (2002) ch 5.

177 Koskenniemi (2002) 410-11, citing H. Lauterpacht, 'Spinoza and International Law' (1927) 8 *BYIL* 89, reprinted in 2 *Collected Papers* 366, 374.

178 Koskenniemi (2002) 407.

most strongly in *Function of Law*, in which Lauterpacht posited the existence of 'a gapless legal order [that] defend[ed] in legal terms the unity of a world that seemed to be headed from fragmentation to collapse'.[179]

A central element of *Function of Law* was to render every event of international policy amenable to legal analysis:[180] were the distinction between the legal and the political in international relations to be upheld, a state's evasion of legal adjudication with respect to international disputes could be seen as the simple application of the distinction. So divided, the binding nature of obligations would be left to the individual state so 'bound', depriving it of the very substance of a legal obligation: '[a]n obligation whose scope is left to the free appreciation of the obligee, so that his will constitutes a legal condition of the existence of the legal duty, does not constitute a legal bond'.[181] *Function of Law* thus posits the existence of an international judiciary with the capacity to preside over essentially political issues, and to fill gaps in the law to ensure that the vital interests of the international community – and the individuals within it – are secured.[182]

Seen within this framework, *Recognition* is the continuation and practical manifestation of the legal order hypothesised in *Function of Law*. In positing recognition as a

---

179 Ibid, 411.

180 *Function of Law*, 165-8.

181 Ibid, 197. This was ironically the very point that Carr made against Lauterpacht – precisely because there cannot be a distinction between law and politics, politics will remain ascendant: Carr (1939; reprinted 2001) 139. Further Koskenniemi (2002) 368.

182 *Function of Law*, 210-49. Lauterpacht's view on this point is now widely accepted by the international judiciary, even if states persist in claiming that the political character of certain issues renders them, if not non-justiciable, then inappropriate for legal adjudication. See, e.g. *Kosovo*, Advisory Opinion of 22 July 2010, paras 26, 27:

> Whatever its political aspects, the Court cannot refuse to respond to the legal elements of a question which invites it to discharge an essentially judicial task, namely, in the present case, an assessment of an act by reference to international law. The Court has also made clear that, in determining the jurisdictional issue of whether it is confronted with a legal question, it is not concerned with the political nature of the motives which may have inspired the request or the political implications which its opinion might have.

Further: *Wall*, ICJ Reports 2004 p 136; *Legality of the Threat or Use of Nuclear Weapons* ICJ Reports 1996 p 226, 234; *Border and Transborder Armed Actions (Nicaragua v Honduras)*, Jurisdiction and Admissibility, ICJ Reports 1988 p 69, 91; *Interpretation of the Agreement of 25 March 1951 between the WHO and Egypt*, ICJ Reports 1980 p 73, 87; *United States Diplomatic and Consular Staff in Tehran (United States of America v Islamic Republic of Iran)*, Provisional Measures, ICJ Reports 1979 p 7, 15; ibid, ICJ Reports 1980 p 3, 20; *Application for Review of Judgment No 158 of the United Nations Administrative Tribunal*, ICJ Reports 1973 p 166, 171-2; *Certain Expenses of the United Nations (Article 17,paragraph 2 of the Charter)*, ICJ Reports 1962 p 151, 155; *Competence of the General Assembly for the Admission of a State to the United Nations*, ICJ Reports 1950 p 4, 6-7; *Conditions of Admission of a State in Membership of the United Nations (Article 4 of the Charter)*, ICJ Reports 1948, p 57, 61. But

predominantly legal act within the political framework of constitutivism, Lauterpacht suggests how international legal order might be brought about: '[w]hat first appears as an act of political will is revealed as an exercise of interpretive discretion'.[183] If, as has been posited, Lauterpacht's interwar works *Analogies*, *Function of Law* and *Development* form a loose thematic 'trilogy' on the place of the judicial process in international organization and the development of international law,[184] then *Recognition* forms a coda to these works, designed to answer the essential preliminary question of how might the politics of international relations be recast so as to make them susceptible to legal analysis and adjudication.

Thus, the perceived excesses identified in *Recognition* by Kunz and others are justified by reference to Lauterpacht's wider project and to progressive interpretation as a legal methodology. Whilst an idealist when considering the *prospects* of international law, Lauterpacht was under no illusions as to the relative weakness of the system at the time he was writing – although he was remarkably reticent as to the details.[185] In terms of an institutional ideal, Lauterpacht may be classified as a Neo-Kantian,[186] in that he saw a comprehensive international organization backed by legal norms as the terminus of international law: '[i]nternational law will not achieve a full measure of reality until it is organically woven into the fabric of a supra-national entity'.[187] This accounts for the emphasis on collective processes in *Recognition*. But Lauterpacht was also aware that international law – at least under the influence of the severe form of positivism that characterised the interwar period – could not be relied upon to reach this goal by itself. It needed to be guided to it, possibly against its own instincts and the internal ordering of the system. *Recognition* represents such a guide, reinterpreting (indeed reimagining)

cf *Haya de la Torre (Columbia v Peru)*, ICJ Reports 1971 p 71, 79.

183 Koskenniemi (2002) 383.

184 Jenks (1960) 36 *BYIL* 1, 36.

185 He seems never to have used the word 'Hitler' in any of his published works. It is not to be found in his *Collected Papers*.

186 See further I. Kant, 'Perpetual Peace: A Philosophical Sketch' (1795), reproduced in H. Reiss (ed), *Kant: Political Writings* (2nd edn, Cambridge University Press, 1992) 93, 105:

> There is only one rational way in which states coexisting with other states can emerge from the lawless condition of pure warfare. Just like individual men, they must renounce their savage and lawless freedom, adapt themselves to public coercive laws, and thus form an *international state* (*civitas gentium*), which would necessarily continue to grow until it embraced all the peoples of the earth. But since this is not the will of the nations, according to their present conception of international right … the positive idea of a *world republic* cannot be realised. If all is not to be lost, this can at best find a negative substitute in the shape of an enduring and gradually expanding *federation* likely to prevent war. The latter may check the current of man's inclination to defy the law and antagonise his fellows, although there will always be a risk of it bursting forth anew.

187 2 *Collected Papers* 47.

state practice with an eye to progressive development of the law, recharacterizing the practice of recognition as fundamentally legal, and setting forth a temporary and ordered solution to the political vicissitudes of the institution until such time as the needs of the international community can be addressed by a supra-national entity.

Such an analysis in effect answers Kunz's criticism that the state practice of recognition – and indeed international law as a whole – ought to be studied in a 'neutral and impartial' way.[188] The meaning of state practice 'is only revealed as international legal doctrine to the extent that it conforms to an immanent understanding of the function of the international legal order'.[189] It was thus Lauterpacht's notion of the wider purpose of international law that enabled *Recognition* to be written. It is, in effect, a proof of concept, an example of how international law could, with relatively few additions, come to represent a complete system of norms, dedicated to the preservation of peace and legal order within the community of nations. Although its vision has not come to pass, its merit has not dimmed.

Cambridge
17 August 2012

188 Kunz (1950) 44 *AJIL* 713, 713
189 Capps (2012) 83 *BYIL* (*forthcoming*), §III(2).

Part One

RECOGNITION OF STATES

Chapter I

INTRODUCTORY

§ 1. *The Problem of Recognition in the Science of International Law.* According to what is probably still the predominant view in the literature of international law, recognition of States is not a matter governed by law but a question of policy.[1] It is urged that recognition is the result of a decision taken not in the execution of a legal duty, but in pursuance of the exigencies of national interest. If this is so, how is it that recognition looms so large in the writings of those very jurists who hold that it is, as such, outside the law? The answer is that, while denying the quality of law to the act of recognition, some of them maintain that this act of policy, once accomplished, entails legal consequences, inasmuch as it is the starting point of international personality with all the rights pertaining thereto; that, in any case, the form and the circumstances of recognition are of legal interest and necessitate the consideration of such questions as the distinction between *de jure* and *de facto* recognition, implied recognition, and conditional recognition; and that important questions of law arise when that act of policy constitutes so-called premature recognition in disregard of the rights of the parent State. But the dominant fact remains that the very commencement of the international personality of States and the question of their legal right to existence as such are declared by these writers to be outside the orbit of international law.

This situation has been obscured by the circumstance that the problem of recognition of States has been identified with the controversy between the rival doctrines of the declaratory and the constitutive character of recognition. The opposition of these two doctrines has for a long time dominated the discussion on the subject. Both have denied that recognition is a matter of legal duty in relation to the community which claims it.

1 It is suggested below, see pp. 158, 240, that in the matter of recognition of governments and of belligerency the political view of recognition can no longer be regarded as predominant.

The constitutive theory, as commonly propounded, culminates in two assertions: the first is that, prior to recognition, the community in question possesses neither the rights nor the obligations which international law associates with full statehood; the second is that recognition is a matter of absolute political discretion as distinguished from a legal duty owed to the community concerned. These two views, it will be shown, are not inconsistent. That much cannot be said of the theory of the declaratory nature of recognition. The latter fully accepts the view of the rival doctrine according to which there does not exist, in any circumstances, a legal duty to grant recognition. At the same time, with some lack of consistency, it maintains that prior to recognition the nascent community exists as a State and is entitled to many of the most important attributes of statehood. This means, upon analysis, that the newcomer is entitled as a matter of legal right to claim what are usually regarded as the normal legal consequences of recognition, but that it is not entitled to claim recognition as such. The difficulty has been thought to be met by dint of the assertion—which is contrary to the practice of governments and of courts—that the only meaning of recognition is a political declaration of willingness to enter into normal diplomatic relations. This questionable solution has been regarded as preferable to accepting the main tenet of the constitutive doctrine according to which a purely discretionary political act of recognition is creative of substantive rights—indeed, of the very existence—of statehood.

The repudiation of the legal nature of recognition, i.e. the denial of the existence of a duty to recognize and of a right to recognition, notwithstanding the presence of requisite factual conditions, is grounded in the same attitude which has brought into being the orthodox constitutive doctrine. It is the attitude congenial to the type of positivism current in the literature of international law. If, in conformity with the positivist teaching, the will of the State is the sole source of its obligations, then it is impossible to concede that the existing States can have fresh duties thrust upon them as the result of the emergence of a politically organized community which they are henceforth bound to recognize as a State.

It would have been natural for those adhering to the declaratory doctrine to feel no hesitation in accepting the view of recognition as a juridical act performed in the fulfilment of a legal duty. For there is but one step—which is certainly not a revolutionary one—between maintaining that an act is merely declaratory of a fact of primary importance in the life of a nation and treating that act as one of legal duty. However, such is the lure of respectability which has attached to the positivist creed that most of those committed to the declaratory doctrine have felt it incumbent upon them to join the opposing doctrine in denying the legal nature of the act of recognition and in finding in that view the hall mark of positivist orthodoxy.[1]

§ 2. *The Place of Recognition in the Relations of States.* The concentration on the controversy between the constitutive and the declaratory doctrines, as well as the tendency to apply the positivist method also in this branch of international law, have been responsible for the present unsatisfactory position of the law of recognition. The practice of States, after allowance has been made for the discrepancies due to the political implication of the function of recognition, supplies a satisfactory basis for conceiving and presenting the process of recognition, in all its manifestations, as an act of law as distinguished from policy. From that practice it is possible to extract legal principles capable of general application. There ought to be no doubt as to the urgency and the intrinsic justification of such principles. For the problem of recognition—not only of States, but also of Governments and of belligerency—touches the life of States in its most vital aspects. It confronts it, in the form of recognition of statehood, at the point of its emergence into the international arena; it faces the State, in connection with recognition of governments, at times of internal and external crises brought about by the revolutionary break in the legal continuity of its constitutional existence; and it confronts it in the shape of recognition of belligerency, at periods of violent commotions when on the battlefield of civil war the nation seeks a solution of intense clashes of creed and interests. Yet, notwithstanding its obvious significance, recognition, as taught by writers, constitutes one of the weakest links in international law. The science of international law can no longer avoid the task of inquiring whether this state of affairs is due to a clear defect of the law of nations as expressed in the practice of States or whether it is attributable to the failure of lawyers to give an accurate account of the practice of States and to analyse it by reference to a jurisprudential principle of order as distinguished from amorphous maxims of policy. An inquiry of this nature is of special urgency at a time when the foundations are being laid of an improved international order.

There is an instructive analogy in this matter between recognition and

1 Kunz, p. 67, goes to the length of maintaining that most of the adherents of the declaratory view are positivists. This is probably an exaggeration. But there are in fact some positivists who incline to the declaratory view of recognition. See, for example, De Louter, *Le droit international public positif* (French translation, 1920), vol. 1, p. 216; Ullmann, *Völkerrecht* (2nd ed. 1908), p. 67; Liszt, *Völkerrecht* (12th ed. by Fleischmann, 1925), p. 91.

the place of war in international law. Thus, prior to the General Treaty for the Renunciation of War of 1928, the admissibility of war as an instrument both for enforcing and for changing the law constituted the principal defect of the law of nations. In time of peace States were rigidly bound to respect the existence, the independence and even the dignity of other members of international society. Recourse to reprisals was regulated by principles circumscribing the conditions and the extent of their application. But by availing itself of its unlimited right to declare war the State could gain full freedom from these restraints and acquire the right to treat its neighbour thus attacked as a veritable *caput lupinum* to the point of legally permissible annihilation through conquest and annexation. The legal admissibility of war showed how unreal was the border-line between law and lawlessness, between the duty to let live and the right to extinguish. It showed that law obtained only so long as States were willing to tolerate it, and that it was left to them to divest themselves of the most fundamental of all duties by one legally authorized arbitrary act.

This glaring gap in the effective validity of international law has been chosen here as an example not only for the reason that it constitutes a weakness much more real than the absence of enforcement or of overriding international legislation. It has been selected because it throws light upon a phenomenon similar to that created by the law of recognition as expounded, at least with regard to recognition of States, by the dominant school of thought. The State is bound by minute rules to respect the sovereignty and independence of other States. But as, in accordance with the traditional view of the function of war, it is left to its free discretion, by availing itself of the unlimited right of war, to assail the very existence of other States, so, in the light of the predominant doctrine of recognition, it is free to decide, according to its unfettered discretion and by consulting its own interests only, whether another community shall enjoy the rights of sovereignty and independence inherent in statehood. By the simple device of refusing—or possibly of withdrawing—recognition, a State is legally entitled, according to a widely adopted view, to deny the right of independent existence to a political community apparently fulfilling the conditions of statehood.

The position is analogous in the case of recognition of governments. A State participates in the benefits of international law largely through the medium of its government. To decline to recognize the government of a State is to refuse, to a substantial extent, to recognize the State itself and to accord it what is its due in the international sphere. Such a refusal results in treating as non-existent the legislative, judicial and administrative acts of the State whose government has been refused recognition; it entails in many cases the suspension of the operation of treaties concluded by former governments; and it has even been suggested that it deprives the government in question of the capacity to wage war.[1] In the case of a civil war the consequences of that alleged right to grant or refuse recognition according to discretion show themselves in an even more glaring manner. A right thus conceived may, in effect, amount to granting to foreign States a licence to withdraw recognition from the lawful government and to bestow it arbitrarily upon the rebels, with all the profound consequences following from that change in the legal status of the two sides.[2] To say, therefore, that the granting of recognition to a new government is a matter of discretion unfettered by legal principle is to maintain that, also in this matter, the line dividing law and arbitrariness is altogether illusory. Similar consequences, in a different sphere, follow from the view that in the case of a civil war the recognition of belligerency, with all the rights attaching thereto, is on the part of foreign States a matter of mere grace and political convenience.

In all these cases the view that recognition is not a function consisting in the fulfilment of an international duty but an act of national policy independent of binding legal principle, has had the further result of divorcing recognition from the scientific bases of fact on which all law must ultimately rest. That basis is the assumption that international personality, governmental capacity, and the competence to exercise the rights of a belligerent in a civil war, must all be determined primarily by reference to the actual conditions of power and effectiveness, evidenced by an adequate expression of the consent of the governed, of the authorities claiming recognition in these various capacities. Law must be based on facts—in so

1 'In view of the fact that the Government of the United States has not recognised the existence in the Republic of Costa Rica of a *de jure* or even a legitimately *de facto* Government, but holds that only the people of Costa Rica can as a moral force set up in that country a government constitutional in character and duly sanctioned by a law, it follows naturally that the Government of the United States could not recognise as legally existent any manifestation of such a Government.

'To declare war is one of the highest acts of sovereignty. The Government of Costa Rica being for the Government of the United States legally non-existent, it follows that so far as the Government of the United States is concerned, no state of war could exist between Costa Rica and the Imperial German Government. Obviously there could be no question so far as this Government was concerned as to signing with Costa Rica the Treaty of Peace of Versailles': Secretary Lansing to President Wilson, 16 August 1919. *U.S. For. Rel.* 1919 (1), p. 853.

2 See, for instance, the recognition of the revolutionary government in Spain by Italy and Germany in November 1936, at the beginning of the civil war. See below, p. 95.

far as such facts are not in themselves contrary to law. Successful secession from the parent State is a fact which is not contrary to international law; the same applies to a rebellion resulting in a revolutionary government or in a civil war. This being so, these events are facts which, if law is to approximate to social reality, must, through the medium of the legally obligatory act of recognition, be permitted to produce the appropriate legal results.

§ 3. *The Principles of Recognition of States.* It is by reference to these general considerations and in anticipation of the results of the survey, to be undertaken in the ensuing chapters, of the practice of governments that the following principles of recognition of States are here provisionally submitted:

To recognize a political community as a State is to declare that it fulfils the conditions of statehood as required by international law. If these conditions are present, the existing States are under the duty to grant recognition. In the absence of an international organ competent to ascertain and authoritatively to declare the presence of requirements of full international personality, States already established fulfil that function in their capacity as organs of international law. In thus acting they administer the law of nations. This legal rule signifies that in granting or withholding recognition States do not claim and are not entitled to serve exclusively the interests of their national policy and convenience regardless of the principles of international law in the matter. Although recognition is thus declaratory of an existing fact, such declaration, made in the impartial fulfilment of a legal duty, is constitutive, as between the recognizing State and the community so recognized, of international rights and duties associated with full statehood. Prior to recognition such rights and obligations exist only to the extent to which they have been expressly conceded or legitimately asserted, by reference to compelling rules of humanity and justice, either by the existing members of international society or by the people claiming recognition.

These principles are believed to have been accepted by the preponderant practice of States. They are also considered to represent rules of conduct most consistent with the fundamental requirements of international law conceived as a system of law. However, although followed in practice with some regularity, they cannot be regarded as having been uniformly acted upon or clearly perceived by governments. Neither have they secured the assent of the majority of writers on the subject.

Chapter II

THE LEGAL NATURE OF RECOGNITION AND THE PRACTICE OF STATES

§ 4. *The Legal Conception of Recognition and Premature Recognition.* The principal feature of the prevalent doctrine of recognition of States is the assertion that recognition is, in its essential aspect, namely, in relation to the community claiming it, an act of policy as distinguished from the fulfilment of a legal duty. It is possible to criticize that view by reference to a compelling legal principle which forbids us to admit that a legal system either fails to determine what are the requirements of legal personality or, what is the same, that it permits that legal personality shall be in the gift of the already existing members of the community acting by exclusive reference to their own interests, to the passing whim of their sympathies, or to considerations of opportunism. We are not at liberty to assume, without overwhelming proof, the existence of a gap so detrimental to the reality of the international legal order.

Does the practice of States suggest that the granting or refusal of recognition is a matter of political expediency and not of binding legal principle? Do States in this matter profess allegiance—and it is their disclosed profession that is of juridical interest, not the surmised political motive and interest behind it—to a compelling rule of law, or do they act as if they were free to follow exclusive considerations of political convenience? In particular, is there any aspect of recognition of States which by general consent is regarded as being governed by rules of law as distinguished from policy, and if so, what is its relevance to the question of the nature of the act of recognition, namely, to the problem of the right to be recognized and of the duty to recognize?

There is no doubt that at least one aspect of the matter is by general agreement governed by international law, namely, what may be called the tortious or delictual aspect of recognition. It is contrary to international law to grant premature recognition. Communities claiming recognition do so, as a rule, following upon secession from the parent State. It is generally agreed that, in relation to the latter, recognition is governed by a duty of restraint the disregard of which entails responsibility on the part of the recognizing State. It is almost exclusively from this point of view that recognition of States has been discussed in the literature of international law and in diplomatic correspondence. The question, which has seldom been seriously denied, whether France committed a breach of international law by her early recognition of the United States in 1778;[1] the protracted controversy concerning the Spanish protests against the recognition of the Latin-American Republics by the United States and Great Britain;[2] the demand of the Confederate States for recognition during the American Civil War, a demand which was discussed mainly not from the point of view of the right of the Confederacy to recognition but by reference to the propriety of such a step in relation to the United States;[3] the recognition of Panama by the United States in 1903, a question which has been debated from the same point of view[4]—all these incidents have occupied writers from the point of view of premature recognition. It is generally[5] agreed that premature recognition is more than an unfriendly act; it is an act of intervention and an international delinquency. The community claiming recognition must fulfil certain conditions of permanency and political cohesion. In particular, the parent State must in fact have ceased to make efforts, promising success, to reassert its authority. Recognition is unlawful if granted *durante bello*, when the outcome of the struggle is altogether uncertain. Such recognition is a denial of the sovereignty of the parent State. It has not the excuse of being dictated by the necessities of intercourse, for international law, notwithstanding the vagaries of the doctrine of implied recognition,[6] permits various forms of intercourse short of recognition of a government or a new State. International law does not condemn rebellion or secession aiming at acquisition of independence. At the same time, save for collective measures of permissible intervention for the sake of humanity or of a general international settlement, as in the case of the recognition of Greek independence in 1830 or of Belgian independence in 1831, it forbids third States to favour insurrection by recognizing the insurgents as a State before they have succeeded in establishing themselves beyond all reasonable doubt. This principle was clearly

1 See below, p. 50.
2 See below, pp. 14–16, 18.
3 See below, p. 17.
4 See below, p. 22.
5 There is practical unanimity among international lawyers about this aspect of the law. But see Anzilotti, *Corso di diritto internazionale* (1928), p. 93, for a clear assertion to the contrary: 'Il riconoscimento non è legato a particolari condizioni o presupposti...il diritto internazionale non conosce casi di riconoscimento lecito o illecito, vietato o imposto; le considerazioni sulla tempestività del riconoscimento... sembrano di natura politica più che giuridica.' This extreme positivist assertion, which is contrary to frequent pronouncements of governments, is a consistent application of the doctrine that the grant or refusal of recognition is the result of a political decision in all circumstances.
6 See below, pp. 388–90.

expressed by a distinguished Secretary of State of the United States as early as 1823, at a time when inclination and policy might have counselled a less restrained course: 'So long as a contest of arms, with a rational or even remote prospect of eventual success, was maintained by Spain, the United States could not recognize the independence of the colonies as existing *de facto* without trespassing on their duties to Spain by assuming as decided that which was precisely the question of the war.'[1]

Premature recognition is a wrong not only because, in denying the sovereignty of the parent State actively engaged in asserting its authority, it amounts to unlawful intervention.[2] It is a wrong because it constitutes an abuse of the power of recognition. It acknowledges as an independent State a community which is not, in law, independent and which does not therefore fulfil the essential conditions of statehood. It is, accordingly, a recognition which an international tribunal would declare not only to constitute a wrong,[3] but probably also to be in itself invalid.

§ 5. *Tests of Premature Recognition.* Whether the recognition is premature is a question of fact. The practice of States is not devoid of useful guidance in this matter. Thus mere protests and assertions of sovereignty unaccompanied by attempts to restore the challenged authority of the mother country can safely be and have been disregarded. Apart from the temporary and futile attempts to introduce the principle of legitimacy, the formal renunciation of sovereignty by the parent State has never been regarded as a condition of the lawfulness of recognition.[4] For parent States are naturally slow in acknowledging the independence of revolted provinces. They often announce, with pathetic finality, that no such

1 Instruction of Mr Adams to Mr Anderson, United States Minister to Colombia, of 27 May 1823: Manning, *Diplomatic Correspondence of the United States concerning the Independence of the Latin-American Nations*, vol. I (Parts I–II) (1925), p. 194.

2 On occasions premature recognition has been described as an unfriendly act. See, for example, President Jackson's Message as to Texas of 21 December 1836: Moore, vol. I, p. 98. See also Fedozzi, *Trattato di diritto internazionale* (2nd ed. 1933), p. 193: 'Tanto un riconoscimento tardato, quanto d' altro lato un riconoscimento prematuro, possono essere considerati come atti non amichevoli.' Actually, such recognition is an illegal, as distinguished from an unfriendly act. It will be noticed that Fedozzi refers in this connection also to tardy recognition.

3 See, for example, Moore, vol. I, p. 73, who regards the recognition of the United States by France in 1778 as an act of intervention; and see ibid. p. 110, as to the Joint Resolution of Congress approved on 20 April 1898 declaring the people of Cuba to be free and independent.

4 For a clear statement to the effect that third States can validly recognize the new State before the mother country has given its recognition see *Deutsche Continental Gas-Gesellschaft* v. *Polish State*, decided by the German-Polish Mixed Arbitral Tribunal: *Annual Digest*, 1929–30, Case no. 5 (*b*).

acknowledgment would ever be forthcoming.[1] The Netherlands declared their independence of Spain in 1576. Before two decades had elapsed that independence was recognized by Great Britain and France. But the Spanish renunciation of her sovereignty did not take place until the Treaty of Münster of 1648. Portugal, which became separated from Spain in 1640, was recognized by her in 1668. Belgium, whose independence was recognized by the European Powers in 1831,[2] was not recognized by the mother country until 1839. The independence of Mexico and other Latin-American States was recognized by the United States in 1822 and by Great Britain soon after, but the mother country did not recognize Mexico until 1836. The independence of Panama was recognized by most States within a year of her secession from Colombia in 1903. But when Colombia joined the League of Nations in 1920, she put on record the fact that her acceptance of Article 10 of the Covenant did not imply the recognition of the independence of the Republic of Panama.[3]

On the other hand, the initial success of the rebellion, even if apparently complete, does not establish the independence of the insurgent community in a manner to make recognition permissible. The shifting fortunes of the war of independence of the South American Republics afford an instructive example of the danger of drawing hasty conclusions from apparently well-established facts.[4] Similarly, occasions may arise when the mother country, because of internal commotions or for similar reasons, is temporarily prostrate and not in a position to assert her authority. This was the case, for instance, with regard to the various States which arose in 1917 and 1918 within the territory of Russia. The United States and, to some extent, Great Britain, refused for a time recognition *de jure* to Esthonia, Latvia and

1 This may on occasions be an imprudent announcement seeing that it supplies third States with a good reason for disregarding altogether the attitude of the parent State: 'For this [Spanish] declaration plainly shows, that the complaint against us is not merely as to the mode or the time of our advances to those States; it shows that the dispute between us and Spain is not merely as to the question of fact....It shows that no extent of forbearance on our part would have satisfied Spain...if the argument on which this declaration is founded be true, it is eternal': Canning's note to the Spanish Minister in London of 25 March 1825: *B.F.S.P.* vol. XII, p. 909.

2 De Louter, a Dutch author, describes this recognition as premature '...sans même attendre que la Holland pût reconnaître le nouvel état de choses, renoncer formellement à son opposition ou s'avouer incapable d'étouffer l'insurrection': *Le droit international public positif* (French translation, 1920), vol. I, p. 222. In this case probably the very fact that the recognition took place through a collective act of the Powers in a manner indicative of an international settlement raises the presumption that the recognition was not premature.

3 *U.S. For. Rel.* 1920 (I), p. 825.

4 The Chilean revolution broke out in 1810. It was suppressed by the Spanish troops in 1814. Not until 1817 did the insurgents gain a decisive victory.

Finland on the ground that the possibility of a united Russia, then in the throes of revolutionary convulsions, was not altogether outside the range of possibilities.[1] This very hesitation, which a hasty estimate may mistake for an infusion of an arbitrary element of politics into the process of recognition, is, on the contrary, an example of the desire to steer clear of the illegality of premature recognition.

§ 6. *Prohibition of Premature Recognition and the Legal Nature of Recognition.* The established rule of international law prohibiting premature recognition of States is not without bearing on the seemingly different question as to the right of a community to claim recognition by third States and as to the duty of the latter to grant recognition. For, upon analysis, the substance of the rule relating to premature recognition is that it gives expression to the objective requirements which make the grant of recognition legally permissible. It formulates the conditions rendering the

1 It appears that as late as October 1920 Great Britain considered the possibility of a reconstituted and unified Russia as a reason for delaying the recognition *de jure* of the Baltic States. It was felt that if *de jure* recognition were granted to the Baltic provinces, their request for admission to the League of Nations could not be refused and that, as a result, members of the League might, in consequence of Article 10 of the Covenant, come into conflict with a reconstituted Russia. The attitude of the United States in the matter was officially stated on a number of occasions. The full independence *de jure* of Esthonia, Latvia and Lithuania was announced by the United States on 28 July 1922, in the following terms: 'The Governments of Esthonia, Latvia and Lithuania have been recognized either *de jure* or *de facto* by the principal Governments of Europe and have entered into treaty relations with their neighbors. In extending to them recognition on its part, the Government of the United States takes cognizance of the actual existence of these Governments during a considerable period of time and of the successful maintenance within their borders of political and economic stability. The United States has consistently maintained that the disturbed conditions of Russian affairs may not be made the occasion for the alienation of Russian territory, and this principle is not deemed to be infringed by the recognition at this time of the Governments of Esthonia, Latvia and Lithuania which have been set up and maintained by an indigenous population' (*U.S. For. Rel.* 1922 (II), p. 873). On the original attitude of the United States with regard to the recognition of Lithuania and other Baltic States see ibid. 1920 (III), pp. 465, 466: 'We are unwilling that while it is helpless in the grip of non-representative government, whose only sanction is brutal force, Russia shall be weakened still further by a policy of dismemberment, conceived in other than Russian interests.' See also ibid. p. 659: 'The Government has held constantly to the belief that Russia—the Russia of 1917—must herself be a party to any readjustments of her frontiers.' For these reasons the United States recognized the independence of Armenia, but refused to recognize that of Georgia and Azerbaijan. The recognition extended to Armenia was 'to the government of the Armenian State as a *de facto* Government on the condition that this recognition in no way prejudges the question of the eventual frontiers': ibid. pp. 777, 778. See also Laserson in *A.J.* vol. XXXVII (1943), p. 242. For some interesting details concerning the early history of the various States and governments which arose within the territory of Russia in 1917 and 1918 see *U.S. For. Rel.* 1918, *Russia*, vol. II.

grant of recognition a step which is in accordance with the requirements of international stability and intercourse, so as to justify what would otherwise constitute an interference with the legal rights of the parent State. This being so, the insistence on the difference between the right to recognize (in relation to the mother country) and the duty to recognize (in relation to the community claiming recognition) may be formally correct, but is not as convincing as appears at first sight. It is not easy to concede that, in substance, the conditions of recognition are one thing when looked at from the point of view of the duty to the parent State and another thing when viewed as a matter of obligation to the community asking for recognition.

When the struggle for independence has obtained a tangible measure of success accompanied by a reasonable prospect of permanency, international law authorizes third States to declare, by means of recognition of the nascent community, that the sovereignty of the parent State is extinct. International law attaches a distinct legal effect to the situation thus created. That effect cannot be limited to the relations between the parent State and the community claiming recognition. It necessarily enures to the benefit of the new State. This explains the interesting phenomenon that while governments in diplomatic correspondence answer the complaints of the parent State by asserting their right, under international law, to recognize the rebellious community, they are often driven to invoke their duty to grant recognition.[1] Similarly, in refusing recognition on the ground that it would be premature, governments often put the matter in such a way as to deny that, in the circumstances of the case, the community which has risen in revolt is entitled to recognition. Thus we find President McKinley in his Annual Message of 11 April 1898, laying down that 'recognition of independent statehood is not due to a revolted dependency until the danger of its being again subjugated by the parent state has entirely passed away'.[2] On a previous occasion he commended to the consideration of Congress the question 'whether the Cuban insurrection possesses beyond dispute the attributes of statehood which alone can demand the recognition of belligerency in its favor'.[3]

§ 7. *The Duty of Recognition and the Practice of States.* (*a*) *The Practice of Great Britain.* What may be described as the tortious aspect of recognition supplies indirect evidence in support of the view that recognition of States is essentially a matter of legal right and duty as between the State granting and receiving recognition. But can we find more direct proof in support of

1 See below, pp. 19, 22. 2 Moore, vol. I, p. 109. 3 Ibid.

the legal view of recognition? Such direct evidence must be sought in the declarations and correspondence of governments in so far as they discuss the question of recognition as a matter of principle. Of these there are two kinds. There are, first, governmental pronouncements defending the right to grant recognition, in the particular case, irrespective of the attitude of the mother country; there are, secondly, pronouncements relating to the duty to recognize. The first are frequent. The second, more directly relevant to the issue here discussed, are rare. They are so because States have as a rule no compelling reason or inclination to expatiate on their duty to the seceding community; on the other hand, they have had occasion to vindicate, as against the complaints of the parent State, their right to grant recognition. It is this last aspect of the matter which has loomed large in diplomatic correspondence. As the result, the impression has gained ground that the question of recognition in relation to the community claiming it is not affirmatively governed by rules of law at all. Yet, although conditions have not been propitious, there is available some substantial evidence bearing on this aspect of the problem. The cumulative effect of that evidence is to make it difficult to understand why, apart from the temporary ascendancy of a theoretical brand of positivism, the predominant political view of recognition has become so firmly established.

There is probably no deliberate pronouncement of a government on record in which the granting or refusal of recognition of statehood is expressly claimed to be a matter of grace or, exclusively, of political expediency. It is not easy to point to any State document which professes to be based on the principle such as is, for instance, laid down by Fauchille (an author who was an adherent of the declaratory view of recognition): 'Les Etats sont libres de reconnaître ou de ne pas reconnaître un Etat récemment formé, de se déterminer selon les convenances de leur politique.'[1] What appears to be the only passage approaching a claim of this nature is the statement by Canning, made in his despatch of 30 November 1822, to the British Minister in Madrid, in which he said: 'The Recognition [of the new States of Latin America] of any other Power [other than Spain] may undoubtedly be given or withholden at its own good pleasure and may be made contingent or conditional.'[2] The context of the passage shows that what was intended was not an assertion of an arbitrary right in relation to the communities which had risen in revolt, but a clear and emphatic reservation of the right to grant or to refuse recognition irre-

1 Vol. I, p. 318.

2 Printed in Smith, vol. I, p. 132, and Webster, *Britain and the Independence of Latin America*, 1812–1830, vol. II (1938), p. 400.

spective of the attitude of Spain. The despatch was sent in connection with the proposed mediation by Great Britain. 'A Power', explained Canning, 'which while undertaking to mediate between the Parties should declare its recognition of the Colonies to be contingent upon that of the Mother Country, would, in truth, be anything but impartial: it would throw its whole weight into the scale of Spain, and would (in case of a failure of the Negotiation) leave the Colonies in a worse situation than it found them.'[1] It cannot be maintained that the element of Great Britain's own convenience and commercial interest did not enter into the matter at all. But these factors were not antagonistic to—they were part of—considerations of a more general nature; they were germane to the convenience and commercial interest of the world at large; they were claimed to have been adopted for reasons of humanity and by reference to general principles of international law;[2] they were dictated by a sense of the practical necessities of the situation in which a mere pretension asserted itself hopelessly against the triumphant independence of the rebellious republics. 'No man', said Canning in the crucial memorandum to the Cabinet of 15 November 1822,[3] 'will say that there is a reasonable hope of her recovering that jurisdiction. No man will say that under such circumstances our Recognition of these States can be indefinitely postponed.' In another communication Canning gave eloquent expression to the underlying facts of the situation. In his despatch of 30 January 1824 to the British Minister in Madrid he said:

'It appears manifest to the British Government that if so large a portion of the globe should remain much longer without any recognized political existence or any definite political connexion with the established Governments of Europe, the consequences of such a state of things must be at once most embarrassing to those Governments, and most injurious to the interests of all European nations. For this reason, and not from mere views of selfish policy, the British Government is decidedly of opinion that the Recognition of such of the New States as have established, *de facto*, their separate political existence, cannot be much longer delayed.'[4]

The discretion which Great Britain claimed for herself was one of the time and of the degree of recognition. That time was hastened by what Canning called the 'overbearing arrogance of Spain' who embarked upon seizing British ships not because they were carrying contraband or were guilty of

1 Printed in Smith, vol. I, p. 132, and Webster, *Britain and the Independence of Latin America*, 1812–1830, vol. II (1938), p. 400.

2 See below, p. 16.

3 Printed in Webster, op. cit. vol. II, p. 393.

4 Ibid. p. 414; Manning, op. cit. vol. III (Parts VIII–XIV), p. 1516.

breach of a blockade but for the reason that they were engaged in trade with her former dependencies.

There was no intention to refuse to consider the situation from the point of view of the right of the insurgent communities to claim recognition. Thus in the final communication of 25 March 1825, addressed to the Chevalier de Los Rios, Spanish Minister to Great Britain, Canning asked: 'Has it ever been admitted as an axiom, or ever been observed by any nation or Government, as a practical maxim, that no circumstances and no time, should entitle a *de facto* government to recognition?'[1] Neither did he show any inclination to refute the idea that the South American Republics could be entitled to recognition when Sir James Mackintosh presented on 15 June 1824 the Petition from the Merchants of the City of London humbly submitting that 'these states have established, *de facto*, their separate political existence; and are, according to the practice of nations in former instances, entitled to be recognized as independent governments'.[2] He agreed with Sir James Mackintosh that 'we have no pretence to be so difficult and scrupulous, as to insist that a new government shall have all the stability of an old one before we acknowledge its independence'; but he urged 'some degree of caution before we can give our fiat'.[3]

In the important despatch of 14 March 1825,[4] addressed to Sir Charles Stuart, British Special Minister to Lisbon, Canning reverted to the same theme. Once, he said, 'that essential requisite', namely, 'the establishment of a substantive political existence with a competent power to maintain it at home and to cause it to be respected abroad' had been ascertained with respect to the several Spanish American provinces, 'there was nothing to prevent our acknowledgment of each as it became entitled to be considered as practically independent'. There followed the statement that 'our interests loudly prescribed the adjustment and cultivation of commercial relations with each of those several States'. Such references to the recognizing State's own interests are a conspicuous feature in the pronouncements of that period in the matter of recognition. They do not seriously affect the view, expressed with equal frequency, that recognition was due for the reason that the rebellious Provinces were 'entitled' to be considered

1 Manning, op. cit. vol. III (Parts VIII–XIV), p. 1544.

2 The Petition is printed in *The Speeches of The Right Honourable George Canning*, edited by Therry (2nd ed. 1830), vol. V, pp. 291–4.

3 Ibid. p. 302.

4 Webster, op. cit. vol. I, p. 264. In the same despatch there occurs (p. 263) the following significant passage: 'The questions to be decided...in each case of a Colony separating itself from the Mother Country were questions of fact and of time rather than of principle, and as to time, the decision of each recognizing State was necessarily to be guided by considerations of its own just interests and of general expediency....'

as independent. They rather tend to show, as in the analogous cases of recognition of belligerency, that recognition was being granted for reasons other than gratuitous interference unrelated to the legitimate interests for the recognizing State.

In general, Canning's utterances clearly indicated the lines of the subsequent practice. That practice is that governments base their attitude in matters of recognition not on any right to follow their own particular interests, but on principles derived from general considerations of international justice and utility. The frequently quoted British Note addressed by Canning to Spain on 25 March 1825, in reply to the Spanish protest against the British recognition of the independence of the Latin-American States, is an instructive instance of this approach to the subject. It relies to a large extent on principles governing State responsibility. It is convenient to quote the relevant passage in full:

'...all political Communities are responsible to other Political Communities for their conduct—that is, they are bound to perform the ordinary international duties, and to afford redress for any violation of the Rights of others by their Citizens or Subjects.

'Now, either the Mother Country must have continued responsible for acts, over which it could no longer exercise the shadow of a controul; or the inhabitants of those Countries, whose independent political existence was, in fact, established, but to whom the acknowledgment of that Independence was denied, must have been placed in a situation in which they were either wholly irresponsible for all their actions, or were to be visited for such of those actions as might furnish ground of complaint to other Nations, with the punishment due to Pirates and Outlaws.

'If the former of these alternatives, the total irresponsibility of unrecognized States—be too absurd to be maintained; and if the latter—the treatment of their inhabitants as pirates and outlaws—be too monstrous to be applied, for an indefinite length of time, to a large portion of the habitable globe:—no other choice remained for Great Britain, or for any Country having intercourse with the Spanish American Provinces, but to recognize, in due time, their political existence as States, and thus to bring them within the pale of those rights and duties, which civilized Nations are bound mutually to respect, and are entitled reciprocally to claim from each other.'[1]

1 *B.F.S.P.* vol. XII, pp. 912, 913. The following passage from Canning's despatch to Wellington, on 15 October 1822, is of interest in this connection: 'In the present situation of Spain with respect to her Colonies, we suffer equally from the maintenance of her claim of sovereignty by herself, and from the violation of it by her lawless subjects. By our determination to abstain from all interference in the internal struggles of Spain, we do not abandon our right to vindicate ourselves against its external violences': printed in Webster, op. cit. vol. II, p. 75.

The combination of the two elements—of the duty of recognition owed to the new community and of reasons of the nature of those adduced by Canning—was

It is from the point of view of the right of the new communities to recognition that Hall summarizes the British attitude with regard to the wars of independence of the Latin-American Republics as governed by 'the principle that recognition cannot be withheld when it has been earned'.[1] He quotes Lord Liverpool's declaration, as coinciding in this matter with the views of Canning, Lord Lansdowne and Sir James Mackintosh, that 'there was no right to recognition while the contest was actually going on...'. The question of the right was not in dispute; what was controversial was whether the contest was still going on. The actual, and not merely verbal, continuation of the struggle was necessary in order, to quote Hall once more, 'to prevent foreign countries from falling under an obligation to recognize as a state the community claiming to have become one'.[2]

In July 1862 the representative of the American Confederacy put before the British Government considerations which, to quote Earl Russell's résumé thereof, 'in the opinion of the Government of the so-called Confederate States, entitle that Government to be recognized of right as a separate and independent Power, and to be received as an equal in the great family of nations'. Lord Russell, in reply, made no attempt to challenge, in principle, the right to recognition. But he pointed to the recent reverses of the Confederacy on the battlefield and to the contradictory reports on the progress of the civil war as showing that the time for recognition had not yet arrived. He said: 'In order to be entitled to a place among the independent nations of the earth, a State ought to have not only strength and resources for a time, but afford promise of stability and permanence.'[3] The French Government, while assuring the United States that no hasty or precipitate action would be taken with regard to the

clearly expressed already in the despatch of 1 January 1819, of the United States Secretary of State to the Minister in Great Britain: '...We wish the British Government and all the European Allies, to consider, how important it is to them as well as to us, that these newly formed States should be regularly recognized: not only because the right to such recognition cannot with Justice be long denied to them, but that they may be held to observe on their part the ordinary rules of the Law of Nations, in their intercourse with the civilized World. We particularly believe that the only effectual means of repressing the excessive irregularities and piratical depredations of armed vessels under their flags and bearing their Commissions, will be to require of them the observance of the principles, sanctioned by the practice of maritime Nations. It is not to be expected that they will feel themselves bound by the ordinary duties of sovereign States, while they are denied the enjoyment of all their rights' (Manning, *Diplomatic Correspondence of the United States concerning the Independence of the Latin-American Nations*, vol. I (Parts I–II) (1925), p. 87).

1 *International Law* (3rd ed. 1890), § 26.

2 Op. cit. § 26.

3 *B.F.S.P.* vol. LV, p. 734.

recognition of the independence of the Confederacy, affirmed that 'the practice and usage of the present century had fully established the right of *de facto* Governments to recognition when a proper case was made out for the decision of foreign Powers'.[1]

(*b*) *The Practice of the United States.* It is in particular in pronouncements of the successive Presidents and Secretaries of State of the United States that the view of recognition conceived as the performance of a legal duty towards the community entitled to claim it has found frequent expression. While, for various reasons, conspicuous changes of emphasis have taken place in the practice of the United States in the matter of recognition of governments,[2] with regard to recognition of States the consistency of its attitude is both impressive and instructive. The utterances in question refer almost exclusively to the situation created by the secession of the Latin-American States. They were undoubtedly influenced by such factors as the revolutionary origin of the United States itself and the disapproval of the principle of monarchic legitimacy involving the possibility of European intervention. But these considerations do not detract from the significance of the legal principle to which they gave rise. Already on 20 April 1818, we find John Quincy Adams, Secretary of State, writing to the United States Minister to Spain: 'None of the Revolutionary Governments has yet been formally acknowledged; but if that of Buenos Ayres should maintain the stability which it appears to have acquired since the Declaration of Independence of 9 July 1816, it cannot be long before they will demand that acknowledgment of right—and however questionable that right may be now considered, it will deserve very seriously the consideration of the European Powers, as well as of the United States, how long that acknowledgment can rightfully be refused.'[3]

In a communication addressed to President Monroe on 24 August 1818, the Secretary of State, Mr Adams, expressed this view in an even more definite form: 'There is a stage in such contests when the parties struggling for independence have...a right to demand its acknowledgment by

1 Mr Faulkner to Mr Seward (in a communication informing the Secretary of State of the attitude of the French Government towards any application of the Confederacy for a recognition of its independence): 15 April 1861, *Parl. Papers*, 1862, vol. LXII, *North America*, no. 2, p. 163. In its note of 17 June 1919, recognizing the independence of Finland the Chilean Government stated that 'a nationality so vigorous, and distinct, a civilization so ancient and developed, had a natural right to complete independence which Finland just attained': as quoted by Graham, *The Diplomatic Recognition of the Border States*, Part I: *Finland* (1936), p. 145. See also below, p. 362, for the assertion of the legal duty of recognition of Finland on the part of the United States in 1919.

2 See below, pp. 124–30.

3 Manning, op. cit. vol. I (Parts I–II), p. 61.

neutral parties, and when the acknowledgment may be granted without departure from the obligations of neutrality. It is the stage when independence is established as a matter of fact so as to leave the chances of the opposite party to recover their dominion utterly desperate.'[1]

In the Message of 30 January 1822, announcing the intention to recognize the independence of some of the South American Republics, the President referred, as being a matter for serious consideration, to the question whether 'their right to the rank of independent nations...is not complete'.[2] In the Message communicated to the House of Representatives on 8 March 1822, the President said once more, referring to the success which crowned the efforts of the insurgent States: 'When the result of such a contest is manifestly settled, the new Governments have a claim to recognition by other Powers, which ought not to be resisted.'[3] He said in the same Message: 'This contest has now reached such a stage, and been attended with such decisive success on the part of the provinces, that it merits the most profound consideration, whether their right to the rank of independent nations, with all the advantages incident to it, in their intercourse with the United States, is not complete.'[4]

Even more explicit is the passage in the reply of the United States of 6 April 1822 to the Spanish protest following upon the announcement of the intention to recognize the independence of the revolted provinces. The Secretary of State affirmed that the Government of the United States, far from consulting the dictates of a policy questionable in its morality, yielded 'to an obligation of duty of the highest order, by recognizing as independent States, Nations which, after deliberately asserting their right to that character, have maintained and established it against all the resistance which had been or could be brought to oppose it'.[5] The recognition, the Note proceeded, was 'the mere acknowledgment of existing facts'.[6] These views were elaborated a year later, with an emphatic insistence on principle, in various instructions sent to the United States representatives in Latin-America. In his instructions of 17 May 1823, to Mr Rodney, United States Minister at Buenos Ayres, the Secretary of State, in an interesting appeal to principle invoked in support of a somewhat controversial claim, wrote:

'The foundation of our municipal Institutions is equal rights. The basis of all our intercourse with foreign powers is Reciprocity. We have not demanded, nor would we have accepted special priviledges of any kind in return for an acknowledgment of

1 Moore, vol. I, p. 78.
2 Ibid. p. 85.
3 Manning, op. cit. vol. I (Parts I–II), p. 147.
4 Ibid.
5 Ibid. p. 157; *B.F.S.P.* vol. IX, p. 755.
6 Ibid.

Independence. But that which we have not desired and would not have accepted for ourselves, we have a right to insist ought not to be granted others. Recognition is in its nature, not a subject of equivalent; it is claimable of right or not at all. You will therefore strenuously maintain the right of the United States to be treated in every respect on the footing of the most favoured...nation.'[1]

He reiterated these views in his Instructions to Mr Anderson, United States Minister to Colombia, dated 27 May 1823:

'The European alliance of Emperors and Kings have assumed, as the foundation of human society, the doctrine of unalienable *allegiance*. Our doctrine is founded upon the principle of unalienable *right*. The European allies, therefore, have viewed the cause of the South Americans as rebellion against their lawful sovereign. We have considered it as the assertion of natural right.'[2]

In his Instructions of 29 November 1823 to Mr Rush, United States Minister to Great Britain, the Secretary of State, after pointing to the fact that in the opinion of both Great Britain and the United States there was no hope for the recovery of the Spanish authority, said: 'Having arrived at that conclusion, we considered that the people of these emancipated Colonies, were, of right, independent of all other nations, and that it was our duty so to acknowledge them.' He urged earnestly upon the consideration of Great Britain that after conceding the hopelessness of the Spanish position she could no longer regard the question of recognition as one of 'time and circumstances'.[3]

The events connected with the recognition of Paraguay in 1845 and 1846 showed the disinclination of the United States to depart from the conception of recognition as a legal duty. In these years Paraguay, after having seceded from Argentina, made repeated approaches to the United States in the matter of recognition. At that time Argentina was confronted by the hostile action of the combined fleets of Great Britain and France attempting to force a passage up the La Plata and the Paraná. In the circumstances, the sympathies of the United States were with the Argentine Republic, exposed, as she was, to foreign armed intervention. An inducement was thus present to delay recognition in order not to create a semblance of solidarity with the European Powers. Actually no departure was made from the established principle; neither was there undue delay in its application. 'You are aware', wrote Mr Buchanan, Secretary of State, to the United States Chargé d'Affaires at Buenos Ayres on 30 March 1846,

1 Manning, op. cit. vol. I (Parts I–II), p. 191. See also ibid. p. 230, for the Instruction of Mr Clay, Secretary of State, to the United States Minister to Mexico, for a similar line of reasoning.

2 Ibid. p. 198.

3 Ibid. p. 211.

'that it is the settled policy of the United States to recognize the independence of all governments which have manifested to the world that they are *de facto* independent. This duty has been eagerly performed towards our sister Republics, on this continent.'[1] The Minister was instructed to prepare the Argentine Government for the recognition of the independence of Paraguay 'in pursuance of the long established and well-settled policy of the American Government'.[2]

There was no change of attitude when during the Civil War the United States were confronted with the attempts by the Confederate States to obtain the recognition of their independence. These attempts were strenuously resisted.[3] Moreover, the experience of the Civil War had the indirect effect of imparting a measure of legitimism to the practice of the United States in the field of recognition of governments. But in the matter of recognition of States the well-established principle was not abandoned in deference to the exigencies of a grave moment. In a communication of 10 April 1861, by Secretary Seward to Mr Adams, there occurs the following passage: 'We freely admit that a nation may, and

1 Manning, *Diplomatic Correspondence of the United States, Inter-American Affairs, 1831–1860, Argentina*, vol. 1 (1932), p. 30. And see generally, Whitaker, *The United States and the Independence of Latin-America* (1941).

2 Ibid. p. 31.

3 In a circular note sent on 28 February 1861, the Ministers of the United States in various capitals were instructed to counteract any suggestion of recognition of the Confederacy and to urge upon the governments concerned that 'it must be very evident that it is the right of this government to ask of all foreign powers that the latter shall take no steps which may tend to encourage the revolutionary movement of the seceding States; or increase the danger of disaffection in those which still remain loyal' (*Diplomatic Correspondence of the United States*, 1861, p. 31). In April 1861 Mr Seward, the United States Secretary of State, wrote as follows in an instruction to the United States Minister in Great Britain: 'To recognize the independence of a new state, and so favor, possibly determine its admission into the family of nations, is the highest possible exercise of sovereign power, because it affects in any case the welfare of two nations and often the peace of the world. In the European system this power is now seldom attempted to be exercised without invoking a consultation or congress of nations. That system has not been extended to this continent. But there is even a greater necessity for prudence in such cases in regard to American States than in regard to the nations of Europe' (ibid. p. 79). The United States were inclined to treat even recognition of belligerency as an unfriendly act and for a time insisted that compensation on account of premature grant of belligerent rights should be included within the purview of arbitral settlement. In a communication addressed to the United States Minister in London Mr Seward treated the recognition of belligerency as interference with the sovereign rights of the United States. Referring to the British proclamation of neutrality he said: 'That proclamation, unmodified and unexplained, would leave us no alternative but to regard the government of Great Britain as questioning our free exercise of all the rights of self-defense guaranteed to us by our Constitution and the laws of nature and of nations to suppress the insurrection' (ibid. p. 97).

even ought, to recognize a new State which has absolutely and beyond question effected its independence....' The Secretary of State added: 'Seen in the light of this principle, the several nations of the earth constitute one great federal republic. When one of them casts its suffrages for the admission of a new member into that republic, it ought to act under a profound sense of moral obligation, and be governed by considerations as pure, disinterested and elevated as the general interest of society and the advancement of human nature.'[1]

The controversy between the United States and Colombia concerning the premature recognition of Panama is particularly instructive in this connection. The Government of the United States, although the temptation was considerable, did not have recourse to the argument that in granting recognition it was entitled to take into account its own interests only. In rejecting the Colombian claim for arbitration in the matter it confined itself to declaring that 'questions of foreign policy and of the recognition or non-recognition of foreign states are of a purely political nature, and do not fall within the domain of judicial decision...'.[2] In a previous note of 5 January 1904, Secretary Hay refrained from supporting the conduct of the United States by any claim of a right to grant recognition by consulting the interest of his country only and irrespective of international principle. After referring to the fact that Panama had been recognized by all the Great Powers and by a number of other States, he said:

'The law of nations does not undertake to fix the precise time at which recognition shall or may be extended to a new state. This is a question to be determined by each state upon its own just sense of international rights and obligations; and it has rarely happened, where a new state has been formed and recognized within the limits of an existing state, that the parent state has not complained that the recognition was premature. And if in the present instance the powers of the world gave their recognition with unwonted promptitude, it is only because they entertained the common conviction that interests of vast importance to the whole civilized world were at stake, which would by any other course be put in peril.'[3]

1 *U.S. For. Rel.* 1861, pp. 76–9.

2 Mr Hay, Secretary of State, to the Colombian Minister, 5 January 1904, as cited in Moore, vol. III, p. 105.

3 Ibid. pp. 90, 91. It is of interest to note that when, eleven years later, Mr Bryan, the Secretary of State, advocated before Congress the adoption of a Bill providing for granting compensation to Colombia, he referred to the action of the United States in 1903 as an instance of the exercise of the right of international eminent domain in the interest of the world. See Callcott, *The Caribbean Policy of the United States* (1942), p. 383. Colombia did not formally recognize the independence of Panama until the Treaty of Bogotá (which was signed on 6 April 1914, but the ratifications of which were not exchanged till 1 March 1922) between the United States

§ 8. *Recognition as a Question of Fact.* In addition to admitting expressly the right of new States to recognition, governments have on occasions voiced the same principle by declaring that the existence of new States is a question of fact. It was in this sense that Canning referred to the question of recognition of the Latin-American States as being one 'of fact and of time rather than of principle'.[1] It was in this sense that on numerous occasions he pointed to the distinction between 'mere acknowledgment' of the existence of the new States—which, he insisted, was a question of fact—and their formal recognition *de jure*, which expressed an opinion as to title and whose grant was a matter for the parent State.[2]

Numerous pronouncements of the Government of the United States express the same attitude. In reply to the Mexican protest against the recognition of the independence of Texas, Mr Forsyth, United States Secretary of State, wrote in 1837: 'The independence of other nations has always been regarded by the United States as question of fact merely, and that of every people has been invariably recognized by them whenever the actual enjoyment of it was accompanied by satisfactory evidence of their power and determination permanently and effectually to maintain it.'[3] In 1875, in a Message concerning the question of the recognition of Cuba, President Grant said: 'In such cases [of recognition of new States] other nations simply deal with an actually existing condition of things, and recognize as one of the powers of the earth that body politic which, possessing the necessary elements, has, in fact, become a new power. In a

and Colombia (Article III): Martens, *N.R.T.* 3rd ser. vol. XII, p. 134. In that Treaty the Government of the United States in its own name and in the name of the people of the United States of America expressed its 'sincere regret that anything should have occurred to interrupt or to mar the relations of cordial friendship that had so long subsisted between the two nations'. The Treaty provided that the Colombian vessels should use the canal toll free and that the U.S. pay $25,000,000. And see above, p. 10 for the Colombian declaration in 1920 on entering the League of Nations.

1 See above, p. 15. And see his speech in the House of Commons of 15 June 1824: 'It [recognition] has clearly two senses, in which it is to be differently understood. If the colonies say to the mother country, "We assert our independence", and the mother country answers, "I admit it", that is recognition in one sense. If the colonies say to another state, "We are independent" and that other state replies, "I allow that you are so", that is recognition in another sense of the term. That other state simply acknowledges the fact, or rather its opinion of the fact' (*Speeches* [as cited above at p. 15], vol. v, p. 299).

2 For an interesting distinction, based on the same reasoning, between acknowledgment of independence and recognition see Wellington's *Observations* on Canning's Notes on Chateaubriand's despatch concerning the recognition of the independence of the South American Republics. Printed in Webster, *Britain and the Independence of Latin America*, vol. II (1938), p. 141, n. 1; also in Temperley, *Foreign Policy of Canning, 1822–1827*, p. 543.

3 Moore, vol. I, p. 102.

word, the creation of a new state is a fact.'[1] The reply, in a similar vein, to the Spanish protest in 1822 has already been noted.[2]

What is the meaning of the principle that the question whether a State exists is a question of fact? It means, negatively, that recognition is not a question of unfettered discretion, of contractual bargain, or of political expediency. It means, positively, that the State called upon to grant recognition must judge whether the required conditions of fact exist, and that it is entitled to exercise its discretion in arriving at that judgment. However, this is a judicial discretion aiming at ascertaining the existence of the relevant facts. When the Declaration of London of 1909 laid down in Article 3 that the effectiveness of blockade is a question of fact, the intention was to lay down that the requirement of effectiveness is an undoubted rule of law and that if the blockade is effective it must be treated by neutrals as valid, though it may be difficult to lay down in advance the precise conditions of the operation of the requirement of effectiveness. To predicate that a given legal result is a question of fact is to assert that it is not a question of arbitrary discretion. This is in general the meaning of the jurisprudential distinction between questions of fact and of law. The emphasis—and that emphasis is a constant feature of diplomatic correspondence—on the principle that the existence of a State is a question of fact signifies that, whenever the necessary factual requirements exist, the granting of recognition is a matter of legal duty.

1 Moore, vol. I, p. 107.

2 See above, p. 19. The connection between the duty of recognition and recognition as based on the ascertainment of the facts of the situation was given clear expression in 1837 by the United States Secretary of State in connection with the overtures of Texas aiming at the annexation of that country by the United States. He pointed out that 'in determining with respect to the independence of other countries the United States have never taken the question of *right* between the contending parties into consideration' and that 'they have deemed it a dictate of duty and policy to decide upon the question as one of fact only'. Before recognizing the independence of Texas, the United States, he said, considered the various political and economic factors militating against recognition. 'A sense of duty and a reverence for consistency, however...left this government no alternative, and it therefore led the way in recognizing Texas' (Manning, *Diplomatic Correspondence of the United States, Inter-American Affairs, 1831–1860, Texas and Venezuela*, vol. XII (1939), pp. 11, 12).

In recognizing in 1861 the new Kingdom of Italy the French Government said: 'C'est une règle de droit public généralement admise que "de la part d'une puissance étrangère reconnaître un autre gouvernement n'est que reconnaître un fait, savoir qu'il est généralement obéi, malgré la libre manifestation qu'un nombre plus ou moins considérable se soit permise d'une opinion contraire. Les puissances étrangères suivent ici la possession si le bien de leurs affaires l'exige"....' It added that in doing so it followed the practice of a great number of governments (*Archives diplomatiques*, 1861, vol. IV, p. 360). The language of the communication seems to refer to recognition of governments. Actually, the case is one of recognition of States.

§ 9. *Governmental Professions and the Creation of Legal Rules.* The preceding examination of the practice of States and of pronouncements of governments showing the acknowledgment of the duty of recognition whenever there exist the requisite conditions of fact is open to the retort that in deducing a legal rule from the practice of States we must not look to the professions of governments but to their motives. Any such retort is probably unsound. Official pronouncements of governments express what in their view are the correct legal rules and principles capable of general application. It is with these alone that the jurist is concerned. The particular legal rule may suit the political interest and convenience of the State enunciating it. But the lawyer abandons his legitimate province once he begins to probe into the motives which have induced governments to express their obligation to act upon a legal rule. Such realism may be appropriate for the historian and the sociologist. The jurist is concerned with the legal rule upon which governments profess to act. The fact that the particular rule has been found to suit the interests of States does not derogate from its legal value; it adds to it. International law is not so rich as to be able to discard, in a spirit of realism of questionable propriety, legal rules acknowledged and acted upon by States.[1]

1 Such attempts at realism have occurred, it will be noted, in other fields of international law. Witness, for instance, the political interpretation of international leases as disguised cessions calculated to spare the susceptibilities of the lessor State. See Lauterpacht, *Private Law Sources and Analogies of International Law* (1927), pp. 184–90. Undoubtedly cases may arise in which a government uses grandiloquent language the insincerity or cynicism of which are so patent as to preclude it from being accepted at its face value. Such contingencies are not a sufficient justification for refusing to treat as a source of law governmental pronouncements which are of considerable uniformity, which have been made in circumstances not offensive to international morality, and which provide a satisfactory basis for a workable and much needed rule of law.

Chapter III

THE LEGAL DUTY OF RECOGNITION AND THE CONDITIONS OF STATEHOOD

§ 10. *The Practice of States and the Essential Conditions of Recognition.* The preceding survey of the practice of States illustrating the legal nature of recognition has shown, at the same time, what are the conditions which give rise to a legitimate claim to recognition of statehood. These coincide with the conditions which permit a State to recognize a seceding community without committing an illegality in relation to the parent State. They are identical with the requirements of statehood as laid down by international law, namely, the existence of an independent government exercising effective authority within a defined area. These requirements will now be considered.

An Independent Government. The first condition of statehood is that there must exist a government actually independent of that of any other State, including the parent State. The independence thus required is one irrespective of the attitude of the mother country. The attitude of the latter is of importance only in so far as the recognition by the mother country of the independence of the rebellious province naturally raises a strong, although not conclusive, presumption that such independence actually exists. On the other hand, the refusal of the mother country to recognize such independence is not conclusive. The legal title of the parent State is relevant to the extent that clear evidence is required showing that the latter has been definitely displaced and that the effectiveness of its authority does not exceed a mere assertion of right. But once such evidence is available, the illegality of origin, from the point of view of the constitutional law of the parent State, is of no consequence. The principle of legitimacy, although proclaimed for a short time by the Powers of the Holy Alliance at the beginning of the nineteenth century,[1] has never become part of

1 These did not include Great Britain, who refused to subscribe to that principle, although a contemporary American critic described the British attitude as not uninfluenced by 'the mystic Virtues of Legitimacy': Mr Adams, United States Minister to Great Britain, to Mr Monroe (Manning, *Diplomatic Correspondence of the United States concerning the Independence of the Latin-American Nations*, vol. III (Parts VIII–XIV), p. 1433). In 1822 Great Britain, at the Verona Conference, formally proposed to the Holy Alliance some measure of recognition *de facto* of the South American Republics as a necessary condition for effectively combating piracy and the slave traffic in those regions. While the attitude of Prussia and Russia was purely negative in their assertion

international law. It has been invoked on occasions by absolutist governments[1] but it has never struck deep roots in the law of nations. When in Article 10 of the Covenant of the League members of the League of Nations mutually guaranteed their territorial integrity and political independence, they limited the guarantee to external aggression as distinguished from internal revolution. A system of law which does not possess the power to impose territorial and political changes within and between States cannot take upon itself the task of perpetuating the existing conditions by refusing to recognize changes of sovereignty effected in violation of the constitutional law of States.

The meaning of independence, however, is not confined to the achievement of actual independence of the mother country. It includes also independence of any State other than the mother country. If a community, after having become detached from the parent State, were to become,

of the imprescriptible rights of the King of Spain (at that time confronted with a civil war within his European possessions), the position taken up by Austria and France was an interesting mixture of legitimism and the *de facto* principle. The Austrian delegate declared:

'1. Que Sa Majesté Impériale, invariablement fidèle aux grands principes sur lesquels repose l'ordre social et le maintien des gouvernements légitimes, ne reconnaîtra jamais l'indépendance des Provinces Espagnoles de l'Amérique tant que S.M. Catholique n'aura pas librement et formellement renoncé aux droits de Souveraineté qu' Elle a jusqu'ici exercé sur ces provinces.

'2. Que plus Sa Majesté Impériale est decidée à ne pas s'écarter de cette ligne de conduite, plus Elle se croira libre, dans l'état actuel des choses, et tant que l'Espagne se trouvera elle-même sous un régime que les Chefs de la révolution ont imposé *de fait* au Roi et à Son pays, d'adopter également vis-à-vis des Colonies Espagnoles telle attitude *de fait* que des considérations d'intérêt ou d'utilité générale pourrant Lui suggérer, toute fois sous la réserve expresse que telle que puisse être cette attitude, elle ne portera aucun préjudice permanent aux droits imprescriptibles du Roi et de la Couronne d'Espagne' (Webster, op. cit. vol. II, p. 80).

The French declaration, after reiterating the principle of legitimacy, proceeded to sacrifice it to more compelling considerations:

'...Néanmoins la France avoue avec l'Angleterre que lorsque des troubles se prolongent et que le droit des nations ne peut plus s'exercer pour cause d'impuissance d'une des parties belligérantes, le droit naturel reprend son empire; elle convient qu'il y a des prescriptions inévitables; qu'un Gouvernement après avoir longtemps résisté, est quelquefois obligé de céder à la force des choses, pour mettre fin à beaucoup de maux et pour ne pas priver un Etat des avantages dont d'autres Etats pourraient exclusivement profiter' (ibid. p. 81).

For these declarations see also Manning, op. cit. vol. III, pp. 1539–41.

---

1 Thus in reply to the request of the United States for assurances that no recognition would be granted to the governments of the Confederate States, Russia answered that 'from the principle of unrelenting opposition to all revolutionary movements, [she] would be the last to recognize any *de facto* Government of the disaffected States of the American Union': as quoted in Bernard, *Neutrality of Great Britain during the American Civil War* (1870), p. 126.

legally or actually, a satellite of another State, it would not be fulfilling the primary condition of independence and would not accordingly be entitled to recognition as a State. This, probably, was the position of Manchuria between 1932 and 1945,[1] following upon its forcible separation from China as the result of invasion by Japan. Apart from the considerations arising out of the principle of non-recognition,[2] that province, controlled politically and strategically by Japan, did not fulfil the primary requirement of statehood, i.e. the possession of sovereignty exercised by an independent government. The same applies to such ephemeral creations as Slovakia or Croatia during the Second World War.

§ 11. *Effective Authority*. The second essential requirement of statehood is a sufficient degree of internal stability as expressed in the functioning of a government enjoying the habitual obedience of the bulk of the population. A community may have succeeded in shaking off the allegiance to the mother country, but if it is in a condition of such internal instability as to be deprived of a representative and effective government, it will be lacking in a vital condition of statehood. This combination of the requirements of external independence and internal stability is shown in an instructive way in the questions formulated by Canning in connection with the proposed recognition of the independence of Mexico and of other American States. These questions were:

'1st. Has the Government so constituted already notified by a publick Act its determination to remain independent of Spain, and to admit no terms of accommodation with the Mother Country?

'2ndly. Is it in military possession of the country, and also in a respectable condition of military defence against any probable attack from Europe?

'3rdly. Does it appear to have acquired a reasonable degree of consistency, and to enjoy the confidence and goodwill of the several orders of the people?'[3]

An identical view was expressed by successive Governments of the United States with regard to the recognition of Cuban independence. Thus President Grant, in his Annual Message of 7 December 1875, while admitting the probability of the Spanish domination having been finally displaced, denied the Cuban claim to recognition on the ground that no effective and stable government had been established. There must exist, he said, 'some known and defined form of government, acknowledged by

1 See below, p. 47.
2 See below, p. 415.
3 Canning's despatch of 10 October 1823, printed in Webster, op. cit. vol. I, p. 435. See also Canning's Note, of 23 August 1824, to Woodbine Parish concerning the conditions of recognition of Argentina, printed in ibid. p. 114.

those subject thereto, in which the functions of government are administered by usual methods, competent to mete out justice to citizens and strangers, to afford remedies for public and for private wrongs, and able to assume the correlative international obligations and capable of performing the corresponding international duties resulting from its acquisition of the rights of sovereignty'.[1] For this reason the recognition of a new State often takes the form of a recognition of its government. Thus when, on 3 May 1919, it was decided that Great Britain and the United States should severally recognize the independence of Finland, the following communication was sent to Finland by Great Britain:

> 'His Majesty's Government seeing in recent elections and in establishment of a new Government a clear expression of the desire of the Finnish people and of their determination to follow the path of order and of constitutional development have decided to recognize the independence of Finland and to enter into formal relations with the present Finnish Government. They desire to congratulate the people of Finland on having vindicated their title to the rights of an independent sovereign State.'[2]

The importance of the requirement of an effective government may be gauged from the fact that the Committee of Jurists, who were asked to give an opinion in the matter of the Aaland Islands, held that notwith-

1 Moore, vol. I, p. 107. See also ibid. pp. 108, 109, respectively, for the statement of the same principle in the messages of President Cleveland in 1896 and President McKinley in 1898.

2 On 5 May 1919, the Department of State of the United States announced that 'in view of the fact that the people of Finland have established a representative Government, the Government of the United States of America declares that it recognizes the Government, so constituted, as the *de facto* Government of an independent Finland': *U.S. For. Rel.* 1919 (II), p. 213. Similarly, the British recognition of Poland on 25 February 1919 was in the form of the 'formal recognition of the Government of Poland'. The French recognition was in the form of the 'official recognition of Poland as an independent and sovereign State and of its government as a regular government'. In December 1884 Great Britain and a number of other States recognized the Association of Congo as a friendly government. The importance of the existence of an effective government explains why some authors maintain that there is no recognition of a State apart from the recognition of its government. See, for example, Kleist, *Die völkerrechtliche Anerkennung Sowjetrusslands* (1934), p. 19; Redslob in *R.I.* (Paris), vol. XIII (1934), p. 433. For a refutation of this view see Scalfati, pp. 488–90, who discusses the recognition of Finland by France in January 1918 and the alleged withdrawal of that recognition in October 1918. He points out—rightly, it is believed—that the recognition in January was one relating to statehood, while the Note of October 1918 intimated the unwillingness to recognize a particular regime. See below, p. 350. See also the case of Albania during the First Assembly of the League; that country, although recognized in principle as a State in 1913 by the Conference of London, was apparently in 1920 in the position of not having a recognized government.

standing the presence of the conditions referred to in the British Note quoted above, Finland was not at that date a State in the contemplation of international law having regard to her unsettled condition and the absence of an orderly administration.[1]

§ 12. *Defined Territory*. The possession of territory is, notwithstanding some theoretical controversy which has gathered round the subject,[2] a regular requirement of statehood. Without it there can be no stable and effective government.[3] On the other hand, it has been held that the fact that the frontiers of a new State have not yet been definitely decided does not constitute an impediment in the way of its statehood.[4] Most of the new States which arose after the First World War were recognized *de facto* or *de jure* before their frontiers were finally laid down in treaties—although as a rule such recognition was accompanied by stipulations relating to the acceptance by the State concerned of the frontiers to be laid down by the Peace Conference. Thus the British recognition of Finland was accompanied by a declaration that 'in recognizing the independence of Finland His Majesty's Government do so with confidence [and] understanding that the Finnish Government accepts the decision to be taken by the Peace Conference as to the drawing of her frontiers...'.[5] However, when the doubts as to the future frontiers were regarded as being of a serious nature, recognition was postponed. Thus when in 1919 Esthonia and Latvia were recognized by the Allied Powers, no recognition was granted to Lithuania on the express ground that owing to the Vilna dispute her frontiers were not yet fixed.[6]

1 See below, p. 50.

2 See, for example, Kelsen, *Das Problem der Souveränität und die Theorie des Völkerrechts* (1920), pp. 70–6; Donati, *Stato e territorio* (1924), pp. 27, 30; Salmond, *Jurisprudence*, § 38.

3 The dispossession of the lawful government by the invader *pendente bello* is no more than an incident of military operations. The fact that Belgium during the First World War and the numerous countries occupied by Germany during the Second World War continued to exist as States with governments functioning in exile (see below, p. 91) is irrelevant to the question of the possibility of the existence of a State without territory.

4 *Deutsche Continental Gas-Gesellschaft* v. *Polish State*, decided on 1 August 1929, by the German-Polish Mixed Arbitral Tribunal: *Annual Digest*, 1929–30, Case no. 5 (*c*). The Tribunal said: 'In order to say that a State exists and can be recognized as such... it is enough that this territory has a sufficient consistency, even though its boundaries have not yet been accurately delimited.... There are numerous examples of cases in which States have existed without their statehood being called into doubt... at a time when the frontier between them was not accurately traced.'

5 For a similar proviso in connection with the recognition by the United States of the Yugoslav State see *U.S. For. Rel.* 1919 (II), p. 900.

6 See also below, p. 360, n. 4.

§ 13. *Irrelevant Tests of Recognition of Statehood.* The existence of the conditions of statehood outlined above—external independence and effective internal government within a reasonably well-defined territory—may be and has often been controversial in reference to particular situations. But, in substance, these conditions are definite and exhaustive. They have nothing to do with the degree of civilization of the new State,[1] with the legitimacy of its origin, with its religion, or with its political system. Once considerations of that nature are introduced as a condition of recognition, the clear path of law is abandoned and the door wide open to arbitrariness, to attempts at extortion, and to intervention at the very threshold of statehood. The legal irrelevance of these various considerations as factors in the process of recognition has not always been perceived. This may be seen, for instance, from Lorimer's treatment of the subject. He begins his exposition by emphasizing the fundamental importance of recognition which, he says, makes of international law a science. He lays down, in an unexceptional manner, that rights and duties have their origin in and are limited by the facts of natural life: 'Any doctrine...which professes to regard it [recognition] as an act of courtesy, comity, or the like, the exercise of which may be jurally withheld—deprives international law of a permanent basis in nature, and fails to bring it within the sphere of jurisprudence.'[2] The question, he says, is one of ascertaining whether there exist the necessary requirements of statehood. He then advances the more debatable contention that in the present state of international law it is for each State to lay down what these conditions are, while the business of the science of international law is to assist States in determining these conditions. Lorimer then proceeds to suggest what the proper tests are. He divides humanity into three concentric spheres: into civilized, barbarous, and savage peoples. The last two are excluded from recognition. They are

1 Modern international law knows of no distinction, for the purposes of recognition, between civilized and uncivilized States or between States within and outside the international community of civilized States. It is therefore unnecessary to discuss this aspect of the question in any detail. In Lorimer's writings the student will find picturesque descriptions of varying degrees of civilization with reference to recognition (see below, p. 32). Fauchille, pp. 327, 328, followed his example. Kunz (pp. 25–34, 105–9) distinguishes between recognition and 'reception into the community of nations'. He describes recognition prior to reception into the international community as partial recognition—as in the case of Turkey with whom various States entertained diplomatic relations and concluded treaties prior to her admission to the benefits 'of the public law and of the Concert of Europe' as the result of Article 7 of the Treaty of Paris of 1856. However, it is probable that the legal position of Turkey remained unaffected by Article 7, whose legal significance is somewhat elusive.

2 *The Institutes of the Law of Nations*, vol. 1 (1883), p. 104.

excluded because they are unable to fulfil the fundamental condition of possessing what Lorimer calls a 'reciprocating will'. That requirement disposes not only of savage or barbarous peoples as candidates for statehood. It eliminates religious creeds whose doctrine renders impossible the presumption of reciprocating will, e.g. the Mohammedan religion.[1] It excludes, further, secular creeds which are devoid of the 'reciprocating will', such as intolerant monarchies ('the very name of monarchy savours of exclusiveness'), intolerant republics (like that of the French Convention of 1793), intolerant anarchies, communities wedded to communism or nihilism (which are 'prohibited by the law of nations'), and communities under personal or class governments (on the ground that their form of government renders them incapable of expressing or reaching a reciprocating will). It is clear that some aspects of Lorimer's treatment of the subject border on absurdity. It has been deemed useful to summarize it at somewhat excessive length as a not unnecessary reminder of the consequences to which may lead the introduction of tests divorced from the solid bases of social reality on which all law must ultimately rest.

§ 14. *The Political Aspect. National Interest and the Duty of Recognition.* It has been submitted in the preceding sections that the legal view of recognition, i.e. of recognition conceived as a declaration, made in the fulfilment of a legal duty, of the existence of the requisite conditions of statehood, can be regarded as being in accordance with the general practice of States. At the same time, it is a fact that the tests of recognition as outlined above, although supported by the bulk of State practice and by cogent legal principle, have often yielded to motives and considerations essentially foreign to the purpose of recognition. This has been so for the reason that governments have not always found it possible to divorce the fulfilment of a duty implied in the act of recognition from the achievement, on that occasion, of specific national advantages. In a properly constituted political society the function—which is perhaps the most important function of any legal system—of ascertaining the presence of the conditions of legal capacity and existence is performed by impartial organs delegated by the law for that purpose. In international society that task is as a rule fulfilled by individual States acting on their own responsibility and endowed with wide discretion in the appreciation of the relevant facts. That discretion is unfettered only in the meaning that, at present, the State which takes a decision on the issue of recognition is not accountable for its acts to any

1 'To talk of the recognition of Mahomedan States as a question of time, is to talk nonsense': Lorimer, op. cit. vol. 1, p. 123.

superior jurisdiction. In essence, it is a discretion determined by international law. In granting or refusing recognition the State administers international law; it does not perform a legally indifferent act of national policy. In the imperfectly developed international society States are often called upon to act in the fulfilment of a legal duty or in the assertion of their legal interest without being directly and immediately responsible to a higher authority. This does not mean that in these matters States are not bound by law at all. They enjoy freedom of decision in ascertaining the facts and assessing their significance. They are not free to assert the liberty to disregard the facts or to act in defiance of them.[1]

However, while the task of ascertaining the existence of conditions of statehood is essentially one of administration of international law, it is at the same time a political act fraught with political consequences involving the interests of the State called upon to grant recognition. In some cases its interests may be identical with those of the international community at large, with the result that their consideration is not incompatible with the loyal application of the objective tests of recognition. That possibility is clearly illustrated by the substance of the British answers, quoted above,[2] in reply to the Spanish protest against the recognition of the Latin-American Republics.

§ 15. *Recognition in Consideration of Benefits.* The identity of national and international interest is, in the matter of recognition of States, by no means a constant phenomenon. In international practice there can be found examples of the function of recognition being abused for the purpose of securing particular national advantages. Even the lofty position assumed by the United States on the question of recognition of the independence of the Latin-American States was not always entirely free from attempts to safeguard the particular interests of the United States. Thus in 1819 the United States made it to some extent a condition of its recognition of Argentina that no special privileges of indefinite duration should be granted to Spain. This, it was said, was not to be interpreted as making recognition an object of bargaining. The reason for the delay in recognition was that if such rights were to be reserved to Spain it would not be quite clear

1 The manner in which the Second Assembly of the League of Nations interpreted the obligations of its members under Article 16 of the Covenant may be referred to as an illustration. It laid down that it is the duty of each member of the League to decide for itself whether a breach of the Covenant has been committed. At the same time the Assembly insisted that the fulfilment of that duty, though dependent upon the member's finding as to the existence of the requisite facts, was a clear legal obligation under the Covenant.

2 See above, pp. 13–15.

whether 'the independence of Buenos Ayres would be complete' [1] There is agreement among historians that the recognition of the United States by France in 1778 was not entirely disinterested. That event, it may be added, showed how shifting and haphazard in their operation may be mere considerations of opportunism in connection with recognition. When the American colonies declared their independence in 1776, Turgot advised the King of France that it was in the French interest that the insurrection be suppressed because the insurgents, when subdued, would require a considerable British force to keep them down permanently and, as a result, Great Britain would become a peaceable or at least a harmless neighbour.[2] In February 1778 France concluded treaties of commerce and alliance with the United States which amounted to recognition and which brought about the war with Great Britain.[3]

Neither are instances lacking in more modern history of attempts to make recognition an object of a bargain or a matter dependent upon political conditions or considerations. In May 1918 the British Minister at Stockholm informed the Finnish Chargé d'Affaires that Great Britain was prepared to recognize provisionally the *de facto* Finnish Government pending final settlement at the peace conference if the Finnish Government would obtain the release of British subjects arrested on Finnish territory by the Germans and give guarantees for the maintenance of neutrality (including the passage of Allied ships through Finnish territorial waters).[4] The attitude of the United States was, for a time, not dissimilar. The instructions to the United States representative at Helsingfors were that 'recognition as a *de facto* government will be given to any properly constituted government established on democratic principles and with a policy not in conflict with the Allies, which may result from the recent Finnish elections'.[5] One of the reasons given by the United States in 1920

1 Mr Adams, Secretary of State, to Mr Monroe: Manning, op. cit. vol. I (Parts I–II), p. 93. 'If Buenos Ayres', wrote Adams to President Monroe in 1818, 'confined its demand of recognition to the provinces of which it is in actual possession, and if it would *assert its entire independence by agreeing to place the United States upon the footing of the most favored nation*...I should think the time now arrived when its government might be recognized without a breach of neutrality' (Moore, vol. I, p. 79).

2 See the letter of Mr Adams, Minister to Great Britain, to Mr Monroe, United States Secretary of State, of 22 January 1816: Manning, op. cit. vol. III (Parts VIII–XIV), p. 1433.

3 See below, p. 36.

4 Communication of the British Ambassador to the United States Secretary of State, 4 May 1918: *U.S. For. Rel.* 1918, *Russia*, vol. II, p. 785. See also, for the statement of the British Foreign Secretary, *The Times* newspaper, 31 January 1918.

5 Acting Secretary of State to the Consul at Helsingfors, 20 March 1919; *U.S. For. Rel.* 1919 (II), p. 213. However, see below, p. 362.

for refusing to recognize Georgia and Azerbaijan was 'the reaction on the minds of the Russians, hitherto friendly to the allied and Associated Governments, of such a recognition'.[1] In October 1920 Poland informed the Latvian Government that she was willing to grant immediate recognition *de jure* to Latvia provided that the latter offered a 99 years' lease of a port, to be declared a free port. When the question of recognition of Albania came before the United States Secretary of State in 1922, the United States Secretary of Commerce pointed to some connection between the grant of recognition by the United States and the grant of oil concessions by Albania.[2] The Secretary of State informed the Secretary of Commerce that there were 'naturally various considerations involved in the question of recognition'.[3] On 28 July 1922, recognition *de jure* was extended. When the United States, on 25 April 1922, recognized the independence of Egypt, it made the recognition 'subject to the maintenance of the rights of the United States of America as they have hitherto existed'.[4] This was done in order not to leave doubts as to the maintenance of the capitulatory and commercial rights of the United States. When in 1928 the Kingdom of Hejaz and Nejd approached the United States with a request for recognition, the Department of State, in a communication to the American Legation at Cairo, expressed the opinion that 'the final decision would be largely influenced by the character and extent of American commercial interests, actual as well as potential, in Hejaz'.[5]

Conditions of recognition have often been exacted which, although not imposed in the selfish interest of the State in question, have been unrelated

1 *U.S. For. Rel.* 1920 (III), p. 778.

2 *U.S. For. Rel.* 1922 (I), pp. 594, 595.

3 Ibid. p. 600. The United States consular representative at Tangier was instructed to enquire, *inter alia*, as to the 'Albanian administration's attitude towards the protection of American interests and its degree and willingness to afford most-favored-nation treatment to the United States': Hackworth, vol. I, p. 197.

4 *U.S. For. Rel.* 1922 (II), p. 105. See also Hackworth, vol. I, p. 209.

5 See Hackworth, vol. I, p. 218. When in April 1909 Germany recognized the independence of Bulgaria, she referred to the '*obligeante communication*' of the Bulgarian Foreign Minister concerning the arrangement arrived at with the view of safeguarding the interests of the Oriental Railways Company: Martens, *N.R.T.* 3rd ser. vol. II, p. 666. See also ibid. vol. IV, p. 22 for the Italian recognition of the annexation of Congo, subject, among others, to the obligation to respect Italian interests. In recognizing the new Republic of Panama on 30 November 1903, Germany noted the formal declaration of the Government of Panama that it recognized the continued validity of the stipulations of treaties existing between the German Empire and Colombia in respect of the territory over which the sovereignty of the Republic of Panama now extends: ibid. p. 797. For an (unsolicited) offer of advantages as a price of recognition—an offer accompanied by threats of discriminating action in case of non-compliance with the request—see the Texan communication to Great Britain in 1840 (Smith, vol. I, p. 248).

to the purpose of recognition. Thus when in 1823 Great Britain admitted in principle the propriety of recognizing the new State of Brazil, she insisted, as a condition of recognition, upon the renunciation of the slave traffic on the part of Brazil.[1] The conditions accompanying the recognition, at the Berlin Congress in 1878, of Bulgaria, Montenegro, Serbia and Roumania,[2] are another instance of the same practice. Yet it follows from the notion of recognition conceived as a declaration of the existence of the requisite conditions of statehood that it cannot properly be granted upon conditions (other than the implied condition that if the essential requirements of statehood cease to exist recognition may be withdrawn).

§ 16. *The Incidental Political Element of Recognition.* The political implications of recognition reveal themselves in the fact that even when it is broached in good faith and in a spirit of impartiality, recognition or its denial may expose the recognizing State to protests, reprisals, and even war on the part of the parent State.[3] The vehemence of the Spanish protest against the recognition of the Latin-American Republics by Great Britain and the United States offers an instructive example of the potential difficulties inherent in the situation.[4] In 1861 the United States contemplated a declaration of war against any State recognizing the independence of the Confederacy.[5] When in 1778 France recognized prematurely the independence of the United States, she adduced general reasons of legal principle and of necessities of peace in support of her action. She was answered by a declaration of war. When Holland in the same year concluded a draft treaty with the representatives of the United States, she made the recognition of the independence of the United States conditional upon its previous acknowledgment by Great Britain—a precaution which did not, in the long run, prevent war with Great Britain. In fact, governments do not as a rule invoke considerations of national policy as a factor in

1 See Canning's despatch of 15 February 1823, printed in Smith, vol. I, p. 187, and Webster, op. cit. vol. I, p. 221.

2 See below, p. 362.

3 There is no such difficulty when the parent State itself informs third States that it has recognized the independence of the new State, as was the case in the Act of Union between Denmark and Iceland of December 1918 (Article 19 of the Act, Martens, *N.R.T.* 3rd ser. vol. XII, p. 6). In recognizing the independence of the Kingdom of Bulgaria in April 1909 Germany expressly referred to the communication informing her that Turkey, the parent State, had recognized the new situation in Bulgaria (ibid. vol. II, p. 666).

4 See as to this the communication of Mr Adams, United States Minister to Great Britain, to Mr Monroe on 22 January 1816: Manning, op. cit. vol. III (Parts VIII–XIV), p. 1434.

5 See Goebel, *The Recognition Policy of the United States* (1915), pp. 171–92.

granting or refusing recognition except when they refer to the danger of being embroiled with the parent State on account of premature recognition.[1] On the other hand, continued refusal to grant recognition is not conducive to friendly relations with the new State. It may lead to measures of retorsion such as the withdrawal of the exequatur of consuls and to inconvenience resulting from the refusal to recognize a *de facto* authority.

In all these cases the infusion into the process of recognition of an element of national interest is not altogether objectionable. When the decision to grant or to refuse recognition is determined by the wish to avoid war or reprisals, it is difficult to condemn the motives of the attitude eventually adopted by the State in question. But these cases do testify to the unsatisfactory nature of the situation resulting from the fact that the task of determining the admission to membership of the international society is entrusted to individual States called upon to combine two incongruous functions in circumstances likely to blur the disinterestedness of judicial detachment.

It is necessary to bear in mind, lest we fail to perceive the wood for the trees, that the decisive infusion of political interest into the process of recognition is not the typical and normal occurrence. Undoubtedly, considerations of national advantage cannot always be divorced from the exercise of the function of recognition which, even when performed in a spirit of detachment and of impartial fulfilment of an international duty, may still have far-reaching political repercussions. This, as will be suggested,[2] is a good reason for effecting a change in the existing machinery in the direction of collectivization of the process of recognition. It is not an adequate reason for misinterpreting the preponderant evidence of the practice of States according to which recognition is conceived in terms of the fulfilment of a legal obligation owed to the community combining the requisite elements of statehood. If we keep that fact in mind, we shall be in a position to approach with a better prospect of success the consideration of the respective merits of the constitutive and the declaratory doctrines of recognition.

1 The case of Georgia shows the possibility of recognition not being in the interest of the community about to receive it. Thus, on 26 January 1921, the Supreme Council of the Allied Powers in Paris decided to recognize *de jure* Esthonia and Latvia and also Georgia 'provided it was clearly established that the latter desired immediate recognition'. It had been pointed out that the Georgians might not welcome immediate recognition as it might expose them to Bolshevik attack.

2 See below, pp. 67, 68.

Chapter IV

THE DECLARATORY AND CONSTITUTIVE VIEWS OF RECOGNITION

§ 17. *The Constitutive View.* The consideration of the theory of recognition in international law has traditionally taken place in terms of the conflict between the constitutive and the declaratory doctrines. The orthodox constitutive view which deduces the legal existence of new States from the will of those already established dates back to Hegel, one of the spiritual fathers of the nineteenth-century doctrines of positivism and of the absolute sovereignty of the State in the international sphere. States, he taught, enter into legal relations with one another in conformity with their own will by virtue of the act of recognition. Prior to that act no relations of a legal nature can exist between them.[1] It was natural that that view commended itself to those wedded to the conception of international law as a loose 'law of co-ordination' based on agreement as distinguished from the overriding command of a superior rule of law. This applies in particular to Jellinek, who gave the first modern formulation of the constitutive doctrine. He insisted that legal relations in the form of legal rights and duties between two entities not subject to a superior legal order can arise only as the result of mutual recognition of legal personality.[2] He admitted that every State which is actually part of organized humanity enters *ipso facto* into the general community of States, but he urged that recognition is necessary in order to make it part of the *juridical* community of States. This confusing distinction between (natural) statehood, which is independent of recognition, and membership of the international community (or full international personality), which alone is a source of rights and which is dependent on recognition, was taken over literally by a number of writers, including Liszt[3] and Oppenheim.[4] The distinction seems to be of little value. There is, in law, no substance in the assertion that a community is a

1 Hegel, *Enzyklopädie der philosophischen Wissenschaften* (1870, ed. by Rosenkranz), § 331. It is, however, significant that at the same time Hegel clearly perceived the importance of recognition as 'the general principle of so-called international law' (§ 547) and insisted that, given the necessary requirements, it is 'the first absolute right of a State' to be recognized by others. See also Trott zu Solz, *Hegels Staatsphilosophie und das internationale Recht* (1932).

2 *Die Lehre von den Staatenverbindungen* (1882), pp. 92–9; *Die rechtliche Natur der Staatenverträge* (1880), p. 48.

3 *Das Völkerrecht* (12th ed. by Fleischmann, 1925), p. 91.

4 *International Law* (3rd ed. 1920), vol. 1, § 71.

State unless we attach to the fact of statehood rights and competencies, within the internal or international sphere, which international law is ready to recognize. It seems irrelevant to predicate that a community exists as a State unless such existence is treated as implying legal consequences.

Subsequently, the theory of constitutive consent as a basis of recognition, clearly foreshadowed by Triepel,[1] was developed by Anzilotti and others as resting on a contract proper. Anzilotti's view may be summarized as follows:[2] Rules of international law are created by the consent of States. Accordingly, a subject of international law comes into being simultaneously with, but not before, the conclusion of the first agreement as expressed by the treaty of recognition or its equivalent. Such recognition is reciprocal and constitutive (i.e. creative of rights and obligations which have not existed so far). Like any other treaty it is, in the last resort, binding by virtue of the fundamental rule *pacta sunt servanda*. This last proviso is a precaution calculated to meet effectively the criticism of those who insist that if the existence of a State is grounded in a treaty, i.e. in the will of another State, then the recognized State can no longer be regarded as anything else than a delegated, and therefore not sovereign, part of the recognizing State. For, says Anzilotti, the operation of the treaty is reciprocal and is supported by the overriding norm *pacta sunt servanda*[3] by virtue of which the treaty is henceforth binding equally upon both States in conformity with a higher rule of law.

The theory of mutual constitutive recognition as based on contract has been assailed on a number of grounds. One of them, which is of some cogency,[4] has been that in actual experience there is no mutuality at all in

1 He regarded recognition as part of a *Vereinbarung* (law-making agreement): *Völkerrecht und Landesrecht* (1899), p. 102.

2 See Anzilotti, *Cours de droit international* (translation from the Italian by Gidel, 1929), pp. 160 et seq.

3 It is useful to reproduce here the wording in the original: 'la personalità internazionale, resa possibile da questa norme, diviene attuale e concreta col riconoscimento. Questo, secondo noi, è puramente e semplicemente l' accordo iniziale a cui si college il sorgere di norme giuridiche per dati subietti e quindi la loro personalità l' uno di fronte all' altro; pel suo stesso concetto è reciproco e costitutivo': *Corso* (1928), p. 148.

For a more recent and occasionally somewhat modified affirmation of the constitutive theory of recognition as based on reciprocal agreement see Knubben, *Die Subjekte des Völkerrechts* (1928), pp. 317 et seq.; Perassi, *Lezioni di diritto internazionale* (1922), pp. 52–5; Redslob in *R.I.* (Paris), vol. XIII (1934), pp. 429–43; Heuss in *Z.V.* vol. XVIII (1934), pp. 37–89, esp. p. 63 et seq. See also Spiropoulos, *Traité de droit international public* (1933), p. 48.

4 The mutuality of advantage is absent only in the sense that recognition is for the new State as a rule of more immediate political, economic and sentimental value. When the news of the recognition of Colombia by Great Britain reached Bogotà, a British observer reported that 'Rockets are flying in all directions, bands of music parading the street, and the Colombians galloping about like madmen, exclaiming

the process of recognition seeing that the recognizing State appears to grant a benefit without a compensating *quid pro quo*.[1] The second, and much more persistent, criticism has been that it is impossible to understand how an entity which does not possess a juridical existence can conclude a treaty which presupposes its personality. This criticism on the grounds of logic has been voiced by numerous writers, including Kelsen,[2] Kunz,[3] Diena,[4] and Cavaglieri.[5] The last named, in order to meet the objection—more formidable in logic[6] than in practice—that a community which does not exist in law cannot take part in a legal transaction establishing its personality, has put forward the view that recognition is a constitutive unilateral act on the part of the recognizing State. Recognition, he says, 'does not declare an already existing quality; it creates and attributes it'.[7] 'It is a manifestation of the will of the already existing States addressing itself to the new State.'[8] The objection that such unilateral conferment of personality is contrary to the principle of State equality receives the somewhat unconvincing answer that the latter principle applies only in the relations of already existing States.[9] These precautions taken by Cavaglieri and others against the charge of logical inconsistency may not be altogether effective seeing that they are open to the retort that a unilateral act, if

"We are now an independent nation!!"': Webster, op. cit. vol. I, p. 385. On the other hand, it is difficult to deny that in requesting recognition or acknowledging it when granted, the new State undertakes, by implication, to comply with rules of international law in relation to the recognizing State. To that extent the transaction is not altogether one-sided.

1 '. . . la tesi della reciprocità e bilateralità del riconoscimento è nettamente smentita dalla pratica, la quale conosce soltanto l' atto di riconoscimento da parte dei vecchi Stati verso il nuovo, senza che questo si sogni di riconoscere i vecchi. . .': Fedozzi, *Trattato di diritto internazionale* (2nd ed. 1933), p. 103.

2 See *Hague Recueil*, vol. XLII (1932) (iv), pp. 268 et seq. But see below, n. 6 and p. 42, n. 6.

3 Op. cit. p. 90. See also Romano, *Corso di diritto internazionale* (2nd ed. 1929), p. 59.

4 *Rivista*, vol. XXIV (1932), pp. 478, 479.

5 Ibid. p. 338; *Corso di diritto internazionale* (1934), p. 213.

6 'To maintain that the legal personality of a State is the result of an act in which it is created by that very State is to put forward an assertion reminiscent of the attempt by Baron Munchhausen to extricate himself with the aid of his pigtail from the morass into which he had fallen': Kelsen in *Hague Recueil*, vol. XLII (1932) (iv), p. 269. However, Kelsen subsequently has adhered to the constitutive view and it is by some such act, though considerably more complicated, that he explains the process of recognition. In the first instance, he says, the new State proclaims itself a State with the effect that it 'becomes a subject of international law for itself'. It is then recognized, with a constitutive effect, by other States. Finally, it, in turn, extends recognition to these States: *A.J.* vol. XXXV (1941), p. 609.

7 *Corso di diritto internazionale* (1934), p. 204.

8 Ibid. p. 214.

9 Ibid. p. 216. Strupp's theory of recognition follows similar lines: *Grundzüge des positiven Völkerrechts* (1932), pp. 75–8; *Hague Recueil*, vol. XLVII (1934) (i), pp. 301 et seq. For a valuable statement of the constitutive view on different grounds see Sander in *Z.ö.V.* vol. I (1919), pp. 132 et seq.

conceived as having juridical effects, must have reference to an entity which already exists within the legal system in question.

The other criticisms of the orthodox constitutive view are discussed below.[1] Whatever may be their merits, they fail to point to the cardinal defect of the constitutive doctrine as generally propounded, namely, that the constitutive act creative of statehood is an act of unfettered political will divorced from binding considerations of legal principle.

§ 18. *The Declaratory View of Recognition.* This can be stated in simple terms. A State exists as a subject of international law—i.e. as a subject of international rights and duties—as soon as it 'exists' as a fact, i.e. as soon as it fulfils the conditions of statehood as laid down in international law. Recognition merely declares the existence of that fact. These propositions are regarded by the adherents of the declaratory view[2] as self-evident. In the words of Mérignhac:

> 'La reconnaissance, en effet, prend l'État déjà existant et se borne à constater qu'il réunit les conditions voulues pour qu'on puisse entretenir avec lui les rapports internationaux ordinaires. Donc l'État existait avant la reconnaissance, car, autrement, il n'aurait pu être question de reconnaissance: on ne reconnaît pas le néant.'[3]

1 See below, pp. 52–8.

2 These, to give what is believed to be a representative selection, include Kunz, pp. 85–95; Ullmann, *Völkerrecht* (2nd ed. 1908), p. 67; Nys, *Le droit international* (2nd ed. 1912), vol. I, p. 74; Heilborn, *Grundbegriffe des Völkerrechts* (1912), pp. 59–69; De Louter, *Droit international public positif* (transl. from the Dutch, 1920), vol. I, pp. 216–18; Bustamante, *Droit international public* (transl. from the Spanish, 1934), vol. I, p. 171; Verdross, *Völkerrecht* (1937), pp. 114–16; Brierly, *The Law of Nations* (3rd ed. 1942), p. 100; Erich in *Hague Recueil*, vol. XIII (1926) (iii), pp. 461 et seq.; Fischer Williams, ibid. pp. 236–8, and see below, p. 50. See also the Resolutions of the Institute of International Law of 1936, below, p. 51. The declaratory view of recognition of States seems also to underlie the Pan-American Convention, of 26 December 1933, on Rights and Duties of States. Article 3 of the Convention laid down as follows: 'The political existence of the state is independent of recognition by other states. Even before recognition the state has the right to defend its integrity and independence, to provide for its conservation and prosperity, and consequently to organize itself as it sees fit, to legislate upon its interests, administer its services, and to define the jurisdiction and competence of its courts.' Article 6 laid down that 'the recognition of a state merely [*sic*] signifies that the state which recognizes it accepts the personality of the other with all the rights and duties determined by international law'. Hudson, *International Legislation*, vol. VI (1937), pp. 622, 623. In signing the Convention the United States added a reservation which described as unfortunate the fact that the Conference did not prepare a definition or interpretation of the fundamental terms used in the Convention so as to 'enable every government to proceed in a uniform way without any difference of opinion or interpretations' (ibid. p. 625). For a judicial affirmation of the declaratory view see *Deutsche Continental Gas-Gesellschaft* v. *Polish State*, decided on 1 August 1929, by the Germano-Polish Mixed Arbitral Tribunal: *Annual Digest*, 1929–30, Case no. 5*b*, as to which see Herz in *R.I.* 3rd ser. vol. XVII (1936), pp. 564–90.

3 *Traité de droit public international*, vol. I (1905), p. 328.

Or, in the more modern formulation of Erich:

> 'Quand un gouvernement étranger reconnaît un nouvel État il constate, par là même, qu'on se trouve devant un fait, un statut organisé dont l'existence lui paraît incontestable. On le reconnaît parce qu'il existe. On ne le reconnaît pas afin qu'il prenne naissance.'[1]

If recognition is purely declaratory of an existing fact, what, then, is its juridical significance? The answer which, granting the premises, seems to be most logical and which is often given is that recognition is a political rather than a legal act.[2] Others maintain that its sole legal effect is to establish ordinary diplomatic relations between the recognizing and the recognized State.[3] This probably is also the intention of that large number of adherents of the declaratory doctrine for whom recognition signifies the acceptance of the new State as a member of the international community.[4] Others still explain the declaratory effect of recognition in the sense that although prior to it the new State possesses all rights which international law grants to States, it is only after recognition that it is assured of enjoying them.[5] Finally, some interpret the function of recognition in a manner suggesting that it is of evidential value in the meaning that the recognizing State is henceforth bound by its own declaration.[6]

1 Loc. cit. p. 461.

2 Brierly, loc. cit.; Miceli in *Rivista*, vol. XIX (1927), pp. 169–86.

3 See, in particular, Kunz, p. 95; Verdross, loc. cit.; Romano, op. cit. p. 98; possibly also Fedozzi, op. cit. p. 191; Balladore Pallieri, *Diritto internazionale publico* (1937), pp. 191, 192; Perassi, op. cit. p. 37; Scalfati, p. 53. See also, for an earlier weighty statement of this view, Strisower in *Grünhut's Zeitschrift für das private und öffentliche Recht*, vol. XVII (1890), pp. 716, 717.

4 See, for example, Nys, op. cit. p. 70; Holtzendorff in *Handbuch des Völkerrechts*, vol. II (1887), p. 18; Rougier in *Revue générale de droit international public*, vol. II (1904), p. 602; Calvo, *Droit international* (5th ed. 1896), vol. I, pp. 240, 241.

5 See, for example, Pradier-Fodéré, *Traité de droit international*, vol. I (1885), p. 237; Fauchille, p. 306; Fiore, *Le droit international codifié* (1911), p. 153; Rivier, *Principes de droit des gens*, vol. I (1896), p. 57; Diena in *Rivista*, vol. XXIV (1932), p. 482, who distinguishes between 'la capacità di diritto' (prior to recognition) and 'capacità di agire' (after recognition).

6 This, possibly, is the intention of Erich in stating that the declaratory nature of recognition 'n'empêche pas que la reconnaissance oblige celui qui reconnaît d'observer une certaine attitude qu'il n'était pas obligé d'observer envers le même État avant la reconnaissance': loc. cit. See also Kelsen, *Das Problem der Souveränität* (1920), p. 231, where he points out that while recognition is juridically of no significance, it may be of some usefulness as introducing an element of certainty and stability. It seems that Kelsen's view on the matter subsequently underwent some modification. Thus in 1929, while denying that recognition is constitutive of international personality, he admits that it may have important juridical (i.e. constitutive) results: in *R.I.* (Paris), vol. IV (1929), p. 617. In a more recent contribution—*A.J.* vol. XXXV (1941), pp. 605–9 —Kelsen, while distinguishing between political and legal recognition, regards the

§ 19. *The Declaratory View and the Practice of Courts.* The preceding survey of the various aspects of the declaratory view of recognition cannot claim the merit of clarity. This is so for the reason that the differences between them are elusive. There is little correspondence between them and the practice of courts and governments. This divorce from practice is strikingly illustrated by some of the main contentions of the adherents of the doctrine of the declaratory nature of recognition. One of them is that courts recognize both the internal competence and the international rights of States prior to recognition. Actually, if, as is often said, the answer to the question as to the nature of recognition lies in the juridical position of unrecognized 'States',[1] then the declaratory doctrine is untenable when gauged by current judicial practice.

It is true that the purely declaratory effect of recognition and the full internal and international existence of the State prior to recognition have on occasions been asserted both by members of international commissions and by judges in municipal courts as a matter of national dignity and interest. This was the case with the American members of the British-American Mixed Commission under Article 6 of the Jay Treaty, when they asserted that the United States were 'in fact...independent so early as 1775, and, on the ever glorious and memorable fourth of July 1776, they solemnly and formally declared to the world they were independent, and from *that* period have maintained their independence with honor and prosperity'.[2] Numerous decisions of the Austrian, Polish, Czechoslovak and other succession States established after the First World War were in similar vein. Thus, for instance, the Czechoslovak courts repeatedly declined to admit the view that the Czechoslovak State came into existence as the result of the coming into force of the Peace Treaties. They held that the sovereignty of the Czechoslovak Republic was established by the revolution of 28 October 1918, on which day the Czechoslovak National Committee assumed sovereignty in all its aspects.[3] The authority of these

latter as constitutive. See above, p. 40. See also Salvioli in *Rivista*, vol. XVIII (1926), pp. 330–66, who maintains that prior to recognition the State possesses the so-called fundamental, i.e. universally admitted, rights under international law, but that in many other respects recognition is constitutive.

1 See, for example, Kunz, p. 42, who says that 'the juridical solution of the entire problem of recognition of States depends on the proper understanding of the legal position of the unrecognized State'.

2 Moore, *International Adjudications, Pre-War Debts*, vol. III (1931), p. 244.

3 See the decision of the Supreme Administrative Court of Czechoslovakia of 29 May 1925: *Annual Digest*, 1925–6, Case no. 8; and see ibid. Case no. 9, and ibid. 1919–22, Cases nos. 4–6. As to Poland see *Republic of Poland* v. *Harajewicz*: ibid. 1923–4, Case no. 1. As to Austria see *A.L.B.* v. *Federal Ministry for the Interior*: ibid. 1919–22, Case no. 7 (where the Court said: '...The Peace Treaty presupposes that

and similar pronouncements is limited. It is natural for municipal courts or arbitrators appointed by their State, especially in the period following the establishment of national independence amidst turmoil and suffering, to use proud and resounding language in relation to the 'glorious and memorable' event of the proclamation of national independence. Moreover, for the purposes of the municipal law of the State concerned, it is reasonable and proper that the autonomous act of the will of its population should be regarded as decisive for fixing the commencement of national independence. But these cases do not decide the question of the *international* validity of the internal acts of the newly established State. In *foreign* courts, the unrecognized State and its acts do not legally exist prior to recognition. English and American courts have been consistent in this attitude to the point not only of refusing to admit the validity of acts of unrecognized States, but also of continuing to apply the law of the parent State,[1] of declining to grant to the unrecognized State the ordinary jurisdictional immunities,[2] of denying to it the right to sue,[3] and even of withholding relief in claims for the maintenance of which it was necessary to allege the existence of a non-recognized State.[4] The attitude of the courts of other countries has, on the whole, been the same—although in most cases it can be gauged indirectly only by reference to the decisions of those courts in connection with unrecognized governments.[5]

the new States already existed legally before it came into force, otherwise the new States could not have been parties. The legal existence of the new Republic of Austria began on 30 October 1918, the moment when she came into life by the fundamental law of the Provisional National Assembly'). The same considerations apply to such cases as *McIlvaine* v. *Coxe's Lessee*, 4 Cranch 214, 215, in which a United States Court found that a person born in New Jersey before the declaration of independence acquired the nationality of that State; or to the decision of the Court of Appeal of Milan of November 1920 (*Foro Italiano*, vol. XLVI (1921), Part V) relating to Fiume.

1 *Gelston* v. *Hoyt*, 3 Wheat. 246, 924; *Rose* v. *Himely*, (1808) 4 Cranch 241; *The Nereide*, (1815) 9 Cranch 388.

2 *The Annette*; *The Dora*, [1919] P. 105.

3 *City of Berne* v. *Bank of England*, (1804) 9 Ves. Jun. 347.

4 *Taylor* v. *Barclay*, (1828) 2 Sim. 213; *Thompson* v. *Powles*, (1828) 2 Sim. 194, *Jones* v. *Garcia del Rio*, (1823) Turner and Russell, 297. See as to all these cases Bushe-Fox in *B.Y.* vol. XII (1931), pp. 63–75. That rigid attitude was to a slight extent modified by common law courts, as distinguished from Chancery, but not to the extent of granting any rights to the unrecognized State or to applying its law: see Bushe-Fox in *B.Y.* vol. XIII (1932), pp. 39–48.

5 See, for instance, as to France, Noël-Henry, *Les gouvernements de fait devant le juge* (1927), pp. 97–9; as to Italy, see, for example, the decision in *Katsikis* v. *Società Fati Svoroni* (ibid. p. 92) where the Court stated that 'political recognition of a foreign State is an essential condition for the exercise of its juridical activity in its relation with other States'; as to Switzerland see the decision of the Civil Tribunal of Berne of

§ 20. *The 'Existence' of a State and the Commencement of International Personality.* The principal feature of the declaratory view is the confident assertion that, as the existence of a State is a fact, recognition is a formal act of political rather than legal relevance. Upon analysis, it seems unhelpful and tautologous to say that recognition is purely formal and declaratory for the reason that a State becomes a subject of international law as soon as it exists or that a State comes into being as soon as there exist the requirements of statehood. For such existence may be and often is the question at issue. In municipal law the beginning of the existence of physical or juridical persons is as a rule determinable by external tests. With regard to physical persons there has been some discussion, especially in the domain of criminal law, as to the precise moment when life begins, but the matter does not on the whole give rise to undue difficulties. Neither is it irrelevant that, apart from the question of its commencement, the mere physical existence of a person does not necessarily carry with it full legal personality. Thus there have been systems of law which, in admitting the institution of slavery, have regarded certain physical persons as incapable, wholly or in part, of possessing legal rights. Legal personality is a creature of law, not of nature. Neither is the rise of juristic persons like corporations an automatic question of fact—although, as in the case of companies, the nature of the various requirements of registration, minimum capital and the like is such as to render their ascertainment comparatively easy.

This is not the case with regard to the determination of the beginning of the existence of States. When we assert that a State exists as a normal subject of international law by virtue of the fact of its existence, we must necessarily have in mind a State fulfilling the conditions of statehood as laid down in international law. In particular, we must be referring to an independent State, i.e. a State with a government independent of any other State. But such independence is often a controversial question which cannot be answered by the tautologous test of existence. In the first instance, in the case of communities aspiring to independent statehood

21 July 1924, relating to non-recognition of the law of Soviet Russia (*Journal du droit international*, vol. LII (1925), p. 491).

The practice of States contradicts also another assertion often propounded by the adherents of the declaratory view, namely, that the effect and purpose of recognition is nothing more than a declaration of willingness to enter into diplomatic relations. The treatment of the immediate effects of recognition (or, what amounts to the same thing, of the effects of non-recognition) before judicial tribunals negatives that view, which is equally inconsistent with the fact that a decision to terminate diplomatic relations with a recognized State—a not uncommon occurrence not only in time of war—has never been regarded as tantamount to withdrawal of recognition. See below, p. 355.

subsequent to secession from the parent State, the sovereignty of the mother country is a legally relevant factor so long as it is not abundantly clear that the lawful government has lost all hope or abandoned all effort to reassert its dominion. It is a self-deception to assume that a difficult problem has been solved by such statements as the one that the Latin-American Republics existed as States as soon as they became independent of the mother country. For the question of actual independence is not one capable of any easy or automatic answer. A temporary success resulting in such independence would not, so long as there exists a reasonable prospect of the mother country reasserting her authority, justify in law the recognition of statehood. The same applies to the assertion that the American Confederacy during the Civil War was, as it claimed to be, a State because it 'existed', or that the United States existed in international law as a State as soon as they declared their independence—as soon as they 'existed'.[1] The fact that the mother country does not, for the time being, make an effort to regain sovereignty may not always be decisive. In all cases in which, on an objective estimate, recognition is premature and as such violative of international law, the seceding community, although actually wielding a substantial degree of independence of the lawful authority, is not a State in international law although it may claim that it 'exists' as such.

Similarly, apart from secession from the mother country, mere 'existence' as a State offers no answer to the question of existence as a State in international law, i.e. as a normal subject of international law. The 'State' in question must be independent of other States. As is clearly shown by the example of Manchukuo, such independence cannot be ascertained by any simple test of 'existence'. Did Manchukuo, established by Japan as a State subsequent to her invasion of the Chinese province of Manchuria in 1932, constitute a State by the very fact of its 'existence'? Apart from the continued claims of the mother country and the so-called principle of non-recognition,[2] the decisive question governing the matter was whether

1 Only a few months before the recognition of the United States by France, the French Ambassador informed the British Government that 'We [France] have repeatedly told them [the United States], you call yourselves an independent State, but you are not so; when Great Britain has *acknowledged* that Independency, then we will treat with you, but not before; at present you are at War with your Sovereign who by no means admits the Independency you assume' (cited in Goebel, op. cit. p. 89).

2 The principle of non-recognition of territorial changes and situations brought about by means contrary to international law was, subsequent to the announcement of the attitude of the United States and of the League of Nations in connection with the invasion of Manchuria, largely responsible for the recrudescence of the declaratory view of recognition. On the part of the opponents of the principle of non-recognition

Manchukuo was independent of the State which purported to detach that province from China. The answer which commended itself to impartial observers was that that province, being under the military occupation and, generally, the controlling domination of Japan in most aspects of its internal and external government, was not independent.[1] The example of Manchukuo shows that it serves no useful purpose to assert that a community is a State because it 'exists' or claims to exist. The question is: Did it exist as a State independent of other States? It is unhelpful to say that Manchukuo existed as a State independently of recognition. For the prior question must be answered, whether it 'existed' as a State in the meaning of international law. When, therefore, it is suggested that Manchukuo existed 'whether the fact is recognized or not',[2] the answer must be that the purported fact was not an independent State in the contemplation of international law. It could not be accurately maintained that, at any time, Manchukuo existed as an independent State, i.e. as a State in international law, and not as a subservient province of Japan endowed for the purpose of deception, which was not even intended to deceive, with flimsy and transparent paraphernalia of a spurious statehood.[3]

there was a tendency to rely on the declaratory view of recognition as suggesting that non-recognition was devoid of legal significance. The principle of non-recognition is not, it will be noted, inconsistent with the legal and constitutive view of recognition as here put forward, namely, the view of recognition as a legal obligation to recognize statehood whenever there exist the requisite conditions of fact not inconsistent with international law (see above, p. 6). See below, pp. 408–20. See also, with reference to Manchukuo, Lauterpacht, 'The Principle of Non-Recognition in International Law' (in *Legal Problems in the Far Eastern Conflict*, ed. by Quincy Wright (1941), pp. 129–56). The facts giving rise to and the situation brought about by the establishment of Manchukuo were in violation of international law. However, in the case of Manchukuo non-recognition followed with equal cogency from the absence of one of the essential conditions of statehood, namely, independence.

1 Yet it is apparently with reference to Manchukuo that Dr Baty (in *A.J.* vol. XXX (1936), p. 378) speaks of a 'perfectly independent community' being denied the rights of a State. Similarly, an Italian writer—Scalfati, p. 215—spoke in 1938 of 'completa dimostrazione della esistenza, nella Manciuria, di tutti gli elementi di uno Stato indipendente'. So, in 1942, does Professor Borchard in *A.J.* vol. XXXVI (1942), p. 109. See also, to the same effect, Cavaré in *R.G.* vol. XLII (1935), pp. 10–39. When, therefore, Erich says: 'les États souverains sont, dans l'organisation actuelle du monde, de par leur nature même, des personnes' (in *Hague Recueil*, vol. XIII (1926) (iii), p. 463), the solution is unhelpful without a prior determination whether the State is 'souverain' or not.

2 Borchard, loc. cit.

3 The following passage occurs in the Protocol between Japan and Manchukuo of 15 September 1932: 'Whereas Japan has recognized the fact that Manchukuo in accordance with the free will of its inhabitants, has organized and established itself as an independent State.' Martens, *N.R.T.* 3rd ser. vol. XXVIII, p. 671. With this may be compared the official French communiqué of 13 March 1778, which, in the result, brought about a state of war between Great Britain and France: 'The United States

In February 1944 Soviet Russia adopted amendments to her Constitution by virtue of which each Republic of the Union acquired 'the right to enter into direct relations with States, to conclude agreements with them and exchange diplomatic representatives with them'.[1] It was maintained by some that by virtue of these amendments the Republics of the Union acquired the position of independent States entitled to full equality and voting at international conferences and that their recognition as such was unnecessary in view of the obvious fact of their 'existence'.

§ 21. *The Automatic Test of 'Existence'*. The reliance on what may be called the automatic test of existence is the gist of the declaratory doctrine, and it is therefore profitable to adduce some further examples showing the degree of helpfulness of that test. Thus the State of the Vatican City as established by the Lateran Treaty of 1929 suggests that not only the independence but also the existence of other requirements may be a subject of controversy. The territory of the Vatican City does not exceed forty acres; one element of statehood is thus reduced to vanishing point. The question whether, notwithstanding the smallness of its territory, a community is entitled to the rank of a State in international law is not one which can be answered by a simple reference to the fact of its existence. The case of the Vatican City also suggests that the second element of statehood, namely, the existence of a population subject to the natural process of renewal and growth, may equally be a subject of controversy. The population of the Vatican City is composed almost exclusively of persons residing there by virtue of their office. It is thus of a radically different nature from the population of any other State, and for this reason also doubts have been expressed whether it can be deemed to be a State. In addition, its statehood has been questioned for the reason that it serves purposes differing fundamentally from those usually associated with temporal States. Finally, its very independence has been put in question on the ground that it is a mere instrument of the Holy See. It is not necessary to express a view as to the justification of these doubts concerning the statehood of the Vatican City. They are conclusively answered, it is believed, by the fact of the almost universal recognition of the Vatican City by other States. But it is that

of North America, which are in full possession of independence, as declared by their Act of the 4th of July, 1776, having proposed to the King to consolidate the connexions that have begun to be established between the two nations, the respective Plenipotentiaries have signed a treaty of amity and commerce.' For an illuminating discussion of the history of the communiqué see Gibbs, *Recognition* (1863), pp. 7–18.

1 Law of 1 February 1944, on the granting to Union Republics of Authority in the Sphere of Foreign Relations.

recognition—not the, hitherto, controversial 'existence' of the Vatican City as a State—which alone is conclusive.

Similarly, a protected State is not a State in international law although it may claim to 'exist' as a State and is as a rule referred to as such. British courts have treated the native States of Johore, of Kelantan, of Baroda, and others, as sovereign and independent States in actions involving jurisdictional immunities, but it would be misleading to assert that they are States in international law because they 'exist'. The question is whether they are independent in the meaning of international law. But this is not a question admitting of a self-evident answer. Three other, somewhat exotic, examples may be mentioned:

In 1871 a certain Sydney Burt and a number of other adventurous British subjects constituted a government in the Fiji Islands, an uncivilized, unrecognized State under King Thakombau, who was in fact the puppet of the government thus set up. Was that community, and its government, a State because it 'existed'? This was not the view of the Law Officers who, in a series of Opinions, reported that notwithstanding any recognition *de facto* of the Fiji authorities, the British subjects in question should not be accepted as subjects of the new State, not yet duly recognized, and that 'Her Majesty's Government may interfere with the acts and engagements of British subjects within Fiji and may declare certain acts and engagements to be legal or illegal in the case of British subjects within Fiji'.[1]

In 1894 a certain Mr Harden Hicky, formerly director of a commercial journal in Paris, purported to establish a State on an island seven hundred miles off the coast of Brazil. He adopted the title of James I and claimed recognition as the ruler of a State. He addressed his request to Switzerland asking for admission to the Universal Postal Union. The Federal Council intimated that in these matters it was proper for the colonial and maritime Powers to take the initiative.[2] It may be assumed that Mr Hicky's commonwealth did not enjoy international personality by virtue of the fact of its asserted 'existence' independently of recognition.

When in 1923 the Six Nations of the Iroquois Indians brought before the League of Nations a complaint against the Canadian Government and

1 Opinion of Law Officers of 9 August 1872 (see Appendix, p. 82). See also to the same effect Opinions of 14 June 1872; 18 July 1872; 9 December 1872. And see the *Fijian Land Claims*, decided on 26 October 1923 by the American-British Claims Tribunal (Nielsen's *Report*, p. 588) with regard to some questions of State succession concerning land grants by native chiefs.

2 *R.G.* vol. I (1894), p. 179; *Le Temps* newspaper, 30 January 1894; Gemma in *Hague Recueil*, vol. IV (1924) (iii), p. 300.

the British Empire, they described themselves as 'a State within the meaning of Article 17 of the Covenant' and offered to accept the obligations of membership of the League for the purpose of the dispute.[1] The question of their existence as a State could hardly be solved by any automatic test of existence.

The above examples may appear unduly numerous and polemical. But a measure of elaboration is perhaps indicated if the discussion of the subject is to be freed of a plausible but unhelpful formula often relied upon by writers.[2] It is not an automatic test of factual existence, but only recognition, given in good faith in pursuance of legal principle, that can answer the question of the legal existence of a State as a subject of international law.[3] Thus there is little force in the argument, often repeated, that France was fully justified in insisting, in her answer to the British protest, that, in 1778, she recognized the United States for the simple reason that the United States 'existed' as a State. The question is whether it existed as an independent State, i.e. whether the recognizing State was justified in its view that the proclaimed independence was effective, in the meaning that the chance of the mother country asserting her sovereignty had disappeared beyond all hope and was no more than a *brutum fulmen*. Neither is it always clear whether the community claiming to exist as a State possesses an effective government of a sufficient degree of stability. The manner in which the authoritative Committee of Jurists in the controversy concerning the Aaland Islands decided that Finland, notwithstanding its recognition by a number of States, was not a State at the crucial date, because of the absence of effective governmental control, is instructive.[4]

1 *Official Journal*, 1924, p. 829. The Canadian Government replied that the Iroquois Indians were not a State. In its view they were 'subjects of the British Crown residing within the Dominion of Canada': ibid. p. 830.

2 We find, for instance, Sir John Fischer Williams lending the weight of his authority to the automatic test of 'existence'. He quotes in support of the declaratory view of recognition the Greek poet's saying: 'This is alone beyond the power of Heaven, to make what has been not to have been.' See *Harvard Law Review*, vol. XLVII (1934), p. 785, and *Hague Recueil*, vol. XLIV (1933) (ii), p. 239. The question that must be answered in the first instance is whether the thing 'has been'. Sir John himself deplores as unfortunate the premature grant of recognition of statehood to some communities after the First World War. Did these communities 'exist'?

3 In the absence of a collective machinery of recognition such a decision has legal effects only in relation to the recognizing State or States—with the unsatisfactory result that a community may exist as a State in relation to some but not to other States (see below, p. 58). This defect is inherent in the existing imperfection of international organization in the matter of recognition. It is not a valid objection to the constitutive view of recognition.

4 The Committee of Jurists, which in 1920 was entrusted by the Council of the League of Nations with the task of giving an Advisory Opinion upon the legal aspects

It follows that there is little substance in the assertion that a State commences its international existence, with the concomitant rights and duties, as soon as it 'exists'.[1] On the contrary, recognition, when given in the fulfilment of a legal duty as an act of application of international law, is a momentous, decisive and indispensable function of ascertaining and declaring the existence of the requisite elements of statehood with a constitutive effect for the commencement of the international rights and duties of the community in question.

of the Aaland Islands question, expressed the view that although Finland was recognized by Soviet Russia on 4 January 1918, by Sweden on the same date, by France on 5 January, by Denmark and Norway on 10 January, by Switzerland on 22 February, and then by numerous other States, 'these facts by themselves do not suffice to prove that Finland, from this time onwards, became a sovereign State' (Special Supplement No. 3 to the *Official Journal*, 1920, p. 8). This was so because, in the view of the Committee, Finland at that time lacked a stable political organization and because the public authorities were not strong enough to assert themselves throughout the territory of the State without the assistance of foreign troops (ibid. p. 9). See also the report of the Mandates Commission in 1931 on the question of the conditions under which a territory can be released from the mandatory regime: *Official Journal*, 1931, p. 2176. These included: (*a*) a settled government and an administration capable of maintaining the regular operation of essential government services; (*b*) capacity to maintain its territorial integrity and political independence; (*c*) capacity to maintain peace throughout the territory.

For a somewhat different formulation of the conditions of statehood see the Memorandum of the Belgian Government on the nationality of the populations of territories placed under mandate: *Official Journal*, 1922, p. 607.

1 These criticisms apply also to the Resolution of the Institute of International Law of April 1936 (*A.J.* vol. xxx (1936), Suppl. p. 185) which lays down that 'recognition of a new State is the free act by which one or more States acknowledge the existence' of certain facts creative of statehood; that 'recognition has a declaratory effect'; and that 'the existence of a new State, with all the juridical effects which are attached to that existence, is not affected by the refusal of recognition by one or more States'. The description of recognition as being a 'free' act apparently means that although it has only a 'declaratory effect' it can be withheld at discretion.

Chapter V

THE DECLARATORY AND CONSTITUTIVE VIEWS OF RECOGNITION (*continued*)

§ 22. *The Criticism of the Constitutive View on Ethical Grounds.* It will be apparent from the preceding analysis of the declaratory view of recognition that it cannot be considered as expressing the correct legal doctrine. For reasons already given and for those to be stated in more detail in this chapter, the constitutive view is here considered to be in accordance with the practice of States and with sound legal principle—though it is not the constitutive view as generally propounded, namely, the view that recognition is an act of policy divorced from any notion of legal duty to the community claiming recognition.

One of the principal grounds of the criticism raised against the constitutive view by the rival doctrine has been that it is offensive to considerations of ethics and humanity. Thus it has been argued that if the community in question does not, in the contemplation of international law, exist prior to recognition, then it is neither protected by international law in the essential aspects of its existence nor bound to respect the equally vital legal interests of States already established. It has been maintained that on the constitutive view of recognition the territory of the unrecognized State could be invaded; that (as in the case of secession from an already recognized State) its subjects, hitherto indirectly protected by international law, would suffer a calamitous *capitis diminutio*; that, in case of war, it could be treated with utter disregard of rules of warfare; and that, in any war in which it may be engaged, third States would not be bound by obligations of neutrality. Similarly, it has been pointed out that all these iniquities may, *mutatis mutandis*, be inflicted by the unrecognized State upon already existing States. These perturbing possibilities have been vividly painted by writers.[1]

It is probable that the prospects involved in this criticism of the constitutive view are not as terrifying as may appear at first sight. The territory of the unrecognized community is liable to invasion, but, under traditional international law,[2] a State may invade the territory of a *recognized* State as soon as it has gone through the formality of declaring war or has otherwise manifested its *animus belligerendi*. Should an un-

1 See, for example, Kunz, p. 89; Fischer Williams in *Hague Recueil*, vol. XLIV (1933) (ii), pp. 237, 238; Brierly, op. cit. p. 100.

2 As distinguished from international law established by the Covenant of the League, the Charter of the United Nations, and the General Treaty for the Renunciation of War.

recognized community become engaged in war, then in all probability the mutual observance of most rules of warfare will naturally follow for reasons of humanity, of fear of retaliation, of military convenience and of conservation of military energy, and, generally, for considerations similar to those for which rules of warfare are observed in a civil war between the lawful government and the rebels declared to be traitors. For the same reason third States will, unless they decide to become belligerents, observe neutral conduct in any wars in which the unrecognized community may be involved. The subjects of the unrecognized community may, it is true, be maltreated in foreign States without international law offering any protection, but here again the legal position represents only inadequately the realities of the situation. If a community is determined to treat some aliens in defiance of the canons of civilization or of generally recognized international law, and if the State affected is a weak State unable or unwilling to protect its subjects by retaliation or otherwise, then recognition will seldom prevent that kind of conduct. On the other hand, if the unrecognized State is in a position effectively to show its displeasure, the absence of recognition will not be likely to cause serious injury to its interests or to those of its subjects. Moreover, absence of recognition does not necessarily render impossible regular intercourse in connection with the protection of nationals abroad and for other purposes;[1] neither does it prevent measures of accommodation calculated to meet the circumstances of the case.[2]

Full recognition is, as a rule, refused for the reason that the conditions of recognition of statehood or governmental capacity are not entirely fulfilled. But it does not follow that the unrecognized community must be ignored altogether—as is convincingly shown by the manifold forms of official and unofficial intercourse with unrecognized governments.[3] The unrecognized community is taken notice of so far as this proves necessary. Thus, for instance, an unrecognized State or government or belligerent cannot, in reliance on the formal logic of its non-recognition, claim the right to commit acts which if done by a recognized authority would constitute a violation of international law. States cannot be compelled to choose between recognition, which they deem themselves rightfully entitled to refuse, and passive toleration of unlawful acts. They can have recourse to remonstrances, protests, retorsion, reprisals, or war. They need

1 See below, pp. 346, 347, 388–95.

2 Similar considerations apply to the converse case, namely, to such acts of the unrecognized community which, if performed by a recognized State, would constitute a violation of international law. Experience does not show that the fact of non-recognition is taken advantage of, by either side, as an opportunity for committing acts otherwise illegal under international law.

3 See below, pp. 346, 347, 388–95.

not be deterred by the argument that that State or government, not being recognized, does not exist as a subject of international rights and duties and that it cannot therefore be saddled with effective responsibility. For there can be no objection to treating the unrecognized State as if it were bound by obligations of international law if these obligations are so compelling as to be universally admitted and if the non-recognizing State acknowledges itself to be bound by them. To that extent the nascent community, although not recognized generally, may be recognized for particular purposes on the not unreasonable ground that the rules in question are general and mutual in their operation. Finally, if the offending authority declines, because it has not been recognized, to act or to be dealt with on the basis of law, it must be dealt with—and suppressed—as a physical evil. There is in cases of this description a discrepancy—an unavoidable one—between law and fact. The seceding community possesses a measure of statehood; it does not possess enough of it to justify full recognition. In such cases the flexible logic of the law adapts itself to circumstances. It refuses to accept the easy dichotomy: either no rights and duties or all rights and duties which follow upon recognition. A situation is thus created in which the unrecognized community is treated *for some purposes* as if it were a subject of international law, namely, to the extent to which existing States elect to treat it as such in conformity with general rules of international law. In many cases substantial rights of statehood have been accorded, notwithstanding the absence of recognition as a State, through recognition of belligerency or insurgency.[1]

1 Similar results may be reached by way of the doctrine of so-called fundamental rights of the individual. It may be argued that, notwithstanding the absence of recognition, a community is entitled to the rights which the conscience of mankind gives to individuals regardless of whether they act in isolation or collectively. For the fundamental rights of the individual are not lost for the sole reason that he acts in conjunction with other individuals. Recognition makes a community a normal subject of international law or, as it is sometimes said, a full member of the international society with all the normal consequences attaching thereto. That does not mean that in the absence of such recognition it is in conformity with the spirit of international law that the individuals composing the community in question should be treated as being altogether outside the pale of law. Similarly, individuals composing a community unrecognized as a State cannot because of that fact acquire an immunity from the fulfilment of duties corresponding to the fundamental rights of the individual. The doctrine of the fundamental rights of the individual protected by international law is, of course, a highly controversial although—it is to be hoped—not entirely discredited doctrine. It acquires a special significance in situations connected with the rise of international personality in cases in which the border line between law and fact as well as between law and morals is necessarily lacking in precision. The repeated recognition, in the Charter of the United Nations, of fundamental human rights and freedoms (see below, p. 173) has a bearing on the subject under discussion.

§ 23. *The 'Right' of Existing States to determine Statehood.* The circumstances which reduce to its true proportions the possible mischief of the constitutive view do not, it must be admitted, dispose altogether of the possibility that, because of the improper exercise of the function of recognition a community may, through no fault of its own, be deprived of the benefits of international intercourse, that the rights acquired under its laws may be without effect abroad, and that its citizens may remain without the usual diplomatic protection. These are weighty considerations. They are only partly met by the suggestion that these rights will be enjoyed in relation to the States which agree to grant recognition—the number of these States will in the long run be in some proportion to the merits of the claim to recognition—and that in relation to the others the weapon of retaliation may prove to be not without effect. In principle the denial of rights of statehood to a community which seems to be entitled to them is an anomaly which it is difficult to justify. But these apparent consequences of the constitutive view are, in fact, attributable to a cause fundamentally different from the merits of the constitutive doctrine conceived in its essential aspect. They are not due to the circumstance that recognition is constitutive, but to the fact that in so far as it is treated as a matter of policy and not of legal duty it may be liable to abuse and arbitrariness. But this defect is an aberration, not an unavoidable consequence of the constitutive view.

These considerations, it may be noted, supply also the answer to a question which is often asked: Why should the mere accident of prior existence give to some States the right to call into being the full international personality of rising communities?[1] The answer is that as such personality cannot be automatic and that as its ascertainment requires the prior determination of difficult circumstances of fact and law, there must be *someone* to perform that task. In the absence of a preferable solution, such as the setting up of an impartial international organ to perform that function, the latter must be fulfilled by States already existing. The valid objection is not against the fact of their discharging it, but against their carrying it out as a matter of arbitrary policy as distinguished from legal duty.

§ 24. *The Logical Argument against the Constitutive View.* We may now consider the various criticisms which have been raised against the constitutive view on logical grounds. The first is directed against that aspect of the constitutive doctrine which considers recognition to be in the nature of

1 See, for example, Fischer Williams in *Hague Recueil*, vol. XLIV (1933) (ii), p. 236.

an agreement between the old and new States. That criticism points to the logical impossibility of the creation of international personality taking place by means of a treaty which presupposes the existence of the State in question.[1] Admittedly, the notion of recognition as a bilateral agreement cannot be accepted. But this is so not for reasons of logic but mainly because that notion finds no support in the practice of States where recognition is as a rule the result of a unilateral request by one party and unilateral compliance by the other.[2] However, it is useful to attempt to meet that particular logical criticism because it has a bearing on the question, previously discussed, whether communities which have not been recognized as States may not have a limited international capacity in so far as it has been expressly conceded to them. From this point of view the cogency of the argument as to the logical impossibility of a new State taking part in its own creation as an international person by means of a treaty which presupposes its existence is more apparent than real. The fact that recognition is provided for in a treaty does not imply that it is due to the treaty. It is not difficult to regard a given treaty as fulfilling two purposes at the same time, namely, as recording the unilateral act of recognition of the new State, which thereupon takes part in the contractual determination of the details of the future relationship. The practice of States shows frequent examples of such treaties preceded or accompanied by recognition in one and the same instrument. This, in fact, is the typical form of treaties of this description. Thus, for instance, Article 1 of the Definitive Treaty of Peace between Great Britain and the United States of 3 September 1783, provided that 'His Britannic Majesty acknowledges the said United States...to be free, sovereign and independent States'; and that 'he treats with them as such, and for himself, his heirs and successors, relinquishes all claims to the Government, propriety and territorial rights of the same and every part thereof'.[3] The same Treaty then laid down the details of the settlement of the principal matters at issue between the two countries. In the Treaty of 29 August 1825, between Portugal and Brazil,[4] Article 1 provided as follows: 'His Most Faithful Majesty recognizes Brazil as an Empire, independent and separate from the Kingdoms of

1 See above, p. 40.

2 Similarly there belongs to the domain of pure theory the contention, occasionally advanced, that in order to establish the plenitude of international rights and duties between the established and the new communities, it is also necessary for the latter to recognize the former. That contention is, upon analysis, a variation of the contractual theory.

3 *Treaties and Other International Acts of the United States of America*, ed. by Hunter Miller, vol. II (1931), p. 152.

4 *B.F.S.P.* vol. XII, p. 675.

Portugal and Algarve....' There followed detailed provisions touching the future relationship of the two States.

In these and similar treaties recognition, although expressed in the treaty, does not form part of the contractual arrangement. The treaty is merely a convenient and suitable opportunity for registering the fact of recognition. If the treaty were to lapse, for instance, as the result of a subsequent declaration of war, the recognition expressed therein would nevertheless remain in full vigour.[1] Recognition is independent of the content of the treaty.

Another objection to the constitutive view on logical grounds is directed against the notion of recognition as a *unilateral* act on the part of the recognizing State. That criticism is based on the contention that juridical effects even of a unilateral act cannot be conceived except between entities already endowed with juridical personality.[2] That objection, even if justified with regard to the unilateral character of the constitutive act of recognition conceived as an act of purely political discretion, does not apply to a constitutive act of recognition regarded as an act of application of international law in pursuance of a legal duty. What happens in the latter case is that the international legal system, as represented by the States already existing, extends its orbit to cover a new component part of the international society. This may, because of the absence of a central organ of recognition, amount to a complicated and baffling procedure inasmuch as the existing States may not all speak with the same voice. Apart from this, the process of recognition thus conceived as a unilateral act is not open to objection. The practice of States shows that recognition is as a rule a unilateral act—unless we regard the request for recognition, which is usually made by the new State, as an offer to recognize the existing State with the implied obligation to respect the rules of international law in relation to it, and unless we regard the actual recognition as acceptance of the offer. But such a construction is artificial and unnecessary. It begs the question inasmuch as it postulates that all obligations of international law must have their source in voluntary agreement.[3]

1 There was little justification, therefore, for the apprehension expressed in *Society for the Propagation of the Gospel* v. *New Haven*, 8 Wheat. 464, that the war of 1812 might be regarded as terminating all former treaties with Great Britain: 'even the treaty of 1783, so far as it fixed our limits, and acknowledged our independence, would be gone, and we should have had again to struggle for both upon revolutionary principles'.

2 See above, p. 40.

3 There are isolated instances of mutual recognition of a semi-contractual nature. See, for example, the official communiqué issued after the ceremony of the signature of the Lateran Treaty of 11 February 1929, stating that the Holy See 'recognizes the

Similarly, it is difficult to accept the view that if recognition is regarded as constitutive it amounts to a kind of subjection of the recognized community to the recognizing State inasmuch as the former becomes, as the result, a delegated authority derived from the law of the recognizing State. Even if it were true that the existence of the new State is derived from the will of the recognizing State, this fact could not leave any permanent stigma of subordination, for recognition, once given, creates an obligation which like any other international obligation owes its continued binding force to international law and not to the will of the State concerned. Moreover, there would be a measure of subjection if recognition were an act of policy as distinguished from one of application of international law. But, as stated, that assumption does not necessarily follow from the constitutive view, although it does follow from the notion of recognition conceived as an unfettered act of policy.

Finally, it is not easy to admit the relevance of the criticism according to which, on the constitutive view, a situation is created in which a new community exists as a State for those States which have recognized it, but not for others. For this is a criticism not of the constitutive doctrine, but of the imperfection of international organization due to the fact that there is no international authority competent to recognize the existence of the new State. The declaratory view, it is true, avoids this particular difficulty, but it does so by the easy device of asserting that a State exists in international law as soon as it exists, and that, accordingly, recognition is a formality. It has been shown that that formula offers no solution of the difficulty. On the other hand, once recognition is conceived not as subject to the vicissitudes of political bargaining and concessions[1] but as an impartial ascertainment of facts in accordance with international law, the likelihood of divergent findings is substantially diminished.

Kingdom of Italy under the dynasty of the House of Savoy, with Rome as the capital of the Italian State' and that 'Italy, on its side, recognizes the State of the Vatican City under the sovereignty of the Supreme Pontiff': *Documents on International Affairs*, 1929, p. 216. There is no such mutual recognition in the text of the Treaty. Mutual recognition in this particular case might also be explained by reference to the necessity of recognition on the part of the Vatican City of the annexation by Italy of the Papal State in 1870.

1 The adherents of the political constitutive view of recognition have attempted to minimise the effects of the resulting divergency of action by maintaining, as does Cavaglieri (*Corso di diritto internazionale* (1934), p. 218), that recognition by the majority of States, especially the most influential Powers, 'sembra avere invece per effeto di investire il nuovo Stato di una qualificazione soggettiva rilevante *erga omnes*' inasmuch as the silence of other States must be regarded as tacit acquiescence. For a criticism of the theory of tacit consent see Kunz, p. 91, and Strupp in *Hague Recueil*, vol. XLVII (1934) (i), p. 444.

§ 25. *The Retroactivity of Recognition and the Traditional Doctrines.* The principle of retroactivity of recognition as acted upon by courts has proved a stumbling block both for the constitutive and for the declaratory doctrines. It is therefore convenient to attempt to assess its place in the field of recognition, although the judicial pronouncements on the matter bear almost exclusively on the question of recognition of governments.[1] Recognition is retroactive in the meaning that, once granted, it dates back to the actual commencement of the activities of the recognized authority, with regard to international rights and duties and, in particular, with regard to the recognition by foreign courts of the validity of its internal acts. That principle is obviously an embarrassment for the declaratory view.[2] For if a State is a subject of international rights and duties as soon as it 'exists', then there is no necessity for a special judicial doctrine sanctioning the validity of those rights and duties *ab initio*. In fact, the principle of retroactivity is an indirect but clear refutation of the declaratory view. It seems equally to be incompatible with the constitutive view, which knows of no rights and obligations prior to recognition.

However, retroactivity may still be conceived as an exception to the constitutive doctrine[3]—an exception adopted for the purposes of convenience and stability, with the object of preserving legal continuity between the old and the new order of things.[4] Inasmuch as the preserva-

1 With regard to recognition of States see the views of the American Commissioners in the *Andrew Allen* case before the British-American Mixed Commission under the Jay Treaty: Moore, *International Adjudications, Pre-War Debts*, vol. III (1931), pp. 238–52, and Lapradelle-Politis, *Recueil des arbitrages internationaux*, vol. I (1905), p. 25. For the suggestion that the principle of retroactivity ought to have been invoked by Chile in the case of *The Macedonian* before the United States-Chilean Commission of 1858, see the *note doctrinale* in Lapradelle-Politis, vol. II (1924), p. 217.

On the other hand, the principle of retroactivity of recognition of governments has received repeated and emphatic application: *Underhill* v. *Hernandez*, (1897) 168, U.S. 250; *Oetjen* v. *Central Leather Co.* (1918) 246 U.S. 297; *Dougherty* v. *The Equitable Life Assurance Society*, (1934) 266 N.Y. 71; *United States* v. *Belmont*, (1937) 301 U.S. 324; *Luther* v. *Sagor*, [1921] 3 K.B. 532; *White, Child & Beney Ltd.* v. *Simmons*, 38 T.L.R. 616; *The Jupiter*, [1927] P. 122, 250; *Kolbin & Sons* v. *William Kinnear & Co.* (1930) S.C. 724; *Princess Olga Paley* v. *Weisz*, [1929] 1 K.B. 718; *In re Marmatscheff* (a French case), *Annual Digest*, 1929–30, Case no. 150. And see below, p. 60.

2 See, for example, Kunz, p. 100.

3 It cannot logically be conceived as an exception to the *declaratory* view. It is logically opposed to it. For a suggestion that it is altogether contrary to juridical logic see Mervyn Jones in *B.Y.* vol. XVI (1935), p. 55. And see Nisot in *Canadian Bar Review*, vol. XXI (1943), pp. 627–43, for a cogent statement of the view that the principle of retroactivity is not a rule of *international* law.

4 Where these considerations do not arise there may be some reluctance to apply the doctrine of retroactivity. See, for example, the observations of the Permanent Court of International Justice in the case of *German Interests in Polish Upper Silesia*, Series A, no. 7, pp. 28, 29. And see Erich in *Hague Recueil*, vol. XIII (1926) (iii), pp. 499–502.

tion of the legal continuity of the municipal system torn asunder by revolutionary convulsions is one of the objects of international law, it is difficult not to approve of that exception. For the same reasons of expediency the principle of retroactivity has been applied not only to *de jure*, but also to *de facto*, recognition.[1] Essentially, the principle of retroactivity is one of convenience. It would not be conducive to the maintenance of friendly relations if, after recognition had been given, courts were to continue to proceed on the theory that, for instance, legislative acts of expropriation prior to recognition were acts of 'thieves and robbers' and conferred no title.[2] There has been no hesitation to abandon that principle of convenience when it was opposed by more cogent considerations. Thus it has been held by the Supreme Court of the United States that the principle of retroactivity was not applicable to transactions in the United States between American nationals and the predecessor of the newly recognized government.[3] To hold otherwise would have meant to frustrate legitimate expectations of persons who relied, as they were entitled to do, on the fact that their government continued to recognize, for a time, the predecessor of the authority newly recognized.

1 See *Luther* v. *Sagor* and some other cases, cited above, p. 59. It will be noted that the principle of retroactivity has been adopted not only with regard to the rights but also with regard to the duties of the recognized authority. In particular it is now clearly established that the recognized State or government originating in revolution is responsible, as from the commencement of civil war, for the obligations undertaken by it as well as for any acts contrary to international law. Thus it has been held in a series of cases decided by the Claims Commission of 1839 and 1849 between the United States and Mexico that the latter was responsible for monies and supplies furnished by citizens of the United States to the leaders of the revolutionary government engaged in revolt against Spain before the independence of Mexico was recognized: see Moore, *History and Digest of International Arbitrations*, vol. IV, pp. 3426–32. A similar Award was given by the United States-Venezuelan Claims Commission of 1885 in the *Idler* case (in respect of supplies furnished to the agents of Bolivar in 1817): ibid. pp. 3491–544. See also the observations in *Williams* v. *Bruffy*, (1877) 96 U.S. 176. As to the governments set up by successful insurgents, see *Puerto Cabello and Valencia Railway* case, Ralston, *Venezuelan Arbitrations of 1903* (1904), p. 455; *Bolivar Railway Co.* case, ibid. p. 388; *Hughes* case, Moore, op. cit. vol. III, p. 2972. See also Moore, vol. VI, p. 992; Ralston, *The Law and Procedure of International Tribunals* (1926) and Supplement (1936), pp. 615, 615*a*; Hyde, vol. I (1922), § 302; Borchard, *Diplomatic Protection of Citizens Abroad* (1916), § 96.

2 This aspect of the matter was stressed by the Supreme Court in *United States* v. *Pink*, (1942) 315 U.S. 203—a case in which the majority of the Supreme Court, in a somewhat drastic manner, assimilated some of the consequences of recognition to those of a treaty.

3 *Guaranty Trust Company of New York* v. *United States*, (1938) 304 U.S. 126—a limitation relied upon by the Appellate Division of the Supreme Court of New York in *Koninklijke Lederfabriek 'Oisterwijk' N.V.* v. *Chase National Bank*, (1941) 32 N.Y.S. 2d, 131 (263 App. Div. 815), where the Court pointed out that 'recognition does not undo the legal consequences of previous recognition'. See also *Union of Soviet Socialist Republics* v. *National City Bank of New York*, (1941) 41 F. Supp. 353.

§ 26. *The Problem of the Legal Nature of Recognition.* It has been submitted that the declaratory view of recognition is inconsistent with the practice of States, that its conception of the function of recognition is over-simplified and devoid of usefulness, and that its criticisms of the constitutive view prove, on analysis, to be without foundation. This being so, what, it must be asked, are the reasons for the wide acceptance of the declaratory view? The answer is that it is the reaction against the conception of recognition as a political act pure and simple which has led most writers to subscribe to the declaratory view of recognition. There is a natural disinclination to regard recognition as constitutive of the international rights and duties of the new State so long as it is felt that recognition is an act of mere policy, a bargain, or a concession of grace on the part of the recognizing State. Professor Brierly's and Sir John Fischer Williams's treatment of this question well illustrates this explanation of the declaratory theory. Thus Sir John, after expressing what is believed to be the accurate view, namely, that 'the Members of the Family [of Nations], acting in the absence of a central authority, when they admit to membership, have a duty to act as in discharge of a duty to the Family and therefore upon some general principle, not in a merely selfish and arbitrary interest',[1] proceeds to say, somewhat unexpectedly, that in the matter of recognition, 'each State cannot be conceived as doing more than declaring its own policy'. It is difficult to see how recognition can at the same time be a matter both of legal duty and of policy unfettered by legal obligation. Apparently it is his belief that recognition is an act of policy, which probably explains his preference for the declaratory view: 'And as each State', he says, 'cannot be conceived as doing more than declaring its own policy, it is also clear that the nature of the act of each State cannot be creative in the sense of making a new international person, but must be limited to a declaration that it personally accepts the fact that a new international person has come into being.'[2] Similarly, Professor Brierly, in a valuable exposition of the subject, seems to start from the proposition that international law delegates to each State the power to decide whether a community claiming the quality of statehood satisfies the necessary requirements.[3] However, from the circumstance that the act of recognition is liable to be abused for political purposes and that the recognizing State is free to take a decision according to its own appreciation of the facts, he draws the conclusion that

1 *Harvard Law Review*, vol. XLVII (1934), p. 780.

2 Loc. cit.

3 *Hague Recueil*, vol. LVIII (1936) (iv), pp. 52 et seq. Professor Brierly agrees that international law prescribes the objective conditions on which States 'are bound to base their decision' in the matter (ibid.).

recognition is merely 'an act of policy and not of law and that no juridical consequences attach thereto'.[1]

It is this negation of the element of legal obligation and the assertion of the State's right to full freedom of action in the matter of recognition which has made the established constitutive view so closely identified with the extreme assertion of sovereignty and so conspicuously open to attack. That denial of the legal nature of recognition is, it is true, common also to the declaratory view. But there it is relatively innocuous. For on the declaratory view recognition is a mere formality or an expression of the wish to enter into diplomatic relations. This being so, the circumstance that recognition is a question of political discretion would be of little consequence. But a theory which makes the very rise of international personality and of the concomitant rights and duties depend on the unrestricted will of sovereign States brings once more into prominence the doctrine of sovereignty in its most uncompromising form. It is not surprising that it has become the subject of disapproval. What is not so easy to understand is why criticism directed against the traditional constitutive view has assailed the sound heart of that doctrine, namely, that recognition is constitutive in its nature, and has associated itself with the objectionable aspect of the constitutive doctrine, namely, with the conception of recognition as an arbitrary function of politics.

Undoubtedly, the refusal or the grant of recognition are acts of political importance. Most legal transactions in the international sphere are of political significance and have political consequences. This naturally applies in particular to matters connected with the rise and the extinction of States. But it does not by any means follow that such transactions are 'acts of policy' not governed by considerations of legal right and duty. It has been shown here that there is no warrant for describing recognition of States as an act of policy in this meaning. Courts[2] and governments have frequently described recognition as being a political—and not a judicial—question. But the intention of such pronouncements is to convey that the grant of recognition is a matter for the political as distinguished from the judicial organs of the State. They are not an authority for the view that in performing the function of recognition the political branch of the government is entitled to act arbitrarily without reference to applicable legal principles.

1 *Hague Recueil*, vol. LVIII (1936) (iv), p. 59.

2 See below, pp. 70, 71, 153, 154. See *Oetjen* v. *Central Leather Co.* (1918) 246 U.S. 297, 302; *Guaranty Trust Company of New York* v. *United States*, (1938) 304 U.S. 126, 137. And see other cases to the same effect cited in Hackworth, vol. I, p. 165.

Once we have assimilated the idea that recognition is not primarily a manifestation of national policy but the fulfilment of an international duty, we shall have removed the principal objection to the acceptance of the view that recognition marks the rise of the international rights and duties of the State. That view is in accordance with the weight of the practice of governments, with decisions of courts, and, in particular, with the requirements of international intercourse. The existing procedural position in the matter of recognition is undoubtedly unsatisfactory. There are, theoretically, two ways of meeting the difficulty. It is possible to approach the subject by minimizing the importance of the act of recognition in its present procedural stage of development and to assert that as recognition is a purely political fact it can be only declaratory of rights and duties. This method of approach has been shown to be both contrary to practice and unworkable. The better method, and one which is more consonant with practice and principle, is to admit the constitutive character of recognition and to bring it—the primary and perhaps the most fundamental aspect of international relations—under the sway of legal right and obligation. This is not what most international lawyers have done.

§ 27. *The Acknowledgment of the Legal Nature of Recognition.* The majority, though not a large one, of writers deny the legal nature of the act of recognition of States. That majority includes the adherents both of the declaratory and of the constitutive view.[1] The first have no difficulty in denying that there is ever a duty to grant recognition. They are in a position to do so without embarrassment for the reason that, in their eyes, recognition is devoid of any legally relevant substance; it is largely synonymous with a political decision to enter into diplomatic relations. The others are compelled to adopt the same view for the reason that it follows inevitably from the positivist attitude which, based in turn on the theories of sovereignty and consent as the foundation of international law, finds it impossible to admit that States may, without their consent, be

1 The following is a selection of those who deny that recognition can properly be regarded as a matter of legal duty to the community claiming it: Kunz, p. 43; Scalfati, p. 232; Verdross, *Verfassung der Völkerrechtsgemeinschaft* (1926), pp. 141, 164, and *Völkerrecht* (1937), p. 116; De Louter, op. cit. vol. I, p. 219; Hershey, *Essentials of Public International Law and Organization* (revised ed. 1927), § 123; Fauchille, no. 203; Oppenheim, *International Law* (4th ed. by McNair, 1928), vol. I, § 71; Strupp in *Hague Recueil*, vol. XLVII (1934) (i), p. 445; Anzilotti, *Corso*, p. 149; Brierly, *The Law of Nations* (3rd ed. 1942), p. 100; Fischer Williams in *Hague Recueil*, vol. XLIV (1933) (ii), p. 238; Balladore Pallieri, op. cit. pp. 193, 194; Noël-Henry, *Les gouvernements de fait devant le juge* (1927), p. 220; Kelsen in *A.J.* vol. XXXV (1941), p. 610.

constrained to be bound by rules of law in relation to a newcomer. In addition, the opinion that recognition, being a political act, can never be demanded as a matter of right, has found support from writers not wedded to any doctrinal view in terms of accepted terminology.[1]

However, that political view of recognition has not remained unchallenged. Alongside the predominant doctrine there has been a substantial body of opinion which has treated recognition from the angle of the fulfilment of a legal duty to the community asking for recognition and to the international society in general. Bluntschli, writing in 1868,[2] put the point with all requisite clearness. He says:

> 'So long as the open struggle for the establishment of the new State lasts and so long as it is doubtful whether a new State has arisen, no other State is bound to recognize the new State.... The newly created State has a right to enter into the international community and to be recognized by other States if its existence is undoubted and secure. It has that right because it exists and because international law unites the States of the world into a common legal system....The existing States can no more arbitrarily exclude a State from the society of States than they can themselves withdraw arbitrarily from that society.'[3]

Hall's emphatic assertion of the right of the new State to recognition has been noted above.[4] Phillimore, who discusses the subject in some detail, considers that when the new State has '*de facto*, achieved an independent existence', recognition is 'a right which other States are under an

1 Thus we find Sir William Harcourt in his *Letters by Historicus on Some Questions of International Law* (1863) saying, at p. 12: 'It is sometimes said that the question of recognition is one of policy—and this is true, if considered with respect to the community which has recently asserted its independence. With respect to such a community, foreign powers have as yet contracted no duties similar to those which are incumbent on them in reference to established Governments with whom they have already entered into relations. It is entirely a matter of discretion and policy how, and how soon, they will admit such communities into the society of nations of which they are themselves members.' Similarly, Sir Travers Twiss in his *The Law of Nations* (1884), p. 20, says: 'Every other State is at liberty to grant or withhold this recognition, subject to the consequences of its own conduct in this respect; as, for instance, if it grants such recognition, it may incur the hostility of the State from which the new State has separated itself; if it refuses such recognition, it may incur the hostility of the new State or its allies.'

2 *Das moderne Völkerrecht der zivilisierten Staaten als Rechtsbuch dargestellt*, pp. 69–70.

3 He adds: 'It is true that the recognition of a true State by other States takes place in the form of a free act of sovereign States, but it is not an absolutely arbitrary act, for international law unites the existing States into a human society even against their will. The view often put forward in the older literature, that it depends on the mere whim of a State whether it will or will not recognize another State, ignores the legal necessity of international law and would be correct only if international law were based solely on the arbitrary will of States, i.e. if it were purely contractual law' (p. 71).

4 See above, p. 17. And see below, p. 75.

obligation to render'.[1] The main reason which he gives in support of this view is that, as recognition is within the province of the government and as the refusal to grant it entails legal consequences highly prejudicial to the community to which it is refused, it is inadmissible that it should be arbitrarily[2] refused. More recently, Hyde says: 'When a country has by any process attained the likeness of a State and proceeds to exercise the functions of one, it is justified in demanding recognition.'[3] Scelle's view is the same: 'La reconnaissance étant constatation est due, ou si l'on préfère obligatoire.'[4]

While those directly admitting the legal nature of recognition in relation to the community claiming it are in a minority, careful examination reveals that it is often indirectly admitted also by those who deny it. This applies even to thoroughly positivist writers wedded to the constitutive view. When, for instance, Anzilotti says that '...one must deny that recognition may depend on any enquiry touching the legitimacy of the new State',[5] that statement must be interpreted as meaning that at least there is a duty not to refuse recognition on the ground of illegitimacy of origin. However, it is mainly from the adherents of the declaratory view that there has come the indirect acknowledgment of the legal nature of recognition. Such indirect admission must be deemed to be inherent in the assertion that statehood in the field of international law—i.e. the quality of a subject of international law—and most consequences of statehood are independent of recognition. That assertion means that the seceding community is entitled as a matter of legal right to demand, and the

1 *Commentaries upon International Law* (3rd ed. 1882), vol. II, p. 37.

2 Ibid.

3 Vol. I, §36.

4 *Précis de droit des gens*, vol. I, p. 56. See also, to the same effect, Klüber, *Europäisches Völkerrecht* (2nd ed. 1851), § 45; Fiore, *International Law Codified* (Borchard's transl. 1918), § 174, where unjustifiable refusal of recognition is described as contrary to international law although in § 169 it is referred to as being in its nature a political act; Ullmann, *Völkerrecht* (2nd ed. 1908), p. 185; Gareis, *Institutionen des Völkerrechts* (1888), p. 57; Pradier-Fodéré, *Traité de droit international*, vol. I (1885), p. 241; Holtzendorff, *Handbuch des Völkerrechts*, vol. II (1887), p. 25. For a clear affirmation of the legal view of recognition conceived as a fulfilment of an international duty which if 'arbitrairement refusée...constituerait une violation du droit, contre laquelle la commune conscience ne tarderait pas à réagir' see Politis in *Mélanges Antoine Pillet*, vol. I (1929), p. 190. Probably there ought to be included in this category writers who emphasize the *judicial* discretion of States granting or refusing recognition. Thus Le Normand, *La reconnaissance internationale et ses diverses applications* (1899), p. 228, says: 'C'est formellement un acte libre de l'État. Mais ce n'est pas un acte arbitraire. Il doit traduire la conviction de l'État qui constate l'existence de certaines conditions matériellement exigées.'

5 *Corso di diritto internazionale* (Gidel's translation, 1929), p. 169.

existing States are bound as a matter of legal duty to concede to it, international rights which according to the constitutive view flow from recognition and are dependent on it. As soon as the conditions of statehood exist, says Kunz, 'the State newly arisen within the territorial domain of the family of nations becomes *ipso facto* and regardless of its consent a member of the international community and from that moment it becomes subject to all international rights and duties'.[1] The declaratory view of recognition postulates that the new State is entitled, as soon as it 'exists', to most of the rights—for instance, jurisdictional immunities—enjoyed by already recognized States. The new State is thus, it would appear, entitled as a matter of law to the normal legal consequences of recognition, but not to recognition as such. The unsatisfactory nature of the solution thus suggested reveals the confusing dilemma resulting from the uncritical repetition of the phrase that there is no right to recognition. From that dilemma the adherents of the declaratory view have attempted to escape by devitalizing the function of recognition, i.e. by reducing it either to a formality, or to a gesture of assurance of enjoyment of already existing rights, or to a declaration of willingness to enter into diplomatic relations. It has been shown that none of these interpretations of the function of recognition can be accepted as being even remotely in accordance with international practice.

1 Op. cit. p. 88. See also Verdross, *Verfassung der Völkerrechtsgemeinschaft* (1926), p. 164, according to whom States are from the moment of their establishment subjects of international law *in posse*, but do not actually become such except by recognition on the ground that in the absence of a positive rule of international law to that effect neither the new State nor the others are bound to entertain international relations and that there is in international law neither an obligation to recognize nor a right to recognition. It is not easy to follow this argument seeing that Verdross asserts at the same time that existing States are bound to treat as valid the internal acts of the unrecognized community. The maintenance of international intercourse does not exhaust the scope of international rights and duties.

Chapter VI

THE PROCEDURE OF RECOGNITION

§ 28. *The Collectivization of the Process of Recognition.* The criticism, formulated in the preceding chapter, of the declaratory view of recognition does not imply that the present position, under which existing States perform the function of recognition with a constitutive effect, is satisfactory and that it ought to be perpetuated. It is true that an acknowledged and decisive infusion of the element of national interest has not been a typical feature of the process of recognition. But, as has been shown,[1] the exceptions are frequent and disquieting. Neither is it possible to ignore the political implications and repercussions of the process of recognition even when it takes place in the conscientious fulfilment of a duty owed to international society and to the community claiming recognition. The dual position of the recognizing State as an organ administering international law and as a guardian of its own interest must reveal itself in a disturbing fashion whenever there is an occasion for successfully using the weapon of recognition for the purpose of achieving political advantages. Situations will arise in which a State may see in the manner of the exercise of the function of recognition an opportunity for securing for itself benefits from the parent State or from the community asking for recognition. The consideration of such benefits cannot be regarded as legitimate, but it cannot always be absent from the decision of the recognizing State. It would be futile to deny either the existence of this aspect of the problem or the fact that it is due to an obvious imperfection of international organization. The solution, which is equally obvious, of that difficulty would seem to lie in transferring that function to an international organ not impeded by a conflict between interest and duty. An innovation of this nature would also abolish the glaring anomaly of a community existing as a State in relation to some but not to other States.[2]

The collectivization of the process of recognition depends clearly upon the achievement of a high degree of political integration of the international community in the form of an international organization of States. Recognition of States, though consisting in the application of a legal principle and in the ascertainment of the existence of conditions of state-

1 See above, pp. 33–7. 2 See below, p. 78.

hood as laid down by international law, could—and in view of its political implications, ought to—be placed within the competence of the highest executive and, to some extent, judicial bodies of the international organization. The thorough collectivization of the process of recognition in this way would be possible only if the international organization were both universal and compulsory, i.e. if it were an organization to which, by a sovereign act of international legislation, all States would be made to adhere and from which there could be neither withdrawal nor expulsion. An international organization which is not universal would make possible the collectivization of recognition only in the mutual relations of its members—though, politically, the authority of such recognition would extend outside the scope of its membership. In a universal international organization on a compulsory basis recognition by an appropriate majority of its highest organs would automatically involve membership. In an international organization which is not universal or in which membership is voluntary, admission by the competent organ of the organization would automatically involve recognition by all the members of the organization. In this respect experience points to the necessity of a clear constitutional provision lifting the question of automatic recognition above the uncertainty and the controversy with which it was surrounded in the Covenant of the League of Nations.[1] No such provision is contained in the Charter of the United Nations.

The development in the direction of collectivization of recognition may be facilitated by the realization that instances of collective recognition are not altogether absent from international practice. These include the recognition of Greece by the Treaty of London of 1830, of Belgium in the Treaty of London of 1831,[2] of some of the Balkan States by the Berlin Treaty of 1878,[3] of the Congo State in the Berlin Treaty of 1885,[4] of Albania by the Conference of London of 1913 as well as the recognition of her independence by the Conference of Ambassadors in 1921,[5] and the

1 See below, pp. 401, 402.

2 The recognition of Greece and Belgium was largely in the nature of intervention by the European Great Powers. For some interesting details see Gibbs, *Recognition* (1863), pp. 38–41. See also *B.F.S.P.* vol. XVIII, pp. 728, 749.

3 See below, p. 362.

4 Protocol 9 of the Act of the Conference: Martens, *N.R.G.* 2nd ser., vol. X, p. 353. But see Nys, *Le droit international* (2nd ed. 1912), vol. I, pp. 99–105 for details showing that recognition was additional to that previously obtained by the International Association of the Congo from various Powers.

5 *Official Journal*, 1921, p. 1195. It is arguable that this was a recognition not of the Albanian State but of the Albanian Government. But see Hackworth, vol. I, p. 196.

various instances of collective recognition of new States by the Allied Powers after the First World War.[1] Moreover, diplomatic practice shows that, as in the case of recognition of governments, recognition of States, even when granted separately, is often preceded by negotiations aiming at establishing a common line of action. The attempts made by Great Britain to secure at the Congress of Verona joint action with other European Powers in the matter of the recognition of the Latin-American States, as well as the efforts of the United States to secure the co-operation of Great Britain in the same matter, may be mentioned as examples.[2]

§ 29. *International Courts as Agencies of Recognition.* There appear to be weighty objections to conferring upon the international judiciary the power to grant recognition on the application of the community claiming it. On the face of it, this would seem to be the rational solution. It would seem that a function consisting in the application of international law through ascertainment of the existence of requisite conditions of fact may and ought properly to be fulfilled by an international judicial organ of the highest authority and impartiality. There is no doubt that, under its Statute, the International Court of Justice would be in a position to act in that capacity. Yet there is substance in the view that it is undesirable to burden the Court with a task whose implications and potential consequences are of capital political significance. This applies in particular to cases in which the question of recognition of States arises in connection with a revolt against and secession from the parent State. In such cases to grant recognition is tantamount to decreeing a radical amputation or dismemberment of the territory of a State. For these reasons it seems more appropriate that that particular function of applying the law should be

1 See, for example, the Note of 26 January 1921, addressed by the President of the Inter-Allied Conference at Paris to the President of the Esthonian Delegation: 'Le Conseil Suprême des Puissances alliées, prenant en considération les demandes présentées à diverses reprises par votre Gouvernement, a décidé, dans sa séance d'aujourd'hui, de reconnaître l'Esthonie comme État *de jure*': *B.F.S.P.* vol. CXIV (1921), p. 558. See also Heumann, *Aspects juridiques de l'indépendance estonienne* (1938). As to Finland see Graham, *The Diplomatic Recognition of the Border States*, Part I: *Finland* (1936). As to Latvia see Laserson in *A.J.* vol. XXXVII (1943), pp. 245. As to Lithuania see below, p. 361 (in connection with conditional recognition). As to Poland see below, p. 381. See also Hackworth, vol. I, § 37.

2 See, for example, the Instructions of Mr Adams to Mr Anderson, United States Minister to Colombia, of 27 May 1823, pointing out that in August 1818 the United States made a formal proposal to the British Government 'for a concerted and contemporary recognition of the independence of Buenos Ayres': Manning, *Diplomatic Correspondence of the United States concerning the Independence of the Latin-American Nations*, vol. I (Parts I–II) (1925), p. 195.

performed not by the judicial but by the highest executive organs of the international community. The Court might still make a useful contribution in pronouncing, by way of Advisory Opinions or in a similar capacity, on any questions of law incidental to recognition.[1]

§ 30. *Municipal Courts and the Function of Recognition.* The foregoing considerations suggest also that no amelioration of the present position can be expected from transferring the function of recognition to municipal courts as distinguished from the executive organs of the State. In addition, there would still remain the contingency of the courts of various countries arriving at divergent views on the question of recognition in any given case.

It is convenient in this connection to consider the criticism which has been levelled against two principles obtaining in Great Britain and in the United States, as well as in some other States, in the matter of recognition. The first principle, which is of unchallenged authority, is that in the matter of recognition, as, indeed, in some other matters relating to foreign affairs, the position taken up by the executive department of government is of decisive weight. The question whether a foreign community exists as a State in the contemplation of international law is answered by the courts in strict reliance upon the statement of the executive informing the court whether and to what extent recognition has been granted. Recognition is a function performed by the executive. The justification, occasionally adduced, of that principle is that it would be inconvenient—for the State and its neighbours—if its various organs were to assume divergent positions in the matter of its external relations.[2] However, the accepted doctrine in the matter is based on considerations more cogent than mere convenience. It is proper that courts should act on the information of the Executive, seeing that the latter is not only particularly qualified to assess

1 Neither do the above-mentioned objections apply to the court giving redress, in the form of compensation for injury actually suffered, for arbitrary delay of recognition by one State in face of practically universal recognition by other States. See below, p. 74.

2 For a clear statement of both practice and principle as applied by British courts see McNair in *B.Y.* 1921–2, pp. 57–67. And see, in general, Jaffe, *Judicial Aspects of Foreign Relations* (1933), for a critical survey and discussion of the existing rule. See also Dickinson in *A.J.* vol. xxv (1931), pp. 214–37; Tennant in *Michigan Law Review*, vol. xxix (1930–1), pp. 708–41; and Makarov in *Z.ö.V.* vol. iv (1934), pp. 1–24. For a thorough judicial treatment of the question see *Duff Development Company* v. *Government of Kelantan*, [1924] A.C. 797. See also *The Annette*; *The Dora*, [1919] P. 105. As to the identical position in France see Noël-Henry, op. cit. pp. 85–7. See also Mann in *Transactions of the Grotius Society*, vol. xxix (1943), pp. 143–70. And see below, pp. 71, 89, 153–6.

the facts of the situation, but also because, as has been shown in the preceding chapters, in reaching a decision on the question of recognition it does not act arbitrarily. In granting recognition of statehood the Executive acts, as a rule, on the applicable principles of international law. This is one of the frequent instances in which the executive organs are entrusted with quasi-judicial functions of administering law. Recognition is, therefore, a political function only in the sense that it is fulfilled by the political department of the State—not in the meaning that it is performed without reference to an applicable rule of law. It is a sound and convenient principle that in some matters pertaining to relations with foreign States the rules of international law should be applied by the Executive, and not by the courts. Recognition is one of them. This being so, it is difficult to assent to the view that the existing rule is open to objection.[1]

The fact that, as a rule, the decision of the executive department on the subject is presumed to be in accordance with international law explains the second principle which governs the attitude of courts in the matter of recognition. That principle is that in the absence of recognition the community in question and the acts of its authorities are legally non-existent. This is a rule the soundness of which is evident so long as the decision as to recognition is a decision taken in conformity with international law, i.e. one which does not arbitrarily ignore the legally relevant facts of the situation. It would be improper and unreasonable if courts were to treat as States communities which are not States—the fact that they are not States being evidenced by the circumstance that recognition has been refused to them by an organ which does not act arbitrarily but which conscientiously takes into consideration the relevant facts in conformity with international law. In view of this it is proper and inevitable that what the executive authority has declared to be non-existent should be so treated by courts.[2]

Adherents of the declaratory doctrine of recognition have occasionally attempted to show, in support of their view, that courts admit the validity

1 In *Duff Development Company* v. *Government of Kelantan*, [1924] A.C. 797, 826, Lord Sumner described the principle that in these matters 'the Courts of the King should act in unison with the Government of the King' as being 'rather a maxim of policy than a rule'. It is believed that that principle is both a rule of law and a sound maxim of policy. The position is different when, in the circumstances of the case, the attitude of the Executive is obscure or indefinite. See the observations of Sir Wilfrid Greene (as he then was) in *Kawasaki Kisen Kabushiki Kaisha of Kobe* v. *Bantham S.S. Co. Ltd.*, [1939] 2 K.B. 544, at pp. 552–6. And see above, p. 70 and below, pp. 153, 154.

2 For an able presentation of the contrary view see Jaffe, op. cit.

of the acts of State authorities prior to recognition.[1] Actually, the courts of practically all countries refuse to recognize the validity of the acts of unrecognized States in the same way as they have declined to treat as valid and enforceable the judicial and legislative measures of unrecognized governments. The uniform practice of courts in this matter has been subject to two exceptions only—both exceptions being more apparent than real. In the first instance, courts have on occasions given effect to the judicial or legislative acts of an unrecognized State or of an unrecognized government when considerations of equity, convenience and fair dealing have required that account should be taken of the acts in question. It appears clearly from the pronouncements of courts that in these cases there is no question of acknowledging the validity of the legal acts of a foreign authority in a manner comparable to that in which effect is given to foreign legislation in conformity with the rules of private international law. Rather is it a case of treating such legislation as mere facts the disregard of which, in relation to private parties, would be contrary to equity and common sense.[2]

1 Verdross—*Verfassung der Völkerrechtsgemeinschaft* (1926), pp. 132 et seq.; *Völkerrecht* (1937), p. 113—has been prominent in this interpretation of the judicial practice. That interpretation has been accepted by many, including Kelsen in *Hague Recueil*, vol. XLII (1932) (iv), pp. 260 et seq. and Kunz. An examination of the decisions enumerated by Verdross shows that—as has already been tentatively suggested by Strupp in *Hague Recueil*, vol. XLVII (1934) (i), p. 434, and Cavaglieri in *Rivista*, vol. XXIV (1932), pp. 305–45—they are not an authority for the view contended for. See above, pp. 43, 59, as to the cases of *Andrew Allen and McIlwain* v. *Coxe's Lessee*. And see next note, below.

2 This is the true import of the often cited decision in *Sokoloff* v. *National City Bank*, 239 N.Y. 158; (1924) 145 N.E. 917 (a case which arose out of the non-recognition of Soviet Russia by the United States but in which the Court relied on a number of judicial decisions in connection with the acts of the Confederate States during the civil war). See below, p. 147. The intention to deny the legal nature of the foreign acts of which account is taken is clearly expressed in *Russian Reinsurance Co.* v. *Stoddard* (240 N.Y. 149; (1925) 147 N.E. 703). The Court said: 'The courts in considering that question assume as a premise that until recognition these acts are not in full sense law. Their conclusion must depend upon whether these have nevertheless had such an actual effect that they may not be disregarded, in such case we deal with the result rather than cause. We do not pass upon what such an unrecognized governmental authority may do, or upon the right or wrong of what it has done; we consider the effect upon others of that which has been done, primarily from the point of view of fact rather than of theory' (147 N.E. at p. 705). This is also the meaning of the decision of the Swiss Federal Court in *Hausner* v. *International Commercial Bank of Petrograd* (*Entscheidungen des Bundesgerichts*, vol. LI, iii, p. 64), where the Court, while admitting that the Bank had in fact ceased to exist as the result of Russian legislation, pointed out that Soviet Russia, not being recognized in Switzerland, 'n'a pas qualité pour représenter la Russie en Suisse, ni en matière de droit public, ni en matière de droit privé'. See also *Wilbuschewitz* v. *Trust Office of the City of Zürich*, decided by the Swiss Federal Court in 1925 (*Annual Digest*, 1925–6, Case no. 75). All these, it will

The second exception, which also refers largely to recognition of governments, has arisen where the decision of the Executive to deny recognition was admittedly due to the adoption of a questionable test of recognition unrelated to the actual existence and the normal functioning of the authority to which recognition has been refused.[1]

CONCLUSIONS

§ 31. *The Meaning of the Legal Duty of Recognition.* The view of recognition which has here been presented as approximating most closely to the practice of States and to a working juridical principle is: (*a*) that recognition consists in the application of a rule of international law by way of ascertaining the existence of the requisite conditions of statehood; and (*b*) that the fulfilment of that function in the affirmative sense—and nothing else—brings into being the plenitude of the normal rights and duties which international law attaches to statehood. Both principles introduce an essential element of order into what is a fundamental aspect of international relations. Both prevent it from being treated as a purely physical phenomenon uncontrolled by a legal rule and left entirely within the precarious orbit of politics.

It is necessary at this stage to push analysis still further at the risk of a

be noted, are cases of recognition of governments. However, it is convenient to refer to them in this context.

For similar reasons governments have on occasions relaxed the consequences following from non-recognition. On 30 December 1919, the Lithuanian Executive Committee in Washington informed the Secretary of State that the Provisional Government of Lithuania constituted that Committee its diplomatic agent in the United States. The Committee were thereupon informed by the Secretary of State that the United States not having recognized the Lithuanian Government, they could not attribute to the Committee any diplomatic character. At the same time it was stated that, within these limitations, the Department was prepared to deal informally with individuals and groups acting disinterestedly on behalf of the Lithuanian people. The Committee were also informed that notwithstanding the refusal to recognize, the United States were ready to co-operate in removing some of the resulting inconveniences. Thus in the matter of passports persons of Lithuanian origin were allowed to depart from the United States on affidavits of identity and nationality approved by the State Department: *U.S. For. Rel.* 1920 (III), p. 643.

1 In *Salimoff and Co.* v. *Standard Oil Company of New York* (262 N.Y. 220; 262 N.Y.S. 693), the State Department of the United States informed the Court that 'Department of State is cognizant of the fact that the Soviet regime is exercising control and power in territory of the former Russian Empire and the Department of State has no disposition to ignore that fact', 262 N.Y. at p. 224. The refusal to recognize was stated to be based 'on other facts'. In view of this clear admission that the unrecognized government actually existed, it was not easy for the Court to act upon the normal implications of non-recognition and to treat the unrecognized authority and its legislation as non-existent. See below, p. 155.

reproach of undue refinement. How is it possible to put forward two apparently contradictory propositions, namely, that recognition is constitutive of the normal rights of statehood of the seceding community and, at the same time, that, given the required conditions of fact, there is a duty of recognition? If there are no rights prior to recognition—and this appears to be the effect and the meaning of the constitutive view—is it permissible to assert the existence of a duty in relation to an entity which is incapable of possessing and asserting rights? It is possible to exaggerate the embarrassment caused by these questions.[1] In the first instance, as the established States act in this matter on behalf of the international community, they may be deemed to owe *to that community* a duty of recognition notwithstanding the fact that the substantive right is not yet fully vested in the beneficiary directly concerned. The law of most States is in many respects based on the principle that certain rules of conduct must be observed in relation to other persons although these do not possess a private right enforceable in their own name. Under the criminal law we are bound by certain obligations of conduct towards others, but to these duties there does not correspond a specific private right of the actual or potential victims of the criminal act or design. From a different angle, the paramount logic of the duty of recognition flows irresistibly from the fact that a society cannot exist without members. When the rise of personality depends, as it does properly on the constitutive view, upon an act of the existing members, that act cannot be the result of arbitrary will but of a duty owed to the society at large.

Secondly, it must be borne in mind that although recognition is constitutive of the international rights and duties of the new State, it consists in the ascertainment—in a declaration, if we wish—that there are present in the particular case the conditions of statehood as laid down by international law. To that extent recognition, while constitutive of the international personality of the new State, is declaratory of an existing physical fact. If this fact is present, the established States fall under a duty to declare its existence and thus to bring into being the international rights and duties of the new State. This means, once more, that although, prior to recognition, the community in question does not possess the ordinary rights of statehood, it is entitled to claim recognition. In the existing state of international law this is indeed, as a rule, an unenforceable and, therefore, imperfect right. But circumstances are conceivable in which that dormant

1 Some embarrassment there must, of course, remain. A certain logical hiatus is inherent in a situation in which the formal rise of legal personality is the result of the acts of the individual members of the community and not of the community as a whole.

and unenforceable right may acquire legal effectiveness. In an international society in which the obligatory jurisdiction of international tribunals will become the rule, the new State, after having been recognized, would be in a position to claim damages for specific losses resulting from unwarranted and arbitrary delay in the granting of recognition. The case of the *Bergen Prizes*, although relating primarily to rights of belligerency, is an instructive example.[1]

§ 32. *Recognition as Declaratory of Facts and as Constitutive of Rights*. The above considerations suggest, in relation to the current terminology in the matter of recognition, that the antinomy of the declaratory and constitutive doctrines, although relevant and important, does not exhaust the legal problem at issue. As we have seen, while recognition is constitutive in one sphere, it is declaratory in the other. It is declaratory in the meaning that its object is to ascertain the existence of the requirements of statehood and the consequent right of the new State to be treated henceforth as a normal subject of international law. It is declaratory in the sense that, in the contemplation of the law, the community in question is entitled to recognition as a matter of right and that we may safely disregard the objection that, not being recognized, it cannot be 'legally entitled' to anything. On the other hand, recognition is constitutive in the meaning that it is decisive for the creation of the international personality of the State and of the rights normally associated with it. It is constitutive in the sense that, provided the existing State acts in good faith in the exercise of the discretion left to it by international law, it is not bound, prior to recognition, to concede to the community in question the normal rights of statehood. A State may exist as a physical fact. But it is a physical fact which is of no relevance for the commencement of particular international rights and duties until by recognition—and by nothing else—it has been lifted into the sphere of law, until by recognition it has become a juridical fact. Recognition declares the existence of a physical, not of a legal, phenomenon. This explains why, although declaratory of a fact, it is at the same time constitutive of legal consequences. It is, if we desire to put it so, merely evidence of facts to which the law attaches importance. But it is indispensable evidence without which the potential international rights are a mere claim. In the absence of a judgment of a higher authority endowed with the requisite jurisdiction, a claim of this nature must remain without effective legal validity. Hall's precise analysis of the process of recognition—an analysis which is perhaps the most valuable contribution to the

1 See below, pp. 191, 192.

subject by any text-book writer—expresses this point of view with all possible clarity.[1]

§ 33. *The Antinomy of the Legal and Political Character of Recognition.* These are the reasons why it may be more conducive to the understanding of the problem of recognition if we treat it not as one determined by the declaratory or the constitutive character of recognition, but as one of a choice between the legal and political, or juridical and diplomatic, view of its function. For, it may be said, the decisive question is whether this fundamental aspect of international relations is one which can be brought within the orbit of the rule of international law, or whether it is and must remain yet another manifestation of the weakness of the law of nations. The correct answer to these doubts is probably that the problem of recognition cannot be properly understood without a clear appreciation of *both* its essential elements, namely, of its constitutive character and of the legal nature of its function. The antinomy between the constitutive and the declaratory nature of recognition is as real as that between the legal and political view of its object. Undoubtedly, the basis of any scientific theory of recognition must be the realization that there exists a law above States; that that law determines the conditions of statehood; that a society cannot exist without members; that those who compose it at any given time must, if there be no other competent organs, apply the law which defines the conditions of membership; and that full international personality is not a concession of grace on the part of the existing States. But the law embodying these principles is not an automatic abstract rule; nor is it pure jurisprudential speculation. It has no reality until it has been applied by a competent organ acting in good faith and in the fulfilment of a duty; and it has no meaning unless, when thus applied, it is the indispensable condition for the rise of statehood as part of the international legal system. The legal character of recognition extricates the process of recognition from the arbitrariness of policy; its constitutive character liberates it from an equally disintegrating element of uncertainty and controversy.

This being so, what is the explanation of the wide acceptance of the

1 He fully adopts what is here described as the legal view of recognition: 'Theoretically a politically organized community enters of right...into the family of states and must be treated in accordance with law, as soon as it is able to show that it possesses the marks of a state...no state has a right to withhold recognition when it has been earned' (*International Law*, § 26). At the same time he adopts the constitutive view of the effect of recognition: 'The commencement of a state dates nevertheless from its recognition by other powers...although the right to be treated as a state is independent of recognition, recognition is the necessary evidence that the right has been acquired' (ibid.). His view on the question has often been described as contradictory. In fact it reveals the true nature of the process of recognition.

declaratory view? Its appeal lies not in any approximation to the practice of governments and courts, but in the fact that it has been a reaction against the constitutive view as commonly propounded—against a doctrine, that is to say, which, basing itself on a radical positivist approach and on an extreme assertion of the sovereignty of existing States, deduces the international personality of new States from the will of those already established. Nowhere is the brand of positivism current in the science of international law more offensive than in its application to recognition of States. It elevates the arbitrary will of States to the authority of the source not only of particular rights, however fundamental, of States, but of their very rise and existence. An attempt has been made here to show that that latter aspect of the constitutive doctrine is in no way essential to it and that its value as a scientific theory receives a refreshing and decisive accession of strength after it has discarded the assertion that the will of States granting or refusing recognition is altogether unfettered by law. Once that blemish—introduced by writers and unsupported by practice —has been removed, the constitutive view reveals itself as being in accordance with positive law and, indeed, as inevitable from the point of view of principle.

§ 34. *The Problem of Recognition and the Political Integration of International Society.* Much of the preceding discussion may tend to create the impression of being of a somewhat abstract nature. However, in assessing the necessity for a detailed analytical examination such as has been here undertaken, it must be borne in mind that the problem of recognition of States, of fundamental significance in itself, is also of importance for a satisfactory treatment of recognition of governments and belligerency. The question of recognition of States is one of the rise of international personality in a legal system which is deprived of the normal and objective means of ascertaining juridical personality and which achieves that end by a precarious process of delegation to not altogether disinterested agencies. It is a question of the application of principles of law to a political phenomenon frequently taking place at times of historical upheavals and international crises. Yet, so long as international law claims the name of law, it is difficult to concede, without overwhelming proof, that that primary aspect of international relations takes place outside the law and that it is in its principal manifestation a matter of politics pure and simple. There is no such proof. On the contrary, much of the available evidence points to what has here been described as the legal view of recognition. Only that view of recognition, coupled with a clear realization of its constitutive effect, permits us to introduce a stabilizing principle into what would otherwise be a pure exhibition of power and a negation of order. The grotesque spectacle of a community being a State in relation to some but not to other States is a grave reflection upon international law. It cannot be explained away, amidst some complacency, by questionable analogies to private law[1] or to philosophical relativism.[2] That paradoxical phenomenon, which more than anything else signifies the negation of the unity of international law as a system of law, may be unavoidable pending the collectivization of the process of recognition. In that intermediate period adherence to the legal view of recognition—i.e. recognition given or refused in accordance with principles of law and in the fulfilment of a legal duty—will naturally tend to reduce the occasions for divergency.

We are not in a position to say either that there is a clear and uniform practice of States in support of the legal view of recognition, or that the process of recognition has invariably taken place, in all its aspects, under the aegis of international law. But the balance of the articulate practice of States enables us to maintain that the imperfections of machinery—i.e. the absence of a central organ of recognition—have not decisively affected its essential nature.[3] That practice permits us to comprehend the process of recognition of States not as a source of weakness of international law but as a substantial factor in its development to a true system of law. It is to be hoped that the political integration of the international community, which, in the long run, is the absolute condition of the full development of the potentialities of man and humanity in general, may, alongside of other improvements, render possible the collectivization of the process of recognition as best in keeping with its nature and purpose. Pending that consummation, it is pre-eminently desirable that recognition of international personality and of governmental capacity should continue to take place—though more uniformly, more consciously, and more conscientiously than has been the case in the past—in accordance with legal principles and in pursuance of a legal duty owed to the community of States.

1 As does Anzilotti—*Corso di diritto internazionale* (Gidel's translation, 1929), p. 168—who points out that in private law a person may be possessed of rights in relation to some persons only. Apart from slavery, private law knows of no cases in which a person, physical or juridical, possesses legal personality in relation to some members of the community but not to others.

2 Kelsen in *A.J.* vol. xxxv (1941), p. 609.

3 A persistent feature of the discussion on the subject is the difficulty which writers experience in comprehending the possibility of a rule of law being administered by the individual members of the society acting as agents of the law. See, for example, Scalfati, p. 229, and Noël-Henry, op. cit. p. 220, who regard the fact that there is no international agency for determining the existence of conditions of statehood as sufficient reason for denying its legal nature in present-day international law.

Appendix

OPINIONS OF THE LAW OFFICERS OF THE CROWN CONCERNING THE STATE OF THE FIJI ISLANDS PRIOR TO THEIR ANNEXATION

The Law Officers' Opinions, printed below, bear on matters of limited compass when compared with the questions discussed in the preceding chapters. The Opinions have not hitherto been published. They are of interest with regard to the position of non-recognized States, in particular in relation to the question whether the subjects of the non-recognizing State can, by purporting to assume the nationality of the non-recognized State, divest themselves of the nationality of the former and release themselves from the operation of its laws (see Opinions nos. I–V). The answers of the Law Officers on these questions are in the negative. On the other hand, the necessity for providing a legal basis for the protection of British interests on the Fiji Islands seems to have moved the Law Officers to assume a measure of implied *de facto* recognition of the Fiji authorities as the result of sending there a consular representative said to have been endowed with a political character[1] (see Opinions nos. VII, VIII). For the same reason the Law Officers advised the Secretary of State that it was the duty of the British local authorities to refrain from interference with the political struggles on the islands except as this was necessary for the protection of British subjects (see Opinion no. IX). The Law Officers were Coleridge, Jessel, and Parker Deane. The Opinions were addressed to Lord Granville, Secretary of State for Foreign Affairs.

I

Temple, *January* 11, 1872[2]

My Lord

We are honoured with your Lordship's commands signified in Viscount Enfield's letter of the 6th instant, stating that, with reference to our Report of the 22nd July last, he was directed by your Lordship to transmit to us the accompanying despatches from Mr March, Her Majesty's Consul at Ovalau, reporting the state of affairs in the Fiji Islands arising out of the assumption of authority by Mr Sydney Burt and certain other British subjects on the Council of Thakombau, one of the native Chiefs, and the complaints of their proceedings made by other white settlers there.

1 For the latter reason the Law Officers did not consider that their Opinion was at variance with a long line of precedents, reviewed in a Memorandum prepared by the Librarian of the Foreign Office and printed in Smith, vol. 1, pp. 251–7, according to which sending of consuls does not in itself imply recognition. And see below pp. 383–7, on Implied Recognition.

2 F.O. 83/2314.

2. That he (Viscount Enfield) was to inclose the correspondence which had passed with the Colonial Office and Admiralty, and the previous papers, from which we would see that the Governor of New South Wales and Her Majesty's naval officers had been instructed that as long as this newly-constituted Government exercised actual authority they should deal with it as a *de facto* Government so far as concerned the districts which might acknowledge its rule....

In obedience to your Lordship's commands we have taken the whole of the correspondence in this matter into consideration, and have the honour to report—

That we think Her Majesty's Consul should not give any formal recognition at present to any authority at Levuka in lieu of the personal authority of King Thakombau; according to Mr Consul March's Reports the so-called *de facto* Government is constituted of British subjects self-appointed, and representing no political community of persons, and in whose hands King Thakombau is a puppet; its members would, under these circumstances, in our opinion, be within the scope of 9 Geo. IV, cap. 83, sec. 4, in respect of any assault committed against British subjects by their direction at Levuka if they should be found within the jurisdiction of the Supreme Court of New South Wales, but how they are to be brought within that jurisdiction we do not see....

II

Temple, 14*th June* 1872[1]

My Lord

We are honoured with your Lordship's commands signified in Viscount Enfield's Letter of the 11th instant, stating that he was directed by your Lordship to transmit to us Despatches, from Her Majesty's Consul in the Fiji Islands, involving questions, in regard to which your Lordship would be glad to have the benefit of our opinion: viz.

1st. To what extent can British Subjects, under the circumstances reported by Mr March, withdraw themselves from British Jurisdiction by assuming the nationality of an uncivilized State, whose independence as a State has not yet been acknowledged by Her Majesty's Government.

2ndly. Can British subjects claiming to have thus divested themselves of their nationality, divest also their hitherto British vessels of their British nationality by placing them under the Flag of the State whose nationality they claim.

3rdly. To what extent are British subjects, under the circumstances already adverted to, amenable to British Laws for acts committed by them, or by their directions, in contravention of those Laws.

And that he (Viscount Enfield) was to state that your Lordship would be glad to be favoured with our opinion upon the above points, together with any observations which we might have to offer as to the instructions which should be given to Her

1 F.O. 83/2314.

Majesty's Consul in the Fijis in the state of things reported by him in the Despatches now laid before us.

In obedience to your Lordship's commands we have taken the Despatches into consideration and have the honour to Report.

That we think your Lordship's questions are to be answered as follows:

1. That British subjects cannot by assuming the nationality of an uncivilized State withdraw themselves from British jurisdiction.

2. That British subjects who claim to have assumed the nationality of an uncivilized State cannot divest vessels owned by them of their British nationality by placing those vessels under the Flag whose nationality they claim.

3. That British subjects under the circumstances referred to in Viscount Enfield's letter remain amenable to British laws notwithstanding their attempted adoption of a foreign national character to the same extent as before their attempted adoption of such national character for such acts subsequently committed by them or by their directions in contravention of British laws.

4. That your Lordship may properly instruct Mr Consul March that he should continue to protect British subjects and their interest taking care not to use force or resort to violent measures in opposition to the *de facto* authorities of the country.

III

Temple, *July* 18*th*, 1872[1]

My Lord

We are honored with your Lordship's commands signified in Lord Enfield's letter of the 13th inst, stating, that with reference to our various Reports on the question of the recognition of the *de facto* government established in the Fiji Islands, he was directed by your Lordship to transmit to us the Draft of a letter, which your Lordship caused to be addressed to the Colonial Office on the subject, together with a letter which had been received from that Department in reply, and he was to request that we would favour your Lordship with our opinion on the question raised by the Colonial Office: namely whether beyond the limit of the new State, British subjects so long as it was not duly recognized, could be accepted as citizens of it, and exempted from British jurisdiction, for acts done or engagements entered into with them.

In Obedience to your Lordship's commands we have the honor to *Report*.

That in our opinion British subjects, beyond the limits of the new State, not yet duly recognized, should not be accepted as citizens of the New State, nor should they be held exempted from British Jurisdiction for acts done by them on British Territory, or on board ships which ought to be navigated under the British Flag.

Nor should they be held exempted from British jurisdiction for engagements entered into with them in cases where the validity or construction of such engagement would properly & in ordinary course be triable before a British Tribunal.

1 F.O. 83/2314.

IV

Temple, *August 9th*, 1872[1]

My Lord

We are honoured with your Lordship's commands signified in Viscount Enfield's letter of the 6th inst, stating, that adverting to our Reports of the date noted in the margin upon questions relating to the jurisdiction over British subjects in the Fiji Islands, he was directed by your Lordship to transmit to us the accompanying letter from the Colonial Office, enquiring whether the recognition by Her Majesty's Government of the Fijian Government as established *de facto* would preclude Her Majesty's Government from interfering with the acts & engagements of British subjects *within* Fiji; and he was to request us to be good enough to enable your Lordship to answer that enquiry.

In obedience to your Lordship's commands we have the honor to *Report*.

We are of opinion that Her Majesty's Government may interfere with the acts & engagements of British subjects within Fiji & may declare certain acts and engagements to be legal or illegal in the case of British subjects within Fiji.

V

Temple, *20th March* 1873[2]

My Lord

We are honoured with your Lordship's commands signified in Lord Enfield's letter of the 15th instant, stating, that with reference to our Report of the 14th instant, he was directed by your Lordship to transmit to us the two accompanying letters from the Admiralty, referring for consideration some embarrassing questions which it was suggested might occur to Naval Officers engaged in the Suppression of the Kidnapping Trade, and he was to request that we would take the papers into consideration, and favour your Lordship at our early convenience with our opinion whether it would be advisable to make any modifications, and, if so, what changes should be introduced in the proposed instructions for the guidance of Naval officers employed in the Suppression of Kidnapping, with the view to meet the difficulties pointed out in the enclosed Letters.

In obedience to your Lordship's commands we have the honor to Report.

That the instructions are framed with reference to 'British Subjects' and 'British Vessels', and upon the principle that neither 'British Subjects' nor 'British Vessels' lose their Nationality, or their responsibility to British Law by assuming to be Fijian Subjects, or carrying the Fijian Flag.

That, in our opinion, the Act passed by the Fiji Legislature Assembly 14 Decr 1871 will not relieve British Subjects from any liability which they may be under by British Law.

1 F.O. 83/2314. 2 Ibid.

And consequently

I. That any officer commanding one of Her Majesty's Ships, who meets a vessel on the High Seas under the Fiji Flag carrying native Labourers without a License, or with a Fiji License only:

a. Will if on his boarding her the owners and crew appear to be foreigners or Fijis immediately quit her....

b. Where the owners appear to be foreigners or Fijis, but some of the Crew appear to be British Subjects, & the Officer has reasonable grounds for suspecting such British Subject or Subjects to have committed any offence enumerated in the 9th or 10th Sections of the Kidnapping Act or any other felony described in Instruction 82 he may with the consent of the person commanding the vessel but not by force arrest such British Subject or Subjects.

c. Where the owners and the crew appear to be British Subjects, the ship and crew may be detained.

II. By instruction 9 Territorial Waters are said to be the waters of any duly recognized State. And by Instruction 8 the powers to be exercised are over British Vessels only.

Therefore

a. In the first two cases where the Vessel in Fiji waters is under Fiji Colours and the owners are foreigners or Fijis, the Naval Officer will not interfere.

b. Where the Vessel in Fiji waters is under British Colours, or is reasonably suspected of being a British Vessel (see Instruction 4) the Naval Officer will apply for permission of the Local Authorities to detain & will detain her.

We are of opinion in answering this second branch or head of questions from the Admiralty that Fiji is a duly recognized State within the meaning of that expression in the Instructions.

III. The Naval Officer is bound to protect British Subjects resident at Fiji when requested to do so by Her Majesty's Consul, or if the case requires his immediate intervention he must do so on his own responsibility. And he must be careful not to offer his protection to any British Subject who has committed wrongs in Fiji, unless the conduct of the Authorities or people in Fiji with respect to the treatment of the British Subject be so excessive or violent that the intervention of force be absolutely necessary for the sake and in the interests of humanity & ordinary justice.

NOTE. See also the Opinion of 19 September 1873 (F.O. 83/2314), in which the Law Officers approved of the following amended Instructions to be sent to the British representative in Fiji.

'Should it come to your knowledge that British subjects are engaged in this traffic you will make known the fact to the nearest British naval authority and furnish them with all the information which you may be able to obtain in Order that they may watch for and apprehend on the high seas or outside Fijian and other territorial waters and jurisdiction the guilty parties and send them to the nearest British Colony for trial.

'You will request the Fijian authorities, using your best endeavours that the request may be effective, to make over to you or to the Commander of the nearest British ship any British subjects, whom you have good and sufficient grounds for believing to have rendered themselves amenable to the provisions of the recent Kidnapping Act....

'In every case in which it may come to your knowledge that kidnapped natives have been brought within Fijian jurisdiction by British subjects, you will in the same manner and by using the same means as above pointed out for obtaining the surrender of British subjects request the Fijian Authorities to deliver such natives over to you in Order that they may be restored to their homes....'

VI

Temple, 15 *Febry* 1873[1]

My Lord

We are honoured with your Lordship's commands signified in Lord Enfield's letter of the 6th inst. stating, that he was directed by your Lordship to transmit to us two despatches from Her Majesty's Consul at Fiji reporting on the proceedings of the Fijian authorities in regard to the estates of deceased British Subjects, & he (Lord Enfield) was to request us to take the matter into consideration & favor your Lordship with our opinion as to the steps which should be taken therein, and also as to any instructions which it might be proper to give to H.M. Consul for his guidance for the future, in the event of circumstances again arising of a similar nature.

In obedience to your Lordship's commands we have the honor to Report.

That in our opinion the state of affairs at Fiji & the conduct of the Fijian *de facto* Government in reference to British Interests as described by Mr Consul March have reached a point, at which for the protection of British Interests your Lordship may properly instruct Her Majesty's Consul to claim the assistance of a Man of War, & to obtain redress by the threat & if necessary by the use of force.

In our opinion strong measures of a similar kind may properly be adopted by H.M. Consul in the event of circumstances again arising of a like kind.

VII

Temple, 10*th March* 1873[2]

My Lord

We are honoured with Your Lordship's commands signified in Lord Enfield's letter of the 5th inst. stating, that he was directed by your Lordship to transmit to us a despatch & its inclosures from Her Majesty's Consul at Fiji relative to the case of

1 F.O. 83/2314.

2 Ibid.

the seizure by the Local Authorities of the 'Volunteer' and the treatment of her Supercargo, Mr Blair.

That he was to enclose a letter from the Board of Trade stating the views of that department on the subject, and he was to request us to take the papers into consideration and favour Your Lordship with our opinion as to the proceedings of the Fijian authorities in that matter and as to the steps, if any, which it might be proper for Her Majesty's Government to take therein.

In obedience to your Lordship's commands we have the honor to Report.

That in our opinion the conduct of the authorities at Fiji in respect to the seizure of the 'Volunteer', and the treatment of Mr Blair was opposed to the rules which are received by and govern civilized nations.

Her Majesty's Government has admitted the existence of a *de facto* Government in Fiji and the actual presence of Mr March as Her Majesty's Consul in Fiji is an acknowledgment of that *de facto* Government.

We are of opinion, subject to your Lordship's consideration, that the time has now come in which strong measures must be resorted to at Fiji and that full redress should be demanded of the Fijian authorities for the seizure of the 'Volunteer', and the treatment of Mr Blair and that demand supported at the time and on the spot by a force sufficient to compel the satisfaction and redress if refused.

VIII

Temple, *May* 6, 1873[1]

My Lord

We are honoured with Your Lordship's commands signified in Viscount Enfield's Letter of the 30th ultimo stating that in our report of the 10th of March we stated that Her Majesty's Government has admitted the existence of a *de facto* Government in Figi *and the actual presence of Mr March as Her Majesty's Consul in Figi is an acknowledgment of that* de facto *Government.*

Viscount Enfield also stated that Your Lordship had caused a memorandum to be prepared showing the practice observed by this Country and by the United States in cases of the withdrawal of diplomatic relations and other instances in which Consuls have continued to reside at their posts without any recognition of the persons there claiming authority as a Government being thereby accorded; And that he was to request that we would take the same into consideration and favour Your Lordship with any further observations which we might have to offer upon the subject.

In obedience to Your Lordship's commands we have the honour to *Report*

That the position of Mr Consul March at Figi is quite anomalous. In the memorandum prepared in the Foreign Office and enclosed in Lord Enfield's letter it is stated that Mr March has received no exequatur from the Government of Figi.

We are not inclined to think that this is of much importance in considering the effect of the relations between Mr March and that Government.

1 Ibid.

Our opinion, to which we adhere, that the actual presence of Mr March as Her Majesty's Consul at Figi was an acknowledgement of that *de facto* Government was formed on the ground that Mr March had for a considerable time carried on official intercourse with members of the *de facto* Figian Government and that his authority so to act had not been repudiated by Her Majesty's Government but on the contrary Mr March had been supported by Her Majesty's Government.

We entirely agree with the observations in the memorandum generally; but, as Your Lordship will have seen we are of opinion that none of the cases cited by Mr Hertslet are really in point and whatever may have been the nature and terms of Mr Consul March's original appointment to Figi, his official acts subsequently have gone far to invest him with a political as well as a commercial character.

IX

Temple, 18 *July* 1873[1]

My Lord

We are honoured with Your Lordship's commands signified in Lord Enfield's letter of the 14th inst stating, that he was directed by your Lordship to transmit to us the accompanying letter from Mr Layard who has been recently appointed Her Majesty's Consul in the Fiji Islands, and that he was to request us to favor your Lordship with any suggestions which we might have to offer in regard to the instructions which it might be proper to give to Mr Layard upon the points raised in his letter.

In obedience to your Lordship's commands we have the honor to Report.

That Mr Layard may properly be instructed to conduct himself in his office of Consul in the Fiji Islands, as he would do in a country of which Her Majesty's Government had recognized the *de facto* Government.

That his duties will be to protect all British interests & British Subjects requesting where the need may occur the assistance of any of Her Majesty's Ships for the protection of such persons and interests.

That he should keep himself entirely aloof from all political disputes and matters of Government, and in no way interfere with the persons constituting the Government, whether those persons be British subjects or not.

And that so far as concerns vessels sailing under the British Flag, or which ought by law to sail under the British Flag, he should act exactly as he would do, if he were a British Consul in any other Foreign Port.

NOTE. See also the Opinion of the Law Officers of 27 June 1873 (F.O. 83/2314), in which, while excusing, in the circumstances of the case, the interference of the Captain of H.M.S. *Dido* in a dispute between certain planters and the *de facto* Government of Fiji, they disapproved of such interference in principle.

1 F.O. 83/2314.

Part Two

RECOGNITION OF GOVERNMENTS

Chapter VII

INTERNATIONAL LAW AND REVOLUTIONARY CHANGES OF GOVERNMENTS

§ 35. *The Principles of Recognition of Governments.* In essence, the principles applicable to the various aspects of recognition are the same—whether it be recognition of States, of governments, or of belligerency. In all of them the choice is between recognition as governed by law and recognition as determined by decisive considerations of national interest. With regard to recognition of States it has been shown how both compelling reasons of principle and the practice of States, viewed in its entirety, leave no option other than the acceptance of the first of these alternatives. To what extent do these principles apply to the recognition of governments?

It is a fundamental rule of international law that every independent State is entitled to be represented in the international sphere by a government which is habitually obeyed by the bulk of the population of that State and which exercises effective authority within its territory. To deny that right to a State is to question its independence. For this reason States are not normally concerned with the changes in the composition or in the form of government which occur in other countries; the international personality of the State is not affected by transformations of that kind. This applies to changes taking place both in conformity with and in violation of the constitutional law of the State in question. However, as in the latter case the replacement of one government by another is often accompanied by revolutionary upheavals in the form of civil wars of differing degrees of intensity and duration and by competing assertions of power on the part of rival authorities, outside States are frequently called upon to take a decision on the question which of the contesting parties must be regarded as being the government of the country concerned. Or, after the hostilities have ceased, they may have to decide whether the authority which for the time being has triumphantly asserted itself over its opponents may properly be considered to be a government. To take a decision of this nature is to recognize—or to refuse to recognize—the government in question. When that government enjoys, with a reasonable prospect of permanency, the habitual and—though this is controversial—willing obedience of the bulk of the population, outside States are under a legal duty to recognize it in that capacity. For this reason, although, according to the law of most countries, recognition of foreign governments falls within the purview of the executive department of the State, it is a function consisting in the application of a rule of international law to given situations of fact. Like recognition of States, recognition of governments is a subject affirmatively governed by international law.

§ 36. *The Legal and Political Views of Recognition of Governments.* This view, which may be called the legal (as distinguished from the political or diplomatic) view of recognition of governments, is not one which is generally accepted. There are many who maintain that States, acting in the exercise of their political discretion and considering their political interests only, are free to refuse recognition to a foreign government of revolutionary origin. On that view a government thus constituted is never entitled to recognition as a matter of law.[1] However, while in the case of recognition of States the upholders of the political conception of recognition represent the opinion of the majority of writers, they are probably in the minority so far as recognition of governments is concerned. It is significant that writers of authority, who deny that there is ever a legal duty to recognize a State, affirm the existence of an obligation of this nature in the matter of recognition of governments.[2] Moreover, some of those who

1 See, for example, Rougier, *Les guerres civiles et le droit des gens* (1903), p. 500; McNair in Oppenheim's *International Law* (4th ed. 1928), vol. I, § 75*b*; Podesta Costa in *R.G.* vol. XXIX (1922), pp. 51, 52; Gemma in *Hague Recueil*, vol. IV (1924) (iii), p. 334; and, in particular, Kunz, pp. 125–7. And see below, p. 160. Professor Hyde (vol. I, p. 67) maintains that 'there is no legal duty imposed upon a State to accord recognition to a new government *at any particular time*' (italics ours). But it appears that he is prepared to justify delay only on account of uncertainty, apparent or presumed, as to the permanence of the new regime. Similarly, Westlake holds that 'when a change of government is effected by violence, a reasonable time must be allowed to other States for judging of the stability of the new government' (*International Law* (2nd ed. 1910), vol. I, p. 58). Does this statement mean that, assuming the stability of the new government, there is a duty of recognition after a reasonable time has elapsed?

2 See, for example, Cavaglieri, *Corso di diritto internazionale. Parte Generale* (1925), p. 187: 'Mentre...uno Stato non ha alcun obbligo giuridico di riconoscere un nuovo Stato, non pùo invece rifiutarsi di riconoscere i mutamenti costituzionali, verificatisi nell' ordinamento interno degli Stati gia riconosciuti'; Fauchille, p. 321; Anzilotti, *Cours de droit international* (transl. by Gidel, 1929), p. 179: 'Si le changement est survenu effectivement et il présente des caractères de stabilité, les autres États ne peuvent pas se refuser à en prendre acte'; Noël-Henry, op. cit. pp. 217–22 (subject to the willingness to fulfil international obligations).

deny that there can ever exist a duty to recognize a government or a right to be recognized as such actually use language which is not easily comprehensible unless on the assumption of the existence of such right and duty.[1] The attitude of governments is equally instructive. Refusal or grant of recognition is as a rule represented by them as having taken place in accordance with a generally applicable test of recognition. These tests vary widely, and in thus varying reveal the unsatisfactory nature of the existing procedure of recognition. But seldom, if ever,[2] has a claim been made by a State that it is free to act in this matter as it pleases. This fact, it will be shown, is in itself an indirect but emphatic acknowledgment of the legal nature of recognition.

Governments and courts have often insisted that recognition of governments is a political function of the executive department of the State.[3] In this sense—but in no other—is recognition of governments, as well as of States, a 'political' question. It is not, according to the existing division of powers within the State, a matter falling within the competence of courts. The act of recognition, as distinguished from its legal consequences, is a branch of international law administered not by the judiciary but by the executive. Nevertheless, it is the law of nations that is administered. In this sense the difference between the judicial and the political function is one of the nature of the organ applying international law. As in the matter of recognition of States, so also with regard to recognition of governments, there is, subject to insignificant exceptions, no evidence to show that governments claim the right to proceed regardless of principle, and to

1 See below, p. 160.

2 In 1921 the United States insisted on negotiating and signing a convention with Mexico before recognizing its government. When Mexico objected to that procedure, the United States answered that 'the question as to whether the United States Government shall not recognize another government is purely a domestic one for the United States'. That assertion was qualified in the following sentence by reference to the principles upon which the United States has 'acted in this respect' and which 'are well known': President Harding to President Obregon, 21 July 1921, *U.S. For. Rel.* 1921 (II), p. 421.

3 In England the subject is governed by the principle of the conclusiveness of acts and statements of the Crown in the field of foreign affairs (a principle less open to criticism than is usually assumed if we bear in mind that, as is submitted here in the matter of recognition, the acts of the Executive, far from being arbitrary, are often acts of application of international law). See *Luther* v. *Sagor*, [1921] 1 K.B. 456; [1921] 3 K.B. 532; *The Gagara*, [1919] P. 95; *The Annette*; *The Dora*, [1919] P. 105; *The Arantzazu Mendi*, [1938] P. 233; [1939] P. 37; [1939] A.C. 256. And see below, p. 154. With regard to the United States, where the position is the same, see the exhaustive enumeration of cases in Hackworth, vol. 1, pp. 165, 166; Hervey, *The Legal Effects of Recognition in International Law* (1928), pp. 25–53; Jaffe, *Judicial Aspects of Foreign Relations* (1933), pp. 207–33. And see above, pp. 70, 71 and below, pp. 153–6.

grant or refuse recognition to foreign governments by way of a bargain, of an act of grace, or of mere expediency.

Apart from the principal reason militating in favour of what may be described as the legal view of recognition, namely, the right of independent States to possess a government chosen or tolerated by their peoples, there are other cogent considerations urging the same view. A State whose government is refused recognition is, for many purposes, deprived of the usual prerogatives of international personality. Thus, for instance, a government from which recognition has been withdrawn or to which it has been refused is deprived of the protection, which it otherwise enjoys under international law, against foreign assistance to forces which have risen in rebellion against it. The acts of its legislative, administrative and judicial organs are treated as invalid; it is often refused jurisdictional immunities; it cannot appear as plaintiff in foreign courts. As is shown elsewhere,[1] these are not the only factors which render non-recognition much more serious than the refusal to entertain normal diplomatic relations (although, in the opinion of writers wedded to the political conception of recognition, absence of diplomatic relations is the sole result of non-recognition).[2] For these reasons, to admit that the grant or refusal of recognition to an authority claiming to be the government of an independent State is a matter of mere political discretion is to concede that some vital aspects of international relations, normally governed by international law, are subject to the vicissitudes of arbitrariness and of changing circumstances of expediency. The conflict, thus conceived, between the legal and political views of recognition is a theme common to recognition of States, of governments and of belligerency. But while the general implications of the problem are more clearly revealed in relation to recognition of States, the question of recognition of governments raises the issue with greater frequency and urgency. For it is largely in this sphere that the political view of recognition constitutes an ever-present inducement to and supplies a justification for action undertaken in disregard of the independence of States and of important rules of international law.

1 See below, pp. 142–4.

2 See, for example, Kunz, p. 163. See also Gemma, who says (in *Hague Recueil*, vol. IV (1924) (iii), p. 334): '...il n'y a pas une règle générale de droit international qui impose aux États le reconnaissance d'un gouvernement dans des conditions déterminées; c'est-à-dire, qui impose la continuation des relations d'auparavant avec un État qui s'est donné un gouvernement revêtu de certaines qualités.' However, he brings even that limited conception of recognition within the orbit of a legal rule by denying the right to refuse recognition on account of lacking legitimacy. And see Basdevant in *R.G.* vol. XI (1904), p. 109; Larnaude, ibid. vol. XXVIII (1921), p. 497; Podesta Costa, ibid. vol. XXIX (1922), pp. 51, 52.

§ 37. *Recognition of Governments and Revolutionary Change.* The guiding juridical principle applicable to all categories of recognition is that international law, like any other legal system, cannot disregard facts and that it must be based on them provided they are not in themselves contrary to international law. In relation to recognition these facts may be either independent statehood, or effective governmental control, or hostilities waged on a large scale between rival factions within a foreign State. With regard to recognition of governments, that principle of the law-creating effect of facts signifies that a government effectively established within national territory and, according to some, sanctioned by adequately expressed popular approval must, notwithstanding its revolutionary origin, be regarded as representing the State in question and as such entitled, in law, to recognition. It is of the essence of the notion of independence of States that changes in the structure or in the composition of their governments are, in international law as at present constituted, an internal question of the States concerned and that foreign States are not, in general, entitled to interfere in the matter by raising the question of recognition or by refusing to grant it.[1] The position is the same when the

1 For this reason no express act of recognition was necessary—and none apparently took place—with regard to the various so-called governments in exile which established themselves in Great Britain in 1940 in accordance with the constitutional law of their countries. These were the Governments of Holland, Greece, Norway, Poland, Belgium, Yugoslavia and Luxemburg (for details of which see Oppenheimer in *A.J.* vol. XXXVI (1942), pp. 568 et seq.). They continued to be recognized by Great Britain and the statements made on behalf of the British Government in connection with cases pending before courts and affirming that the governments in question were recognized by Great Britain do not mean that any specific and deliberate act of recognition had taken place. This applies to the statement made by the Attorney-General in *In re Amand* ([1941] 2 K.B. 239) that His Majesty's Government recognized 'Her Majesty Queen Wilhelmina and her Government as exclusively competent to perform the legislative, administrative and other functions appertaining to the Sovereign and Government of the Netherlands', as well as to the statement in *Lorentzen* v. *Lydden* ([1942] 2 K.B. 202) to the effect that the Norwegian Government was recognized by Great Britain as 'the *de jure* government of the entire Kingdom of Norway' and that no other government was recognized 'as either the *de jure* or the *de facto* government of Norway or any part thereof'. In a similar case the government of the United States stated that it 'continues to recognize as the Government of the Kingdom of the Netherlands the Royal Netherlands Government, which is temporarily residing and exercising its functions in London': *Anderson* v. *N.V. Transandine Handelsmaatschappij* (289 N.Y. 7; *Annual Digest*, 1941–2, Case no. 4). See also, to the same effect, *Re de Bruijn*, decided in 1941 by the British Columbia Supreme Court ([1942] 1 *Dominion Law Reports*, p. 249), and *Haak and Others* v. *Minister of External Affairs*, decided in 1942 by the Appellate Division of the Supreme Court of South Africa: *The South African Law Reports*, [1942] Appellate Division, p. 318. The position with regard to Czechoslovakia was different. In this case a special act of recognition was necessary in view of the apparent break in legal continuity. It was given by Great Britain on 21 July 1940, when the Foreign Minister informed the

change is of a revolutionary character and accompanied by violence—although in that case the question often arises whether the new government, based as it is on force in the first instance, is an effective government with a reasonable prospect of permanency and although it is that question which makes recognition necessary. Apart from this, the nature of the change is of no legal relevance. This is so for the simple reason that, so far as international law is concerned, the legality or otherwise of the revolution is a matter of indifference. If revolution were an unlawful act in international law, it would produce no results valid in the international sphere; its factual success could not prevail against the unlawfulness of its origin. But international law does not prohibit revolution as a means of constitutional or purely governmental change within the State. From the point of view of foreign States and of international law generally, there is, in principle, no difference between a constitutional and a revolutionary change of government. Within the State the revolution destroys irrevocably the continuity of the legal system; the former law subsists only in so far as it is adopted by the new, revolutionary order. It is, in fact, international law which preserves the legal continuity of the State. It does so by laying down the rule that the State and its obligations remain the same

President of Czechoslovakia that 'His Majesty's Government in the United Kingdom are happy to recognize and enter into relations with the provisional Czechoslovak Government established by the Czechoslovak National Committee to function in this country.' 'Full recognition to the Czechoslovak Government' was given on 18 July 1941. In the Exchange of Notes between H.M. Government in the United Kingdom and the Government of Czechoslovakia of 5 August 1942 (*Treaty Series*, no. 3 (1942)) the British Foreign Secretary described the letter of 18 July 1941 as a formal act of recognition. It was explained in that letter that the decision to accredit an Envoy Extraordinary and Minister Plenipotentiary to Dr Benesh as President of the Czechoslovak Republic 'implied that His Majesty's Government in the United Kingdom regarded the juridical position of the President and Government of the Czechoslovak Republic as identical with that of the other Allied heads of States and Governments established in this country'. For the relevant documents, including acts of recognition by other countries, see *Czechoslovak Year Book of International Law*, 1942, pp. 229–31. See also *H.C. Debates*, vol. CCCLXIII, col. 614, and vol. CCCLXX, col. 1150. The recognition of a government which did not exercise effective control within national territory was apparently based on the view, which is believed to be unimpeachable, that the German annexation of Czechoslovakia was a legal nullity; that Czechoslovakia, whose government declared war on Germany on 16 December 1941, as from 15 March 1939 (the date of the German invasion), must be considered as being under enemy occupation; that her last freely elected Head of State, present in England, and the government formed under him constituted the requisite link in legal continuity; and that that government, not able to function freely in Czechoslovakia, was therefore in the same category as the other governments in exile. For a valuable discussion of the issues involved in the recognition of the Czechoslovak Government in London see Táborsky, *The Czechoslovak Cause* (1944), pp. 70–101. As to the French Committee of National Liberation see below, p. 164.

notwithstanding constitutional or governmental changes, revolutionary or other. This is a principle which goes back to Grotius.[1]

It is possible that in the ultimate rational development of the political organization of mankind rebellion against national authority will appear in an altogether different light. When that happens international law will fulfil functions of a scope infinitely wider than it does at present. It will render unlawful not only international but also civil war in a way comparable to the suppression of civil war within the component territories of the member States of a Federal State as the result of the guarantee, in the Federal Constitution, of the fundamental rights of the individual. The final political organization of mankind will signify the incorporation of these rights as an organic part of the constitution of the international commonwealth in a manner similar to that in which Section 4 of Article IV of the Constitution of the United States provides that the latter 'shall guarantee to every State in this Union a republican form of government, and shall protect each of them against invasion; and on application of the Legislature, or of the Executive (when the Legislature cannot be convened) against domestic violence'. In so far as civil war is due to a disregard or suppression of those rights, it will be eliminated as the result of the constitutional guarantees provided by the *civitas maxima* and enforced by judicial review and executive action. In the meantime, the rules of international law relating to recognition of governments cannot be framed on the assumption that that consummation has already come to pass.[2]

§ 38. *Presumption in Favour of Established Governments.* Although international law does not stigmatize revolutions as unlawful, it does not ignore altogether the distinction between the revolutionary forces and the established government. So long as the revolution has not been fully successful, and so long as the lawful government, however adversely affected by the fortunes of the civil war, remains within national territory and asserts its authority, it is presumed to represent the State as a whole.[3]

1 Book II, ch. IX, § VIII ('*Neque refert quomodo gubernetur idem enim est populus Romanus sub regibus, consulibus, imperatoribus*').

2 See below, pp. 233, 245, 246.

3 Thus, for instance, during the Spanish Civil War of 1936–9 the lawful government, deprived of the major part of national territory, continued to represent Spain in the Council and the Assembly of the League of Nations and before the Permanent Court of International Justice. See the Judgment of 6 November 1937, in the *Borchgrave* case between Belgium and Spain (*P.C.I.J.* Series A/B, no. 72). But, as in other matters, so also in this case good faith prescribes limits to the operation of a general rule. Thus it is doubtful whether political or commercial treaties of a far-reaching character may properly be concluded with a government thus situated. There is force in the contention that, notwithstanding the general rule as to the continuity of the

How far these presumptions extend to granting to the lawful government privileged treatment in the course of a civil war in the matter of supply of munitions and otherwise is a controversial question which it is more convenient to discuss in connection with recognition of belligerency.[1]

In one respect, however, the presumption in favour of the lawful government is above controversy: the latter is entitled to continued recognition *de jure* so long as the civil war, whatever its prospects, is in progress. So long as the lawful government offers resistance which is not ostensibly hopeless or purely nominal, the *de jure* recognition of the revolutionary party as a government constitutes premature recognition which the lawful government is entitled to regard as an act of intervention contrary to international law.[2] For such recognition amounts to recognizing the rebels either as the government of the entire State or as the government of a new State. An authority cannot be recognized, *de jure*, as a

State, the successful revolutionary government would not be bound by such treaties concluded *durante bello* as being *in fraudem* of the general interests of the nation. When in 1858 and 1859 the United States recognized the Constitutionalist Government of Juarez in Mexico, while refusing recognition to the insurrectionist Miramón Government established in the capital, they were negotiating—and eventually concluded—important political treaties of alliance and of cession with the Constitutionalist Government. This they did notwithstanding the grave doubts entertained in the matter by the United States Minister to Mexico. He said: 'The cession of territory is the gravest and the most important act of sovereignty that a government can perform; it is therefore questionable whether it should be performed at a moment when it is in conflict with another government for the possession of the empire, even though it may be *de jure* and *de facto* much more entitled to respect than that with which it is struggling in civil war, and this consideration is as important to the party purchasing as to the party ceding the territory': Mr McLane, United States Minister to Mexico, to the United States Secretary of State, 25 June 1859: Manning, *Diplomatic Correspondence of the United States, Inter-American Affairs, 1831–1860, Mexico*, vol. IX (1937), pp. 1093, 1094. For the treaties in question see ibid. pp. 1137–41.

1 See below, pp. 230–3.

2 Sir William Harcourt, in *Letters by Historicus on Some Questions of International Law* (1863), expressed that principle in emphatic terms: 'While the issue can be still considered in any degree *in ambiguo*, the presumption is necessarily in favour of the former Sovereign. And a friendly State is bound to exact very conclusive and indisputable evidence that the sovereignty of a government with which it has existing relations over any parts of its former dominions has been finally and permanently divested. It is not at liberty during the pendency of an actual struggle to speculate on the result, or to assume the probability of the ultimate failure of the ancient Sovereign, however plausible may be the grounds for such an inference' (at pp. 7, 8). Le Normand, op. cit. p. 250, disapproves of premature recognition with even greater emphasis: 'Ce n'est une reconnaissance que de nom; c'est, en soi, une intervention... l'État cache, sous la dénomination trompeuse de reconnaissance, une pression sur la volonté de l'État ancien pour l'amener à modifier son droit public.' See, to the same effect, Hall, op. cit. § 26; Moore, vol. I, p. 73; Baty, *The Canons of International Law* (1930), pp. 206, 207; Gemma, op. cit. pp. 365 et seq.; Jessup in *Foreign Affairs*, January 1937, p. 279; Raestad in *R.I.* 3rd ser. vol. XIX (1938), p. 617.

government without being recognized as the government of a State. In either case recognition of the revolutionary party as a *de jure* government constitutes a drastic interference with the independence of the State concerned. The illegality of such action is so generally admitted that, as in the corresponding case of recognition of States,[1] even those who adhere to the political view of recognition admit that at least this particular aspect of it is governed by international law. Premature recognition is a tortious act against the lawful government; it is a breach of international law. If States could proceed in this matter regardless of what is now a well-established legal principle, the result might be that in case of a civil war in a foreign country or, for that matter, even before actual hostilities have taken place there on a large scale, there would be nothing to prevent any State so minded from withdrawing recognition from the established government and transferring it to the rebellious party, with all the far-reaching consequences of the change thus affected in the legal position. The result, in international law, would be to reduce the established government to the status of a rebellious group and to raise the newly recognized authority to the position of the legitimate government to which support and encouragement may lawfully be given. Such abuse of the power of recognition is vividly illustrated by the recognition by Germany and Italy of the Spanish insurgents in the early stages of the Spanish Civil War in 1936, two and a half years before the termination of the civil war, at a time when the issue of the struggle was altogether uncertain.[2]

1 See above, pp. 11, 12.

2 The civil war in Spain broke out in July 1936. On 18 November of that year Germany and Italy recognized the insurgent government of General Franco as the *de jure* government of Spain. That recognition, being in violation of the law of nations, could not subsequently regularize what would have been clearly unlawful in the absence of premature recognition, namely, the rendering of assistance to the rebellious authorities. This was so although as a result of the premature recognition the roles were reversed and the lawful government transformed into a rebellious body. This, in fact, was the view taken by a German court which referred in 1938 to the government of General Franco as 'the only lawful Government of Spain' and to its opponents as 'the Red Spanish authority' which 'must be regarded as an insurgent authority'. The Court said of that 'insurgent authority': 'They are not subjects of international law. They cannot conclude or denounce international conventions; neither can they pass valid laws for the territories occupied by them': *Spanish Republican Government (Security for Costs)* case, Court of Appeal of Frankfurt-on-the-Main: *Annual Digest*, 1938–40, Case no. 28. In December 1939, Soviet Russia, following upon her invasion of Finland, recognized as the government of Finland a somewhat artificial regime whose power extended over an insignificant fraction of Finnish territory occupied by Russian forces and which she pretended to assist in its efforts to suppress the hitherto lawful Government of Finland. At that time the latter was in possession of practically the entire Finnish territory. It continued to be recognized by all States except Russia.

Some of the consequences of the accepted rule prohibiting premature recognition of governments[1] can, in practice, be mitigated by a substantial measure of intercourse—amounting to, or expressly given in the form of, *de facto* recognition—with the insurgent authority which has established itself within a substantial portion of the national territory. Thus at a later stage of the Spanish Civil War of 1936–9 Great Britain recognized 'the Nationalist [Franco] Government as a government which at present exercises *de facto* administrative control over the larger portion of Spain'.[2] But care was taken to state expressly that 'His Majesty's Government recognized the Republican Government as *de jure* government of Spain and no other government as *de jure* government of any part of Spain'.[3] In this matter, as in others, the distinction between *de jure* and *de facto* recognition is not a mere matter of form.[4]

The continued refusal of recognition *de jure* to an insurgent party about to emerge successful from the struggle undoubtedly involves some diminution of prestige and inequality of status as compared with the lawful government still recognized *de jure*, but it is not for outside States to administer to the *de jure* government the *coup de grâce* by transferring full recognition to the victorious opponent. In so far as such withdrawal of recognition from the lawful government has the result of hastening the final victory of the insurgents, it may commend itself for humanitarian reasons, but it is open to the charge of abandonment of the attitude of impartiality and, more generally, of an unlawful act of intervention. This was the apparent reason for the criticism levelled against the action of Great Britain and other States in recognizing *de jure*, in February 1939, the insurgent government in Spain at a time when the lawful government was still in possession of about one-third of national territory, but when its defeat became probable in the highest degree. On the other hand, it is

1 The British attitude towards the Venizelos revolution in Greece in 1916 furnishes an instructive example of the reluctance to grant premature recognition although the revolutionary government in question proclaimed itself an ally of the Powers asked to grant recognition. In 1916 M. Venizelos set up a provisional government in Crete and Salonica and organized a corps of volunteers to assist the cause of the Allies. He repeatedly asked for recognition. The British local representative was instructed to inform the Foreign Minister of the Venizelos Government that he (the Consul-General) was authorized to recognize the *de facto* government, the recognition being purely local, and to maintain cordial relations with it.

2 A formula used by the Foreign Office in a certificate issued in connection with the proceedings in *The Arantzazu Mendi*, [1938] P. 233; [1939] P. 37; [1939] A.C. 256. Similar, though not identical, expressions were used in other cases which came at that time before British courts. See below, pp. 365–8.

3 *The Arantzazu Mendi*, ubi supra.

4 See below, pp. 284–93.

clear that the traditional rule of international law in the matter contains an element of rigidity, favouring the lawful government, which may on occasions render its application difficult and artificial. These difficulties induced Great Britain to recognize the Spanish Serrano Government in 1874, after a delay of more than a year, notwithstanding the continuance of the Carlist war in some parts of Spain. The reasons for this action were persuasively stated by Lord Derby in the House of Lords.[1] There is no compelling necessity to interpret the existing rule in a pedantic manner. To maintain that the lawful government holding out in one isolated fortress is entitled to continued recognition *de jure* is to strain to breaking point an otherwise unimpeachable rule. Outside States, in granting recognition in such cases, may honestly assert that, in their view, the lawful government has—in the words of Sir William Harcourt—been 'finally and permanently' divested of its sovereignty. In so far as the existing rule errs on the side of rigidity the statesman may be justified in wielding the sharp knife of policy to prevent it from being reduced to an absurdity.

1 On 8 March 1875: *H.L. Debates*, vol. CCXII, col. 1382. On the other hand, in 1868 Great Britain adhered strictly to the rule prohibiting premature recognition. When in September 1868 the Queen fled from Spain, the British Minister in Spain acted on instructions ordering him to regard his mission to the Queen as being in abeyance but to abstain from recognizing the *de facto* government set up in Madrid. He was instructed to remain at his post 'not formally recognizing indeed any *de facto* Government that may be set up, nor holding official Intercourse with them, but still not altogether abstaining from communicating with them in regard to Matters affecting the Interest of British Subjects': Smith, vol. I, p. 199. Recognition was withheld for some considerable time. It is clear that the mere fact of the departure abroad of the nominal Head of the State is of little importance in this connection.

Chapter VIII

THE TESTS OF RECOGNITION OF GOVERNMENTS

§ 39. *Effectiveness of Governmental Power as the Standard of Recognition.* Apart from the limited presumption in favour of the established government and the prohibition of premature recognition, international law disregards the internal illegality of the revolutionary change. As has been submitted before,[1] there is nothing in international law which compels or permits States to treat a revolution in a foreign country as an event which is unlawful in itself and which entitles them to raise on that account the issue of the recognition of the revolutionary government—save in relation to the question of its effectiveness and its representative character. The problem of recognition of governments arises not because of any unlawfulness of the change, but because the accompanying violence and the resulting period of unsettlement demand an answer to the question whether the new government claiming to represent the State is in fact the government of the country. The rule of international law on the subject is based on the principle that the revolutionary government which wields effective power, with a reasonable prospect of permanency, over the whole—or practically the whole—territory of the State is entitled to recognition.

The principle of effectiveness—either in its literal meaning or as conditioned by the consent of the nation adequately expressed—conceived as the test of recognition of governments must, it will be shown, be regarded as expressing most accurately the general practice of States. Other tests of recognition have undoubtedly been adopted from time to time, such as legitimacy in its primary meaning as referring to the lawful origin of the new government in relation to the constitutional law of the country; the manner of the revolutionary change; and, above all, the willingness and the ability of the new government to fulfil its international obligations. These various tests of recognition will be examined in this and the following chapters. It will be shown that some of these tests have now been largely abandoned and that there are persuasive reasons why they ought to be definitely discarded in so far as they depart from the principle of effectiveness (in its literal or in its wider sense). For it is that latter test of recognition which amidst the apparent diversity of practice emerges as the predominant and governing principle.

1 See above, p. 93.

The foundations of the principle of effectiveness were laid down with some clarity, although within a limited compass, in the seventeenth century in the writings of the founders of international law. They discussed the matter mainly under two aspects: as a question of the duty of obedience to the revolutionary authority of the 'usurper' or of 'rebel', and as a question of the right of the usurping authority—the '*de facto* government', as it would now be called—to send diplomatic representatives. Grotius[1] affirmed that the acts of the usurper who is in possession have binding force—although he based that view on the necessities of peace and order rather than on legal considerations. The duty of obedience, he said, arises 'not from a right possessed by him, for no such right exists, but from the fact that one to whom the sovereignty actually belongs...would prefer that measures promulgated by him should meanwhile have the force of law, in order to avoid utter confusion which would result from the subversion of laws and suppression of the courts'.[2]

Pufendorf, who relied in this matter on Grotius, developed the subject in greater detail and introduced the international element. He regarded it as 'highly probable that he who actually holds the supreme sovereignty should, despite the fact that he seized it by base methods, be held for the time by the citizens as a lawful prince, so long as there is none who can lay a better claim to the sovereignty'.[3] After citing various authorities in support of that view, he adds: 'These conclusions are all the more to the

1 *De jure belli ac pacis libri tres* (1625), Book I, ch. IV, § XV.

2 Ibid. The whole subject is treated by Grotius from the point of view of the paramount necessity of avoiding the calamities of civil war. In the first instance, he restricts severely the right of rebellion (Book I, ch. IV, §§ I–VII). But once the rebellion has been successful, there is, in his view, a clear duty to obey the command of the otherwise unlawful authority; the occasions when force may be used against the usurper are rigidly circumscribed, namely, 'by virtue of a right of war still continuing' (ibid. § XVI), 'by virtue of a pre-existing law' (ibid. § XVII), and 'by virtue of a mandate of one possessing sovereign power' (ibid. § XVIII). Apart from these cases, force must not be used against the usurper: 'For it may happen that he who holds the sovereign power by right would prefer that the usurper should be left in possession rather than that the way should be opened for dangerous and bloody conflicts...' (ibid. § XIX) (translation by Kelsey in *Classics of International Law*, 1925).

3 *De jure naturæ et gentium*, Book VII, ch. VIII, 9. This, he says, is also the position when the usurper has driven out the lawful prince and acts as king: 'Here our decision must be that the matter may come to such a pass that it is not only lawful but also obligatory to obey as one's sovereign him who has possession, no matter how secured, of the kingdom, it being understood that the lawful lord is reduced to such a state that he can no longer fulfil any of his duties as a prince toward his subjects.... Since one's country cannot do without some sort of sovereignty, and the possessor is after a manner guarding the public safety, a good citizen, and one who loves his country, should not furnish the cause for still further turmoil by useless stubbornness' (ibid. 10) (translation by C. H. and W. A. Oldfather in *Classics of International Law*, 1934).

point with respect to foreigners, who have no concern in examining the title whereby a man secures sovereignty, but merely follow along with the possession, especially when the usurper of the sovereignty can rely upon great resources.'[1]

Fifty years later, Bynkershoek dealt with the matter in almost modern terminology by reference to the question of diplomatic representation in the course of a civil war. The party, he says, which is entitled to exercise the right of legation is the one which actually performs the functions of a government.[2] This solution is not necessarily helpful in cases in which the two factions purport to exercise the prerogatives of government in separate portions of national territory,[3] but Bynkershoek discusses the question of legation from a wider angle. Those, he says, 'who require that a ruler must be an independent sovereign in order to send envoys, do not customarily distinguish whether he holds his sovereignty by just title, or whether he has acquired it unjustly, and, in fact, such a distinction would be impossible. It is sufficient for those who receive the embassy that he is in possession of sovereignty.'[4] He quotes with approval Paschalius (*Legatus*, XII), who points out that there are few kingdoms and empires 'quorum initiis libera Gentium suffragia causam dederint'[5] and that 'plura Imperia vis enixa est, quam electio'[6]. Bynkershoek himself adds pithily: 'In

1 Book VII, ch. VIII, 9.

2 *Quaestionum juris publici libri duo*, Book II, ch. III (On the Right of Legation). In the last chapter, 'Variae Quaestiunculae', he discusses the question of the international validity of the acts of the *de facto* government. His view is that it is politically expedient that 'the acts and agreements of all rulers whatsoever be considered valid' subject to the somewhat vague exception of those 'quae occupando vel defendendo impie Imperio causam praebuerunt' (ch. XXV, iii).

3 Grotius's reference, in this connection, to the situation in which 'gens una pro tempore quasi duae gentes habetur' (Book II, ch. XVIII, § II) is of little assistance as he is speaking of the right of legation of the parties to the civil war *inter se*. It is in this context also that Gentilis (*De legationibus libri tres*, Book II (1594), ch. VII) discusses the question whether rebels engaged in a revolt against a tyrant have the right of embassy. He denies to them that right on the ground that a tyrant who has supplanted the lawful king is in this matter in the same position as the (lawful) king: 'Each of them is master, and law perhaps is the basis of each one's sovereignty. A king rules over his subjects because they want him to do so, a tyrant in spite of them.' He quotes Plato (*Politica*, 3, 10, 11, 12) as saying that just as we give the name of physician both to those who cure us against our will and at our request, so we must not distinguish between tyrant and king provided that both govern satisfactorily. The chapter is full of spirited defence of efficient government, as distinguished from government by consent. Indirectly, his treatment of the subject may not have been without some influence on weakening the authority of legitimism.

4 *Quaestionum juris publici libri duo*, Book II, ch. III (Frank's translation in *Classics of International Law*, 1930, p. 157).

5 'Whose origin rests upon the free vote of the people.'

6 'Violence has brought forth more empires than has election.'

causis publicis utique expedit, *uti possidetis, ita possideatis*; alioquin omnium Imperiorum origines essent excutiendae, justae nempe sint, necne, & sic demum pronunciandum, qui Legatos mittunt, jure an injuria mittant. Quod valde esset inutile, & Gentium tranquillitati turbandae insignem causam praeberet.'[1]

The *de facto* principle was once more given clear expression by Vattel about twenty years later.[2] As in the case of his predecessors, he discussed the matter in answer to the question whether 'ministers may be received from and sent to the usurper'. His answer was clear: Foreign powers are entitled to look to the sovereign in actual possession. This rule he regards as fully in accordance with international law. 'Since foreigners have no right to interfere in the domestic affairs of a State, they are not obliged to examine or to pass upon the justice or injustice of its conduct in the management of them; they may, if they think fit, presume that the sovereign in possession is the lawful one. When a Nation has driven out its sovereign, other powers which do not wish to declare against and thereby expose themselves to war with it or arouse its enmity, consider it thenceforth as a free and sovereign State, without taking it upon themselves to judge whether it has acted justly in throwing off the sovereignty of its former prince.'[3] He points, as an example, to the fact of the reception by France of the ambassador of Cromwell and of her refusal to entertain relations with either Charles II or his ministers. This also, he says, was the position with regard to the recognition, by the majority of the European Powers, of King Charles of Sweden who assumed the crown in derogation of the rights of his nephew Sigismund, King of Poland: 'The King of France was neither the judge nor the guardian of the Swedish nation, so as to be warranted in refusing, *contrary to the interests of his own Kingdom*, to recognize the King which Sweden had chosen, on the ground that a competitor to the throne regarded Charles as an usurper. Even though there were grounds for thinking so, the question was not one for foreigners to decide.'[4] Similarly, he was of the opinion that England was justified in

1 Ibid. Mr Tenney Frank's translation (in *Classics of International Law*, 1930) is as follows: 'In political matters, at any rate, it is expedient that possession be nine points of the law. Otherwise we would be compelled to examine into the origins of all states to find whether or not they were based upon justice [the better translation would probably be: "whether or not they were lawfully established"], and then ultimately to decide whether or not they had the right to legation. This, however, would be utterly futile, and would provide an excellent excuse for disturbing the peace of nations' (ibid. p. 158).

2 *Le droit des gens* (1758), Book IV, ch. v, § 68.

3 Ibid. (Fenwick's translation in *Classics of International Law*, 1916, p. 366).

4 Ibid.

regarding as a cause of war the continued recognition by France of the successor of James II.[1] While he thus rejects the dogma of legitimacy, it will be noted from the italicized passage above that Vattel regards action in accordance with the principle of effectiveness not so much as a matter of duty to the revolutionary government as a right given by international law, a right of which the recognizing State may avail itself in accordance with its interests. This is not surprising in view of the respect customarily shown by Vattel for the claims of the sovereign State.

We find in the same period unimpeachable positivist authority for the same view of recognition. Thus Moser, writing in 1778, is emphatic that the recognition of a newly elected sovereign on the part of other States is a duty.[2] The question of the legitimacy of the new regime, he says elsewhere, is irrelevant;[3] if the latter is accepted by those directly affected, third States have no reason to interfere.

The persistent voicing of the principle of effectiveness in the seventeenth and eighteenth centuries is instructive, seeing that it took place at a period when a legitimist outlook would have found strong support in the patrimonial conception of the State and in the theory of the divine rights of kings. These ideas were not alien to the founders of international law. There is, accordingly, significance in the fact that they perceived the value of the principle of effectiveness as a convenient test of recognition.

§ 40. *The Test of Legitimacy*. Legitimacy of origin as a criterion of recognition was rejected, as we have seen, in various quarters already in the seventeenth and eighteenth centuries in favour of the principle of effectiveness of governmental power. At the beginning of the nineteenth century the test of legitimacy became prominent once more in connection with the events which followed upon the French Revolution. It loomed large in the debates of the Congress of Vienna and in Talleyrand's discourses.

1 As early as the year 1601 the Cardinal of Ossat, Ambassador of Henry IV, in a letter to the Minister Villeroy rejected as irrelevant the question of legitimacy with regard to the right of a prince to send and receive envoys (Merlin, *Répertoire universel et raisonné de jurisprudence*, vol. VIII (1908), p. 240).

2 He says: 'Die Erkennung eines neu-erwählten Souveränen an Seiten derer übrigen Staaten ist eine Schuldikeit': *Beyträge zu dem neuesten europäischen Völckerrecht in Fridens-Zeiten*, Part I (1778), p. 329.

3 *Grundsätze des jetzt üblichen europäischen Völcker-Rechts in Fridens-Zeiten* (1763), ch. V: Von Erkennung und Garantierung, oder nicht-Erkennung, der Thronfolge in Erb-Recht durch Andere, p. 84. On p. 254 of *Beyträge* (see above), he says: 'Dritte Souverainen pflegen ordentlicher Weise dergleichen Dinge als blosse Haussachen des Staats, darin sie vorgehen, anzusehen, darin also Andere sich nicht zu mengen haben; machen mithin auch keine Schwürigkeit, die Thronfolge zu erkennen.'

Attempts were made to extend it to recognition of States.[1] However, with the passing of the Holy Alliance legitimacy, both in the dynastic and in its wider sense, conceived as a test of recognition was definitely discarded.[2] Apart from some provisions of the Treaty of 1923 between the Central American Republics,[3] there are in the last hundred years no instances of irrevocable refusal of recognition on the sole ground that the government in question originated in a revolution. Whenever revolutionary origin has been regarded as a reason for refusing recognition, it has been treated as a defect which can be cured by subsequent popular approval. Even the declaration of the three Powers of the Holy Alliance (Russia, Austria and Prussia) of 13 November 1820 did not ostensibly go further than that. It said: 'Any state forming part of the European Alliance which may change its form of interior government through revolutionary means, and which might thus become a menace to other states, will automatically cease to form a part of the Alliance, and will remain excluded from its councils until its situation gives every guarantee of order and stability.'[4]

Arbitral decisions have rejected the doctrine of legitimacy as having no place in international law. They have discarded it as a test both of the international obligations of the State in question and of recognition in general.[5] Thus, in the *Dreyfus* case before the Franco-Chilean Arbitral

1 See above, p. 26.

2 Even at the time of the Holy Alliance the uncompromising principle of legitimacy was interpreted out of existence by writers of conservative tendencies. There are only remnants of legitimacy in the third edition of the treatise of G. F. de Martens. He says, with regard to recognition of States, that though actual possession of independence is in no way decisive for its legality, foreign nations may, in case of doubt, rely on the fact of possession and, except 'when the injustice of the rebellion is obvious', treat as independent of its former government the State or province which actually enjoys independence; by the same token, they may regard as the lawful monarch the ruler who actually governs the country (*Précis du droit des gens moderne de l'Europe* (1831), p. 193). See also Klüber, *Droit des gens*, vol. 1 (1831), § 23, who asserts that the recognition of an usurper would be an outrage upon the lawful sovereign: 'tant qu'il n'a pas renoncé ou *qu'il ne doit être censé* avoir renoncé à ses droits de souveraineté'.

3 See below, p. 129.

4 As translated in Cresson, *The Holy Alliance* (1922), p. 99. However, the above interpretation of Article 1 must be read in the light of the concluding passage of Article 2 which provided as follows: '...In the case of States where such changes have already taken place and such action has thereby given cause for apprehension to neighbouring states (if it lies within the ability of the powers to take such useful and beneficent action) they will employ every means to bring the offenders once more within the sphere of the Alliance. Friendly negotiations will be the first means resorted to, and if this fails, coercions will be employed, should this be necessary.'

5 See below, p. 104.

Tribunal of 1901, Peru denied liability in respect of a claim arising out of a contract concluded by the revolutionary Pierola Government on the ground that that Government was unconstitutional. The Tribunal rejected that contention. It found that as the Pierola Government exercised *de facto* authority to the exclusion of any other government, its acts bound Peru irrespective of the legitimacy of its origin. 'A solution', said the Tribunal, 'which would deny under pretext of illegitimacy legal effect to contracts had with a government *de facto* at a moment when such government was the only recognized organ of the nation, would imply the very negation of the idea of a state.'[1] The same principle was expressed, with even greater emphasis, by Taft, former Chief Justice of the Supreme Court of the United States, in the arbitration between Great Britain and Costa Rica in 1923:

> 'To hold that a government which establishes itself and maintains a peaceful administration with the acquiescence of the people for a substantial period of time does not become a *de facto* government unless it conforms to a previous constitution would be to hold that within the rules of international law a revolution contrary to the fundamental laws of the existing government cannot establish a new government. This cannot be, and is not, true.... The issue is not whether the new government assumes power or conducts its administration under constitutional limitations established by the people during the incumbency of the government it has overthrown. The question is, has it really established itself in such a way that all within its influence recognize its control....'[2]

Moreover, the Arbitrator held that as the Tinoco Government had been refused recognition by the Powers not on account of any absence of effectiveness but because of its revolutionary origin, the fact of non-recognition did not constitute decisive evidence as to the existence of that Government for the purposes of international law. This was so because, in the view of the Arbitrator, the refusal to recognize was due to the revolutionary origin of the Government. That particular reason for non-recognition, he commented, 'certainly has not been acquiesced in by all

1 Descamps et Renault, *Recueil international des Traités du XXe siècle* (1901), p. 294. This case, it must be added, is only partly germane to the issue under discussion for, it appears, the Pierola Government *had been* recognized by foreign Powers, and the main point before the Tribunal was whether, notwithstanding such recognition, the internal illegitimacy of that Government vitiated, or rendered unenforceable, contracts made with it. This the Tribunal refused to admit. See also, to the same effect, the decision of an English Court in *Republic of Peru* v. *Dreyfus Brothers and Co.*, (1888) L.R. Ch.D. 348, 355. And see Lecharny, *La validité des actes internes des gouvernements de fait à l'égard des étrangers* (1929).

2 As reported in *Annual Digest*, 1923–4, Case no. 15.

the nations of the world, which is a condition precedent to considering it as a postulate of international law'.[1]

In view of the fact that the rigid principle of legitimacy is now a matter of the past, it is unnecessary to discuss in detail its merits or shortcomings. Its application is clearly illogical in a world in which all governments owe their origin to a revolutionary event in a more or less distant past.[2]

1 *A.J.* vol. XVIII (1924), p. 153; *Annual Digest*, 1923–4, Case no. 15. In essence, this case is an affirmation of the rule—which is a controversial one—that a State is responsible for the acts and omissions of a defeated revolutionary *de facto* government even if the latter is not recognized by outside States. See, to the same effect, the *Georges Pinson Claim*, decided in 1928 by the French-Mexican Mixed Claims Commission (*Annual Digest*, 1927–8, Case no. 164) and, subject to some qualifications, the *George W. Hopkins* case, decided in 1926 by the United States-Mexican General Claims Commission (ibid. 1925–6, Case no. 170).

2 This aspect of the matter was brought out clearly in a memorandum submitted by Bismarck in 1857 on the question of the relations between Prussia and Napoleon III. The following passage may be usefully cited:

'Aber wie viel Existenzen gibt es in der heutigen politischen Welt, welche mit voller Kontinuität im Rechte wurzeln? Spanien, Portugal, Brasilien, alle amerikanischen Republiken, Belgien, Holland, die Schweiz, Griechenland, Schweden, das noch heute mit Bewusstsein in der Revolution von 1688 fussende England können ihre dermaligen Rechtszustände auf keinen legitimen Ursprung zurückführen. Selbst für das Terrain, welches die deutschen Fürsten teils ihren eigenen Landständen abgewonnen haben, lässt sich kein vollständig legitimer Besitztitel nachweisen.

'Ein Prinzip kann man aber nur insoweit als ein allgemein durchgreifendes anerkennen, wenn es sich unter allen Umständen und zu allen Zeiten bewahrheitet, und der Grund: quod ab initio vitiosum, lapsu temporis convalescere nequit, bleibt der Doctrin gegenüber richtig, wird aber durch die Bedürfnisse der Praxis unaufhörlich widerlegt.

'Die meisten der oben berührten Zustände sind eingealtert, wir haben uns an sie gewöhnt und deshalb ihre revolutionäre Geburt vergessen. Aber auch dann, wenn sie noch nicht diesen Grad von Verjährung hatten, stiess man sich früher nicht an ihrer revolutionären Natur. Cromwell wurde von den europäischen Potentaten "Herr Bruder" genannt und seine Freundschaft gesucht, wenn sie nützlich erschien. Mit den Generalstaaten waren die ehrbarsten Fürsten im Bündnis, bevor sie von Spanien anerkannt wurden; Wilhelm von Oranien und seine Nachfolger in England hatten, auch während die Stuarts noch prätendierten, nichts an sich, was unsere Vorfahren von den intimsten Beziehungen mit ihnen abgehalten hätte; den Vereinigten Staaten haben wir schon in dem Haager Vertrage von 1785 ihren revolutionären Ursprung verziehen. In neuster Zeit hat unser Hof den Besuch des Königs von Portugal empfangen, und mit dem Hause Bernadotte hätten wir uns verschwägert, waren nicht zufällige Hindernisse eingetreten.

'Wann und nach welchen Kennzeichen haben alle diese Mächte aufgehört, revolutionär zu sein?' (*Fontes Juris Gentium, Digest of the Diplomatic correspondence of the European States*, 1856–71, p. 160).

For a significant comparison, on the *tu quoque* basis, of the merits of the principle of effectiveness as-against that of legitimacy see the argument adduced in 1861 by the new Kingdom of Italy in its communications to Spain: '...ce ne sera certes par l'Espagne qui voudrait méconnaître le droit fondé sur le fait de la volonté nationale, fait sur lequel pose également le droit de sa dynastie actuelle, droit qu'au surplus, ici moins qu'ailleurs, on ne saurait considérer comme dépendant d'une reconnaissance étrangère, n'oubliant pas combien celle-ci s'y est fait attendre sans qu'on ne crût pas pour cela moins légitime le droit de S.M. Isabelle II, que la nation avait proclamé' (ibid. p. 132).

International society would be entitled to discourage revolutions by wielding the weapon of non-recognition if at the same time it provided methods guaranteeing and ensuring individual rights and government by consent within the territories of all States.[1] When that consummation comes to pass, revolutions will be subject to suppression as being subversive of the constitution of the international commonwealth. Until this happens, international law must be satisfied with a different function, namely, that of ensuring a measure of continuity—otherwise radically broken—between the revolutionary and the old order. 'I hold that a little rebellion now and then is a good thing, as necessary in the political world as storms in the physical', wrote Jefferson to Madison in 1787.[2] 'We recognize the right of revolution...', wrote the United States Secretary of State in 1923 when reviewing the reasons which prompted the refusal to recognize the Government of Soviet Russia.[3]

§ 41. *The Method of the Revolutionary Change as a Test of Recognition.* Similar considerations apply to the test of the method of the revolutionary change as distinguished from its illegitimate source. The inhumanity and ruthlessness which often accompany the emergence and maintenance in power of revolutionary governments has frequently given rise in foreign countries to indignation and disapproval which have found expression in the refusal to recognize the new authority. The attitude of Great Britain to the Government of the French Convention of 1793, to the Serbian Government in 1903, and to the Greek Government in 1922, and the refusal of a number of countries to recognize the Government of Soviet Russia after 1917, may be mentioned as examples.[4] This policy has occasionally been supported by writers.[5] But there are weighty objections

1 See above, p. 93.

2 *Works* (4th ed.), vol. IV, pp. 362, 363. He added later: 'God forbid, we should ever be twenty years without such a rebellion' (ibid. p. 467).

3 Hackworth, vol. I, p. 177. In 1902 we find a United States Secretary of State saying: 'To deny to an insurgent the right to prevent the enemy from receiving material aid cannot well be justified without denying the right of revolution' (Mr Secretary Hay, as quoted by Wilson in *A.J.* vol. I (1907), p. 56).

4 See, for example, the outspoken declaration of Colby, United States Secretary of State, referred to in *Russian Socialist Federated Soviet Republics* v. *Cibrario*: 235 N.Y. 256; 139 N.E. 259, 262.

5 An eloquent justification of both these tests will be found in the treatise of Professor Hyde, who suggests that 'in the interest of the society of nations the members thereof should habitually manifest extreme reluctance in recognising as a new government one which acquires power in the teeth of popular opposition and by inhuman methods' (vol. I, § 43). He explains the practice of the United States,

to the application of a test of this nature. So long as international law does not stigmatize revolutions as being in the nature of crimes against the law of nations, it cannot condemn the means, necessarily violent, by which revolutions are achieved. Respect for the sanctity of human life is not a natural concomitant of revolutionary upheavals. When the revolutionary regime lends itself to acts of cruelty and savagery which shock the moral sense of the civilized world, mere refusal of recognition is an ineffective and inadequate substitute for immediate suppression of the evil by a determined act of intervention. Short of that radical remedy, refusal to recognize is a stimulus to rather than a check upon barbarity. It deprives States adopting that attitude of the opportunity for intercession and for appeal to the sense of humanity and pity of the revolutionary authorities. Finally, unless humanitarian intervention is made a rule of international practice to a larger extent than it is at present, it is difficult to see why drastic disapproval on the part of foreign nations by means of non-recognition or withdrawal of recognition should be restricted to cases of inhuman conduct in the course of a revolution, and leave untouched barbarous suppression of opponents and minorities by an apparently well-established regime.

These are probably the reasons why this particular test of recognition has been applied only on rare occasions, and even then somewhat hesitatingly. Thus, although the final breaking off of diplomatic relations with the French Minister in London on 24 January 1793 was decisively influenced by the execution of King Louis XVI, the principal reason for the refusal to recognize the new government was the determination of the National Convention to assist the cause of revolution in other countries.[1] Similarly, the atrocities accompanying the revolution were only one of the numerous reasons why recognition was refused to the Government of

at that time, as based on the view that 'normally a government, which by force has won the ascendancy in opposition to the will of the people and with contempt for rights created under a local constitution, is internationally a menace because its very supremacy sows seeds of discord bound to ripen into a conflict which, however localized, may fairly be deemed hurtful to the maintenance of the general peace' (ibid. § 73).

1 On 19 November 1792, the National Convention passed a decree in the following terms: 'La convention nationale déclare, qu'elle accordera secours à tous les peuples qui voudront recouvrir leur liberté, et elle charge le pouvoir exécutif de donner des ordres aux généraux des armées françaises pour secourir les citoyens qui auraient été, ou qui seraient vexées, pour la cause de la liberté.' See Laurent, *Histoire du droit des gens et des relations internationales* (1st ed. 1869), vol. xv, pp. 161–97; Basdevant, *La révolution française et le droit de la guerre continentale* (1901), pp. 161–76. For the exchange of notes between Great Britain and France see *Annual Register*, 1793, pp. 115 et seq.

Soviet Russia after 1917. In the case of Serbia in 1903[1] and Greece in 1922,[2] the reaction of foreign States was more in the nature of a suspension of diplomatic relations than of refusal of recognition.

1 On 23 June 1903, a telegram was sent to various British representatives abroad instructing them to inform the governments of the countries in which they were resident that Great Britain had suspended diplomatic relations with Serbia. In a statement made in the House of Commons on 17 June 1903, the Prime Minister, Mr Balfour, said: 'Diplomatic relations between this country and Servia came to an end with the death of King Alexander and have not been renewed. His Majesty's Government have considered whether they should mark their reprobation of the crime which has disgraced the Servian capital by withdrawing His Majesty's representative at Belgrade. It has, however, been thought that, for the present, Sir G. Bonham should remain at his post, in order that he may watch and report upon events and that he may take whatever steps are necessary to protect British interests. He will not be accredited to the new Government nor will any steps be taken to accord official recognition to it until we are in possession of fuller information as to the circumstances under which it has come into power' (*H.C. Debates*, vol. CXXIII, col. 1171). On 22 June 1903, the Under-Secretary of State for Foreign Affairs made the following statement in the House of Commons: 'The formal official functions of Sir George Bonham as His Majesty's Representative at the Servian Court are suspended. He remains for the present at Belgrade as the unofficial Agent of His Majesty's Government.... The protection of British subjects continues to be entrusted to His Majesty's Legation which is authorized to make such unofficial communications to the *de facto* authorities as may be necessary for that purpose' (ibid. vol. CXXIV, col. 64). According to the Foreign Office List, diplomatic relations were resumed in 1906. For further details see *British Documents on the Origins of the World War* (edited by Gooch and Temperley), vol. IV, pp. 124–48.

2 The Greek revolution in 1922 resulted in the restoration of the monarchy and in the execution of the principal members of the former Government. In consequence of these events Great Britain suspended, on 28 November 1922, her diplomatic relations with Greece. On that day the British Representative sent a note to the Greek Foreign Office announcing the rupture of diplomatic relations, and left Athens. At the same time Great Britain continued to be represented at Athens by a Chargé d'Affaires. She declined to recognize the King. To what extent she refused to recognize the new government is not quite clear. It appears that she recognized the new authority as the *de facto* government. This was the information given by the Foreign Office on 18 June 1923 to a party engaged in litigation. On 11 June 1923, another party was informed that the Greek Government was not then recognized, apparently *de jure*, by His Majesty's Government. In reply to a further question when recognition had been withdrawn, there came the answer that the British Minister had been withdrawn from Athens on 28 November 1922. For an inconclusive case bearing on the matter see *King of the Hellenes* v. *Brostrom and Others*, (1923) 16 *Lloyd's List Law Reports*, p. 168, where Rowland J. held, somewhat summarily, that there was 'nothing' in the defendants' plea that the Greek Government had not been recognized by the Government of the United Kingdom. In the House of Commons on 11 April 1923, it was stated on behalf of the Government that there was no reason to assume that British commercial interests suffered as the result of the interruption of normal diplomatic relations. But, it was added, recognition must await proof of the stability and good faith of the Greek Government. It was apparently assumed in official quarters that courts would recognize the laws and decrees of the government to which recognition was thus refused.

The American Chargé d'Affaires was formally accredited to the Greek Government

§ 42. *Willingness to fulfil International Obligations.* Recognition has often been refused on the ground that the new government has been unwilling either to give an undertaking to fulfil international obligations contracted by its predecessor or to desist from its own illegal conduct. This particular test of recognition, which must be distinguished from that of *ability* to fulfil international obligations,[1] is of comparatively recent origin. Apparently it was first given clear expression by the United States in 1877 in connection with the recognition of the Diaz Government in Mexico. In a Message to Congress President Hayes stated that it had been 'the custom of the United States, when such [revolutionary] changes of government have heretofore occurred in Mexico, to recognize and enter into official relations with the *de facto* government as soon as it should appear to have the approval of the Mexican people and should manifest a disposition to adhere to the obligations of treaties and international friendship'.[2] The theory underlying this test was developed two years later in some detail in connection with the recognition of the Blanco Government in Venezuela. After admitting that that Government seemed to be wielding effective authority and that there was therefore under the general usage of nations no obstacle to its recognition on that score, the Secretary of State continued as follows:

> 'But the capacity of a state, in itself, for recognition, and the fact of recognition by other states, are two different things. Recognition is not an act wholly depending on the constitutionality or completeness of a change of government, but is not infrequently influenced by the needs of the mutual relations between the two countries. When radical changes have taken place in the domestic organization of the country, or when they seem to be contemplated in its outward relations, it is often a matter of solicitude with this government that some understanding should exist that the rights acquired by our citizens, through the operation of treaties and other diplomatic engagements, shall not be affected by the change. In other words, while the United States regard their international compacts and obligations as entered into with *nations* rather than with political *governments*, it behooves them to be watchful lest their course toward a government should affect the relations to the nation.'[3]

on 19 January 1924, after regular elections had been held in December 1923. Prior to that date the United States were represented in Greece by a Chargé d'Affaires *ad interim*, who was not accredited to any Greek authority. See Dulles in *Proceedings of the American Society of International Law*, 1924, pp. 101–6; Hackworth, vol. 1, pp. 286–90. Previously, the American Chargé d'Affaires joined the representatives of other States in impressing upon the Greek authorities the unfortunate effect which the execution of the Greek ministers had on public opinion.

1 It would seem that ability to fulfil obligations is merely one aspect of the question of effectiveness discussed in the next chapter.

2 Moore, vol. 1, p. 148. 3 Ibid. p. 151.

It is doubtful whether there was anything in the former practice of the United States to warrant either the above view of recognition or the particular test adopted, but the latter seems to have since gained a firm foothold in the United States. When in 1913 the Assistant Secretary of State was making a weighty pronouncement in the matter, he thought himself justified in laying down the following conditions of recognition, which he described as having been valid since the American revolution: 'The control of the administrative machinery of the State; the general acquiescence of the people; and the ability and willingness of their government to discharge international and conventional obligations.'[1] One of the principal reasons for the refusal of the United States to recognize the Soviet Government of Russia after 1917 was its unwillingness to fulfil what the United States (and other countries) regarded as its international obligations in the matter of certain treaties and financial commitments of the Czarist Government, of compensation for expropriation of American property, and of revolutionary propaganda abroad.[2] In general, it does not appear that, apart from the practice of the United States and from the innovation introduced in the British practice after the First World War in connection with the abandonment of the requirement of evidence of constitutional approval of the revolutionary change, that particular test of recognition has gained wide acceptance.[3]

The soundness and propriety of the test of willingness to fulfil inter-

1 *U.S. For. Rel.* 1913, p. 100. But see Mr Hay's note to Lord Pauncefote of 16 November 1899, ibid. 1899, p. 344 (where the recognition of the Government of Bolivia was made dependent upon that Government being 'in control of the machinery of administration and *in a position* to fulfil its international obligations'), and the statement of policy of the United States on the subject of 8 September 1900, ibid. 1900, p. 412. In both cases the reference was not to the willingness but to the ability to fulfil international obligations.

2 For a series of statements of successive American administrations on this matter see *A.J.* vol. XXVIII (1934), pp. 89–94. See also Houghton in *International Conciliation*, 1929, Pamphlet no. 247. On 10 August 1920, the United States Secretary of State wrote to the Italian Ambassador: 'It is not possible for the Government of the United States to recognize the present rulers of Russia as a government with which the relations common to friendly governments can be maintained. This conviction has nothing to do with any particular political or social structure which the Russian people themselves may deem fit to embrace. It rests upon a wholly different set of facts. These facts, which none dispute, have convinced the Government of the United States, against its will, that the existing regime in Russia is based upon the negation of every principle of honour and good faith, and every usage and convention, underlying the whole structure of international law.' Reference was also made to the Russian attitude to the binding force of treaties and revolutionary propaganda against other States: *U.S. For. Rel.* 1920 (III), p. 465.

3 See below, p. 136. Smith (vol. I, p. 239) considers it to be a feature of the British practice, but there is not sufficient evidence to warrant that contention.

national obligations as a condition of recognition are questionable for a number of reasons.[1] It is difficult to see why, in law, the mere fact of the advent of a new government should cause other States to raise the issue of the fulfilment of obligations incurred by or binding upon its predecessor. These obligations are in any case binding, within reasonable limits,[2] upon the new government by virtue of the well-established principle of the continuity of the State regardless of changes in the composition of its governments. It does not, in law, lie within the power of the new government to repudiate the obligations of its predecessor.[3] Recognition in face of any attempted repudiation of obligations does not amount to acquiescence in what is clearly a breach of international law. At the same time, the refusal of recognition on that account deprives the injured State of the opportunity of seeking legal redress through the ordinary channels. The more satisfactory course would appear to be to grant recognition and then to insist by such means as international law permits on the fulfilment by the new government of its international obligations.

This particular test of recognition is open to a further objection inasmuch as it involves the danger, which practice has shown to be not purely

1 There is some support among writers for this test of recognition—not only among those who assert the political nature of recognition of governments but also from those who regard it as a legal duty. Thus Cavaglieri (*Corso*, p. 187) regards it as a legitimate ground for delaying recognition, while Anzilotti (*Corso*, p. 199) considers it a good ground for refusing recognition altogether. For an able criticism of this test see Spiropoulos, *Die de facto Regierung im Völkerrecht* (1926), pp. 32–9.

2 It is probable that in order to preserve the vitality and usefulness of the generally accepted rule postulating the continuance of the international obligations of the State notwithstanding any internal changes in the composition or the form of its government, it may be necessary to mitigate in appropriate cases the rigidity of the general principle. There may be room for far-reaching modifications of obligations undertaken by the former regime—not because of a change, revolutionary or otherwise, in the government, but for the reason that the change has brought about or has been accompanied by such fundamental alterations in the political, social or economic conditions of the nation as to produce a vital change in circumstances requiring a reconsideration of the obligations in question. For a statement of the view of Soviet Russia on the matter see the Memorandum presented by the Russian Delegates to the Genoa Conference on 20 April 1922 (reproduced in Taracouzio, *The Soviet Union and International Law* (1935), p. 415), and 11 May 1922 (adequately summarized by Houghton in *International Conciliation*, 1929, Pamphlet no. 247, p. 70).

3 In 1912, when revolution broke out in China, Japan and Russia suggested that the Powers should not recognize the new government until they had secured from it adequate guarantees for safeguarding their common interests. The United States, while communicating, rather cautiously, 'its agreement in principle to the policy of concerted action in the recognition of the Republic of China in accordance with the accepted principles of international law', expressed the view that 'the established obligations of China held irrespective of the form of government and passed automatically in turn to the *de facto* Provisional Government and to such ultimate government as might merit formal recognition': *U.S. For. Rel.* 1912, p. 76.

theoretical, of its being used as a means of exacting promises and concessions in return for recognition.[1] Whenever this is done the process of recognition is being abused for purposes alien to its true function. The alacrity with which revolutionary governments, based on force, often proclaim their desire to fulfil the international obligations of their country is a disconcerting reminder of the danger inherent in that practice. A dictatorial regime will have little hesitation in acknowledging a doubtful obligation at the valuable price of recognition. As a means of inducing conduct conforming to international law, the refusal to recognize a government may be effective only in exceptional cases, for instance, in the relations of a powerful State and a weak neighbour. Otherwise, the refusal to recognize is a mere gesture unsound in law and futile in practice. In 1918 and in the following years a considerable number of States refused to recognize the Government of Soviet Russia on account of its unwillingness to give guarantees of the fulfilment of the contractual obligations of the former Russian regime as well as of its own obligations in the matter of compensation for confiscation of foreign property and of revolutionary propaganda against foreign States.[2] The Government of Soviet Russia was subsequently recognized by most of those States without being obliged to give assurances not given reciprocally by the recognizing States.[3]

From the test of willingness to fulfil international obligations there must be distinguished the test of ability to fulfil them. The latter would seem to be free of the objections to which the former is open. For ability to fulfil obligations is merely one of the several aspects of the test of effectiveness.

1 See below, p. 162.

2 For a detailed account see Toynbee, *Survey of International Affairs*, 1924, pp. 228 et seq.; Lagarde, *La reconnaissance du gouvernement des Soviets* (1924); Hackworth, vol. I, pp. 298–305; Harriman in *Proceedings of the American Society of International Law*, 1924, pp. 84–97; Houghton, 'Policy of the United States and Other Nations with respect to the Recognition of the Russian Soviet Government, 1917–1929', in *International Conciliation*, February 1929, Pamphlet no. 247.

3 See, for example, the Exchange of Communications of 16 November 1933, between the United States and Soviet Russia, printed in *A.J.* vol. XXVIII (1934), Suppl. pp. 2–4. Both parties gave identical assurances in the crucial matter of revolutionary propaganda. In his letter of 16 November 1933, addressed to M. Litvinoff, the President of the United States, after reciting the four undertakings given by Soviet Russia with regard to revolutionary propaganda, said: 'It will be the fixed policy of the Executive of the United States within the limits of the powers conferred by the Constitution and the laws of the United States to adhere reciprocally to the engagements above expressed' (ibid.). This was also the case in connection with the recognition by the Little Entente in 1934 (*Documents on International Affairs*, 1934, p. 403). For the correspondence relating to this matter and preceding the British recognition of the Government of Soviet Russia see Cmd. 1602 (1922); 1846, 1874, 1890 (1923); 2216, 2261 (1924).

The ability and the willingness to fulfil international obligations are, as a rule, coupled in official pronouncements, but occasionally it is the former alone which is referred to.[1]

The test of willingness to fulfil international obligations is, it has been submitted, of doubtful juridical soundness and of controversial practical value when conceived as a condition of recognition. But it is a test which, though not figuring prominently in British practice, has often been applied and which constitutes a uniform feature of the practice of some States, in particular of the United States.[2] In view of this, the question arises how far it amounts to a denial of the legal nature of recognition, i.e. of recognition viewed as the fulfilment of a legal duty as determined by international law. On the face of it, that test may seem to make recognition dependent exclusively upon considerations of national interest. However, although the motive and the immediate occasion of the refusal of recognition in such cases lie in an injury to the national interest and in the desire to obtain satisfaction through the use of the weapon of non-recognition, the denial of recognition is at the same time intended to do away with a violation of international law. To that extent the State refusing recognition deems itself to be acting in conformity with the wider interests of international law. It bases its action on legal grounds thought to be capable of general application. It says in effect: it is useless to recognize as representing the State a government which at the very threshold of its existence refuses to abide by rules of international law; it is futile to concede the enjoyment of international rights to a government which declines to be bound by the

1 See above, p. 109. See, in particular, the frequently quoted instruction issued in 1900 by the American Acting Secretary of State summarizing the practice of the United States as favouring postponement of recognition until it appears that the new government 'is in possession of the machinery of the state, administering government with the assent of the people thereof and without substantial resistance to its authority, and that it is in a position to fulfil all the international obligations and responsibilities incumbent upon a sovereign State under treaties and international law': Moore, vol. I, p. 138. See also President Taft's Message to Congress in 1912 with regard to the recognition of the Republican Government of China (*U.S. For. Rel.* 1912, p. 21).

2 When in 1908 the parties to the Treaty of Algeciras recognized collectively Sultan Moulai Hafid of Morocco they did so following upon assurances asked from and given by the Sultan as to the fulfilment of provisions of treaties bearing upon Morocco. For the exchange of correspondence see *B.F.S.P.* vol. CII, pp. 932–8. For numerous instances see Hackworth, vol. I, §§ 47–51. See also ibid. p. 176, where it is pointed out that in nearly all recent instances of recognition of governments by the United States 'the ability and willingness of the new government to discharge its international obligations has been stressed as pre-requisite to recognition' and that in those cases in which it has not been expressly referred to it has probably been considered implicit in the requirement of stability and effectiveness of the new government.

accepted duties of the law of nations; it is consistent with legal principle and it is beneficial to the rule of international law to deny recognition to a government exhibiting such disposition.[1] This argument is not, it has been suggested, one which commends itself by its soundness. But it is not necessary to interpret this particular test of recognition as amounting to the assertion of a right to refuse recognition arbitrarily or by exclusive reference to considerations of national policy.

1 For an explanation of the test of willingness to fulfil international obligations by reference to some such general considerations see the statement of Secretary Hughes on 19 July 1923, with regard to Russia. He pointed out that recognition is an invitation to intercourse, that it is 'accompanied on the part of the new government by the clearly implied or express promise to fulfil the obligations of intercourse', and that the Government of Soviet Russia could not be recognized because of 'a repudiation of the obligations inherent in international intercourse and a defiance of the principles upon which alone it can be conducted' (*U.S. For. Rel.* 1923 (II), p. 760).

Chapter IX

THE PRINCIPLE OF EFFECTIVENESS AND THE CONSENT OF THE GOVERNED

§ 43. *Consent of the Governed as Evidence of Effectiveness.* It has been submitted in the preceding chapter that the tests of legitimacy, of humanity of revolutionary methods, and of willingness to fulfil international obligations, while not necessarily inconsistent with a legal view of recognition, are open to serious objection. They are not the predominant feature of international practice. That practice is dominated, in addition to and as part of the overriding principle of effectiveness, by the requirement of the subsequent legitimation of the revolutionary government through an adequately expressed act of popular approval. The requirement of such consent may be described, with some plausibility, as yet another manifestation of the principle of legitimacy. It may, more accurately, be regarded as insistence on proper evidence of effectiveness. This is so although its evidential value for that purpose is, in the present state of international organization, open to criticism.

While dynastic or similar legitimacy of origin, in so far as it played any part at all in the practice of States, has now been definitely discarded as a test of recognition, the practice of the majority of States, in particular of Great Britain and the United States, has been to take into account the unconstitutional character of and the violence accompanying the change of government to the extent of requiring that, as a condition of recognition, the authority of the new rulers shall be confirmed by the people. That practice is, in substance, not a denial but an affirmation of the principle of effectiveness. In the turmoil and uncertainty following upon the upheavals of the revolution, popular approval, properly expressed, is deemed to be evidence of the true authority of the government, of the obedience accorded to it, and of its probable permanence and stability. For when Jefferson wrote in 1792 that it was in accordance with the principles of the United States to acknowledge as rightful any government which is formed 'by the will of the nation substantially declared',[1] he was stating a principle which was less self-explanatory than appeared at first sight. The *de facto* principle originally helped to elevate to the dignity of a legal rule the reality of the national will as against the fictional encroachments of

1 See below, p. 125.

monarchical legitimism. But subsequent experience showed that the principle of mere effectiveness may supply a sanction for ruthless regimes inimical to the true will of the nation. That experience has provided the origin of the practice according to which, as a condition of recognition, the will of the people sanctioning the new scheme of things must be substantially declared in an orderly way and in accordance with the provisions of the constitution.

§ 44. *The British Practice.* It has been shown in connection with recognition of States that, although the circumstances at the beginning of the nineteenth century were favourable to the adoption of the principle of legitimacy, Great Britain had consistently refused to identify herself with it.[1] The same attitude was followed with regard to recognition of governments. We find Canning stating in 1825 that even the refusal to recognize the Government of the French Convention up to 1796 was due exclusively to 'the unsettled state of the French Government', and that this was the

1 See above, pp. 12–18, 26. For an early example of somewhat nominal legitimism tempered by practical considerations of convenience see the answer given in 1680 by Charles II to the Portuguese Ambassador sent by Prince Don Pedro after Alfonso VI had been removed from the throne. The reply was signed by Sir Leoline Jenkins:

'His Majesty therefore having as perfect a Tenderness and Concern, as any Christian Prince can have for the Honour and Safety of all Crowned Heads, most especially of so near an Ally, from all Violences among their own Subjects, and having espoused the Interests of that Royal Family by choosing out of it our most gracious Queen his Consort, can do no less (whatever other Princes his Neighbours, either out of Interest or Indifferency may have done in this Case) than expect, and resolve to be fully satisfied in his own Royal Judgment, that the present Possession which the Prince *Don Pedro* has taken of the Kingdom of Portugal, and the Dominions thereunto belonging, is such as the Law of Nations, and the Constitutions of that Kingdom, do warrant, before your Excellency be received to any Publick Audience. I do therefore, by the King my Master's most express and special Command, and in his Royal Name and Behalf, hereby declare, that nothing can be more welcome to his Majesty, than an Opportunity to demonstrate the sincere Affection he hath for his dear Brother-in-law the Prince *Don Pedro*; and for the Grandeur of his Estate and Dignity; and also for the establishing of the strictest Commerce and Conjunction possible between the Two Crowns: And that in order thereto, his Majesty is most willing to receive and treat with your Excellency, as Ambassador from the Crown of Portugal, and as a Person qualified in all Things suitable to his Majesty's Affections and Desires; but I do likewise declare and protest, in His Majesty's Name, that His Majesty intends not to admit of your Excellency, to represent the Person of any other, than that of his dear Brother *Alphonso* VI. King of Portugal, in this Court; unless it be first made appear to his Majesty, either that the King *Don Alphonso* has freely and voluntarily resigned, renounced, and divested himself of his Kingdom and Government, and without any Fear, Constraint, or Surprize; or else, that the Prince *Don Pedro* his Brother, pretends to no more at present, than a necessary Curatorship and Lieutenancy in the said Government, during the King his Brother's Absence, or other Impediment allowable by the Law of Nations, and the ancient fundamental Laws of that Government, and no longer or otherwise': Wynne, *Life of Sir Leoline Jenkins*, vol. II (1724), p. 688.

reason alleged 'in Parliament and in State Papers for that abstinence'.[1] But this rejection of legitimism was not accompanied by the adoption of the *de facto* principle pure and simple. The practice was to exact some formal evidence of the effectiveness of the new government. That evidence was sought in various manifestations, in a form provided by law, of popular consent to the new rule.

The attitude which various British Governments adopted in relation to the successive revolutions in France illustrates the persistent adherence to the principle of subsequent legitimation. After the revolution broke out in France on 24 February 1848, the British Ambassador was informed that as his credentials had been addressed to King Louis Philippe, who had now abdicated, his official functions were for the time suspended, but that he was free to enter into such unofficial communications as he might think useful so long as he made it clear that such unofficial communications did not commit the British Government. Subsequently he was instructed that the British Government could not send new credentials to an Ambassador placed in the circumstances in which he then stood 'until it should be seen that there was a Government sufficiently settled and well supported by the nation at large to be considered by foreign Powers as the real organ of the nation'.[2] In August 1848 the credentials of Lord Normanby, the British diplomatic representative, were addressed to 'the President of the Council of Ministers, charged with the Executive Power of the French Republic'. He was accredited 'in the character of our Ambassador Extraordinary and Plenipotentiary on a Special and Temporary Mission'. Even this concession was not forthcoming until, in the view of Great Britain, a firmer and more permanent government had been established.

When in December 1852, after a *coup d'état*, a popular vote on the 21st of that month expressed itself in favour of the re-establishment of the Empire, Lord Cowley, the British Ambassador, was instructed that 'it had long been the policy of England...to acknowledge without hesitation the practical results of those decided demonstrations of opinion by which the French people have so often of late years changed their rulers and internal institutions'. It was pointed out that 'Her Majesty saw no reason to deviate from that principle', and that 'they were, therefore, prepared to recommend Her Majesty to recognize both the Empire and the Imperial Dignity...which had been conferred on the person of Louis Napoleon by

1 Manning, *Diplomatic Correspondence of the United States concerning the Independence of the Latin-American Nations*, vol. III, p. 1546.

2 This account is to a large extent based on a Foreign Office Memorandum of 1 October 1874. See also the documents printed in Smith, vol. I, pp. 106–12.

an immense majority of the votes of French people'.[1] The principle underlying these instructions was clearly stated by Lord Malmesbury on 6 December 1852, in the House of Lords. He said: 'It has been...our usual policy for a period of 22 years—since the revolution of 1830 in Paris—to acknowledge the constitutional doctrine that the people of every country have the right to choose their own sovereign without any foreign interference; and that a sovereign having been freely chosen by them, that sovereign, or ruler, or whatever he may be called, being *de facto* the ruler of that country, should be recognized by the sovereign of this.'[2]

The same attitude was adopted when the Second Empire fell on 4 September 1870 and after a provisional government of the newly proclaimed Republic was established on 5 September. On 14 September, M. Thiers visited England and, in an interview with Earl Granville, urged the recognition of the French Republic by Great Britain. He was informed that 'it is contrary to precedent to do so at present', and that the new government had no legal sanction so long as it had not been elected by the Constituent Assembly.[3] The attitude of the British Government was clearly expressed in the despatch, of 1 October 1870, of Earl Granville to Lord Lyons, the British Ambassador in Paris:

> 'I stated to them [the Cabinet] that I had said to M. Thiers that the course which Her Majesty's Government were pursuing in this respect, was in strict conformity with that heretofore observed in analogous cases; and that I had pointed out to him that the Government, though administering *de facto* the affairs of France, itself recognized that the voice of France speaking in a Constituent Assembly could alone determine the form and character of the Government to whom the destinies of France should be finally committed. I had added that I believed Her Majesty's Government would at once advise the Queen to recognize any such Government, and to enter into formal and official relations with it.'[4]

1 See F.O. Memorandum of 1 October 1874.

2 *H.L. Debates*, vol. CXXIII, col. 971.

3 *B.F.S.P.* vol. LXI, p. 751.

4 *Parl. Papers*, 1871, vol. LXXI, no. 166, p. 111; *B.F.S.P.* LXI, p. 802. In January 1871 the French Government, in an emphatic communication, pressed once more for recognition (*Archives diplomatiques*, 1871–2, vol. IV, p. 1296). The British Government adhered to its point of view. On 20 January 1871, Earl Granville insisted that 'the first element of recognition was still wanting, and that as the Government of National Defence itself admitted that it did not possess that stability which a formal vote of a Constituent Assembly could alone bestow upon it, it would be premature in Her Majesty's Government to recognize, as the national Government of France, a Government which is only administering the affairs of the country pending its decision as to the form of government under which it may ultimately elect to live' (*Parl. Papers*, 1871, vol. LXXI, I, no. 328, p. 258; *B.F.S.P.* vol. LXI, p. 995). The final part of the despatch merits quotation: 'It is fully admitted that France, by her heroic and patriotic co-operation with the Government of National Defence, has fully recognized that Government in the capacity which it has claimed for itself by the name it has adopted.

On the occasion of the London Conference of 1871, convened in connection with the Russian denunciation of the Black Sea clauses of the Treaty of Paris, the French Chargé d'Affaires again urged recognition on the ground that the 'Government of National Defence' had been approved by the vote of many provinces and that it had been recognized by a number of States, including Italy, Spain, the United States and Switzerland. He was given a reasoned reply to the effect that the principal condition of recognition was absent, seeing that, as the Government of National Defence itself admitted, it did not possess the stability which only a formal vote of the Constituent Assembly could bestow upon it; that the confirmation by the several provinces referred only to the provisional capacity which the Government claimed for itself by the name it had adopted; that recognition at that moment would be open to construction as an intimation on the part of Great Britain that she would view with favour any particular government; and that 'it had been the ruling principle of England scrupulously to abstain from interfering in the internal affairs of foreign nations, and from indicating a preference as to the particular form of government to which the nation would do best to confide its interest'. On 15 February 1871, the British Ambassador, in reply to an enquiry, was instructed to recognize at once whoever was placed at the head of the Government by the Assembly.[1]

...Her Majesty's Government, however, are not satisfied that it would be for the interest of France herself at the present moment, as regards foreign Powers, to comply with the request for recognition on the part of England; but such a measure on their part would seem to prejudge the ultimate decision of the French nation, and admit of the construction that it carried with it an intimation on the part of England that she would view with special favour one particular form of Government. But it is the ruling principle of this country scrupulously to abstain from interfering in the internal affairs of foreign nations, and from indicating a preference as to the particular form of Government to which the nation would do best to confide its interests' (ibid.). The United States formally recognized the Government of National Defence on 7 September 1870 (*Archives diplomatiques*, 1871–2, vol. II, no. 422, p. 517).

1 As quoted in the F.O. Memorandum, ubi supra. See also Smith, vol. I, pp. 113–15. It is of interest to note that Austria-Hungary insisted, though in a less emphatic manner, as a matter of principle and of international practice, on the necessity of confirmation by a popular vote. In his despatch of 3 October 1870, Count de Beust said: 'Nous n'avons pas de préjugé hostile contre la République et nous n'hésiterons pas à la reconnaître officiellement, aussitôt qu'elle aura reçu la consécration d'un vote national. Aujourd'hui, avant que la France ait été consultée et se soit prononcée, il serait contraire aux usages qui régissent les relations des Puissances entr'elles de devancer la décision du pays' (*Archives diplomatiques*, 1871–2, vol. II, no. 573, p. 703). The refusal to grant formal recognition was accompanied by nearly complete recognition in practice, including the maintenance of full diplomatic relations. In his despatch, quoted above, Count de Beust went on to say: 'Quant au Gouvernement actuel de la France, nous l'avons reconnu autant que sa nature toute provisoire nous a permis de le faire. Nos relations diplomatiques n'ont pas été interrompues un seul instant; nous avons laissé à Paris et nous maintenons à Tours dans la personne de Votre

The practice with regard to the successive revolutions in Spain followed the same lines. After the revolt headed by Marshal Serrano broke out on 18 September 1868, Queen Isabella fled from Spain and sought refuge in France. In October the new Provisional Government informed Sir J. Crampton, the British Minister, of the fact of its establishment and of the appointment of a new Secretary of State. Sir J. Crampton thereupon received instructions to the effect that as his credentials were addressed to the Queen, whose government had left Spain, his official functions were for the time being suspended; that he should not on that account abstain from unofficial communication with the persons having direction of affairs; and that he should explain to the Spanish Secretary of State that official intercourse was dependent on the receipt of new credentials which could not be sent until it was clear that there was in Spain a government sufficiently strong and well supported by the population at large so that it could be considered as the real organ of the nation. When the Spanish Government declared itself dissatisfied with this arrangement, it was explained to it that the lack of formal recognition, while in conformity with precedent, need not prevent discussion and settlement of any pending question. It was subsequently intimated to the Spanish Government that the British Government was prepared to receive agents appointed by the former for diplomatic purposes—a course which proved satisfactory to the Spanish authorities. In June 1869, after the new constitution providing for a hereditary monarchy had been promulgated and Marshal Serrano elected Regent of the Kingdom, Great Britain recognized the Government.

In February 1873, after the abdication of King Amadeus who had been elected in 1870, the Cortes proclaimed a Republic and convened the Constituent Assembly for 1 June. Great Britain declined the request for recognition of the Republic before that date: 'Until this Assembly had declared its views, it would be impossible to do more than he, Lord Granville, had already stated that Her Majesty's Government was willing to do. Whatever Government was formally confirmed and accepted by the Spanish nation would be recognized by Great Britain.'[1] The subsequent

Altesse un Représentant revêtu du caractère diplomatique le plus élevé. Nous avons accueilli et continuerons de même à accueillir avec le plus grand empressement toutes les communications du Gouvernement de la défense nationale, absolument comme s'il était muni des pouvoirs les plus réguliers' (ibid.). Switzerland recognized without delay, on 8 September, the French revolutionary Government of 1870. The Swiss Minister, in informing the French Government of the decision of the Federal Council, stated: 'La Suisse a toujours reconnu le droit de libre constitution des peuples. La France s'étant constituée en République aux acclamations du pays tout entier, le Conseil fédéral n'hésite pas un instant à appliquer ce principe au nouveau Gouvernement de la France' (ibid. no. 434, p. 529).

1 F.O. Memorandum of 1 October 1874. See also Smith, vol. 1, pp. 198–205.

history of the revolution and of the efforts to obtain recognition show that, in the view of Great Britain, even formal confirmation by the constituent body, if not accompanied by the general stabilization of the country pointing to true popular support, was not sufficient to warrant recognition. For although on 1 June the Constituent Cortes proclaimed with practical unanimity a Federal Republic and invested Señor Castelar with the title of President of the Executive Powers of the Republic until 2 January 1874, recognition was withheld because of the anomalous and provisional character of the government and the continuing state of disorder in Spain. In fact, in the same month Castelar was defeated in the Cortes and replaced by Marshal Serrano. It was only on 11 August 1874 that Great Britain recognized the Spanish Government thus constituted.[1]

In relation to the frequent revolutions in the Latin-American countries, Great Britain for a long time acted on the same principle.[2]

After the outbreak of the revolution in Portugal in October 1910, Sir F. Villiers, the British Minister, received instructions to transact business with the Provisional Government as being the government of a country with whom it was desired to maintain existing friendly relations. This was done in consultation with and with the concurrence, in the first instance, of France and Spain, in order to avoid any action which might embarrass Portugal's nearest neighbours. The concurrence of Austria-Hungary,

1 Prior to that date the German Government, in a communication to the British Government, urged speedy recognition on the ground, *inter alia*, that recognition would be instrumental in putting an end to the civil war in Spain and that by granting it foreign States would be fulfilling a duty to humanity by discouraging Carlist activities. With regard to the recognition of Marshal Serrano, Lord Derby said in the House of Lords: 'It was natural that we should wait until we saw that it was a Government in a position—I will not say permanent, for it is very difficult to say what Government will be permanent in Spain as Spain now is—but in a position in which it could hold its own, and in which it should be recognized *de facto* by the great majority of the people' (*H.L. Debates*, vol. CCXXII, col. 1382).

2 The following communication of 23 September 1891, from the Foreign Office to Señor Ross, appointed by the revolutionary Government in Chile, illustrates the British practice:

'Lord Salisbury desires me to say, in reply to the inquiry you made of me to-day, that Her Majesty's Minister at Santiago has recognized provisionally the new Government of Chile, and has entered into unofficial relations with it. According to the usage observed by this country in such cases, formal and full recognition with the establishment of official relations will follow as soon as a President has been constitutionally elected and installed.

'In the meanwhile, as Mr Kennedy reports that you have been gazetted to the appointment of Chilean Envoy Extraordinary and Minister Plenipotentiary in this country, Lord Salisbury, though unable as yet, for the above reason, to recognize you officially in that capacity, will be happy to receive from you any communications which you may wish to make to him on behalf of the Chilean Government' (*State Papers*, vol. XCV (1892), *Chile*, no. 1).

Germany, Italy and Russia was subsequently secured. Sir F. Villiers was further instructed to make a verbal communication in the following terms:

> 'His Majesty's Government feel bound to govern their action according to the precedents by which the policy of this country has been guided in regard to the recognition of provisional governments which have at various times been established in foreign countries. According to the practice of the British Constitution, the King cannot address letters to or receive letters from any government that is not, at least ostensibly, established as a permanent government. As soon as Portugal shall, by a formal vote of a constituent assembly, or in some other unambiguous manner, have determined the form and character of the future government of the country, His Majesty's Government will be prepared to advise the King to recognize it, and will be happy to enter into official relations with it when established in accordance with popular vote.'[1]

After the constitution had been voted and the president elected, the Government was recognized, on 11 September 1911, by Great Britain, Austria, Germany, Italy and Spain in a joint declaration,[2] stating that as the new Constitution had been voted the Governments concerned were glad to join in the recognition of the new Government. In the interval between the fall of the old regime and the recognition of the new Government, correspondence was transacted unofficially with the diplomatic representative left in London.[3] It was intimated to him that 'he would be able to transact business'.[4]

1 F.O. Portugal, 1910, 1911.

2 Which, however, was accompanied by individual declarations of recognition. See, for instance, that communicated by the German Embassy in Lisbon on 11 September 1911, to the Portuguese Minister of Foreign Affairs. The declaration was in the following terms: 'L'Assemblée Nationale Constituante ayant sanctionné le Régime actuel j'ai l'honneur de faire savoir à Votre Excellence que je suis autorisé à Lui déclarer que le Gouvernement de Sa Majesté l'Empereur d'Allemagne est heureux de pouvoir reconnaître officiellement la République Portugaise' (Martens, *N.R.T.* 3rd ser. vol. VIII, p. 348).

3 'He was addressed as "Sir"; no official designation was appended to his name; he was not invited to receptions or other functions of an official character. When in March 1911 the Portuguese Government proposed to appoint another representative in London and enquired whether the nominee would be a *persona grata*, they were informed that the person concerned could not be received officially until the provisional Government in Portugal had been confirmed by the country and had been recognized by His Majesty's Government' (F.O. Portugal, 1910, 1911). In reply to an enquiry in the House of Commons Sir Edward Grey, Secretary of State for Foreign Affairs, said on 13 July 1911: 'It would be contrary to precedent for His Majesty's Government to recognize the Portuguese Republic before a new Constitution had been definitely set up' (*H.C. Debates*, vol. XXVIII, col. 472).

4 British Consuls in Portuguese territories were instructed, on 15 November 1910, that they might transact business with local authorities but should not take steps implying official recognition of the new Government. Portuguese Consuls in Great Britain were allowed informally to continue the discharge of their functions.

When in February 1912 Japan took the initiative in the matter of recognition, by collective action, of the new revolutionary government in China, the view of the British Government, as well as that of other Powers, was that recognition should be deferred until a Chinese constitution had been definitely adopted by a representative national assembly and a government set up in accordance with the new constitution.[1]

Neither was the requirement of evidence of popular consent altogether abandoned in the period following the First World War when dictatorial forms of government made their appearance on an increased scale. When the Albanian Government of Fan Noli, which came into power in 1924, asked for recognition, its request was refused on the ground that 'the usual practice of His Majesty's Government in these matters is to refuse formal recognition of Governments which have attained power by revolutionary methods until it is clearly demonstrated that these Governments have the support, or, at any rate, the consent of the majority of the population'.[2] It appeared that the new government dissolved parliament and refused to summon its successor. On 28 July 1924, the British Minister in Durazzo was instructed as follows:

> 'In view of the fact that the present Government reached power by violence, and contemplates taking measures of reprisal against the former Government we are not prepared to depart from ordinary precedent in this matter. If therefore you are further pressed by the Albanian Government you should inform them that until His Majesty's Government are satisfied by some clear expression of national will that the Albanian Government enjoys the confidence of the country you are not authorized to accord the formal recognition of His Majesty's Government but are instructed merely to transact with them such routine business as is necessary.'[3]

In the same year the British Government, after an interval of two years, recognized the Greek Government established in 1922. The British Minister at Athens informed the Greek Government that 'His Majesty's Government accept the verdict of the plebiscite as representing the wishes of the Greek people, and they formally recognize the regime thus established'.[4] An account of the circumstances in which Great Britain adopted the pure *de facto* principle in 1924 and in subsequent years is given

1 *U.S. For. Rel.* 1912, pp. 82–6; 1913, pp. 109–15.

2 F.O. Albania, 1924. In August 1920 France recognized General Wrangel's Government as the *de facto* Government of South Russia and appointed a French diplomatic agent at Sevastopol with the title of High Commissioner. This took place after General Wrangel had given 'assurance regarding the democratic form of his administration and respect for previous engagements of the Russian State': as reported in *U.S. For. Rel.* 1920 (III), p. 611.

3 Ibid.

4 F.O. Greece, 1924.

below.[1] The previous practice, however, was not totally discarded. When in April 1931 Great Britain recognized, without undue delay, the new regime in Spain, she did not furnish the British Ambassador in Spain with new credentials until the regime had been confirmed by popular vote and a constitutional president elected.

§ 45. *The Practice of the United States.* It is not easy to characterize in a simple formula the practice of the United States in the matter of recognition of governments. Isolated pronouncements—of which there is an abundance—provide material for contradictory conclusions. But a comprehensive survey of the practice of more than a century and a half justifies the view that, on the whole, that practice has been essentially the same as that of Great Britain. It has been based predominantly on the principle of effectiveness evidenced by an adequate expression of popular consent. Occasionally language has been used which seemed to adopt the bare fact of effectiveness as a test of recognition—as, for instance, when President Van Buren was laying down in 1829 that 'that which is the Government *de facto* is equally so *de jure*';[2] or when Secretary Clay stated in 1818 that 'for us, the sovereign *de facto* is the sovereign *de jure*';[3] or when Secretary Fish said in 1875: 'The practice of the United States in recognizing that government of a people which is the *de facto* one, is founded upon the only true and wise principle and policy.'[4] These and similar statements are likely to prove—and have proved[5]—to be a source of confusion, which may well obscure the true significance of the American contribution, unless we realize that the emphasis on *de facto* existence of a government does not refer in this connection to the bare circumstance of effectiveness regardless of the consent of the population. It refers to the factual existence of a government, based on the consent of the population, irrespective of any legitimacy of origin. Thus the United States Minister at Paris was instructed, in September 1870, to recognize the new French Provisional Government provided it 'has actual control and possession of power, and is acknowledged by French people so as to be, in point of fact, *de facto* government'.[6] It will be noted that the *de facto* character of the government is conceived here as resulting from and as dependent upon the consent of the people. This was also the case in connection with the recognition of the French revolutionary Government in 1848: 'In its

1 See pp. 133–6.
2 Moore, vol. I, p. 137.
3 Mallory, *Life and Speeches of Henry Clay*, vol. I, p. 391.
4 *U.S. For. Rel.* 1878, p. 1115.
5 See, for example, Baty, *The Canons of International Law* (1930), pp. 214–16.
6 Moore, vol. I, p. 127.

intercourse with foreign nations the Government of the United States has, from its origin, always recognized *de facto* governments. We recognize the right of all nations to create and re-form their political institutions according to their own will and pleasure. We do not go behind the existing Government to involve ourselves in the question of legitimacy.'[1] The consent of the people, and not the circumstance that the government is actually in power, confers upon it the character of a *de facto* government. In explaining the reasons of the refusal to recognize the Rivas Government of Nicaragua in 1855, the Secretary of State did not deny that that Government was actually in power; yet he declined to admit that it was a *de facto* government. He said: 'The knowledge we have of their proceedings does not authorize the President to recognize it as the *de facto* government of Nicaragua.... It appears to be no more than a violent usurpation of power, brought about by an irregular self-organized military force, as yet unsanctioned by the will or acquiescence of the people of Nicaragua.'[2] A year later President Pierce, in a message to Congress, said: 'It is the established policy of the United States to recognize all governments without question of their source, or organization, or of the means by which the governing persons attain their power, provided there be a government *de facto* accepted by the people of the country.'[3]

These instances—and many others could be adduced—show that when it is affirmed that for the United States a government *de facto* is also a government *de jure*, this does not mean that a government *de facto* is one with regard to which the question of the consent of the people is irrelevant. On the contrary, that latter requirement is the predominant and constant feature of the practice of the United States. It was natural that the rejection of the dogma of legitimacy should have become the decisive consideration in the conduct of a State which itself arose out of a revolution and which championed the cause of revolution in other American countries struggling for independence. But it soon became apparent that rigid adherence to the unadulterated principle of effectiveness—conceived as undisputed paramountcy of physical power—might have the result of substituting the tyranny of ruthless and adventurous dictatorships for that of monarchic legitimacy. Instead, the United States adopted and adhered, on the whole with impressive uniformity, to what may be called the principle of subsequent legitimation by the people. The new government, in addition to being stable and effective, must exercise its authority with the properly expressed consent of the people. As Jefferson said in 1792: 'It accords with

1 Mr Buchanan to Mr Rush, Moore, vol. I, p. 124.

2 Ibid. p. 140.

3 Ibid. p. 142.

our principles to acknowledge any government to be rightful which is formed by the will of the nation, substantially declared.'[1] This insistence on the substantial nature of the declaration of popular approval remained the guiding principle of the practice of the United States for the next hundred and thirty years. It was a formula permitting of some elasticity. Occasionally, though not frequently, it was reduced to the barest minimum by being interpreted as compatible with mere passive submission to the successful government.[2] At times it was interpreted rigidly in the sense of a requirement of regular elections in accordance with the provisions of the national constitution. This was so particularly during and after the civil war, when the United States, for obvious reasons, attached increased

1 *Works* (4th ed.), vol. III, p. 489.

2 See, for example, the following passage in the Note of 30 April 1833, of Mr Livingston, Secretary of State, to the British Minister: 'It has been the principle and the invariable practice of the United States to recognize that as the legal Government of another nation which by its establishment in the actual exercise of political power might be supposed to have received the express or implied consent of the people' (Moore, vol. I, p. 129). In 1870 Secretary of State Fish said: 'We have always accepted the general acquiescence of the people in a political change of government as conclusive evidence of the will of the nation' (*U.S. For. Rel.* 1871, p. 792). See also Mr Hill's instruction, in 1900, referring to the regime 'administering government with the assent of the people thereof and without substantial resistance to its authority': Moore, vol. I, p. 139; or Mr Evart's statement in 1880 on the election of General Blanco by the Venezuelan Congress to be as sufficient evidence of the assent of the people of Venezuela 'as can be reasonably expected in countries so subject to sudden and violent political change as are those of Spanish America': ibid. p. 152. And see Prèsident Pierce's reference, in 1856, to the 'positive action or ascertained acquiescence' of the people of Nicaragua: ibid. p. 142. This passage is the more instructive as, six weeks prior to the Presidential Message, the United States representative was expressly instructed not to recognize the new regime on the ground that it owed its existence to 'a band of foreign adventurers' who had invaded the country and, after gaining recruits from the resident inhabitants, 'has by violence overturned the previously existing government and now pretends to be in possession of the sovereign authority', a regime '...as yet unsanctioned by the will or acquiescence of the people of Nicaragua' (ibid. p. 140; Manning, *Diplomatic Correspondence of the United States, Inter-American Affairs, 1831–1860, Central America*, 1851–1860, vol. IV, p. 74). The principle of constitutional approval was applied in that period with some laxity for, as stated in a Presidential Message in 1856, within a few months the United States recognized five successive Mexican Governments (Moore, supra). In 1857 Mr Dana, United States Minister Resident in Bolivia, writing to the Foreign Minister of that country, referred to the 'fixed principles, uninfluenced by circumstances', which guided the United States in the matter of recognition of governments: 'During the whole period of its existence, the Government of the United States has acted, uniformly and invariably, upon the principle of recognising in every country with which it had diplomatic relations whatever Government might exist, without questioning its character, or origin, and without waiting any length of time for evidence of its permanency—the only question, which its decision ever involved was the question of its being, *at the time*, the Government *de facto*' (Manning, op. cit. *Bolivia, Brazil*, vol. II, p. 53). This was hardly an accurate account of the practice of the United States.

importance to notions of legality and constitutionality. Thus in 1868 we find Secretary Seward laying down that 'revolutions in Republican States ought not to be accepted until the people have adopted them by organic law; with the solemnities which would seem sufficient to guarantee their stability and permanence'.[1] In general, this was the attitude of the United States in the matter of recognition of governments until the period following the First World War.[2]

During the administration of President Wilson[3]—apart from cases in which the bare fact of the replacement of an autocracy by an apparently democratic form of government prompted speedy recognition[4]—the test

1 *U.S. Diplomatic Correspondence*, 1866, vol. II, p. 630. And see generally, for a lucid account of Seward's policy of recognition, Goebel, *The Recognition Policy of the United States* (1915), pp. 198 et seq.

2 See, for example, with regard to the revolution in Brazil in 1899 where, notwithstanding the general welcome extended to the substitution of a republican for the monarchical form of government, recognition was made dependent upon the approval of the change by the majority of the people of Brazil: Moore, vol. I, p. 161; with regard to the restoration of constitutional government in Peru in 1881: *U.S. For. Rel.* 1883, p. 709; as to the postponement of the recognition of the Bolivian Government in 1899 until the Constitutional Assembly shall have been convened: ibid. 1899, p. 344; as to the requirement of the 'general consent of the people' in Ecuador in 1895: ibid. 1895, vol. I, p. 249; as to the 'approval of the Mexican people' with regard to the Diaz Government in 1877: ibid. 1877, vol. XII; on the recognition of the Colombian Government in 1867 in view of the 'universal acquiescence of the people': Moore, vol. I, p. 138; as to the postponement of the recognition of the Portuguese Government in 1917 until 'after elections shall have been held and the government established in accordance with the constitution': Hackworth, vol. I, p. 293; with regard to the 'obvious re-establishment of constitutional order' and 'conditions showing that the freely expressed wish of the Portuguese people accepts and gives national sanction to the proclaimed republic' as a condition of the recognition of the Portuguese Government in 1911: *U.S. For. Rel.* 1910, pp. 825–8, and 1911, pp. 689–92; as to Honduras in 1907: ibid. 1907, Part II, pp. 601–6; as to Haiti in 1914: ibid. 1914, pp. 359–67. And see above, p. 125, as to the meaning of a *de facto* government.

3 For an instructive survey of that policy and of its subsequent development see Hackworth, vol. I, pp. 180 et seq. See also Goebel, op. cit.; Cole, *The Recognition Policy of the United States since* 1901 (1928). And see Notter, *The Origins of the Foreign Policy of Woodrow Wilson* (1937), pp. 224–30, and McMahon, *Recent Changes in the Recognition Policy of the United States* (1933).

4 The United States granted prompt recognition, on 2 May 1913, to the new Chinese Republic without waiting for the concerted action proposed by the British, German and Japanese Governments (*U.S. For. Rel.* 1913, pp. 96–8, 100–3, 173–4). Previously, the Acting Secretary of State addressed an enquiry to the American Minister in China as to 'how far is the situation in China responsive to the conditions of recognition of governments under international law?' He answered that 'the Government was established by the political manœuvres of a few, not by general demand of the people'. 'But', he added, 'it is the only government in sight, and recognition would strengthen its hold on the country, particularly if given by concerted action of the powers.' Some governments regarded the United States' action as

of constitutionality was insisted upon with special vigour as a manifestation both of attachment to democratic principles and of the desire to promote stability and order within the American Republics. But although President Wilson pursued with characteristic consistency the policy of actively encouraging constitutional habits in Latin-American countries, the requirement of a proper expression of popular consent was based on a long line of precedent and went back to Jefferson's insistence on 'the will of the nation substantially declared'[1] as a condition of recognition.[2] The same principle was occasionally adopted with regard to non-American States, both before and after President Wilson's administration.[3] In the case of some American States, notably Cuba and Haiti, special treaties had created a relation approaching in many ways that of tutelage and of guarantee of the constitution. The result was that the requirement of the observance of constitutional procedure was to some extent indistinguishable from intervention permitted by treaty.

premature (*U.S. For. Rel.* 1913, pp. 110–13). Similarly, almost immediate recognition was granted, on 22 March 1917, to the Provisional Russian Government on the ground that it was clearly established by consent of the governed (ibid. 1917, pp. 1205–8, 1211). In his report to the Department of State the American Ambassador in Russia said: 'This revolution is the practical realization of that principle of government which we have championed and advocated, I mean government by consent of the governed' (Hackworth, vol. I, p. 298).

1 See above, p. 125.

2 In view of this it seems difficult to accept the interpretation which Mr Stimson, as Secretary of State, put in 1931 both on the novelty of the practice followed by President Wilson and on the meaning of the principle of recognition formulated by Jefferson. Mr Stimson, in explaining the acceptance of the *de facto* principle in 1930 (see below, p. 132), said: 'The present administration has refused to follow the policy of Mr Wilson and has followed consistently the former practice of this Government since the days of Jefferson' (*The United States and the Other American Republics*, Department of State, Latin-American Series, no. 4 (1931), p. 8). Jefferson's doctrine of recognition was clearly inconsistent with the mere *de facto* principle. The practice emphasized, though not inaugurated, by President Wilson was, unlike the policy initiated in 1931, fully in keeping with the Jeffersonian tradition. What was to some extent novel was President Wilson's determination to use recognition as a means of encouraging constitutional development and democratic habits. This was an object which, while not unworthy in itself, was not germane to the true purpose of recognition—namely, a declaration of the existence of the requisite conditions of governmental capacity—though it was incidental to the legitimate application of the test of popular approval in accordance with the constitution.

3 After the revolution in Portugal in 1911 the Secretary of State wrote to the American Chargé d'Affaires in Portugal on 6 June 1911: 'So soon as the Constituent Assembly, which meets on the 19th instant, shall have expressed the voice of the people and settled upon the form of government to be adopted by Portugal, you are instructed to inform the minister for foreign affairs of its official recognition by the Government of the United States of America' (*U.S. For. Rel.* 1911, p. 690). And see above, p. 122.

Moreover, without becoming a party to the Central American Treaties—embodying the so-called Tobar doctrine—of 1907 and 1923, the United States acted for a time upon the principles enunciated in those treaties.[1] The Treaty of 20 December 1907 between the five Central American Republics not only provided that the parties 'shall not recognize any other Government which may come into power in any of the five Republics as a consequence of a *coup d'état*, or of a revolution against the recognized Government, so long as the freely elected representatives of the people thereof have not constitutionally reorganized the country'.[2] In the Treaty of 7 February 1923, the Central American Republics extended the obligation of non-recognition, apparently irrespective of any subsequent approval by the people, to any person who should be chosen in the free election as President, Vice-President or Chief of State (*a*) 'If he should be the leader or one of the leaders of the *coup d'état* or revolution, or through blood relationship or marriage, be an ascendant or descendant or brother of such leader or leaders'; (*b*) 'If he should have been a Secretary of State or should have held some high military command during the accomplishment of the *coup d'état*, the revolution, or while the election was being carried on, or if he should have held this office or command within the six months preceding the *coup d'état*, revolution, or the election.'[3] The United States, though not a party to that treaty, formally associated itself with its purpose and expressed its intention to act in accordance with its provisions. When, in 1925, a revolution headed by General Chamorro broke out in Nicaragua, the United States formally announced that, in pursuance of its proclaimed policy with regard to the recognition of revolutionary governments in Central America, it would refuse recognition to the Chamorro Government.[4] The same principle was applied to Costa Rica in 1917 when Tinoco, the leader of the revolution, was informed that 'even if he is elected he will not be given recognition by the United States',[5] and in 1924 to Honduras.[6] A similar practice was followed with regard to

1 For a defence of this policy against the reproach that it may result in perpetuating existing autocracies see the address of Mr Stimson before the Council on Foreign Relations of 6 February 1931 (*The United States and the Other American Republics*, Department of State, Latin-American Series, no. 4 (1931)).

2 Malloy, *Treaties of the United States*, vol. II (1910), p. 2397.

3 Hackworth, vol. I, p. 188. The Convention of 1923 was denounced, as from 1 January 1934, by Costa Rica and Salvador. See Woolsey in *A.J.* vol. XXVIII (1934), pp. 325–9. It remained in force as between the other three parties.

4 Hackworth, vol. I, pp. 190, 266.

5 Ibid. p. 234.

6 Ibid. p. 255. The Acting Secretary of State wrote to the Provisional Minister for Foreign Affairs of Honduras on 23 August 1907: 'Being advised of the competency of the provisional government to perform international obligations, and being satisfied with the steps taken to revive the constitutional regime in Honduras and to

States other than those bound by the Treaties of 1907 and 1923.[1] Even when in 1930 the United States, in recognizing the new Governments of Argentina, Peru and Bolivia on a purely *de facto* basis, abandoned the principle of constitutional approval,[2] it seemed to attach importance to the expression of intention on the part of each of the new governments 'to hold in due course elections to regularize its status'.[3]

§ 46. *The Abandonment of the Traditional Test of Recognition after the First World War.* The test of recognition based on effectiveness and evidenced by an expression of popular consent was abandoned temporarily, by both Great Britain and the United States, in the period following upon the First World War. That period witnessed the establishment, in Europe and elsewhere, of systems of government which did not provide for free expression, in the generally accepted sense, of national opinion. As a result, the view gained ground that, with regard to some countries, adherence to the traditional test of recognition was not practicable. In 1920 the Government of the United States still gave as one of the reasons for its refusal to recognize the Soviet Government the fact that it denied self-determination to the Russian people in violation of the principles of democracy.[4] But only two years later the United States Secretary of State abandoned that particular ground of non-recognition. He said: 'We recognize the right of revolution and we do not attempt to determine the internal concerns of other States.... But while a foreign regime may have securely established itself through the exercise of control and the submission of the people... there still remain other questions to be considered.'[5]

provide for the election of the executive thereof, the President has directed the recognition of the provisional government' (*U.S. For. Rel.* 1907 (II), p. 605). On 19 April 1920 we find the United States Secretary of State instructing the Minister in Guatemala to obtain information as to the constitutionality of the action of the Assembly declaring the candidate for the Presidency insane and, in case the new government is not organized in accordance with the Constitution, not to take, for the time being, any action regarding its recognition (ibid. 1920 (II), p. 708).

1 Thus we find on 24 August 1920 the Secretary of State writing to the Minister in Bolivia: 'The Department does not feel that it has yet had sufficient opportunity of determining whether the *de facto* Government represents the will of the people, and does not at present consider that satisfactory evidence on this point can be obtained until after the general elections to be held next December' (*U.S. For. Rel.* 1920 (I), p. 379). In December 1920 it was decided to extend recognition *de facto* as soon as the Congress had elected the provisional President (ibid. p. 385).

2 See below, p. 133.

3 *A.J.* vol. XXV (1931), p. 121.

4 *U.S. For. Rel.* 1920 (III), pp. 466–8.

5 Statement by Mr Hughes, Secretary of State, as quoted in Hackworth, vol. I, p. 177.

The Secretary of State continued to elaborate what was in fact a change in the attitude of his Government in a passage which merits quotation:

'...while this Government has laid stress upon the value of expressed popular approval in determining whether a new government should be recognized, it has never insisted that the will of the people of a foreign State may not be manifested by long-continued acquiescence in a regime actually functioning as a government. When there is a question of the will of the nation it has generally been regarded as a wise precaution to give sufficient time to enable a new regime to prove its stability and the apparent acquiescence of the people in the exercise of the authority it has assumed. The application of these familiar principles, in dealing with foreign States, is not in derogation of democratic ideals cherished by our people, and constitutes no justification of tyranny in any form, but proceeds upon a consideration of the importance of international intercourse and upon the established American principle of non-intervention in the internal concerns of other States.'[1]

Much of this argument was controversial. The right of revolution and adequately expressed popular approval of the results of the revolution are not irreconcilable. Neither did the insistence, as a condition of recognition, on such popular approval constitute, at least according to the well-established practice of the United States, intervention in the internal concerns of other States. Possibly the reference to 'long-continued acquiescence in a regime actually functioning as a government' was, at that juncture, premature. The recognition of the Soviet regime could have been based on the more cogent ground that the fact of the absence of a normal democratic expression of popular approval was the accompaniment, not necessarily enduring, of a social revolution of a fundamental nature, and that it was not comparable with the revolutionary situations in Latin-America and elsewhere in relation to which the requirement of popular approval had become a constant feature of the practice of the United States. There was accordingly no compelling necessity, in the case of Soviet Russia, to make any apparent departure from the previous practice of recognition the starting point for a more general abandonment—or, at least, radical relaxation—of the principle that an effective government is one which is based on the consent of the people. However, this was what in fact happened.

A decisive step towards abandoning the requirement of subsequent legitimation by constitutional methods was taken in 1930. Acting in conjunction with Great Britain,[2] Mr Stimson, the Secretary of State, announced the recognition of new Governments in Argentina, Peru and

1 Hackworth, vol. 1, p. 177. 2 See below, p. 135.

Bolivia on satisfactory evidence that these Governments 'are *de facto* in control of their respective countries and that there is no active resistance to their rule'.[1] He stated that in acting in this way the United States was following 'the regular rules of international law, and the regular policy which has characterized this country' ever since Jefferson announced it. He described as exceptional the special policy followed with regard to the Central American Republics.[2] Inasmuch as that statement referred to the regular policy of the United States in the matter of recognition, it probably erred on the side of over-simplification. It ignored the insistence, frequently exhibited in the preceding seventy years and not limited to the Central American Republics, on evidence of popular control. In fact, in the same statement Mr Stimson proceeded to qualify the unconditional character of the *de facto* principle by announcing that each of the three Governments had made clear 'its intention to fulfil its respective international obligations and to hold in due course elections to regularize its status'. But there was no doubt as to the significance of the change adopted. The decision to grant recognition in return for a *promise* to furnish evidence of popular consent constituted a departure from numerous precedents and signified a decision to adopt the principle of effectiveness pure and simple.

About the same time, the United States recognized the revolutionary Vargas Government in Brazil, in reliance, largely, on the assurance that a reform of the electoral system would be introduced to provide means for a free expression of the will of the people and for guaranteeing individual liberty.[3] These assurances never materialized. The case of Brazil showed also in a different way that there was taking place an imperceptible but significant change in the practice of the United States. Instead of enquiring whether the revolutionary Government had received confirmation by a freely expressed popular vote, the enquiries were directed to the question whether there was a likelihood of a successful counter-revolution and whether there was active resistance to the rule of the new authority.[4] When what was in fact a revolutionary Government was installed in Chile in 1924 importance was still attached, though in a somewhat attenuated form, to the consent of the people. There was no question of insisting on a general popular vote or that of a constituent assembly. What was required, in the words of the Secretary of State to the Ambassador in Chile, was evidence that the new Government 'is in a position to maintain stability and retain

1 *A.J.* vol. XXV (1930), p. 121; Hackworth, vol. I, p. 223.
2 See above, p. 129.
3 Hackworth, vol. I, p. 229.
4 Ibid.

its power through the acquiescence of the people'.[1] No recognition was in fact granted to the revolutionary government in question. In 1932, on a similar occasion, the question of acquiescence was not raised. The new Government was merely expected to show 'that it is in control of the country and that there is no active resistance to it'.[2] In 1925 recognition was still refused to the new revolutionary Government of Ecuador until 'it regularizes its position or until a legally constituted government is set up';[3] it was not until 1928 that that condition was deemed fulfilled and *de jure* recognition granted. In 1935 recognition was given to a revolutionary government of that country on the ground that 'apparently it is firmly established'.[4] In 1937, on a similar occasion, the questions which were asked in this connection were whether the new Ecuadorian Government 'has the substantial support of public opinion in Ecuador, whether it is able to discharge the normal functions of Government, whether it is capable of maintaining public order...'.[5]

A similar development, in an even more marked manner, took place in Great Britain. After the First World War, at a time when she was still acting in accordance with the test of subsequent legitimation by constitutional methods,[6] that country began to adopt a practice based on the pure *de facto* principle. As in the case of the United States, the impetus for that change was supplied largely by the advent, in various parts of Europe, of authoritarian regimes having their origin in revolution. Thus in 1921 Great Britain recognized *de facto* the Soviet Government of Russia. The reason given was that that Government 'have as complete control over that vast territory as any Government could possibly have under present conditions, and therefore they have to be recognized as the *de facto* Government of that Empire'.[7] In 1924 recognition *de jure* was accorded to the Soviet Government. It has been suggested above that the circum-

1 Ibid. p. 230. It is significant that while the Secretary of State reiterated that 'the attitude of the Government of the United States so far as the recognition of the new regime is concerned must be guided not simply by the sincerity and objectives of those in control but also by those general principles which must govern our policy in extending recognition to any administration which may come into power in another nation by extra-constitutional means', he explained the temporary withholding of recognition on the ground that the new regime was not yet sufficiently established to warrant formal relations. There was no reference to the assent of the people (*U.S. For. Rel.* 1924 (I), p. 360).

2 Hackworth, vol. I, p. 231.

3 Ibid. p. 244.

4 Ibid. p. 246.

5 Ibid.

6 See above, p. 123, as to Albania.

7 Statement by the Prime Minister, *H.C. Debates*, vol. CXXXIX, col. 2506.

stances which prompted that step were such that no considerations of consistency or uniformity necessarily called for a generalization of that departure from accepted practice.[1] But that is what actually took place. In 1924, in connection with the revolution in Chile, a significant change was accomplished in relation to some Latin-American countries with regard to which the requirement of subsequent legitimation by popular approval had hitherto been part of the established practice. As the event marked an important departure it may be useful to give an account of the facts accompanying the change.

After the President of Chile left the country on 10 September 1924, nominally on six months' leave of absence—he left under pressure from the military junta—the Cabinet dissolved the Congress. In consequence, the civilian members of the Cabinet resigned, and the government remained in the hands of a military and naval junta of three. It promised elections in due course and accepted the resignation of the President. The Foreign Minister informed the diplomatic corps of these measures and expressed the wish of the junta that diplomatic relations should be maintained. At a meeting of the diplomatic corps, on 14 September, it was decided by a large majority that relations should be confined to semi-official treatment of urgent questions pending the receipt of instructions. The question before the British Government was whether the change, although a bloodless one, did not in fact constitute a revolution calling for the application of the principle hitherto followed of confining intercourse to semi-official exchanges pending confirmation of the regime by a popular vote. On the part of the Chilean representative in London it appears to have been urged that the Government was not strictly speaking revolutionary or militarist, and that its purpose was to save the country, in response to the appeal made to the army by both the conservative and the radical parties, from the rule of a corrupt government which came to power as the result of an election made on the basis of false registers. On 22 September the Chilean Minister was informed that in the view of the British Government the change of government in Chile in no way affected the diplomatic relations between the two countries.[2]

1 See above, p. 131.

2 At the outset, the French Government had decided to maintain with the new Government semi-official relations only; similarly the United States Government took the decision, on 18 September, not to recognize the new Government and to maintain with it merely 'unofficial relations of a frank and friendly character'. Germany and Spain, while deciding to continue diplomatic relations with the new Government, stated that they did not regard that as recognition. From a report sent by the British Minister at Santiago it appeared that the Junta Government, 'while so far orderly and generally supported throughout the Republic, is unconstitutional in its

The meaning of the important decision taken on 22 September to the effect that the diplomatic relations were unaffected was not free of doubt. In particular, it was not clear whether it amounted to *de jure* recognition. However, as at the same time the new British Minister was due to arrive in Santiago, it was thought that it might be necessary for him to present his credentials in the usual way, and that it was to be left to the Chilean Government to decide whether the wording of the communication of 22 September was to be treated as recognition *de jure* or whether it would be preferable to wait until the Constituent Assembly met and then to endeavour to obtain recognition in some definite form.[1]

Although this was not quite clearly perceived at the time, there is no doubt that a drastic departure from previous practice had taken place. It was followed on the next occasion of recognition in similar circumstances. When in July 1925 a military junta was established in Ecuador, the Chilean precedent—including the formula of recognition—was adopted without much hesitation. This was also done when at the beginning of September 1930 a revolution broke out in Peru. On 18 September the new Government was informed that the change which had taken place did not affect the cordial relations between the two countries. On the same day similar recognition was extended to the new revolutionary Government of Argentina. The phrase that the revolutionary change 'did not affect the relations between the two countries' was becoming the accepted formula

very nature, and that an entirely new order of things is contemplated as announced in the proclamation of the Junta Militar'. F.O. Chile (1924). The incident of the Chilean revolution in 1924 provides an instructive instance of the elasticity of the border-line between constitutional and revolutionary change. In his first report on what was in fact a revolutionary change of government the United States Ambassador in Chile said: '...Everything has been done according to constitutional forms. The exertion of pressure has been by intimation rather than by direct threats. No act of violence has yet occurred, but if compliance had not been given force would undoubtedly have been used' (*U.S. For. Rel.* 1924 (I), p. 358). As the Ambassador had reported to the effect that constitutional forms had been observed, he was originally instructed that the Government of the United States did not desire to raise the question of recognition. However, next day (13 September), in view of the report, received by the State Department from another quarter, that the President of Chile had stated that he had been banished and that there was no constitutional government in Chile, the Ambassador was instructed to avoid any formal relations with the new regime until the situation had cleared up. It did not clear up till March 1925, when the President returned from his enforced leave of absence and when the Ambassador was instructed to resume formal relations without making any special communication.

1 The ensuing months did not substantiate the hopes of the stability of the regime, and shortly after his arrival the new Minister was once more troubled by the question of the constitutionality of the regime. He was instructed to avoid, if possible, the question of recognition—although it had been previously assumed by many that full recognition had been granted.

with regard to recognition of revolutionary governments.[1] There was no reference to the consent of the people when in 1939, at the close of the Spanish Civil War, Great Britain recognized *de jure* the Nationalist Government of General Franco.[2]

§ 47. *The Value of the Principle of Subsequent Legitimation through Popular Consent as a Test of Recognition.* There is no sufficient reason for assuming that the relaxation by Great Britain and the United States, in the period between the two World Wars, of their traditional attitude in the matter of recognition was more than a measure of adaptation to what, in retrospect, must be regarded as a retrogressive phase in the general political development of modern States. It would not be accurate to regard that attitude as expressive of a judgment with any claim to finality on the merits of the requirement, as a condition of recognition of governments, of the subsequent legitimation of the revolutionary government by a satisfactory expression of the consent of the governed. Undoubtedly, apart from the advent of dictatorial forms of government on a large scale, that particular test, unaccompanied as it is by adequate international safeguards, is open to criticism. For the 'will of the nation substantially declared' has proved to be a notion of considerable elasticity. Instead of the effectiveness of the governmental power being deduced from the assent of the people, that consent has often been implied from the fact of unchallenged exercise of authority. There is a wide range of possible ambiguity in the statement that governments must be recognized which '*might be supposed* to have

1 On 3 November 1930, the Secretary of State for Foreign Affairs, after giving an account of the revolutionary changes in Bolivia (in June), in Peru (in August) and in Argentina (in September), said: 'In all three countries the Provisional Governments are exercising effective control, and have declared that they will abide by their international obligations. These Governments have been informed that His Majesty's Government consider that the change of government in the countries concerned in no way affects the relations between them and His Majesty's Government' (*H.C. Debates*, vol. CCXLIV, col. 458). An almost identical statement was made on 10 November with regard to Brazil (ibid. col. 1304). This was in reply to the assurance previously received from the Brazilian Government that 'they recognize and respect all national engagements contracted abroad, existing treaties with foreign Powers, all public debt contracts in force, and other obligations legally enacted' (ibid.).

2 Recognition of that Government by the United States took the form of a communication announcing willingness to establish diplomatic relations. The Spanish Government, not satisfied with that unequivocal method of implied recognition, asked for an express assurance that that communication 'signifies full recognition on the part of your Republic of the National Government as the sole and legitimate one of Spain'. The United States confirmed that its step signified '*de jure* recognition of Your Excellency's Government as the National Government of Spain' (Hackworth, vol. I, p. 297).

received the express or *implied* assent of the people'.[1] The same realization of the inadequacy of a rigidly conceived test of popular approval underlay the reference to the 'general'[2] consent of the people as a condition of recognition.

What are the difficulties which have impeded the full and consistent application of the test of effectiveness as expressed in the requirement of subsequent legitimation? It would appear—though this is not necessarily a decisive consideration—that the insistence on subsequent legitimation goes beyond the mere affirmation of the requirement of effectiveness which it proposes to implement. A tyrannical and despotic regime may be—and usually is—effective so long as it lasts. The obedience which it enjoys may be imposed, passive, and resentful. But there is no sufficient warrant for maintaining that an authority based on that kind of obedience is necessarily short-lived and therefore not 'effective' from the point of view of permanence and stability.[3] Moreover, there is substance in the suggestion that a government wielding absolute powers may be based on the acquiescence of the majority of the population, although the constitution of the State and its political system do not allow of an unhampered and truly free expression of the approval of the nation. Also, when it is said that the consent of the population must be given in accordance with the provisions of the constitution, do we mean the constitution of the old or of the new regime? It is not practicable to insist on an expression of popular approval in forms provided for by the constitution which has been overthrown. A revolutionary dictatorship will not be easily persuaded to allow the will of the people to be ascertained in a way prescribed by the constitution which it has supplanted. If, on the other hand, we mean the constitution enacted by the new regime, what guarantee is there that its provisions render possible a truly free popular verdict?

The main defect of the principle of subsequent legitimation by popular vote, when not accompanied by appropriate safeguards, is the assumption of the likelihood of a free expression of popular opinion in circumstances in which the use of force has supplanted the normal constitutional avenues of political development and in which the ordinary channels of information and discussion are absent. For this reason the requirement of subsequent

1 See above, p. 126, n. 2.

2 Mr Secretary Olney to the United States Minister in Ecuador (*U.S. For. Rel.* 1895 (1), pp. 248–9).

3 Actually, writers of authority have interpreted insistence on popular approval as being one of the aspects of the test of effectiveness seeing that governments notoriously opposed to democratic rule are likely to be short-lived—an assumption which events have not invariably tended to substantiate. See, for example, Hyde, vol. 1, p. 67.

popular confirmation has often tended to become a matter of mere form. In the language used by the Department of State of the United States in connection with changes of government in Mexico, the United States were 'accustomed to accept and recognize the results of a popular vote in Mexico and not to scrutinize closely the regularity or irregularity of the methods' by which the results were brought about.[1] The spectacle of overwhelming majorities confirming a revolutionary *coup* is not a novel one. The *coup* of Louis Napoleon of 2 December 1851 was confirmed by a vote of 7,439,216 to 640,737. Successive votes in Germany after the advent of the National-Socialist regime in 1933 showed an even more baffling approximation to unanimity. In circumstances such as these only a vote accompanied by effective, i.e. internationally supervised, guarantees of electoral freedom both before and during the voting could afford some assurance of reflecting the considered wishes of the majority of the people and thus afford a satisfactory test of popular approval.[2] There is no reason why, once collective recognition based on the principle of consent of the governed has become a rule of international law, the international organization of States should not develop organs and procedures for achieving that object. The practice of internationally supervised plebiscites provides some useful lessons in this respect.[3] Pending that consummation, the test of subsequent legitimation will often remain deficient in its operation.

1 Moore, vol. I, p. 148.

2 For an interesting expression of scepticism about the value of the popular vote in such circumstances see Lord Russell's despatch, of 21 January 1861, to Sir John Hudson in Turin concerning the vote following upon the annexation of Naples, Sicily, Umbria and the Marches: 'In fact the votes by universal suffrage which have taken place in those Kingdoms and Provinces appear to H.M.'s Government to have little validity. These votes are nothing more than a formality following upon acts of popular insurrection, or successful invasion, or upon Treaties, and do not in themselves imply any independent exercise of the will of the nation in whose name they are given' (*Parl. Papers*, 1861, vol. LXVII, *Further Correspondence relating to the affairs of Italy*). The recommendations, in the matter of recognition of governments, of the Conference of international lawyers held in London in July 1943 apparently revert to the test of subsequent legitimation: '3. *De jure* recognition should be granted to new governments whose authority is not only effective, independent, and apparently stable, but has been acquired with the general acquiescence of the people or has been confirmed by them in the appropriate way, which *in countries of modern civilization* implies *in normal circumstances* a free election or vote by the people or their representatives' (*A.J.* vol. XXXVIII (1944), p. 294). The italicized passages reveal some of the difficulties of the test adopted.

3 In April 1945, Great Britain, the United States and France agreed at the request of the Greek Government and the party in opposition to supervise, through observers, the elections to be held in that country. The Government of Soviet Russia declined to participate in the supervision on the ground that they 'were opposed in principle to the supervision of national elections by foreign States' (Foreign Office announcement of 20 April 1945; *The Times* newspaper, 21 April 1945). See below, pp. 173–4, n. 2.

There is, in this connection, a further difficulty for the solution of which some international procedure may be equally indicated. Experience shows that in so far as a change of regime effected in an apparently revolutionary fashion is regarded as raising the issue of recognition, there often arises the question whether the change was in fact of a revolutionary nature. A revolutionary change in the legal and social system may be ingeniously concealed behind apparent adherence to constitutional forms. A revolution may be effected as the result of a successful show of force without actual recourse to violence. A revolution involving fundamental changes in the law and the constitution may be brought about by the government in power while adhering to the letter of the constitution.[1] This being so, to confine the requirement of express popular approval to cases of a violent substitution of one government for another may often amount to the adoption of a test which is somewhat unreal.

These, then, are the factors which, apart from the circumstances of the period between the two World Wars, have interfered with the successful and consistent application of the principle that effectiveness must be proved by free popular approval of the authority which has come to power by way of revolution. These factors are not inherent in that principle. They can be removed by means of appropriate machinery. They do not warrant a condemnation of the principle of subsequent legitimation as intrinsically unsound. That principle has behind it a substantial body of practice. It is the most persistent and conspicuous feature of the British and American practice of recognition. There is no compelling reason to assume that its abandonment after the First World War was more than a temporary adaptation to a transient period of political retrogression. Its re-emergence, when accompanied by appropriate international safeguards, must be regarded as a rational development deeply rooted in history.

Finally, it must be borne in mind that, although the requirement of the subsequent confirmation of the revolutionary regime is, in some respects,

1 The revolutions in Italy in 1922 and Germany in 1933 took place, in form, without a break in the legal continuity of the constitution. As to the former see Raestad in *R.I.* 3rd ser. vol. XIX (1938), p. 609. In Germany, the National-Socialist revolution was realized without a formal break in the legal continuity of the Weimar Constitution of 1919, which was never expressly abolished. The Enabling Act of 24 March 1933, which superseded the legislative powers of the Reichstag, was passed by a majority of two-thirds as required by Article 76 of the Weimar Constitution. For an example of the elasticity of the border-line between a constitutional change and a revolution see above p. 134, n. 2, with regard to the revolution in Chile in 1924. For a discussion of this question in connection with the revolutions in France in 1830 and 1848 see Gemma in *Hague Recueil*, vol. IV (1924) (iii), p. 318. See also Loewenstein, *Political Reconstruction* (1946), pp. 220 et seq.

reminiscent of the test of legitimacy, it is essentially a negation of that test inasmuch as it rejects the view that the revolutionary character of the change renders the new regime irrevocably invalid. Similarly, whatever its merits, the test of subsequent legitimation must be regarded as an affirmation of the legal view of recognition, i.e. of the view that there is a duty of recognition, as distinguished from the purely optional right to recognize, as soon as there is present the primary condition of effectiveness of governmental power. For the test of subsequent legitimation of the revolution by an expression of popular consent is not a denial of the test of effectiveness. It is a combination of the test of effectiveness with the requirement of specifically conceived evidence of the effectiveness of the revolutionary regime.

Chapter X

THE LEGAL EFFECTS OF NON-RECOGNITION OF GOVERNMENTS

§ 48. *The Principle of Effectiveness and the Duty of Recognition.* It has been shown in the preceding chapter that while willingness to fulfil international obligations, legitimacy of origin, and the method of the revolution have occasionally been adopted as tests of recognition, they have not constituted the predominant feature of the practice of recognition of governments. Effectiveness of power, accompanied by a sufficient degree of stability and a reasonable prospect of permanence—this is the most frequently followed standard of recognition. That standard has been adopted either without qualifications or, more frequently, subject to the requirement of the consent of the population as evidence of the effectiveness of governmental authority. Amidst the diversity of tests thus applied there has been no denial of the principle that, as in the case of recognition of States or of belligerency, recognition of governments is, given the required conditions of fact, a matter of legal duty. Once the new authority has definitely established itself after utterly defeating the former government beyond any reasonable prospect of re-establishment, and once, according to a widely adopted qualification of the test of effectiveness, the revolutionary change has been approved by a substantial expression of national will, the course of other States is clear. They must follow the fact—subject to their right and duty to exercise the legal discretion called for by the nature of events.[1] They are bound to accord recognition in fulfilment of the duty not to withhold the benefits of international personality from a State represented by a government whose rule is accepted by the population. For in so far as the test of effectiveness has become part of international

1 The exercise of such discretion may not always be an easy matter. For effectiveness and stability are relative questions. When during the Mexican revolution in 1858 the United States Minister urged the recognition of the constitutionalist government which had been driven out from the capital, he admitted that although sixteen out of twenty-one provinces were in favour of that government, the general authority which it exercised was weak and that he took a grave responsibility 'in pronouncing it such an authority as promises stability'. But he counselled its recognition on the ground that 'it offers a far better prospect of stability than that which is established in the City of Mexico' (Mr McLane, United States Minister to Mexico, to the United States Secretary of State, 7 April 1859: Manning, *Diplomatic Correspondence of the United States, Inter-American Affairs, 1831–1860, Mexico*, vol. IX (1937), p. 1041). The advice was acted upon. For the protest of the Miramón Government see ibid. p. 1047.

law, it is expressive of a right of the effective government to claim recognition. This is so not only because that test is supported by the bulk of international practice in the last hundred and fifty years; it is so also because the right to recognition follows from the overriding principles of independence of States and of prohibition of intervention. But for the departure from that principle and the introduction of extraneous tests, the question of recognition of governments would never have gained the prominence which it has in fact acquired.

The subjection of the function of recognition of governments to a legal rule is, as has been pointed out above, a necessary consequence of the principle of State independence. To deny recognition to a government possessing the necessary qualifications is not only to question the independence of the State concerned; it is to deprive that State, to a substantial extent, of its status as a subject of international law.[1] This result manifests itself mainly with regard to the position of the unrecognized government before foreign tribunals—a matter which is discussed more fully in this chapter.[2] But the consequences of non-recognition show themselves in many other ways; they are, for most practical purposes, identical with the refusal to recognize the State as such. Existing treaties, it is true, remain in force. However, as their operation presupposes normal intercourse between the States in question, they remain in most instances inoperative;[3]

1 Respect for the independence of States has been frequently referred to as a relevant factor in granting recognition. In 1862 Earl Russell wrote to the British representative at Athens in the following terms with regard to the change of dynasty in Greece: 'The Kingdom of Greece having by the transactions of 1832 been acknowledged as an independent State, the people of Greece are entitled to exercise the rights of national independence; and of the rights which belong to an independent nation, and the exercise of which the history of Europe affords many examples is that of changing its governing dynasty upon good and sufficient cause' (*State Papers*, vol. LXXIII (1863), *Correspondence relating to the Revolution in Greece*, p. 617, no. 20, p. 20). In reply to the communication by Marquis d'Azeglio informing him that Victor Emmanuel II assumed the title of 'King of Italy', Lord Russell stated that 'Her Majesty, acting on the principle of respecting the independence of the nations of Europe' would receive him 'as the Envoy of Victor Emmanuel II, King of Italy' (30 March 1860: *State Papers*, vol. LXVII (1861), *Correspondence relating to the assumption by King Victor Emmanuel of the title of the King of Italy*, p. 353, Cmd. 2799, no. 2, p. 2).

2 See below, pp. 145–53.

3 See McNair, *The Law of Treaties* (1938), pp. 383–6, who gives detailed information on the subject of treaties between Great Britain and Soviet Russia prior and subsequent to recognition *de jure*. In a Note addressed on 1 February 1924 to the Russian Government it was stated that 'recognition of the Soviet Government of Russia will, according to accepted principles of international law, automatically bring into force all the treaties concluded between the two countries previous to the Russian Revolution, except where these have been denounced or have otherwise juridically lapsed' (ibid. p. 384). See also above, p. 111, and below, p. 143. The Committee of Jurists appointed by the Council of the League of Nations in connection with the question of the Aaland Islands held that although, because of the non-recognition of the Soviet

on occasions they have been expressly denounced by the State refusing recognition.[1] As treaties regulate most of the current relations of States, the refusal to recognize a government amounts to a considerable extent to exclusion from the benefits of international intercourse. The unrecognized government is, before foreign courts, denied access to and the right to dispose of State property situated abroad.[2] Its agents, if it attempts to send

Government by the signatories of the Treaty of 1856, Russia could not for the time being participate in any agreement relating to that Treaty, this fact could 'hardly prevent the other States interested from undertaking the settlement of a question which also affects them and which requires as speedy a settlement as possible'. The Commission added that 'Russia, as soon as it possesses a recognized Government, will be free to give its adherence to the agreement' (*Official Journal*, Special Supplement, no. 3, 1920, p. 14). In connection with the binding force of the obligations imposed upon the signatories, including Russia, by the Treaty of Paris of 1856, the same Committee of Jurists stated in its report that notwithstanding the non-recognition of the Soviet Government by the other contracting parties Russia remained one of the contracting parties to the agreement of 1856 and that the non-recognition of the Soviet Government 'in any case can only amount to a mere interruption of the exercise of Russia's legal capacity' (ibid. p. 18).

1 Thus, for instance, the French Government in 1921 denounced the Consular Convention with Russia of 1874. As, owing to the refusal to recognize the Soviet Government, the denunciation could not be addressed to the latter, a declaration to that effect was published in the *Journal Officiel*, 19 May 1921, p. 5890, col. 1. See the decision of the Paris Court of Appeal of 2 February 1921, in *Aidov* v. *Bode* (Clunet, vol. XLVIII (1921), p. 228), to the effect that although the refusal to recognize the Russian Government did not result in the cancellation of the treaties with Russia, they could be denounced. And see below, p. 150. On the other hand, some conventions, especially those the application of which favoured the cause of Russian refugees, continued to be applied notwithstanding the absence of reciprocity. See Lagarde, op. cit. pp. 117–22.

2 The legal position thus created may on occasions produce curious consequences. Thus in 1938 the Supreme Court of the United States held that as the Soviet Government was not recognized by the United States from 1917 to 1933, and as the State of Russia was validly represented during that period by the diplomatic representatives of the former Russian Government (which continued to be recognized by the United States) who failed to prosecute a certain claim, the Government of Soviet Russia was barred by a United States statute of limitations from proceeding with the action (*Guaranty Trust Co. of New York* v. *United States*, (1938) 304 U.S. 126: *Annual Digest*, 1938–40, Case no. 69; and see comment by Jessup in *A.J.* vol. XXXII (1938), pp. 542–5). See also *Spanish Government* v. *Campuzano*, decided in November 1938 by the Supreme Court of Norway, to the effect that because of the continued recognition by Norway of the Spanish Republican Government the latter was entitled to the sole possession of property belonging to the Spanish State in Norway (*Annual Digest*, 1938–40, Case no. 27). In 1921 in connection with the question of the Russian refugees the British Government considered the question whether it could use for that purpose part of the sum of £5,000,000 lying at a London bank and belonging to the former Imperial Russian Government. Acting on legal advice, the Government decided that the money could not be touched seeing that it would ultimately become the property of the legal successor of the Imperial Government. It was decided to hold the money in a Suspense Account pending the formation of a government recognized by Great Britain (*Russian Refugees*, British Memorandum, League of Nations, *Official Journal*, 1921, p. 1014).

any, are treated like ordinary individuals.[1] The unrecognized government does not enjoy that measure of protection in case of civil war which international law grants to recognized governments.[2] At least, according to the British practice, it is denied the right to ordinary jurisdictional immunities; in practically all countries it is denied the right of access to courts. Legal effect is refused to the acts of its legislative and other authorities. It is prevented from obtaining loans and other economic facilities.[3] Its right to declare war and to conclude peace has been questioned.[4] On occasions these legal consequences of non-recognition have been amplified by announcements issued by the executive department to the effect that no diplomatic protection would be granted to nationals in respect of their

1 On 19 March 1920, a Mr Martens presented to the Secretary of State a certificate of his appointment as the representative in the United States of the Russian Socialist Federated Soviet Republics. The letter remained unacknowledged. On 29 March he was served with a warrant demanding his appearance before the immigration authorities in connection with impending deportation proceedings against him. On 16 December 1920, an order was signed for his deportation and he left the United States on 22 January 1921. See *U.S. For. Rel.* 1920 (III), pp. 455 et seq. For a memorandum of the Department of State on the status of representatives of unrecognized governments or of representatives who have not been duly accredited see ibid. pp. 457–61. See also ibid. pp. 478, 479. And see Moore, vol. IV, p. 557; *Hollander* v. *Baiz*, 135 U.S. 403, 432; *Rose* v. *Himely*, (1808) 4 Cranch 239. On occasions immunity has been granted in such cases as a matter of courtesy and without prejudice as to the future course of action.

2 See above, p. 93 and below, p. 229.

3 See *U.S. For. Rel.* 1922 (II), p. 456, with regard to the proposed flotation of a loan to the Government of Greece which at that time was not recognized by the United States. The firm in question was informed that the Department of State could not look with favour upon such a loan. A loan of 14,000,000 dollars was stated to be available to Finland in May 1919 for food purchases in the United States of America provided that the United States granted provisional recognition (as a State) (*U.S. For. Rel.* 1919 (II), p. 211). The following extract will illustrate the practical importance of recognition in this and other matters: 'They [the Constitutionalist Government of Mexico] are daily gaining in popularity throughout the Republic. All they have required for the last six months, in order to secure their certain success and the complete triumph of liberal and constitutional principles, has been the recognition of their Government by the United States. By such recognition they would be enabled to raise money, concentrate their forces and take possession of the capital' (Mr Churchwell, Special Agent of the United States to Mexico, to Mr Cass, Secretary of State, 8 March 1858: Manning, *Diplomatic Correspondence of the United States, Inter-American Affairs, 1831–1860, Mexico*, vol. IX (1937), p. 1035). We find on 23 June 1921 the United States Minister in Poland informing the Secretary of State that the Minister of Mexico in Austria approached the Government of Poland with an offer of colonization privileges and concessions if it would recognize the Government of Mexico (*U.S. For. Rel.* 1921 (II), p. 434).

4 See above, p. 5. Apparently one of the consequences of recognition is to legalize the display of the flag of the recognized government. See the decision of the French Court of Cassation in *Public Prosecutor* v. *Liefquin* (*Annual Digest*, 1933–4, Case no. 31).

dealings with the unrecognized authority.[1] Those who deny the legal duty of recognition and who assert that recognition is a purely political function find themselves compelled to identify it with a declaration of willingness to maintain normal diplomatic relations.[2] But that is a view which is conspicuously at variance with the practice of governments and courts. The practice of the latter may best be considered in connection with the position of unrecognized governments.

§ 49. *Unrecognized Governments before Judicial Tribunals. (a) Anglo-American Practice.* The grant or the refusal of recognition as a government is shown both by international practice and by considerations of legal principle to be a matter affirmatively regulated by international law. In view of this, the well-established attitude of courts in the matter of unrecognized governments, far from justifying criticism, reveals itself as sound and, as will be shown, inevitable. That attitude has been that, subject to certain exceptions, no juridical existence can be attributed to an unrecognized government and that no legal consequences of its purported factual existence can be admitted. The practice of English courts in the matter has been uniform to the point of rigidity. They have declined to grant relief invoked with regard to a contract made with an unrecognized government.[3] They have denied to the unrecognized

1 Such warnings were issued by the Government of the United States in 1917 in connection with the revolution in Costa Rica (see Hackworth, vol. 1, p. 234) and in 1920 with regard to Soviet Russia. In the latter case the Department of State said: 'The assistance which the United States can normally extend to its citizens who engage in trade or travel in some foreign country whose government is recognized by the United States cannot be looked for in the present case since there is no official or representative Russian authority with which this Government can maintain those relations usually subsisting between nations' (Instructions to the Ambassador in France, as quoted in Hackworth, vol. 1, p. 300). Conversely, a further effect of non-recognition of the new Government is to give to nationals an assurance, enforced by courts, that they may safely deal with the representatives of the last recognized government (*Guaranty Trust Company of New York* v. *United States*, (1938) 304 U.S. 126; *Annual Digest*, 1938–40, Case no. 69). This is also the gist of the decision in *The Republic of Peru* v. *Dreyfus Bros. and Co.* (1888) L.R. 38 Ch.D. 348, where it was held that one of the results of the recognition by Great Britain of the revolutionary Pierola Government in Mexico was that an English court would give effect to a contract made with that Government.

2 See, for example, Kunz, p. 163. This is also the view of Gemma, cited above at p. 139. However, the latter expresses, in the same work at p. 163, an altogether contrary opinion in maintaining, rightly it is believed, that 'le gouvernement, pour les Etats qui ne l'ont point reconnu, est sans existence juridique...par la reconnaissance une profonde transformation se produit: c'est-à-dire que le gouvernement reconnu acquiert vis-à-vis de l'Etat reconnaissant une existence légale qu'il n'avait pas auparavant'.

3 *Taylor* v. *Barclay*, (1828) 2 Sim. 213, 221; *Jones* v. *Garcia del Rio*, (1823) Turner and Russell, 297.

government (including the government of an unrecognized State) the right to sue in English courts, the right to claim jurisdictional immunities, and the right to the acknowledgment of the validity of the legislative, administrative and judicial acts of its organs.[1] Subject to some exceptions formulated in connection with the conditions which arose during and after the civil war, and apart from the question of jurisdictional immunities, the practice of the courts of the United States was, until recently, the same.

The exception which the practice of American courts has engrafted upon the refusal to admit the legal existence of unrecognized governments, with all the consequences attaching thereto, is that effect will be given to the acts of the unrecognized authority whenever justice and public policy so require. That principle was formulated by the courts of the United States in connection with a number of cases which arose after the civil war and which concerned the validity of various legislative and judicial acts in the territory of the rebel States. The recognition thus extended related to acts of normal administration within what was, in the eyes of the law, national territory. For the same reason recognition was consistently refused to acts going beyond the normal administration of the country or derogating from the fundamental principles of the Constitution. In the words of Mr Justice Field, in *Williams* v. *Bruffy*, 'as far as the acts of the States do not impair or tend to impair the supremacy of national authority, or the just rights of citizens under the constitution, they are, in general, to be treated as valid and binding'.[2] Or, as pointed out in *Baldy* v. *Hunder*, such acts may be treated as valid 'if they were not hostile in their purpose or mode of enforcement to the authority of the national government, and did not impair the rights of citizens under the constitution'.[3] Thus the courts admitted the validity of transactions in conformity with legislation relating to the creation of corporations, the sale of property, currency matters, marriage and descent, and the like.[4] It may be said that the acts of the rebellious authority were treated as valid only in so far as they could be regarded as giving effect to the letter or the purpose of the law of the Union. It was clear throughout that there was in the acts of the rebellious body no inherent authority resulting from its *de facto* status.[5]

1 See above, p. 44.

2 (1877) 96 U.S. 176.

3 (1898) 171 U.S. 388. See also *Horn* v. *Lockhart*, 17 Wallace 570; *Stevens* v. *Griffith*, 111 U.S. 48.

4 *United States* v. *Insurance Companies*, (1874) 22 Wallace 99; *Thorington* v. *Smith*, (1868) 8 Wallace 1; *Texas* v. *White*, (1868) 7 Wallace 700; *Delmas* v. *Merchants' National Insurance Co.* (1871) 14 Wallace 661.

5 'The validity of its acts...depends entirely upon its ultimate success; if it fail to establish itself permanently, all such acts perish with it. If it succeed and become recognized, its acts from the commencement of its existence are upheld as those of an independent nation' (Mr Justice Field in *Williams* v. *Bruffy*, supra).

In 1924 and in subsequent years the courts of the United States extended the doctrine of 'justice and public policy' to cover acts of unrecognized foreign governments. They interpreted the civil war cases as suggesting, in the words of Mr Justice Cardozo in *Sokoloff* v. *National City Bank*, 'the possibility that a body or group which has vindicated by the course of events its pretensions to sovereign power, but which has forfeited by its conduct the privileges or immunities of sovereignty, may gain for its acts and decrees a validity quasi-governmental, if violence to fundamental principles of justice or to our own public policy might otherwise be done'.[1] In the same judgment Mr Justice Cardozo, while affirming the principle that 'juridically, a government that is unrecognized may be viewed as no government at all, if the power withholding recognition chooses thus to view it', qualified the general rule by the statement that 'in practice, however, since juridical conceptions are seldom, if ever, carried to the limit of their logic, the equivalence is not absolute, but is subject to self-imposed limitations of common sense and fairness, as we learned in litigations following our Civil War'.[2] It will be noted that the acknowledgment of the validity of the acts of an unrecognized government is described in this bold pronouncement as permissible only by way of exception. In the case in which that pronouncement was made, as well as in most of the other cases which approved of it, it was in fact followed by a refusal to treat as valid, with regard to the matter in hand, the legislation of the unrecognized government.[3] Yet so unsatisfactory was the situation resulting from the continued refusal to recognize an admittedly effective government, namely, the Government of Soviet Russia, on the ground that it had forfeited by its conduct the privileges of sovereignty, that some have been led to treat the exception as the rule accurately defining the status of the unrecognized government. The correct and reasonable rule is that both the unrecognized government and its acts are a nullity.

That rule, it must be admitted, would cease to be reasonable if it became customary to refuse recognition to governments not on the ground that they are not effective but for such reasons as that they are 'unworthy of a place in the Society of Nations'. Had any such practice become a permanent feature of the policy of recognition, there would be room for reconsideration of a well-established and sound principle of law. This

1 239 N.Y. 158; (1924) 145 N.E. 917 at p. 918.

2 Ibid.

3 See also the emphatic opinion of Crane, J., in *Joint Stock Co. of Volgakama Oil and Chemical Factory* v. *National City Bank*, (1925) 240 N.Y. 368. On the other hand see, for an application of the doctrine, the final judgment of the Court of Appeals in *James and Co.* v. *Second Russian Insurance Co.* (1925) 239 N.Y. 248.

happened in the case of *Salimoff* v. *Standard Oil Company*,[1] where the Court refused to follow the principle laid down in *Luther* v. *Sagor*[2]—the leading English case on the matter—as well as in numerous decisions of courts in the United States[3] according to which the acts of an unrecognized government must be treated as a nullity. But the decision in the *Salimoff* case was given at a time when it had become widely admitted in the United States that the refusal to recognize the Soviet Government was based on grounds other than absence of effectiveness of the Soviet regime, whose growing stability could no longer be ignored. In fact, the wording of the certificate issued by the Secretary of State for the purposes of that case was such as almost to invite a clear judicial pronouncement departing from previous practice.[4] The Court said: 'The courts may not recognize the Soviet Government as the *de jure* government until the State Department gives the word. They may, however, say that it is a government, maintaining internal peace and order, providing for national defense and the general welfare, carrying on relations with our own government and others. To refuse to recognize that Soviet Russia is a government regulating the internal affairs of the country is to give to

1 Decided in 1933 by the Court of Appeals of New York (262 N.Y. 220; 186 N.E. 679).

2 [1921] 3 K.B. 532.

3 See, for example, *Petrogradsky Mejdunarodny Kommerchesky Bank* v. *The National City Bank of New York*, (1930) 253 N.Y. 23, 38–40; *Annual Digest*, 1929–30, Case no. 20, where the Court said with regard to Russian nationalization decrees: 'They are exhibitions of power. They are not pronouncements of authority.' Following *Sokoloff* v. *National City Bank*, supra, the Court was prepared to recognize the legal consequences of these decrees if to ignore them 'would bring hardship or confusion to the helpless and the innocent without compensating effect. On the other hand, there is no shelter in such exceptions for rapine or oppression'.

4 The certificate of the Department of State was as follows:

'1. The Government of the United States accorded recognition to the Provisional Government of Russia as the successor of the Russian Imperial Government, and has not accorded recognition to any government in Russia since the overthrow of the Provisional Government of Russia.

'2. The Department of State is cognizant of the fact that the Soviet Regime is exercising control and power in territory of the former Russian Empire and the Department of State has no disposition to ignore that fact.

'3. The refusal of the Government of the United States to accord recognition to the Soviet regime is not based on the ground that the regime does not exercise control and authority in the territory of the former Russian Empire, but on other facts.'

For a more direct intimation from the Executive to the courts see the declaration made before the Belgian Senate by the Belgian Minister of Foreign Affairs on 6 April 1933 in the following terms: 'Si les Tribunaux belges, jugeant dans la plénitude de leur indépendance, décidaient que la législation de la Russie d'aujourd'hui peut produire certains effets en Belgique, le gouvernement n'y verrait pas une opposition a la politique suivie par lui, de non-reconnaissance du Gouvernement de l'U.R.S.S.' (as quoted by Stoupnitzky, *Statut international de l'U.R.S.S.* (1936), p. 228).

fictions an air of reality which they do not deserve.'[1] The decision of the Court may be regarded as a response, possibly not unwelcome to the Executive, to an invitation to relieve an embarrassment brought about by the continued adherence, about to be abandoned, to an inadequate test of recognition. But there are obvious limits to the capacity of courts to interpret away an otherwise sound juridical principle which has been rendered difficult of application owing to the attitude of the Executive.

Possibly, in the *Salimoff* case the Court found it less difficult to commit itself to a departure from a well-established practice seeing that the courts in the United States had previously refused to extend the consequences of non-recognition to the point of denying jurisdictional immunities to unrecognized governments. Thus in *Underhill* v. *Hernandez*[2] the Supreme Court held that 'acts of legitimate warfare cannot be made the basis of individual liability', that 'the courts of one country will not sit in judgment on the acts of the Government of another done within its own territory', and that that principle cannot 'be confined to lawful or recognized Governments, or to cases where redress can manifestly be had through public channels'. In *Wulfsohn* v. *Russian Socialist Federated Soviet Republic*[3] the New York Court of Appeals, reversing decisions of two lower courts, held that the unrecognized Government of Soviet Russia could not be sued, by means of an action for conversion of personal property, for an act of confiscation done within its territorial jurisdiction. The same course was followed in *Nankivel et al.* v. *Omsk All-Russian Government et al.*[4] This was an action against the Omsk All-Russian Government under General Koltchak to recover the value of certain automobiles requisitioned by it within the territory under its control in 1918 and 1919. The Court held that, although unrecognized, the latter was a *de facto* government in the international sense. It expressly adopted the principle acted upon in the *Wulfsohn* case. It said: 'Lack of recognition by the United States Government, we have recently held, does not permit an individual suitor to bring a *de facto* Government before the bar.... To sue a sovereign State is to insult it in a manner which it may treat with silent contempt. It is not bound to come into our courts and plead its immunity.'[5] And although some passages in the *Wulfsohn* case suggested that the grant of jurisdictional immunity was limited to acts of sovereignty proper and that the Court merely refused to allow its process to be used for the redress of wrongs for

1 *Salimoff* v. *Standard Oil Company*, ubi supra.
2 (1897) 168 U.S. 250, 252–3.
3 (1923) 234 N.Y. 372; *Annual Digest*, 1923–4, Case no. 16.
4 (1923) 237 N.Y. 150; ibid. Case no. 70.
5 At p. 156.

which the usual remedy is a political one,[1] no such limitation can be read into a subsequent decision bearing on the matter.[2] Similarly, courts in the United States and elsewhere have refused to extend the consequences of non-recognition so as to interfere with the principle that although the government is not recognized, the international entity of the State, with the rights attaching thereto, continues.[3]

On the other hand, the rule established by decisions of English courts at the beginning of the nineteenth century that an unrecognized government cannot sue seeing that refusal of recognition amounts to denial of juridical capacity,[4] has been repeatedly acted upon in the United States. This was the case, for instance, in *Russian Socialist Federated Soviet Republics* v. *Cibrario*, an action brought by the Soviet Government and arising out of the alleged fraudulent non-fulfilment by the defendant of a contract for the purchase of moving-picture machines.[5]

1 The Court said: 'Whenever an act done by a sovereign in his sovereign character is questioned, it becomes a matter of negotiation or of reprisals or of war' (at p. 375).

2 *Voevodine* v. *Government of the Commander-in-Chief of the Armed Forces in the South of Russia et al.*, (1931) 232 App. Div. (N.Y.) 204, 249 N.Y. Suppl. 644; (1931) 257 N.Y. 557, 178 N.E. 793; *Annual Digest*, 1931–2, Case no. 25. This was an action in respect of goods sold to the unrecognized Denikin Government of Russia. The Court admitted that the Denikin Government was 'a *de facto* Government, which existed for a short time in the southern part of European Russia, and was not recognized by the Government of the United States as either a *de facto* or a *de jure* Government'. But, the Court said, 'during its life no enforceable right or remedy in the courts of this country existed against that *de facto* Government, for it could not be required to submit itself to our laws and to the jurisdiction of our courts. This is true, irrespective of whether or not such Government were recognized by the Government of the United States'. For the, controversial, suggestion that the unrecognized government does not enjoy immunity from suit when it is not directly impleaded (e.g. in an action against a ship) see Preuss in *A.J.* vol. XXXVI (1942). The suggestion is advanced on the ground that, in the case of an unrecognized government, the State Department would refuse to request immunity and that the unrecognized government would, in the absence of diplomatic representation, be unable to intervene in order to claim immunity.

3 *Lehigh Valley R. Co.* v. *State of Russia*, (1927) 21 F. (2d) 396, 400, 401; *Annual Digest*, 1927–8, Case no. 35. In the same line of reasoning Dutch courts have held that the non-recognition of the Soviet Government did not affect the rights of Russian nationals under treaties concluded with the former Russian regime (*Lowinsky* v. *Receiver in Bankruptcy*; ibid. 1931–2, Case no. 16). But in *Shipoff* v. *Elte Ltd.* (ibid. Case no. 17), another Dutch court held that the absence of normal diplomatic relations resulting from non-recognition rendered provisionally inoperative an otherwise binding treaty.

4 See above, p. 44.

5 (1923) 235 N.Y. 255; *Annual Digest*, 1923–4, Case no. 17. See also *The Penza*, (1921) 277 Fed. 91; *The Rogdai*, (1920) 277 Fed. 133; and other cases referred to in *Guaranty Trust Co. of New York* v. *United States*, (1938) 304 U.S. 126, 137 (*Annual Digest*, 1938–40, Case no. 69), in which the Court fully endorsed the principle followed in those cases. The tendency to a restrictive interpretation of the consequences

(*b*) *Continental Practice.* In the countries of the European continent the courts, with slight exceptions, have adopted the view that prior to recognition the unrecognized authority and the acts emanating from it are a mere nullity. In France, so long as the Soviet Government was not recognized, French courts refused to give effect to Soviet legislation and regarded the law of the former regime as continuing.[1] In the leading case of *Héritiers Bouniatian* v. *Société Optorg*,[2] the Civil Tribunal of the Seine followed closely the decision and the reasoning in *Luther* v. *Sagor*. The Court pointed out that in the eyes of the French Government the Soviets were a mere accumulation of force without international standing; that the expropriations for which they were responsible were acts of usurpation and violence showing all the features of fraudulent conversion in terms of Articles 379 and the following of the Civil Code; and that the apparent passing of property in such circumstances was irregular and inoperative.

The Belgian Civil Court of Liége refused, in 1929, to recognize a divorce decree obtained in Russia on the ground that Soviet Russia was not at that time recognized by Belgium. The Court said: 'Seeing that the country in which the above act [divorce at Odessa] has taken place is not politically recognized by Belgium, it follows that the officials of that country have according to the laws of Belgium no recognized authority. It follows also that according to the same law the acts of such officials do not possess the character of authentic and obligatory acts. In the case in question the signature of the act has not been validly certified and is, for this reason, lacking in the necessary conditions of authenticity.'[3] The Brussels Civil Court gave an identical decision in the *Digmeloff* case.[4] It said: 'Belgium

of non-recognition, without discarding the accepted principles in the matter, manifested itself in the decision of the Federal Court of Appeals in *Amtorg Trading Corporation* v. *United States*, (1934) 71 F. (2*d*) 524 (*Annual Digest*, 1933–4, Case no. 30), to the effect that the plaintiff, a Russian corporation under the control of the Russian Government, was a person distinct from that Government and accordingly entitled to sue in the courts of the United States even prior to the recognition of the Soviet Government by the United States.

1 *Chiger* v. *Chiger* (ibid. 1925–6, Case no. 18). In that case an action for divorce was brought in 1920 on grounds recognized by Soviet law. The action was dismissed on the ground that the Soviet Government was not recognized. But the divorce was granted in 1926 after recognition had been given. See also *Basil and Alexander Bessel* v. *Cools* (ibid. 1929–30, Case no. 24) and *In re Marmatscheff* (ibid. Case no. 150).

2 *Gazette du Palais*, January 1924, pp. 96 et seq.; Clunet, vol. LI (1924), p. 133.

3 *Krimtschansky* v. *Officier de l'Etat Civil de Liége* (*Annual Digest*, 1929–30, Case no. 26).

4 Ibid. 1927–8, Case no. 45. See, to the same effect, *Bekker* v. *Willcox*, decided by the Civil Tribunal of Brussels in November 1923 (ibid. 1923–4, Case no. 22); *Jelinkowa* v. *Serbouloff* (ibid. 1925–6, Case no. 20).

has not given either *de jure* or *de facto* recognition to the Soviet Government; hence, Belgian tribunals are not competent to recognize or enforce any decrees of that Government. The personal status of Russian refugees on Belgian soil is, therefore, governed by the legislation last in force before the coming of the Soviet regime.' Similarly, Belgian courts refused to draw a distinction between the Russian commercial representation and the Russian Government, and as the latter had not been recognized they declined to allow the former to bring an action in Belgian courts.[1]

The position in Italy is the same. In *Nonis* v. *Federation of Seamen*, the Court of Appeal of Genoa held that as the Soviet Government was not recognized by Italy in 1920, changes of property purported to have been effected by Soviet legislation could not be recognized and that the juridical status of the ship in question sailing under the Imperial Russian flag was unchanged.[2] The Court of Appeal of Rome refused to the Russian Commercial Delegation the status of a representative of a foreign State protected by the special provisions of the Italian Code.[3] When the Italian Court of Cassation, in a case arising out of the same transaction, affirmed the right of the Union of Soviet Socialist Republics to sue in Italian courts, it did so on the ground that the Soviet Government had been recognized by Italy.[4]

The Swedish Supreme Court, notwithstanding an able Opinion to the contrary, fully associated itself with the view that the Soviet Government, not being recognized by Sweden, could not sue in Swedish courts.[5] The Czechoslovak Supreme Court held that although a provisional treaty had been concluded with the Soviet Government in 1922 in commercial matters, there had been no recognition *de jure* and that accordingly 'the quality of juridical persons was accorded to the Governments of these Republics and to their organs only for a strictly limited sphere of activity'.[6] The position taken by the Egyptian Mixed Courts was very much the same. In the case of *Consorts Gregorian* the Civil Court of Alexandria refused to apply the law of Soviet Russia and applied instead the old law of Imperial Russia on the ground that, as the Soviet Government was not recognized by Egypt, neither the new laws enacted by the Soviet Government nor the abrogation by it of the old Russian law could be recognized. The Court said: 'It would be a juridical heresy to deny a State international

1 *Société Despa et Fils* v. *U.S.S.R.* (*Annual Digest*, 1931–2, Case no. 26).

2 Ibid. 1929–30, Case no. 23.

3 *In re Serventi* (ibid. 1919–22, Case no. 211).

4 *Cibrario* v. *Russian Trade Delegation in Italy and the National City Bank of New York* (ibid. 1931–2, Case no. 26).

5 *Soviet Government* v. *Ericsson* (ibid. 1919–22, Case no. 30).

6 *Soviet Representation in Czechoslovakia Case* (ibid. 1925–6, Case no. 44).

personality, including the legitimate exercise of its sovereign powers, and yet, at the same time, to recognize its legislative enactments, that is to say, the most significant manifestation of the power which has been denied to it.'[1] In *Gross* v. *Gretchenko*, the Mixed Commercial Tribunal of Alexandria gave expression to the same view. It said:

> 'When by the principles of international law the national law of Russians is to be applied to their claims, the foreign court cannot have recourse to the new Soviet law, save where the State has recognized the Government of the Soviets. In States such as Egypt, which have directly or indirectly refused to recognize the actual Russian Government, it is the old Russian law which must be applied in such case. The existence and independence of Russia as a sovereign State constitute a material fact which cannot be contested after the Bolshevik Revolution. The negation of power of the Soviets as embodying legitimately that sovereign State, while leading necessarily to the ignoring of the legislation issued by it, cannot have the effect of making the Russians lose their national character and of submitting them to a kind of natural law or to the law of the country where they happen to be; and they continue to be governed by their national statute, which is the old law that is still deemed to be in force.'[2]

Holland and Switzerland seem to be the only countries in which Russian decrees were to some extent given the effect of law notwithstanding non-recognition of the Soviet Government.[3]

§ 50. *The Current Criticism of the Attitude of Courts in the Matter of Recognition.* The propriety of the principle upon which courts have acted in the matter of the legal position of unrecognized governments, namely, their refusal to admit the juridical existence of such governments with all the rights appertaining thereto, ought not to be open to doubt. There are good reasons why after one organ of the State has decided that a body claiming to be a foreign government does not legally exist as such, it should not lie with another organ of the same State to treat that foreign authority as

1 Ibid. 1929–30, Case no. 27.

2 Ibid. 1923–4, Case no. 23. See also, to the same effect, *Ichlenedjian and Others* v. *Gregorian* (ibid. 1931–2, Case no. 27). And see *Dahan and Dorra Brothers* v. *Paul Tchoureff* (ibid. 1935–7, Case no. 34), where the Court of Appeal held in 1936 that the acts of the Ural Cossack Government and those of its Trade Board in 1918 ought to be treated as valid on the ground that the Government, 'far from repudiating the laws of the Imperial regime, was in fact, if not in law, merely the continuation of that Government, the recognition of which by Egypt had never been withdrawn'.

3 In February 1935 the District Court of Amsterdam held in *Exportchleb Ltd.* v. *Goudeket* that although the Russian Government was not recognized by Holland it could 'appear for Russia in matters of civil law in the Courts of Holland' (*Annual Digest*, 1935–7, Case no. 36). As to Switzerland see *Schinz* v. *High Court of Zürich* ibid. 1925–6, Case no. 23. See also *In re Héritiers de Dame Pribiloff*, ibid. 1931–2, p. 58.

legally existing. Courts take no notice of unrecognized governments not because of any subservience to the Executive or because of any misplaced importance attached to the desirability of the Executive and the judiciary speaking with one voice on matters pertaining to the external relations of the State. They take no notice of unrecognized governments for the reason that what 'exists'—if it exists—is not a government in the meaning of international law as understood by the Executive. Not every instrumentality of power is a government; it may not be truly effective; it may be purely local, unstable, or altogether precarious; or, though actually in operation, it may fall short of that conception of effectiveness as based on consent which the practice of many States has legitimately associated with the idea of government. To say that an unrecognized government nevertheless exists is to beg the question both as to the meaning of 'government' and of 'existence'. Neither is there substance in the view that a State may have no government, and yet may possess laws which can be given effect by the courts of foreign countries.[1] Laws are the instrument of an enforceable social order; there is no such order without a government enforcing them. The principles laid down in *Luther* v. *Sagor*[2] are sound and inescapable—so long as recognition is not withheld arbitrarily for political reasons. They become artificial and productive of hardship when the test of effectiveness, in its wider or its narrower sense,[3] is abandoned, and when other considerations, which have here been subjected to criticism, are relied upon in disregard of the actual existence of the foreign authority.

A situation of this kind was created after the First World War with regard to the Soviet Government of Russia, which many States refused to recognize on account of the apparent ruthlessness of the revolutionary change, the unwillingness of the Soviet Government to abide by international obligations of its own and those of its predecessors, and even on account of the political creed of the new regime.[4] The result was either that the courts, following well-established precedents, were compelled to

1 See, for example, Mann, cited below, p. 158.

2 For a criticism of the decision in *Luther* v. *Sagor* and, generally, of the attitude of courts in treating as non-existent an unrecognized government and in refusing to recognize its laws, see Dickinson in *A.J.* vol. XIX (1925), pp. 268 et seq.; ibid. vol. XXVII (1933), pp. 743–7; and in *Michigan Law Review*, vol. XXII (1922), pp. 29–45, 118–34; and Borchard in *A.J.* vol. XXVI (1932), pp. 262–4.

3 Namely, whether based on evidence of popular consent or not.

4 See, for example, the statement by President Wilson in 1919 with regard to recognition of the Soviet Government: 'In the view of this government there cannot be any common ground upon which it can stand with a Power whose conceptions of international relations are so entirely alien to its own, so utterly repugnant to its moral sense' (as quoted in *A.J.* vol. XXVIII (1934), p. 90). And see above, p. 110.

render decisions of a pronounced degree of artificiality inasmuch as they denied the existence of the *de facto* authority; or that they felt moved to rectify the consequences of the executive departure from the test of effectiveness by introducing exceptions by reference to considerations of equity and of general convenience; or, finally, that, as in the *Salimoff* case, acting as it were on an indirect intimation on the part of the executive authorities, they resorted to judicial legislation jettisoning the accepted principles. The situation thus created was undoubtedly unsatisfactory. However, instead of directing their criticisms to the questionable exercise of the power of recognition on the part of the Executive, writers have criticized the courts for drawing from the fact of non-recognition conclusions which they found it difficult to avoid having regard both to sound legal principle and to previous decisions on the matter.[1] There may be room for the opinion that the function of recognition conceived as the ascertainment of the existence of the requisite elements of governmental capacity ought to be entrusted to courts. But, for reasons stated, there is probably no merit in the view that after one organ of State has declared that an authority claiming to be the government of a foreign country does not in fact exist and is therefore not entitled to recognition, another organ of the State should attribute a legal existence to that body and should treat it as entitled to the rights ordinarily enjoyed by a foreign government. Admittedly the existing position is on occasions productive of unsatisfactory results. But the remedy lies not in an appeal to the courts to rectify the conduct of the Executive by ignoring its legal consequences and by reducing refusal of recognition to a mere denial of diplomatic intercourse.

1 This line of criticism seems to be the principal drawback to the able monograph by Jaffe (*Judicial Aspects of Foreign Relations* (1933)), who charges courts with having proceeded in respect to recognition with undue 'deference and subserviency' to executive policy, and who suggests that although the executive, by refusing recognition, considers a foreign government to be non-existent in law, courts should give effect to their laws and allow them to sue. The author probably simplifies the issue by reducing the consequences of such divergence of views to an 'embarrassment' (p. 235) the only result of which may be that 'the effectiveness of a particular foreign policy as conceived by a given group of persons [i.e. the government] may be diminished' (ibid.). Dr Mann seems to follow the same line of criticism (*Transactions of the Grotius Society*, vol. XXIX (1943), pp. 156–63). Some writers have adopted an easier method of asserting that courts actually do, as a broad rule, recognize the juridical existence, and its consequences, of unrecognized governments. See Kunz, pp. 154–7; Spiropoulos, *Traité de droit international public* (1933), pp. 55–8. On the other hand, see Hervey, *The Legal Effects of Recognition in International Law* (1928), pp. 157 et seq., for suggestions calculated to mitigate some of the consequences of non-recognition. See also Jessup in *A.J.* vol. XXXVI (1938), p. 545, who—rightly, it is believed—directs his criticism not to courts but to a recognition policy conducted in conspicuous disregard of the principle of effectiveness.

The remedy lies in the adherence of the Executive to a practice, sanctioned by the bulk of precedent and by considerations of legal principle, in which recognition is determined by the standard of effectiveness, in either of its accepted senses,[1] as distinguished from the other tests and from shifting considerations of national policy.

§ 51. *The Necessity for Recognition of Governments.* The necessity, in law, for the recognition of governments arises not from the fact of the revolution preceding the establishment of the new authority. That necessity is due mainly to the uncertainty, brought about by the events of the revolution, as to who is the holder of effective power. But for that circumstance, recognition of governments would occupy only a limited place in international law. However, so long as revolutionary changes within States take place, recognition of governments is a substantial and necessary act. It is no solution of the difficulty to suggest that, without any declaration of recognition, foreign States ought to confine themselves to maintaining relations with the authority actually in power. For a decision must often be made—though it can frequently be deferred without undue inconvenience—as to which of the rival authorities is in power with a reasonable prospect of permanency. In the absence of such decision contact may still be maintained with one or both of the competing factions for a variety of purposes.[2] In the long run, however, the international position of the State in question cannot be regularized without a clear finding on the part of other States as to who is competent and authorized to represent the country.

For this reason the so-called Estrada doctrine of recognition enunciated on 27 September 1930 by the Mexican Foreign Minister[3] is less helpful than may appear at first sight. In that communication, sent to the Mexican diplomatic representatives abroad, it was announced that henceforth the Mexican Government would issue 'no declarations in the sense of grants of recognition, since that nation considers that such a course is an insulting practice and one which, in addition to the fact that it offends the sovereignty of other nations, implies that judgment of some sort may be passed upon the internal affairs of those nations by other governments'; and that in the future the Government of Mexico would confine itself 'to the maintenance or withdrawal as it may deem advisable of its diplomatic agents'.[4] It is this latter aspect of the Estrada doctrine, rather than abstention from formal

1 I.e. effectiveness in its primary meaning or effectiveness as evidenced by the adequately expressed consent of the nation.

2 See below, pp. 388–90.

3 *A.J.* vol. XXV (1931), Suppl. p. 203.

4 Ibid.

recognition, which reveals the source of difficulty. For the questions still remain: With which of the rival factions shall diplomatic relations be maintained? In what circumstances are they to be suspended? With whom shall they be resumed after they have been interrupted? These questions were hardly solved by the Mexican declaration.[1] As in the case of recognition of States, it is unhelpful to say that recognition is unnecessary, or purely declaratory, or merely political, on the ground that the new government is internationally entitled to its position as such as soon as it is 'effective'.[2] For it is the question of the effectiveness of the new government which is often at issue. It may be argued that, if foreign States are willing to wait long enough, the course of events will decide the question of the effectiveness of a government in an unequivocal manner making unnecessary an express finding by way of recognition. But this is a counsel of perfection. The disadvantages of waiting long enough may be greater than those of the risks and the responsibility of an express decision.[3] When such a decision is made, it is as 'constitutive' of the rights and duties of the new government as is, in a different sphere, the recognition of States.

1 In August 1945 Mexico recognized as the *de jure* government of Spain a group of Spanish exiles in Mexico headed by President Barrio, the last President of the Spanish Cortes before the Spanish revolution. Extra-territorial privileges were granted to what purported to be a meeting of the Cortes and the legation and other property of the Spanish State were handed over to the Government thus recognized. In view of the fact that Mexico had not previously recognized the Nationalist Government which arose after the Civil War of 1936–9 and that there was a distinct element of legal continuity between the last lawful government and the newly recognized authority, the recognition thus given, while unorthodox, could not be regarded as an abuse of the power of recognition (for some details see *The Times* newspaper, 22 and 31 August 1945). But the incident points to some of the inherent limitations of the Estrada doctrine.

2 For an interesting contribution to this aspect of the question of recognition of governments see Scelle in *R.G.* vol. XXI (1914), pp. 117–32, who points out that given the effectiveness of the new authority recognition is due as a matter of legal duty. Indeed, it would appear that in his view the legal duty is so imperative that recognition is unnecessary seeing that the change of government, whether revolutionary or peaceful, is an internal matter of the State. The only remedy open to foreign States for marking their disapproval or doubts is, says Scelle, to refuse to enter into diplomatic relations.

3 See the judicious observations on this subject by Fenwick in *A.J.* vol. XXXVIII (1944), p. 449.

Chapter XI

THE LEGAL NATURE OF RECOGNITION AND THE DUTY OF RECOGNITION

§ 52. *The Right to Recognition as a Government.* In the matter of recognition of governments the insistence, on the part of writers, on the political character of recognition and on the complete freedom of action said to be enjoyed by States in granting or refusing it has been less emphatic and less widespread than in the case of recognition of States.[1] But there is still a substantial body of jurists who adopt the political interpretation of the process of recognition and who deny the existence of a right to recognition as a government. It is not easy to understand the reason of that attitude. In principle the right to recognition of the government freely chosen or, according to some, tolerated by the population of the State, would appear to be the very minimum of those rights of independence and sovereignty which States enjoy under international law. If that is so then the pretended right to refuse recognition to an effective government of a foreign State without assigning legally valid grounds for such action constitutes a denial of the independence of that State. The majority of writers now admit that this is so, and the denial of the 'right to recognition' as a government is no longer a hall-mark of sound scientific approach. The practice of States, almost without exception, shows that they do not deem themselves free to act arbitrarily in granting or refusing recognition. On the contrary, the student of the practice of States, in particular that of Great Britain and the United States, must be impressed with the importance which has been attached to following precedent and principle. That practice shows the inaccuracy of the plausible assertion that recognition of governments is a matter of policy pure and simple. Undoubtedly, the act of recognition permits and necessitates the exercise of discretion in ascertaining the existence of the requisite conditions of recognition in situations which are complicated and liable to sudden changes. But to exercise discretion of this nature is not to perform an act of policy.[2]

1 See below, p. 160.

2 The necessity of combining the exercise of discretion with action based on precedent and principle was forcibly stated by the Earl of Malmesbury in connection with the Italian request for recognition in 1859. He said: 'The Marquis d'Azeglio quoted precedents, and referred to the principle generally acted upon in this country in regard to the recognition of *de facto* Governments, in support of his assertion that the captain of the "Conqueror" should at once have acknowledged the Tuscan re-

The outstanding fact in the situation is that States attempt to relate their action in the matter of recognition of governments to some objective test for which they claim general validity—an attempt which is in itself proof of the legal character of the function of recognition. It is true that there has been no uniformity in the matter of the tests of recognition acted upon by States. Some of these tests, it has been suggested, are open to criticism. But none of them has been enunciated as exclusively calculated to promote the interests of the State granting or refusing recognition. They have all been based on considerations capable or alleged to be capable of general application—whether it be the stability and effectiveness of the new authority, or the consent of the governed as evidence of such effectiveness, or the method of the revolutionary change, or the willingness and ability to fulfil obligations. They have been put forward as embodying or capable of embodying a rule of international law. It is also true that as the application of these tests—in particular the determination as to when the new authority must be deemed to be in possession of the requisite degree of effectiveness and stability—is a matter left to the judgment of the recognizing State, considerations of national interest must occasionally influence the exercise of the judicial discretion thus left to it. However, this is a remediable defect of the machinery of recognition. Essentially, the function of recognition is a political matter only in so far as, in addition to its legal aspect, it is exercised by the political, i.e. executive, branch of the State and in so far as it has a political significance and political consequences.

In fact, many of those who deny that there is ever a duty to grant recognition express views which in fact amount to bringing recognition within the orbit of a legal duty. Thus, for instance, Dr Kunz, who in his thorough monograph repeatedly denies the existence of the duty to recognize or of a right to obtain recognition, is emphatic that it is unlawful to refuse to grant recognition in certain cases or for certain reasons. 'Third States', he says, 'have no right to object [i.e. to refuse recognition] to a government merely because of the manner of its establishment or the

volution. I observed to him that, although I admitted that such was the general principle on which this country acted, and which we had carried out in recognizing successive *de facto* Governments in France and other States, yet the application of it must always be a question of discretion, and must depend upon the circumstances of each case. If Her Majesty's Government had at once, and without waiting for further information, recognized the revolutionary Government set up in Parma simultaneously with the establishment of the new Government in Tuscany, their recognition of it on arriving at Parma would have found that, in the interval, a counter-revolution had taken place, and that the Government of the Grand Duchess had been restored.' (*State Papers*, 1859, 2nd session, vol. XXXII, p. 443 (*Further correspondence respecting the affairs of Italy*, Earl of Malmesbury to Sir J. Hudson).)

nature of its regime.'[1] The same, in his view, applies to the use of recognition as an instrument for securing economic advantages or for supporting a particular regime. 'These', he says, 'are undoubtedly acts of illicit intervention; they are an international delinquency.'[2] But, clearly, if there is no duty of recognition in any circumstances, what is the relevance of the enquiry into the legality of a refusal of recognition for any particular reason? If, so far as the new authority is concerned, the entire process of recognition is outside the province of legal right and duty, it seems futile to probe into the legality of certain of its aspects. If the new authority has no right to recognition even if it fulfils all requisite conditions, what is the meaning of the assertion that recognition must not be refused on certain specified grounds—unless it is suggested that while a State is completely free to refuse recognition altogether, it must exercise caution in selecting the ostensible grounds on which it bases its action?

Undoubtedly, the task of substantiating the legal conception of recognition such as is here put forward is not an easy one. For it is not enough to show that the political view of recognition is contrary to the principle of independence of States inasmuch as it denies to them, in effect, the right to possess a government enjoying the obedience of the bulk of the population. What is more important is to discover in the baffling flux of seemingly discretionary tests of recognition the constant and ever-recurring element of legal obligation. This is the proper task of juridical science. It is the task of revealing the persistent working of a legal principle in apparently discon-

1 Op. cit. p. 161. Other writers who equally deny the right to recognition adopt the same inconsistent reasoning. Thus, according to Podesta Costa (op. cit. p. 51), recognition is 'un acte facultative', not 'un acte obligatoire'. But, he says, the decision of third States in the matter must be 'ni arbitraire ni capricieuse'; it ought not to be given or refused under the influence of political sympathies or interests. Are these qualifications principles of law or of politics? If, as we must assume, they are principles of law, then recognition is no longer optional. Spiropoulos states categorically that there is no 'legal duty to recognize' (*Die de facto Regierung im Völkerrecht* (1926), p. 46), but, he says, the use of recognition as an instrument of political pressure or sympathies is 'questionable from the point of view of international law' as offending against the prohibition of intervention. See also the same, *Théorie générale du droit international* (1930), pp. 140–3. He points out there that to adopt tests of recognition other than those of effectiveness is to adopt a political as distinguished from a legal test. But a legal test is one which the law prescribes as a matter of legal duty. Professor Brierly (*Law of Nations* (3rd ed. 1942), p. 106) says—rightly, it is submitted—that as in the case of recognition of States so also with regard to recognition of governments, the question which other States have to decide is a question of fact. He then expresses the view that recognition of a government, like recognition of a State, is a 'political rather than a legal act' (ibid.). It is submitted that the ascertaining of a fact is a legal, not a political, act. Admittedly that act may have political consequences, and it may be influenced by or abused for political purposes. But there is a disadvantage in identifying the nature of an act with the aberrations of its exercise.

2 Ibid.

nected manifestations of political action. This task has been attempted here. We have analysed the various tests of recognition in order to ascertain how far they depart from the principle of effectiveness. It has been shown that all these tests are based on considerations of principle of general application. These principles may be inadequate and open to criticism, but their indirect and cumulative result is to demonstrate that States, in granting or refusing recognition to governments of revolutionary origin, do not claim the right to proceed according to arbitrary discretion based on an exclusive consideration of their own interests. The refusal of recognition on such grounds would constitute a legal wrong. This means—and we must not shrink from this conclusion—that an international tribunal endowed with the requisite jurisdiction and confronted with a clearly arbitrary refusal of recognition would be acting in accordance with its judicial duty if it were to find that international law is not without a remedy against a wrong of this nature. Admittedly, in a matter in which international law leaves to States full discretion in ascertaining the existence of the necessary conditions of recognition, it may not be easy to find that the discretion has been exercised arbitrarily. But the mere affirmation that it is a legal wrong to withhold recognition without good cause would go far towards securing for the process of recognition its legitimate place as a factor of international order. In the meantime it is proper that the science of international law, in deference to both principle and practice, should hasten and not retard that development.

§ 53. *The Abuse of the Power of Recognition.* The general adherence to what may be described as the legal view of recognition is not inconsistent with the fact that, as in the case of recognition of States, the power of recognition has occasionally been used for ends foreign to its true purpose. Diplomatic practice shows instances—far less numerous than is generally assumed—of recognition being used for the purpose of securing advantages to the recognizing State. At times it has been sought to achieve that purpose by cloaking it in the garb of an objective test of recognition, in particular that based on the willingness to fulfil international obligations. For there is only one step between proclaiming the latter as a condition of recognition and the insistence on the fulfilment of what is claimed to be a particular obligation to the recognizing State; and there is often only one further step between the latter and the requirement of compliance with an arbitrary political demand unrelated to any true claim of right. The practice of recognition on the part of the United States, with regard to which the published record is in this respect fuller than that of any other country and which shows deliberate adherence to general standards of recognition,[1] supplies occasional examples of that spurious use of the weapon of recognition. Although in 1913 the Huerta Government of Mexico was, according to the information received by the American ambassador, 'installed and evidently in secure possession', the United States demanded, as a condition of recognition, concrete evidence of the disposition to fulfil 'the general duties to foreigners and foreign governments incidental to international intercourse'.[2] In conformity with that requirement the Mexican Government was expected, *inter alia*, to settle the long-standing controversy concerning the Chamizal boundary, to agree, in a separate convention, to the equitable distribution of the waters of the Colorado River, and to settle various claims arising out of revolutionary disturbances and maladministration of justice in Mexico. When in 1923 there arose the question of the recognition of the Obregón Government in Mexico, the conditions of recognition included the obtaining of satisfactory assurances against confiscation of subsoil interests in lands owned by American citizens and the restoration of or reparation for the taking of lands owned by them.[3] When the question of the recognition of the new revolutionary Government of Bolivia arose in 1937 there were included among the conditions of recognition not only willingness to fulfil international obligations (which were stated to comprise the recently concluded Chaco protocols in the matter of the territorial dispute with Paraguay), but also to protect 'legitimate rights of private property'.[4] The latter figured among the conditions of recognition of the Chilean Government in 1932.[5] In connection with the recognition of the Albanian Government

1 See, for instance, the memorandum addressed by the diplomatic representatives of the United States in connection with the proposed recognition of the Chinese Government in 1912 in which the question was asked 'whether the present Chinese Government may not be regarded as so far substantially conforming to the accepted standards of international law as to merit formal recognition?' (quoted in Hackworth, vol. I, p. 314). See also instructions sent to the American Minister at Bogotá in 1900 and quoted by Moore, vol. I, p. 138.

2 Hackworth, vol. I, pp. 257, 258.

3 *U.S. For. Rel.* 1913, pp. 728, 741, 747. For the lengthy correspondence on the subject see Hackworth, vol. I, pp. 261 et seq. When, subsequently, Mexico proceeded to expropriate certain property rights owned by American nationals an American writer expressed the view that that act was a 'bald repudiation of Mexico's own official assurances solemnly given to the United States in consideration of the recognition of the Obregón Government in 1923' (Woolsey in *A.J.* vol. XXXII (1938), p. 525).

4 Hackworth, vol. I, p. 228.

5 Ibid. p. 232. With regard to the recognition of the Estrada Government in Nicaragua by the United States in 1910 subject to that Government undertaking, *inter alia*, to abolish monopolies, to guarantee rights of foreigners, and to make itself responsible for the punishment of persons responsible for the death of certain American citizens, see *U.S. For. Rel.* 1910, pp. 763–7.

in 1924, the assurance of most-favoured-nation treatment[1] as well as the prosecution of persons involved in the death of certain American citizens[2] figured prominently in the negotiations. The recognition of the Liberian Government in 1931 was made dependent to a considerable extent upon the attitude of Liberia concerning the report and recommendations of the experts appointed by the Committee of the League of Nations concerning slavery and forced labour.[3] There are similar examples in the practice of Great Britain and of other States.[4] In time of war the inducement to depart from accepted standards of recognition is particularly strong, and it is then that the function of recognition often assumes the complexion of belligerent policy and action.[5] However, even in this sphere the conduct of belligerents

1 Hackworth, vol. I, p. 192.

2 Ibid. p. 283.

3 Ibid. p. 306.

4 In 1861 Great Britain agreed to recognize the new Juarez Government in Mexico provided that the latter agreed to suitable redress and reparation in connection with outrages committed against the British Legation (*State Papers*, 1861, vol. LXV, p. 263 (Encl. I, no. 24, p. 66)). The British Minister at Athens, in informing, on 5 October 1862, the Provisional Government that, as he was accredited to King Otho, he could maintain only unofficial relations with it, at the same time claimed 'immediate compensation' for some acts of pillage of British property (*B.F.S.P.* vol. LVIII, p. 1021). See also the answer given in the House of Commons, on 14 May 1919, by the Foreign Secretary to the effect that in view of the attitude taken up by the Mexican Government with regard to the treatment of British property, His Majesty's Government were not disposed 'to accord the recognition implied by the resumption of diplomatic relations' (*H.C. Debates*, vol. CXV, col. 1472). When Russia recognized in 1862 the new Kingdom of Italy, Count Gortshakow, in explaining to Russian representatives abroad the reasons for this step, referred to two 'points essentiels' which influenced the decision: 'd'abord que la cour de Turin aurait la ferme intention de reprimer toutes tentatives des parties extrêmes qui pourrait troubler la paix générale, et ensuite qu'elle avait en mains la force nécessaire' (*Archives diplomatiques*, 1863, vol. I, p. 156).

5 Thus during the Second World War Great Britain and the United States, alongside of other United Nations, refused for a time to recognize the revolutionary Governments formed in Bolivia in December 1943 and in Argentina in February 1944. The refusal of recognition in these cases constituted a departure from the purely *de facto* principle which Great Britain and the United States had followed for a period of nearly twenty years. There was no allegation that recognition was withheld because of any instability of the Governments in question in a part of the world in which stability has not, as a rule, been judged by exacting standards. Recognition was denied because of doubts as to the sincerity of the anti-Axis attitude of these Governments. Probably the more appropriate procedure and one more in accordance with principle would have been to refrain from entering into diplomatic relations with governments whose attitude was regarded as inconsistent with the general interest of the United Nations engaged in a struggle for the preservation of international law. See, however, Kunz in *A.J.* vol. XXXVIII (1944), pp. 436–41. Actually, especially in the case of Great Britain, the non-recognition of the Argentine Government bore the character of a limited suspension of diplomatic relations rather than of non-recognition proper.

has often been marked by restraint and regard for the general principles of recognition of governments.[1]

1 In June 1918 the Czechoslovak National Council asked the United States for '*de facto* recognition [of the Council]...as constituting the lawful Government of that state'. The recognition extended by the United States was recognition of the Council 'as a *de facto* belligerent government clothed with proper authority to direct the military and political affairs of the Czecho-Slovaks'. The United States Government declared that it was 'prepared to enter formally into relations with the *de facto* government thus recognized for the purpose of prosecuting the war against the common enemy' (Hackworth, vol. 1, pp. 203 et seq.). Great Britain recognized in August 1918 'the unity of the three Czecho-Slovak Armies as an allied and belligerent army waging regular warfare against Austria-Hungary and Germany' as well as 'the right of the Czecho-Slovak National Council, as the supreme organ of the Czecho-Slovak national interests, and as the present trustee of the future Czecho-Slovak Government, to exercise supreme authority over this allied and belligerent army' (*Annual Register*, 1918, p. 217). The British recognition given in the same month was in the following terms: 'His Majesty's Government will...be prepared to recognize the Czecho-Slovak National Council as the supreme organ of the Czecho-Slovak movement in Allied Countries, and they will also be prepared to recognize the Czecho-Slovak Army as an organized unit operating in the Allied cause and to attach thereto a British liaison officer as soon as the need for this may arise. His Majesty's Government will at the same time be prepared to accord to the National Council political rights concerning the civil affairs of Czecho-Slovakia similar to those already accorded to the Polish National Council' (as to the latter see this note below). In June 1918 France recognized 'publicly and officially the [Czechoslovak] National Council as the governing organism of the general interests and as the just basis of the future Czecho-Slovak Government' (*History of the Peace Conference at Paris*, ed. by Temperley, vol. v (1921), p. 159). There was no recognition of the Council as a government in the detailed agreement with the United States of 14 October 1918 (for the text of which see *U.S. For. Rel.* 1918, Suppl. 1, vol. 1, pp. 813 et seq.). The British recognition, in October 1917, of the Polish National Committee was even more guarded (see Smith, vol. 1, p. 235). In October 1918 there took place the recognition of the Polish army as an autonomous and co-belligerent army under the supreme political authority of the Polish National Council. On the limited effect of that recognition see the Judgment of the Permanent Court of International Justice in the *Case concerning Certain German Interests in Polish Upper Silesia* (*P.C.I.J.* Series A, no. 7, pp. 27–9). See also Táborský, *The Czechoslovak Cause* (1944), pp. 86–9.

As to the recognition of the Czechoslovak Government in exile during the Second World War see above, p. 92.

Conspicuous caution, significant in the circumstances, marked the limited recognition which Great Britain granted in 1940 to the so-called Free French Movement. In the exchange of letters of 7 August 1940, between the British Prime Minister and General de Gaulle, the former said: 'You were good enough to give me your ideas as to the organization, employment, and conditions of service of the French volunteer force now being assembled under your command, in your capacity, in which you are now recognized by His Majesty's Government in the United Kingdom, of leader of all free Frenchmen, wherever they may be, who rally to you in support of the Allied cause' (Cmd. 6220 (1940)). On the other hand, it was in accordance with the test of effectiveness that the French Committee of National Liberation, formally set up at Algiers on 3 June 1943, was recognized by Great Britain in August 1943 'as administering those French oversea territories which acknowledge its authority and as having assumed the functions of the former French National Committee in respect

In fact, the instances of the improper use of the faculty of recognition, through so-called conditional recognition[1] or otherwise, are not typical of the normal conduct of States. But the occurrence is of sufficient importance to bring to mind the imperfections of the present position where the function of recognition is wielded by individual States.

§ 54. *The Collectivization of Recognition of Governments.* The disadvantages of the existing decentralization of the function of recognition of governments are almost the same as in the case of recognition of States. The possibility of the abuse of the power of recognition for the direct purpose of obtaining national advantages; the occurrence, whose frequency in no way diminishes its absurdity, of an authority being recognized as a government by some States but not by others;[2] the responsibility, which is often

of territories in the Levant'. Similarly, the United States recognized the Committee 'as administering those French oversea territories which acknowledge its authority'. Neither was there a substantial difference in the British recognition of the Committee 'as the body qualified to ensure the conduct of the French effort in the war within the framework of inter-allied co-operation' and the declaration of the Government of the United States that it 'takes note, with sympathy, of the desire of the Committee to be regarded as the body qualified to ensure the administration and defence of French interest', but that 'the extent to which it may be possible to give effect to this desire must...be reserved for consideration in each case as it arises'. (For the text of the Declarations see *The Times* newspaper, 27 August 1943.) No recognition of the Committee as the Government of France took place at that time. When the claim of the Committee to recognition as the Provisional Government of France was under discussion in 1944, prior to the liberation of French territory from German occupation, two factors were relevant to the issue: the first was the principle of effectiveness, which militated against recognition. The French Committee at Algiers did not at that time exercise effective control over the population of French metropolitan territory; nor, unlike the governments in exile, was it in a position to rely on legal continuity as being identical with or the constitutional successor of a previously recognized government. The second relevant factor was that as France was under enemy occupation there did not exist in France a government in a position to act freely on her behalf and that to that extent the recognition of a provisional French government as trustee of French interests would not have been improper. While some of the United Nations recognized the Committee as the Provisional Government of France, the United States was not willing to grant such recognition. In July 1944 the United States recognized the Committee as 'the *de facto* authority for the civil administration of France'.

1 See below, p. 360.

2 For an outspoken criticism of the existing position see the observations of Sir John Fischer Williams, *Aspects of Modern International Law* (1939), pp. 109–10. He says: 'The whole doctrine of recognition...is a doctrine leading to chaos rather than to order so long as there is no central machinery for determining the attitude of the world as a whole to the new developments. What greater absurdity can there be than a position in which a state exists for some of its fellow states but not for others, or in which for one state one set of people constitute the lawful and only rightful government of another state whereas for other members of the international community quite another set of persons are the lawful representatives of the state in question?'

an invidious one,[1] of determining which of two rival factions is entitled to recognition; the difficulty of forming an accurate judgment as to the facts of the situation[2]—all these factors point to a measure of collectivization of the process of recognition as a rational and desirable development. That process of collectivization of the procedure of recognition of governments may be visualized in three ways.

(*a*) *Recognition by or upon Recommendation of the Diplomatic Corps.* In so far as the proper exercise of the function of recognition depends upon the ascertainment of the principal relevant facts of the situation, namely, whether the new government wields effective power with a reasonable prospect of permanency, the diplomatic representatives in the capital of the country concerned would seem, when acting jointly, to be a useful instrument for that purpose. A measure of international co-operation in this matter has on occasions been achieved in the course of revolutions in some Latin-American countries in the form of a joint pronouncement of the diplomatic body. Thus in December 1908 the diplomatic corps in Haiti expressed the unanimous opinion that 'the situation is not opportune to recognize the present existing authority'.[3] When a revolutionary change of government took place in China in November 1924, the Chiefs of Foreign Mission expressed the unanimous opinion that the newly constituted Government of Tuan Chi-jui 'was the *de facto* government', and they authorized the senior Minister to communicate with the Chinese Minister of Foreign Affairs with the view to expressing a measure of recognition as a

1 As in the case of recognition of States so also recognition of governments has occasionally given rise to acts of retaliation. In 1867 the Mexican Government refused to admit to their functions consuls of States which recognized the overthrown Government of Maximilian and considered that such recognition put an end to the treaties between Mexico and those States (*B.F.S.P.* vol. LVIII, pp. 683–704).

2 It may be argued that outside States are as a rule under no imperative necessity to arrive at a prompt decision. When civil war is still raging, they are assisted by the principle, which is now clearly established by international law, that so long as the lawful government maintains resistance on national territory recognition of the insurgents as a *de jure* government is, as a rule, unlawful. They are helped by the rule that they may without impropriety establish such relations with the insurgent authorities as are necessary for the protection of their interests and the maintenance of ordinary commercial intercourse. Such limited intercourse cannot in the long run be a satisfactory substitute for recognition.

3 *U.S. For. Rel.* 1908, p. 444. On the part of the United States there has occasionally been reluctance to participate in such common action in order to avoid the appearance of international entanglement. In December 1943, with reference to the new revolutionary Government of Bolivia, the Advisory Committee for the Political Defence of the Western Hemisphere recommended to the countries of the western hemisphere which had declared war or broken off relations with the Axis Powers that for the duration of the war they should not recognize governments created by force without prior consultation between one another (*The Times* newspaper, 29 December 1943).

de facto, but not *de jure*, government.[1] Diplomatic practice shows instances of the revolutionary government addressing itself to the diplomatic corps on the question of recognition.

It is highly improbable that the diplomatic corps as a whole can ever be a direct instrument of recognition. It is an amorphous organism which, although occasionally acting in unison in connection with ceremonial and for the purpose of protecting diplomatic privilege, can hardly function as an organ acting on its own responsibility in matters of importance. But it may be practicable to use a standing committee of the diplomatic corps, specially set up for the purpose, as a fact-finding and advisory body to assist in the decision any international political or judicial agency endowed with jurisdiction on the subject of recognition.

(*b*) *Recognition of Governments by Collective Action of States*. International practice offers examples of collective recognition (usually by the Great Powers) and of consultation with a view to parallel, if not joint, action. These include the collective recognition of the Portuguese Government in 1911 by a number of European Powers;[2] the recognition in 1908, by the Powers signatory to the Act of Algeciras, of Moulai Hafid, Sultan of Morocco, after the violent overthrow of his predecessor Abd el Aziz;[3] and the *de facto* recognition, in December 1924, of the Chinese Government in a joint note signed by the diplomatic representatives in Pekin of Great Britain, Japan, France, Italy, Belgium, the Netherlands and the United States.[4] In a number of cases consultation took place between governments with a view to common action. This was the case in 1912 and 1913, at the instance of the United States, with regard to China;[5] in connection with the recognition of the Paraguayan Government in 1936, though on that occasion the United States declined the suggestion that recognition should be given by a joint act of the six States participating in the peace conference which followed the war between Paraguay and

1 Hackworth, vol. I, p. 316.

2 See above, p. 122. As to the attempts at concerted action of Great Britain, France and Russia with regard to the recognition of the Provisional Government of Greece in 1862 see *B.F.S.P.* vol. LVIII, p. 1037.

3 For the communication addressed on 5 January 1909 by the Dean of the Diplomatic Corps to Moulai Hafid informing him that the signatories of the Act of Algeciras 'have decided to recognize Moulay Hafid as the legitimate Sultan of Morocco and that they have charged the Dean of the Diplomatic Corps at Tangiers to communicate that recognition to the representatives of His Majesty, the Sultan', see Martens, *N.R.T.* 3rd ser. vol. II, p. 15. See also *U.S. For. Rel.* 1909, p. 433, and ibid. 1908, pp. 646–55. And see *B.F.S.P.* vol. CII, pp. 932–8.

4 Hackworth, vol. I, p. 317.

5 Ibid. p. 315.

Bolivia;[1] and in connection with the recognition of the Bolivian Government in the same year.[2] The difficult question of recognizing in 1915 the revolutionary Government of General Carranza in Mexico was settled as the result of previous consultation and concerted action of the United States, Brazil, Chile, Argentina, Bolivia, Uruguay and Guatemala, which extended *de facto* recognition on 19 October 1915.[3] The recognition of the Provisional Polish Government in Warsaw was the result of the decision of Great Britain, the United States and Russia reached in 1945 at the Conferences of Crimea and Potsdam.[4] These instances show in a rudimentary fashion the possibilities of collective action in the matter of recognition. Collective acts of recognition by groups of States are possible independently of the existence of an universal international organization of States, but it is only within and through some such organization that the function of recognition can be properly exercised in accordance with its true nature and free from the inconsistencies and abuses inherent in the present position. In fact, the idea of membership of a comprehensive international organization presupposes and calls for some collective machinery of recognition of governments. For it is clear that after a revolutionary change in government has taken place in a State which is a member of the organization there must be some organ to determine whether the new authority can be regarded as properly representing the State in question within the international organization. The rational development of the procedure of recognition would lie in a provision in the Charter of the Organization to the effect that recognition by the Organization shall be binding upon all its members.[5] Assuming the

1 Hackworth, vol. I, p. 272. The following significant passage occurs in the instructions from the Department of State to the Embassy in Brazil: 'From every point of view it seems better that recognition be accorded by each of the governments involved as an independent act of individual sovereignty.' 2 Ibid. p. 226.

3 See *U.S. For. Rel.* 1915, p. 771. See also Finch in *A.J.* vol. X (1911), pp. 357–67. As to the consultations on the subject between Great Britain and the United States see the statements in the House of Commons on 2 and 8 November 1915 (*H.C. Debates*, vol. LXXV, cols. 482 and 1042 respectively). 4 See below, p. 173.

5 The recommendations of a meeting of a number of international lawyers in London in July 1943 provided, *inter alia*, that 'a new government to which recognition *de jure* has been granted by a certain number of governments shall be allowed to apply for general recognition before an international authority having competence for that purpose, such decision to be binding on all States' (*A.J.* vol. XXXVIII (1944), p. 294). The recommendation is open to criticism on the general ground that it leaves room for individual recognition and also that it fails to consider the effect of an adverse decision of the international authority upon individual recognitions already given. In case of an adverse decision, given in conformity with the legal principles governing recognition, it would follow that the individual acts of recognition have been without legal foundation and must therefore be regarded as void.

universality of the Organization, this would mean the solution of the problem of recognition of governments—a solution which, if it is to be commensurate with the magnitude of the task, would necessitate the creation of a permanent organ of the Organization, such as a standing Committee of the General Assembly or of the Security Council combining a high degree of authority with the faculty of expeditious action. The incorporation of some such machinery in the Charter of the United Nations must be regarded as one of the principal objects of its contemplated revision.[1]

(*c*) *Determination by International Judicial Authority*. As the function of recognition of governments consists in the exercise of a legal judgment as to the existence of the requisite conditions of governmental capacity and as the ascertainment of facts falls properly within the province of judicial activity, the development of the procedure of recognition might, in theory, take the form of the exercise of that function by the highest international judicial authority. By a general international treaty States could agree to accept the decision on the subject pronounced by the court at the instance of the authority claiming to be the government. However, the political implications of recognition as well as the necessity for expeditious action would seem to favour the exercise of that function by a political organ subject to the assistance of the court on such matters of law as may be relevant to the issue.

Any improvement in the procedure of recognition in the direction of its collectivization must depend, to a large extent, upon the measure of agreement on the substantive law of recognition and, in particular, on the tests of recognition to be applied by the political or judicial international organs. It is therefore convenient to define once more, by way of a summary of conclusions reached in these chapters, both the nature of the function of recognition and its wider significance as a problem of legal philosophy both in the international and municipal spheres.

§ 55. *Conclusions—Recognition of Governments and the Right to Government by Consent.* From the apparent divergence of practice and from the diversity of tests of recognition of governments reviewed in the preceding chapters there emerge two principal conclusions:

The first conclusion which may be drawn from the consideration of the various tests of recognition is that all of them—whether based on the requirement of effectiveness or otherwise—have, as a rule, been followed in pursuance of generally applicable principles laid down by international

1 Articles 108 and 109 of the Charter.

law. States do not claim to be entitled to act in this matter by exclusive reference to considerations of national interest and convenience. Like recognition of States, recognition of governments can properly be regarded as part of international law. There is no warrant for confining it to the sphere of international politics. As recognition of States consists in a declaration, which is constitutive of far-reaching legal effects, that the community in question possesses the requisite conditions of statehood, so also the recognition of a government arising out of the abnormal circumstances of a revolutionary change amounts to a declaration that the new authority fulfils the requisite conditions of governmental capacity. Thus conceived, recognition consists in the ascertainment, in conformity with a legal duty, of an existing fact. To use that fact-finding function as an occasion for promoting the interests of the recognizing State is to misuse the power of recognition and to deny to the State affected the right of independence.

Secondly, it has been shown that, among the various tests of recognition, that of effectiveness—either in its literal meaning or as evidenced by adequately expressed popular approval—has become the predominant standard of recognition. A government enjoying the obedience of the bulk of the population must be regarded as representing the State and as such, to be entitled to recognition. Although the test of willingness to fulfil international obligations has been widely adopted in practice—though not as widely as the test of effectiveness—it has been shown here to be unsatisfactory in many respects and unrelated to the true purpose of recognition.

While the test of effectiveness has been most prominently and consistently associated with the practice of States in the matter of recognition of governments, there remains unsolved the question which conception of effectiveness is to form the basis of the law of the future: effectiveness pure and simple, or effectiveness as evidenced by freely expressed popular approval? Both have been widely followed for nearly a century and a half, and although the latter suffered an eclipse during the period of the rise of authoritarian regimes, there is little to suggest that that setback was more than a temporary adaptation to what must be regarded as a retrogressive and transient phase in the constitutional history of nations. Undoubtedly, what has been called the test of subsequent legitimation is open to some searching questions: Is not the insistence, as a condition of subsequent legitimation, on a manifestation of the will of the people under safeguards accepted in democratic countries tantamount to the assertion of democratic legitimacy as distinguished from monarchic legitimacy? Does it not, in fact, amount to intervention? Unless international law should provide means for ensuring the reality of the democratic idea not only in form but also in substance, is there any justification for the protection of the democratic system of government by way of a rule sanctioning refusal of recognition to revolutionary dictatorships not confirmed by a free popular vote? If the inalienable right of man to government by consent were thus to become part of the enforceable law of mankind, would not mere refusal of recognition be an inadequate and illusory way of enforcing it?

These are weighty questions. Yet it is probable that they do not go to the root of the matter. They ignore the fact that that particular test of recognition has already to a large extent become part of international law. It was acted upon—probably we are justified in saying that it *has been* acted upon—for a long period by Great Britain and the United States, the two countries which have made the greatest contribution to the development of the law of recognition. To that limited extent the right of man to government by consent has become, through the doctrine of recognition, part of international law. Where, in solemn declarations, such as that enshrined in the Atlantic Charter,[1] made in the course of the Second World War, States have proclaimed the principle that peoples must be left free to determine their own form of government, those pronouncements have been subsequently qualified by the insistence that such freedom of choice implies not only effective freedom of decision in adopting a form of government, but also in the continuing freedom of choice as a permanent principle of the national constitution. Thus interpreted the declarations are in accord with a prominent feature of the law of recognition of governments as applied in the past.

Moreover, these questions ignore the fundamental nature of the relation between the law of recognition and the wider jurisprudential problem of the validity of the positive law within the State. What is the legal—as distinguished from the moral and political—foundation of the duty to obey the law within the State? The legal source of validity of any particular legal rule as enacted by the State or ascertained by courts is the constitution of the State. The constitution is, in law, the irreducible source of legal obligation. Beyond that legal enquiry cannot go. There is no legal answer to the question why the constitution should be obeyed—unless it be reliance on the fact that it is generally and actually obeyed. In the final

1 In the Joint Declaration of 14 August 1941 of the President of the United States and the Prime Minister of Great Britain—a Declaration commonly referred to as the Atlantic Charter—expression was given to the principle of respect for 'the right of all peoples to choose the form of government under which they will live'.

analysis the validity of the law is grounded in the existence of an order, based on force, which is actually in operation. Law is what is in fact obeyed and enforced as an external rule of conduct. But is it not possible to endow the primary source of legal obligation with an authority transcending the physical phenomenon of social reality within the State? Some such result may be achieved if the juridical basis of the validity of the municipal legal order is, not its effectiveness pure and simple—an effectiveness partaking of the nature of a physical phenomenon—but its recognition by a higher and more comprehensive legal order.[1] On that hypothesis there is a legal duty to obey the constitution because it is recognized by international society as the penultimate source of legal obligation—by international society acting not through the disjointed and essentially anarchical procedure of individual recognition, but through proper organs impartially ascertaining the existence of the requisite test of recognition. Admittedly, the answer to the question why a constitution recognized by international society must be obeyed cannot, in the nature of things, be of a legal character. Yet there is an advantage, which is a fundamental one, in that change of emphasis. It lies in shifting the source of the obligation from the reality of force within the State to a juridical act performed by the society of States acting in its collective capacity.

However, this advantage must in the long run be merely formal if that juridical act of international society is no more than a regularization of force actually in operation within the State, i.e. if it is based on effectiveness only. That contingency is avoided if, in accordance with substantial British and American practice in the matter of recognition, effectiveness is interpreted as government with the consent, adequately proved, of the people. It has been shown that the difficulties in the application of that test are not of a permanent nature. They are a matter of machinery. In an international society in which the right of man to political freedom and to government by consent will become part of the law of nations, recognition will be denied—in addition to other means of enforcement—to a dictatorial regime which has come to power by way of revolution and which, even if to all appearances effective, declines to submit its rule to the test of clearly expressed popular approval. That consummation may be far off. Yet we are not at liberty to regard it as lying in the infinite future. In fact, we are entitled to say that in so far as effectiveness based on and evidenced by the

1 In Professor Kelsen's *Das Problem der Souveränität und die Theorie des Völkerrechts* (1920)—a work whose classical stature will grow with the passage of years—there will be found not only the most authoritative exposition of the jurisprudential basis, as outlined in the text above, of the validity of the municipal legal order, but also, somewhat tentatively, of the relevance of its recognition by international law (pp. 235–41).

consent of the governed has become part of international practice, the right of man to government by consent has, to that extent, become part of international law. That connection is revealing in its significance inasmuch as it brings to mind the ultimate place of the law of recognition in the system of jurisprudence. It is independent of the significant, though still indefinite and elastic, acknowledgment of 'human rights and fundamental freedoms' in the various provisions of the Charter of the United Nations. Of these rights and freedoms the right to government by consent is not the least fundamental. We are not likely to do justice to a weighty issue by the plausible retort that the insistence on an international plane and through the medium of the weapon of recognition based on the test of democratic legitimacy constitutes intervention in denial of the self-determination and of the independence of nations. There is no self-determination and no independence under the rule of tyranny, and there is no intervention, except in a sense dangerously approaching an abuse of language, when, by means of procedure which is international and disinterested in character, safeguards are provided for ensuring freedom from a rule of violence which may be more destructive of national independence than any foreign intervention.[1]

During and after the Second World War the requirement of freely expressed consent to a free form of government regained its place as a test of recognition.[2] This has not been an *ad hoc* device adopted for coping with novel situations in a disturbed world. Although it was abandoned

1 For an eloquent elaboration of this theme see Sir James Mackintosh's *A View of the Reign of James II* (1835), pp. 300, 301. 'What foreign enemy', he asked, 'could do a greater wrong to a community than the ruler who would reduce them to hold these interests by no higher tenure than the duration of his pleasure?' (ibid.).

2 When, in July 1941, Great Britain recognized the Czechoslovak Government in London, this was made subject to the understanding that that Government would, after the war, 'at once submit to the regulations of a democratic Czechoslovak constitution'. The attitude of Great Britain and the United States to the question of new governments in liberated parts of Europe after the Second World War was, in general, based on the same principle. When, in July 1945, the United States and Great Britain recognized the Provisional Government of Poland, they did so after receiving formal and solemn assurances that that Government would submit itself to the test of a national election based on an universal suffrage and a secret vote. In the Report of the Potsdam Conference in August 1945, the United States, Great Britain, and Russia noted that 'the Polish Provisional Government, in accordance with the decisions of the Crimea Conference, has agreed to the holding of free and unfettered elections as soon as possible on the basis of universal suffrage and secret ballot'. In the course of that year Great Britain and the United States, alongside of other States, refused to recognize the Governments of Bulgaria, Greece, Hungary, Roumania, and Austria until satisfactory free elections had been held in these countries or satisfactory assurances had been given of the intention to hold such elections. The following communication sent on 21 April 1945 by Great Britain to the Bulgarian Prime

for a time in a period of ascendancy of forms of government based on force only, it is a test of recognition deeply rooted in the past. It is pre-eminently capable of application within the orbit of that legal conception of recognition of governments which has been shown here to be most in accordance with the practice of States and with the principles of international law.

Minister may be cited as an illustration: 'His Majesty's Government have had under consideration the announced intention of the Bulgarian Government to hold general elections in the near future. While His Majesty's Government would welcome elections which gave full and free opportunity for the expression of the opinion of the Bulgarian people, they are unable to believe that such an opportunity will result from elections held under the present Bulgarian electoral law and in the conditions now obtaining in Bulgaria. They consider that the form of this law is designed to operate to the advantage of the Government now in power and to the disadvantage of its opponents. Very recent concessions which have been made are proof that freedom of expression was previously denied to the opposition and His Majesty's Government can have no confidence that these tardy concessions are in any sense adequate. They have now also received reports which they consider reliable that persistent efforts have been made to intimidate supporters of the opposition and to influence voters in a manner entirely inconsistent with democratic principles. I am accordingly instructed to inform you that His Majesty's Government will be unable to recognize as democratic or representative any Bulgarian Government formed as a result of elections held under these conditions' (*The Times* newspaper, 22 April 1945). The United States sent a similar note. On 21 August 1945, the Foreign Secretary declared in the House of Commons that the United Kingdom did not recognize the Governments which had been set up in Bulgaria, Hungary, and Roumania on the ground that they did not represent the majority of the people and that they amounted to a substitution of one kind of totalitarianism for another. See also above, p. 138, n. 3, as to Greece. And see the *Report of the Allied Mission to observe the Greek election*, issued in Athens on 10 April 1946 (Cmd. 6812) and, in the words of the report, 'made after analysis of factual information gathered in all parts of Greece by 240 trained observation teams throughout the period of pre-election campaigning'. The report constitutes a significant example of the possibility, as previously shown in the practice of territorial plebiscites, of an international supervision and guarantee of the freedom of expression of the national will. The development of a machinery of this nature must be regarded as one of the most important constructive tasks in the field of international organization.

Part Three

RECOGNITION OF BELLIGERENCY AND OF INSURGENCY

Chapter XII

THE PRINCIPLES OF RECOGNITION OF BELLIGERENCY

§ 56. *The Duty of Recognition of Belligerency.* The basic principle governing the recognition of States and governments applies also to recognition of belligerency, i.e. to the declaration, express or implied, that hostilities waged between two communities, of which one is not or, possibly,[1] both are not sovereign States, are of such character and scope as to entitle the parties to be treated as belligerents engaged in a war in the sense ordinarily attached to that term by international law. The essence of that principle is that recognition is not in the nature of a grant of a favour or a matter of unfettered political discretion, but a duty imposed by the facts of the situation. Given the required conditions of belligerency as laid down by international law, the contesting parties[2] are legally entitled to be treated as if they are engaged in a war waged by two sovereign States. This view is accepted by what is probably the majority of writers. It has the support both of the practice of governments and of considerations of principle. The law cannot refuse to acknowledge the legal consequences of facts which are not in themselves unlawful and which, as between sovereign States, normally give rise to legal rights and obligations. Armed rebellions and civil wars which create the occasion for recognition of belligerency are not acts or situations prohibited by international law.

There is general agreement as to the nature of the conditions which impose the duty of recognition of belligerency—or which, according to

1 See below, p. 205.

2 The question will be examined below (see pp. 193–9) whether the lawful government is entitled to exercise belligerent rights without any act of recognition on the part of third States. For there is room for the view that these are bound to acquiesce in the exercise of belligerent rights thus unilaterally asserted—with the further consequence that by so doing they automatically concede belligerent rights to the insurgents.

others, justify recognition of belligerency.[1] These conditions are as follows: first, there must exist within the State an armed conflict of a general (as distinguished from a purely local) character;[2] secondly, the insurgents must occupy and administer a substantial portion of national territory; thirdly, they must conduct the hostilities in accordance with the rules of war and through organized armed forces acting under a responsible authority; fourthly, there must exist circumstances which make it necessary for outside States to define their attitude by means of recognition of belligerency. Recognition of belligerency is in essence a declaration ascertaining the existence of these conditions of fact.

To grant recognition of belligerency when these conditions are absent is to commit an international wrong as against the lawful government. The same applies to the premature recognition of belligerency. To refuse to recognize the insurgents as belligerents although these conditions are present is to act in a manner which finds no warrant in international law. The fact that the parent State has recognized or treated the insurgents as belligerents constitutes a strong presumption that there are present the first three conditions referred to above; these, when combined with the fourth requirement, impose upon outside States the duty of recognition.

Of these principles the only one which is generally admitted is that relating to the duty owed by outside States to the parent State not to grant recognition when the four conditions referred to above, or any one of them, are absent. Others are controversial. They will be examined here by reference to the not inconsiderable practice of States as well as to the general principles of recognition and of international law.

So far as outside States are concerned, the question of the duty of recognition arises, it is believed,[3] only in relation to insurgents. It will be submitted that the lawful government may exercise belligerent rights at its option, and that, so long as it does so in conformity with international law, outside States are under a duty to submit to the normal incidence of their operation—such incidence including the obligation to treat the insurgents in the same manner as the lawful government, i.e. as belligerents.

§ 57. *The Practice of States in the Matter of Recognition of Belligerency. (a) The British Practice.* On the face of it, the practice of States seems to

1 See below, pp. 240–3, for a survey of authorities on the subject.

2 For examples of refusal of recognition on account of the absence of that condition see below, p. 271. In 1894, during the revolution in Brazil, the Great Powers refused to recognize the belligerency of the insurgent forces of Admiral de Mello on the ground, mainly, that they were limited to units of the navy. See *R.G.* vol. I (1894), pp. 53–7, 161–7.

3 See below, p. 193.

give little guidance on the subject. This is so, in the first instance, because of the relative rarity of unequivocal instances of recognition of belligerency. In contradistinction to recognition of States and of governments, recognition of belligerency does not, as a rule,[1] take place by means of a formal declaration to that effect. It occurs either through the express adoption or the actual pursuance of an attitude of neutrality identical with that obtaining in ordinary wars—an attitude of which the essence is impartiality of treatment and submission to measures of interference necessitated by the conduct of the war. In particular, acquiescence in the exercise of the right of blockade may, in the absence of indications to the contrary, not improperly be regarded as recognition of belligerency.

A formal proclamation of neutrality, as distinguished from limited municipal enactments or announcements enjoining upon individuals an attitude of restraint and non-interference,[2] constitutes an unequivocal mode of recognition of belligerency. Such a formal proclamation of neutrality, clearly coupled with the intention to recognize belligerency, was issued by Great Britain on 13 May 1861, during the American Civil War.[3] In this case recognition of belligerency was regarded by the British

1 Recognition of belligerency *expressis verbis* is in the nature of a rare exception. We find, in May 1891, the British representative informing the Marquis of Salisbury that the Government of Bolivia recognized the Chilean insurgents as belligerents (*State Papers*, vol. XCV (1892), *Chile*, no. 1). In 1869 the Government of Peru announced that it 'recognized as a belligerent the political party engaged in a struggle for the independence of Cuba' (Rougier, *Les guerres civiles et le droit des gens* (1903), p. 400). See below, pp. 403–5, on implied recognition.

2 See, for example, the proclamations of the President of the United States of 12 June 1895 (*B.F.S.P.* vol. LXXXVII, p. 733) and 27 July 1896 (ibid. vol. LXXXVIII, p. 844) calling attention to the disturbances in Cuba and to the neutrality laws of the United States; or the British announcement of 1937 calling attention to the provisions of the Foreign Enlistment Act as applying to the Spanish Civil War (see below, pp. 235, 273).

3 In view of its importance the text of the opening passages of the proclamation may be usefully reproduced here (*B.F.S.P.* vol. LI, p. 165):

'Whereas we are happily at Peace with all Sovereigns, Powers, and States:

'And whereas hostilities have unhappily commenced between the Government of the United States of America and certain States styling themselves the Confederate States of America:

'And whereas we, being at Peace with the Government of the United States, have declared our Royal determination to maintain a strict and impartial neutrality in the contest between the said contesting Parties:

'We, therefore, have thought fit, by and with the advice of our Privy Council, to issue this Royal Proclamation:

'And we do hereby strictly charge and command all our loving subjects to observe a strict neutrality in and during the aforesaid hostilities, and to abstain from violating or contravening either the laws and statutes of the realm in this behalf or the law of nations in relation thereto, as they will answer to the contrary at their peril.'

There followed a textual reproduction of most of the provisions of the Foreign Enlistment Act.

Government as the inevitable consequence of the recognition of the belligerency of the Confederate States by the Government of the United States—a recognition expressed by implication in the Presidential proclamation of a blockade of some of the ports in the disaffected States 'in pursuance of the laws of the United States, and of the law of nations in such case provided'.[1] In fact, British Governments and Law Officers of the Crown on numerous occasions described the proclamation by the lawful government of a blockade *jure gentium* against the insurgents as a recognition of a state of belligerency.[2]

In many cases of what may properly be regarded as recognition of belligerency there was no formal declaration of neutrality.[3] Thus there was no such proclamation in the case of the Greek revolution in 1821 and in the subsequent years.[4] Moreover, the events connected with the Greek struggle show that even the explicit announcement of the intention to preserve impartiality does not necessarily amount to a recognition of belligerency. A proclamation was issued on 6 June 1823,[5] calling attention to the provisions of the Foreign Enlistment Act and announcing the intention of the Government to observe strict neutrality in the contest, but it is clear from the conduct of the authorities and from Opinions of the Law Officers delivered at the time that that measure was not intended to and did not imply recognition of belligerent rights on the high seas.[6] It was only at the end of 1824, after the struggle had been in progress for some time, that the British Government in its declarations and despatches disclosed an attitude amounting to a recognition of belligerency with

1 *B.F.S.P.* vol. LI, p. 185. And see below, pp. 195, 200, 203.

2 See below, pp. 202 et seq.

3 A declaration of neutrality was issued on 7 June 1821, in connection with the Greek rebellion, by the Senate of the Ionian Islands at the suggestion of the High Commission (*B.F.S.P.* vol. VIII, p. 1282).

4 See below, pp. 179, 188.

5 *B.F.S.P.* vol. x, p. 648. See also the Proclamation by the Ionian Government of 17 November 1824, communicating the Greek announcement of the establishment of a blockade of the ports of Patras and Lepanto by a naval force 'consisting of Ships regularly commissioned, and according to the Law of Nations', and ordering all ships bearing the Ionian flag 'to respect the same in the most strict and exact manner' (ibid. vol. XII, p. 304). But when in the same year the Provisional Government of Greece issued an order to the effect that ships of European nationals chartered by the Turkish Government shall 'be attacked, burnt or sunk, together with their Crews, by the Ships of the Greek Fleet or by any other armed Greek Force that may fall in with them', the reply of the Ionian Government was to order the commander-in-chief to seize and detain all Greek vessels so long as the offending Order had not been revoked (ibid. vol. XI, p. 829).

6 For a collection of some of the relevant documents and comment thereon see Smith, vol. I, pp. 282–94.

all its implications. Thus, we find Canning saying in a despatch of 31 December 1824 that 'we have openly and uniformly, from the time when the Greek struggle assumed the shape of a regular contest on the sea, professed an impartial Neutrality between the two belligerent Parties, having allowed to each the free exercise of belligerent rights, such as the Law of Nations warrants—and specifically we have expressed our determination to respect the blockades of either party, when instituted and maintained according to the practice of civilized War'.[1] There was in that statement a distinct element of exaggeration which Canning found it necessary to explain. He referred to the fact that 'we denied the validity of certain of their blockades, on account either of want of due notice, or of the insufficiency of the force appropriated to maintain them'.[2] Nevertheless, from this and other pronouncements[3] there could be unmistakably deduced the intention, at that stage, to grant belligerent rights and a clear perception of the significance of recognition of belligerency.

A similar development occurred during the war of independence of the Latin-American Republics in 1813 and the following years. No express recognition of belligerency or proclamation of neutrality took place. At the same time a series of measures were adopted showing the intention to assume an attitude of impartiality. Thus in November 1817 a proclamation was issued forbidding British subjects to serve in the armed forces of either side in South America;[4] in 1819 the Foreign Enlistment Act was passed;[5] in the same year Spain and her colonies were put on an equal footing in the matter of the prohibition of the export of munitions.[6] It was only in the later stages of the struggle, between 1821 and 1823, that the attitude of neutrality became articulate and coupled with a measure of recognition of

1 Ibid. p. 295. On 15 July 1822, the Marquis of Londonderry announced in the House of Commons that instructions had been issued to the Government of the Ionian Islands that the strictest neutrality be preserved in all transactions between the Greeks and the Turks (*Parl. Deb.* vol. VII (1822), col. 1653). On 1 December 1824, he wrote to M. Rodios, Secretary to the Greek Government: 'With respect to the Contest between Spain and the several Countries of Spanish America, Great Britain has professed and maintained a strict neutrality; and the like neutrality has been observed by Great Britain in the Contests now raging in Greece. The Belligerent Rights of the Greeks have been uniformly respected' (*B.F.S.P.* vol. XII, p. 902). For a suggestion that recognition of belligerency was merely preliminary to the recognition of independence, described as an act of intervention pure and simple, see *Letters by Historicus on Some Questions of International Law* (1863), p. 6.

2 *B.F.S.P.* vol. XII, p. 902.

3 See below, p. 188.

4 *B.F.S.P.* vol. VI, p. 488.

5 59 Geo. III, c. 69.

6 *B.F.S.P.* vol. VI, p. 519. In February 1823, by a further Order-in-Council (ibid. vol. X, p. 646), the export of munitions was permitted to both parties.

the belligerent rights of the insurgents on the high seas.[1] But it is indicative of the gradualness of the development of the notion of belligerency and of its consequences that in *De Wutz* v. *Hendricks*, a case decided in 1824 and arising out of attempts to raise a loan for the Greek rebels, Best C. J. was of the opinion that 'it was contrary to the law of nations...for persons in England to enter into engagements to raise money to support the subjects of a government in amity with our own, in hostilities against their government'.[2]

The cases of Greece and of the Latin-American Republics are typical of the absence of formality in the procedure of recognition of belligerency. Alongside these major examples of recognition of belligerency, British practice shows numerous instances in which, without a proclamation of neutrality having been issued, an attitude of neutrality was in fact assumed or belligerent rights granted in part or in full or in which the advice of the Law Officers was tendered to that effect. Thus, to give some examples in the period from 1865 to 1885, we find that a 'state of hostilities' existed and, in the words of the Queen's Advocate, was 'recognized in the correspondence of Her Majesty's Government to exist, in the Bonny River, which would invest the rival chiefs with the rights of belligerents'[3]—an exotic, but significant, example. We find recognition of the belligerent right of blockade and of other war measures of the Venezuelan insurgents and of the lawful government in 1871 and 1879,[4] of the Uruguayan insurgents in 1871,[5] of the Dominican rebels against Spain in 1864,[6] of the insurgents in Haiti in 1876, 1883 and 1884,[7] and of the Colombian revolutionaries in 1885.[8] We see the British Government adopting, in principle, the same attitude with regard to the Spanish revolution in 1874,[9] and in the case of the exiled Kerais fighting against Japan in 1879.[10] In some of these cases the recognition of insurgent belligerent rights was described as incidental to the recognition of rights of blockade proclaimed by the

1 It is maintained by some—see, for example, Smith, vol. I, p. 119—that recognition of belligerency was granted by implication as the result of the single act of extending to Spanish metropolitan territory the prohibition of the export of munitions which hitherto applied only to the rebellious States. As is pointed out elsewhere (see below, pp. 403–5), recognition of belligerency is a matter of intention and cannot be implied from any single measure. It is possible for equal treatment of both parties in the matter of munitions or for a declaration rendering applicable the Foreign Enlistment Act to be combined with a clear refusal of recognition of belligerency.

2 S.C. 9 Moore, 586.

3 See below, pp. 205, 206.

4 See below, pp. 202, 208.

5 See below, p. 204.

6 See F.O. 83/2373 and Smith, vol. I, p. 319.

7 See below, pp. 203, 211–13.

8 See below, p. 205.

9 See below, pp. 208, 209.

10 See below, p. 214.

lawful government—a kind of recognition which is a frequent phenomenon in British practice.[1]

(*b*) *The Practice of the United States.* As in the case of Great Britain, the practice of the United States shows only few examples of express recognition of belligerency. During the revolutions in South America directed against the Spanish rule there was no express recognition of belligerency by means of a proclamation of neutrality. In September 1815 President Madison issued, under the neutrality laws, a proclamation in respect of hostile expeditions against Spain, but that step did not in itself constitute recognition of belligerency. Neither was such recognition implied in the decision of the Government of the United States to admit into its ports the merchant vessels of the rebellious provinces.[2] As events progressed, the idea of neutrality took more definite shape. In July 1817 we find an acknowledgment of neutrality and of the equal belligerent status of both parties. Referring to the claim of Spain to impose upon foreign Powers conditions applicable to a mere state of rebellion against the constitutional authority, the United States Secretary of State said: 'This pretension has not been acceded to by this government, which has considered the contest in the light of a civil war, in which the parties are equal.'[3] In his Message of 2 December 1817, President Monroe stated: 'Through every stage of the conflict the United States has maintained an impartial neutrality.... They have regarded the contest not in the light of an ordinary insurrection or rebellion, but as a civil war between parties nearly equal, having as to neutral powers equal rights.'[4] Relying upon this and similar declarations, the United States courts repeatedly refused to consider as criminal captures made by the rebellious governments; they regarded them as captures *jure belli*.[5]

In fact, the practice of the United States in connection with the wars of independence of the Latin-American States shows that the conception of belligerency of bodies other than States did not spring up at once in the

1 See below, pp. 194–9.

2 'There is no principle of the law of nations which requires us to exclude from our ports the subjects of a foreign power, in a state of insurrection against their own government' (Instructions to the United States Treasury, as cited by Moore, vol. I, p. 170). See also the Note of the Secretary of State to the Spanish Minister of 19 January 1816 (Manning, *Diplomatic Correspondence of the United States concerning the Independence of the Latin-American Nations*, vol. I (Parts I and II) (1925), pp. 20, 21), rejecting the Spanish claim for the exclusion of the flag of the provinces which had risen in revolt.

3 Manning, op. cit. p. 43.

4 Moore, vol. I, p. 173.

5 See *United States* v. *Palmer*, (1818) 3 Wheat. 610, 643; *The Divina Pastora*, (1819) 4 Wheat. 52, 63.

form in which we know it to-day. It began with the admission of rebel merchant vessels into ports; it continued with the admission of their war vessels and prizes; gradually, it assumed the form of a grant of equal and impartial treatment (subject, at the outset, to existing treaty obligations); the deliberate concession of belligerent rights to both sides on the high seas was the last stage in the process of the hardening of the conception of recognition of belligerency. It was only in the later stages of the contest that, although there had been no express grant of belligerency by a proclamation of neutrality or otherwise, the intention to treat the rebels as belligerents in all respects was given clear expression.[1] The proclamation of neutrality in 1836 in the course of the Texan rebellion against Mexico is perhaps the nearest approach to a formal recognition of belligerency by the United States.[2] On the other hand, the practice of the United States shows numerous instances of express refusal of recognition.[3] In some cases, like that of the Cuban insurrection, the refusal of recognition formed for a number of years the theme of repeated and elaborate pronouncements which throw instructive light on the subject.[4]

§ 58. *The Reasons for the Relative Infrequency of Recognition of Belligerency.* Notwithstanding the fact that recognition of belligerency and of belligerent rights has been more frequent than the absence of formality in the relevant pronouncements seems to suggest, it has not become the usual concomitant of civil wars. It constitutes an exception rather than the rule. The explanation of this phenomenon lies, first, in the fact that the conditions warranting recognition of belligerency are seldom realized to their full extent. While rebellions and revolutions, with resulting changes of governments, are a frequent occurrence, prolonged civil wars are comparatively rare. Even when the civil war is of considerable magnitude and duration, one of the

1 This explains, for instance, the divergencies in the statements of the date of the recognition of the belligerency of the South American Republics by the United States. Lord Russell in his Note to the United States Minister in 1865 assumed that date to be 1815—apparently in reliance upon President Madison's proclamation relating to hostile expeditions; Fauchille, no. 200, gives 1816 as the proper date; Moore, vol. I, p. 173, attaches decisive importance to President Monroe's Annual Message of December 1817 in which he refers to the 'impartial neutrality' of the United States and to the fact that 'they have regarded the contest not in the light of an ordinary insurrection or rebellion, but as a civil war between parties nearly equal, having as to neutral powers equal rights'.

2 Moore, vol. I, p. 176.

3 See, for example, as to Colombia (1885), Haiti (1889) and Brazil (1893), ibid. pp. 200–2.

4 Ibid. pp. 192–200. For a survey of the more recent practice of the United States which shows instances of recognition of belligerency see Hackworth, vol. I, pp. 319–27.

several requirements of recognition may be missing. Thus the rebels, although powerful and persistent, may not possess sufficient cohesion to establish governmental agencies of some stability. The successive Presidential Messages during the two Cuban insurrections bring out with particular clarity[1] this aspect of the matter. The refusal of France and of other Powers to recognize the belligerency of the Polish insurgents in 1863 was due to the same cause.[2]

Secondly, although other conditions may be present, recognition may be unjustified and incapable of being the subject of a valid claim for the reason that the conflict does not affect outside States to a degree warranting recognition. This was the position, for instance—so far as Great Britain and the United States were concerned—in the case of the Polish rebellion against Russia[2] in 1831 and of the Hungarian revolution in 1848.[3] That there was no lack of general interest on the part of Great Britain in the fate of the Polish insurrection may be seen from the continued British efforts to find a solution of the conflict in accordance with humanity and existing treaties. Similarly, the animated correspondence between the United States and the representative of the Emperor of Austria arising out of the sending of an American agent to Hungary suggests that the absence of recognition of belligerency was not due to mere disinterestedness.[4] But there was absent in these cases such direct interest as would make it necessary to define the mutual relations of the parties concerned by means of recognition of belligerency. This was not the position with regard to the contiguous countries on the continent of Europe.[5]

1 'The insurgents hold no town or city; have no established seat of government; they have no prize courts; no organization for the receiving and collecting of revenue....The existence of a legislature representing any popular constituency is more than doubtful. In the uncertainty that hangs around the entire insurrection there is no palpable evidence of an election, of any delegated authority, or of any government outside the limits of the camps occupied from day to day by roving companies of insurgent troops': President Grant's Message of 13 June 1870 (Moore, vol. I, p. 195). 'The mere existence of contending armed bodies, and their occasional conflicts, do not constitute war in the sense referred to': President Cleveland's Message of 2 December 1895 (ibid. p. 196).

2 For this reason there may be some difficulty in accepting Professor Wehberg's statement to the effect that there existed all the conditions required for recognition of the belligerency of the Polish insurgents (*Hague Recueil*, vol. LXIII (1938) (i), p. 23). See also Geffcken in *R.I.* vol. XXIII (1891), p. 578.

3 For the details of which see Wehberg, loc. cit. pp. 25, 26, and Moore, vol. I, pp. 218–34. It appears that no government recognized either the Polish or the Hungarian insurgents.

4 Moore, loc. cit.

5 When in May 1831 Polish troops crossed into Austrian territory, the Austrian Government handed over to Russia their guns and war material. Russia's attitude during the Hungarian revolution in 1848 took the form of direct intervention.

Finally, as the Spanish Civil War of 1936–9 showed, notwithstanding the apparent existence of all the requisite conditions, there may be no room for recognition for the reason that the struggle, although primarily partaking of the character of a civil war, has acquired the characteristics and the significance of an international contest.[1]

§ 59. *The 'Tortious' Aspect of Recognition of Belligerency.* In addition to the relative rarity of recognition of belligerency, another factor has tended to blur the comprehension of what is believed to be its principal aspect, namely, the legal right to recognition of belligerency and the legal duty to grant it. The discussion of the problem of recognition of belligerency has been concentrated mainly on what may be called the 'tortious' aspect of recognition, i.e. on the question when recognition may be granted without committing a wrongful act in relation to the lawful government. The recognition of the belligerency of the Confederate States by Great Britain in 1861 has been the most widely discussed case of recognition of belligerency. It has been responsible, more than any other similar event, for the development and formulation of the law on the subject. Attempts at justification or condemnation of the British action underlay much of subsequent references to that matter by writers and governments. The question was discussed almost exclusively from the point of view of the right of Great Britain to recognize the belligerency of the Confederate States without committing a breach of international law against the United States. On the part of the writers in the United States there has been, for obvious reasons, no inclination to stress the legal right of insurgents to recognition; on the part of the British writers there has been some tendency to emphasize the element of absolute discretion in the matter both in order to refute the American complaint of unlawful action and as a justification for the British refusal to agree to the arbitration of the American claim to damages on account of alleged premature recognition of belligerency.

However, while the emphasis placed on the question of the right of outside States to recognize the belligerency of insurgents without committing a wrong against the lawful government tended to obscure the more fundamental question of the true nature of the function of recognition, it had the merit, at the same time, of clearly defining the objective conditions justifying the grant of recognition of belligerency. The conditions of this aspect of recognition of belligerency—i.e. the right to recognize as distinguished from the duty to recognize—have been

1 See below, p. 252.

repeatedly laid down with clarity and authority and may be regarded as being covered by an undisputed rule of international law.[1] They have been summarized at the beginning of this chapter.[2] As in the analogous case of recognition of States,[3] these requirements, expressing as they do the basic factors of belligerency, are not irrelevant to the determination of the question of the right to and the duty of recognition as between the insurgent community and outside States. Whenever conditions are present which make the grant of recognition permissible and lawful in relation to the lawful government, their existence renders recognition obligatory in relation both to that government and to the rebellious community.

1 See in particular the Resolutions of the Institute of International Law of 1900 printed on p. 159 of the volume under that title, published in 1916 by the Carnegie Endowment; Olivart, *Del reconocimiento de beligerancia* (1895); Dana's note in § 23 of his edition of Wheaton's *International Law* (p. 29 of the *Classics* edition of 1936); and the diplomatic correspondence between the United States and Great Britain in 1865 concerning the claims of the United States arising out of the British recognition of the belligerency of the Confederate States (Moore, vol. 1, pp. 188–90).

2 See above, p. 176.

3 See above, pp. 11, 12.

Chapter XIII

THE RIGHT OF THE INSURGENTS AND OF THE LAWFUL GOVERNMENT TO RECOGNITION OF BELLIGERENCY

§ 60. *The Right of Insurgents to Recognition of Belligerency.* (*a*) *The British Practice.* There is only slender support in the practice of States for the view that governments regard recognition of belligerency as an act of grace or of political convenience. On occasions governments emphasize the wide element of discretion open to them in the matter. But the discretion which they invoke is discretion in estimating the existence of the conditions of recognition as postulated by international law. They do not appeal to an arbitrary liberty of action after the presence of those conditions has been clearly ascertained.[1] The British practice with regard to the three principal instances of recognition of belligerency—of the South American Republics in the second and third decades of the nineteenth century, of Greece in 1825, and of the Confederate States during the American Civil War—as well as in the case of some minor instances, illustrates with some clarity this conception of recognition.

At the time when the South American provinces declared their secession from Spain and embarked upon the war of independence, neither the principle nor the conception of recognition of belligerency had acquired any degree of precision. The hands of the British Government were tied by an additional article of the Treaty with Spain concluded in 1814 in which Great Britain engaged to prohibit the export of arms and war material to the rebellious Spanish colonies in America.[2] Neither was the attitude of Great Britain entirely unhampered, at that time, by a measure of regard for the legitimist frame of mind of her allies and by her own disapproval of

1 This, and no other, is the true meaning of the statement by an American Secretary of State that 'every sovereign power decides for itself, on its responsibility, the question whether or not it will, at a given time, accord the status of belligerency to the insurgent subjects of another power'. In fact, the same statement proceeds as follows: 'But the rightfulness of such an act depends on the occasion and the circumstances... national belligerency, indeed, like national independence, being but an existing fact, officially recognized as such, without which such a declaration is only the indirect manifestation of a particular line of policy' (Instructions by Mr Fish to Mr Motley, Minister to England, of 25 September 1869, in connection with the *Alabama* claims (*U.S. For. Rel.* 1873 (III), p. 336)).

2 *B.F.S.P.* vol. III, p. 292.

revolutions—an attitude which was counterbalanced, in turn, by a disinclination to intervene in the struggle and by the prospects of economic advantages from the growing trade with the South American States. However, as with the progress of time the hostilities assumed a wider scope, Great Britain, notwithstanding the existing Treaty, regarded it as her duty to grant to the insurgents the first essential privilege of recognition of belligerency, i.e. impartial treatment. Canning's speech of 16 April 1823 on the repeal of the Foreign Enlistment Act of 1818 merits quotation in this connection: 'In process of time, as those colonies became more powerful, a question arose...to be decided on a due consideration of their *de jure* relation to Spain on the one side, and their *de facto* independence of her, on the other. The law of nations was entirely silent with respect to the course which, under a circumstance so peculiar as the transition of colonies from their allegiance to the parent state, ought to be pursued....It became necessary, therefore, in the Act of 1818, to treat the colonies as actually independent of Spain; and to prohibit mutually, and with respect to both, the aid which had hitherto been prohibited with respect to one alone.'[1] No express proclamation of neutrality was issued, but in official pronouncements and declarations both the term and the principle of neutrality were repeatedly alluded to not only as the right line of conduct for British subjects but also as a matter of legal duty, on the part of Great Britain, to the contesting parties. 'The repeal of the Act of 1818', said Canning, would be 'an infraction of neutrality'.[2] Already in November 1817 a proclamation had been issued prohibiting British subjects from enlisting in the armed forces of either side in America.[3] While there was no hesitation in conceding what is a vital consequence of belligerency, namely, impartial treatment, there was originally, as appears from successive Opinions of the Law Officers of the Crown,[4] some reluctance to allow the exercise of belligerent rights on the high seas. However, that consequence of belligerency eventually also became recognized.[5]

1 *The Speeches of The Right Honourable George Canning*, ed. by Therry (2nd ed. 1830), vol. v, p. 40.

2 Ibid. p. 43.

3 *B.F.S.P.* vol. VI, p. 488.

4 Printed and commented upon in Smith, vol. I, pp. 268–81.

5 Thus Sir Christopher Robinson says in one of his Opinions: 'Considering the principles of neutrality that have been professed on the part of this country, the asserted independent Governments would have a right to exercise the ordinary privileges of War in maritime capture' (ibid. p. 279). Similarly, in another Opinion, he says, with reference to the repeated British declarations of neutrality: 'I do not imagine that the circumstance that such Blockades were established by Insurgent Provinces not formally recognized and acknowledged by His Majesty's Government as Independent Governments would alone invalidate such Blockades' (ibid. p. 278).

In the course of the Greek rebellion against Turkey the right of the insurgents to recognition of their belligerency was fully acknowledged. In 1825 the Foreign Secretary, in a despatch to the British Ambassador in Constantinople, wrote that 'a certain degree of force and consistency acquired by any mass of population engaged in war entitled that population to be treated as a belligerent'.[1] There had already been established a certain continuity in the British practice, for we find the following passage in Castlereagh's Instructions, which he drew up for his own guidance and which were handed over to Canning: 'Considering the course pursued by Great Britain now for so many years towards the local Governments exercising dominion in South America, and her avowed neutrality as between the Greeks and the Turks, it may be difficult for this country, if a *de facto* Government shall be actually established in the Morea, and the Western provinces of Turkey, to refuse it the ordinary privileges of a belligerent....'[2] The British Government acted fully on that view very soon after the beginning of the insurrection. In June 1821 the Senate of the Ionian Islands, acting at the suggestion of the High Commissioner, issued a Proclamation of Neutrality. As appears from the Opinion of the King's Advocate of September 1821, the British Government put itself already in 1821 in a position to apply the Foreign Enlistment Act so as to make unlawful the arming and equipping of a Turkish ship.[3] As the insurrection progressed, the recognition of belligerency developed from mere factual adherence to an attitude of impartiality to a mere explicit acknowledgment of the rights of maritime warfare appertaining to the insurgents.[4]

The view that, when the necessary conditions of fact are fulfilled, the insurgents are entitled to recognition, was also adopted in 1861 by the British Government as one of the reasons justifying the recognition of the belligerency of the Confederate States in that year. The passage in Canning's despatch referring to rebellious bodies as being entitled to recognition was relied upon and cited with approval in the House of Lords

1 Cited by Hall, *International Law* (3rd ed. 1890), p. 33, n. 1. There is probably no convincing reason for doubting (see, for example, Hall, loc. cit. and McNair in *Law Quarterly Review*, vol. LIII (1937), p. 481) whether the intention was to state that the insurgents were legally entitled to recognition. The pronouncement states a principle, and importance need not therefore necessarily be attached to the fact that the statement was made by one British authority to another. Its character as a statement of legal principle is emphasized by the fact that it was relied upon once more in 1861. See below, p. 188.

2 *Cambridge History of British Foreign Policy*, vol. II (1923), p. 45.

3 F.O. 83/2358.

4 See above, pp. 178, 179.

by Lord Russell when he explained the British position.[1] When the British Law Officers summarized in 1867 the British attitude to the American complaints of premature recognition, they pointed out that 'to these arguments of the United States it has been repeatedly replied, and we think rightly replied, that this recognition was in accordance with principle and practice'.[2] On a previous occasion they said: 'With respect to the repetition by Mr Adams of the old complaint, that Her Majesty thought fit upon the original commencement of hostilities, to recognize the status of belligerents in both the parties to this unhappy contest, we can but repeat the observation, which we have had occasion to make on many former occasions, that any other course would have justly exposed this Country to a charge of violating the clearest principles and soundest precedents of international law.'[3]

In Appendix I[4] there are reprinted a number of hitherto unpublished Opinions of Law Officers between 1869 and 1885 bearing on civil wars of a minor character but showing that also in those cases there was no inclination to regard recognition of belligerency or acquiescence in the exercise of belligerent rights on the part of insurgents as a matter of politics unrelated to legal principle. They include the exotic incidents of the war of the rebellious Kerais against Japan in 1868, when, although recognition of belligerency was refused, belligerency was treated as a matter of 'pure fact' by reference to the unusual circumstances of the case,[5] and of hostilities between the rival African chiefs in the Bonny River.[6] In the main, they illustrate the acknowledgment of the duty to concede to the insurgents the right to exercise belligerent rights following upon the exercise of those rights by the legitimate government. Thus in the course of the rebellion in Venezuela in 1871, the Government was advised—and acted on the advice—that from the recognition of a state of war and of the blockade proclaimed by the Venezuelan Government it followed that 'the insurgents will be also entitled to the exercise of belligerent rights against neutral commerce, subject to the responsibility of making compensation, where the capture shall prove to be unjustifiable'.[7] During the rebellion in

1 *H.L. Debates*, vol. CLXII, cols. 1563–6.

2 F.O. 83/3225; also printed in Smith, vol. I, p. 309.

3 Opinion by Roundell Palmer, Collier and Phillimore of 2 February 1864 (F.O. 83/2220).

4 See below, pp. 202–14.

5 See below, p. 214.

6 See below, p. 206. For a somewhat quaint correspondence between the British representative in China, Sir George Bonham, and the insurgent chiefs in the civil war in 1853 not recognized as belligerents see *B.F.S.P.* vol. XLIV, pp. 476–527.

7 See below, p. 203.

Uruguay in the same year the Government was advised that it could not properly interfere with the activities of the insurgents in connection with their military operations.[1] In the course of the Haitian rebellion in 1883 the Government was informed that as the rebels had been recognized as belligerents by their own Government they were entitled to the same treatment at the hands of outside States.[2] In an Opinion given in 1864 the Law Officers expressed the view that once the British Government had granted to the Spanish Government the rights of a belligerent power they could not, consistently with the principles and practice of international law, refuse to recognize the Dominican insurgents as belligerents.[3] The Government acted fully on that advice. Similarly, during the Carlist revolution in Spain in 1874, the British Government, acting on the advice of the Law Officers,[4] took the view that, while they were bound to recognize the blockade proclaimed by the Government, the automatic result of such recognition would be the conferment of belligerent status on the insurgents.[5] The British practice, as well as that of other States, leaves no doubt that, apart from other aspects of the question, the insurgents are entitled to recognition inasmuch as acquiescence in the exercise of belligerent rights by the lawful government confers corresponding rights upon the insurgents.

(*b*) *The Practice of the United States.* The practice of the United States has adopted what may be called the legal view of recognition of belligerency largely in the form of the frequent expression of the view that the question is essentially one of fact. This principle has been voiced with particular emphasis in various declarations of the Government of the United States.[6] In some of its pronouncements the Government of the United States, while

1 See below, p. 211.

2 See below, p. 203.

3 F.O. 83/2373; also printed in Smith, vol. I, p. 318.

4 See below, p. 208.

5 See also the circular Note of the Duc de Broglie to French diplomatic representatives abroad on the question of the recognition of the belligerency of the Spanish insurgents in 1873: 'Jusqu'à ce jour aucun des parties qui se sont déclarés contre l'administration issue du vote des Cortès n'a pu remplir les conditions nécessaires pour être considéré pour les puissances tierces comme un véritable belligérent et pour revendiquer de leur part les égards dus à ce titre' (*Fontes Juris Gentium, Digest of the Diplomatic Correspondence of the European States*, 1871–8, Part I (1937), p. 109). And see, for a statement of reasons for the French refusal in 1864 to recognize the belligerency of the Polish insurgents, Rougier, op. cit. p. 391. The reason was the absence of a government, of a central military authority, and of territory permanently occupied by the insurgents. See also above, p. 186.

6 See, for example, the Note of Mr Cass, Secretary of State, to the Peruvian Minister, 22 May 1858 (Moore, vol. I, p. 183); and President Grant's Annual Message of 7 December 1875 (ibid. p. 196).

insisting that the ascertainment of the facts in question is a matter of free appreciation by the Government concerned, took pains to show that, in the case before it, the conditions justifying the grant of belligerent status were not fulfilled and that the claim to recognition could not therefore be conceded. The Messages to Congress delivered by President Grant in connection with the Cuban insurrection are a good example of the meticulous care with which these facts were scrutinized.[1] They were so examined not from the point of view of the propriety of recognition in relation to the lawful government, but in relation to the claim, on the part of the insurgents, to recognition. In one important instance the right to recognition was expressly admitted. In his Message of 8 March 1822, President Monroe said: 'As soon as the (revolutionary) movement assumed such a steady and consistent form as to make the success of the provinces probable, the rights to which they are entitled by the law of nations, as equal parties to the civil war, were extended to them.'[2]

The practice of the United States is also instructive as providing an example of a State putting forward a claim based on a right to be recognized as a belligerent. Thus the United States for a time pressed against Denmark a claim for compensation on account of the action of the latter in denying to the United States belligerent rights at a time when, during the War of Independence, Denmark had not recognized it as a belligerent. That action consisted in the restoration to Great Britain of some prizes captured by the United States and brought into the Danish port of Bergen. Denmark at one time pleaded that she acted under a threat of compulsion on the part of Great Britain; at another time she offered to pay compensation which the United States rejected as inadequate. Eventually, Denmark denied legal liability altogether. But the United States insisted to the end on the juridical correctness of its claim.[3] In the case of *The Macedonian*, decided in May 1863, the United States seems to have adopted a different view. It

1 See ibid. pp. 194 et seq. See also ibid. p. 202, for the refusal of the request for recognition on the part of the Brazilian insurgents in 1893 on the ground that they had not 'up to date established and maintained a political organization which would justify such recognition on the part of the United States'.

2 Ibid. p. 174. Woolsey, in his *International Law* (Appendix III, note 19), criticized this passage on the ground that the insurgents have no *right* under the law of nations and that 'the concession of belligerency is not made on their account, but on account of considerations of policy on the part of the state itself which declares them such, or on grounds of humanity'. Professor Hyde (2nd ed. 1945, vol. I, p. 199) says with regard to the legal duty to accord recognition to insurgents as belligerents that the 'Department of State feels that there is none'. It is submitted that that statement requires modification.

3 See Moore, vol. I, § 60; and Lawrence's edition of Wheaton, *International Law* (1863), p. 41.

challenged the validity of the capture by Chilean forces in 1821 of American goods as contraband on the ground, *inter alia*, that at that time Chile had not been recognized by the United States either as a State or as a belligerent.[1] But in the case of *Georgiana and Lizzie Thompson*, decided in 1864, the United States again advocated the view that insurgents are entitled to exercise certain belligerent rights as against third States even without express recognition as belligerents.[2] In his Opinion bearing on the matter Attorney-General Black expressed the view that while the right of insurgents to exercise, prior to recognition, belligerent rights against outside States on the high seas was controversial, there was no doubt as to their right 'to conduct it [the war], with all the incidents of a lawful war, within the territory to which they both belong'.[3]

The attitude of the United States in combining the grant of belligerent rights as a matter of legal duty owed to the insurgents with scrupulous respect for the rights of the parent Government was clearly put in the communication of Mr Adams, Secretary of State, to the United States Minister in London on 1 June 1819:

> 'To this War, the avowed and real policy of the United States has been to remain neutral; and the principles of Neutrality which we consider as applicable to the case are these. First; that the parties have, in respect to Foreign Nations, equal rights, and are entitled as far as is practicable, to equal and the same treatment. Secondly; that while the contest is maintained, on both sides, with any reasonable prospect of eventual success, it would be a departure from Neutrality to recognize, either the supremacy contended for by Spain, or the Independence contended for by the South-Americans. For to acknowledge either would be to take the side of that party, upon the very question at issue between them.'[4]

There are numerous pronouncements of American courts laying down that hostilities on a large scale conducted by organized communities in possession of a substantial part of national territory automatically bring

1 The Arbitrator did not pronounce on this aspect of the matter as he found that the seizure was in any case contrary to international law. This aspect of the dispute is discussed with great clarity by A. Rolin in Lapradelle-Politis, *Recueil des arbitrages internationaux*, vol. II (1923), pp. 215–17. He disapproves of the American contention and asserts that insurgents have a right to recognition as belligerents.

2 See the *note doctrinale* in Lapradelle-Politis, op. cit. p. 401, affirming that while recognition of belligerency must be regarded as a governmental function, it must be determined by the actual situation of fact, and not by arbitrary considerations. And see Moore, *History and Digest of International Arbitrations*, vol. II, pp. 1599–1614.

3 Ibid. p. 1604.

4 Manning, *Diplomatic Correspondence of the United States concerning the Independence of Latin-American Nations*, vol. I (Parts I and II) (1925), p. 85.

into play the operation of international rules of war.[1] These decisions apparently refer only to the relations between insurgents and the lawful government, but they are not irrelevant to the matter at issue.

§ 61. *The Right of the Lawful Government to Recognition of Belligerency.* We have discussed so far the nature of recognition from the point of view of the right of the insurgent community to the recognition of its belligerent status on the part of outside States. With this question there is closely connected that of the right of the lawful government to claim belligerent status for itself (and, incidentally,[2] for the insurgents). In the course of the Spanish Civil War of 1936–9 the British[3] and other Governments declared repeatedly that belligerent rights had not been granted to either side in the civil war. In the Preamble to the Nyon Agreement of 14 September 1937, relating to the suppression of attacks by submarines, the Parties expressly stated that they did not in any way admit 'the right of either party to the conflict in Spain to exercise belligerent rights or to interfere with merchant ships on the high seas even if the laws of warfare at sea are observed'.[4] Inasmuch as these and similar declarations implied that it is open to outside States to refuse, at their discretion, belligerent rights to the lawful government after it has decided to claim them and when it is able to exercise them

1 See, for example, *Ford* v. *Surget*, 97 U.S. 611: '...the contest though it originated in rebellion, must in the progress of events, when it assumes such proportions as to be justly denominated civil war, be recognized as entitling both parties to the rights of war just as much as if it was waged between two independent nations'. In *Williams* v. *Bruffy*, 96 U.S. 191, it was said: '...in a civil war the contending parties have a right to claim the enforcement of the same rules which govern the conduct of armies in wars between independent nations...'. See also *Prize Cases*, 2 Black 666, 667. On the other hand, there are some decisions of inferior courts which are based on the view that notwithstanding the fact that the rebels were treated as belligerents by the government, they remained criminals so far as the courts were concerned. In a number of cases, reported by Dana in Wheaton's *International Law* (p. 377), the courts held that individuals in the naval service of rebels were pirates. Dana's seemingly approving but controversial comment on these cases is that the government never recognized the rebels as belligerents *de jure* with the resulting legal status of belligerents: 'It was a course of policy from day to day, and from place to place, held under political discretion all the while; liable to be discontinued as to persons or places, or altogether abandoned in that discretion.' This view seems to be inconsistent with the decisions of the Supreme Court in the three cases cited above.

2 See above, p. 190.

3 The Secretary of State for Foreign Affairs informed the House of Commons, on 8 December 1937, that 'His Majesty's Ambassador at Hendaye has been instructed to inform the Salamanca authorities that as belligerent rights have not been recognized to either party in the Spanish conflict, His Majesty's Government are not prepared to admit their right to declare any such blockade': *H.C. Debates*, vol. CCCLVII, col. 330.

4 Cmd. 5568 (1937).

in accordance with international law, such statements are believed to be unsound as a matter of legal principle and contrary to practice. The fact that the insurrection has reached dimensions compelling the lawful government to recognize the rebels, at some risk to its prestige and at the cost of conferring corresponding advantages upon them, supplies persuasive evidence that the necessary conditions of recognition of belligerency are present. The right to wage war is, in the absence of obligations to the contrary, an undoubted right of the State. If the lawful government, after having considered all the circumstances, arrives at the conclusion that the position is such as to make it necessary to treat the hostilities on the same footing as war in the ordinary sense, with all the concomitant rights and obligations of warfare, it does not lie with outside States to deny to it that right.[1] The British practice in the matter seems to be well settled with regard to its crucial aspect, namely, the right of the lawful government to proclaim a blockade. According to that practice, the blockade proclaimed by the lawful government will be recognized as valid so long as it is maintained, from the point of view of effectiveness and otherwise, in conformity with international law. The proclamation of a blockade by the lawful government amounts to an assertion of belligerent rights which must be recognized subject to the further consequence that such rights are thus automatically conferred upon the insurgent party. On the other hand, a mere decree of the lawful government purporting to close ports occupied by the insurgents without the maintenance of an effective blockade will not be treated as valid inasmuch as it constitutes an attempt to secure the rights of war without regard to the conditions which international law attaches to the exercise thereof. It cannot be recognized as a blockade in the sense of international law.

During the American Civil War it was not suggested that it was open to Great Britain to deny to the United States the right to proclaim an internationally valid blockade of the coast of the Southern States or, generally, to exercise belligerent rights. As Lord Russell wrote to Lord Lyons on 19

1 In the important case of *The Amy Warwick and Other Vessels* decided by the Supreme Court of the United States, the Court had no hesitation in holding that—in the words of Dana, who was counsel in the case—'it was settled in the practice of nations, and necessary in the nature of things, that a nation should have the right to meet a rebellion by the exercise of those acts of force commonly known and classified as belligerent rights, or war powers; that among them there are included blockade and capture of enemy's property at sea; that if an insurrection or civil war reaches the dimensions requiring their exercise, neutral nations must acquiesce' (Wheaton, *International Law* (Dana's edition), p. 376). The cases are conveniently reported in *Prize Cases Decided by the United States Supreme Court*, 1789–1918, published by the Carnegie Endowment, vol. III (1923), pp. 1413–59.

July 1861, in connection with some proposed measures of the United States Government:[1] 'In the present case, Her Majesty's Government do not intend to dispute the right of blockade on the part of the United States with regard to the ports in the possession of the Confederate States; but an assumed right to close any ports in the hands of insurgents would imply a right to stop vessels on the high seas without instituting an effective blockade. This would be a manifest evasion of the necessity of blockade in order to close an enemy's port.' In 1864 we find Sir Robert Phillimore advising that the blockade proclaimed by the Central Government of Venezuela against the State of Ciudad Bolivar must be recognized provided that it was effective.[2] The same view was expressed in 1871 by Sir Travers Twiss with regard to the blockade of the coast of the Orinoco River by the Government of Venezuela.[3] In 1876 the Law Officers advised the Government that the Haitian Government was entitled to blockade the ports in the occupation of the insurgents and that 'by such blockade that Government creates a state of war, giving neutral as well as belligerent rights'.[4] Similar Opinions were expressed with regard to Haiti in 1883.[5] During the Carlist Revolution in Spain in 1874 the British Government was advised by its Law Officers—and acted on the advice—that, assuming that the blockade proclaimed by the Spanish Government was effective, Great Britain was bound to recognize the blockade *de facto* and *de jure*. The relevant despatch of Lord Granville to the British Minister at Madrid may be quoted verbatim:

> 'H.M.'s Govt. . . . are advised that, assuming the Blockade to be effective,—they must recognize the fact that it exists *de facto* and *de jure*.
>
> 'The result however will be that the Carlists henceforth become belligerents. . . .
>
> 'I have therefore to instruct you to warn the Spanish Govt. that the establishment of the proposed Blockade must lead to the issue by H.M.'s Govt. of a proclamation of neutrality. . . .'[6]

On a previous occasion, in connection with the revolt of San Domingo against Spain, the Law Officers, in urging the concession of belligerent rights to the insurgents, pointed out that the Spanish Government had in 1863 declared a blockade of the Dominican coast and that 'Her Majesty's Government, in the course of the subsequent correspondence, never disputed the right of the Spanish Government to establish and maintain

1 *B.F.S.P.* vol. LI, p. 206.
2 See below, p. 207.
3 See below, p. 208.
4 See below, p. 210.
5 See below, pp. 203, 210.
6 Printed in Smith, vol. I, p. 321.

such a blockade; but only insisted, that it must be a real and effective, and not a mere paper blockade'.[1]

The *London Gazette* and the *British and Foreign State Papers* abound in notifications of blockades instituted by the lawful government.[2] Its right to institute a blockade—as distinguished from the closure by decree of ports actually in the control of the insurgents[3]—has not been questioned so

1 Smith, vol. I, p. 314. They said: '...the question, whether a state of war does or does not exist between insurgents holding possession of a particular territory, and a Government claiming their allegiance and attempting to subdue them, is one of fact, quite as much as of law: and, if the facts are such, as really to constitute a state of war between the contending parties, according to the law of nations, it is not, we think, competent, by law, to any neutral Power, to withdraw its ships and subjects, upon the high seas, from the operation of the ordinary laws incident to that state of things, merely by declining to acknowledge its existence' (ibid.).

2 See, for instance, in addition to others referred to in this chapter, the notification of the Spanish blockade of the coast of Galicia in 1846 (*B.F.S.P.* vol. XXXV, p. 860); of the Turkish blockade of insurgent ports in Albania in 1847 (ibid. p. 1154); of the Venezuelan blockade of the coasts of the States of Camaná and Maturin on 6 July 1871 (ibid. vol. LXVI, p. 939); of the blockade of the mouth of the Orinoco River on 12 December 1871 (ibid. vol. LXVII, p. 520); of the French blockade of part of the Gold Coast on 24 April 1872 (ibid. vol. LXII, p. 1215) (it was announced that the coast was effectively blockaded, and all British subjects were warned not to attempt to violate the said blockade); of the Dutch blockade of a portion of the west coast of Acheen (*London Gazette*, 11 April 1884); of the blockade of the port of Monte Christi by the Dominican Government on 6 September 1886 (*B.F.S.P.* vol. LXXVII, p. 1029) (raising of the blockade announced on 25 November 1886; ibid. p. 1030); of the Portuguese blockade of Quissembo on the west coast of Africa on 26 June 1888 (ibid. vol. LXXIX, p. 234); of the French blockade of the Dahomey coast on 16 June 1892 (ibid. vol. LXXXIV, p. 687); of the blockade of Puerto Plata by the Dominican Government on 23 May 1914 (ibid. vol. CVII, p. 304).

For examples of British blockades of this kind see the blockade in 1826 of the ports of part of the Gold Coast by the Governor-General of Sierra Leone 'according to the usages of war acknowledged and allowed in similar cases', the blockade being 'necessary for the more vigorous prosecution of the war which we are thus forced to wage and declare against the chiefs and people of the Gallinas, and all rebels now in arms against our lawful authority' (ibid. vol. LXIII, p. 1164). See also the British blockade of parts of the Gold Coast, notified on 15 December 1873, and described as maintained by a competent force, 'all measures...authorized by the law of nations' to be taken against all vessels which may attempt to violate the blockade (ibid. vol. LXV, p. 1290).

3 Which, according to practically uniform practice and opinion, has no claim to recognition by foreign governments. In 1861, in connection with the announcement by the Government of New Granada of a closure, but not of blockade, of ports occupied by the insurgents, Lord Russell said: '...The opinion of Her Majesty's Government, after taking legal advice upon the question, was that it was perfectly competent to a Government of a country in a state of tranquillity to say which ports should be open to trade and which be closed. But in the event of insurrection or civil war in that country it was not competent for its Government to close ports which were *de facto* in the hands of the insurgents; and that such a proceeding would be an evasion of the international law relating to blockade' (*H.L. Debates*, vol. CLXIII, p. 1645). That statement was relied upon and fully approved in 1885 by the American Secretary of State (*U.S. For. Rel.* 1885, pp. 256–7). See also the case of

long as the blockade has been effective. It is probable that notification, in an official government publication, of a blockade by a foreign authority amounts, if unaccompanied by a simultaneous or subsequent statement to the contrary, to recognition of the blockade.[1] In cases in which the notification is not intended as a recognition of the blockade the intention not to recognize it is made clear, as a rule, in the published announcement. Thus, for instance, when in 1902 Great Britain notified the blockade by the Venezuelan Government of certain ports in Venezuela, the announcement was accompanied by the following rider: 'His Majesty's Government have ascertained from the reports of His Majesty's Minister at Carácas, from those of the Senior Naval Officer of His Majesty in those waters, and from other trustworthy sources, that no effective blockade of the stretch of coast and ports comprised in the Decrees of 28 June and 19 July is, or has ever been, maintained. It is, therefore, further notified that the blockade so declared is held by His Majesty's Government to be, and to have been, *ab initio*, null and of no effect.'[2] (It is of interest to note in this connection that the British Government were advised that their withdrawal of recognition of the blockade did not take away the right of the insurgents to maintain that as a result of the original proclamation of the blockade they acquired

Compagnie Générale des Asphaltes de France before the British-Venezuelan Claims Commission (*Venezuelan Arbitrations of* 1903 (Ralston's *Report*), p. 95). And see Wheaton, op. cit. p. 34, n. 15, and Westlake (*International Law* (2nd ed. 1910), vol. I, p. 71), who suggest, somewhat ingeniously, that the refusal to recognize the validity of such decrees amounts to a recognition of belligerency. See also Dickinson in *A.J.* vol. XXIV (1930), pp. 69–78; the *Oriental Navigation Company* case decided by United States-Mexican Claims Commission, *Annual Digest*, 1927–8, Case no. 361; Hackworth, vol. I, pp. 142, 359; and Nielsen in *Proceedings of the American Society of International Law*, 1937, pp. 147–52.

There are a number of Opinions of Law Officers of the Crown relating to the question of exaction of customs duties from British subjects who had already paid such duties in the territory which, for a time, was under the control of *de facto* insurgent authorities. The view uniformly expressed has been that the lawful government is not entitled to exact repeated payment of customs duties. See, for example, the Opinion of 24 August 1885 in which the advice of the Law Officers was: 'Her Majesty's Government are entitled to object to the exaction of such second payment by British subjects of import duties, and of an additional duty in case of refusal, in respect of the importation of goods into territory which was not under the *de facto* sovereignty of the Colombian Government at the time of such importation.' See also the despatch of the Marquis of Salisbury to Mr J. G. Kennedy of 11 April 1891, instructing him to inform the Chilean Government that their right to exact export duties from British ships for cargoes on which such duties had already been paid under protest and compulsion to the insurgent authorities in possession of the port of export was not admitted by Her Majesty's Government (*State Papers*, vol. XCV (1892), *Chile*, no. 1, p. 71).

1 Such notification is as a rule, in cases of civil wars, preceded by a consultation of the Law Officers who often prepare a draft of the notification of the blockade.

2 14 November 1902 (*B.F.S.P.* vol. XCV, p. 472).

the status of belligerency as against the Venezuelan Government, but that such implied recognition did not bind the British Government.) On other occasions we find recognition and notification[1] of the blockade followed by withdrawal of such recognition on the ground that the blockade had ceased to be effective. Thus the Haitian blockade decrees of November 1888 were originally recognized by Great Britain and published in the *London Gazette*. Subsequently, on 11 July 1889, a notice was published by the British Government that the blockade previously announced,[2] 'had plainly ceased to be effective' and that the Haitian Government had been informed that 'it could no longer be respected by Her Majesty's Government'.[3]

This right of the lawful government to proclaim a blockade—the most usual object[4] of the assumption and of the grant of belligerent rights—is

1 From a notification of blockade there must be distinguished a notification, not amounting to recognition of a belligerent right, more limited in scope. During the revolution in Chile in 1891 the British Government, acting on legal advice, inserted in the *London Gazette* of 23 February a notification to the effect that His Majesty's Government had been informed by the Chilean Government that the importation into Chile of 'arms, ammunition and war material is absolutely prohibited during the continuance of the present civil disorders in Chile'. The original instruction was to use the expression 'the present civil *hostilities*'. The change was made in order to avoid the implication of recognition of belligerency. But see a telegram of the Foreign Office of 24 January 1891 to Messrs Smith and Service, a private firm, informing them that according to reports a Chilean squadron was blockading Valparaiso and Iquique and that 'assuming effective blockade to exist, escort through it cannot be given' (*State Papers*, vol. XCV (1892), *Chile*, no. 1, p. 8).

2 *B.F.S.P.* vol. LXXIX, p. 235.

3 Ibid. vol. LXXXI, p. 165. The British naval authorities were instructed to intervene in that sense if necessary.

4 But not, of course, the only object. The absence of recognition of belligerency may have results of an altogether different nature in war on land. In 1907 in the course of the rebellion of the Hottentot and other native inhabitants of the Protectorate of German South-West Africa, the Government of Cape Colony interned a number of rebels who crossed the frontier. Serious doubts were subsequently expressed in authoritative quarters in Great Britain whether this was the proper procedure in the case of natives who had not been invested with belligerent character. The view was expressed that they partook rather of the character of political refugees who had sought asylum on British soil. There was strong support to the view that the question was not so much whether the Cape Government were justified in not releasing the refugees as whether in continuing to keep them 'interned' they would not be merely prolonging an illegal situation. On the other hand, the view was expressed that the Cape Government was bound to take reasonable steps to prevent the use of Cape territory as a base for hostile operations against a friendly Power and that for that purpose, though not bound to intern, the Cape Government were entitled to do so if they thought fit. It was also thought that the Cape Government had no legal or equitable claim to have their expenses reimbursed by the German Government, unless they could show some express or clearly implied promise on the part of that Government to do so.

When in January 1908 a revolution broke out in Haiti, the Government proclaimed a blockade of certain ports. There had been no recognition of belligerency,

indirectly admitted in the many cases in which Great Britain has refused to recognize a mere decree closing ports in the possession of the insurgents. Some of the Opinions of the Law Officers elaborating this point are printed in the Appendix below.[1]

§ 62. *The Right of Insurgents and of the Lawful Government contrasted.* It has been shown that, given the necessary factual requirements, outside States are bound to recognize the belligerency both of the insurgents and of the lawful government and that there is a substantial body of practice in support of that proposition. There is, nevertheless, a considerable difference between the right to recognition of belligerency in the case of the lawful government and in that of the insurgents. With regard to the latter, outside States are in law bound to grant recognition as soon as they have satisfied themselves as to the presence of the necessary conditions of recognition. In doing so they are entitled and bound to exercise judicial discretion in weighing the circumstances of the situation. On the other hand, so far as the lawful government is concerned, it is for the latter to decide whether circumstances warrant the transformation of the struggle into a war governed by rules of international law. If it takes an affirmative decision in the matter, outside States are bound to recognize a condition of belligerency and to acquiesce in the exercise of belligerent rights by the lawful government provided that the struggle bears the character of a civil war and that the lawful government is able and willing to exercise those rights in accordance with international law. Thus the lawful government is entitled to proclaim a blockade of the coast occupied by the insurgents and, by implication, to assert its belligerent status. But outside States, while not at liberty to question its right to belligerent status, are entitled to examine whether the blockade thus proclaimed is from the point of view of its effectiveness and otherwise in conformity with international law. If it is not, then the belligerent rights asserted by a legally ineffective means cannot be recognized as validly operative in the particular situation. The British and American refusal to recognize the belligerent right of blockade claimed by the Spanish Government in 1936 was based to a large extent on the fact that that blockade was not effective.[2]

but the Government was informed by the Diplomatic Corps that the blockade would be recognized if it complied with conditions of international law concerning blockade, in particular with respect to effectiveness and notification: see *U.S. For. Rel.* 1908, pp. 425 et seq.

1 See pp. 214–22.

2 When in August 1936 the Spanish Government notified the United States and other States that entry into some ports occupied by the insurgents was forbidden, the United States Government replied that 'with the friendliest feelings toward the Spanish Government, it cannot admit the legality of any action on the part of the Spanish Government in declaring such ports closed unless that Government declares

Similarly, if the lawful government were to claim belligerent rights whilst denying them to the insurgents, such illogical and one-sided conduct would invalidate its continued recognition as a belligerent. Thus, for instance, during the American Civil War the United States for a time claimed to be entitled to refuse to recognize the prize courts set up by the Confederate States and to disregard their sentences. The British Government successfully resisted that attitude, which, it was advised by the Law Officers, 'is as much at variance with the most important principles of International Law, as it is destructive of the Belligerent Rights and status, on which the conduct of the United States Government throughout the War has been founded....'[1] The Law Officers strongly urged that the British Government, in conjunction with other governments, should issue a declaration to the effect that it would refuse to continue to accord to the United States the belligerent rights hitherto enjoyed by them unless they were prepared to recognize the obligations which accompany those rights and, in particular, 'unless they also concede to their enemy the *status* of a belligerent for all *international* purposes...'.[2] These qualifications must not obscure the fact that according to both principle and practice it is normally not open to outside States to deny to the lawful government the exercise of belligerent rights so long as it exercises them in conformity with international law. So great is the cogency of the underlying principle and practice that even those writers who in general make recognition of belligerency dependent upon the discretionary will of outside States admit, to quote the author of an able monograph on the question, that 'recognition of the insurgents as a belligerent party by their own State confers upon it belligerent rights which must be respected by third States'.[3]

and maintains an effective blockade of such ports' (quoted in *Proceedings of the American Society of International Law*, 1937, p. 149). When in 1902 the *de jure* government of Venezuela proclaimed a blockade of the coastline the British view was that they were entitled to do so provided the blockade was effective and provided it was understood that by doing so they were giving the insurgents belligerent status. (The view was expressed that the blockade, in order to be valid, must apply to territory in the possession of the insurgents; the Government could not legally blockade a territory or river in their own control merely because it gave access to territory or waters in the hands of the insurgents.)

1 F.O. 83/2216.

2 Ibid. For an earlier example see the objections of the United States to the proclamation of the blockade of the Spanish coast in South America in 1816, on the ground that it did not comply with the conditions of blockade as then understood (Manning, *Diplomatic Correspondence of the United States concerning the Independence of the Latin-American Nations*, vol. I (Parts I and II) (1925), pp. 26–8 (Note of the Secretary of State to the Spanish Minister)).

3 Kunz, p. 185. Yet on the preceding page Dr Kunz declares that recognition by the lawful government produces in principle legal results only as between the latter and the insurgents. See also Rougier, op. cit. p. 222.

If outside States have legally no option but to acquiesce in the exercise of belligerent rights by the lawful government as soon as it cares to claim them in conformity with international law, it follows that the insurgents, too, are in such case entitled to the rights of belligerency not only in relation to their own State but also as against outside States. The lawful government cannot claim or exercise belligerent rights without acknowledging a state of war; similarly, outside States cannot acquiesce in such claim unless they are prepared to admit the existence of a state of war. But a state of war in which only one party is allowed to exercise belligerent rights is a logical absurdity—unless we assume that the concession of belligerent rights to the governmental side only is a form of intervention in the internal affairs of the State prompted by the view that it is the business of international law to favour actively the established government. This untenable view is by no means altogether obsolete. It underlies, for instance, the Resolution of the Institute of International Law of 1900 on the rights and duties of foreign Powers, in case of insurrectionary movements, in relation to established and recognized governments. There, in Article 5 (1), it is expressly laid down that 'a third State is not bound to concede to insurgents the status of belligerency for the mere reason that it has been conceded to them by the State in which the revolution has broken out'.[1] It seems to be assumed in the Resolution that there is no such discretion concerning belligerent rights claimed by the lawful government. On the contrary, while in Article 5 (2) it is expressly provided that in the absence of recognition blockades instituted by insurgents need not be respected, nothing is said about blockades proclaimed by the lawful government in similar circumstances. However, there is no escape from the conclusion that, by claiming to exercise belligerent rights as against the insurgents, the lawful government not only acquires those rights as against outside States but also automatically confers belligerent rights upon the insurgents in relation to itself and others. This appears also to be the view of the great majority of writers.[2] It was in such deduction from the conduct of the lawful government that Great Britain, in recognizing the belligerency of the American insurgents in consequence of the proclamation of the blockade by the President of the United States on 19 April 1861, was able to find unimpeachable support for her action.

1 *Annuaire*, vol. XVIII (1900), p. 228.

2 See Wiesse, *Le droit international appliqué aux guerres civiles* (1898), p. 224; Rougier, op. cit. p. 226; and Kunz, p. 187, who, however, seems to think that insurgents recognized by their own State may in such case exercise belligerent rights against outside States without having the right to claim recognition of belligerency.

Appendix to Chapters XII and XIII

I

OPINIONS OF THE LAW OFFICERS OF THE CROWN RELATING TO THE RIGHT OF INSURGENTS TO RECOGNITION OF BELLIGERENCY AND OF BELLIGERENT RIGHTS

The following two Opinions are amongst the many which affirm the right of the insurgents to exercise belligerent rights as the result of the assertion of belligerent rights by or their concession to the lawful government.[1] They show also that the fact of the acquisition of belligerent rights renders the insurgents internationally liable for the manner of their exercise.

Opinion of the Queen's Advocate of 28 June 1871[2]

Temple

My Lord

I am honoured with Your Lordship's commands signified in Mr Hammond's letter of the 19th instant, stating that with reference to my report of the 25th ultimo upon the subject of the Blockade by the present Government of Venezuela of part of the coast of that Republic, which remains in the hands of the party opposed to the Government, he was directed to transmit to me the accompanying letter from the Colonial Office, enclosing further correspondence relating to this matter, and also to the seizure by a Ship of War of the Venezuelan Government of the British Vessel 'Unison' for alleged infraction of the Blockade, and of the British Vessels 'Helen' and 'Sophie' by the Insurgent Government. That the Despatch from Mr Middleton already submitted to me is also enclosed together with some further correspondence relating to the same subject, Mr Hammond was pleased to request that I would take these papers into my consideration and furnish Your Lordship with my opinion as to the course which should be pursued in the matter.

In obedience to Your Lordship's commands I have the honour to *Report*

That I am of opinion that a state of War exists between the Republic, of which the President has issued a Notification of the blockade of certain Venezuelan ports, and the Insurgents, who are in possession of those ports, and that the Government of the Republic has made known the existence of hostilities to Her Majesty's Chargé d'Affaires at Caracas in a manner sufficient to entitle it to the exercise of Belligerent rights against British Commerce. Her Majesty's Government will consequently not be justified in objecting to the capture of British Vessels on the high seas by the blockading Squadron, but it may properly insist upon such Vessels being sent forthwith before a Prize Court for the purpose of Judicial enquiry,

1 See below, p. 245.

2 F.O. 83/2403.

whether they have in any way infringed the Belligerent rights of the Captors. It follows also that the Insurgents will be also entitled to the exercise of belligerent rights against neutral commerce, subject to the responsibility of making compensation, where the capture shall prove to be unjustifiable....The Insurgents are the parties responsible to neutral powers for any abuse of belligerent right by persons acting under their authority. With regard to the capture of the 'Unison', upon the statements submitted to Her Majesty's Government her capture was clearly unjustifiable, and unless clear evidence is forthcoming from the Venezuelan Captors to rebut the affidavit made by the Master and Owner of the Vessel at the Harbour Master's Office at Port of Spain Her Majesty's Government will be justified in my opinion in demanding from the Venezuelan Government the restitution of the Vessel and full compensation for any losses incurred by the Owners of the Vessel and of her cargo, and by Her Master and Crew....

I have the honour to be, My Lord,

Your Lordship's most obedient, humble Servant,

TRAVERS TWISS

To The Right Honble The Earl Granville, K.G.

Opinion of the Law Officers of the Crown and Dr Deane to Earl Granville of 23 October 1883[1]

Royal Courts of Justice

My Lord

We are honoured with your Lordship's commands signified in Mr Currie's letter of the 10th instant, stating that he was to transmit to us a letter from the Admiralty, inquiring, with reference to the case of the 'Eider', what status a ship purchased by rebels in those circumstances would have if met with on the high seas....

In obedience to your Lordship's commands we have the honour to report—

That it is not possible to express a positive opinion upon the point raised by the Admiralty without further information than we possess.

The vessel purchased was an unarmoured merchant-vessel, and she, no doubt, became the lawful property of those who purchased her. She appears to be now flying the Haïtian flag, and if, as is presumably the case, she is the property of Haïtian subjects, she is entitled to the status of a Haïtian vessel. If she should hereafter be used for belligerent purposes on the high seas, her status would depend upon the position of those who so used her.

We gather that the rebel party in Haïti are recognized and treated by the Haïtian Government as belligerents, and in that case they, and any vessels they may employ, should be so treated by us, just as the Confederate Government and their cruizers were during the time of the civil war in the United States.

We have, &c.

(Signed) HENRY JAMES, FARRER HERSCHELL, J. PARKER DEANE

1 F.O. 35/121.

The following Opinion is of interest as showing the recognition of the right of the insurgents to conduct operations deemed necessary for the success of the rebellion.

Opinion of the Queen's Advocate of 19 *August* 1871[1]

My Lord

I am honoured with Your Lordship's commands signified in Mr Odo Russell's letter of the 12th instant stating that he was directed to transmit to me the accompanying letter and its inclosures from the River Plate Telegraph Company, claiming the interference of Her Majesty's Government in consequence of the alleged unjustifiable proceedings of the Uruguayan Government with regard to the Representatives and property of the Company in that Republic, and he was to request that I would take the same into my consideration, and furnish Your Lordship with my opinion as to any steps which should be taken in the matter.

In obedience to Your Lordship's commands I have the honour to *Report*

That I am not perfectly informed as to the present condition of political affairs in the State of Uruguay, but I infer from the Declaration of Mr John Oldham of 29th Novr. 1870 that there is a rebellion against the Government recognized by Her Majesty, and that the Rebels are in possession of the 'Campana', and have interrupted the working of the line of Telegraph between Monte Video and Buenos Ayres. Under these circumstances the Telegraph Company have requested Her Majesty's Government to protect them, on the ground that they are a British Company with British Representatives, and they rely on the 4th Article of the Concession granted to the Company by the Monte Videan Government, by which it undertook to protect the property of the Company 'as far as lies in its power.' I do not find any good grounds in the correspondence for supposing that the Monte Videan Government is able to protect the property of the Company from the Blanco party, which has evidently the Command of the Country between Monte Video and Colonia, and Her Majesty's Government cannot in my opinion properly interfere to control the action of the Blancos in The Campana, if it be thought necessary by them in the interests of the Rebellion to interrupt the Telegraph wires in order to prevent the use of the Telegraph by the Monte Videan Government for political purposes.

I have the honour to be, My Lord,

Your Lordship's most obedient, humble Servant,

TRAVERS TWISS

To The Right Honble The Earl Granville, K.G.

NOTE. See also, for an interesting example of affirmation of full belligerent rights of insurgents, the 'Opinion of the Law Officers of the Crown and Dr Deane to Earl Granville of 23 June 1885'.[2] In this Opinion

1 F.O. 83/2309. 2 F.O. 55/318.

the Law Officers express their concurrence with the view of Captain Curtis, of H.M.S. *Canada*, with regard to the legality of convoying into the port of Cartagena British vessels containing provisions for the forces of the National Government of Colombia. The proposition as stated by Captain Curtis and approved by the Law Officers was 'By the constitution of the Republic of Colombia each State is entitled to sovereign rights, and as a *de facto* Government has been established in the State of Bolivar by the insurgents after successes in the field I maintain that they are entitled to all the rights of belligerents, and to convoy British vessels into the port of Cartagena, if it is still being besieged, would be a direct interference with those rights, for by so doing the siege might be indefinitely prolonged.'

The following two Opinions do not refer to recognition of the belligerency of insurgents. They illustrate in an interesting manner the affirmation of belligerent rights of non-civilized communities.

Opinion of the Queen's Advocate to Earl Granville of 29 September 1870[1]

Temple

My Lord

I am honoured with your Lordship's commands signified in Mr Otway's letter of the 21st instant, stating that with reference to my report of the 19th instant upon the subject of the questions raised by the Company of African Merchants with respect to the hostile measures alleged to be contemplated by the African Chiefs at Bonny and by their rival Ja Ja, he was directed to transmit to me, in compliance with my request, the correspondence that has taken place upon the subject of this quarrel, in order to enable me to form an opinion as to whether a state of war can be said to exist in the Bonny River which would invest the rival Chiefs with the rights of belligerents, and to advise your Lordship as to the proper answer to return to Mr Tobin's letter....

In obedience to your Lordship's commands I have the honour to report...

That I am of opinion that a state of hostilities exists, and has been recognized in the correspondence of Her Majesty's Government to exist, in the Bonny River, which would invest the rival Chiefs with the rights of belligerents, and which would expose any persons within Her Majesty's dominions to proceedings under the Foreign Enlistment Act of 1870, if they should dispatch any vessel of war to be employed in the naval service of Ja Ja and his confederates against the King of Bonny, and that Mr Tobin should be informed that he cannot safely engage in any such enterprise.

I have, &c.

(Signed) TRAVERS TWISS

1 F.O. 83/2362.

Opinion of the Queen's Advocate to Earl Granville of 7 October 1870[1]

Temple

My Lord

I am honoured with your Lordship's commands signified in Mr Otway's letter of the 30th ultimo (received this day) stating that with reference to my report of the 29th ultimo upon the subject of the war in Bonny, he was directed to transmit to me three further despatches from Consul Livingstone reporting the steps he has taken to bring the quarrel between the rival Chiefs to arbitration, and to request that I would furnish your Lordship, at my earliest convenience, with my opinion whether the proceeding of Her Majesty's Consul in temporarily stopping the trade of the River Opobo under the circumstances stated in his despatches, is inconsistent with the promised neutrality of Her Majesty's Government, or with the recognition which, I advised, was implied in their correspondence of a state of hostilities between the rival Chiefs.

Mr Otway was pleased to add that it must be borne in mind that the trade is reported to be entirely in the hands of British subjects, who have doubtless assisted one of the belligerent parties, and continued to trade, notwithstanding the advice and remonstrances of the Consul and Her Majesty's Government....

In obedience to your Lordship's commands I have the honour to report—

That it would be difficult to say that the course adopted by Her Majesty's Consul has been in accordance with strict neutrality on the part of Her Majesty's Government as between the contending parties on the Opobo River. The intervention of Her Majesty's ship 'Pert' has been rather an act of armed mediation, the propriety of which can hardly be measured by the ordinary European standards.

If it was the intention of Her Majesty's Government to remain strictly neutral between Ja Ja and the Bonny Chiefs, and to allow them to fight their quarrel out, no matter with what injury to British subjects trading in those parts, Her Majesty's Consul has not carried out that intention, but it appears to me that the circumstances under which this quarrel was fomented by rival traders on the Opobo for selfish purposes, coupled with the fact that Ja Ja voluntarily accepted the mediation of Her Majesty's Consul, and then repudiated it, warranted Her Majesty's Consul in putting some pressure on Ja Ja, sufficient to counteract the influence of those traders who were thriving upon the quarrel and interested in preventing the restoration of peace....

I have, &c.

(Signed) Travers Twiss

1 F.O. 83/2362.

II

OPINIONS OF THE LAW OFFICERS OF THE CROWN ON THE RIGHT OF THE LEGITIMATE GOVERNMENT TO PROCLAIM AN EFFECTIVE BLOCKADE AND, GENERALLY, TO EXERCISE BELLIGERENT RIGHTS

Report of the Queen's Advocate of 21 October 1864[1]

Doctor's Commons

My Lord

I am honoured with Your Lordship's commands, signified in Mr Hammond's Letter of the 19th Instant, stating that he was directed by Your Lordship to transmit to me a Despatch and its Inclosures from the Acting British Chargé d'Affaires at Carácas reporting that the Central Government of Venezuela have employed force to coerce the State of Ciudad Bolivar to be in a state of Blockade; and Mr Hammond was to request that I would take these papers into consideration, and furnish Your Lordship with my opinion as to the validity of this Blockade, and whether or not Her Majesty's Government should recognize it.

In obedience to Your Lordship's commands, I have taken these papers into consideration, and have the honour to *Report*

That as far as I can judge from the papers laid before me the Government of Carácas does not appear to have exceeded its power in notifying the existence of a Blockade of the Coasts of the Country during a period of insurrection. I observe that the 3rd Article of the Proclamation provides that no Vessel is to be seized unless it persist in approaching the Coast, after due notice not to do so has been given to it on the spot by the blockading Force. Such a provision of course renders necessary the actual presence of a Blockading Force off the Coast, which Mr Mathison seems to think did not exist at the time when he wrote his Despatch to Your Lordship. Upon the whole, I think that the Blockade must be recognized by the Government of this Country.

I have the honour to be, My Lord,
Your Lordship's most obedient, humble Servant,
ROBERT PHILLIMORE

To The Right Honble The Earl Russell, K.G.

1 F.O. 83/2402. Reference may also be made to the Opinion of 19 April 1869, concerning the capture by a Spanish ship of an American vessel. It was not clear whether the capture was made in British waters or on the high seas. The Opinion is of interest because of its concluding passage: 'Meanwhile it will be open to the Government of the United States to claim the restitution of the Ship on the finding of the Court, "that she was captured on the High Seas", inasmuch as the Proclamation of the Spanish Governor is an implicit negation of the existence of a state of war, which would entitle Spanish Cruizers to exercise belligerent rights on the high seas against Neutral Vessels' (F.O. 83/2376). The assumption apparently was that it was within the election of Spain to bring about a state of belligerency with resulting belligerent rights.

Report of 13 *November* 1871[1]

Temple

My Lord

I am honoured with Your Lordship's commands signified in Mr Hammond's letter of the 9th Instant stating that he was directed to transmit to me the accompanying Despatch from Her Majesty's Chargé d'Affaires at Caracas, inclosing a Decree with a translation, which has been issued by the Provisional President of Venezuela, establishing a blockade of the Coast embraced by the mouths of the Orinoco, Mr Hammond was pleased to request that I would take this Decree into my consideration, and furnish Your Lordship with my opinion thereupon.

In obedience to Your Lordship's commands I have the honour to *Report*

That I am of opinion that there is nothing in the Decree of the Provisional Government of Venezuela, which would render the blockade invalid, provided it is effectively maintained in accordance with the Declaration of Paris of 1856.

I have the honour to be, My Lord,
Your Lordship's most obedient, humble Servant,
TRAVERS TWISS

To The Right Honble The Earl Granville, K.G.

Report of the Law Officers of 6 *February* 1874[2]

Temple

My Lord

We are honoured with your Lordship's commands signified in Lord Tenterden's letter of the 2nd inst stating that he was directed by your Lordship to transmit to us the accompanying copies of two telegrams from Her Majesty's Minister at Madrid reporting that a great part of the North Coast of Spain has been declared in a state of blockade to commence from the 20th inst....

Lord Tenterden also stated that he was to request that we would favour your Lordship at our earliest convenience with our opinion as to the course that should be followed by Her Majesty's Government with regard to the blockade now declared bearing in mind that the Carlists have not been recognized as Belligerents.

In obedience to your Lordship's commands we have the honour to *Report*

That assuming the blockade to be effective Her Majesty's Government must in our opinion recognize the fact that it exists *de facto* and *de jure*.

The result however will be that the Carlists henceforth become belligerents.

The parts of the Coast to which the blockade is applied was we presume in the hands of the Carlists, for the Madrid Government cannot establish a Municipal blockade of its own ports or coast.

1 F.O. 83/2403. In an Opinion of 11 December 1871 (F.O. 83/2403), Sir Travers Twiss advised the Government that they may properly publish in the *London Gazette* a notification of the Decree of the President of Venezuela announcing the blockade of the mouths of the Orinoco River.

2 F.O. 83/2379.

It would be well that Mr Layard should be instructed to inform the Spanish Government that such a course must lead to the issuing of a proclamation of neutrality.

We have the honour to be, My Lord,
Your Lordship's most obed' humble Servts'.
HENRY JAMES, W. V. HARCOURT, J. P. DEANE

The Right Honble The Earl Granville, K.G., etc., etc., etc.

Opinion of the Law Officers of 14 *February* 1874[1]

Temple

My Lord

We are honored with your Lordship's commands signified in Lord Tenterden's letter of the 11th instant stating that with reference to his letter of the 7th instant relative to the proposed Blockade of the Northern Coast of Spain he was directed by your Lordship to transmit to us to be taken into our consideration together with papers already before us a further despatch from Her Majesty's Minister at Madrid enclosing a copy of Blockade regulations issued by the Spanish Government on November 26, 1864 and referred to in the decree enclosed in Mr Layard's No. 106.

In obedience to your Lordship's commands we have the honor to *Report*

That if the Spanish Government is prepared to accept the consequences which will follow of raising the Carlist insurgents to the status of recognized belligerents by a declaration of belligerent blockade we see no objection to the regulations of November 26th 1864 so far as they relate to the matter of blockade. Upon other points however the regulations contain serious errors against which we think Her Majesty's Government should at once protest if it is proposed to put these regulations in force....

We have the honor to be, My Lord,
Your Lordship's most Obedt. humble Servants
HENRY JAMES, W. V. HARCOURT, J. P. DEANE

The Right Honble Earl Granville, K.G., etc., etc., etc.

Opinion of the Law Officers of the Crown and Dr Deane to the Earl of Derby of 6 *May* 1876[2]

Temple

My Lord

We are honoured with your Lordship's commands signified in Lord Tenterden's letter of the 12th ultimo, stating that he was directed by your Lordship to transmit to us the accompanying despatches from Her Majesty's Minister at Port-au-Prince, relative to the measures adopted by the Haytian Government in consequence of the outbreak of an insurrection in that Republic; and that he (Lord Tenterden) was to

1 Ibid. 2 F.O. 83/2290.

request that we would favour your Lordship with our opinion as to the instructions that should be sent to Major Stuart upon the subject of the blockade of Jacmel.

We are also honoured with a letter from Mr Lister, dated the 17th ultimo, stating that he transmitted to us, by direction of your Lordship, a letter from the Atlas Steamship Company, calling attention to the loss which would be caused to them by the action of the Haytian Government in blockading the port of Jacmel....

In obedience to your Lordship's commands we have the honour to report—

That the Haytian Government have the right to blockade the port of Jacmel, but by such blockade that Government creates a state of war, giving neutral as well as belligerent rights.

It appears from the letter of Messrs Leech that the blockade was established and existed *de facto*.

So long, therefore, as the blockade is maintained, British subjects have no legal right to complain of, and no redress to claim for, any loss which they may suffer through the blockade.

Major Stuart may therefore, in our opinion, properly be instructed to point out to the Haytian Government that Her Majesty's subjects are entitled to claim, and will be protected in, the exercise of their rights as neutrals.

We have, &c.

(Signed) John Holker, Hardinge S. Giffard, J. Parker Deane

Opinion of the Law Officers of the Crown and Dr Deane to Earl Granville of 24 October 1883[1]

Royal Courts of Justice

My Lord

We are honoured with your Lordship's commands signified in Mr Currie's letter of the 28th ultimo, stating that, with reference to the letters from the Foreign Office of the 10th and 21st ultimo, he was to transmit to us, by direction of your Lordship, the letter from the Colonial Office, forwarding a despatch from the Officer Administering the Government of the Bahamas relative to the proceedings of a Haïtian war-vessel in boarding and searching the schooner 'Research', belonging to the port of Nassau, commanded by a British subject named Erskine J. Stuart, when 10 miles distant from the port of Jeremie, the schooner being at the time on a voyage from Jamaica to Nassau.

That Mr Currie was to request that we would take that paper into our consideration with those then before us relating to the blockade of the Haïtian ports, and that we would favour your Lordship with our opinion as to what action, if any, should be taken in the matter.

In obedience to your Lordship's commands we have the honour to report—

That the rebel force appears to be in complete possession of a part of Haïti, and to have acquired such a position as to be treated by the Government of Haïti as belligerents.

1 F.O. 35/120.

If such a state of war exists, the vessels of war belonging to the Haïtian Government would have a right to seize any contraband of war destined for the enemy, and to search any vessel near the enemy's shores which might be supposed to contain such contraband.

The Haïtian officers seem to have acted with unnecessary rudeness, and to have made use of unjustifiable threats; but their action in searching the vessel was probably, in strictness, warranted by international law.

It would be well, however, to call the attention of the Government of Haïti to the matter, and ask for an explanation.

We have, &c.

(Signed) HENRY JAMES, FARRER HERSCHELL, J. PARKER DEANE

NOTE. See also to the same effect the 'Opinion of the Law Officers of 16 July 1883' approving the terms of the following instruction sent by the Foreign Office to the British local representative:

'I have therefore to instruct you to inquire and report at once whether the blockade is (as I presume it is intended to be) one *jure gentium*, and, if so, whether it is effectively maintained by the presence of ships of war in sufficient number to prevent ingress and egress.

'If the blockade should not be effective, Her Majesty's Government could not recognize its validity; nor could they do so if the Decree is intended to operate only as a municipal blockade closing the port of Jérémie to foreign commerce by a municipal law. Jérémie being in possession of the insurgents, the only valid blockade that can be lawfully established as against neutrals is one recognized by international law as a blockade *jure gentium*, and such blockade must be effectively maintained as a condition of its validity.'

Opinion of the Law Officers of the Crown to Earl Granville of 29 September 1883[1]

Royal Courts of Justice

My Lord

We were honoured with your Lordship's commands signified in Mr Currie's letter of the 10th instant, stating that with reference to the letter from the Foreign Office of the 14th July, and to our reply of the 16th of the same month, relative to the blockade of the port of Jeremie in Haïti, he had the honour to transmit to us, by direction of the Secretary of State, the despatch, noted in the margin of his letter from Her Majesty's Representative at Port-au-Prince, forwarding a notification received by him from the Haitian Government of the blockade of Jacmel, and stating that it was not likely to be an effective one, and that the port of Jeremie was still open. That Mr Currie was at the same time to transmit to us, as by the accom-

1 Ibid.

panying list, a correspondence which had taken place with the Atlas Steamship Company, and also a letter, which, by your Lordship's direction, had been addressed to the Board of Admiralty, requesting them to instruct the British officer commanding Her Majesty's ships in Haitian waters to report whether the blockade of Jacmel and Jeremie was effective or not, and if it was clearly not effective to warn the Haitian authorities that Her Majesty's Government protested against any interference with British vessels proceeding to those ports.

In obedience to your Lordship's commands we have the honour to report—

That, in our opinion, Her Majesty's Government would not be justified, under the circumstances, in preventing by force the seizure of British vessels. If the Haitian Prize Courts should act in clear defiance of law and justice, Her Majesty's Government would be entitled to insist upon redress on behalf of any British subjects injured by such action.

We think the reply to the Atlas Steamship Company is a sufficient one.

We have, &c.

(Signed) Henry James, Farrer Herschell

Note. In the 'Draft of Letter to the Atlas Steamship Company' the Foreign Office said: 'If the blockade of the ports of Jeremie and Jacmel, notification of which has been received from the Haitian Government, is not effective, it must be held to be invalid. But there is no reason, because the blockade is not effective on one day, that it should not be effectively carried out on the next day.

'The fact of the proper maintenance of the blockade can only be ascertained at the time, when the question arises, and on the spot, and in case of capture of a vessel for breach of the blockade, it is a question for the decision of a Prize Court.

'Meanwhile, instructions will be sent to the officer in command of Her Majesty's forces in Haitian waters, to report whether the blockade of these ports is effective or not effective, or doubtful, and, if clearly not effective, to warn the Haitian authorities, both civil and naval, that Her Majesty's Government protest against any interference with British vessels proceeding to those ports.'

Opinion of the Law Officers of the Crown and Dr Deane to Earl Granville of 22 January 1884

Royal Courts of Justice[1]

My Lord

We are honoured with your Lordship's commands signified in Sir Julian Pauncefote's letter of the 14th instant, stating that, with reference to the Foreign

1 F.O. 35/124.

Office letter of the 28th September last, and to previous correspondence upon the subject of the blockade of Haïtian ports, he was to transmit to us papers relative to the blockade of Jacmel.

That Her Majesty's Consul at Port-au-Prince forwarded copies of two communications which he had received from the Haïtian Government: the first, requesting him to notify to the agents of the Royal Mail Steam Packet Company that the blockade of Jacmel was then effective by the presence before that port of the Haïtian war-vessel 'Dessaline', which had orders to sink any ship trying to force the blockade; and the second, stating that the President had received information that two British men-of-war were about to proceed to Jacmel in order to protect the Royal Mail steamer, which it was reported intended to force the blockade of that place on the 26th ultimo, and requesting that Mr Hunt would take measures to prevent their interference.

That Sir J. Pauncefote was to request our opinion as to the reply which Mr Hunt should be instructed to make in regard to the threat of the Haïtian Minister for Foreign Affairs, that vessels attempting to force the blockade would be sunk, a measure which it was conceived would not be warranted by international war....

In obedience to your Lordship's commands we have the honour to report—

That if the blockade of Jacmel be effective, a Haïtian vessel of war would no doubt be entitled to capture any vessel attempting to break the blockade, and to prevent its being broken. And we apprehend that if a vessel persisted, in defiance of the opposition of the war-vessel, in its endeavours to reach the port, and refused to surrender, such conduct would justify hostile action. But we do not think a vessel of war would be justified in sinking a merchant-vessel, except as an extreme measure, in the case where such vessel was acting in defiance of the rights of the blockading force, and by its own action rendered such an extreme act of hostility absolutely necessary.

We have, &c.

(Signed) HENRY JAMES, FARRER HERSCHELL, J. PARKER DEANE

The following Opinion relating to a rebellion in Japan in 1869 counsels the denial of belligerent rights both to the lawful government and to the insurgents. The reason, as suggested in the Opinion, is that the situation did not reveal the features of a civil war as understood in Europe.

Opinion of the Law Officers of 19 April 1869[1]

Temple

My Lord

We are honoured with your Lordship's commands signified in Mr Hammond's letter of the 13th instant, stating that he was directed by your Lordship to transmit to us, together with the previous papers, a Despatch from Sir H. Parkes, inclosing

1 F.O. 83/2299.

copies of a correspondence, which has passed between him and Admiral Sir H. Keppel respecting the denial of belligerent rights to the exiled Kerais, who had made a descent in the Island of Yezo: and Mr Hammond was pleased to request that we would take the same into our consideration, and favour your Lordship with our opinion thereupon, at our earliest convenience.

In obedience to the commands of your Lordship, we have taken these papers into consideration, and have the honor to *Report*.

That whether civil war exists or not is a question of pure fact, to be decided from the condition of the country where it is alleged to exist. In Europe civil war means such a substantial suspension of the powers of the central Government, as prevents its arm being felt, or its law administered by the ordinary Tribunals. But this definition is essentially European, and can not be strictly applied with exactness or rigour to communities where the action of the central Government is different, probably more irregular, than our own, certainly quite unlike it, and the question of civil war or not is a question to be decided with special reference to local circumstances.

We think Sir Henry Parkes is the most competent person to judge of this question of fact; and his opinion as to the non-existence of anything, which can properly be called civil war, is clear. Nor is there anything in the voluminous papers sent to us to make us doubt the soundness of his opinion.

We may observe that the refusal of belligerent rights to the exiled Kerais implies that no war in fact exists; and that the Japanese Government have no more than the Kerais the right as against neutrals, like ourselves, to assume the exceptional rights of belligerents; but must confine their action, as far as our shipping and commerce are concerned, to their rights in time of peace, as modified (if they are modified) by express Treaty.

We have the honor to be, My Lord,
Your Lordship's most obedient humble servants,

R. P. COLLIER, J. D. COLERIDGE, TRAVERS TWISS

The Right Honble The Earl of Clarendon, K.G.

III

OPINIONS OF THE LAW OFFICERS OF THE CROWN ON CONDITIONS OF CLOSURE OF PORTS OCCUPIED BY INSURGENTS

The following Opinions illustrate the principle that the conditions of blockade cannot be avoided by a decree closing ports occupied by insurgents and purporting to have an effect outside the territorial limits of the State.

Opinion of the Law Officers of 25 June 1861[1]

Doctors Commons

My Lord

We were honoured with your Lordship's commands signified in Lord Wodehouse's letter of the 20th June instant, stating that he was directed by your Lordship to transmit to us the accompanying Despatches from Her Majesty's Minister at Washington, relative to the measures which it is proposed to ask Congress to adopt at its meeting on the 4th of next month.

That among those proposed measures, is said to be one giving to the President the right to declare the Ports of the Seceded States to be no longer Ports of entry, and to confiscate any Vessel which shall attempt to resort to them; the apparent object of this measure, (as stated by Her Majesty's Minister,) being to free the United States Government from the obligation of observing the Rules of International Law respecting the Blockade, but especially to do away with the necessity of keeping at all times a Force on the coast sufficient to render it effective.

Lord Wodehouse was pleased to request that we would take into our consideration the project said to be entertained by the United States Government for closing the Southern Ports by the means above indicated.

In obedience to your Lordship's commands we have the honor to *Report*.

That any attempt on the part of the Northern (United) States to close by an act of Congress all the ports in the Southern (Confederate) States against British Commerce, would be inconsistent with the pacific and commercial relations at present existing between the 'United States of America' and this Country.

Further we are of opinion that no belligerent power has a right, by mere prohibitory enactment, to require neutral nations to abstain from all commercial dealings with another belligerent power; which would be the result of the expected enactment. Such a right can extend only to ports of which the belligerent is in actual possession, and into which he can therefore not only forbid entry, but by competent force upon the spot, give effect to such prohibition. We are, therefore, of opinion that any paper enactment by Congress, to the effect anticipated by Lord Lyons, may be treated as nugatory by the Law of Nations; and any attempt to enforce it by the seizure and confiscation of a neutral ship may be justly regarded as an act of hostility.

We would suggest the expediency of this country and other European powers concurring in a representation to this effect to the Government of the (Northern) United States.

We have the honor to be, My Lord,
Your Lordship's obedient Humble Servants,

J. D. Harding, Richard Bethell, Wm. Atherton

The Right Hon: Lord John Russell, M.P., &c., &c., &c.

1 F.O. 83/2211.

Opinion of the Queen's Advocate of 1 July 1870[1]

Temple

Sir

I am favoured with your Letter of the 30th ultimo stating that you were directed by the Secretary of State to transmit to me the accompanying Despatches from Her Majesty's Chargé d'affaires in Venezuela relating to the closing to Foreign Trade of the Ports of Maracaibo, La Véla, and Precerto Cabello, by the Venezuelan Government.

That the Representatives of France, Spain, Italy, and the North German Confederation, had, it would be seen, joined Her Majesty's Chargé d'affaires in protesting against the legality of the measure adopted by the Venezuelan Government, on the ground that no effective blockade of the Ports in question has been established; and you were pleased to request that I would take the enclosed Papers into my consideration and Report to the Secretary of State my opinion upon the proceedings of the Venezuelan Government in this case, and also as to the legality of the Protest on the part of the Foreign Representatives.

In obedience to the commands of the Secretary of State I have taken these papers into consideration and have the honor to Report.

That I am not aware of the precise character of the insurrectionary movement in Venezuela but I gather from the correspondence, that the contest between the insurgents and the Government hitherto recognized by Her Majesty, has not at present the attributes of a Civil war, so as to impart to that Government as regards the intercourse of foreign nations with Venezuela the rights attaching to belligerency. The closing therefore by a decree of that Government of certain ports occupied by the Insurgents against foreign commerce can only be regarded as a municipal regulation, which Venezuela would have the right to enforce as part of her revenue laws within a marine league from her coast by vessels stationed in the neighbourhood of the ports, but not by vessels cruizing on the high seas beyond that distance. It will be important for Her Majesty's Chargé d'affaires to ascertain what orders the Venezuelan Government proposes to give to its armed vessels in pursuance of its decrees, as if it should order them to interrupt by force the navigation of foreign vessels on the ocean beyond the limits above mentioned under plea either of intercepting all commercial communications with the specified ports, or of confiscating all vessels which have contravened its decrees; I should be of opinion that such an interference with the commerce of Foreign nations might be rightfully resented by them, and would give just cause for reprisals—and that Her Majesty's Chargé d'affaires may properly intimate to the Venezuelan Minister of Foreign Affairs that Her Majesty's Government would not be disposed to acquiesce in any such vexatious interference with peaceable British Merchant Vessels.

How far I may be in error in the limited view, which I have taken of the insurrectionary movement in Venezuela, it is for Her Majesty's Government to decide. It may be that the laws of Venezuela are *de facto* suspended in the ports in

1 F.O. 83/2403.

question, and it is possible, that the protest of the diplomatic body is grounded on the view that the revolutionary party is supreme over the ports, of which it holds possession: If this be the view entertained by those who have joined in the Protest, other considerations of Public Law will govern the question of right, as regards foreign vessels frequenting such ports. It would be their duty upon entering such ports to obey the authorities there established in all questions of internal administration touching the public revenue, and their obedience to such authorities could justly work no forfeiture of the vessels on leaving the ports, and passing into waters still under the controul of the recognized Government of the Republic. Whether the events of the contest justify this view of the ascendancy of the insurrectionary forces in the ports in question must be determined by the facts which are presented in each case, respecting which there is very little light in the papers, which have been forwarded to me, as the collective note of the Diplomatic body referred to in Mr Middleton's Despatch No. 7. Commercial of 4th of June 1870, does not accompany it. I infer however from Mr Middleton's Despatch to the Diplomatic Body laying stress upon there being 'no effective blockade of the ports', that they consider the contest to have the attributes of a civil war, in which case foreign vessels would have a right to enter any port under the *de facto* Government of the Insurgents, which was not blockaded by the forces of the *de jure* Government, and it would be the duty of the Masters of such vessels, upon entering such ports, to obey such authorities as they might find established there in all matters of fiscal or Custom House regulations. Upon this latter supposition the Protest might be justifiable.

I have the honor to be, Sir,
Your most obedient Servant,
TRAVERS TWISS

Arthur Otway, Esq., M.P.

Opinion of the Law Officers of the Crown and Dr Deane to the Marquis of Salisbury of 31 May 1878[1]

Temple

My Lord

We were honoured with your Lordship's commands signified in Sir Julian Pauncefote's letter of the 25th ultimo, stating that he was directed by your Lordship to transmit to us a despatch from the British Vice-Consul at Santo Domingo forwarding a Decree issued by the Provisional Government of that Republic ordering the closing of the harbour of Puerto Plata to foreign commerce.

That that Decree had not been officially notified to Her Majesty's Government, and was perhaps intended to operate as a Municipal Act only; but, from the terms of the Decree, it would seem to be intended that the closing of the ports should be enforced by the rules of blockade.

1 F.O. 23/69.

That your Lordship would therefore be glad to be favoured with our opinion whether, the port of Puerto Plata being in the hands of the rebels, it was competent to the Government of Santo Domingo to close it to foreign commerce otherwise than by establishing a belligerent blockade, duly notified to neutral Powers and effectively maintained....

In obedience to your Lordship's commands we have the honour to report—

That, taking the words of the Decree, we are of opinion that the act of closing the port to foreign commerce is a belligerent act, and must be taken to mean a blockade in the proper sense of the word, and requiring due notice and efficient maintenance before vessels arriving at the port could be legally seized and condemned.

We have, &c.

(Signed) JOHN HOLKER, HARDINGE S. GIFFARD, J. PARKER DEANE

NOTE. See also to the same effect the 'Opinion of 6 January 1885' relating to the closure of the ports of Peru. The Law Officers said:

'We do not understand what is meant by a closing of the ports "in furtherance of fiscal interests,"...and as the "closing" of them was an act of hostility, we think it could only be valid as against other Powers if the blockade were effectively maintained and duly notified.'

The view which underlies these Opinions was expressed with similar emphasis in 1889 when the Government of Peru once more closed by Decree ports occupied by insurgents. They were informed that 'when a port is in the *de facto* possession of forces in open rebellion against the recognized Government of the country, that Government cannot claim to close such ports to commerce by Municipal Decree, but can only do so, according to international law, by means of an official blockade *jure gentium* the existence of which in itself constitutes an admission on the part of the Government instituting it that a state of belligerency exists.'

When in 1891 the Chilean Government refused to grant clearances to British vessels for foreign ports or the high seas unless a written pledge was given that they would not call at ports in the possession of insurgent forces, they were informed by the British Government that their right to exact a pledge was not admitted and that they would be held liable for resulting losses (*Correspondence relating to the Revolution in Chile*, 1891, pp. 156, 157).[1]

1 See also the interesting correspondence in connection with the proposed Spanish blockade of Sulu in 1876: 'Blockade is a belligerent right, and can only be exercised against a State with which the blockading Power is at war. A Power may prohibit foreign trade with its own ports; but such prohibition does not carry with it the same rights of interference with foreign vessels as are conferred by a regularly-constituted blockade' (Earl of Derby to Lord Odo Russell, 17 January 1876 (*B.F.S.P.* vol. LXXIII, p. 965)).

The following despatch of the Marquis of Salisbury of the same year is in line with the preceding pronouncements.

The Marquis of Salisbury to Mr J. G. Kennedy

Foreign Office, April 10, 1891

(Telegraphic)

APPLICATIONS are being received at this Office from Steamship Companies and others with reference to the Decree which you reported in your telegram of the 5th instant had been issued by the Chilean Government closing to commerce all ports north of Caldera which are in possession of the party opposed to the President.

I have to instruct you to inform the Chilean Government, without delay, that Her Majesty's Government cannot admit their right to close by Municipal Decree ports in the effective possession of the Congressional party, or to impose fines or penalties on ships which, in the ordinary and regular course of trade, have visited such ports, or, generally, to inflict penalties under the Decree.

You will further state that the Chilean Government will be held responsible by Her Majesty's Government for any loss or damage which may be caused to British subjects by any action of the Government of Chile in the above respects, and that instructions have been sent to the officers in command of Her Majesty's ships in Chilean waters to protect British vessels from molestation on such grounds.[1]

The following Opinion shows that the objection to closing ports by decree does not apply when they do not purport to operate beyond the territorial limits of the State or, as in the last two Opinions, when special circumstances justify a measure of this nature.

Opinion of the Queen's Advocate of 4 *September* 1866[2]

Doctors Commons

My Lord

I am honoured with Your Lordship's commands, signified in Mr Egerton's Letter of the 1st Instant stating that he was directed to transmit to me two Despatches from Her Majesty's Minister at Mexico inclosing copies of decrees which have been issued by the Mexican Government closing certain Ports of that Country against both internal and Foreign Commerce: and Mr Egerton was pleased to request that I would take these papers into consideration, and furnish Your Lordship with my opinion as to the legality of the above-mentioned proceeding.

In obedience to Your Lordship's commands, I have taken this case into consideration and have the honour to *Report*

That the Decree in question prohibits all commerce between places subject to the Imperial Government and the Department of Chihuahua which is under the control of the enemy of the Emperor, and it also contains a Regulation with respect to

1 *State Papers*, vol. XCV (1892), *Chile*, no. 1.

2 F.O. 83/2307.

Passports as to persons travelling in that Department.—That it is to be remembered that Her Majesty though neutral in the Civil War now existing in Mexico has recognized the Emperor as the lawful Sovereign of that State.—No question it will be observed as to the validity of any blockade is raised by this Decree. I see no reason to doubt the competence of the Emperor of Mexico to make the Decree in question which is to have effect only within his own dominions.

I have the honour to be, My Lord,
Your Lordship's most obedient, humble Servant,
ROBERT PHILLIMORE

To The Right Honble The Lord Stanley

NOTE. See also to the same effect the 'Opinion of the Law Officers of 5 August 1869'[1] with regard to a Cuban Declaration, one Article of which provided that 'vessels attempting to enter the Ports which are closed or to communicate with the Coast will be chased, and if captured will be tried'. The Law Officers advised that 'the right of chase and capture of the Spanish Government is confined to their own territorial limits, viz 3 miles from the shore, and that it may be well, (to prevent misapprehension) that they should be informed that Her Majesty's Government cannot permit that any British vessel, even if she should have violated the Spanish regulations, should be chased and captured on the High Seas.'

In a previous 'Opinion of 15 July 1869'[2] the Law Officers said: 'The Cuban Insurgents have not been declared or recognized as belligerents, they are not in actual possession (as far as we are aware) of any ports, no blockade has been proclaimed by Spain; under these circumstances the Spanish Government are entitled to prohibit foreign ships entering their ports, possibly to capture such as disregard the prohibition, and to deal with those on board them by the Spanish Municipal Law; but we are of opinion that they are not entitled to pursue vessels beyond the limits of their local jurisdiction and to exercise the belligerent right of capture on the high seas.'

Opinion of the Queen's Advocate of 13 *August* 1870[3]

Temple

My Lord

I am honoured with Your Lordship's commands, signified in Mr Otway's Letter of the 9th Instant stating that with reference to my Report of the 1st Ultimo he was directed to transmit to me together with the previous papers two Despatches from Mr Middleton relative to the course pursued by the Venezuelan Government in closing certain Ports of the Republic: and to request that I would again take this

1 F.O. 83/2376. 2 Ibid. 3 F.O. 83/2403.

matter into my consideration, and report to Your Lordship any further observations I might have to offer thereupon.

In obedience to Your Lordship's commands, I have the honour to *Report*

That assuming the Government established at the present time at Caracas to be recognized by Her Majesty's Government, as the Government of the Republic of Venezuela, I am of opinion that Her Majesty's Government is bound in comity to respect its decrees for the regulation of the Commerce of British Subjects with any of the Ports of Venezuela, unless those Ports are not only not in the Possession, but also not under the Dominion of the Republic. Whether the three Ports, to which the Decree of the Venezuelan Government applies, are, or are not, in the possession and under the Dominion of the Republic, is a question partly of fact, partly of Law. That they are not in the actual possession of the forces of the Republic is apparent, but the Government of the Republic asserts its right of dominion over them, and it appears from the Protocol of the Diplomatic Body signed at Caracas on 22nd June 1870, to which the signature of Her Majesty's Chargé d'Affaires is attached, that the Powers, whom they represent, hold the so-called Government, in whose name General Hernandez claims to act within those Ports, to have ceased to exist since 27th April last, and refuses to recognize any state of War between him and the Government of the Republic, which would entitle him to establish a belligerent blockade of the three Ports. Under these circumstances I am of opinion that Her Majesty's Government will be consistent, if it recognizes the right of the Government of the Republic to close for a time the three Ports against Foreign Commerce on the alleged ground that it is unable to prevent the Customs on Foreign Commerce in those Ports being wrongfully diverted from the Treasury of the Republic, to which they of right belong.

I have the honour to be, My Lord,

Your Lordship's most obedient, humble Servant,

TRAVERS TWISS

To The Right Honble The Earl Granville, K.G.

Opinion of the Law Officers of the Crown and Dr Deane to the Marquis of Salisbury of 18 April 1879[1]

Temple

My Lord

We were honoured with your Lordship's commands signified in Sir Julian Pauncefote's letter of the 1st March ultimo, stating that he was directed by your Lordship to transmit to us the accompanying despatch from Her Majesty's Minister at Carácas (No. 8 of the 16th January, 1879) relative to an order recently issued by the Venezuelan Government prohibiting all intercourse with the port of Puerto Cabello, in consequence of that place having fallen into the hands of a revolutionary force, and requiring all vessels touching at La Guayra with merchan-

1 F.O. 80/261.

dise or correspondence for Puerto Cabello to discharge their goods and deliver up their letters at the first-named port....

In obedience to your Lordship's commands we have the honour to report—

That circumstances may justify a Government in closing a particular port. The Government, in whose country the port is, is the proper judge of the circumstances which may make the closing of the port necessary or expedient.

We assume that Puerto Cabello is closed to the ships of all nations.

We are, therefore, of opinion that Mr Bunch (the British representative) may be instructed to remonstrate no further with the Venezuela Government.

We have, &c.

(Signed) JOHN HOLKER, HARDINGE S. GIFFARD, J. PARKER DEANE

IV

OPINIONS OF THE LAW OFFICERS OF THE CROWN ON RECOGNIZED BELLIGERENTS IN RELATION TO PROPERTY RIGHTS OF ALIENS

The following three Opinions, which are not altogether consistent, are of interest as showing the degree of acquiescence in the exercise of belligerent rights with regard to the property of aliens on land. The first refers to the prohibition of trading with the enemy issued by the Government of the United States; the second to the legitimacy of penal legislation in respect of dealings with the insurgents; the third to measures taken by the Confederate States recognized as belligerents.

Opinion of the Queen's Advocate of 27 September 1861[1]

Doctors Commons

My Lord

I am honored with Your Lordship's Commands signified in Mr Hammond's letter of the 10th September Instant, stating that he was directed to transmit to me a despatch from Her Majesty's Minister at Washington, inclosing a copy of a Proclamation issued by the President of the United States, prohibiting commercial intercourse with the Seceded States.

Mr Hammond was also pleased to enclose, for reference, a copy of the Act of Congress under which it is stated that this Proclamation has been issued; And to request that I would take the Proclamation into consideration, and furnish Your Lordship with such observations as I might have to offer thereupon.

In obedience to Your Lordship's Commands, I have taken this Proclamation into consideration, and have the honor to *Report*,

1 F.O. 83/2212.

That this Proclamation appears to me, to be within the competence of the President, and in conformity with the Law and usage of Nations. The existence of a war between two Governments implies and involves, in theory and contemplation of international Law, the existence of a war between all the individuals voluntarily domiciled within the territory of either Government, which is supposed to represent and act for all such persons; and one of the immediate consequences of war, is the entire interdiction of all commercial dealing between the subjects, citizens, or domiciled inhabitants, of the belligerents, excepting by the formal and special license or permission of their Government. With this exception, 'war' places every individual living within the territory of either Government, as well as the Governments themselves, in a state of hostility, legally and internationally, and trading with the inhabitants of the enemy's territory, is 'trading with the enemy'. These principles have been constantly applied 'inter gentes', by this Country, and other Foreign Powers, when belligerents.

The fact that the war now existing in North America, may in a certain sense be viewed as a civil war, and that the President speaks of 'the insurrection' of the particular States named in the Proclamation, does not appear to me to make any very material or practical difference; more especially as Her Majesty's Govt and all other Governments have treated both parties as 'belligerentes inter se in justo bello', and consider themselves as 'neutrals' internationally. It does not appear to me therefore that the issuing of this Proclamation requires any international notice on the part of Her Majesty's Government. It remains to be seen how the 'forfeiture to the United States' (imposed by the Proclamation) is to be enforced, and carried out in practice; whether by legal proceedings in Court, or otherwise; upon which point Lord Lyons will doubtless send further information.

I have the honor to be, My Lord,
Your Lordship's most obedient humble Servant,
J. D. Harding

To The Right Honble Earl Russell

Opinion of the Law Officers of the Crown of 3 February 1866[1]

Lincoln's Inn

My Lord

We are honoured with your Lordship's commands signified in Mr Hammond's letter of the 24th ultimo, stating that with reference to our Report of the 6th ultimo, he was directed by your Lordship to transmit to us the accompanying despatch from Her Majesty's Consul at Charleston (No. 11, January 5), and its inclosures, respecting cotton purchased for British subjects by agents in the so-styled Confederate States during the late civil war.

And Mr Hammond was to request we would take the same into consideration, and furnish your Lordship with our opinion thereupon....

1 F.O. 97/47.

In obedience to your Lordship's commands we have taken these papers into consideration, and have the honour to report—

That we do not find any new facts stated in these papers which at all affect the Report which we have already had the honour to make upon the general subject of the seizure of cotton belonging to British subjects, purchased from Confederate owners.

In our opinion the seizure of this cotton now is an act scarcely justifiable; the confiscation of it would be an act wholly unwarrantable by any principles of jurisprudence, private or public, with which we are acquainted.

To treat the dealings of foreigners with persons in the Confederate States as bound by the Acts of Congress of the United States during the time while the *de facto* Government of the Confederate States continued, would be a most questionable course of proceeding; but to hold *bonâ fide* transactions of this kind, which took place in 1862 and 1863, defeated *ex post facto* by an Act of Congress passed in 1864, would be nothing less than monstrous.

The circumstances as stated appear to place the case of Messrs Gibbs on a most favourable footing; but we do not advise that Her Majesty's Government should at present intervene exceptionally on behalf of any individual British purchaser of this cotton. We think that the strongest official remonstrance as to the whole of this class of cases should be pressed upon the United States' Government.

Messrs Gibbs' case, and its circumstances, may (of course) be referred to, as illustrating the nature of the injustice complained of.

We have, &c.

(Signed) ROUNDELL PALMER, R. P. COLLIER, ROBERT PHILLIMORE

Opinion of the Law Officers of the Crown of 13 *November* 1861[1]

Doctors Commons

My Lord

We were honored with your Lordship's commands signified in Mr Hammond's letter of the 7th instant, stating that he was directed by your Lordship to transmit to us a correspondence with Messrs Copestake Moore and Co, and a despatch and its inclosures from Her Majesty's Consul at New York, respecting an Act of Congress of the so-styled Confederate States, confiscating the property and debts of alien enemies.

That to this act was appended a letter of Instructions issued by Mr Benjamin, the Attorney General of the Confederate Government, from which it would appear that the subjects of Her Majesty, and of other neutral powers, having their domicile in the Northern States, were comprised in that designation.

That it was Your Lordship's intention to have deferred consulting us upon the subject until it had been ascertained whether the act of the Confederate Govern-

1 F.O. 83/2212.

ment had been put into active operation, but, as that measure had produced some excitement among British Subjects owning property in the South, and Mr Dennistoun, of Glasgow, having requested an interview with your Lordship in regard to it, your Lordship was pleased to request that we would at once take these Papers into our consideration, and favour your Lordship with such observations as we might have to offer thereupon.

In obedience to your Lordship's commands, we have considered these Papers, and have the honor to *Report*.

That, we understand your Lordship's question to refer to the confiscation, in the Confederate States, of property and debts belonging and due to British Subjects resident, or having a commercial domicile, in the United States. In our opinion, no distinction can, in strictness of international law, be taken, for the purposes of this question, between such British subjects, and citizens of the United States. The general question, whether belligerents may, by the law of nations, confiscate the property of, and debts owing to, private persons, subjects of the Enemy, within its territory, has been the subject of controversy: and a decision of the Court of Queen's Bench, in the time of Lord Ellenborough, is adverse to the existence of this right.[1] It appears to us, however, that this decision is outweighed by a considerable preponderance of authority among the writers on international Law; and that the power of confiscating such property and debts is, in the abstract, recognized by the Law of Nations. The instances, however, of its exercise, in modern and civilized times, are so rare, and have been so generally condemned, that it may almost be said to have become obsolete. The conclusion of Wheaton (*Elements*, 6th ed. p. 369) is thus expressed—

'It appears, then, to be the modern rule of International usage, that property of the enemy found within the territory of the Belligerent state, or debts due to his subjects by the Government or individuals, at the commencement of hostilities, are not liable to be seized and confiscated as prize of war. This rule is frequently enforced by treaty stipulations, but, unless it be thus enforced, it cannot be considered as an inflexible, though an established, rule. The rule [as it has been beautifully observed[2]], like other precepts of morality, of humanity, and even of wisdom, is addressed to the Judgment of the Sovereign—it is a guide which he follows or abandons at his will; and although it cannot be disregarded by him without obloquy, yet it may be disregarded. It is not an immutable rule of law; but depends on political considerations, which may continually vary.'

These observations assume the existence of an ordinary state of war between 2 independent and foreign nations—The present case is infinitely stronger against the exercise of the right in question, being one of civil war between the different parts of one Confederation, during whose union the citizens of Foreign States were invited and induced to settle indiscriminately in its various States, without the

1 *Wolff* v. *Oxholm*, (1817) 6 M. & S. 92.

2 Mr Chief Justice Marshall in *United States* v. *Brown*, Cranch's Reports, vol. VIII, p. 110.

possibility of their contemplating such a disruption as has occurred. No notice has been given to them, or time allowed which would enable them to prepare for such an emergency, or to separate their affairs from those of the citizens of either belligerent: and, though liable, technically, to be deemed enemies, it is impossible to treat them as such, in this respect, without gross injustice, and a breach of that faith to which every State of the American Union was originally a party. We think, under these circumstances, that the case is one for urgent remonstrances; in which it would be, of course, desirable to secure the concurrence of the other great Powers; who, in common with Great Britain, are deeply interested in the question.

We have the honor to be, My Lord,
Your Lordships obedient, humble Servants,
J. D. Harding, Wm. Wharton, Roundell Palmer

To The Right Honble Earl Russell, etc., etc., etc.

Chapter XIV

RECOGNITION OF BELLIGERENCY AND THE PRINCIPLES OF INTERNATIONAL LAW

§ 63. *The Humanitarian Aspect.* The practice of States surveyed in the preceding chapter shows that, as a rule, they acknowledge a legal duty of recognition of belligerency as soon as the requisite conditions of recognition are present. We may now enquire what are the general principles of international law which, in addition to international practice, lead to the same result. What are the considerations of legal principle which compel us to accept the view that, given certain conditions of fact as expressed in the accepted requirements of belligerency, recognition follows as a matter of legal obligation?

These considerations must be kept apart from the arguments of an ethical or humanitarian nature which have often been adduced in support of recognition of belligerency. It is often maintained that recognition of belligerency by outside States is an important factor in securing compliance with rules of warfare and in helping to infuse into an otherwise savage and irregular combat an indispensable measure of restraint and humanity. The following passage from a despatch sent by Canning in 1824 for the use of the British Minister in his conversations with Metternich well illustrates this argument:

> 'The doctrine of Prince Metternich, that the Greeks, as *rebels*, are not entitled to the same rights of war, as legitimate belligerents, is one, of which, we think His Highness would do well to weigh all the consequences, before he promulgates it to the world. The practical enforcement of that doctrine could have no other effect than to convert the contest which has been brought, in a great measure by our exertions, into one of a regular and civilized character, into one of indiscriminate rapine and massacre. It cannot be expected that men should scrupulously discharge the duties of a situation, the ordinary rights of which are denied to them. Those rights we acknowledge, not out of any partiality to the Greeks, but because we think it for the Interest of humanity to compel *all* belligerents to observe the usages by which the spirit of civilization has mitigated the practice of War.'[1]

During the Spanish Civil War of 1936–9 considerations of this character were adduced in favour of recognition of the belligerency of the insurgents.

1 Printed in Smith, vol. 1, p. 296.

This humanitarian argument is to a large extent deceptive. Subject to isolated exceptions,[1] experience shows that, after an initial stage of severity prompted by stern assertions of outraged legality and by the reprisals of the revolutionaries, the parties to the civil struggle tacitly accept and act upon most of the rules of war which have secured general consent. This has been so even in cases in which the lawful government has refused to recognize the belligerent status of the rebels. In most of these cases rules of warfare have been adhered to for reasons of convenience and for fear of reprisals.[2]

The other humanitarian argument which has often been put forward in favour of recognition of belligerency is that in its absence the maritime (and, possibly, other) operations of the rebels must be tainted with illegality and expose them to treatment which outside States mete out to pirates.[3] That argument, too, has been unduly exaggerated. States have often claimed the right to treat foreign unrecognized insurgents as pirates. However, almost without exception, that right has been asserted only in the case of ruthless interference with the ships of foreign States.[4] Even then the assertion of the right thus claimed has fallen short of drastic enforcement.

§ 64. *The Duty of Recognition of Belligerency and the Independence of States.* The reasons militating in favour of recognition of belligerency as a matter of legal duty to the insurgents, whenever the requisite conditions of recognition are present, are of a character more persuasive than humanitarian considerations. They follow from accepted rules of international law. Their cogency reveals itself as soon as we cut ourselves adrift from the formalistic way of thinking which bids us insist that unrecognized insurgents are not subjects of international law and that they are not therefore entitled to claim a right under it. In case of a war between

1 See below, p. 244.

2 As Mr Justice Harlan said in *Ford* v. *Surget* (97 U.S. 594): 'To the Confederate Government was conceded, in the interest of humanity, and to prevent the cruelties of reprisals and retaliations, such belligerent rights as belonged, under the law of nations, to the armies of independent Governments engaged in war against each other.' In *Thorington* v. *Smith* (8 Wall. 1) the concession of belligerent rights was described as having been given 'from motives of humanity and expediency'. Although there had never taken place an express recognition of belligerency during the War of Independence, nevertheless, in the words of James Monroe writing in 1816, 'the rights of war were observed on both sides, flags passed between them, discussions took place, cartels were settled and exchanges made, from the commencement' (Manning, *Diplomatic Correspondence of the United States concerning the Independence of the Latin-American Nations*, vol. I (Parts I and II) (1925), p. 28).

3 Canning, in his frequently quoted Note of 25 March 1825, addressed to Los Rios, Spanish Minister in London, used the same argument with respect to the recognition of the independence of the South American Republics (*B.F.S.P.* vol. XII, p. 909). See above, p. 16.

4 See below, pp. 298–300.

sovereign States, international law imposes upon outside States, if they remain neutral, certain obligations of abstention and acquiescence. They must neither aid the belligerents nor permit their subjects to do such acts as would constitute the national territory a base of military or naval operations. They must acquiesce in certain restrictions upon their own freedom of action and that of their nationals, in particular in respect of commerce on the high seas. With regard to the latter that acquiescence is, upon analysis, an acknowledgment of what is in the last resort the right of self-defence. It is the right to prevent activities which amount to indirect participation in the war by rendering assistance to the adversary in the form of supply of articles of military importance. These obligations of abstention and acquiescence follow from the duty of non-interference. They are the consequence of the existence of hostilities on a large scale between foreign communities. In the case of civil war the duty of non-interference follows from the obligation to respect the independence of the State affected by the civil war. That independence would be denied if the ordinary obligations of neutrality were to be disregarded.[1]

However, it is only in consequence of the recognition of belligerency that these obligations come, in law, into being. For this reason the refusal, in disregard of the actual situation, to recognize the insurgents as belligerents may work in such a way as to amount in fact to a denial of the independence of the State concerned. So long as recognition is withheld, the lawful government may—and in the view of some ought to—be given support and facilities the grant of which to the insurgents would be unlawful.[2] The resulting situation must in the long run constitute actual interference—in fact, intervention[3]—in the affairs of the State in question so as to prevent its population from determining the outcome of the struggle and, with it, the political fate of the country. For it is impossible, in the long run, without actually intervening in the civil war, to attach decisive importance

1 The true nature of recognition of belligerency as based on the duty of non-interference was clearly perceived already in 1822, as is shown by Mr Justice Story in *The Santissima Trinidad* (7 Wheaton 283, 337). In answer to the objection that the Government of Buenos Ayres had not been recognized by the United States as an independent government and that therefore its ships could not be treated as national ships, Mr Justice Story said: 'The government of the United States has recognized the existence of a civil war between Spain and her colonies, and has avowed a determination to remain neutral between the parties, and to allow to each the same rights of asylum and hospitality and intercourse. Each party is, therefore, deemed by us a belligerent nation, having, so far as concerns us, the sovereign rights of war, and entitled to be respected in the exercise of those rights. We cannot interfere to the prejudice of either belligerent without making ourselves a party to the contest, and departing from the posture of neutrality.'

2 See below, pp. 231–3.

3 See below, p. 233.

to and to act on the distinction between the established government and the insurgents. Once the contest has assumed the complexion of widespread hostilities, the continued differentiation, because of the absence of recognition of belligerency, between the lawful government and the rebels must result in the granting to the lawful government of advantages and facilities which are being withheld from the insurgents. So long as there are good grounds for the refusal to recognize the belligerency of the insurgents such conduct is not open to objection.[1] When recognition is refused notwithstanding the existence of the requirements of recognition of belligerency, it amounts, when coupled with discrimination against the insurgents, to intervention denying to a State what is the essence of its sovereignty and independence, namely, the right of political self-determination. As such it must be deemed to be contrary to international law.

§ 65. *The Duty of Non-Interference prior to Recognition of Belligerency.* It is generally accepted that prior to recognition of the belligerency of the insurgents the lawful government is entitled to privileged treatment as compared with the insurgents. The Resolutions adopted in 1900 by the Institute of International Law expressed this tendency in clear terms:

'International law imposes upon third Powers, in case of insurrection or civil war, certain obligations towards established and recognized governments, which are struggling with insurrection.

CHAPTER I.—Duties of Foreign Powers toward the Government which is Fighting the Insurrection

Article 2. Section 1. Every third Power, at peace with an independent nation, is bound not to interfere with the measures which this nation takes for the re-establishing of internal peace.

Section 2. It is bound not to furnish the insurgents with either arms, munitions, military goods, or financial aid.

Section 3. It is especially forbidden for any third Power to allow a hostile expedition against an established and recognized government to be organized within its domain.'[2]

1 See below, p. 233. The principles applicable to the situation were lucidly stated by Lord Halifax before the Council of the League of Nations in May 1938 in connection with the civil war in Spain. He said: 'One of the fundamental principles governing the relations of States to one another is that each independent State has the right to determine for itself its own form of Government.... It follows from the right of self-determination that when a dispute arises in one State as to how the people should be governed, other States should refrain from exercising any pressure upon the people of that State in one direction or in the other' (*Off.J.* 1938, p. 330). Speaking of the provisions of the Non-Intervention Agreement he said: 'Whether under neutrality or non-intervention, the principle of showing no favour to one side as against the other is upheld' (ibid.).

2 *Resolutions of the Institute* (Carnegie Endowment, 1916), p. 156.

In the Pan-American Convention of 20 February 1928 concerning the Duties and Rights of States in the event of Civil Strife the principle of preferential treatment for the lawful government, so long as belligerency is not recognized, plays a prominent part.[1] In that Convention the Contracting Parties undertook, *inter alia*, 'to disarm and intern every rebel force crossing their boundaries, the expenses of internment to be borne by the State where public order may be disturbed',[2] and 'to forbid the traffic in arms and war material, except when intended for the Government, while the belligerency of the rebels has not been recognized, in which latter case the rules of neutrality shall be applicable'.[3] Indirectly, the same principle underlay the Convention of 17 June 1925 on Supervision of International Trade in Arms and Ammunition and in Implements of War, which provided, in Article 2 (1), that 'the Contracting Parties shall not export or permit the export of the articles covered by the Convention unless the export shall be for a direct supply to the Government of the importing State or, with the consent of such Government, to a public authority subordinate to it'.[4] When in 1930 a revolution broke out in Brazil, the United States, apparently in pursuance of the Convention of 1928, prohibited the export of arms to that country with the exception of arms destined for the lawful government. The Department of State justified that action as dictated by an elementary international duty. 'Until belligerency is recognized', said the Secretary of State, 'and the duty of neutrality arises, all the humane predispositions towards stability of government, the preservation of international amity, and the protection of established intercourse between nations are in favor of the existing government.'[5]

1 See Hudson, *International Legislation*, vol. IV (1931), p. 2416. By January 1941 the Convention was ratified by the following States: Brazil, Colombia, Costa Rica, Cuba, Ecuador, Salvador, Haiti, Mexico, Nicaragua, Panama, the Dominican Republic, the United States, and Uruguay.

2 Article 1 (2).

3 Article 1 (3).

4 Hudson, op. cit. vol. III (1931), p. 1640. In 1919 Great Britain, Spain, Portugal, the United States, Brazil, France and Japan agreed to restrain their nationals from exporting to or importing into China arms and munitions 'until the establishment of a government whose authority is recognized throughout the whole country' (*U.S. For. Rel.* 1919 (I), p. 670). For a recommendation to the same effect by the diplomatic corps in Peking in October 1922, see ibid. 1922 (I), pp. 742–3.

5 Mr Stimson's address before the Council on Foreign Relations, 6 February 1931 (*The United States and the Other American Republics*, Department of State, Latin-American Series, no. 4 (1931)). See also *A.J.* vol. XXV (1931), p. 125. In 1869 Hoar, United States Attorney-General, expressed the opinion that the United States Neutrality Act of 1818 would extend to the fitting out and arming of vessels for a revolted colony whose belligerency had not been recognized, but would not apply to vessels for the parent State against a revolted colony whose independence (or, probably, belligerency) has not been recognized by the United States (Moore, vol. VII, p. 1079). See also, to the same effect, the Opinion of the British Law Officers of 28 October 1873, concerning the revolution in Spain. See below, p. 232.

Writers who insist that there is an inalienable right to revolution and that the grant of preferential treatment to the lawful government amounts to intervention, nevertheless maintain that prior to recognition of belligerency the lawful government is entitled to privileges—especially with regard to importation of arms and munitions*—which must be withheld from the insurgents.[1]

* It is necessary to scrutinize such statements with some care. States are not bound to permit the supply of munitions for the lawful government. The latter is not entitled to unrestricted freedom in buying munitions—unless such freedom is stipulated by treaty. Even then the provisions of the treaty may have to be read subject to the implied condition of its fulfilment not involving the danger of international complications following upon interference, implied in an unilateral grant of advantages, in a civil war of considerable dimensions. It is natural for the lawful government, when thus cut off from the foreign supply of arms and munitions, to complain and to assert that it is inadmissible that it should be deprived of such facilities, hitherto open to it, at a time when it stands desperately in need of them. However, once civil war on a larger scale has broken out, the lawful government cannot properly rely, for the purpose of the conduct of war, on the fact that it is the lawful authority. To do so would mean in effect to invite the help of other States and to ask them to abandon impartiality. The British practice in the last three quarters of the nineteenth century was not to interfere with the sale of munitions to the parties engaged in a civil war in a foreign country. In an Opinion given on 1 December 1873, in connection with the civil war in Spain, the Law Officers pointed out that when the Foreign Enlistment Bill was under discussion in 1870 the House of Commons deliberately declined to introduce any provision as to the exportation of arms (F.O. 83/2378). They admitted that prior to 1826 Orders in Council prohibiting export of arms and munitions to certain foreign countries were occasionally issued under 33 Geo. II, c. 2.

The question arose in an acute form during the Spanish Civil War in 1937 and 1938 when the lawful Spanish Government claimed that it was entitled to continue to buy munitions in countries to which it had hitherto had access for that purpose. In the so-called Non-Intervention Agreement, originating in the Exchange of Notes of 15 August 1935 between Great Britain and France, the parties to the Agreement undertook to prohibit the export or re-export, directly or indirectly, of 'arms, munitions and materials of war as well as all airplanes mounted or dismantled, and all ships of war' from their countries to Spanish territories. The accurate answer to the Spanish complaint was probably that the question whether at that time it possessed a right to buy munitions was a matter governed by existing treaties. There is normally no such right apart from treaty. In the relations between Great Britain and Spain the question was regulated by the Commercial Treaty of 3 October 1922 and the Exchange of Notes of 4 and 5 April 1927 (Hertslet's *Commercial Treaties*, 1931, pp. 624, 637) which, while providing in general terms for the duty to abstain from prohibitions on importation and exportation, expressly reserved to the contracting parties freedom of action with regard to weapons, ammunition and war material and, generally, for reasons of public safety and on sanitary grounds. It is believed that the prohibition of export of munitions was covered both by the specific exception of the Treaty referring to war material and by considerations of public safety. Even if the Treaty had contained no special provisions relating to munitions, the prohibition might still have been justified on the ground of a vital change of circumstances if the govern-

---

1 See, e.g. Scelle in *R.G.* vol. XLV (1938), pp. 268–70 and 272. See also McNair, loc. cit. p. 497; Raestad in *R.I.* 3rd ser. vol. XIX (1938), p. 632.

The presumptions in favour of the established government are based on the view that, so long as the lawful sovereign authority has not been definitely supplanted, it alone can be regarded and treated as the subject of the rights ordinarily enjoyed by a State. However, these presumptions do not go beyond the duty not to grant to the insurgents premature recognition as a government,[1] and not to permit foreign territory to become a basis of operations against the lawful government. Apart from this, any unilateral and extended grant of advantages to the lawful government amounts, even prior to the recognition of the belligerency of the insurgents, to interference and to a denial of the right of the nation[2] to decide for itself—by a physical contest, if necessary, between the rival forces—the nature and the form of its government. This is so especially when some but not all of the requirements of recognition of belligerency are present. In such cases the formal distinction between the lawful government and the insurgents is particularly undesirable.

§ 66. *The Non-Intervention Agreement during the Spanish Civil War, 1936–9.* For these reasons the so-called Non-Intervention Agreement concluded at the beginning of the Spanish Civil War in 1936,[3] while novel in the use of terminology,[4] was not devoid of value for evolving a workable

ment responsible for the prohibition acted in the belief that it was preserving its country from the danger of international complications. By a Joint Resolution of Congress of 8 January 1937 (50 Stat. 3) the United States prohibited the export of arms and munitions to Spain. For the legislative measures of other States in the matter see Spain, no. 2, Cmd. 5300 (1936). See on this question McNair in *Law Quarterly Review*, vol. LIII (1937), pp. 472–4. See also *International Conciliation*, March 1939, Pamphlet no. 348, for a discussion by various writers of the position in the United States. During the American Civil War a proclamation was issued in Great Britain on 4 December 1861, prohibiting the export of arms, ammunition and military stores from Great Britain (*B.F.S.P.* vol. LI, p. 171). And see Atwater, *American Regulation of Arms Exports* (1941), Finch in *A.J.* vol. XXXI (1937), pp. 74–81, and Hackworth, vol. I, pp. 356–8. In 1912 a Joint Resolution of the Congress of the United States provided that 'whenever the President shall find that in any American country conditions of domestic violence exist which are promoted by the use of arms or munitions of war procured from the United States, and shall make proclamation thereof, it shall be unlawful to export except under such limitations and exceptions as the President shall prescribe any arms or munitions of war from any place in the United States to such country until otherwise ordered by the President or by Congress' (37 Stat. 630). A similar Resolution was adopted in January 1922 (42 Stat. 361).

1 See above, pp. 93–5.

2 See, to the same effect, Wiesse, *Le droit international appliqué aux guerres civiles* (1898), p. 86; Wehberg in *Hague Recueil*, vol. LXIII (1938) (i), p. 57.

3 See above, p. 232.

4 That terminology is believed to be essentially correct. There is good reason for extending the traditional notion of intervention (as meaning dictatorial interference, in relation to an existing and unchallenged government, with its external or internal freedom of action) to cover interference with the right of a nation to determine its political regime.

rule of international law on the subject. In that Agreement the parties undertook, in effect, to refrain from acts prohibited by international law (i.e. from supplying munitions to the insurgents) and to forgo what was hitherto a right enjoyed under international law (i.e. the right to supply munitions to the lawful government).[1] The exercise of the latter right, if accompanied by observance of the prohibition of supply to insurgents, would have amounted to intervention in the struggle and, in substance, to interference with national independence. The Non-Intervention Agreement went beyond that prohibition inasmuch as the parties undertook to forbid the passage of munitions through their territory and their supply by private individuals—a measure going beyond the obligations of the ordinary law of neutrality. In view of the fact that some of the contracting parties were States in which the manufacture or control of exports of munitions were entirely in the hands or under the control of the government, the observance of the traditional distinction between supply of munitions by individuals and by governments may not have been altogether easy in a situation calling for a rapid adjustment. In general, although the Non-Intervention Agreement was conceived as an instrument for meeting an international emergency of exceptional complexity, it gave expression to a rule which is more consistent with the principle of independence of States than the tendency to favour the established government. The prohibition of intervention is of a significance more decisive than any leaning to stability to be ensured by a preferential treatment of the lawful government. In so far as any such tendency implies disapprobation of the conduct of the insurgent party responsible for initiating the civil war, it cannot—as has already been pointed out[2]—be regarded as a sound rule in the present stage of international organization. There must be definite limits to presumptions in favour of established governments so long as the international community has no such control over them as to secure effectively the fundamental rights of the individual and decent administration of the law.

The rigidity[3] of the rule authorizing—or, according to some, enjoining—

1 As international law does not *oblige* States to give the lawful government preferential treatment, it cannot be said that the Non-Intervention Agreement was in violation of international law. For the suggestion that it was contrary to international law see O'Rourke in *A.J.* vol. XXXI (1937), p. 409, and Smith in *B.Y.* vol. XVIII (1937), p. 28. And see generally the judicious treatment of the subject by Padelford in *A.J.* vol. XXXI (1937), pp. 578–603 and the same *International Law and Diplomacy in the Spanish Civil Strife* (1939).

2 See above, p. 93.

3 The attempt to maintain the formal distinction between the lawful government and the unrecognized insurgents with regard to the conduct of hostilities may constitute a dangerous inducement to outside States in sympathy with the insurgents to

privileged treatment of the lawful government has often been relaxed as the result of recognition of insurgency.[1] Thus, during the Cuban War of Independence the United States, while refusing to recognize the rebels as belligerents, brought into effect its neutrality legislation and thus secured the operation of one of the principal consequences of recognition of belligerency, namely, of a distinct measure of impartiality and non-interference in relation to both contesting parties.[2] During the Spanish Civil War of 1936–9 the main provisions of the Foreign Enlistment Act were declared to be applicable in Great Britain on 10 January 1937,[3] although the refusal to recognize belligerency was maintained to the end. The recourse to these measures operating within a limited sphere was not either in fact or in intention a substitute for recognition of belligerency.[4]

escape from the dilemma by committing the illegality of recognizing prematurely the rebellious authority as the lawful government with the result that they may henceforth deem themselves free to grant all the necessary facilities to the newly recognized authority. This probably was the position in which Germany and Italy found themselves in 1936 when, soon after the beginning of the civil war in Spain, they recognized the insurgents as the lawful government of Spain (see above, p. 95). The reasoning adopted was false seeing that the recognition thus given, being illegal *ab initio*, could not validate conduct which was otherwise unlawful.

1 See below, pp. 270 et seq.

2 See below, p. 272. See also the observation of Secretary of State Hay as cited by Wilson in *A.J.* vol. 1 (1907), p. 56: 'To deny to an insurgent the right to prevent the enemy from receiving material aid cannot well be justified without denying the right of revolution.'

3 See below, p. 273.

4 Municipal enactments are often wide enough to cover the case of unrecognized insurgents. This applies, for instance, to the British Foreign Enlistment Act of 1870, Section 30 of which for most purposes assimilates unrecognized insurgents to 'a foreign State' (see below). Thus it was rightly held at the beginning of 1937, in connection with the Spanish Civil War, that the wording and intention of that section made it possible to regard the insurgents as being 'at war' with the Government of Spain. Doubts arose as to whether the insurgents were, as required by the Act, 'at peace' with Great Britain seeing that there were, at that time, no normal diplomatic relations between Great Britain and the insurgents. These doubts, too, were rightly resolved in the affirmative on the ground that in the past Great Britain had often had no diplomatic relations with countries with which she was 'at peace' and that the latter expression meant the absence of a state of war. On the other hand, it would appear that the elasticity of the Foreign Enlistment Act may not always be sufficient for the purpose. In 1925, during the rebellion of the Riff tribes against the Government of the Spanish Zone of Morocco, the question arose as to the means by which the British Government could prevent the purchase of an aeroplane in Great Britain for the use of the rebels. There seemed to be agreement that the matter could not be dealt with under the Foreign Enlistment Act of 1870 without recognizing the Riffs as belligerents, except under Article 11 (relating to military expeditions), if it could be shown that: (*a*) the aeroplane was to fly direct to Morocco; (*b*) if it was equipped with arms, bombs, etc.—as otherwise it might be difficult to call it a military expedition.

When in 1889 a British subject, a certain Lewis, was recruiting forces against the Damane region, a German protectorate, it was assumed that although a German

It showed that the tendency to favour the lawful government does not always represent a workable principle and that its consequences must in such cases be obviated by *ad hoc* measures, including the elastic device of recognition of insurgency. For the same reason, notwithstanding the absence of recognition of belligerency, outside States have acted on occasions as if they were bound by the formal obligations of neutrality. Thus, during the revolution in Chile in 1891, Peru interned a detachment of the forces of the Government of Chile which found themselves compelled to take refuge in Peruvian territory.

§ 67. *The Formal Argument against the Duty of Recognition of Belligerency.* The duty to grant recognition of belligerency in cases where there exist the requisite conditions follows from accepted principles of international law. So cogent are these principles that, as has been shown,[1] the practice of States reveals a tendency, expressed in the recognition of insurgency or otherwise, to treat the contesting parties in many respects as belligerents on a footing of equality even before recognition of belligerency has been granted. In fact we are not likely to do justice to the complexity of the subject unless we divest ourselves of the purely formal way of thinking on

protectorate was not part of the dominions of Germany within Section 11 of the Foreign Enlistment Act, it was a friendly foreign State within the meaning of Section 11 taken together with Section 30.

During the hostilities in 1895 between France and Madagascar (a French protectorate over which was recognized by Great Britain in the Franco-British Declaration of 5 August 1890), the question arose whether Madagascar was 'a foreign State' within the meaning of the Foreign Enlistment Act. The view was expressed in some quarters that there existed a state of hostilities which might justify the issue of a proclamation of neutrality if the struggle developed on a sufficiently large scale; that such a proclamation would constitute the recognition of Madagascar as 'belligerent'; that recognition by a neutral of belligerency between a protected State and a protecting State, especially when the former is uncivilized, might be interpreted as an unfriendly act towards the protecting State unless clearly required by the legitimate interests of national commerce; that the legitimate interests of British trade could properly afford a test of the propriety of recognition; and that if France proposed to exercise belligerent rights (i.e. with respect to contraband) she could not properly object to the issue of such a proclamation. It was argued that in view of the recognition of the protectorate Great Britain could not treat the rebellious protectorate as a 'foreign State'. The argument was open to question seeing that a protectorate cannot be in a position different from that of an integral part of the State affected by a rebellion. Eventually no recognition of belligerency took place on the ground that the existing hostilities did not touch British interests and that they did not assume proportions different either in degree or quality from similar hostilities in which Great Britain had been engaged in the past and of which foreign nations had not taken any public notice. For some questions on this matter see *H.C. Debates*, 7, 19 and 21 February 1895. See also Holland's letter to *The Times* newspaper of 22 February 1895.

1 See above, p. 235.

the lines of the argument that a duty to recognize presupposes a right, and that a community which does not exist in law can have no rights. The argument begs the question.[1] For the point to be decided in the first instance is whether the fact of insurgency, when accompanied by certain well-established conditions, does not, by the operation of the law, give to the parties to the struggle international rights and duties which make them *pro tanto* subjects of international law. These rights and duties may not be operative so long as recognition of belligerency has not been granted. But this circumstance, as in the corresponding case of recognition of States, merely signifies that recognition, while constitutive of the rights and duties of belligerency, is declaratory of an existing fact and, so far as outside States are concerned, of a corresponding legal duty. The insurgents are entitled to recognition although prior to the declaration of recognition they have no rights or duties of belligerency. To that extent theirs is an imperfect right. The case of the *Bergen Prizes*[2] shows that it is not necessarily a purely theoretical right. Given the requisite jurisdiction of an international tribunal there is no reason why it should not be invoked by the insurgents in the form of a claim for damages after they have achieved the status of a recognized government with acknowledged international capacity.

Even if we adopt the purely analytical view that the insurgents, not being subjects of international law, have no right to recognition, we are not necessarily precluded from maintaining that outside States are under a duty to grant recognition. In the domain of public law the duty owed by a private person need not correspond to a private right. Criminal law imposes duties upon the individual; but to these duties there does not correspond any specific private right. In the field of public law the corresponding right is in such cases vested in the community as a whole. In fact most, if not all, cases in which belligerency has been recognized can be understood—if we disregard the appeal to considerations of humanity—only on the assumption that it was felt that there was a duty to grant recognition. What else could be the reason for submitting to the onerous duties of neutrality and, on occasions, for incurring the odium of disapproval by the lawful government? It is not the necessity of providing the national authorities with legal means for prohibiting citizens from meddling in the quarrel of others by enlisting in their forces or otherwise.

1 This would not, in any case, be an argument applicable to the right of the lawful government to be recognized as belligerent—assuming, as some do (see above, p. 200), that the lawful government cannot assume belligerent rights without recognition by other States.

2 See above, p. 191.

For such prohibition can be and has often been based on enactments applying not only to a state of belligerency but also to a condition of insurrection.[1] Neither can it be accurately asserted that the burdens resulting from recognition of belligerency are adequately compensated by the advantages accruing from putting the relations between the insurgents and outside States on a regular basis for the purpose of trade or of protection of nationals.

Undoubtedly, in the case of recognition of belligerency the legal view—as distinguished from the political or diplomatic—of the nature of recognition is put to a severe test. To maintain that, given the necessary requirements of fact, insurgents are entitled to recognition as of right, is to expect outside States to acquiesce in far-reaching restrictions upon their commerce and shipping. Yet international law shows other situations in which outside States have to submit to inconveniences resulting from events over which they have no control. In particular, this applies to the case of a war between independent States.

1 See below, pp. 272, 273.

Chapter XV

PROBLEMS OF RECOGNITION OF BELLIGERENCY

§ 68. *The Interest of Outside States as a Legally Relevant Factor.* In the accepted enumeration of the requisite conditions of recognition we find one element which, on the face of it, appears to be inconsistent with the view of recognition conceived as a legal duty to the insurgents independently of any particular national interest of outside States. That condition, voiced with practical unanimity, is that recognition is unjustifiable and wrongful if the interests of the recognizing State are not directly affected so as to call for a definition of its position through the act of recognition. They are directly affected when, for instance, the parties to the struggle purport to exercise belligerent rights on the high seas and when outside States have commercial maritime interests likely to be interfered with by the naval operations.[1] If a distant continental State in no way directly concerned with the hostilities at sea were to recognize the insurgents as belligerents, it would lay itself open to the charge of a gratuitous gesture unfriendly to the lawful government and merely calculated to encourage the rebellion.

1 The urgency of the definition of the attitude of outside States was expressed in emphatic terms by Historicus in his letter to *The Times* on 22 March 1865, in a manner meriting quotation. He said, with regard to the situation created by the American proclamation of a blockade on 19 April 1861: 'Was an English merchantman, sailing peaceably in pursuance of his ordinary trade, to be left in ignorance whether an armed vessel which overhauled and captured him was regarded by his own Government in the light of a pirate committing a robbery on the high seas, or whether it was a lawful belligerent exercising the recognized rights of war? What was the position of the English navy, who are posted in every corner of the habitable globe, to protect by their presence, and if necessary to vindicate by their arms the security of our mercantile marine? Were they or were they not to be informed whether they were "to sink, burn and destroy" as pirates or to respect as lawful belligerents the cruisers of either party who exercised against our merchantmen those acts of force which the rights of war alone could justify?'

For an example of recognition of belligerency admittedly prompted by overriding national interest see the Bolivian Decree of 29 May 1891, recognizing the Chilean insurgents as belligerents. The British Minister in Lima informed Lord Salisbury that 'President Aice declares that, on the part of Bolivia, such recognition is unavoidable, owing to the fact that the Revolutionary Government hold Antofagasta and Arica, the first of which ports is open for the free transit of Bolivian exports and imports, whilst from the Customs of the second Bolivia derives a considerable portion of her revenue' (*State Papers*, vol. xcv (1892), *Chile*, no. 1).

This does not signify that recognition of belligerency is, in law, determined solely by the interests of the recognizing State. The fact that the interests of the latter must be involved before recognition can properly be granted means that the insurgents are not entitled to ask for recognition—even assuming the existence of the other necessary conditions—so long as they have no interest in recognition other than that accruing from a political declaration of sympathy and encouragement. That direct interest substantially corresponds to and constitutes the measure of the interest of outside States in defining their relations with the insurgents. However, to say that outside States must have a direct interest in defining their relations with the conflict is not to predicate that in granting or refusing recognition of belligerency they are entitled to consider their own interests only. Recognition of belligerency is permissible and—given the existence of other factual requirements—obligatory when the interests of outside States are involved in such a manner as to necessitate a definition of relations. But it is conceivable that recognition thus given may not be directly beneficial to the commercial and other national interests. Normally, when a State recognizes belligerency it submits to inconvenience and restrictions. It will thus be seen that the particular condition of recognition here discussed, far from constituting a refutation of the legal view of the nature of recognition of belligerency, actually affirms it. It prevents recognition of belligerency from being used as a political gesture of sympathy and encouragement unrelated to the true purpose of recognition.

§ 69. *Opinions of Writers and the Duty of Recognition.* The considerations, based both on practice and on principle, in favour of the legal character of recognition of belligerency—i.e. in particular, in favour of the legal right of the insurgents to recognition—are so cogent that, notwithstanding the contrary tendency in matters of recognition generally, the legal view of recognition of belligerency is supported by what is probably the majority of writers.[1] There are only a few publicists who, having discussed the matter in any detail, give a categorical negative reply to the question whether the insurgents may have a legal right to recognition. These

1 Wehberg (*Hague Recueil*, vol. LXIII (1938) (i), p. 107) believes that there is a majority in favour of the other view, but there may be difficulty in accepting that estimate seeing that he includes among the majority writers such as Brierly (*Law of Nations* (1st ed. 1928), p. 79) and Garner (*A.J.* vol. XXXII (1938), p. 112) who express no opinion on the subject, and Wheaton who, in fact, holds the contrary view (see below, p. 243, n. 3).

include Wiesse,[1] Rougier,[2] Nys,[3] Gemma,[4] Woolsey,[5] Kunz,[6] McNair,[7] Noël-Henry,[8] and Hall.[9]

Hall's view expresses most clearly the attitude of this school of thought. For this reason and also because, in a sense, his opinion marks a transition to the contrary view, it is useful to refer to it in some detail. He states emphatically that a belligerent community 'cannot...demand to be recognized on legal grounds, and recognition, when it takes place, either on the part of the foreign government, or of that against which the revolt is directed, is from the legal point of view a concession of pure grace'.[10] The argument is purely formal: 'As a belligerent community is not in itself a legal person,[11] a society claiming only to be a belligerent, and to have permanently established its independence, can have no rights under that [international] law.'[12] He admits that there may be a moral claim to recognition, but that 'has nothing to do with international law'. And yet, after quoting those who maintain that 'humanity requires that the members of such a community shall be treated as belligerents, and if so there must be a point at which they have a right to demand what confessedly must be granted', he adds that 'so far, the correctness of this view may at once be granted'.[13]

Bernard, writing in 1870 on the *Neutrality of Great Britain during the American Civil War*, goes a considerable step further in the affirmation of a legal right to recognition. He says (at p. 115):

'It is sometimes said that recognition [of belligerency]...is due as of right to any body of people whose number and organization enable them to carry on regular warfare, and who are actually engaged in it....I am averse to the use of language which appears vague and abstract. But this, I think, cannot be denied—that recognition in such cases has been sanctioned by the practice and opinion of nations, not solely with a view to the protection of the neutral, but on wider grounds of general expediency. It is generally expedient that the ordinary rules of war should extend, as far as possible, to civil wars. The restraints which they impose are here as wholesome, their influence in making war regular and humane and in confining its range are as useful....These considerations appear to show not only that recognition may be conceded, but that it ought not to be withheld.'

1 Op. cit. pp. 20 et seq.
2 *Les guerres civiles et le droit des gens* (1903), p. 383.
3 *Le droit international* (2nd ed. 1912), vol. III, p. 21.
4 Op. cit. p. 409.
5 See above, p. 191, n. 2.
6 Op. cit. p. 192.
7 *Law Quarterly Review*, vol. LIII (1937), p. 483.
8 Op. cit. p. 221.
9 See below, this page.
10 *International Law* (3rd ed. 1890), p. 35.
11 Upon which passage Westlake's comment (*International Law* (2nd ed. 1910), vol. I, p. 55) is: 'does not this beg the question?'
12 Hall, op. cit. p. 34.
13 Ibid.

Sir William Harcourt, in laying down that the claim of the insurgents to exercise belligerent rights was the inevitable result of the assertion of these rights by the lawful government, was defending essentially the same doctrine. He said, with reference to the American Civil War:

'The North created belligerent rights in both parties by making war on the South. The North have enjoyed their rights and we have endorsed them. They have seized our merchantmen and crippled our trade, and they have a right to do it. If the South had not had belligerent rights it could only be because there was no war.... In order to exercise belligerent rights yourself you must have an antagonist, and that antagonist must have belligerent rights also.'[1]

Westlake was not altogether disinclined to accept the same view:

'We think it must be said that a right of insurgents to claim the recognition of their belligerency as distinct from the recognition of their independence has not yet become a legal one, either by the consent of approved authorities or by custom, though much may be said for it on the ground of reason when even those who deny its legal character can represent the consequences which might follow from its refusal as being inhuman.'[2]

He admits the reasonableness of the legal view of recognition and makes no attempt to describe it as illogical on the ground that insurgents, not being legal persons in the contemplation of international law, can claim no right. It is probable that Westlake underestimated the volume both of State practice and of legal opinion in favour of the view which he regarded as a reasonable one. Prior to Westlake writers in various countries asserted that the right of insurgents to recognition is, in appropriate circumstances, a legal one. These included Vattel,[3] Bluntschli,[4] Fiore,[5]

1 Letter to *The Times* newspaper, 22 March 1865.

2 *International Law* (2nd ed. 1910), vol. I, p. 55.

3 He says in § 293 of Book III, ch. XVIII: 'Civil war breaks the bonds of society and of governments, or at least suspends the force and effect of them; it gives rise, within the Nation, to two independent parties, who regard each other as enemies and acknowledge no common judge. Of necessity, therefore, these two parties must be regarded as forming thenceforth, for a time at least, two separate bodies politic, two distinct Nations.' And he proceeds in § 295: '...when the Nation is divided into two absolutely independent parties, who acknowledge no common superior, the State is broken up and the war between the two parties falls, in all respects, into the class of a public war between two different nations' (Fenwick's translation in the *Classics* edition, 1916).

4 *Völkerrecht* (1868), § 512, n. 1.

5 He says (in *Nouveau droit international public* (French translation, 1886), vol. III, p. 39): '...on ne peut nier à la lutte ainsi engagée le caractère d'une guerre, ni refuser d'appliquer aux combattants de chacun des belligérants le droit de la guerre'. In his *International Law Codified* (Borchard's translation, 1918, p. 550) he lays down that insurgents are entitled, as against outside States, to the recognition of rights and duties of belligerents as soon as they have been recognized by their own State.

Lorimer,[1] Kent,[2] and Wheaton.[3] During the Spanish Civil War of 1936–9 the great majority of writers were in the same category.[4]

§ 70. *The Duty of the Lawful Government to grant Recognition.* It remains to consider the question as to how far insurgents are entitled to recognition as belligerents by their own State. It would appear that this is a purely domestic question and there is therefore no occasion for international law to attempt to answer it. Those who discuss the matter are emphatically of the view that, as against the legitimate government, there can be no question of international law conferring a right of recognition upon the insurgents or imposing a corresponding duty upon the lawful government.[5] They are in a position to adduce some impressive historical instances in support of that view. During the civil war the United States claimed the full exercise of belligerent rights. Its courts and its government frequently expressed and acted upon the view that the hostilities had by their dimensions acquired the character of an international war.[6] At the same time both the government and the courts frequently acted on the view

1 *Institutes of the Law of Nations* (1883), vol. I, p. 141, where he speaks of the concession of belligerent rights as an acknowledgment of the right of the inchoate State to contend for recognition.

2 See *Commentaries* (Abdy's edition, 1878), p. 94, approving of Canning's statement cited above, p. 188.

3 *Elements of International Law* (1st ed. 1836), vol. I, pp. 92, 93. He lays down that in case of civil war foreign States, if they choose to remain neutral, are 'bound to allow impartially to both belligerent parties the free exercise of those rights which war gives to public enemies against each other; such as the right of blockade, and of capturing contraband and enemy's property'. In another place (vol. II, p. 11) he says even more clearly that 'the general usage of nations regards such war as entitling both parties to all the rights of war as against each other, and even as respects neutral nations'. See also Rolin in Lapradelle-Politis, *Recueil des arbitrages internationaux*, vol. II (1923), pp. 215–17. And see Benton, *International Law and Diplomacy of the Spanish-American War* (1908), p. 41, who expresses the view that, when the necessary conditions are present, 'recognition becomes almost mandatory on the neutrals'.

4 See Scelle in *Friedenswarte*, vol. XXXVII (1937), p. 65; Wehberg, ibid. p. 398; Padelford, ibid. p. 192; the same in *Proceedings of the American Society of International Law*, 1937, p. 155; Smith in *B.Y.* vol. XVIII (1937), pp. 17–31. See also O'Rourke in *A.J.* vol. XXXI (1937), pp. 405–7; and in particular Wehberg in *Hague Recueil*, vol. LXIII (1938) (i), pp. 108–11. Politis states what is believed to be the correct rule with all requisite clarity. He says: 'La reconnaissance de belligérance n'est pas discrétionnaire. Elle ne peut être accordée ou refusée selon le bon vouloir des États. Elle est subordonnée à certaines conditions, sans la réunion desquelles elle ne saurait être accordée —de même qu'elle ne peut, en droit, être refusée si elles sont réunies' (*Mélanges Antoine Pillet*, vol. I (1929), p. 183).

5 Kunz, p. 177. Hall (*International Law* (3rd ed. 1890), p. 35) refers to it as 'a concession of pure grace'; Olivart (*Del reconocimiento de beligerancia* (1895), p. 89) refers to it as an 'acto de absoluto, libre y revocable arbitrio del Govierno legitimo'. See also Rougier, op. cit. p. 178.

6 See above, p. 228.

that the belligerent rights of the rebels were of a purely factual character, that they were liable to be withdrawn at any moment, that they could not be relied upon before courts (which continued to regard them as traitors), and that foreign States were not entitled to admit them to the equal exercise of belligerent rights.[1] The Hungarian insurgents in 1848 were treated as traitors and their leaders executed as such by the Austrian authorities. In the initial stages of the hostilities between Spain and her revolting colonies the mother country claimed the right to treat the rebels as traitors and pirates. In fact, in most civil wars the legitimate governments have declared the ships operated by the insurgents to be piratical.[2] Neither can the numerous cases in which recognition has been granted by the lawful government—including those of a solemn treaty, as between the Spanish General Morillo and Bolivar on 26 November 1820[3]—be cited in support of the contrary view. For these instances show merely that the lawful government may, if it so wishes, grant belligerent rights to the insurgents.

Even apart from the current argument that insurgents lack international personality, it would, at first sight, appear difficult to defend a view according to which international law imposes upon the lawful authorities of the State, faced with an armed rebellion against its fundamental law and institutions, the duty to relinquish the deterrent of the law of treason and to smooth the path of the rebellion by subjecting itself to the restraints of the laws of war. Yet—once we have abandoned the uncertain ground of the predominant view of the limitations of international personality—it is difficult to regard as final the accepted view on the matter. We must have

1 The courts of the United States did not regard the assertion of the criminality of the civil war (from the point of view of the Constitution of the United States) and the assumption of belligerent rights as mutually exclusive. This was the view taken by Dunlop J. on 13 June 1861, in *The Tropic Wind* (printed in *B.F.S.P.* vol. LI, p. 207), who quoted with approval the dictum of Chief Justice Marshall in *Rose* v. *Himely* (4 Cranch 272): 'It is not intended to say that belligerent rights may not be superadded to those of sovereignty.' See also the Opinion of the British Law Officers of 23 May 1865 (F.O. 83/2723) referring to an Opinion of the United States Attorney-General on certain questions arising out of the terms of capitulation accorded to General Lee and the Army of Virginia by General Grant: 'It [the Opinion of the Attorney-General] places the recognition of the Confederates as belligerents upon the most exact and formal footing, and deduces from it, very strictly, its rigorous consequences. If it were possible to suppose that any demands or complaints founded on the recognition of the Belligerent status of the Confederates by this country would hereafter be pressed by the United States' Government, this document might advantageously be referred to, in any answer, which it might become necessary to return to such demands or complaints.'

2 See below, pp. 296–300.

3 Martens, *N.R.* vol. v, p. 540; see also Article 10 of the Treaty between Spain and Buenos Ayres of 4 July 1822 (ibid. vol. VI, p. 277).

recourse to the wider principle on which alone the international doctrine of recognition can satisfactorily be based. The governing principle in the matter of recognition is that of the law-creating consequences of facts not prohibited by international law. A clearly ascertained state of hostilities on a sufficiently large scale, willed as war at least by one of the parties, creates *suo vigore* a condition in which the rules of warfare become operative. Such hostilities constitute a fact creating legal consequences in international law between the parties to the contest (whether States or not) and outside States. Are we inescapably bound to accept the view that that fact creates no legal consequences between the parties themselves? In practice belligerent rights as between the parties are in fact conceded and respected whenever the hostilities assume the complexion of a drawn-out struggle of wide dimensions and a degree of permanency and coherence assimilating them to a war between independent States. Until matters have reached that stage there is nothing save considerations of humanity to limit the lawful government's freedom of action. But once a situation has been created which, but for the constitutional law of the State concerned, is indistinguishable from war, practice suggests that international law ought to step in in order to fulfil the same function which it performs in wars between sovereign States, namely, to humanize and regularize the conduct of hostilities as between the parties. The restraining power of the internal law of the State has, provisionally at least, broken down; unless revengeful ruthlessness is to multiply the ravages of war, regulation by international law is indispensable. It would not be accurate to urge that such regulation by international law must have the result of encouraging rebellion. For it is the already accomplished initial success of the rebellion which brings into operation the rule of international law to the mutual advantage of both parties. International law thus makes possible a regime of moderation without loss of face to the lawful government. This is not the only case in which international law claims to introduce an element of order destroyed by the breakdown of the constitutional law of the State. Thus as between the old and the finally successful new revolutionary regime within the State there is not—and cannot conceivably be—any legal continuity so far as that State is concerned. It is international law which bridges the gap by proclaiming the principle of State continuity unaffected by revolutionary changes.

The practice of legitimate governments in relation to the insurgents has, as we have seen, varied. On some rare occasions governments have treated the rebels as traitors up to the end of the civil war and have insisted that other States should treat them as criminals. More often, they have departed from that attitude in the course of the hostilities and have treated the insurgents as if they had been actually recognized as belligerents. It is true that in thus acting governments have not been animated by a sense of legal obligation. More probably, they have been guided by considerations of humanity and convenience. However, these considerations are not irrelevant to the creation of a legal rule. That more enlightened practice, which is in conformity with the principal object of the laws of war, offers a satisfactory basis for the rule that once conditions have been brought about which entitle the insurgents to claim recognition of belligerency from outside States, they are entitled to claim recognition as such from the lawful government. As the law stands at present, a State which denies the character and the rights of belligerents to insurgents who have risen against it and who are in fact possessed of the attributes of belligerency does not act contrary to a clear rule of international law. But it does disregard the principles which underlie the law of war and which are in their essence independent of the formal status of the parties to the struggle. So long as international law has not eliminated the possibility of civil wars, it is reasonable that it should regulate them not only with respect to the relations of the lawful government and the insurgents with outside States, but also with regard to the relations between the lawful government and the insurgents. The sovereignty of the legitimate government is not so sacrosanct and the claims of human personality involved in the struggle not so negligible as to permit international law to stand aside. Once we have revised the current notions of recognition as being an arbitrary act of political discretion and of insurgents as not being 'entitled' to recognition for the reason that they are not subjects of international law, we shall have gained sufficiently firm ground to assert more effectively than we can hope to do at present the legally regulated right of the insurgents to recognition, not only by outside States but also by the legitimate government against which they have risen with an initial success assimilating the hostilities to ordinary warlike operations.

§ 71. *Effect of Recognition of Belligerency by Outside States and by the Lawful Government.* Recognition of belligerency, like any other kind of recognition, is an act performed by each State on its own responsibility in the judicial exercise of discretion in ascertaining the existence of the necessary requirements of fact. This means that recognition by one State has no compelling effect upon the decisions of other States. At the same time, however, it is clear that recognition by a considerable number of States is not without weight inasmuch as it supplies persuasive evidence as to the existence of the required conditions of recognition. Recognition by a large number of States is therefore a factor which other States (including the legitimate government) cannot lightly disregard.

Similarly, although the fact that the lawful government has expressly or by clear implication recognized the insurgents as belligerents does not impose any similar obligation upon outside States, it is nevertheless a weighty factor in the situation. If the lawful government, which is entitled to regard the rebellion as a criminal act of treason, finds itself compelled to admit, by the act of recognition, the existence of hostilities on a wide scale, outside States cannot without good reason brush aside what appears to be highly persuasive evidence in the matter.

§ 72. *Recognition of Belligerency and Responsibility for Acts of the Insurgents.* It is often stated that recognition of the belligerency of the insurgents by the legitimate government has the effect of relieving it of the responsibility for their actions. It is also frequently maintained that this is the result of such recognition by foreign States as between these States and the legitimate government. Neither of these views is correct. There is no warrant for the opinion that, normally, the lawful government is responsible for the acts of the insurgents or for losses suffered by foreigners as the result of the insurrection.[1] That opinion is the result of somewhat unguarded expressions of British and American statesmen on various occasions. The source of the confusion can be traced to Canning's despatch to Lord Granville of

1 The same applies to the responsibility of successful insurgents for losses suffered by foreigners in the course of military operations conducted in accordance with the rules of international law. There is no such responsibility. On the general question of responsibility for acts of insurgents see Silvanie in *A.J.* vol. XXXIII (1939), pp. 78–103.

After having gained independence Cuba announced that she declined to accept responsibility for losses suffered by aliens during the rebellion, on the ground that the claims were for acts of the insurgents at a time when they were not recognized as belligerents, and that the Cuban Republic was only subject to international rights and duties from the date of its constitution as a sovereign State, i.e. from 20 May 1902. Her constitution of 21 February 1901 laid down that 'the Republic of Cuba does not recognize any other debts and obligations than those legitimately contracted on behalf of the revolution by the Corps Commanders of the liberating army'. That clause was interpreted by Cuba as limiting her responsibility to contracts formally entered into. In authoritative quarters in Great Britain there was the impression that it might not be easy to establish the identity, in all cases, of the government with the leaders of the insurgents. The view was expressed that there was no rule of international law establishing the liability of the Cuban Government for requisitions or damage done by the insurgents, but as the Cuban Government represented the party who conducted the insurrection there was a strong moral claim under this head—to the exclusion, however, of damage done incidentally in the course of military operations as distinguished from requisitions or damage done for the purpose of enforcing requisitions.

22 June 1826, in which he asserted that if, as contended by the Turkish Government, the Greek insurgent Government had no international rights or duties, then the Turkish Government was responsible for the acts of the insurgent authorities. He pointed out that a time must arrive when foreign States would have to decide whether to hold the parent government responsible for the acts of the insurgents or whether to deal with the latter as a *de facto* government.[1] When in 1861 Great Britain recognized the belligerency of the Confederate States the Government of the United States seemed to find partial consolation in the reflection that 'at any rate, there was one compensation, the act had released the Government of the United States from responsibility for any misdeeds of the rebels towards Great Britain. If any of their people should capture or maltreat a British vessel on the ocean, the reclamation must be made upon those who had authorized the wrong. The United States would not be liable.'[2]

This view has since been adopted, with some uniformity, by most writers who have discussed the subject.[3] Yet there is no international award on record in which a State has been held responsible for the failure, in Hall's words, 'to perform its international obligations in such parts of its dominions as are not under its actual control'.[4] There is no warrant for holding a State liable for injurious events which it could not prevent. This principle was clearly stated by the Tribunal in the Case of the *Home Missionary Society*, decided in 1920 under the Arbitration Agreement of 1910 between Great Britain and the United States. 'It is a well-established principle of international law that no government can be held responsible for the acts of rebellious bodies of men committed in violation of its authority, where it is itself guilty of no breach of good faith, or of no negligence in suppressing insurrection.'[5] The matter is, in fact, governed by the overriding principle that in the absence of fault there is no international responsibility. International law does not, apart from exceptional cases, favour the doctrine of absolute responsibility. To hold a State

1 See also above, p. 188.

2 Mr Adams, Minister to Great Britain, to Mr Seward: in Moore, vol. I, p. 185.

3 See Rougier, op. cit. pp. 219–21; Strupp, *Das völkerrechtliche Delikt* (1920), p. 101; Kunz, p. 185; Gemma, in *Hague Recueil*, vol. IV (1924) (iii), p. 409; McNair in *Law Quarterly Review*, vol. LIII (1937), p. 477.

4 *International Law* (3rd ed. 1890), p. 32.

5 *Annual Digest*, 1921–2, Case no. 117: See also the *Solis* case, decided in October 1928 by the United States-Mexican Claims Commission, in Nielsen, *International Law applied to International Adjudications* (1933), p. 277; *Coleman* case, ibid. p. 286; Ralston, *Venezuelan Arbitrations of 1903* (1904), p. 38, where most of the authorities are collected and analysed. See also, for a more emphatic qualification of the principle of non-liability, Dunn, *The Protection of Nations* (1932), pp. 159–63.

responsible for the acts of organized rebellious bodies which it is engaged in suppressing by military action is to impose upon it an intolerable and unjustified burden. A State fighting an insurrection by a supreme military effort is clearly doing its best to secure the operation of the normal conditions of State responsibility.[1] It is interesting to note that Hall, who, as we have seen, attributes to recognition of belligerency the result of freeing the lawful government from responsibility for the acts of insurgents, expresses elsewhere a contrary view.[2] He says: 'When a government is temporarily unable to control the acts of private persons within its dominions owing to insurrection or civil commotion, it is not responsible for injury which may be received by foreign subjects in their person or property in the course of the struggle, either through the measures which it may be obliged to take for the recovery of its authority, or through acts done by the part of the population which has broken loose from control.' Recognition of belligerency on the part of outside States may be of some evidential value as showing the degree of independence achieved by the insurgents and the resulting inability of the lawful government to control their actions. But international law does not postulate the organized and semi-permanent character of insurgency, evidenced by recognition of belligerency, as a condition of the absence of liability on the part of the lawful government.[3]

In the Appendix below there are printed a number of Opinions of

1 Professor Borchard, who has made an exhaustive study of the subject, says: 'These theories [of absolute liability], however interesting, have all been abandoned, and the doctrine which has now received general support is that on principle the state is not responsible for the injuries sustained by aliens at the hands of insurgents in civil war unless there is proven fault or want of due diligence on the part of the authorities in preventing or in suppressing the revolution' (*Diplomatic Protection of Citizens Abroad* (1916), p. 229). See also, to the same effect, Articles 12 and 13 of the Harvard Research Draft of 1929 on *The Law of Responsibility of States for Damage Done in their Territory to the Person or Property of Foreigners, Harvard Research in International Law* (1929), pp. 193–6.

2 *International Law* (8th ed. 1924), p. 274.

3 When in 1858 the United States recognized the constitutionalist Government of Juarez in Mexico—after having withdrawn recognition from the insurrectionary government established in the capital—she held the constitutionalist government responsible, in principle, for the injuries done to the life and property of the citizens of the United States in the territory occupied by the rival government. But it appears that that responsibility was not pressed beyond a claim for permission to be given to the United States to take steps to abate the injury. 'On that [constitutionalist] government rests the responsibility to vindicate its own dignity and protect the lives and property of American Citizens in Mexico, and when it fails in that duty from inability to discharge it, every practical assurance should be afforded that it is ready to do what is possible in that direction, and to accept the aid and assistance of the government of the United States to the same end' (Manning, *Diplomatic Correspondence of the United States, Inter-American Affairs, 1831–1860, Mexico*, vol. IX (1934), p. 1059).

British Law Officers of the Crown on the question of responsibility for the acts of insurgents.[1] These Opinions substantiate the view put forward on the subject in this chapter.

§ 73. *Recognition of Belligerency and the Spanish Civil War of* 1936–9. A discussion of the nature of recognition of belligerency, especially when viewed as a matter of legal duty to the insurgent community, would be incomplete without an examination of what is perhaps the most important recent case bearing on this aspect of the question, namely, the refusal of Great Britain, France and other States to recognize the belligerent status of the insurgents in the Spanish Civil War of 1936–9. Recognition of belligerency was refused both to the lawful government and to the insurgents. The British Government stated on a number of occasions that it had not granted belligerent rights to either side in the struggle.[2]

It is not certain whether in the view of the governments which refused recognition of belligerency the position of the two parties to the struggle was identical. When in August 1936 the Spanish Government published decrees announcing that the territories in the occupation of the insurgents were to be 'considered as war zones and subject to blockade', the attitude of the British and United States Governments was that they were not in a position to recognize the blockade on the ground that it was not effective.[3] It is not clear whether belligerent rights in this respect would have been refused if the lawful government had been in a position to institute an effective blockade. As already suggested, it does not lie with outside States to refuse to the legitimate government the legal faculty of exercising belligerent rights in conformity with international law.[4] Be that as it may, this aspect of the question remained largely theoretical for the reason that the lawful government, having early in the struggle lost the initiative on the high seas, did not insist on recognition of belligerency which, had it been granted, would, in the circumstances of the case,[5] have conferred a superior advantage upon its adversary.

1 See below, pp. 256 et seq.

2 See above, p. 192.

3 See above, p. 199.

4 See above, p. 194.

5 In theory, recognition of belligerency by all interested Powers would, in consequence of the resulting obligation of neutrality, have conferred upon the Spanish Government the benefits of the cessation of direct assistance hitherto afforded by some States to the insurgents. This seems to have been the reason why some international lawyers—e.g. Scelle in *Friedenswarte*, vol. XXXVII (1937), p. 65—urged such recognition. However, there was no compelling reason to assume that States which violated their international obligations by a clear act of intervention prior to recognition of belligerency would have scrupulously observed their obligations of neutrality after recognition of belligerency had been granted.

For these reasons, during the Spanish Civil War of 1936–9 the question of recognition of belligerency was discussed mainly from the point of view of the right of the insurgents to recognition. The insurgent authorities insisted on it as a matter of clear and unconditional right. Their view, emphatically stated in reply to the plan for recognition of belligerency conditional upon the evacuation of foreign volunteers,[1] merits quotation:

'The National Government...deem the grant of belligerent rights to be a right. There exist to a full extent in National Spain the conditions necessary to request that it may be recognized:

(*a*) The possession of, and full sway over, a portion of the national Spanish territory which greatly exceeds that held by the enemy.

(*b*) A legal and regular Government which *de facto* exercises over the said portion of territory the rights inherent in sovereignty.

(*c*) A regular land and air army, perfectly organized and subject to a strict military discipline, which affords a guarantee of order...respecting and causing to be respected with the utmost scrupulousness the laws and customs of warfare....'[2]

The insurgents urged that the grant of belligerent rights, 'which is the consecration of an undoubted fact', should be made 'in all its fullness and not subject to conditions, since there is no question of a favour capable of discussion, but of a well-founded right, without the previous recognition of which, free from any restriction, the National Government of Spain would lack sufficient personality to enter into an agreement, such as the one now offered to them'.[3]

The insistence of the insurgents on recognition as a matter of clear right would—but for one vital factor—have been in accordance with what is here submitted to be the sound principle of international law. The factor in question was that, almost from the very inception, the contest in Spain had lost the character of a civil war, to which alone are applicable the principles of recognition of belligerency as here propounded. As the result of the direct

1 5 July 1938, Spain, no. 1, Cmd. 5793 (1937).

2 The Note, of 2 August 1938, is printed in *The Times* newspaper, 22 August 1938, and in Padelford, *A.J.* vol. XXXI (1937), p. 596. The only reason for which, at that stage, the Spanish Government objected to recognition of belligerency by foreign States was the alleged employment by the insurgents of 'methods of warfare contrary to principles of humanity' (ibid. p. 595). See also, for an interesting exposition of the right of insurgents to recognition of belligerency, the application, made on 26 March 1891, by the Chiefs of the Revolutionary Party in Chile to the Commander-in-Chief of the British Fleet in the Pacific (*State Papers*, vol. XCV (1892), *Chile*, no. 1).

3 Ibid. The reference to lacking international personality resulting from an incomplete and conditional concession of belligerent rights was obviously somewhat pedantic inasmuch as it assumed that recognition of belligerency confers upon the insurgents full international personality.

participation of outside States in the struggle, the hostilities had assumed a character differing radically from that of an ordinary civil war. So-called volunteers, sent and equipped by foreign governmental agencies in direct violation of international law as well as of expressly assumed obligations, served on both sides—in particular on the side of the insurgents. Although various European States concluded in August 1936 the so-called Non-Intervention Agreement in which they pledged themselves to prohibit the export of munitions to either side in Spain,[1] it soon became a matter of common knowledge that a number of States had failed to adhere to the terms and to the spirit of the Agreement. Thus, for instance, Italy, while still formally adhering to the Non-Intervention Agreement, officially identified herself, on repeated occasions, with the cause of the Italian volunteers and explained the export of certain quantities of war material on the ground that it was needed for Italian volunteers already present in Spain. A situation was thus created in which the principles of recognition of belligerency in a civil war could not be applied for the reason that the contest had ceased to a large extent to be a civil war in the accepted meaning of the term. The refusal on the part of Great Britain, France and some other States to recognize the belligerency of the insurgents was not therefore in the nature of an illegality consequent upon the illegality of the intervention on the part of other States. It was a refusal to apply to a situation both illegal and unprecedented legal rules devised for an altogether different set of conditions. When, therefore, in July 1938 Great Britain and other Powers made the granting of recognition conditional upon the withdrawal of foreign armed forces, that condition, far from constituting an attempt to make the duty and right of recognition the object of a bargain, was a legitimate effort to restore to the contest the character of a civil war which alone would have rendered possible and proper the granting of belligerent rights.[2] It was an attempt to secure in advance that minimum

1 See above, p. 232. For a detailed account of the working of the Non-Intervention Committee see *Survey of International Affairs*, 1937 (II), pp. 289–329. As to the execution of the Resolution relating to the scheme of observation of the Spanish frontiers by land and sea, adopted by the Committee in March 1937, see Spain, no. 1, Cmd. 5399 (1937).

2 It was repeatedly admitted by the British Government (see, for example, the statement by Mr Eden on 25 June 1937: *H.C. Debates*, vol. CCCXXV, col. 1608) that if the circumstances had been normal 'every precedent would be in favour of granting belligerent rights as was done in the American Civil War'. In May 1938 Lord Halifax stated before the Council of the League of Nations: 'The position was rapidly reached where a state of belligerency existed in fact if not in name, and the normal procedure would have been for other States to assume the rights and obligations of neutrality and for them to recognise that the two parties to the civil war were possessed of the rights and obligations of belligerents' (*Off.J.* 1938, p. 330). See also, to the same effect,

of neutral conduct which is the necessary corollary of recognition of belligerency. At no stage did the British Government attempt to justify its refusal to recognize the belligerency of the insurgents on the ground that insurgents can in no case have a legal right to such recognition.[1]

§ 74. *The Collectivization of the Process of Recognition of Belligerency.* As in the corresponding cases of recognition of States and governments so also in the case of belligerency, recognition, while declaratory of existing conditions of fact, is constitutive of the rights and duties of belligerency. Because of its constitutive character it must, as a matter of principle, be regarded as taking place in fulfilment of a legal duty as distinguished from an act of policy ministering exclusively to the interests of the State concerned. It has been shown that the practice of States is not inconsistent with that principle. However, the same considerations which in the matter of recognition of States and governments militate in favour of the collectivization of the process of recognition apply also to recognition of belligerency. The drawbacks of the phenomenon of an insurgent authority being recognized as a belligerent by some States but not by others are obvious. The same applies to the unavoidable infusion into the process of recognition of considerations of national interest. These must necessarily be present in the minds of governments, and they have often been adduced not indeed as a factor of decisive and exclusive importance but as a circumstance counselling caution even when the presence of the required conditions of belligerency did not appear to be in doubt. It is sufficient to recall the place which the charge, and the vastness of the claims connected with it, of 'unprecedented and precipitate' haste in the British recognition of the belligerency of the Southern States occupied in the negotiations preceding the *Alabama* arbitration. The same charge was levelled with similar emphasis, though unaccompanied by claims for reparation, against France, who recognized belligerency one month after Great Britain.[2] Neither can

the British statement before the Non-Intervention Committee on 16 July 1937 (*Survey of International Affairs* (1937 (II)), p. 328). For a criticism of the attitude of the British Government see Smith in *B.Y.* vol. XVIII (1937), pp. 17–31, who considers the British refusal to grant belligerent rights as a departure from the principles of international law in the matter. The writer does not discuss the question whether these principles were applicable to hostilities which by virtue of the participation of foreign forces in violation of international law had lost the complexion of a civil war.

1 See, for an exposition of this point of view, McNair in *Law Quarterly Review*, vol. LIII (1937), pp. 479–84.

2 Secretary Seward described the French action as being 'in derogation of the law of nations and injurious to the dignity and the sovereignty of the United States' (*United States, Diplomatic Correspondence*, 1864, vol. III, p. 55).

considerations of national interest be ruled out as an inarticulate factor in the process of reaching a decision left to the free discretion, to be exercised in a judicial spirit, of the governments concerned. As in other cases of recognition, the judicial disinterestedness of the finding is here put to a severe test.

For these reasons the rational development of the process of recognition of belligerency lies in the conferment upon an international authority of the right to determine, on the application of any interested State or of the insurgents, whether the objective requirements for recognition of belligerency exist in any particular case. The practice of States is not devoid of examples approaching some such collectivization of the process of recognition of belligerency. Of these the plan propounded by the States signatories to the Non-Intervention Agreement of 1936 in the course of the Spanish Civil War is the most instructive.[1] It might be said that in view of the rule that recognition of belligerency is unlawful unless the interests of the State in question necessitate a definition of its relations to the contest, it does not lend itself to uniform collective action.[2] The answer is that the collectivization of recognition would to a large extent render obsolete that particular test of recognition. Its generality would render it immune from the charge of having as its sole purpose a gratuitous manifestation of support for the cause of the insurgents.

Although the collectivization of the process of recognition of belligerency must be viewed as a rational and desirable consummation, it cannot be regarded as the final achievement at which international law ought to aim in this matter. The ultimate development cannot fall short of the attitude of international law to war in general. If and when war is effectively renounced between States as an instrument of national policy, recognition of the full belligerent status of the parties to civil wars will become an incongruous anachronism. On the other hand, the elimination of civil wars as an institution regulated by the law of nations is conditioned by such a measure of international supervision over and of protection of constitutional systems of States, in pursuance of an effective international recognition of the fundamental rights of man, as seems remote at present.

1 See above, p. 251. For an instance of collective action accompanying refusal to recognize belligerency and calculated to curb the claims of insurgents see the announcement by Sir Edward Grey in the House of Commons on 1 March 1894, to the effect that the commanders of naval units of France, Italy, Holland, Portugal and the United States stationed in Brazilian waters had received orders from the governments to concert with the British naval authorities in Brazil with a view to protecting foreign nationals against the insurgent forces of Admiral de Mello.

2 See, for example, Wiesse, *Le droit international appliqué aux guerres civiles* (1898), p. 23.

Yet we are not at liberty to relegate the possibility of that development to the domain of an unattainable ideal. The Charter of the United Nations has constituted 'human rights and fundamental freedoms' a matter of international concern.[1] The way has thus been opened for the ultimate acknowledgment of these rights and freedoms—including the inalienable right of man to government by consent[2]—as an effective part of international law. When that consummation comes to pass, the present attitude of indifference of international law towards civil wars will be deprived of its moral and legal foundations. Civil war will become the object of international condemnation and suppression in the same way as war between sovereign States. The law relating to recognition of belligerency will then become a subject of legal history.

1 See the Preamble to the Charter and Articles 1 (3), 13 (1) (*b*), 55 (*c*), 62 (2), 68, 76 (*c*).

2 See above, p. 173.

Appendix to Chapters XIV and XV

I

OPINIONS OF THE LAW OFFICERS OF THE CROWN ON THE RESPONSIBILITY OF THE LAWFUL GOVERNMENT FOR LOSSES SUFFERED BY ALIENS IN THE COURSE OF A REVOLUTION

The following seven Opinions give uniform expression to the view that, in principle, the lawful government bears no responsibility for losses sustained by aliens as the result of a civil war. All these Opinions have been included in view of the varying circumstances in which that principle was relied upon by the Law Officers.

Opinion of the Law Officers of 7 June 1866[1]

Lincolns Inn

My Lord

We are honoured with your Lordship's commands signified in Mr Hammond's letter of the 31st Ultimo, stating, that he was directed by your Lordship to transmit to us the accompanying despatch from Sir Frederick Bruce, reporting that he had been informed by Mr Seward, that in the opinion of the United States' Judge Advocate General, no claim on account of losses sustained during the Civil War could be entertained by the United States' Government, unless such claim originated in a *loyal* State; and to request that we would take the same into our consideration, and favour your Lordship with any observations we might have to offer thereupon.

In obedience to your Lordship's commands, we have taken this matter into our consideration, and have the honour to *Report*

That we are of opinion, that the subjects of Her Majesty, resident and possessing landed property in the territory of the United States, cannot, generally speaking, claim to be placed on a better footing, with respect to compensation, than native citizens. There may be particular cases, the circumstances of which may justify the official intervention of the Government of the foreign subject; but such cases would be exceptions to the general rule. In the absence of information that the case referred to by Sir F. Bruce is such an exceptional one, we are not able to say,

1 F.O. 83/2223. See also, to the same effect, the Opinion by Roundell Palmer, R. P. Collier and Robert Phillimore dated 10 March 1866, concerning Mr O'Connor's claims; the Opinion, by the same lawyers, dated 11 May 1866, concerning Mrs Molyneux's claim; the Opinion dated 13 December 1866, concerning Mr Cox's claim, by John Bolt, John B. Karslake and Robert Phillimore; and the Opinion by the same lawyers dated 31 May 1867, concerning Mr Carmalt's claim: all F.O. 83/2225.

that there is any ground for the remonstrance of Her Majesty's Government against the decision of the Judge Advocate: which is adverse to the British claimant in this case.

We have the honour to be, My Lord,

Your Lordship's most obedient, humble Servants,

ROUNDELL PALMER, R. P. COLLIER, ROBERT PHILLIMORE

The Right Honourable The Earl of Clarendon, K.G., etc., etc., etc.

Opinion of the Queen's Advocate of 3 *May* 1871[1]

Temple

My Lord

I am honoured with Your Lordship's commands signified in Mr Hammond's Letter of the 29th ultimo, stating that he was directed to transmit to me the accompanying Despatch and its inclosures received from Her Majesty's Ambassador in France, with reference to the arrest of Mr George J. Spelman, a British Subject by the Communist Authorities in Paris, whilst, as he states, he was proceeding to give an English Lesson to one of his pupils in that City. That Mr Spelman, as I should perceive claims a pecuniary indemnity on account of this outrage, and the punishment of the principal parties concerned. Mr Hammond was pleased to request that I would take this case into my consideration and furnish Your Lordship with my opinion thereupon.

In obedience to Your Lordship's commands I have the honor to *Report*

That I am of opinion that Her Majesty's Ambassador at Paris has taken a correct view of Mr Spelman's case, and that Your Lordship cannot properly make any demand against the French Government for a pecuniary indemnity to be made to Mr Spelman for the indignities to which he reports himself to have been exposed at the hands of the Insurgents in Paris. With regard to his suggestion that Her Majesty's Government should make a demand for compensation on his behalf against the Commune of Paris, I am of opinion that Your Lordship cannot properly make any such demand, unless Her Majesty's Government has recognised the Government of the Insurgents in Paris as a *de facto* Government, which I apprehend not to be the case.

I have the honour to be, My Lord,

Your Lordship's most obedient, humble Servant,

TRAVERS TWISS

To The Right Honble The Earl Granville, K.G.

1 F.O. 83/2276.

Opinion of the Queen's Advocate of 7 August 1871[1]

Temple

My Lord

I am honoured with Your Lordship's commands signified in Mr Odo Russell's letter of the 31st ultimo stating, that with reference to my report of the 21st of February last, he was directed to transmit to me the accompanying further Despatches as marked in the margin, to and from Her Majesty's Chargé d'Affaires at Buenos Ayres, upon the subject of the refusal of the Argentine Government to grant compensation to British Subjects, who have settled in Entre Rios, for losses sustained by them in consequence of the Revolution which took place in that Province. Mr Odo Russell was pleased to request that I would take these Despatches into my consideration, and furnish Your Lordship with my opinion as to the proper course for Her Majesty's Government to pursue in this matter.

In obedience to Your Lordship's commands I have the honour to *Report*

That Her Majesty's Government would not be justified in my opinion, in the absence of any Treaty securing to British Subjects established in the Argentine territory a privileged *status*, in claiming for them any greater measure of compensation for losses incurred by them during the Civil War, than is accorded by the Argentine Government to loyal Argentine citizens. Unless therefore the Argentine Government should determine to compensate its own loyal citizens for losses incurred by them from requisitions made on their property, by the rebel armies, I am of opinion that the proper course for Her Majesty's Government to adopt would be to limit its interference on behalf of British Subjects, established in the Argentine territory, to cases where the troops of the Government hitherto recognised by Her Majesty's Government have made requisitions on their property. It would appear, however, that the Argentine Government is not indisposed to listen favorably to claims of this latter description, subject however to certain conditions as to proofs, which it may be impossible for British Subjects in many cases to comply with. Under such circumstances Her Majesty's Government would be in my opinion justified in interfering to obtain more equitable conditions for British Subjects, as regards the production of proofs to establish the integrity of their claims. In what particular manner the rules laid down by the Argentine Government should be modified is rather a matter of detail, upon which I cannot venture to advise Your Lordship, and which Your Lordship may probably think fit to entrust to the discretion of Her Majesty's Chargé d'Affaires at Buenos Ayres.

I have the honour to be, My Lord,

Your Lordship's most obedient, humble Servant,

TRAVERS TWISS

To The Right Honble The Earl Granville, K.G.

1 F.O. 83/2229.

Opinion of the Law Officers of 9 May 1874[1]

Lincolns Inn

My Lord

We are honored with your Lordship's commands signified in Lord Tenterden's letter of the 29th April ultimo stating that he was directed by your Lordship to transmit to us the accompanying despatches from Her Majesty's Minister at Madrid, respecting the claims of British subjects, arising out of the recent bombardment of Carthagena, and that he Lord Tenterden was also to enclose to us a Report upon those claims by Mr Pauli, Her Majesty's late Consul at Carthagena then in this Country, to whom Mr Layards despatches were referred; and to request that we would take the papers into our consideration and favor your Lordship with our opinion as to the instructions which should be addressed to Mr Layard in the matter.

In obedience to your Lordship's Commands we have taken the papers into our consideration

And have the honor to *Report*

That in our Opinion your Lordship cannot properly instruct Mr Layard to make any representation to the Government at Madrid which would place British Subjects who may have suffered loss at Carthagena in a better or different footing for compensation than that in which Spanish Subjects similarly situated may stand.

As a matter of international right and a subject for diplomatic interference, a government cannot be held responsible for injuries inflicted on the property or persons of foreigners resident in the Country by insurgents engaged in armed hostility to the government, and which injuries the Government had not the power to prevent.

We have the honor to be, My Lord,
Your Lordships Most Obedt. Hble Servts,

RICHARD BAGGALLAY, JOHN HOLKER, J. PARKER DEANE

The Right Honble Earl Derby, etc., etc., etc.

Opinion of the Law Officers of 9 May 1874[2]

Lincolns Inn

My Lord

We are honored with your Lordship's commands signified in Lord Tenterden's letter of the 6th instant stating that with reference to his letter of the 29th ultimo, enclosing for our opinion, certain papers relative to the claims of British Subjects against the Spanish Government, on account of losses sustained by them during the insurrection at Carthagena: he was directed by your Lordship to transmit to us two despatches from Her Majesty's Minister at Madrid showing the steps that have been taken with regard to similar claims brought forward by German and Italian

1 F.O. 83/2379. 2 Ibid.

Subjects. And to request that we would take the enclosed papers into our consideration, together with the correspondence already before us

In obedience to your Lordship's commands we have the honor to

Report

That we have taken into consideration the letters of Her Majesty's Minister at Madrid, showing the steps that have been taken by the Spanish Government with respect to the claims brought forward by German and Italian Subjects on account of losses sustained by them during the insurrection at Carthagena, but it appears to us that there were special circumstances in connection with each of such cases which led to the claims being recognised by the Spanish Government and we see no reason to alter the opinion expressed by us in our Report bearing even date with this and made in answer to your Lordships letter of the 29th ultimo.

We have the honor to be, My Lord,

Your Lordships most obedt. humble Servants,

RICHARD BAGGALLAY, JOHN HOLKER, J. PARKER DEANE

The Right Honble The Earl of Derby, K.G., etc., etc., etc.

Opinion of the Law Officers of 7 December 1874[1]

Lincolns Inn

My Lord

We are honoured with your Lordship's commands signified in Lord Tenterdens letter of the 19th November Ultimo stating that he was directed by your Lordship to transmit to us the accompanying Despatches from Her Majesty's Minister at Madrid, relative to the claims of certain British Firms at Bilbao to be compensated by the Spanish Government for losses occasioned to them by the Civil War in Spain, which losses appear to have been caused partly by Government Troops and partly by Carlists.

Lord Tenterden was also to inclose a Memorandum drawn up in the Foreign Office upon the question of the liability of the Government of a Country, in which War is being carried on, to make good such losses, together with various other papers, as marked in the margin, relating to the subject—and Lord Tenterden was to request that we would take all these Papers into our consideration and favour your Lordship with our opinion as to the Instructions that should be sent to Mr Layard with regard to the claims of the British Firms above referred to

In obedience to your Lordship's commands we have taken these papers into consideration and have the honour to *Report*

That we have carefully considered the papers transmitted to us and we are of opinion that British Subjects carrying on their business or resident in Spain have no claim upon the Spanish Government for compensation for the losses which they may have sustained by the Acts of the Troops and Insurgents during the Civil War, except in the event of the Spanish Government compensating Spanish Subjects who may have incurred similar losses

1 F.O. 83/2379.

That Mr Layard may therefore properly be instructed that Her Majesty's Government cannot interfere on behalf of the British Firms and Subjects referred to in his Despatches.

We have the honour to be, My Lord,
Your Lordships most Obedt. humble Servants,
RICHARD BAGGALLAY, JOHN HOLKER, J. PARKER DEANE

The Right Honble The Earl of Derby

Opinion of the Law Officers of 28 *August* 1873[1]

Temple

My Lord

We are honoured with your Lordship's commands signified in Mr Hammonds letter of the 14th inst. stating, that he was directed by your Lordship to transmit to us a Despatch with its inclosures from Her Majesty's Charge d'Affaires in Madrid respecting the publication by the Municipality of Malaga, of a Tariff of Export Duties, in contravention of Spanish Law & that he (Mr Hammond) was to request us to take the papers into consideration & favor your Lordship at our early convenience with our opinion as to the instructions which should be addressed to Her Majesty's Charge d'Affaires in this matter.

In obedience to your Lordship's commands we have the honor to Report.

That it is not the duty of the English Charge d'Affaires to interfere as to any breach of the Constitutional Law of Spain by any Spanish Municipality except so far as British interests or existing Treaties between Great Britain & Spain may be affected thereby. The present condition of Spain is no doubt anarchical yet while there exists a central Government claiming authority over the whole country, that Government is bound by Treaties and to that Government only recourse must be had for the purpose of enforcing them and to obtain redress for the breach of them. Mr Macdonnell can under the peculiar circumstances of the country do no more than persistently call the attention of the Central Government to the illegal exactions threatened or enforced by the Municipality of Malaga & distinctly inform the Central Government that Great Britain holds it responsible for the consequences of such illegality. Mr Macdonnell has in our opinion rightly advised the payment of these exactions under protest by British subjects. Beyond this nothing can be done by them until, if ever, the independence of various portions of Spain is recognised by this country, and separate diplomatic relations are entered into with those portions.

We have the honor to be, My Lord,
Your Lordship's Most Obt, humble Servants,
J. D. COLERIDGE, G. JESSEL, J. PARKER DEANE

The Rt. Hon. The Earl Granville, K.G.

1 F.O. 83/2378. This Opinion is not inconsistent with those printed above. It refers to acts within territories over which the Central Government claimed control.

II

OPINION OF THE QUEEN'S ADVOCATE ON THE RESPONSIBILITY OF THE LAWFUL GOVERNMENT FOR THE CONTRACTUAL OBLIGATIONS OF INSURGENTS RECOGNIZED AS BELLIGERENTS

The Opinion which follows is printed in full having regard both to the standing of its author and to the scholarly manner in which the subject is treated.

Opinion of the Queen's Advocate of 13 *February* 1867[1]

Doctors Commons

My Lord

I am honoured with Your Lordship's commands, signified in Mr Hammond's Letter of the 9th Instant stating that he was directed to transmit to me a Letter from Messrs. Iewell and Chamberlain forwarding a memorial from the holders of the Confederate Cotton Loan together with a legal opinion which they have obtained on the subject of their claims; and to request that I would take these papers into consideration and furnish Your Lordship with my opinion thereupon.

In obedience to Your Lordship's commands, I have taken this case into consideration and have the honour to *Report*

That the positions for which the Petitioners contend appear to be these:

(1) That the late Confederate States have been recognised as *de facto* belligerent by Her Majesty's Government and by the Tribunals of the United States, and are to be considered exactly in the same light as a Foreign Enemy whose Territory has been conquered and passes *cum onere* to the conqueror that is with the obligation to discharge its debts contracted with the other Foreign States, binding upon him.

(2) That the debts in this case were contracted on behalf of separate States which had independently of their temporary Union under a Confederacy, by their prior original political constitution as acknowledged by the United States power to contract such debts, and that the Confederate Government was only the Agent of each or all of these States separately competent to contract *per se* the Loan.

(3) That these States have been prevented from discharging their debts by the Conqueror, the United States and have been forced to repudiate them.

(4) That the United States has possessed itself as Conqueror of all the resources of the States available for the discharge of the debt, and even of the Cotton which was especially pledged for the payment of the Foreign Creditor.

Upon these grounds principally, if not exclusively, the Memorialists apply to Her Majesty's Government to intervene on their behalf with the Government of the United States and obtain from them payment of the bonds issued by the late *de facto* Confederate Government. The Memorial raises two distinct questions:

1 F.O. 83/2225.

(i) Whether the United States are bound by the principles rules and precedents of International Law to pay to the Foreign Creditor debts owing to him from the Confederate Government?

(ii) Whether, whatever may be the true answer to this question, the case of the Memorialists is made out for the official intervention of Her Majesty's Government on their behalf with the Government of the United States?

The second question alone calls for any remarks from me. I am of opinion, that Her Majesty's Government ought not to accede to the request of the Memorialists. It might be enough to say that Her Majesty's Government could not do so without to a certain extent pronouncing judgement upon the difficult question of Foreign constitutional Law with respect to the limits of the Sovereignty of each State and their relation to the Supreme Government of the United States which in great measure gave rise to this very war.

The Memorialists take their stand upon the language of the Confederate Constitution previous to the war of the United States (Page 5 in line 6) with respect to the Sovereignty of each State composing the Union, and protest against the 'charge that the Bonds which we hold were issued by insurgents or by a Government having its origin in insurrection'.

Her Majesty's Government must therefore necessarily assume as the basis of their right to intervene that the very proposition of American Constitutional Law as to which this fierce controversy has arisen, and which has practically been solved by force and conquest after a bloody civil war, is nevertheless incontrovertible in the sense contended for by the Confederates and their Creditors.

In other words Her Majesty's Government must found their application to the United States Government on the ground that the War which they have waged, and in which they have conquered, was unlawful, and contrary to the principles and laws of their own internal constitution.

It is obvious that it is not competent to Her Majesty's Government to take this course. The United States Government would be entitled to treat it in the same spirit as Her Majesty's Government would have treated the intervention of the United States Government, on behalf of a subject, who had lent money to a Native Indian Prince, during the late rebellion in India, to enable him to levy war against the Queen of England. The United States Government might by a like process of reasoning contend that the original contract subsisting between the East India Company and the Native Prince had been broken, that he being an independent Sovereign had a right to borrow money of a Foreign Creditor, and that the Conqueror took his territory *cum onere* and was bound to discharge the debt.

The argument from the recognition of the Confederates as *de facto* belligerents fails altogether as an argument for the interference of Her Majesty's Government.

Her Majesty proclaimed a strict neutrality and enjoined it upon her subjects admonishing them that if they aided either belligerent they would do so at their own peril and without any claim upon her assistance, if evil consequences ensued to them therefrom.

To furnish a belligerent with money is to render him the most material aid, to supply him with the very sinews of war. Let me moreover suggest some tests by which both the duty of the Neutral Government towards its subjects, and the *jus victoris* may be tried.

If the money, *in specie*, advanced by the Memorialists to the Southerners had been captured on its way out to them? If the United States Army had seized the money *in specie* in the Treasury of the Confederates? If instead of money munitions of war, Ships, cannons, and the like had been furnished by the Memorialists, and the United States Army had seized these articles for which Cotton Bonds had been given as a security, and afterwards the very Cotton itself which was pledged for their payment? In any or all of these instances the unfitness of any intervention on the part of Her Majesty's Government would be apparent: but it would not be easy to distinguish, in principle, the right of Her Majesty's Government to demand, on behalf of the Memorialists, from the United States repayment of the money, which had actually reached the hands of the Confederate Government, and been expended by them; from the right to do so, when the money had been captured on the high seas, or on land, or when the loan has been contracted by an exchange immediate or promised, of commodities (e.g.—so much munitions of war for so much Cotton) and these commodities had been seized *jure belli* by the Conqueror.

I do not think that Her Majesty's Government is bound to consider the remaining question—namely, as to the obligation of the United States, towards the private British Creditor of the late Confederacy: if my opinion be well founded, that the creditor has no claim to the official intervention of Her Majesty's Government on his behalf.

But I will offer upon this part of the case also a few observations. The United States Government may not unfairly contend that the general obligation of the conquering State to discharge the debts, previously contracted with foreign creditors, by the conquered State, does not extend to the case, where these debts have not been the subject of an engagement previous to the war, but have been contracted during, and for the express purpose of carrying on, the war: inasmuch as this doctrine would compel the Conqueror to defray the costs not only of his own conquest, but of the resistance of his enemy.

But that at all events it cannot be said to apply to the case of a debt contracted by Provinces or States, which before the War, were subject to the authority of the Power from which they revolted, and by which they have been, after a short struggle, by force of arms, recovered.

This War (the United States Government may observe) was not closed by a Treaty which contained stipulations that the conqueror should, either altogether or in a specified proportion, pay the debts of the conquered, according to the usage which has long prevailed on this subject. No Foreign State intervened in the war, or made any demand at the close of it, that a Foreign debt should be recognised by the Conqueror. The Creditors, in this case, entered of their own free-will into a speculation which, if the Confederates had prospered, would have been lucrative, but which their failure has rendered the reverse.

Whether they have any right to complain that their debtors, the States of the late Confederacy, yielded without making terms, on their behalf, with the Conqueror; or that they accepted the repudiation of the debt as a condition of their being restored to the union, or that they do not now contrive some means of fulfilling their engagements with their creditors, are questions which the Government of the United States may well refuse to entertain.

The importance of the subject has led me to report at greater length than I could have wished, but, for the reasons which I have stated, I am clearly of opinion that Her Majesty's Government ought not to comply with the prayer of the Memorial from the holders of the Confederate Cotton Loan.

I have the honour to be, My Lord,

Your Lordship's most obedient, humble Servant,

ROBERT PHILLIMORE

To The Right Honble The Lord Stanley

III

OPINIONS OF THE LAW OFFICERS OF THE CROWN ON INSURGENCY AND MUNICIPAL LEGISLATION OF THIRD STATES

The following two Opinions illustrate the application of the Foreign Enlistment Act in cases of insurgency unaccompanied by recognition of belligerency.

Opinion of the Law Officers of 10 *October* 1876[1]

My Lord Temple

We were honored with Your Lordship's commands, signified in Sir Julian Pauncefote's letter of the 5th of September, ultimo, stating that he was directed by Your Lordship to transmit to us the accompanying letter and its enclosures from the Colonial Office relative to the expected arrival in Bahama Waters of a Steamer named the 'Amazona' said to fly the British Flag,—to have on board four guns ready for Mounting, and to be intended for use by the Cuban Insurgents against the Spanish Government.

That we would see that the Attorney General of the Colony in his Report to the Governor raised doubts as to whether the provisions of clauses 4 to 10 of the 'Foreign Enlistment Act 1870' were applicable to a Vessel in the service of the Cuban Insurgents,—those Insurgents not being recognised as Belligerents—and therefore not constituting in his opinion a 'Foreign State', at war with a Foreign State at peace with Her Majesty.

That as the question thus raised by the Attorney General of the Bahamas, was one of great general importance, apart from the special question of the 'Amazona' he was to request that we would favor your Lordship with our opinion thereon.

1 F.O. 83/2379.

Sir Julian Pauncefote was pleased to enclose a copy of the Judgment of the Privy Council on the case of the 'Salvador' which was of a somewhat similar nature but which arose under the old Foreign Enlistment Act (59 Geo: III. c. 69), and to add that your Lordship would also be glad to be favored with our opinion as to whether the Colonial Attorney General was correct in supposing that the 'Amazona' is proved to be fitted out as a privateer to be used in the service of an unrecognised Nationality might be dealt with as a piratical Vessel.

In obedience to Your Lordship's commands we have the honor to *Report*

That in our opinion the Attorney General of the Colony has not given due weight to the Interpretation Clause s. 30 of the Foreign Enlistment Act 1870.

If therefore the 'Amazona' is in the employment or intended to be employed in the service of the Insurgents in Cuba, although those Insurgents may not be in the strict sense of the word 'belligerents', the case is brought within the statute. The case of the 'Salvador' though under the former Foreign Enlistment Act, was decided upon words almost if not quite the same with the words in the 30th section of the Act of 1870; and is a clear authority upon the point that as in the 4th section of the Act of 1870 the Insurgents are a 'Foreign State' at war with a Foreign State at Peace with Her Majesty.

We doubt if the 'Amazona' fitted out as a privateer and to be used in the service of an unrecognised Nationality could be dealt with as a piratical Vessel.

The proceedings proper to be taken against her if the facts should justify any proceedings when she comes to the Bahamas will be, in our opinion, under the Foreign Enlistment Act 1870.

We have the honor to be, My Lord,
Your Lordship's most obedient, humble Servants,
JOHN HOLKER, HARDINGE S. GIFFARD, J. PARKER DEANE

The Right Honorable The Earl of Derby, etc., etc., etc.

Opinion of the Law Officers of the Crown and Dr Deane to the Earl of Derby of 7 December 1877[1]

Temple

My Lord

We are honoured with your Lordship's commands signified in Sir J. Pauncefote's letter of the 3rd July last, stating that he was to transmit to us a letter from the Lords of the Admiralty forwarding a despatch from the Commander-in-chief on the Pacific Station, in which Admiral de Horsey applied for instructions as to the course he should pursue in the case of British ships hired by a foreign State for the conveyance of troops dispatched to suppress a rebellion, and reporting the case of the Pacific Steam Navigation Company's steam-ship 'Limena', which was recently chartered for that purpose by the Peruvian Government at Callao.

That it would seem that Admiral de Horsey took a right view of his duties in abstaining from any interference with that vessel, as the provisions of the Foreign

1 F.O. 61/304.

Enlistment Act relating to the dispatch of vessels 'in the military or naval service of a foreign State at war with a friendly State,' even if they should apply to such a transaction as that referred to, were limited to acts committed within Her Majesty's dominions.

That as regards the question whether the dispatch of a vessel from a British Colony in the service of a foreign State for the purpose of suppressing a rebellion was an offence against the Act, the reply would seem to depend on the construction of the words 'a foreign State at war with any friendly State.'

That Sir J. Pauncefote was to inclose our Report of the 10th October, 1876, on a question which arose at the Bahamas with reference to the rebellion in Cuba, and in which we advised that, having regard to the interpretation clause of the Act, the Cuban rebels came within the definition given 'of a foreign State at war with a foreign State at peace with Her Majesty,' and that the dispatch of a vessel from the Bahamas in the service of the Cuban insurgents, for the purpose of committing hostilities against the Spanish Government, would be a violation of the Act.

That the converse case now presented itself for consideration, and your Lordship desired to be favoured with our opinion as to whether, on the right construction of the Act, where a rebellion occurs in a foreign State at peace with Her Majesty, and the rebels assume to exercise the powers of government over part of a province or people, the rebels must be considered as 'a foreign State at peace with Her Majesty,' or as a 'friendly State' (which expressions are declared synonymous by section 4), so as to render illegal the dispatch of a British ship from Her Majesty's dominions to be employed in the military or naval service of the foreign State for the purpose of suppressing the rebellion.

That that would appear to be the effect of the definition of 'foreign State' in the interpretation clause, 'if not inconsistent with the context.'

That Sir J. Pauncefote was also to request that we would be good enough to advise your Lordship as to the reply which should be given to the inquiry made by the Lords of the Admiralty both as regards the case of the 'Limena' and the general question raised.

In obedience to your Lordship's commands we have the honour to report—

That the granting the use of a ship to convey troops is clearly an accepting of an engagement (see section 4 of the 'Foreign Enlistment Act, 1870') in the military or naval service (see section 30 of the same Act for the meaning of these words).

This section 4 provides that if any person, being a British subject, within or without Her Majesty's dominions, accepts an engagement in the military or naval service of any foreign State at war with a foreign State at peace with Her Majesty, he shall be guilty of an offence against the Act, although the engagement was made and carried out not within Her Majesty's dominions.

Then, referring to the definition of a 'foreign State,' in section 30, that term includes 'part of any province or people, or any person or persons exercising or assuming to exercise the powers of government in or over any foreign country, Colony, province, or part of any province or people.'

The use of a ship to convey troops belonging to a friendly Power to act against rebels to the foreign Power would, under sections 4 and 30, be, in our opinion, an offence against the 'Foreign Enlistment Act, 1870.'

In reference to the conduct of Admiral de Horsey in the particular case, and the reply which should be given to the Lords of the Admiralty, their Lordships may, in our opinion, properly be informed that, as long as the 'Limena' was in Peruvian waters, he was quite right in not detaining her, and in confining himself to the caution which he gave to the master and crew of that vessel.

We think, however, that, as the master and crew of the 'Limena' were engaged in the commission of a breach of neutrality, Admiral de Horsey would, on the high seas, have been justified in stopping the vessel and preventing her proceeding on her voyage whilst the Peruvian troops remained on board.

We have, &c.

(Signed) JOHN HOLKER, HARDINGE S. GIFFARD, J. PARKER DEANE

NOTE. See also the Opinion of the Law Officers of the Crown and Dr Deane to Earl Granville of 10 October 1883, given in the course of the rebellion in Haiti and bearing on the question whether the Foreign Enlistment Act can be enforced against subjects or ships of foreign States. They said: 'The Foreign Enlistment Act contains no provisions expressly dealing with such a case, and we think that neither British naval officers nor civil officials would have any right to interfere with the vessels or subjects of a foreign Power though acting in concert with a vessel and subjects of Her Majesty engaged in a breach of the Foreign Enlistment Act. But inasmuch as any British ship engaged in an expedition prepared in Her Majesty's dominions in contravention of that Act is by section 11 forfeited to Her Majesty, we think that the officers of one of Her Majesty's ships would be warranted in resisting the object of such expedition being attained, and could interfere upon the high seas and compel the vessel to return to a British port.'

IV

OPINION OF THE LAW OFFICERS OF THE CROWN ON SUPPLY OF MUNITIONS TO THE LAWFUL GOVERNMENT AND TO THE INSURGENTS

Opinion of the Law Officers of the Crown of 28 October 1873[1]

Temple

My Lord

The Right Honble The Earl Granville, K.G., etc., etc., etc.

We are honoured with Your Lordship's commands signified in Lord Tenterden's letter of the 21st instant, stating that with reference to his letter of that day's date, he

1 F.O. 83/2378.

was directed by Your Lordship to transmit to you a copy of the Letter from the Admiralty referred to in that already sent to us.

That we would perceive from Captain Phillimores Telegram that the Spanish Fleet were taking in coals at Gibraltar, presumably from the ordinary Commercial sources, and that the object of his second Telegram was to ask instructions as to supplying the Spanish admiral with Welsh Coal from Her Majesty's stores.

That if coals were supplied in either manner to the Spanish Government Ships, it was possible that the Insurgents might also request to be furnished with them upon similar terms, and that the decision come to upon that point might involve very difficult and delicate questions.

That Lord Tenterden was therefore to request that we would give our most careful consideration to the points raised by the papers before us and that we would favour Your Lordship with our opinion as to the rules which should be laid down with respect to the supply of coals to either, both, or neither of the contending Spanish Fleets, and also as to the grounds upon which those rules should be maintained.

In obedience to Your Lordship's commands. We have the honor to *Report*.

The principle, which in our opinion should be the foundation of any rule with respect to the supply of coals to the contending Spanish Fleets is that Her Majesty's Government has no concern with the political state of Spain and the conflicts between opposite parties in that country.

This condition of things and the consequences following from it will continue as regards the Fleet under the Madrid Government until that Government shall cease to treat the Insurgents as Insurgents, or 'Pirates' as it has we believe hitherto called them, and recognises them as Belligerents, or until if ever Her Majesty's Government think fit to recognise the insurgents as belligerents.

Then Her Majesty's Government will be bound to strictly observe the duties of Neutrals in War and neither supply nor allow the supply of coals for the purposes of carrying on war to either party.

In the meanwhile we are of opinion that coals may be supplied to the ships belonging to the Madrid Government as a Government *de facto*, and may properly be refused to the ships of the Insurgents as they carry no national Flag and are officered by persons who hold no commission under either a *de facto* or a *de jure* Government.

We have the honor to be, My Lord,
Your Lordship's most obedient humble servants,

J. D. Coleridge, Henry James, Jas. Parker Deane

Chapter XVI

RECOGNITION OF INSURGENCY

§ 75. *Recognition of Insurgency as distinguished from Recognition of Belligerency*. Insurgency, as conceived in relation to foreign States, is the sum total of rights and privileges which these States concede to the rebellious party during a civil war. It is not a well-defined status resulting from an express declaration in the form of recognition or an implied equivalent thereof. The difference between the status of belligerency and that of insurgency in relation to foreign States may best be expressed in the form of the proposition that belligerency is a relation giving rise to definite rights and obligations, while insurgency is not. Insurgency, so far as foreign States are concerned, results, on the one hand, from the determination of those States not to recognize the rebellious party as a belligerent on the ground that there are absent one or more of the requirements of belligerency. On the other hand, recognition of insurgency is the outcome both of the unwillingness of foreign States to treat the rebels as mere law-breakers[1] and of the desire of those States to put their relations with the insurgents on a regular, although clearly provisional, basis. Situations may arise, and have arisen, in which some of the legal conditions of recognition of belligerency are absent, but in which it is nevertheless impracticable to act as if the civil war in a foreign State were entirely an internal matter of that State. Thus it may become necessary to apply municipal enactments intended to prevent nationals from participating in a foreign civil war. It may prove expedient to enter into contact with the insurgent authorities with a view to protecting national interests in the territory occupied by them, to regularizing political and commercial intercourse with them, and to interceding with them in order to ensure a measure of humane conduct of hostilities. Finally, the disinclination to assume an attitude of partiality in the contest by denying to rebels the rights exercised by the lawful government against foreign States may lead the latter to acquiesce in a certain amount of interference with their own rights on the part of the insurgents.

This factual recognition of the existence of limited international personality of the insurgents may somewhat inaccurately but conveniently be referred to as recognition of insurgency. Actually, international law

1 See below, p. 278.

knows of no 'recognition of insurgency' as an act conferring upon insurgents international rights flowing from a well-defined status. That insurgency has been recognized in any given case means that specific rights have been conceded or particular municipal enactments brought into being. It does not create a status from which further and more general rights can be deduced. The two principal cases of recognition of insurgency as distinguished from recognition of belligerency provide an instructive illustration of the difference between these two kinds of recognition. They are the cases of the Cuban War of Independence and of the Spanish Civil War of 1936–9.

§ 76. *Recognition of Insurgency during the Cuban War of Independence.* During the Cuban insurrection against Spain from 1868 onwards the United States consistently refused to recognize the belligerent status of the insurgents. It did so on the ground that, in the words of the Message of President Grant to Congress of 7 December 1875, it did not 'find in the insurrection the existence of such a substantial political organization, real, palpable, and manifest to the world, having the forms and capable of the ordinary functions of government toward its own people and to other states...as to take the contest out of the category of a mere rebellious insurrection, or occasional skirmishes, and place it on the terrible footing of war, to which a recognition of belligerency would aim to elevate it';[1] or, in the words of President McKinley's Message of 6 December 1897, because the United States was not of the view that 'the Cuban insurrection possesses beyond dispute the attributes of statehood, which alone can demand the recognition of belligerency in its favour'.[2] At the same time, however, the Government of the United States in a series of pronouncements addressed to its own nationals recognized the existence of a condition of insurrection in Cuba. On 12 June 1895 the President of

1 Moore, vol. I, pp. 196–7. See also Benton, *International Law and Diplomacy of the Spanish-American War* (1908), pp. 21–64.

2 Moore, vol. I, p. 198. It must be noted that the United States also refused to concede belligerent rights to Spain. In a communication addressed to the Secretary of the Navy on 18 May 1869, the Secretary of State said with regard to the civil war: 'Those hostilities must be regarded as strictly of a domestic character. As such they can not impart to Spain...any belligerent rights on the high seas, nor have we recognized any such rights anywhere as possessed by those who are in arms against Spanish authority in that island. The right of search for contraband is a right to be exercised against a public enemy only on the high seas. It can not therefore be lawfully exercised against a neutral who has not recognized both parties as belligerents' (ibid. p. 193). For a similar British pronouncement, in connection with the case of *The Virginius* in 1873, see *B.F.S.P.* vol. LXV, p. 145. On the question of the right of outside States to refuse belligerent rights to the lawful government see above, p. 243.

the United States issued a proclamation declaring that Cuba was 'the seat of civil disturbances, accompanied by armed resistance to the authority of the established Government of Spain' and admonishing all persons within the jurisdiction of the United States to refrain from acts prohibited by the neutrality laws.[1] The Courts of the United States regarded these pronouncements and declarations as sufficient authority for applying the United States neutrality laws and for assuming the existence of a condition of insurgency as distinguished from belligerent status. Thus in the well-known case of *The Three Friends* the Supreme Court of the United States said:

'The distinction between recognition of belligerency and recognition of a condition of political revolt, between recognition of the existence of war in the material sense and of war in the legal sense, is sharply illustrated by the case before us. For here the political department has not recognized the existence of a *de facto* belligerent power engaged in hostility in Spain, but has recognized the existence of insurrectionary warfare prevailing before, at the time and since this forfeiture is alleged to have been incurred.... We are thus judicially informed of the existence of an actual conflict of arms in resistance to the authority of a Government with which the United States are on terms of peace and amity, although acknowledgment of the insurgents as belligerents by the political department has not taken place; and it can not be doubted that, this being so, the act in question [the neutrality statute] is applicable.'[2]

§ 77. *Recognition of Insurgency during the Spanish Civil War of* 1936–9. The Spanish Civil War of 1936–9 is an instructive example of what may be regarded as recognition of insurgency for the purpose both of the application of relevant municipal enactments and of maintaining intercourse with and conceding certain rights to the insurgent authorities. Recognition of the belligerency of the insurgents was withheld on the part of Great Britain and of many other States until the end of the civil war for the reason that the struggle had assumed a complexion different from that of a civil war in the ordinary meaning of the term.[3] At the same time, however, no attempt was made to interfere with the naval or aerial operations of the insurgents either on the high seas in so far as they were confined to their adversary, or in territorial waters, even if, in the latter case, they were directed against ships of foreign States, provided that such operations were not contrary to international law. Official intercourse was maintained with the insurgents for the purpose of protecting nationals, of safeguarding commercial interests and of securing a mitigation of the conduct of the war

1 29 Stat. 871. Similar proclamations were issued in 1876: see 29 Stat. 881.

2 (1897) 166 U.S. 1, 63.

3 See above, p. 252.

by offers of good offices in the exchange of prisoners and the like. After a time, agents were exchanged who, while not formally endowed with diplomatic status, in many ways fulfilled the functions of diplomatic representatives.[1] Finally, Great Britain, while still refusing to concede rights of belligerency, took the unprecedented step of recognizing the insurgents as the 'insurgent'[2] or 'nationalist'[3] *de facto* government of the portion of Spain under their control, with the result that British courts accorded to them treatment to a large extent identical with that accorded to governments of sovereign States. Thus in *Banco de Bilbao* v. *Rey*[4] it was held that as the result of the recognition *de facto* the courts were bound to recognize the legislation of the insurgent government within the territory under its control and to treat, so far as that territory was concerned, the legislation of the lawful government as a mere nullity. In *The Arantzazu Mendi*[5] it was decided that the Nationalist (insurgent) Government thus recognized must be regarded as the government of a foreign sovereign State with the result that it was entitled to claim the ordinary jurisdictional immunities even against the lawful government which continued to be recognized *de jure*. The Court set aside a writ *in rem* issued by the Republican (lawful) Government on the ground that the action impleaded the Nationalist Government of Spain, a foreign sovereign State, which was in possession of the vessel by its duly authorized agent. Some of the consequences which British courts drew from that form of recognition are controversial,[6] but they show that, notwithstanding the refusal to grant recognition of belligerency, what may be properly called recognition of insurgency may make possible a substantial measure of regular intercourse analogous to that mutually obtaining between established governments. At an early stage in the civil war, in a warning issued on 10 January 1937, the Foreign Enlistment Act was declared to be applicable. The warning referred specifically to enlistment in the armed forces of either side.[7] At the same

1 See below, p. 390. 2 See below, p. 280. 3 See below, p. 365.
4 See below, p. 284. 5 See below, pp. 279 et seq.
6 See below, p. 290. And see Padelford, *International Law and Diplomacy in the Spanish Civil Strife* (1939), pp. 3–7.
7 The declaration in question contained a warning that persons enlisting in the service of either side to the civil war in Spain would be contravening the Foreign Enlistment Act of 1870, in particular Sections 4 and 5 of that Act. Section 4 of the Act provides that it is illegal for any British subject, without the King's licence, to accept, or agree to accept, or for any person, whether a British subject or not, to induce any other person to accept or agree to accept any commission or engagement in the military or naval service of a foreign State at war with a State at peace with his Majesty. Section 5 makes it an offence to leave or to induce to leave British territory with the intention of engaging in any such war. The effect of the interpretative Section 30 of the same Act is to assimilate insurgents, whether recognized or not, to a

time British courts attached decisive importance to the absence of recognition of belligerency and declined to attach legal consequences to measures of blockade adopted by the insurgent authorities.[1]

§ 78. *Other Examples of Recognition of Insurgency*. The minor instances of 'recognition' of insurgency show once more the combination of a refusal to recognize full belligerent status with the concession of some belligerent rights and with the maintenance of a measure of official intercourse. Already in 1886 Dr Wharton, Solicitor to the Department of State of the United States, insisted, in connection with the revolution in Colombia, on the clear distinction in the practice of the United States between recognition of belligerency and recognition of insurgency.[2] During the revolution in Brazil in 1893 the demand for recognition of belligerency was expressly refused by the United States and other States. Representatives of foreign

foreign State, and there seemed therefore to be little doubt that the Act was applicable although the insurgents were not a 'State'. See also above, p. 235. The question whether there was 'war' in the meaning of the Act was accurately answered in authoritative quarters to the effect that for the Act to become operative it was not necessary for the struggle to be a war in the technical meaning of the term. See the statement by Sir John Simon in the House of Commons on 21 January 1937, to the effect that the Government had been 'advised not long after the outbreak of the civil war in Spain that it had from the beginning been illegal for any British subject to take service in the combatant forces of either of the parties engaged in that war or for any person to induce them to take such service' (*H.C. Debates*, vol. CCCXVII, col. 323). The provisions of the Foreign Enlistment Acts of 1819 and 1870 had previously been applied to cases in which there was no recognized state of belligerency: *The Salvador*, (1870) 3 P.C. 218, where it was decided that the provision of a ship to Cuban insurgents was contrary to the Act (*R.* v. *Sandoval*, 3 T.L.R. 411). See also *Burton* v. *Pinkerton*, 2 Ex. 340; *The Harrier*, (1921) 8 *Lloyd's List Law Reports*, p. 488; *Annual Digest*, 1919–22, Case no. 122. For a discussion of this question see McNair in *Law Quarterly Review*, vol. LIII (1937), pp. 494–6.

1 See *Spanish Government* v. *North of England Steamship Company*, (1938) 54 T.L.R. 852; *Annual Digest*, 1938–40, Case no. 30, where Lewis J. held that 'the "blockade" declared by General Franco never was a blockade' and did not therefore justify reliance on a clause in the charter-party giving the defendants the right, in case of a blockade, to discharge the cargo in a safe port. See also *Tatem* v. *Gamboa*, [1939] 1 K.B. 132; *Annual Digest*, 1938–40, Case no. 31, where Goddard J. rejected the view that in the circumstances there was a risk of capture in the meaning of the contract. Capture meant lawful capture. The latter presupposed a lawful blockade recognized by Great Britain. As belligerent rights had not been granted, no lawful blockade could be held to have been established.

2 He wrote: 'While in very many cases we have recognized foreign insurgencies, we have never recognized such insurgencies as belligerent until they have shown themselves, by long and enduring exhibition of strength, to be on something like a parity with the state against which they revolt. The government of the United States unquestionably recognized the *insurgency* of the forces arrayed in April last against the Colombian titular government. But it expressly declares that it did not recognize their *belligerency*...': as cited in Moore, vol. II, p. 1100.

Powers, including Great Britain and the United States, informed the rebel commander that any attempt to bombard Rio de Janeiro or to interfere with commercial operations in the port would be resisted by force.[1] At the same time, however, there was a disposition to concede to the insurgents the right to blockade Rio de Janeiro provided that the blockade was effective.[2] Similarly, in the somewhat inconclusive case of the Chilean revolution in 1891, the British and other governments, while refusing recognition of belligerency, apparently acquiesced in the exercise of certain belligerent rights by the insurgents.[3] In 1899 the Secretary of State of the United States instructed the Minister to Bolivia to have no diplomatic relations with the insurgents which might imply their recognition 'as the legitimate Government of Bolivia', but, short of recognition, 'to deal with them as the responsible parties in local possession' with a view to

1 Moore, vol. I, p. 203. On 21 September 1893, the British representative in Brazil informed the home authorities that the insurgent admiral communicated to the French admiral his intention to search all foreign merchandise placed in cargo boats and that a collective note had been sent to the former by the foreign Naval commanders stating that they considered that, not being a belligerent, he had no right to conduct a search (*Correspondence relating to the Revolution in Brazil*, 1893, p. 50). The British representative was advised by his Government that the collective note was in order, that the insurgents had no right to enforce the proposed measure, and that should they try to do so the question would become one of 'the prudent exercise of right against might' (ibid. p. 55). 'The insurgents', it was said, 'have no doubt an interest in preventing the landing of munitions of war, but they have no status entitling them to prevent it' (ibid. p. 57). On the other hand, the British Government is believed to have acted on the view that foreign ships of war would not be justified in preventing the insurgents from firing on batteries or other posts such as the Arsenal established in Rio de Janeiro for the purpose of attack on the insurgent fleet. However, when on 21 July 1893, the British representative informed the Earl of Rosebery of the proposed blockade of Rio de Janeiro he received on the same day the reply that 'His Majesty's Government cannot recognize a blockade instituted by persons who have no legal status as belligerents'. The Secretary of State followed the Opinion of the Law Officers who said: 'Until there are two recognized belligerent forces, and a state of war between them, no blockade intended to interfere with neutral vessels can legally be enforced. We therefore think that Lord Rosebery's telegram of the 21st July is correct, namely, that, in the existing circumstances, His Majesty's Government cannot recognize the so-called blockade; and, further, we think that the Senior British Naval Officer would be justified in resorting to force if necessary to prevent such blockade becoming effective against British merchant vessels' (ibid.). See also Hackworth, vol. VII, pp. 166–73 for more recent examples of refusal of belligerent rights to non-recognized insurgents.

2 Moore, vol. I, p. 203. The United States Secretary of State wrote to the United States Minister in Brazil on 11 January 1893: 'The insurgents have not been recognized as belligerents, and should they announce a blockade of the port of Rio the sole test of its validity will be their ability to make it effective' (ibid. p. 204). The meaning of this statement was, apparently, that if the blockade were effective its exercise would be permitted although no recognition of belligerency had been given.

3 Ibid. vol. II, § 333.

ensuring the protection of the life and property of American citizens.[1] The numerous cases, referred to above,[2] in which outside States, notwithstanding the absence of recognition of belligerency, have recognized a blockade if effectively maintained, point again to a measure of recognition of a condition of insurgency. Occasionally American courts have construed the conduct of their Government as amounting to a recognition of the existence of a condition of 'actual war' which, notwithstanding the absence of recognition of belligerency, invested the acts of insurgents with a degree of legality sufficient to effect the passing of title with respect to contributions levied by them.[3]

§ 79. *Insurgency as a Status.* In the preceding instances of recognition of insurgency the admission of the existence of a state of hostilities on a large scale has been combined with a refusal to recognize belligerent status and the concomitant rights of war normally attaching to the status of belligerency. That refusal has in turn been modified by the acknowledgment of certain governmental and belligerent capacities and rights of the insurgents. It is permissible to describe the situation thus brought about as recognition of insurgency so long as it is clear that such 'recognition' does not go beyond what has actually and expressly been conceded. It does not confer a formal status. There is no such thing as express or implied recognition of insurgency as a status, with rights and duties of its own following upon such recognition.[4] There exist only such rights and duties as have been conceded or agreed upon.

Accordingly, it is difficult to define in exhaustive legal terms the rights attendant upon recognition of insurgency as distinguished from belligerency. It is not a relation the elements of which are determined by the law in advance. So far as outside States are concerned it may range from a simple decision to abstain from treating the rebels as law-breakers pure and simple to a measure of regularized intercourse indistinguishable from that maintained with the lawful government. For this reason, any attempt to lay down the conditions of recognition of insurgency lends itself to mis-

1 *U.S. For. Rel.* 1899, p. 105.

2 See above, pp. 194 et seq.

3 *O'Neill et al.* v. *Central Leather Company et al.* (1915) 87 N.J.L. 552, 555–8. This judgment of the New Jersey Court of Errors and Appeals was approved by the Supreme Court in *Oetjen* v. *Central Leather Company*, (1918) 246 U.S. 297, but on the ground of the retroactive effect of the subsequent *de facto* and *de jure* recognition of the Carranza Government by the United States. In *Compañia Minera Ygnacio Rodriguez Ramos* v. *Bartlesville Zinc Co.* (1925) 115 Tex. 21, the Supreme Court of Texas expressly dissociated itself from the grounds of the decision in the *O'Neill* case.

4 It is therefore only by way of description and not of exhaustive definition of a status that writers speak of recognition of insurgency.

understanding.[1] Recognition of insurgency creates a factual relation in the meaning that legal rights and duties as between insurgents and outside States exist only in so far as they are expressly conceded and agreed upon for reasons of convenience, of humanity, or of economic interest.

At the same time, however, to the extent to which legal rights and duties as between insurgents and outside States are mutually agreed upon or expressly conceded, they form the substance of a legal relation between those States and the insurgents. Such concessions are by their nature revocable. For it is of the essence of a well-founded refusal to grant belligerent rights that the States refusing recognition retain freedom of action. Subject to such freedom of action, States may go very far in imposing upon themselves restraints indistinguishable in substance from duties of neutrality and in conceding to the contesting parties rights usually associated with belligerency proper. In that sense, but in no other, recognition of insurgency may be regarded as a *de facto* recognition of belligerency, i.e. recognition of belligerency granted for limited purposes and distinguished from its recognition *in toto*. There is a temptation to regard such comprehensive concession of privileges of belligerency as implied recognition of belligerency pure and simple.[2] The impropriety of inferring recognition in cases where the intention to recognize is expressly disclaimed is discussed below.[3] As in the case of recognition of States and of governments so also in the matter of belligerency, so-called implied recognition is often an exhibition of wishful political thinking and might well disappear from the dictionary of international law. The fact that international

1 For an enumeration of these conditions see Wilson in *A.J.* vol. I (1907), p. 51. See also R. R. Wilson in *Proceedings of the American Society of International Law*, 1937, pp. 136 et seq.

2 See, for instance, the article by Smith in *B.Y.* vol. XVIII (1937), pp. 17–31, on the Spanish Civil War of 1936 in which an attempt was made to show that by her conduct, i.e. by maintaining intercourse with the insurgents and by the concession to them of certain rights, Great Britain had actually recognized a state of war in Spain and that the refusal to grant belligerent rights was therefore illogical. The author did not refer to the possibility that there may have taken place recognition of insurgency. See also Walker in *Transactions of the Grotius Society*, vol. XXIII (1938), p. 208.

Similarly, no results other than those directly at issue follow from the insistence of outside States that the lawful government is not entitled to close by decree, as against foreign shipping, ports occupied by the insurgents unless the decree is accompanied by a blockade effectively maintained (see above, pp. 194 et seq.). It might be argued that if outside States claim the right to deprive the lawful government of its ordinary powers on the ground that these powers have in effect been usurped by the insurgents, then they cannot at the same time blow hot and cold and refuse to grant to the insurgents the rights pertaining to their status. The answer to this is that insurgents enjoy no rights other than those specifically granted.

3 See below, p. 403.

practice has developed the intermediate instrument of recognition of insurgency is an additional reason for avoiding the fiction of implied recognition of belligerency.

§ 80. *Wrongs committed by Rebels not recognized as Insurgents.* In accepted theory, prior to the acknowledgment of a condition of insurgency, the rebellious bodies are in the eyes not only of their own State but also of foreign States law-breakers pure and simple. As it is often put, they are in the same category as robbers and pirates. However, it is useful to scrutinize this somewhat picturesque language more closely in order to avoid unnecessary exaggeration. Thus with regard to the acts of the insurgents on land, when such acts do not cause injury to foreign States or their subjects but are merely manifestations of a revolt against the constituted authority, outside States have no reason to express an opinion or to adopt an attitude. They are not bound or entitled to co-operate in the suppression of the treasonable acts of the insurgents against the lawful authority. In so far as the acts of insurgents in the territory occupied by them amount to such injury to the interests of foreign States or their subjects as would constitute a violation of international law if the insurgents were the government of a recognized State, these States may, of course, hold the insurgent authorities responsible and take appropriate action. They may, if this is practicable, enforce immediate reparation and, generally, apply such means of pressure as are calculated to cause the cessation of the injury. They are justified in disregarding the unsubstantial objection that it is impossible to exact from the insurgents reparation for breaches of international law by which they, not being in any way recognized, are not bound. For such measures of protection are legitimate acts of self-defence which, so long as they are resorted to in conformity with the principles of international law applicable to recognized States, are not open to criticism. Acts of violence committed against foreign States or their nationals on the high seas are clearly unlawful and may be assimilated to acts of piracy.[1] Except in cases of proved ruthlessness and inhumanity, enlightened practice has been limited to resistance to such unlawful acts without an attempt to treat the offenders with the extreme severity applied to *hostes generis humani*.[2]

1 See below, pp. 298 et seq. 2 See below, p. 304.

Chapter XVII

RECOGNITION OF INSURGENTS AS A GOVERNMENT

§ 81. *Recognition of Insurgents as a* de facto *Government.* It has been shown that the refusal to recognize the status of belligerency is fully consistent with the concession to the insurgents of a substantial measure of freedom of action and of extended intercourse with their authorities.[1] The latter is compatible with their recognition as a *de facto* government. It is clear, on the other hand, that to recognize them as a *de jure* government, while the contest is still in progress, is to take a step which is contrary to international law.[2] Moreover, to recognize the insurgents as a *de jure* government (even if only in respect of the territory under their control) would amount to creating a situation in which there are two *de jure* governments entitled to full belligerent rights irrespective of any recognition of belligerency.[3] In view of this, the question arises as to the consequences and the limits of the *de facto* recognition of insurgents as a government. Such recognition is lawful only if it is not in practice identified with *de jure* recognition. This means that courts, when confronted with *de facto* recognition of insurgents as a government, remain within the orbit of international law only if they stop short of identifying *de facto* recognition thus given with *de jure* recognition. This, however, was not the view taken by English courts during the Spanish Civil War of 1936–9 in the important case of *The Arantzazu Mendi*[4]—a case which raises questions of significance not only as to recognition of insurgents as a government but also as to certain important aspects of the judicial function in the matter of interpretation of international law.

The Arantzazu Mendi was registered at Bilbao. She had left Spain before May 1937. In June 1937, in the course of the Spanish Civil War, Bilbao was captured by the insurgent forces. On 23 March 1938 the owners of the ship were served in London with a notice of requisition on the part of the Republican Government under a decree of requisition of 28 June 1937; on 5 April 1938 the accredited agent of the insurgent Nationalist Government in London served on the owners a notice of requisition under a decree issued on 2 March 1938. On 13 April the managing director of the

1 See above, pp. 270 et seq. 2 See above, pp. 94, 95, and below, pp. 290–3.

3 See above, pp. 194–9.

4 [1938] P. 233 (Probate Division); [1939] P. 37 (Court of Appeal); [1939] A.C. 256 (House of Lords).

owners' firm declared that he freely submitted to the provisions of the Nationalist decree of 2 March. On the same day the Republican Government issued a writ asking for possession of the ship to be adjudged to them. The Nationalist Government appeared conditionally under protest and moved that the writ be set aside on the ground that it impleaded a foreign sovereign State, namely, the Nationalist State which was in possession of the ship by its duly authorized agents. Mr Justice Bucknill in an interim judgment held that the Nationalist Government was in possession of the ship. On the question whether that Government was the government of a foreign sovereign State his Lordship sought the usual information from the Foreign Office. The answer received was as follows:

'(1) His Majesty's Government recognizes Spain as a foreign sovereign state. (2) His Majesty's Government recognizes the government of the Spanish Republic now having its seat in Barcelona as the *de jure* government of Spain. (3) No government other than that referred to in the preceding subparagraph is recognized by His Majesty's Government as the *de jure* government of Spain or any part thereof. (4) The Nationalist Government of Spain is a government in conflict with the government of the Spanish Republic established at Barcelona. It claims to be the government of Spain and is seeking to overthrow the government of the Spanish Republic and to establish its authority over the whole of Spain. (5) His Majesty's Government recognizes the Nationalist Government as a government which at present exercises *de facto* administrative control over the larger portion of Spain. (6) His Majesty's Government recognizes the Nationalist Government as a government which at present exercises *de facto* administrative control over all the Basque provinces of Spain. (7) His Majesty's Government has not accorded any other recognition to the Nationalist Government. (8) The Nationalist Government is not a government subordinate to any other government in Spain....'

In reliance upon this letter Mr Justice Bucknill held that the Nationalist Government was for the purposes of the case a government of a foreign sovereign State and that the writ must be set aside seeing that it tended to implead the government of a foreign sovereign State. The Court of Appeal unanimously upheld the decision of the trial judge on both points—that of the status of the Nationalist Government as the government of a foreign sovereign State and that of its being in possession of the ship. The House of Lords unanimously confirmed the decision of the Court of Appeal.

At the time of the judgment the Nationalist authority in Spain had not been recognized as a belligerent. It was an insurgent government. The condition of insurgency in international law is, as has been shown,[1] one of considerable elasticity. It is a factual relation in the meaning that legal

1 See above, pp. 276–8.

rights and duties as between insurgents and third States exist only in so far as they are expressly conceded and agreed upon for reasons of convenience, of humanity, or of economic interests. Great Britain maintained official intercourse with the Nationalist authorities for the protection of British subjects, for safeguarding commercial interests, and for securing a relaxation of severity in the conduct of war by appeals of various kinds and offers of good offices in the exchange of prisoners and in similar matters. Agents had been mutually appointed for these purposes. They had been granted certain privileges calculated to facilitate the execution of their duties, but were denied the diplomatic immunities enjoyed by representatives of sovereign States.[1] At the time when these arrangements were made the British Government repeatedly denied that there was an intention to recognize the sovereignty of the insurgent authority.[2] This being so, the decisions of the Court of Appeal and of the House of Lords laying down that the insurgent government was the government of a foreign sovereign State seem, on the face of it, to go so far beyond the declared intentions of the British Government as well as beyond what international law associates with an insurgency or with recognition of a government during a civil war that, but for the statement of the Foreign Office, it might have

1 Answering a question in the House of Commons on 4 April 1938, concerning a letter sent to a local authority and referring to the 'Spanish Nationalist Government' the Under-Secretary of State for Foreign Affairs said: 'The use of the phrase "Spanish Nationalist Government" in this letter, which was in fact only of a semi-official character, implies no sort of modification of the attitude of his Majesty's Government in regard to the recognition of General Franco's administration. Under the agreement made with the latter for the exchange of agents, diplomatic status was not to be claimed for them, and no such claim has in fact been made or conceded by either party to the agreement. It was, however, felt desirable to secure for the British Agent and his staff certain privileges of a kind which are commonly enjoyed by diplomatic officials in order to facilitate the discharge of their duties. It was thus found necessary to concede corresponding privileges such as the one in question to General Franco's Agent and his staff. Such concessions made by either side involve no admission that the recipients possess diplomatic status, in proof of which it should be sufficient to say that certain reliefs which could be granted only on the basis of such status are withheld from the Duke of Alba and his staff, and the privileges accorded to them are of a limited character' (*H.C. Debates*, vol. CCCXXXIV, col. 5). The position had not changed at the time when the judgment of the Court of Appeal was given. See also below, p. 390, where the question of implied recognition is discussed in detail.

2 On 22 November 1937 the attention of the Secretary of State for Foreign Affairs was called to an official communiqué issued by General Franco's headquarters claiming that the conclusion of the agreement concerning agents implied recognition of the sovereignty of the Franco administration. In reply the Secretary of State for Foreign Affairs stated that he was 'unable to find any phrase therein which might be interpreted as claiming that the agreement implies recognition of sovereignty'. He then agreed that His Majesty's Government 'do not accept any suggestion of that kind' (ibid. vol. CCCXXIX, col. 834).

been difficult to follow the judicial pronouncements in question. The question is whether the nature and degree of recognition as described in the communication of the Foreign Office irresistibly led to the conclusion arrived at by the courts.

§ 82. *Recognition of Insurgency and Premature Recognition of a Government.* The principle that in questions relating to the status of foreign States and governments courts rely on the information received from the Executive is a well-established rule of judicial practice. But that principle does not relieve the courts of the substantial duty both of interpreting the answer of the Executive and of drawing from it the appropriate legal consequences. Thus on questions of recognition courts must, in the first instance, interpret the statement of the Executive in order to determine what degree of recognition has been granted. For on this point the communication may be—and often is—obscure or ambiguous. Moreover, once the task of interpreting the statement has been accomplished, courts are called upon to determine the legal consequences of such degree of recognition as may have been given. With regard to either, their function must be guided by the consideration that in matters involving the international relations of the country results must be avoided which are inconsistent with its international obligations. In particular, with regard to the communication from the Foreign Office it is incumbent upon courts, if only possible, to interpret it so as not to impute to the Crown the intention to disregard international law. This is a rule which is generally regarded as applicable to the interpretation of statutes.[1] It must be applied *a fortiori* to the interpretation of the pronouncements of a department of the Executive which is specially concerned with the international relations of this country. In *The Arantzazu Mendi* the answer of the Foreign Office did not purport to constitute a clear exposition of the situation. But the Secretary of State was explicit on one point, namely, that the British Government had not accorded to the Nationalist Government any recognition other than that deducible from the terms of the letter—an expression of caution which would have had little meaning if recognition identical with that of a foreign sovereign State had been intended.

This being so, it is appropriate to enquire what was the kind of recognition which the British Government could not, consistently with its international obligations, have intended to grant. It is proper to ascertain what manner of recognition would be so inconsistent with international

1 *Mortensen* v. *Peters*, [1906] Sc.L.T. 227. See also *Croft* v. *Dunphy*, (1933) 1 D.L.R. 225; [1933] A.C. 156; Cockburn C.J. in *Queen* v. *Keyn*, 7 Ex.D. 63, 210; Marshall C.J. in *The Charming Betsey*, 2 Cr. 64, 118.

law as to impose upon the court the duty to do its utmost in order to avoid the necessity of attributing to the Crown a desire to set aside the applicable rules of international law. In the present case it would have been fitting to interpret the letter from the Foreign Office by enquiring what were the rules of international law in the matter of recognition of insurgent governments *durante bello*.

This particular question is not an unduly difficult one. For while some problems of recognition of States, governments, and belligerency are controversial—for instance, whether recognition is constitutive or declaratory or whether it is a diplomatic or a legal function—there are some which are clearly and generally acknowledged. Thus it is universally admitted that in the case of a civil war or a war of secession it is contrary to international law to grant to the insurgent community full recognition as a government or a State. So long as the issue has not been definitely decided in favour of the rebellious party, recognition is premature and unlawful. As Hall says: 'Until independence is so consummated that it may reasonably be expected to be permanent, insurgents remain legally subject to the state from which they are trying to separate. Premature recognition therefore is a wrong done to the parent state; in effect indeed it amounts to an act of intervention.'[1]

The passage quoted refers to the recognition of insurgents attempting a secession from the existing State, but the position is the same in the case of rebellions aiming at setting up an alternative government, seeing that the recognition of the insurgents as a sovereign State results in the separation of the State in question into two units. There is, for instance, no doubt that if in the course of the American Civil War Great Britain had recognized without qualification the Confederate States as the government of the part of the United States under their control in such a manner as to oblige the courts to treat it as a foreign sovereign State, such recognition would legally have been a wrong committed against the lawful government and politically a probable cause for war with it.

Recognition pure and simple of the Spanish insurgent government as a government of Spain or even as a government of a part of Spain, at the time when these cases were decided, would not have been in conformity with an established principle of international law. It might conceivably have been open to the British Government to form the view that the established rule of international law was too rigid and that it was no longer possible to adhere to it in the unprecedented conditions of the Spanish

1 *International Law* (8th ed. 1924), § 26. And see the authorities cited above, pp. 94, 95.

Civil War, but nothing short of a very clearly expressed determination to effect a change of that nature can properly be regarded as sufficient. No such determination appeared in the letter of the Foreign Office in *The Arantzazu Mendi*. On the contrary, there was a clear expression of intention to grant a limited recognition only, as distinguished from full recognition *de jure*—'His Majesty's Government has not accorded any other recognition to the Nationalist Government'. The recognition granted was to 'a government which at present exercises *de facto* administrative control' over the larger portion of Spain. It did not partake of the formality of the *de facto* recognition such as, for instance, was accorded to Soviet Russia in 1921.[1] But assuming that the intention was to grant full *de facto* recognition, the question arises: Is such recognition indistinguishable in its legal results from full *de jure* recognition—with the result that the prohibition of premature recognition ceases to be a rule of international law?

§ 83. *Effects of* de facto *and of* de jure *Recognition*. The decision of the Court of Appeal in *Luther* v. *Sagor*[2]—a much overworked case—has tended to foster the view that there is 'a diplomatic distinction between recognition *de jure* and recognition *de facto*, but [that] there is no legal difference between these two forms'.[3] Actually, the decision in that case went no further than to lay down that there is no difference between *de facto* and *de jure* recognition for the purpose of acknowledging the validity of the legislative or executive acts of the government recognized *de facto*. It was to that extent—and no further—that the Court of Appeal relied upon *Luther* v. *Sagor* in its decision in *Banco de Bilbao* v. *Rey*.[4] In that case the Court held that, in view of the *de facto* recognition of the insurgent authorities by the British Government, it was bound to treat as valid the decrees of the Spanish Nationalist authorities in the territory under their control while treating as a mere nullity the decrees of the Republican Government in respect of that territory. The communication of the Foreign Office in that case approximated closely to that in *The Arantzazu Mendi* except that it was stated in the crucial passage that 'His Majesty's Government recognized the Government of General Franco as an *insurgent* Government exercising *de facto* control over a considerable portion of

1 In the letter of the Foreign Office in *Luther* v. *Sagor* it was stated that 'His Majesty's Government recognize the Soviet Government as the *de facto* Government of Russia'.

2 [1921] 3 K.B. 532.

3 Brierly, *The Law of Nations* (2nd ed. 1935), p. 110—a view somewhat modified in the third edition (1942), p. 109.

4 [1938] 2 K.B. 176; [1938] 2 All E.R. 253.

Spain'. It is not clear how far the qualification of the recognized authority as an 'insurgent' government was intended to reduce the import of the recognition. Similarly, it may be a matter for discussion how far the principle of *Luther* v. *Sagor*, originally applied to an authority in unrivalled possession of the entire territory of the State, can be applied without modification to the case of an insurgent administration in the course of a civil war waged against a government enjoying recognition *de jure*. But apart from the not unnecessary warning against using the decision in *Luther* v. *Sagor* as covering all possible aspects of *de facto* recognition,[1] there are weighty reasons of convenience and common sense which render acceptable the true principle of *Luther* v. *Sagor* as followed in *Banco de Bilbao* v. *Rey*—the principle, that is to say, that recognition *de facto* carries with it the acknowledgment of the validity of the acts of the recognized authority within its territory. It is not inconsistent with the legitimate interests of the lawful government that outside States should be in a position to maintain some intercourse with the insurgent administration without treating the insurgents as a sovereign State in the international arena. Recognition *de facto* serves that very purpose. A rule of law which compels third States to regard as invalid, for a prolonged period of time, the laws and administration of a *de facto* authority and to regard as valid within the territory of that authority the laws and administration of the *de jure* government, is not one which commends itself to sound principle (unless, perhaps, in particular cases, the *de facto* authority is established in violation not only of the constitutional law of the State concerned but also of international law[2]). A State cannot be called upon to disregard persistently facts which are not in themselves contrary to the law. Revolutions and rebellions are not contrary to international law. For this reason the rule of international law prohibiting premature recognition of governments during the civil struggle applies only to recognition *de jure*, but not to recognition *de facto* as interpreted in *Banco de Bilbao* v. *Rey*. This means that

1 See below, p. 294, as to *The Gagara*.

2 This latter consideration might conceivably have been adduced in criticism of the decision in *Bank of Ethiopia* v. *National Bank of Egypt and Liguori* ([1937] Ch. 513), discussed below, p. 286. In that case the principle of *Luther* v. *Sagor* was applied to the internal effects of a decree of the Italian *de facto* Government, recognized as such by Great Britain, putting into liquidation the Bank of Ethiopia. It might have been argued that as the *de facto* recognition was accomplished in violation of international law courts could not attach to it any legal effects whatsoever. Probably the accurate answer to that line of reasoning is that the grant of *de facto* recognition validated the effects of the illegal act to the extent covered by the *de facto* recognition. For a criticism, from a different point of view, of the decision in this case, see McNair, *Legal Effects of War* (2nd ed. 1944), pp. 340–2.

international law permits such a measure of recognition as is necessary for the acknowledgment of the validity of the acts of the *de facto* authority within its territory. But the permission does not go to the length of denying its own premises by making recognition *de facto* extend to all purposes, i.e. by assimilating it to full recognition *de jure*. It does not go to the length of permitting the treatment of the *de facto* authority as a foreign sovereign State for all purposes.

The circumstance that international law permits recognition *de facto* but not *de jure* means that there is a substantial difference between these two kinds of recognition. Recognition *de facto* goes so far and no farther. But a hasty reading of *Luther* v. *Sagor* is apt to lead to the facile generalization that the distinction between these two kinds of recognition is a mere formality so far as courts are concerned. This seems to have been the view adopted in *Bank of Ethiopia* v. *National Bank of Egypt*,[1] where the Court said (*per* Clauson J.):

> 'The recognition of the fugitive Emperor as a *de jure* Monarch, appears to me to mean nothing but this, that while the recognized *de facto* Government must for all purposes, while continuing to occupy its *de facto* position, be treated as a duly recognized foreign Sovereign State, His Majesty's Government recognizes that the *de jure* Monarch has some right (not in fact at the moment enforceable) to reclaim the Governmental control of which he has in fact been deprived. Where, however, His Majesty's Government has recognized a *de facto* Government, there is, as it appears to me, no ground for suggesting that the *de jure* Monarch's theoretical rights (for *ex-hypothesi* he has no practical power of enforcing them) can be taken into account in any way in any of His Majesty's Courts.'

It would have been sufficient for the purposes of the case to hold that as the British Government regarded the Italian Government as the government *de facto* of the parts of Ethiopia which they controlled, the Court was bound, on the analogy of *Luther* v. *Sagor*, to recognize as valid the decree of the Italian authority placing the Bank of Ethiopia in liquidation. But there was no warrant for suggesting that the *de facto* authority was to be treated for *all* purposes as a duly recognized foreign sovereign State. In fact, in the Foreign Office certificate which was laid before the Court in that case it was stated that an Envoy Extraordinary and Minister Plenipotentiary of the Emperor of Ethiopia had been received at the Court of St James and that he continued to be accorded recognition in that capacity.

Neither is the above quoted *dictum* of Mr Justice Clauson acceptable in so far as it suggested that the *de jure* sovereign had as such no rights enforceable before English courts. In a case decided a year later, *Haile Selassie* v. *Cable*

1 [1937] Ch. 513.

and Wireless Company Limited (no. 2), it was expressly held that the continued recognition *de jure* of the Emperor of Abyssinia had decisive consequences for the enforcement of the property rights of the Emperor outside Abyssinia. The Court refused to consider as applicable the principle laid down in *United States of America* v. *McRae*[1] that a successful government succeeds to the property of the defeated government. The Court pointed out that in *United States of America* v. *McRae* the question of rival claims of a *de jure* and a *de facto* government was not at issue—a timely reminder that continued *de jure* recognition is not a meaningless fiction. Similarly, the Court refused to follow the easy path of accepting the authority of *Luther* v. *Sagor* as covering the point. Mr Justice Bennett said:

> 'I think that the only point established by the decision in that case is that, when the Government of this country has recognized that some foreign Government is *de facto* governing some foreign territory, the law of England will regard the acts of the *de facto* Government in that territory as valid and treat them with all the respect due to the acts of a duly recognized sovereign State. It is clear, I think, that the acts so treated are acts in relation to persons or property in the territory which the authority is recognized as governing in part.'[2]

The learned judge attempted, not without some difficulty, to explain the wide statement, quoted above, in Mr Justice Clauson's judgment in *Bank of Ethiopia* v. *National Bank of Egypt*. He suggested that Mr Justice Clauson was merely concerned to demonstrate that as the plaintiff had no governmental control of any kind in Ethiopia he had no means of enforcing control *there*. Mr Justice Bennett then referred to *Banco de Bilbao* v. *Rey* as an authority for the limited proposition that recognition *de facto* has legal consequences only with regard to property and acts within the territory under the control of the *de facto* authority. Having thus set a limit to the seemingly uncontrollable influence of *Luther* v. *Sagor*[3] Mr Justice Bennett held that in view of the continued recognition *de jure* of the Emperor of Ethiopia the plaintiff was entitled to recover a debt which had accrued to him in his capacity as Emperor of Ethiopia before his country had been occupied by Italian troops. The juridical consequences of the distinction between *de jure* and *de facto* recognition were thus clearly asserted. The relation between the claim of the plaintiff and his continued recognition *de jure* was demonstrated several months later when the case came before the

1 (1869) L.R. 8 Eq. 69. 2 (1938) 54 T.L.R. 1087, 1089.

3 In the first phase of *Haile Selassie* v. *Cable and Wireless Company Limited* the Court of Appeal (54 T.L.R. 996) reversed the order of Mr Justice Bennett (54 T.L.R. 628) who, relying, *inter alia*, on *Luther* v. *Sagor*, stayed the proceedings in this case on the ground that the Italian Government made a claim to the sum in question.

Court of Appeal which, in view of the impending recognition *de jure*, stayed the proceedings until a date after the probable date of recognition in order to prevent unnecessary recourse to judicial process. Subsequently, after recognition *de jure* had been granted in due course and certified in a communication from the Foreign Office, the Court of Appeal held that, in view of that recognition, the situation which obtained at the time when the appeal had been lodged was changed, and that the King of Italy, as the Emperor of Ethiopia, was entitled to the sums claimed by the plaintiff.[1]

§ 84. *Recognition of Insurgency and the Distinction between* de facto *and* de jure *Recognition.* In *The Arantzazu Mendi* the trial judge and the Court of Appeal reverted to *Luther* v. *Sagor* as a source of judicial inspiration. They held that an insurgent government recognized as a *de facto* authority was entitled to jurisdictional immunity in England in respect of property situated in England, not only in general but also as against the rival claim of the lawful government which His Majesty continued to recognize *de jure*. The Court of Appeal in *The Arantzazu Mendi* was free to overrule the decision in *Haile Selassie* v. *Cable and Wireless Company Limited* (no. 2), but some distinguishing reference to this case would have been appropriate. The decision in *The Arantzazu Mendi* raises issues wider than the matter which was immediately before the Court and it is therefore permissible to scrutinize it in some detail. In none of the judgments was there an attempt to approach the problem, which, on the face of it, was one pertaining to the international relations of the Crown, from the point of view of the question whether the measure of recognition as assumed by the Court was in accordance with international law and, if it was not, whether it was unavoidable to impute to the Crown the intention of committing an international wrong by recognizing the Nationalist authority as a foreign sovereign State.[2]

1 [1939] Ch. 182.

2 An attempt was made by some members of the Court of Appeal to explain why it was deemed necessary to extend the principle of *Luther* v. *Sagor* to cover the position of the *de facto* authority abroad. Thus Slesser L.J. discussed the suggestion that the principle enunciated in *Luther* v. *Sagor* was limited to the validity of the acts of the *de facto government within its territory*, but he confined himself to quoting extracts from *Luther* v. *Sagor* asserting that the government *de facto* is one which is actually in possession of power while a government *de jure* is one which ought (apparently in law) to possess it. However, it is possible that in the view of the recognizing power there follow *some* legal consequences from the fact that the *de jure* government *ought* to possess authority. Otherwise the insistence on the part of the recognizing State on the difference between the two kinds of recognition would be meaningless. In the eyes of international law recognition *de facto* may *for some purposes* be tantamount to recognition *de jure*, but this does not mean that it is so for *all* purposes.

The substantial difference between the recognition of the Soviet Government in *Luther* v. *Sagor* and the recognition of the Nationalist Government in *The Arantzazu Mendi* was not that, in the former case, the whole territory of Russia was under the control of the recognized authority while this was not so in the case of Spain. The essential distinction was that, in the case of the Soviet Government of Russia, a measure of recognition which would have amounted to full recognition obliterating the difference between the *de jure* and the *de facto* variety would not have been inconsistent with international law seeing that the civil war was then at an end (the circumstance that the whole Russian territory was under the sway of the Soviet Government was, from this point of view, not immaterial in the sense that it was evidence of the fact that the *de jure* authority had actually ceased to exist). On the other hand, in the case of Spain the *de jure* authority was still a *de facto* power over a considerable portion of Spain, the civil war was raging, and a full measure of recognition assimilating in effect *de facto* and *de jure* recognition would have constituted premature recognition and as such be contrary to international law.

In *The Arantzazu Mendi* Justice Slesser had no hesitation in holding that the recognition of an authority as a *de facto* government pointing to an orderly and organized constitution was a recognition that the authority thus recognized possessed the powers of a State.[1] But there are governments which are not governments of a State in the meaning of international law. International conventions, especially those of a technical character, are often signed and ratified by a large number of 'governments'; but only a portion of these are governments of sovereign States in the meaning attached to the term by international law. The fact that an authority does 'possess the powers of a State' does not mean that it is a State in international law with the full prerogatives of statehood attaching to it. It may mean that it possesses sufficient power to make it incumbent upon courts to recognize the internal validity of its laws and decrees. There is no potency in the words 'government'[2] or 'recognition' irrespective of the context in which they are used or of conditions to which they refer.[3] The term '*de*

1 [1939] P. at p. 45.

2 Earl Russell, writing to Mr Adams, Minister of the United States, on 26 November 1861—at a time when Great Britain refused to recognize the Confederacy as a government of a State—was referring to it throughout as a *de facto* government. He said: 'Her Majesty's Government hold it to be an undoubted principle of international law that when the persons or the property of the subjects or citizens of a state are injured by a *de facto* government, the state so aggrieved has a right to claim from the *de facto* government redress and reparation' (Moore, vol. 1, p. 209).

3 In *The Charkieh* (4 Adm. and Eccl. 59) the certificate of the Foreign Office affirmed that 'he [the Khedive] is recognized by Her Majesty's Government as the

facto government' is often used in international law with reference to a temporarily successful local authority which has risen in opposition to the central government. When English courts in a number of cases arising out of the American Civil War referred to the Government of the Confederate States as a *de facto* government, they did not intend to imply that it was the government of a sovereign State.[1]

§ 85. *Recognition of Insurgency and the Limits of* de facto *Recognition.* The judgment of the House of Lords in *The Arantzazu Mendi*, confirming the judgment of the Court of Appeal, was given at a time when the overwhelming realities of the political and strategic situation would have imparted an appearance of unreality to a decision denying, in effect, the full international sovereignty of the insurgent government. However, an artificiality of this nature may on occasions be of the very essence of the proper application of international law. Neither can the judgment of the House of Lords, and of the courts below, be explained by any compelling necessity of acting upon the statement of the Executive. Undoubtedly, when the terms of the latter are clear, it must not be questioned on legal grounds, but it may be doubted whether in the case under discussion the statement was sufficiently clear or 'precise'[2] to render unnecessary its interpretation by reference to principles of international law. It was not a communication which suggested irresistibly that recognition had been granted to the government of a foreign sovereign State.

While, as has been shown, in some matters there is no distinction, in the eyes of the courts, between mere *de facto* and full *de jure* recognition, there

hereditary ruler of the province of Egypt under the supremacy of the Sultan of Turkey', but the same certificate stated that 'the Khedive has not been and is not now recognized by Her Majesty as reigning sovereign of the state of Egypt'. Probably recognition as a hereditary ruler of the province would have been sufficient for acknowledging the validity of the legislative acts done under the authority of the Khedive, while the absence of recognition as a sovereign was deemed a good reason for not granting him immunity from jurisdiction.

1 Thus we find the Vice-Chancellor saying in *United States* v. *Prioleau*, (1865) L.J.Ch. 7: 'If the case had been that of a body of mere robbers devastating and plundering the territories of the United States, our courts might have interfered to restore property so acquired; but then the rightful claimants would have been not the United States Government, but the persons who had been robbed. It is only because the money was raised by a *de facto* Government that the United States can come here to claim at all. Had the money been obtained by mere robbery it would have never become public property. It only acquired that character because it was levied by an authority exercising rights of Government.'

2 Lord Wright, in his concurring judgment, expressed the view that the 'Foreign Office stated the precise facts as then existing in regard to the recognition of His Majesty's Government' and that the contents of the statement of the Foreign Office were not 'open to be discussed by the court on grounds of law' (at p. 724).

exists such a distinction for some purposes. Recognition *de facto* means, *inter alia*, that courts are bound to treat as lawful the internal acts of the insurgent authority within its territory; it does not signify that that authority must be treated in every other respect like a sovereign State.[1] Once it is so treated, the distinction between *de facto* and *de jure* recognition —a distinction to which clearly the recognizing State attaches importance and which is of considerable usefulness in international relations—is obliterated.

There are no overwhelming reasons *ab inconvenienti* militating against the view denying to a *de facto* insurgent government the ordinary jurisdictional immunities to which the *de jure* government is entitled. This undoubtedly places the latter in a favoured position in comparison with the former. But the advantage is hardly as far-reaching as may appear at first sight. It is certainly not an advantage which may have the result of interfering appreciably with the maintenance of an attitude of impartiality in relation to a civil war. The denial of the privilege of jurisdictional immunity does not mean the impairment of the substantive rights of the government concerned. If that government is in possession of the subject-matter of the action—and *The Arantzazu Mendi* and other authorities show that very nominal possession may on occasions be sufficient—then it is in a position to proceed to prove such title as it possesses, and the mere claim of the *de jure* government will not be regarded as depriving it of that right. It may or may not have difficulty in establishing its title. It may attempt to show, not without considerable prospect of success, that the decrees of the *de jure* government requisitioning ships registered in territory occupied by the *de facto* government are invalid in the eyes of foreign courts. In case of rival requisition decrees relating to ships in foreign waters the difficult questions may have to be faced as to the relevance of the place of registration and as to the extraterritorial effect of decrees. It may be possible in such cases to avoid the necessity of solving a thorny problem by relying on the fact of actual or constructive possession and of conceding immunity to the government which happens to be in such possession. This is a solution which may recommend itself because of its simplicity. But it is not one which, in the case of the *de facto* government—especially in a claim against the *de jure* government—can be resorted to consistently with the applicable rules of international law.

A solution of this nature, shifting, as it does, the determination of the rights of the parties from a legal basis to the accidents of possession, may lead to strange and unexpected results. The rival governmental claims over

1 See below, pp. 336 et seq.

the ship may be made dependent on the attitude of the owners or the master or the crew or on the results of a physical contest between them.[1] It may be embarrassing for the courts of a third State to decide quarrels between a *de jure* and a *de facto* government, but if the necessity for such a decision arises it is preferable that it should be made in reliance on a substantive rule of law rather than by reference to the accidents of possession as determined by the changing attitudes of the owners of the ship, of the master, or of the crew. In *The Arantzazu Mendi* the owners and master declared themselves to hold the ship on behalf of and at the order of the Nationalist Government. This fact, in the view of the Court of Appeal, determined the issue. What would be the position if the master or the owners, subsequent to a final decision of the Court, were to change their allegiance and proceed to hand over the ship to the Republican Government? What would be the position if the master of a ship which is rightly in the possession of the Republican Government were to offer her to the Nationalist Government? What is the legal situation if the ambassador representing the lawful government decides to change his allegiance and, after having declared in favour of the insurgent government, hands over to that government the embassy building and other national property? On the reasoning of *The Arantzazu Mendi*, the lawful, the *de jure*, government

1 This was what happened in *The Abodi Mendi* (reported in *The Times* newspaper, 10 December 1938) where the master—who, apparently, favoured the Nationalist cause—after having left the ship for a walk, found that the crew had removed the gangway and had since prevented him from returning on board. The Republican authorities then appointed a new captain who held the ship at their disposal. In view of this the Republican Government moved that the warrant of arrest, under which the ship had been as the result of a writ previously issued by them, should be set aside, while the owners, assisted by the Nationalist Government, asked that the master be reinstated. The President ordered the summons to stand over pending the appeal to the House of Lords in *The Arantzazu Mendi* on the question of the status of the Nationalist Government. He thought that the plaintiffs should not be allowed to obtain possession of the vessel in the way described above. It will be noted that in *The Cristina*, (1938) 54 T.L.R. 512, Lord Wright thought that it was 'unnecessary to consider by what mode the respondents obtained possession' (at p. 518). Lord Maugham said: 'It seems to me that the claim by the Spanish Government for immunity from any form of process in this country may extend to cases where possession of ships or other chattels had been seized in this country without any shadow of right' (at p. 521). But see the judgment of the Supreme Court of the United States, delivered on 31 January 1938, by Mr Justice Stone in *Compañia Española de Navegacion Maritima* v. *The Navemar*, 303 U.S. 68, where possession acquired as the result of the forcible seizure of the ship by the crew was not deemed sufficient to found a claim for immunity. See also the same case: 18 F. Suppl. 153, 158; 24 F. Suppl. 495, 497. And see *Ervin* v. *Quintanilla*, 99 F. (2d) 935. And see on the relevance of the concurrent recognition of the *de jure* and *de facto* government: *The Arraiz*, (1938) 61 *Lloyd's List Law Reports*, p. 39; *Annual Digest*, 1938–40, Case no. 89; *The El Neptuno*, (1938) 62 *Lloyd's List Law Reports*, p. 7.

would have no remedy because of the jurisdictional immunity said to appertain to the insurgent *de facto* government. These consequences cannot be lightly admitted. They are inconsistent with what are believed to be established rules of international law in the matter and they are contrary to the clearly declared determination of governments to insist that there is a difference between *de facto* and *de jure* recognition. The practical results of that distinction may not be considerable in relation to the conduct of the civil war, but they are of importance in the eyes of international law. One of them is that the *de jure* government is entitled to a measure of immunity to which the *de facto* authority can have no claim. This may mean in practice that the *de jure* government is entitled to rely on possession (unless, probably, effected in breach of the peace or otherwise in violation of the law of the land), while the *de facto* government must be prepared to prove its title to possession even when it is actually or constructively in possession. This is undoubtedly an inconvenience for and a derogation from the dignity of the *de facto* authority. But these drawbacks are inherent in the situation of a power attempting to dislodge the lawful government.[1]

§ 86. *Conclusions.* Even if the principles adopted in *The Arantzazu Mendi* had not been unanimously endorsed by the Court of Appeal and the House of Lords, anything in the nature of emphatic criticism of these decisions[2] would be misplaced seeing that it had been held—and rightly held—in other cases that a recognized *de facto* government is in the same position as a government recognized *de jure* with regard to the validity of its internal legislation, and that even in the matter of jurisdictional immunities a State recognized *de facto* is in the same position as a State recognized *de*

1 For these reasons there may be some hesitation in accepting Lord Atkin's view that there existed in *The Arantzazu Mendi* 'all the reasons for immunity which are the basis of the doctrine in international law as incorporated into our law', namely, 'the same necessity for reciprocal rights of immunity, the same feeling of injured pride if jurisdiction is sought to be exercised, the same risk of belligerent action if Government property is seized or injured' ([1939] A.C. 256 at p. 265). An insurgent group which has not yet succeeded in dislodging the lawful authority is not entitled to insist on the same consideration for its pride as the *de jure* government. The risk of belligerent action can, in the circumstances of the case, be disregarded. Even fully established governments do not go to war because a foreign State assumes jurisdiction over their property. On the contrary, they have usually accommodated themselves to the consequences of the fact that the extent of jurisdictional immunities of States is by no means well-defined in international law; witness, for instance, the position with regard to the activities of the State in the domain of private law. As to the necessity for reciprocal rights of immunity, these may not improperly be left in abeyance pending the transitional period of the civil war.

2 See, for example, Briggs in *A.J.* vol. XXXIII (1939), pp. 689–99. See also Jaenicke in *Z.ö.V.* vol. IX (1939), pp. 354–82.

jure.[1] These questions are a matter of degree for the obvious reason that *de facto* recognition is a question of degree and circumstances.[2] But a line must be drawn somewhere—unless we decide to obliterate altogether the distinction, which is firmly embedded in international practice, between *de facto* and *de jure* recognition. Reasons have been given for the view that that line must be drawn at a point when an insurgent authority which is recognized as a *de facto* government, and which it would be contrary to international law to recognize *de jure*, claims jurisdictional immunities as against the government still enjoying *de jure* recognition. This being so, notwithstanding the impressive authority of the successive decisions in *The Arantzazu Mendi*, the following conclusions are submitted as an exposition of an accurate rule of international law:

(*a*) It is an established principle that so long as the civil war lasts the recognition of the insurgents, whether recognized as belligerents or not, as a *de jure* government is contrary to international law.

(*b*) A communication of the Executive Department relating to the recognition of insurgents as a government must be interpreted in the light of that principle.

(*c*) It is not contrary to international law to recognize the insurgents as a government exercising *de facto* authority over the territory under its control.

(*d*) Such recognition is limited in its effect and cannot properly be assimilated to recognition *de jure*.

(*e*) While obliging courts to acknowledge the validity of the legislation of the *de facto* insurgent authority within its territory, it does not transform the authority thus recognized into an independent government of a foreign sovereign State entitled outside its territory to jurisdictional immunities, in particular as against the government recognized *de jure*, in respect of its property or its representatives.

1 *The Gagara*, [1919] P. 95. This case is perhaps the strongest authority in support of the decision in *The Arantzazu Mendi*. The decisive distinguishing feature is that in *The Gagara* there was no rival *de facto* authority either generally or in the case before the Court.

2 See below, pp. 329 et seq.

Chapter XVIII

INSURGENCY AND PIRACY

§ 87. *The Nyon Agreements of* 1937. Insurgency is a status of a conspicuous degree of elasticity. This fact explains the circumstance that while on occasions insurgents not recognized as belligerents have been treated in most respects as the government of an independent State,[1] the question has often been raised whether, in certain contingencies, insurgents may not be treated as pirates. The latter feature of insurgency was illustrated during the Spanish Civil War of 1936–9 which brought into prominence the question whether and in what circumstances ships duly commissioned by the authorities of the unrecognized insurgents may be treated as piratical. The Nyon Agreement of 14 September 1937,[2] concluded between the United Kingdom, Belgium, Egypt, France, Greece, Roumania, Turkey, the Union of Soviet Socialist Republics and Yugoslavia, provided for certain collective measures 'against piratical acts by submarines' in the course of the civil war in Spain. These acts, for which no government was prepared to take the responsibility, were described as 'acts contrary to the most elementary dictates of humanity which should be justly treated as acts of piracy'. It was provided that any submarine attacking vessels not belonging to either of the parties to the Spanish Civil War in a manner contrary to the rules of Part IV of the Treaty of London of 1930 which is encountered in the vicinity of the occurrence 'in circumstances which give valid grounds for the belief that the submarine was guilty of attack' shall be counter-attacked and, if necessary, destroyed by the forces of the parties to the Agreement. The Supplementary Agreement of 17 September 1937 extended the provisions of the former Agreement to cover similar acts by surface vessels and aircraft.[3] The propriety of using the term 'piracy' in connection with naval operations in a civil war was subsequently questioned by some international lawyers,[4] and it is therefore useful to attempt to

1 See, for example, *The Arantzazu Mendi*, above, pp. 279 et seq.

2 Cmd. 5568 (1937).

3 Cmd. 5569 (1937).

4 See, for example, Anonymous in *B.Y.* vol. XIX (1938), pp. 198–208; Genet in *A.J.* vol. XXXII (1938), pp. 253–63; Mirwart in *R.I.* 3rd ser. vol. XIX (1938), pp. 341–52. But see Padelford in *A.J.* XXXII (1938), pp. 271–9. See also Finch, ibid. vol. XXXI (1937), pp. 659–65, and Schmitz in *Z.ö.V.* vol. VIII (1938), pp. 641–71. Prior to the Nyon Agreement, in March 1937, the Dutch Government announced that the seizure of Dutch vessels by the vessels of the Spanish insurgents would be regarded as an act of piracy (*Survey of International Affairs*, 1937 (II), p. 309).

formulate the rule underlying the judicial and governmental practice in the matter.

At the time when the attacks which led to the Nyon Agreements were made, it was not known which State or authority was responsible for the outrages. Both parties to the civil war, as well as the governments of other States, disclaimed responsibility for the acts in question. The subject indicated in this chapter is therefore discussed here on the assumption that the responsible authority was that of the Spanish insurgents. In fact, the matter has been debated largely from the point of view of the question whether the ships of unrecognized insurgents may be treated by third States as piratical. So far as the Nyon Agreements are concerned the discussion was largely one about terminology, for there were few who denied that the Agreements were a proper answer to a situation which was repeatedly and officially described as intolerable. It was not suggested that the severity of the measures contemplated in the Agreements was the result of the adoption of the consequences flowing from piracy *jure gentium*. The treatment of the offenders under the Agreements was to be more severe than that meted out to pirates; the drastic punishment was to be instantaneous and there were no judicial safeguards of its application.

§ 88. *Declaration of Piracy by the Lawful Government.* It is now a rule established with a substantial degree of uniformity that foreign States refuse to regard as binding upon them the decrees of the lawful government declaring the rebels to be pirates. Such decrees are frequent; they are the almost invariable accompaniment of civil wars in which the insurgents attempt to conduct operations on the high seas.[1] The rule that outside States are in no way bound by the declaration of piracy issued by the lawful government is clearly brought out in a number of Opinions of British Law Officers in connection with various declarations of piracy issued on such occasions.[2] Foreign States have invariably refused to regard themselves as

1 On 27 July 1936, the Spanish Government published in the *Gaceta de Madrid* a decree declaring the rebel warship *Almirante Cervera* to be a piratical vessel which must be treated according to 'international laws which punish piracy and according to the criminal law of the states which may effect the capture'. The United States Department of State confined itself to a mere acknowledgment of the communication of the Spanish Government informing it of the Decree (Hackworth, vol. II, p. 696).

2 These Opinions are instructive having regard to the variety of situations which gave rise to them, and as they have not hitherto been published they are printed at the end of this chapter (pp. 311–28). Pretensions of this nature have been put forward in various forms by other States. See, for instance, the Opinion of Phillimore of 14 February 1867, rejecting the contention of the United States that ships of insurgents

under a duty to participate in the struggle by treating as pirates insurgents committing depredations upon their own government.[1] Neither, as shown in the well-known case of *The Virginius*, have they been prepared to recognize such decrees of the lawful government as authorizing it to treat as pirates their own subjects found on insurgent vessels declared to be piratical.[2]

On occasions third States, while refusing to admit the duty to treat rebel ships as piratical in these circumstances, have asserted the right to do so. As the United States Secretary of State said in 1869 with reference to the Haitian insurgent ships: 'We may, or may not, at our option, as justice or policy may require, treat them as pirates in the absolute and unqualified sense.'[3] It would also appear that if such ships take refuge in a port of a third State they may be handed over to the lawful government whose property they are.[4]

must be treated as piratical unless commissioned in a belligerent port (*Law Officers' Opinions*, United States, 1867). See also the Opinion of 9 June 1866, concerning *The Shenandoah* to the effect that the contention of the United States was opposed to universally recognized principles of law 'if Mr Seward means to contend that the Commander and crew of a vessel, commissioned as a public ship of war by a Revolutionary Government, which has been recognized as a belligerent Power by neutral nations, can be charged with piracy in a neutral country merely for capturing and destroying the ships of the other belligerent'. As to the Act of Congress of 5 August, 1861, bearing on the matter, see the Law Officers' Opinion of 18 November 1861 (F.O. 83/2212).

1 What is probably the best and fullest statement of the legal position on the matter is that issued by Mr Bayard, the United States Secretary of State, in connection with the Colombian insurrection in 1885 (Moore, vol. II, pp. 1089–96). For a collection and discussion of precedents see Gidel, *Le droit international public de la mer*, vol. I (1932), pp. 320–9 ('La notion de piraterie et les insurrections ou guerres civiles'). See also the circular of the Duke de Broglie to diplomatic agents of France of 11 August 1872, referring to the notification of the Madrid Government to the effect that the insurgents ought to be considered as pirates: 'Une semblable communication ne pouvait nous lier par elle-même, et tant que les rebelles n'avaient pas commis un acte constituant, en point de vue de droit international, un véritable fait de piraterie, nous ne pouvions prêter notre appui aux mesures ainsi décrétées' (*Fontes Juris Gentium, Digest of Diplomatic Correspondence of the European States*, by Schmitz and Makarov, Part I (1937), p. 110).

2 For a detailed account of this case involving Cuban insurgents and a number of British and American nationals executed by Spain in 1873, see Moore, vol. II, pp. 967–8, and Hall, *International Law* (8th ed. 1924), pp. 319–21.

3 Moore, vol. II, p. 1085.

4 See, for example, the Opinion given by Sir Travers Twiss on 6 September 1870, advising the British Government with regard to certain insurgent Venezuelan vessels declared by the Venezuelan Government to be piratical. The advice was that every facility should be given to the Venezuelan Consul if the vessels in question should enter a British port and the Consul should wish to arrest them in the British Vice-Admiralty Court with a view to recovering possession of them as the property of his Government (F.O. 83/2403).

§ 89. *Insurgent Interference with Foreign Vessels. British and American Practice.* The preponderant practice of governments, weighty judicial decisions, as well as the majority of writers, seem to favour the view that unrecognized insurgents, if they interfere with the ships of third States or their subjects, may be treated by them as piratical. In the course of the correspondence arising out of the recognition of the belligerency of the Confederate States, one of the reasons adduced by Great Britain for her action was that it was necessary for her to decide whether the letters of marque or the public ships of the rebels should be treated as pirates or lawful belligerents. In September 1874 we find an instruction by the British Government to the naval authorities to the effect that 'if an attack is made at sea upon any foreign vessel by a ship belonging to no recognized national Government who can be made responsible for such act, such attack is piracy; but that as regards an attack by a ship in possession of insurgents against their own domestic Government, upon the ships of that Government at sea, or upon its cities, ports, or people, within the territorial limits of their own nation, such attack is not piracy'.[1] In 1873 the Foreign Office, relying on the Opinion of the Law Officers,[2] advised the Admiralty that 'Her Majesty's Government consider that if Spanish ships of war which have revolted commit any acts of piracy affecting British subjects or interests they should be treated as pirates, the decree of the Spanish Government having deprived them of the protection of the Spanish flag'.[3] In an Opinion given by the Law Officers concerning privateers equipped by the Cretan insurgents in 1867 the view was expressed that 'if they are not entitled to the status of belligerents, and these Privateers sail upon the high seas under no Flag or any *de jure* or *de facto* Government, they would be liable to be treated generally as Pirate Vessels, and especially to be treated as such, if they should attempt to interfere in any way with the Vessels of any foreign State'.[4] They expressed a similar view in 1870 in the case of *The Maparari* acting under the orders of the Venezuelan insurgents[5] and in 1877 in the case of *The Montezuma*, a ship armed by the Cuban insurgents.[5] In the well-known case of *The Huascar* the Law Officers expressed approval of the conduct of the commanding admiral in treating as piratical a cruiser of unrecognized insurgents which attacked British property.[5]

1 Mr Hammond to the Secretary to the Admiralty (*Fontes Juris Gentium, Digest of Diplomatic Correspondence of the European States*, by Schmitz and Makarov, Part 1 (1937), p. 111).
2 F.O. 83/2378.
3 F.O. 72/1391.

4 Smith, vol. 1, p. 265. In 1860 in an Opinion by Sir J. Harding (ibid. p. 301) it was denied that Garibaldi could be treated as a pirate *jure gentium*, but the Opinion apparently assumes that Garibaldi had been recognized both by the King of the Two Sicilies and by the British naval authorities.

5 The Opinions are printed at the end of this chapter, pp. 312 et seq.

The attitude of the United States on a number of occasions has been similar. Thus, while refusing in 1885 to regard as binding upon them the Colombian decree declaring insurgent ships to be piratical, the Secretary of State affirmed that 'the piratical character of such acts, and the consequent jurisdiction of any sovereign power in respect thereof, must depend on the circumstances of the individual case'.[1] He pointed out that that view underlay the orders issued to the United States men-of-war, one of which had just captured a Colombian insurgent vessel, *The Ambrose Light*, which was on her way to the United States for submission to the jurisdiction of the courts of the United States. The Court, as we shall see, had no hesitation in laying down that in the absence of recognition of belligerency the vessel would have been piratical. Previously, during the Haitian insurrection in 1869, the United States refused to pay attention to similar decrees issued by the Haitian Government. But they asserted the right 'to capture and destroy the vessels in question, and others of similar character, if any aggression upon persons or property entitled to the protection of this Government shall recommend such action'.[2]

In the course of the hostilities between Spain and Venezuela in 1823 the United States protested against what they described as the piratical activities of Spanish privateers supplied with some kind of commission. In his instructions of 28 April 1823 to the United States Minister to Spain, the Secretary of State wrote:

> 'The privateers from Porto Rico and Porto Cabello have been, by their conduct, distinguishable from pirates only by commissions of most equivocal character, from Spanish officers, whose authority to issue them has never been shown; and they have committed outrages and depredations which no commission could divest of the piratical character.'[3]

He said in the same document: 'Acts of *piratical* aggression and depredation may be committed by vessels having lawful commissions as privateers....'[4]

When in 1832 a group of persons off the Falkland Islands, seemingly acting on behalf of the Government of Buenos Aires, committed depredations upon the ships of the United States apparently for the purpose of enforcing Argentinian laws, a United States sloop of war attacked the offenders and brought some of them to trial in the United States. When the Government of Buenos Aires protested, the United States Ambassador was instructed to justify the acts of the American commander 'in

1 Moore, vol. II, p. 1096.

2 Ibid. p. 1086.

3 Manning, *Diplomatic Correspondence of the United States concerning the Independence of the Latin-American Nations*, vol. I (Parts I–II) (1925), p. 167.

4 Ibid. p. 176.

seizing and sending to the United States the persons most active in the outrage against our citizens to be tried as pirates—the acts of which they were guilty coming strictly within the definition of that crime'. The Secretary of State wrote: 'Even if they had (which they had not) authority to seize vessels which had infringed the laws of the Republic for the protection of their fisheries, they are pirates for making them the color for an unlawful appropriation to their own use without the form of trial.'[1]

During the revolution in Brazil in 1893, the admiral in command of the fleet of the United States in Brazilian waters, acting upon his instructions, addressed a warning to the admiral commanding the naval units of the unrecognized insurgents to the effect that interference with the ships of the United States would be resisted as an act of piracy. He said: 'Until belligerent rights are accorded to you you have no right to exercise any authority whatever over American ships or property of any kind. You can not search neutral vessels or seize any portion of their cargoes, even though they be within the class which may be clearly defined as contraband of war, during hostilities between two independent governments. The forcible seizure of any such articles by those under your command would be, in your present status, an act of piracy.'[2] In general, the attitude of governments is that they will refuse to treat ships of unrecognized insurgents as piratical—so long as the molestations are confined to the parent State. As the Brazilian Government said in the case of *The Montezuma*, in refusing to treat the insurgent Spanish vessel as a pirate: 'Les hostilités qu'elle dénonce et prévoit ne sont pas dirigées contre toutes les nations, mais uniquement contre l'Espagne.'[3]

§ 90. *Judicial Decisions.* Such judicial decisions as bear on the matter point in the same direction. Of these *The Ambrose Light*,[4] decided in 1885 by a United States District Court, is the most instructive. The vessel in question operated on behalf of the Colombian insurgents; she was intended to assist in the blockade and siege of the port of Cartagena, which was under the control of the lawful government. There was no evidence of any hostilities or depredations actually committed against the United States or its nationals. After a full discussion of the contrary view, the Court had no hesitation in holding that

1 Manning, *Diplomatic Correspondence of the United States, Inter-American Affairs, 1831–1860, Argentina*, vol. 1 (1932), p. 14.
2 *U.S. For. Rel.* 1893, p. 122.
3 As quoted in Calvo, *Le droit international* (5th ed. 1896), vol. 1, § 503.
4 (1885) 25 Fed. 408.

'in the absence of recognition by any government of their belligerent rights, insurgents that send out vessels of war are, in legal contemplation, merely combinations of private persons engaged in unlawful depredations on the high seas; that they are civilly and criminally responsible in the tribunals for all their acts of violence; that such acts are therefore piratical, and entitle the ships and tribunals of every nation whose interests are attacked or menaced, to suppress, at their discretion, such unauthorized warfare by the seizure and confiscation of the vessels engaged in it.... The right to treat unlawful and unauthorized warfare as piratical, seems to me, therefore, clearly imbedded in the very roots of international law.... In the absence of any recognition of these insurgents as belligerents, I therefore hold the *Ambrose Light* to have been lawfully seized, as bound upon an expedition technically piratical.'[1]

However, after expressing this clear view on the question of principle, the Court held that there had taken place implied recognition of belligerency and that for that reason the vessel could not be deemed to be piratical.[2] In *The Three Friends* the Supreme Court associated itself with the view that in the absence of recognition of belligerency 'the vessels of the insurgents, if molesting third parties, may be pursued as pirates'.[3] The case of *The Magellan Pirates*,[4] decided in 1853 by Dr Lushington, does not constitute direct authority on the question at issue as the learned Judge found that the depredations in question were acts of plunder in no way connected with the insurrection.[5] But the general language used by him deserves quotation. He said:

'I think it does not follow that, because persons who are rebels or insurgents may commit against the ruling power of their own country acts of violence, they may not be, as well as insurgents and rebels, pirates also.... Even an independent state may, in my opinion, be guilty of piratical acts.... I am well aware that it has been said that a state cannot be piratical; but I am not disposed to assent to such dictum as a universal proposition.'

1 Ibid.

2 The Court expressly rejected the view that in order to constitute piracy the depredations must be done *animo furandi*, for the sake of plunder, as distinguished from acts of war.

3 (1897) 166 U.S. 1, 63.

4 *Spink's Eccl. and Adm. Rep.* 81. See also the early case of *Marches*, (1615) 1 Rolle 175; *Eng. Rep.* vol. LXXXI, p. 411. This case was a prosecution for piracy instituted by the Spanish Ambassador. Marches, a subject of the King of Morocco who pretended to be ambassador to the United Provinces, seized on the seas a Spanish ship, Morocco then being at war with Spain. The civilians, while holding that an ambassador is according to the law of nature and nations immune from suit, were of the opinion that he loses his privileges if he commits an offence against the law of nature or reason, but not against the positive law. The common law judges 'disoint que les civillians fuerunt beside le matter, car cestuy que est destre trie icy pur piracie est destre trie sur l'estatute de 28 H. 8. cap.'

5 The same applies to *United States* v. *Smith*, (1820) 5 Wheaton 153.

The question whether action under a commission issued by an unrecognized insurgent authority constitutes piracy came, in peculiar circumstances, before an English court in 1693 and was answered in the affirmative. In that year proceedings took place, before the Lords of the Council and the Admiralty, against John Golding and others on a charge of piracy for having acted as privateers under a commission issued by the deposed King James II. Dr Oldish, the Queen's Advocate, and other civilians, who had been ordered to proceed against them as pirates, declined to do so on the ground that the accused acted under a commission issued by a person who waged war against the government and who was treated by the King of France as still possessed of royal prerogatives.[1] However, the Court were against him. He was thereupon removed from office and, after another Queen's Advocate had been appointed, the accused were condemned and some of them executed.[2] The prosecution, it will be noted, was not for high treason, but for piracy. The status of the late king was that of an insurgent whose belligerency had not been recognized. However, as a rule there has been no disposition on the part of English courts to assume piracy *jure gentium* when there was no *animus furandi*.[3]

1 He said: 'Pirates are common enemies to all mankind, having no legal authority for what they do; but they shew a commission signed J.R. dated at the court of St Germaine's, together with articles and instructions annexed, in the same form as privateers have, giving caution and security to bring prizes...this does no way agree with piracy, or the character of a pirate, who is a robber, and has thereby lost his right in the law of nations' (12 How. St. Tr. 1269).

2 A detailed account of the proceedings and a spirited defence of the decision of the Court will be found in Dr Tindall's *Essay concerning the Laws of Nations and the Rights of Sovereigns. With an account of what was said at the Council-Board by the Civilians upon the Question, Whether their Majesties Subjects taken at Sea acting by the late King's Commission, might not be looked on as Pirates* (2nd ed. 1694). Dr Tindall, who was one of the civilians consulted by the Court, also refers in the essay to the case of certain privateers, French subjects, commissioned by Antonio, the deposed King of Portugal, who when captured by the Spaniards were treated as pirates. It appears from the account of Connestagio, in his work on the Union of the Kingdoms of Castile and Portugal (*Dell' Unione del Regno di Portogallo alla Corona di Castiglia*), that they were treated as pirates on the ground that the King of France without declaring war sent them to the assistance of Antonio. This case is also referred to by Gentilis, *De Jure Belli Libri Tres* (1612), Book I, ch. IV (*in fine*), who disapproves of the Spanish action.

3 See *In re Ternan and Others*, 33 L.J.M.C. 201, a case decided in May 1864 in the Court of Queen's Bench. This was a request by the United States for extradition for piracy of persons purporting to act on behalf of the Confederate States. It was not clear whether the acts with which they were charged were acts of war or acts of robbery *animo furandi*, but the view of all the judges seems to have been that if the accused acted with the sole intention of helping one of the belligerents such acts did not constitute piracy *jure gentium* (see Cockburn C.J. at p. 213, and Blackburn J. at

The great majority of writers are of the view that ships of unrecognized insurgents which do not confine their activities to their own State are and may be treated as piratical.[1]

p. 216). See also the observation of Holt L.C.J. in 1696 in the *Trial of Captain Thomas Vaughan*, 13 How. St. Tr. at pp. 503 and 525, to the effect that Dutch subjects who had received a commission from the King of France could not be treated as pirates. Similarly, about the same time Sir Lionel Jenkins held that a privateer who had exceeded his commission could not be treated as a pirate—although he was subject to the jurisdiction of the State which commissioned him (Wynne, *The Life of Sir Leoline Jenkins*, vol. II (1724), p. 714). *The Republic of Bolivia* v. *Indemnity Mutual Marine Insurance Co.* [1909] 1 K.B. 785—an insurance case involving seizure of goods by Bolivian revolutionaries operating on the river Amazon—is only of limited interest seeing that it was decided largely on the ground that the acts in question were not committed on the high seas and that, in any event, the expression 'piracy' used in the insurance policy referred not to piracy *jure gentium* but to piracy according to municipal law. In connection with the controversy with the United States in 1841 concerning the *McLeod* case Great Britain repeatedly referred to the naval depredations of the insurgents as 'piratical' (see Manning, *Diplomatic Correspondence of the United States, Canadian Relations*, 1784–1860, vol. III (1943), pp. 141, 422, 454, 616).

1 Some writers go further than that and regard as piratical ships of unrecognized insurgents generally. Thus Dana in his edition of Wheaton says: 'If it is a war [i.e. if belligerency has been recognized], the insurgent cruisers are to be treated by foreign citizens and officials, at sea and in port, as lawful belligerents. If it is not a war, those cruisers are pirates, and may be treated as such' (*Classics* edition, p. 30). Calvo, whose views are less loyalist than those of Dana, says: 'If the rebel ships do not limit themselves to attacking the government or the forces of the government against which they have rebelled, but commit acts of hostility or of damage against the ships of other nations, these nations have the right to obtain direct satisfaction by seizing them and inflicting the customary punishment on them, in conformity with the law of nations, or indirect, by handing them over to the government whose allegiance they have thrown off by rebellion' (as quoted by Wharton in Moore, vol. II, p. 1101). See also Brierly, *The Law of Nations* (2nd ed. 1936), p. 193 ('...an act cannot be piratical if it is done under the authority of a state or even of an insurgent community whose belligerency has been recognized'); McNair in *Law Quarterly Review*, vol. LIII (1927), p. 471; Pitt Cobbett, *Cases on International Law*, vol. I (5th ed.), p. 301; De Louter, *Le droit international public positif*, vol. I, p. 424. Professor Hyde, vol. I, § 233, believes that when interference with foreign shipping is incidental to the revolutionary struggle such acts should not be treated as piratical, but he does not assert that the practice is in accordance with the suggestion. According to Hall, *International Law*, § 81, the political character of insurgent activity takes it necessarily out of the category of piracy. The *Report of the Sub-Committee of the League of Nations Committee of Experts for the Progressive Codification of International Law*, p. 117, seems merely to register two opposing views: 'The regular Government sometimes treats such ships as pirates, but foreign Powers ought not to do so unless these ships commit acts of violence against vessels belonging to the Powers in question. Third Powers, on the other hand, may consider such ships as pirates when they commit acts of violence and depredations upon vessels belonging to those Powers, unless the acts are inspired by purely political motives, in which case it would be exaggeratedly vigorous to treat the ships as declared enemies of the community of civilized States.'

§ 91. *Enforcement of the Penalties of Piracy as against Unrecognized Insurgents.* While there is thus evidence in the form of governmental declarations, judicial pronouncements and opinions of writers to the effect that ships of unrecognized insurgents interfering with the vessels of third States or their subjects can properly be treated as piratical, there are no cases of the officers or the crews of such ships being put to trial and sentenced as pirates—though the case of *The Ambrose Light* came dangerously near it. However, there are good reasons for this absence of direct judicial authority. One of them is that unrecognized insurgents as a rule take heed of the drastic warnings addressed to them and refrain from interfering with the ships of third States. The second is that in cases in which such interference is attempted the convenient and necessary course is to meet the molestations and depredations not by judicial proceedings but by instantaneous and summary measures of resistance and suppression. This does not mean that the acts which occasioned these measures were not acts of piracy.

It is sometimes maintained that a regular trial and sentence are essential in cases of piracy *jure gentium*;[1] but there is no good reason for any such assertion. The mode of suppression depends upon the circumstances.[2] Originally, when piracy was rampant, not a judicial trial but instantaneous punishment was the rule. The principal consequence of piracy so far as international law is concerned is that every State is entitled to suppress it regardless of the nationality of the criminal. But the fact that every nation has jurisdiction over a pirate does not mean that that jurisdiction must be in the form of judicial proceedings. Neither need the suppression of the crime go to the length of capital punishment. Once we have disabused our minds of the idea that an *animus furandi* for private purposes is essential to constitute the crime of piracy *jure gentium*, there is room for taking into consideration the motive and the nature of the unlawful act of violence committed on the high seas. If the object of the piratical act is political and its means not inhuman and confined to interference with property, then it would be cruel to press the customary consequences of piracy *jure gentium* to their logical conclusion. *The Huascar* was attacked and chased by the British squadron after she had interfered with British steamers. But there was no prosecution for piracy. 'In strictness they were pirates', said the Attorney-General in reply to a question by Sir William Harcourt in the House of Commons concerning the officers and the crew of *The Huascar*, 'and might have been treated as such, but it is one thing to assert that they

1 See Anonymous in *B.Y.* vol. XIX (1938), p. 208.

2 See below, p. 308.

have been guilty of acts of piracy, and another to advise that they should be tried for their lives and hanged at Newgate.'[1] On the other hand, if the acts in question are brutal and ruthless acts of a criminal character directed against the life and person of nationals of third States, then there may be room for drawing the full conclusions from the absence of recognition and inflicting upon the culprits the exemplary measure of retribution. It does not really matter what label we attach to that act of retribution or in what manner the penalty is exacted. We may describe it as an act of self-defence. Or the offending insurgents may be handed over to the authorities of their own State—in which case they will probably be tried for both piracy and treason.[2]

§ 92. Animus furandi *as an Essential Element of Piracy*. The almost uniform trend of practice and opinion on the matter could be successfully questioned only if it could be shown that an *animus furandi* for the purpose of private gain is an essential element of piracy. No such proof can be adduced. Opinion on the matter is almost equally divided. It is probable that originally the use of that term was limited to acts of robbery and violence for private purposes. But there is no doubt that since then it has often been used in a wider connotation.

When in 1870 negotiations were in progress for the conclusion of a convention for the protection of submarine cables it was at first proposed to obtain an international declaration to the effect that the destruction of submarine cables shall be dealt with as an act of piracy. The British Government were of the view that this was the proper course, and their view received the approval of the Law Officers.[3] This is a not unusual example of extension of the scope of a legal term to cover acts other than those for which it was originally intended. It is sufficient to recall the history of the use of the term 'piracy' in municipal law. Far from being confined to acts of violence committed *animo furandi*, it now covers in many systems of law a multitude of offences including the engaging in slave traffic or the acceptance without national authorization of letters of marque from a foreign government. Already in the seventeenth century treaties were concluded authorizing the parties to treat as pirates those of

1 *H.C. Debates*, vol. CCXXXVI, pp. 787 et seq.

2 See, for example, the Pan-American Convention of 20 February 1928, on the Duties and Rights of States in the Event of Civil Strife, which provides in Article 2 that if the offending insurgent vessel is a warship it may be captured and returned to the lawful government; if it is a merchantman it may be captured by the injured State and punished according to its penal laws (Hudson, *International Legislation*, vol. IV (1932), p. 2418).

3 *Law Officers' Opinions*, United States, no. 279, Opinion of 18 May 1870.

their subjects who take letters of marque from the other belligerent.[1] In general, the accepting of letters of marque in a manner contrary to international law is often regarded as piracy not only according to municipal law but also according to international law.[2] In the instruction issued to the French naval authorities in January 1916 we read as follows: 'The captain, officers, and crew of every privateer commissioned by a Government signatory of the Declaration of Paris, 1856, being liable to punishments provided for the crime of piracy, must not be considered as prisoners of war but must be sent to the nearest French authority to be proceeded against according to the laws of the Republic' (Article 117).[3] The use of the term 'piracy' in connection with the suppression of the slave traffic is a frequent occurrence. In view of this it is impossible to regard as accurate or justified the criticism of those who appeal to an accepted meaning of the term 'pirate' as rendering impossible or improper its application to acts of insurgents not committed *animo furandi*.

§ 93. *The Development of the Conception of Piracy*. The above considerations provide also the answer to the criticism raised against the use of the terms 'piracy' and 'piratical' in the Nyon Agreements. In so far as the criticism was based on the view that piracy is conditioned by the existence of an *animus furandi*, it cannot be regarded as well founded. Neither, it has been shown, was it justified in so far as it proceeded on the assumption that ships of unrecognized insurgents cannot be treated as piratical.[4]

1 See, for example, the Treaty of 1686 between England and France or the Treaty of 1825 between Colombia and the United States—both referred to in Wild, *Sanctions and Treaty Enforcement* (1934), p. 195. On 24 October 1827, the British, French and Russian admirals addressed to the Committee of the Legislative Assembly of Greece a letter concerning the interference by ships under the Greek flag with allied commerce after the armistice with Turkey had been accepted. The letter referred to illegal pillage by these ships and stated clearly that they [the admirals] 'will not suffer these piracies to continue under any pretext'. They announced that they would regard as void all letters of marque given to privateers outside certain limits and that orders had been given to arrest them (*Annual Register*, 1827, p. 326).

2 For an impressive collection of authorities on the subject see *Harvard Research in International Law, Piracy* (1932), pp. 857–66. See also ibid. pp. 893–1013, for a survey of the municipal law of various countries.

3 As quoted in Hall, *International Law* (8th ed. 1924), p. 317, n.

4 In a sense the case of the submarines against which the Nyon Agreement was directed was worse than the case of submarines of unrecognized insurgents. With regard to the latter, there is some semblance of lawful commission originating from a responsible although not recognized authority. In the case of the former, there was no government which was prepared to take the responsibility for the acts of the submarines in question. In fact, all governments which might conceivably have been connected with the outrages expressly disclaimed any connection with the incidents. Accordingly, the persons in charge of the submarine would have been unable, if apprehended, to point to governmental commission or authority—a situation which is regarded by most writers as decisive for assuming piracy *jure gentium*.

In the method of punishment adopted in the Nyon Agreements the parties reverted to—and possibly exceeded in severity—the original practice which obtained in the early days of the history of piracy. The method was one of instant and drastic retribution. In the Supplementary Agreements made in February 1938 between Great Britain, France and Italy, even stricter measures of suppression were adopted. While under the Nyon Agreements the suspected submarines were to be attacked only if recently a neutral vessel had been attacked and there was reason to believe that the submarine was responsible, henceforth mere presence in the prohibited area was to be regarded as indicative of criminal intent and criminal action. We may, if we wish, give to this method of suppression the name of self-defence. But it is not a name which is obviously more accurate than that used in the Agreement. Regular judicial trial has never been an essential concomitant of piracy *jure gentium*.[1] Its distinguishing feature is the subjection of the offender, as a matter of course,[2] to the jurisdiction of States other than that of which he is a national. Other elements are more or less controversial. There would therefore seem to be little force in the criticism of the provisions of a treaty on the ground that it does not conform with such supposedly indispensable requirements as the existence of an *animus furandi* on the part of the offenders, or the absence of a proper commission from a government (or even from unrecognized insurgents) and, on the part of the captor, of provision for a proper trial. For all these conditions are controversial.

The criticisms of the terminology of the Nyon Agreements assumed not only that the notion of piracy *jure gentium* is clear and non-controversial, but also that it is not a term the use of which can legitimately be extended and developed. There is no warrant for any such assumption. Piracy, conceived as organized robbery for the purpose of private gain, is now largely obsolete. It has ceased to be the evil which it was before the advent of modern means of communication and information. As the notion of piracy *jure gentium* has never been rigidly confined to one type of unlawful

1 'If Piracy be committed on the *Ocean*, and the Pirates in the Attempt there happen to be overcome, the Captors are not obliged to bring them to any port, but may expose them immediately to punishment, by hanging them up at the Main-yard end before a Departure; for the old natural liberty remains in places where are no Judgments' (Molloy, *De Jure Maritimo et Navali*, vol. I, ch. IV, § XII). The right to inflict the extreme penalty for the crime of piracy, without resorting to the procedure of a regular trial, is almost unanimously asserted by modern writers in cases where circumstances render the bringing into port dangerous and impracticable.

2 There are other instances in which international law permits a State to assume jurisdiction over an alien for crimes committed abroad, but these instances are limited to what may be called protective jurisdiction, whereas in the case of piracy a State is entitled to assume jurisdiction regardless of whether its interests are directly affected.

action and as the kind of lawlessness with which it was at the beginning predominantly connected is now becoming a historical survival, it would not seem improper to describe and treat as piratical such acts of violence on the high seas which by their ruthlessness and disregard of the sanctity of human life invite exemplary punishment and suppression.[1]

If the essential aspect of piracy in international law is not the quality of the act of violence in question or the kind of punishment following in its wake but the jurisdictional right of States other than that of the criminal to suppress the unlawful act of violence on the high seas, then the use of terminology extending the conception of piracy beyond its original connotation cannot be regarded as improper. Neither can the validity of such criticism be admitted in so far as it rests on the assertion that acts committed on behalf of a public authority cannot or ought never to be made the subject of punishment of the individual directly responsible for them. The plea of superior orders is not an absolute defence—although for a time this was, somewhat inconsistently,[2] the view of the British *Manual of Military Law*[3] and of those of some other countries. As stated by the German Supreme Court in the case of *The Llandovery Castle*, where the accused were charged with firing on the boats of sinking British hospital ships: 'It is certainly to be urged in favour of the military subordinates that they are under no obligation to question the order of their superior officer, and they can count upon its legality. But no such confidence can be held to exist, if such an order is universally known to everybody, including the accused, to be without any doubt whatever against the law. This happens only in rare and exceptional cases. But this case was precisely one of them....'[4]

1 Story J. in *United States* v. *The Malek Adhel*, 2 How. 211, at p. 232: 'If he wilfully sinks or destroys an innocent merchant ship without any other object than to gratify his lawless appetite for mischief, it is just as much piratical aggression, in the sense of the law of nations and of the act of congress, as if he did it solely and exclusively for the sake of plunder, *lucri causa*. The law looks at it as an act of hostility, and being committed by a vessel not commissioned and engaged in lawful warfare, it treats it as the action of a pirate, and of one who is emphatically *hostis humani generis*.'

2 Inconsistently from the point of view of British constitutional law, where the plea of superior orders does not constitute a valid defence of illegal actions of officials, and inconsistently from the point of view of the disregard of the plea of superior orders with regard to some war crimes, e.g. spying or breach of parole.

3 § 443 of *The Laws and Usages of War*, in which it was said: '...members of the armed forces who commit such violations of the recognized rules of warfare as are ordered by their Government or by their commander are not war criminals and cannot therefore be punished by the enemy'. The contrary view was adopted in §443 as revised in 1944.

4 *Annual Digest*, 1923–4, Case no. 235. For a detailed discussion of the plea of superior orders see Lauterpacht in *B.Y.* vol. XXI (1944), pp. 69–74, and in Oppenheim (6th revised ed. 1945), § 253 (and the literature cited there). See also Glueck, *War Criminals* (1944), pp. 140–58.

The modern conditions and instrumentalities of warfare are such as to make us pause before subscribing, without reservation and for the purposes of a passing terminological controversy, to the view that the plea of superior orders is in all circumstances a good defence. There may be acts so inhuman and so violative of accepted standards of civilization that neither the fact that they are perpetrated in time of war nor that they are committed at the order of superior authority can shield them from punishment inflicted both as a deterrent and as retribution. Article 3 of the unratified Washington Treaty of 1922 provided for the punishment 'as if for an act of piracy' of persons directly responsible for attack upon merchant vessels in a manner contrary to international law. That particular provision was omitted in the corresponding rules of Part IV of the Naval Limitation Treaty of London of 1930. But the fact that in 1922, after the passions of wartime had ceased to exert their influence, governments and their advisers thought it proper to use the term in question in relation to the forces of recognized belligerents in time of ordinary war is not without instruction. When in September 1941 orders were issued to the naval forces of the United States to fire at sight upon German and Italian submarines and surface vessels, that measure was described by President Roosevelt as being one in defence against piratical attacks in violation of international law. No question of superior orders was entertained. In the Agreement of 8 August 1945, between Great Britain, the United States, Soviet Russia and France for the prosecution and punishment of major war criminals of the European Axis it was provided, in Article 8, that 'the fact the Defendant acted pursuant to order of his Government or of a superior shall not free him from responsibility, but may be considered in mitigation of punishment if the Tribunal determines that justice so requires'.[1]

§ 94. *Conclusions.* With regard to the specific question of the treatment of insurgents not recognized as belligerents, the weight of governmental and judicial practice seems to warrant the following conclusions:

(1) So long as unrecognized insurgents refrain from interfering with the ships of neutral States, the weight of practice and the principle of non-interference seem to favour the view that third States have no occasion to treat their activities as piratical. Domestic treason is not an international crime.

(2) When unrecognized insurgents molest the ships of third States they may be treated as pirates, although even in this case the political motives of the act and the absence of an *animus furandi* suggest punishment less severe and drastic than that ordinarily meted out to pirates.

1 Misc. No. 10 (1945) Cmd. 6668.

(3) When to the illegality of the insurgent depredations upon the shipping of third States there is added criminal and callous ruthlessness resulting in actual loss of life, the perpetrators of the piratical act, if they fall into the hands of the injured State, may justly be subjected to the customary penalties which the law of nations reserves for pirates *jure gentium*.[1]

1 The recent judicious treatment of the question by Professor Hyde, vol. I (2nd ed. 1945), p. 775, seems to arrive on the whole at the same conclusions. See also Hackworth, vol. II, p. 690. With regard to the criticism levelled against the terminology of the Nyon Agreements, the proper conclusion from the discussion undertaken in this note appears to be that the Agreements, far from creating a new crime in the garb of a faulty terminology, were declaratory of the existing law of piracy in relation to an unprecedented situation. That declaration could properly be made as between the signatories with regard to their nationals. In so far as the signatories represented a substantial portion of maritime powers they could claim for that declaratory treaty a measure of more general validity. It is submitted that the terminology of the Nyon Agreements in so far as it related to piracy does not seem to be unscientific; that, in accordance with a well-established principle of interpretation, whenever an international document makes use of a technical term it is not permissible to reduce that term to a mere manner of speech; and that the term 'piracy' as used in the Nyon Agreements is in accordance with the widely held view as to the essential conditions of piracy and the proper method of its repression.

Appendix to Chapter XVIII

OPINIONS OF THE LAW OFFICERS OF THE CROWN ON THE TREATMENT OF UNRECOGNIZED INSURGENTS

Of the Opinions printed below the first four assert the right of outside States to treat as piratical such vessels of unrecognized insurgents as commit depredations upon the ships of States which have declined to grant recognition of belligerency. Opinions V–X, on the other hand, give uniform expression to the principle that a proclamation of piracy issued by the lawful government against insurgents is not binding upon outside States.

I

Temple, August 11 1870[1]

My Lord

We are honoured with your Lordship's commands signified in Mr Hammond's letter of the 2nd instant stating, that he was directed by your Lordship to transmit to us, therewith, the accompanying despatch and its inclosures from Her Majesty's Chargé d'Affaires at Caracas detailing the circumstances, under which the British Schooner 'Clemencia' which was employed as a packet between Puerto Cabello and St Thomas, had been fired upon and damaged by the 'Maparari' a war vessel in the service of the party in hostility to the Government of the Republic of Venezuela, and reporting the steps he had taken to obtain compensation for that outrage, and he was to request that we would take the papers into our consideration and favour your Lordship with our opinion thereupon.

In obedience to your Lordship's commands we have taken the said papers into consideration and have the honour to *Report*

That we are of opinion that the firing upon the British Merchant vessel 'Clemencia' whilst peaceably at anchor in the seaport of 'Borburata' and subsequent plunder of her, if the Maparari had no 'Commission of War' or 'Letters of Marque', was an Act of piracy, the cognisance of which is within the Admiralty Jurisdiction of Nations, and as the Republic of Venezuela has declined to exercise her territorial jurisdiction, which is concurrent with that of the Admiralty of Nations, Great Britain may properly exercise the latter, and direct the 'Maparari' to be seized wherever she shall be found upon the seas by a British Cruizer, and carried for adjudication on a charge of piracy before the most convenient British Court of Vice Admiralty.

1 F.O. 83/2403.

We assume that there has been no recognition on the part of Her Majesty of the insurgents, who are in possession of Puerto Cabello, as belligerents.

We have the honour to be, My Lord,
Your Lordship's most Obedt. humble Servants,
R. P. Collier, J. D. Coleridge, Travers Twiss

The Right Honble The Earl Granville, K.G.

II

Temple, February 3, 1877[1]

My Lord

We are honoured with your Lordship's commands signified in Sir Julian Pauncefote's letter of the 29th January ultimo, stating that he was directed by your Lordship to transmit to us the accompanying correspondence... relative to the case of a Spanish steamer named the 'Montezuma' or 'Mortezama', which vessel was forcibly seized on the 7th November last while on the high seas, on a voyage between Porto Rico and Havana, by a party of armed persons who were on board the vessel as passengers, and are presumed to be Cubans.

That they are stated to have killed the captain, helmsman, and a steward who attempted resistance, and to have wounded at least one other of the crew.

That we should see by the inclosure in the Admiralty letter of the 25th January that the Commander-in-chief of Her Majesty's naval forces on the North American and West Indian Station had directed the Commodore at Jamaica to issue orders to Her Majesty's ships on his division of the station to capture the 'Montezuma', should she be fallen in with by them, flying the Cuban flag, either on the high seas or in British waters, and to take her into a British port for trial.

Sir Julian Pauncefote also further stated that it would appear from the judgment of the Privy Council in the case of the 'Attorney-General of Hong Kong *v.* Kwok Asing' (5 L. Rep. P.C. 179), and from that of the Court of Queen's Bench in the case of 'Reg. *v.* Terman' (33 L.J.M.C. 201), that the Commander-in-chief was right in treating the case of the 'Montezuma' as one of piracy, *jure gentium*.

That he was, however, to request that we would take the inclosed papers into our consideration, and favour your Lordship, at our earliest convenience, with our opinion as to whether the orders given by Rear-Admiral Cooper Key should be approved.

In obedience to your Lordship's commands we have the honour to report—

That, in our opinion, the orders given by Rear-Admiral Cooper Key may properly be approved.

We have, &c.
(Signed) John Holker, Hardinge S. Giffard, J. Parker Deane

The Right Honble The Earl Derby

1 F.O. 72/1486.

III

Temple, July 21, 1877[1]

My Lord

We are honoured with your Lordship's commands signified in Sir Julian Pauncefote's letter of the 17th July instant, stating that he was directed by your Lordship to lay before us the papers noted in the margin relating to the naval engagement which had taken place between Her Majesty's ships 'Shah' and 'Amethyst' and the Peruvian iron-clad 'Huascar' while in the possession of rebels.

That the facts of the case, and the grounds upon which Admiral de Horsey considered his action justified under the circumstances, were so fully and clearly set out in his despatch of the 3rd June that it was only necessary to draw our attention to the Decree of the President of the Republic of Peru inclosed in Mr Graham's despatch No. 22 of the 12th of May last, and to request that we would favour your Lordship with our opinion as to whether the proceedings of Admiral de Horsey reported by him in his despatch above referred to were open to any objection in point of law.

That the attention of Parliament had been drawn to that case; and Sir Julian Pauncefote was to request that we would be good enough to report upon it at our earliest convenience.

In obedience to your Lordship's commands we have the honour to report—

That the papers transmitted to us show that the 'Huascar' had been taken out of the hands of her lawful officers, that the Peruvian Government had disavowed any liability for the acts of the 'Huascar', and that the vessel was consequently sailing under no national flag, and no redress could be had for any acts which she might commit.

The papers further show that the 'Huascar', whilst so sailing and officered, and after the Peruvian Government had disavowed all liability for the acts of the 'Huascar', stopped two British mail steamers on the high seas and demanded their mails; took by force a passenger from a ship under British colours, and a quantity of coals out of another British vessel; and lastly, that a British subject was forced to act as engineer on board the 'Huascar', and was by violence prevented from communicating with the British authorities.

In this state of things, we are of opinion that Admiral de Horsey was bound to act decisively for the protection of British subjects and British property, and that the proceedings resorted to by him were in law justifiable.

We have, &c.

(Signed) John Holker, Hardinge S. Giffard, J. Parker Deane

The Right Honble The Earl Derby

1 F.O. 61/304.

IV

Temple, March 5, 1878[1]

My Lord

We were honoured with your Lordship's commands signified in Sir Julian Pauncefote's letter of the 15th February ultimo, stating that with reference to our Report of the 21st July last[2] on the subject of the attack on the Peruvian iron-clad 'Huascar' by Her Majesty's ships 'Shah' and 'Amethyst', he was directed by your Lordship to transmit to us the accompanying letter from the Peruvian Minister at this Court,[3] inclosing a memorandum which he had been instructed by his Government to place in the hands of Her Majesty's Government.

That that memorandum contained an exposition of the case from the point of view in which it was regarded by the Peruvian Government, and concluded with a demand of satisfaction for the acts of Rear-Admiral de Horsey, which they consider an outrage on the rights of Peru.

That the inclosed draft of reply had been drawn up by your Lordship's directions, and Sir Julian Pauncefote was to request that we would take it into our consideration, and inform your Lordship whether it met with our concurrence, or whether we would suggest any modifications in it.

In obedience to your Lordship's commands we have the honour to report—

That the draft reply meets with our concurrence, but we submit, for your Lordship's consideration, that the word 'reprisals' in the third line from the foot of page 2 of the draft is objectionable.

The word 'reprisals' is a term of art, and in our opinion not applicable to the 'Huascar', and the circumstances in which that vessel was attacked.

We suggest the words 'immediate and severe treatment' in the place of the word 'reprisals'.

We have, &c.

(Signed) JOHN HOLKER, HARDINGE S. GIFFARD, J. PARKER DEANE

The Right Honble The Earl Derby

1 F.O. 61/309.
2 Confidential No. 4216, p. 44.
3 Señor Galvez, 27 November 1877.

Annex

Draft of Letter from the Earl of Derby to Señor Galvez

Foreign Office, , 1878

M. le Ministre

Her Majesty's Government have had under their consideration your letter of the 27th November last, inclosing a memorandum which you state contains the exposition of the 'Huascar' question addressed to them by you in the name of your Government, and expressing the hope that the demand of your Government for satisfaction on account of the proceedings of Rear-Admiral de Horsey in relation to the 'Huascar' will be received with those sentiments which are characteristic of the equity of the British Government.

Her Majesty's Government have given to this memorandum the careful attention which it deserves, with every desire to treat the question in that spirit of justice which you so courteously recognize as guiding their relations with foreign States in the discussion of international difficulties. They find it, however, impossible to reconcile their views of international law and of justice with the arguments advanced by the Peruvian Government in this case, and although they deeply regret that circumstances should have arisen which necessitated a recourse to the measures complained of, it appears to them that the memorandum entirely fails to establish the proposition that the proceedings of Rear-Admiral de Horsey constitute an outrage on the rights of Peru.

There can be no dispute as to the main facts of the case, which are fully and accurately set out in the papers laid before Parliament, a copy of which I have the honour to inclose for convenience of reference.

The 'Huascar' was a rebel ship, and the Peruvian Government, by a public Decree dated the 8th May, 1877, which was officially communicated to Her Majesty's Minister at Lima and to the other foreign Representatives, declared that the Republic would not be responsible for the acts of the rebels in whose possession she had fallen, of whatsoever nature those acts might be. By the same Decree they publicly authorized the capture of the 'Huascar', and offered to recompense properly all those who, not belonging to the crews of the vessels forming the squadron of operations, should bring her under the authority of the Government, or who might contribute to do so.

After the promulgation of this Decree, the 'Huascar' committed a series of outrages on the British flag. She boarded and detained the 'John Elder' at sea. She boarded and demanded despatches from the 'Santa Rosa'; she forcibly took coal from the 'Imuncina'; she removed a Peruvian officer from the 'Columbia', and she compelled the engineer of the latter ship,[1] a British subject, to serve against his will.

The 'Huascar' having been taken out of the hands of her lawful officers, and the Peruvian Government having disavowed any liability for her acts, it follows that she was sailing under no national flag, and that no redress could be obtained from that Government for any acts which she might commit.

Under these circumstances Her Majesty's Government consider that Rear-Admiral de Horsey was bound to act decisively for the protection of British subjects and British property by visiting upon the vessel herself and her crew the consequences of her unwarrantable proceedings, and they cannot admit the right of the Peruvian

1 Should be, 'the engineer of the "Huascar"' (see Admiralty letter of 27 March 1878).

Government, whilst disclaiming, by a public Decree, all responsibility for the acts of the 'Huascar' as a rebel ship, to regard her at the same time as a national vessel, and to resent as a national injury the reprisals[1] which she brought upon herself by the outrages which she committed on a foreign flag.

It is argued, however, in the memorandum, that Rear-Admiral de Horsey cannot justify his action by an appeal to the Decree of the 8th May, as that Decree did not authorize the capture of the 'Huascar' in Peruvian waters; and that from the fact that he did not intimate to the Peruvian Government that he intended to act under the Decree, as well as from the character of the attack made upon the monitor, it must be inferred that he could have had no intention to co-operate in her recovery, but was bent only on her destruction.

Her Majesty's Government dissent altogether from those views.

Having regard to the general terms of the Decree, they are at a loss to perceive how the exercise of the authority thereby conferred, whether on the high seas or in Peruvian or any other waters, can afford any legitimate ground of remonstrance or complaint on the part of the Peruvian Government. There is nothing whatever in the Decree to indicate that the authority to capture the 'Huascar' did not extend to Peruvian waters, or that any previous notice to the Government of an intention to act upon the Decree was necessary. On the contrary, the vessel and the rebels on board of her were declared outlawed, and the natural presumption, as well as the only practical purpose of the Decree, was that the vessel should be seized wheresoever and whensoever she could be found.

With reference to the character of the attack on the 'Huascar', and to the intention attributed to Rear-Admiral de Horsey, I would observe that neither the 'Shah' nor the 'Amethyst' being armour-plated vessels, the capture of so powerful a monitor as the 'Huascar' could not reasonably be attempted without the employment of all the force at their command; and that the intention of Rear-Admiral de Horsey to deliver her into the hands of the Peruvian Government, if he should effect her capture, is evidenced by the terms of the letter which he addressed to her rebel commander on the 16th May, and to which reference is made in the early part of the memorandum. In that letter he distinctly stated that any further interference with British subjects or property would cause him to capture the vessel 'and deliver her to the lawful authority'.

As regards the strictures contained in the memorandum respecting the use of torpedoes by Her Majesty's ships on that occasion, the necessity for this proceeding and its propriety under the circumstances must be left to the appreciation of those best qualified to form a judgment thereon from a professional point of view; and I need only express the satisfaction of Her Majesty's Government that no casualty resulted therefrom.

The exact meaning and effect of the Decree of the 8th May having given rise to discussion, it may not be out of place to invite your attention to the following remarks:

The intention of the Peruvian Government in promulgating that Decree, if it admitted of any doubt, was very clearly manifested in the correspondence which passed between Señor Zegarra, the Peruvian Chargé d'Affaires accredited to Chile, and the Chilean Minister of Foreign Affairs, and which is published in the Chilean official 'Gazette'.

It appears from this correspondence that on the occasion of the mutiny and escape of the 'Huascar' from Callao, Señor Zegarra, acting under telegraphic instructions from his Government, addressed a note to the Chilean Minister for Foreign Affairs, requesting that if the 'Huascar' should enter a Chilean port, she should be seized by the authorities and placed at the disposal of the Peruvian Legation.

1 Alteration suggested by the Law Officers: 'the immediate and severe treatment'.

On the 17th May, it having become known that the 'Huascar' had entered the port of Caldera, Señor Zegarra renewed most formally his demand for the detention of the vessel, which he stated was then in Chilean waters, and in fulfilment of the decisive orders of his Government, he required that the Chilean Minister should telegraph with the least possible delay the necessary instructions for the carrying out of such action.

Señor Zegarra on the 22nd May again addressed a note to the Chilean Government remonstrating against their refusal to comply with the wishes of his Government, and criticizing the grounds put forward by them in justification of their refusal, namely, that the 'Huascar' was not a pirate, that there was no reason to fear that she would interfere with Chilean commerce, and, therefore, that Chile had no right to assume a hostile attitude towards her.

In this note Señor Zegarra used the following language, which, being addressed under instructions from his Government, is deserving of special attention:—'If a vessel under such conditions is not a pirate, I confess I do not know what to term her; she navigates without a commission from any Government, acknowledges no territorial authority, and to establish more precisely her position has detained on the high sea a commercial packet, forcibly compelling the delivery of the correspondence on board; if such a vessel is not a pirate, at the least she has placed herself completely outside international right; the flag she flies does not belong to her.'

Señor Zegarra concludes his note by repeating his protest against the Chilean Government for not having arrested the 'Huascar'.

Her Majesty's Government, concurring as they do in the views above expressed as to the status and condition of that vessel at the time of her engagement with Her Majesty's ships 'Shah' and 'Amethyst' and considering the terms of the Decree of the 8th May, are of opinion that the demand of the Peruvian Government is not sustainable on any principle of law or justice. Although Rear-Admiral de Horsey did not succeed in capturing the 'Huascar', it is incontestable, from the fact of her surrender to the Peruvian Government immediately after her encounter with the British ships, that he contributed to her recovery in the manner contemplated by the Decree, and while discharging his duty in the protection of British interests, he intended to render, and did actually render, material service to the Government of Peru.

Her Majesty's Government cannot but believe that the popular excitement which has been caused by the event in question is to be attributed to an imperfect knowledge of the true facts of the case, and they trust that the friendly explanations which I have given in this letter will satisfy your Government that Rear-Admiral de Horsey is quite innocent of the charge imputed to him in the memorandum, of having violated the rights of Peru, and that he has committed no act which can justly be construed as an offence against the dignity of the Republic.

I avail myself of this occasion to renew the expression of the friendship and goodwill with which Her Majesty's Government are animated towards the Government which you so worthily represent.

I have, &c.

V

Lincoln's Inn, March 21, 1866[1]

My Lord

We are honoured with your Lordship's commands signified in Mr Hammond's letter of the 1st of March instant, stating that he was directed by your Lordship to transmit to us the accompanying translation of a note addressed by the Spanish Minister at this Court, dated the 16th ultimo, and communicated to him by the latter, containing the views of the Spanish Government in regard to the conditions under which Chilean privateers would be treated as pirates.

Mr Hammond was also pleased to state that, for our convenience, he was to inclose to us the paper referred to in the above note; and to request that we would take these papers into our consideration, and favour your Lordship with any observations we might have to offer thereupon.

In obedience to your Lordship's commands we have taken these papers into our consideration, and have the honour to report—

That it is necessary to state clearly the difference of opinion between Her Majesty's Government and the Government of Spain upon this important subject.

The Spanish Government maintain that they have a right to treat as pirates all Chilean privateers duly commissioned by and carrying the flag of that State, unless the captain and the majority of the crew be composed of Chilean subjects.

Her Majesty's Government, on the other hand, maintain that the privateer derives her authority from the commission and flag, and that the condition required by the Spanish Government with respect to the composition of the crew is not warranted by international law; and that though it is competent to Spain or any other State to treat as pirates its own subjects serving on board a duly-commissioned foreign privateer, it is not competent to Spain, or any other State, so to treat the subjects of a foreign country; that, in fact, the regulation as to the number of the crew, who are to be the subjects of the State which commissions the privateer, is a regulation of municipal and not of international law.

These positions Her Majesty's Government have supported by arguments derived from principle, from practice, and from the authority of accredited writers upon international jurisprudence.

The Spanish Government, in this last despatch, allege that upon all these grounds Her Majesty's Government have failed to support their opinion.

It is proposed to examine the arguments upon which this assertion rests, in the order in which they are stated in the despatch.

1. The first argument is, that to deny to Spain the right of treating as pirates foreign subjects so serving on board privateers, is to deny to her the exercise of that jurisdiction which is the essential attribute of independent sovereignty.

It is very difficult to understand this argument. It is not contended by Her Majesty's Government that foreign subjects in the dominions or in the ships of

1 F.O. 83/2374.

Spain are not subject to the jurisdiction of that State. It is not contended that Her Majesty's subjects serving in the armies or fleets of the enemies of Spain are not subject, when captured by Spain, to be treated as prisoners of war. Either of these contentions would indeed be derogatory to the sovereignty of Spain; but it is contended that Spain cannot, by a private law of her own, whether that law be or be not identical with the private law of another State, change the character and alter the condition of a prisoner of war into the character and condition of a pirate.

It seems to be admitted by Spain that she is bound to treat foreign subjects taken in the army or navy of her enemy as what she calls 'milites', as prisoners of war; but she contends that a different rule applies to foreign subjects serving in the privateers of the enemy. But upon what principle? When it is admitted that the privateer herself is entitled to be treated as a vessel of war: it is said that otherwise the foreign subject would be the subject of two Powers at once, namely, that of the State to which his original allegiance was due, and that of the State under whose commission he was fighting. But this is a transparent fallacy. So far as affects the belligerent, which is Spain in this instance, it has been already stated that he must be considered as a subject of the State of whom he is the military servant. And here must be noticed a confusion into which the writer of the despatch has fallen with respect to the bearing of the English Foreign Enlistment Act upon this question. It has never been argued by Her Majesty's Government that this municipal law in any way affected the rights of Spain in peace or in war; but it was argued that Spain could not insist upon the regulations of this municipal law as a reason for treating English subjects on board Chilean vessels as pirates.

While reasoning upon a mistaken view of this statute, and maintaining, justly, that no municipal law can affect international law, the writer of the Spanish despatch says: 'Although England might declare those English subjects to be pirates who should form part of the crew of a foreign privateer, if such privateer were an enemy of Spain, and were captured, it is clear that Spain would not consider as pirates the English subjects she might find on board, if the captain and the majority of the crew were subjects of the Power which issued the commission.'

To this proposition Her Majesty's Government entirely assent, but it is fatal to the whole argument of the writer upon the main subject of his despatch; for the position, that when a majority of foreigners form the crew of a privateer they are to be treated as pirates, is just as much the creature of municipal law as the position, that foreigners forming a minority of the crew may be treated as pirates by the State of which they are subjects. For, in fact, the former position is simply a provision contained in the Spanish and French Ordinances, the latter of which, it may be observed in passing, has varied from time to time as to the requisite number or proportion of the foreigners. Such provisions are not a portion of international law, and the legislation of a particular nation has no authority beyond its own territory. Then what are the other authorities? It will be found, when they are examined, that they rest upon the statement of Ortolan, a respectable modern writer, but not of the first class, nor a jurist by profession, and who founds his proposition upon the French Municipal Ordinance. It is true that De Pistoye et

Duverdy express the same opinion; but, as has been already observed in a former Report, they cite, in support of it, no other authority than that of Ortolan.

It was stated, on the other hand, by Her Majesty's Government that no such position was to be found in the writings of any English or American jurists, or in the Orders issued by those Governments with respect to privateers, and this statement appears to be uncontradicted by the Spanish Minister.

It was further stated that the authority of many other writers—among whom were enumerated the older jurists Bynkershoek and Abreu, and the modern Spanish jurists Pando and Riquelme,—was, directly or indirectly, opposed to this doctrine. It is replied that this is an error; and first, with regard to Bynkershoek, a passage is cited from one of his chapters (lib. i, chap. xvii) in his 'Quæstiones Juris Publici', to the effect that the commander of a privateer sailing 'sine codicillis sui Principis' is a pirate; and also another passage (though not expressly cited) is referred to, that one who sails under the orders 'externi Principis' is in the same category.

It will be found, on examination of the chapters, and the context of the passages referred to, that Bynkershoek laid down no such doctrine as is contended for; but that his general reasoning, as well as his particular language, is most clearly adverse to it.

He has three chapters bearing on the subject; one (chap. xvii) upon piracy—who are pirates? and three upon the subject of privateering. The passage, 'sine codicillis', &c., is in the first of these chapters (page 127); and it is hardly too much to say, that if the whole chapter had been read, it never would have been cited.

The author begins by propounding the question, 'Who are pirates?' and immediately answers by this definition: 'Qui autem *nullius* Principis auctoritate, sive mari, sive terrâ, rapiunt, piratarum praedonumque vocabulo intelliguntur.' This is the true international doctrine upon the subject. He proceeds to say that, according to the Dutch law, a Dutchman may not sail from a Dutch harbour or coast with the commission of a foreign Prince, 'cum mandato externi Principis'; and continuing his argument, he adds that those who, under the authority of a foreign ('externi') Prince, 'ad prædandum exeunt, piratarum nomine censendos esse; quia sic possent et non hostes deprædari, et alios Principes contra suum suscitare'. He is here speaking of the case of a privateer belonging to a neutral subject (a thing not unknown in the times when he wrote), and not of a privateer belonging to the belligerent, and carrying the commission of the belligerent State.

In another part of the chapter (page 127) he deals with the question whether a foreign vessel, taken without a commission, while acting as a privateer, can be tried and punished by the country of the captor, and expresses his own opinion in the affirmative; and then he adds the passage cited by the Spanish Government, namely, 'et nemo contradixerit, si sine codicillis Principis sui in nostros rapinam egerit; sed si ex mandato, cujus fines egressus dicitur, simile quid fecerit, magis dubitari posset'.

He then refers to a dispute in 1667 between England and Holland, which had arisen in the case of vessels which, having letters of marque, continued, *after peace was proclaimed*, to act as belligerents. England contended that they should be tried by the State which gave the letters of marque; Holland contended that the State of the captor might deal with them; and he ends this discussion by the words, 'Sed pirata quis sit, nec ne, inde pendet, an mandatum prædandi habuerit; si habuerit, et arguatur id excessisse, non continuo habuerim pro pirata.'

In his next chapter, 'De Prædatoriâ privatâ' (chap. xviii), after describing the privateer as a vessel which individuals equip and arm, he says: 'Quod autem *Albericus Gentilis* in libris "De Advocatione Hispanicâ," variis locis, etiam cum de jure, quod usu servatur ipsi sermo est, ejusmodi homines passim appellat piratas, nec alio, quam piratarum, loco habet, utique absurdius est, quam ut constitutâ disputatione refutari oporteat; quicquid enim illi agunt, agunt auctoritate publicà, neque enavigant nisi ex mandato ordinum generalium,' &c. The rest of the chapter is occupied with the law of prize as to the rights of privateers. The next chapter treats of the case of a ship without a commission, as privateer, making a prize, and considers to whom the prize shall belong. At the close of the chapter he again refers to the distinction between those 'qui sine auctoritate publicâ' and 'sine codicillis prædatum enavigant,' and those who have a commission; upon the possession of which, duly granted, he throughout, from first to last, considers the lawful character of the privateer to depend.

The next authority impugned is that of Abreu.

The averment on the part of Her Majesty's Government was that in no part of the work of this Spanish writer was the position to be found, that a lawfully commissioned privateer could be treated as a pirate, because the captain and majority of the crew had been by birth subjects of a foreign State; and that the fact was remarkable because the question of a privateer, under a double Commission from two distinct States, was treated of (cap. 12, page 151), in which he speaks of the Commission as giving the authority to the privateer. No such position is now cited by the Spanish Minister. The passage referred to by him (cap. 1, N. 11, p. 9) merely asserts that it is not lawful for a subject, without a commission from his Prince, to make war, on account of the many inconveniences which would otherwise result, and that, according to the Spanish Ordinance, among the vessels which are lawful prize are those 'which traverse the sea without the authority of *any* Prince or Sovereign State'; which is the 'nullius Principis auctoritate' of Bynkershoek.

Next, with respect to Pando. It is said that he called the foreigners who commanded the South American privateers 'Filibusters,' and said that no other name could be given to them. This is a strong instance of the evil of partial citation. What he really does say (page 427) is, that a privateer with two commissions was considered a pirate by the French Ordinances; and he adds that one of the abuses committed by the Republic of Buenos Ayres in her war with her ancient mother country, Spain, was entrusting the command of her privateers to foreigners, whose conduct, in the exercise of their authority, was such that they deserved no other character than that of Filibusters. At page 429 this author says, 'It is competent to each nation to give to its own privateers whatever rules it pleases. So far as these rules relate exclusively to subjects, no one can dispute the competency of the Sovereign to establish them; but this does not apply to foreigners: it has no authority to subject them to requisitions of any particular kind, except so far as the rules which it imposes are conformable to the universal law of nations, to general custom, or to Treaties.'

Next, the authority of Riquelme (Wheaton, by Lawrence, vol. i, p. 225). This author, Riquelme, refers to the Ordinances of Spain as being extremely severe upon the subjects of Spain; but, so far from recognizing the rule contended for as one of international law, he observes, 'Besides, the taking of a commission for privateering from a foreign State, though its object be making prizes by incurring the risks of war, cannot be esteemed a proof of high morality, still it is very far removed from the crime of piracy.'

Massé and even Hautefeuille are of the same opinion. But there is another author (De Martens) of much continental celebrity (though adverse to many opinions of English jurists), who wrote, besides his great work upon international law, a special treatise upon privateering, 'Essai concernant les Armateurs.' He says, section xi, 'At present all the Powers of Europe agree in these three points: 1. That whoever wishes to fit out a privateer must provide himself with letters of marque, or with a commission from one of the belligerent Powers, for want of which he may be treated and punished as a pirate, as well by those on whom he commits violence as also by his own Sovereign. 2. That a lawful privateer has, in strictness, a right to demand his prize to be adjudged to him, inasmuch as it is lawfully made; but also (3), That he can in no wise regard it as his property till it has been adjudged to him by a competent tribunal.' And, at section xiii, 'There is nothing that prevents the granting of letters of marque, even to the subjects of neutral or allied Powers who are able to solicit them; but, since it is contrary to neutrality to suffer neutral subjects to contribute by this means to the reinforcement of one of the belligerent Powers, and to the annoyance of the other, States generally prohibit their subjects from taking letters of marque from a foreign Power without the permission of their Sovereigns; and many Treaties oblige them also to prohibit their subjects from doing it, as well as to forbid every species of armaments on the enemy's account in their ports. However, the enemy is not justified in punishing them as pirates when they have letters patent (commissions) from one of the Powers with whom it is at war, although their ships may be confiscated' (pp. 43, 44).

To pass from the topic of authorities to that of Treaties.

The object for which the Treaty between England and the United States of America, and that of the United States of Mexico, was cited, seems to have been misunderstood by the Spanish Minister. The object was to prove that, when this particular composition of the privateer's crew was to be treated as imparting to the vessel the character of a pirate, it was necessary to make it the subject of this specific Convention between the nations by whom it was to be so considered, and that, accordingly, this was done in the Treaties referred to, which, if the doctrine had been universally recognized by international law, would have been unnecessary.

Then as to the practice.

It is no longer asserted that England assented, by tacit acquiescence, to this doctrine when propounded by the French Admiral in 1839, because the evidence that England then promptly and formally protested against the application of this doctrine to Her Majesty's subjects cannot be gainsayed.

The conclusion, therefore, to which these premises lead Her Majesty's Government is:

1. That no infringement ('attentorio') of the sovereign rights of Spain is intended or attempted by Her Majesty's Government.

2. That the proposition for which the Spanish Government contend is opposed to the authority of jurists, considered *numero vel pondere*.

3. That it is a part of the municipal law of Spain applicable to the subjects of that kingdom only, by virtue of its own legislation.

4. That wherever it has been extended to the subjects of other States, it has been necessary to embody it in the specific provisions of Treaties, entered into for limited periods.

5. That it is not competent to Spain, in this war with Chile, to alter the law of nations and treat any duly commissioned privateers as pirates, to the injury of the subjects of neutral States who, if found on board commissioned ships of either belligerent, are liable to be treated as prisoners of war, as serving under the Government which issued the commission, but not as robbers upon the high seas.

We have, &c.

(Signed) Roundell Palmer, R. P. Collier, Robert Phillimore

The Right Honble The Earl of Clarendon

VI

Lincolns Inn, 1st December 1865[1]

My Lord

We are honoured with Your Lordship's commands, signified in Mr Hammond's Letter of the 30th Ultimo, stating, that he was directed by Your Lordship to call our special attention to the 9th Article, respecting Privateers, of the instruction sent therewith for Spanish Cruizers in the present war with Chile, and to the interpretation or extension, stated to be given to that Article of the Instruction, by a Circular of the Spanish Minister of Marine, ordering the Commanders of Spanish Ships to treat as Pirates all Vessels of which the Captain, the Officers, and the majority of the Crew are not Chilians, or, who may not have received their Commission direct from the Chilian Government: and that Mr Hammond was pleased to request that we would acquaint Your Lordship, at our earliest convenience, whether such Instructions as are stated to have been issued by the Spanish Minister of Marine, as well as those issued by the Spanish Admiral, are consistent with the Law of Nations, and therefore to be acquiesced in by Foreign Governments, any of whose subjects may under them be proceeded against as Pirates.

1 F.O. 83/2373.

In obedience to Your Lordship's commands, we have taken this case into consideration, and have the honour to *Report*,

That we think both these Instructions are inconsistent with the Law of Nations; which has never regarded the enlistment of the subjects of one nation in the war-service of another, as piracy, and which draws no distinction between Commissions given direct by a belligerent Government, and Commissions given by persons acting as its Agents for that purpose, by its authority. We think, therefore, that these Instructions cannot properly be acquiesced in by Foreign Governments, any of whose subjects may, under them, be proceeded against as Pirates.

We have the honour to be, My Lord,
Your Lordship's most obedient, humble Servants,
ROUNDELL PALMER, R. P. COLLIER, ROBERT PHILLIMORE

To The Right Honble The Earl of Clarendon

VII

Lincolns Inn, 20th June 1866[1]

My Lord

We are honored with your commands, signified in Mr Hammond's letter of the 2nd of June, instant, stating, that he was directed by Your Lordship to transmit to us a copy and translation of a Despatch from the Spanish Minister for Foreign Affairs to the Spanish Minister in London, in reply to the Despatch, which, in accordance with our Report of the 21st of March, Your Lordship addressed to Her Majesty's Minister at Madrid, in regard to the intention of Spain to treat as Pirates, Chilian Privateers under certain conditions; and Mr Hammond was pleased to request, that we would take this Despatch into our consideration, and favor Your Lordship at our earliest convenience with our opinion thereon.

In obedience to Your Lordship's commands, we have taken this matter into consideration, and have the honor to *Report*

That it is apparent that the Spanish Minister is determined to persist in ascribing to certain commentators, on this branch of International Law, a meaning, which we think we have conclusively shown to be at variance alike with the general reasoning which pervades their treatises, and, with the particular passages, read with their legitimate context, which they contain. It would scarcely appear to us, that any advantage can accrue from the continuance of this controversy: more especially as the Spanish Minister is obliged to admit, that Martens, the most considerable of writers on this particular subject (and, it may be added, the least inclined to English expositions of International Law), maintains in the clearest terms, the opinion which Her Majesty's Government consider to be correct. But it may be as well to offer the following observations upon the general subject, in addition to those which we have already addressed to Your Lordship.

1 F.O. 83/2374.

There is a master fallacy, which appears to us to pervade the whole contention of the Spanish Minister: namely, That, because the Queen of England has by proclamation forbidden her subjects to take any part in the war, which Spain is now waging against Peru and Chile, England is not entitled to interfere on behalf of any of her subjects, if they, being found on board Peruvian or Chilian Privateers, are treated as Pirates by Spain. But the answer is obvious:

In the first place, the Law of Great Britain, with respect to her subjects, is municipal only; and the vindication of that law belongs to Her Majesty, and not to any foreign State: In the second place, it does not visit those who transgress it with the penalties of Piracy. Thirdly: Such persons do not cease to be Her Majesty's subjects, though engaged at a particular time in the service of either belligerent.

The Law of Spain, with respect to the character and composition of the Crews of Privateers, is municipal, and applicable to her own subjects only; but the crime of Piracy on the high seas is a matter of International Law; the character of which it is not competent to any individual State to vary: and Her Majesty is certainly entitled to protect her subjects from any arbitrary oppression, at variance with the principles of the law of nations, though they may have transgressed her command, by taking part with either belligerent. She is, therefore, entitled to protect them from the treatment of Pirates, when they ought to be treated only as Prisoners of War.

It is not contended, that England, or the United States of America, have ever allowed this new doctrine, that, without reference to the specific terms of any particular Treaty, it is competent to any one State to declare, that the fact of a particular number of foreigners being on board a Privateer, duly Commissioned, shall convert that legitimate Vessel of war into a Pirate, whom it is the duty of every one if possible to capture and destroy.

It is obvious to observe, among other objections to this novel proposition of International law, that any State might from time to time vary the number, or alter the composition of the crew, from which (and not from the Flag and Commission, as hitherto received according to the general maritime Law), it is now contended, that the character of a Vessel on the high seas is to be determined. Such has been the case in former days with respect to France, as we mentioned in our former Reports; and, so far as the subjects of that State were concerned, the Ordinance may have been perfectly legitimate; but it could have no effect upon the subjects of States not owing allegiance to Spain or France, in a place, like the high seas, where no one State has exclusive jurisdiction.

Lastly, it is of no avail to attack the general character of Privateers. It is competent to any State, which has not formally renounced the use of Privateers, to carry on at sea, as in the case of volunteers by land, public war, offensive or defensive, in some degree by the aid and instrumentality of the exertions of its private subjects. No Country has more fully recognized this right than Spain, and it might be, that otherwise a newly constituted State, like one of the South American Republics, might be absolutely defenceless against its enemy at Sea. But, be this as it may, it cannot be denied, that the present belligerents are entitled to have recourse to this ancient and recognized means of warfare; and, that being the case, it is no more competent to Spain to declare a duly commissioned Privateer to be a Pirate, because Foreigners constitute a certain portion of her Crew, than it would be competent to her to ascribe the same character, in the like circumstances, to a regular ship of war.

We have the honor to be, My Lord,
Your Lordship's most obedient, humble Servants
ROUNDELL PALMER, R. P. COLLIER, ROBERT PHILLIMORE

The Right Honorable The Earl of Clarendon

VIII

Temple, 17th April 1869[1]

My Lord

I am honoured with your Lordship's commands signified in Mr Hammond's letter of this days date, stating that he was directed by your Lordship to transmit to me a Despatch from Her Majesty's Consul General at Havana, enclosing a copy of a Decree issued by General Dulce, the Captain General of Cuba, with regard to vessels captured off the coast of that Island, having on board men, arms, ammunition or any article which could in any way contribute to the aid of the insurrection; and Mr Hammond was pleased to request that I would favour your Lordship with my immediate opinion on that Decree.

In obedience to your Lordship's commands I have the honor to *Report*.

That whatever warrant the Spanish authorities in Cuba may have in right of the territorial sovereignty to exclude from Spanish waters, under pain of death against the crews, all Foreign vessels, which are laden with supplies calculated to promote or encourage the insurrection, there can be no doubt that it will be a glaring violation of the Law of Nations, if they capture any such vessels on the High Seas, and treat the crews as Pirates.

I think your Lordship may properly lose no time in protesting against the enforcement of the edict against British vessels captured on the High Seas, and may properly represent to the Spanish Government, that Her Majesty's Government will regard with the deepest concern the enforcement of the edict against the crew of any British vessel captured within Spanish waters, where the crew has had no warning of its promulgation.

I have the honor to be, My Lord,
Your Lordship's most obedient, humble servant,
TRAVERS TWISS

The Right Honble The Earl of Clarendon

1 F.O. 83/2376.

IX

Temple, 24th July, 1873[1]

My Lord

We are honoured with your Lordship's commands, signified in Mr Hammond's letter of the 23rd inst. stating, that it appeared from a Telegram from Her Majesty's Chargé d'Affaires at Madrid, although imperfectly transmitted, that a large number of Spanish Ships of War have been declared by a Decree of the *de facto* Government of Madrid to be in a state, which has led to their being denounced as Pirates, and that by the same Decree the vessels of war of friendly Powers are authorized to treat them as such.

That he (Mr Hammond) was to enclose a copy of the telegram—No copy had yet been received of that decree; but as it is very probable that the vessels so denounced as Pirates may be met with at Sea by British Ships of War or may enter the waters of Gibraltar, your Lordship would be glad to receive our opinion at our earliest convenience, whether any and what instructions could properly be issued to Her Majesty's officers for the guidance of their conduct in such contingencies.

In obedience to your Lordship's commands we have the honor to Report.

That, in our opinion, Her Majesty's Government cannot properly take any action with respect to the Ships, which the Government at Madrid appears by the Telegram to have declared to be Pirates, and that Her Majesty's officers at sea and in the waters of Gibraltar may properly be instructed to conduct themselves towards such Ships of war as belonging to a Friendly Power.

We have the honor to be, My Lord,
Your Lordship's Most Obt, humble Servants,
(Signed) J. D. Coleridge, G. Jessel, J. P. Deane

The Rt. Hon. The Earl Granville

X

Temple, 4th Augt. 1873[2]

My Lord

We are honored with your Lordship's commands signified in Mr Hammond's letter of the 1st inst, stating, that he was directed by your Lordship to transmit to us therewith a Despatch from Her Majesty's Ambassador at Paris reporting a conversation with the Duc de Broglie on Spanish Affairs, and, with reference to that passage in it from which it appeared that the French Government considered that Foreign Powers had the right of treating the rebel Spanish Ships as Pirates; if they chose to do so, under the general Law of Nations, but not as a duty imposed upon them by the Spanish Government, he (Mr Hammond) was to request that we would

1 F.O. 83/2378. 2 Ibid.

favor your Lordship at our earliest convenience how far we agree with the opinion of the French Government.

In obedience to your Lordship's commands we have the honor to Report.

That we do not agree with the opinion of the French Government.

The Spanish rebel Ships are sailing under circumstances entirely different from those under which piratical vessels in the legal & well known sense of the term 'piratical' are found at Sea. The Spanish Rebel Ships have not committed and are not cruizing, with the intent to commit any act which a foreign nation can properly call or treat as a piratical act & needing therefore capture and punishment in the one case or seizure & detention in the other case.

These Spanish ships are manned by crews whose only alleged crime or offence is that they are in revolt against the Government at Madrid & in our opinion they cannot properly be visited or detained or seized unless the Government which orders or approves of such visit, detention or seizure is prepared to support the Government at Madrid against all persons and parties who may be in insurrection against that Government.

We have the honor to be etc.

J. D. Coleridge, G. Jessel, J. Parker Deane

The Rt. Hon. The Earl Granville

Part Four

PROBLEMS OF RECOGNITION

Chapter XIX

DE FACTO RECOGNITION, WITHDRAWAL OF RECOGNITION AND CONDITIONAL RECOGNITION

I. *DE FACTO* RECOGNITION

§ 95. *Recognition* de facto *as a Legal Act.* The subject of *de facto* recognition is a somewhat elusive topic of the law of recognition. There is no consensus of opinion as to its precise legal meaning. There are some who doubt whether, in law, it is at all distinguishable from *de jure* recognition. They regard it as a political nuance of the latter.[1] Some identify it with tacit recognition; others see its distinguishing feature in the circumstance that it results in an international capacity more limited than that following upon *de jure* recognition; others regard it as conditional, or provisional, or both; others consider its essential feature to lie in its revocability; others still reduce its effect to the absence of ordinary, or complete, diplomatic intercourse.[2]

We cannot hope to do justice to the question of *de facto* recognition unless we bear in mind: (*a*) that it is not a modern innovation but a frequent feature of the practice of States in the last century and a half; (*b*) that, far from constituting a mere diplomatic device of no other than political significance, it is a formal act the legal consequences and character-

1 Fischer Williams in *Hague Recueil*, vol. XLIV (1933) (ii), pp. 261, 262; Anzilotti, *Corso* (1934), p. 203; Knubben, *Die Subjekte des Völkerrechts* (1928), p. 340; Redslob in *R.I.* (Paris), vol. XIII (1934), p. 438.

2 The following is a selection from the literature on the subject of *de facto* recognition: Wiesse, *Le droit international appliqué aux guerres civiles* (1898), pp. 237–43; Rougier, *Les guerres civiles et le droit des gens* (1903), pp. 478–560; Spiropoulos, *Die de facto Regierung im Völkerrecht* (1926); Noël-Henry, *Les gouvernements de fait devant le juge* (1927); Kunz, pp. 50–3, 132–69; Stille, *Die Rechtstellung der de facto Regierung in der englischen und amerikanischen Rechtsprechung* (1932); Schlüter, *De facto Anerkennung im Völkerrecht* (1936); Hershey in *A.J.* vol. XIV (1920), pp. 499–518; Larnaude in *R.G.* vol. XXVIII (1921), pp. 457–503; Podesta Costa, ibid. vol. XXIX (1922), pp. 47 et seq.; Baty in *Yale Law Journal*, vol. XXXI (1922), pp. 469–88; Dickinson in *Michigan Law Review*, vol. XXII (1923), pp. 29–45, 118–34; Briggs in *A.J.* vol. XXXIII (1939), pp. 689–99.

istics of which clearly distinguish it from recognition *de jure*; (*c*) that it must not be confused with informal intercourse, even when accompanied by an exchange of agents and representatives not amounting to and not intended as recognition. For these reasons, which will be here considered in some detail, *de facto* recognition has a distinct place in the law of recognition and must be treated accordingly. In particular, it must be remembered that both *de facto* and *de jure* recognition are legal acts. They are convenient abbreviations for 'recognition as a *de facto* Government (or State)' and 'recognition as a *de jure* Government (or State)'—'*de facto*' and '*de jure*' being, in this connection, terms expressive not of any judgment upon the legitimacy of the recognized authority from the point of view of the constitutional law of the State concerned, but upon its claim to be considered as validly and effectively representing the State or territory in question in the field of international law. It is possible that the customary and convenient abbreviation—recognition *de jure* and recognition *de facto*—has been responsible for obscuring the legal nature of *de facto* recognition and for relegating the distinction between *de jure* and *de facto* recognition to the province of politics. In so far as recognition is of interest for international law it must be an act intended or calculated to give rise to legal rights and obligations. This applies to both '*de jure*' and '*de facto*' recognition.[1]

§ 96. *The Practice of States and* de facto *Recognition*. The exigencies of international life, especially those relating to the different aspects of recognition, do not admit of simple and categorical solutions. It is tempting to invoke formal logic and to say: A State, or a government, or a belligerent either does exist or does not; *tertium non datur*.[2] Such logic may or may not be deceptive. The practice of States does admit of legally relevant degrees of recognition.

The beginning of *de facto* recognition may be traced back to the first quarter of the nineteenth century when the secession of the Latin-American Republics confronted Great Britain and other States with the problem of reconciling the practical necessity of recognition with the legitimist pretensions of Spain and Portugal. The solution was found in a measure of *de facto* recognition, the distinguishing feature of which was that it did not

1 See, to the same effect, Verdross in *Strupp's Wörterbuch*, vol. I, p. 51, and in *Verfassung der Völkerrechtsgemeinschaft* (1926), p. 140; Fedozzi, *Trattato di diritto internazionale*, vol. I (1933), p. 194; Brierly, *The Law of Nations* (3rd ed. 1942), p. 107; McNair, *Legal Effect of War* (2nd ed. 1944), p. 353, n. 1; Redslob in *R.I.* vol. XIII (1934), p. 438.

2 For an outspoken rejection of *de facto* recognition see Dr Baty's remarks in *Yale Law Journal*, vol. XXXI (1921–2), p. 470.

purport to express an attitude with regard to the legal merits of the claim to independence and to the title of the parent State. Canning, his predecessors, and his immediate successors, spoke of recognition *de facto* in this sense.[1] It is with reference to *de facto* recognition thus conceived that Phillimore asserts that the 'virtual and *de facto* Recognition of a new State gives no just cause of offence to the old State, inasmuch as it decides nothing concerning the asserted rights of the latter'.[2] He identifies *de facto* recognition with virtual recognition, e.g. with the recognition of the commercial flag and the appointment of consuls to the new State.

In the further course of the nineteenth century, while frequent reference is made to '*de facto* governments', there appear to be no clear instances of *de facto* recognition. Repeated pronouncements of the government of the United States use the expression '*de facto* governments', but only in order to emphasize the practice of the United States to grant full recognition to '*de facto* governments' once they have been firmly established in accordance with the will of the nation.[3] In the words of the instructions sent in 1829 by Mr Van Buren, Secretary of State: 'So far as we are concerned, that

1 See, for example, a Memorandum, approved in 1822 by the British Cabinet, in which a clear distinction was drawn between three kinds of recognition in relation to the Latin-American Republics:

'1st. The Recognition, *de facto*, which now substantially subsists;

'2ndly. The more formal Recognition by diplomatic agents;

'3rdly. The Recognition, *de jure*, which professes to decide upon the title and thereby to create a certain impediment to the assertion of the rights of the former occupant.'

The view was expressed that while there was no doubt that the first kind of recognition had already been granted, there was no occasion to commit Great Britain as to the third. The question to be decided was how far the second kind of recognition was to be granted. (Earl Bathurst to the Duke of Wellington, 14 September 1822: Webster, *Britain and the Independence of Latin America*, 1812–1830, vol. II (1938), p. 71.) For another example of dialectical skill on the same lines see Wellington's *Observations* on a circular despatch sent in 1824 to British representatives abroad and printed in Webster, op. cit. vol. II, p. 141, n. 1. See also Canning's speech of 14 June 1824, printed in *The Speeches of the Right Honourable George Canning*, ed. by Therry (2nd ed. 1830), vol. I, pp. 294–302. He spoke of the extent of the commerce between Great Britain and the Spanish colonies which led to 'another *de facto* recognition of their separate political existence', namely, the recognition of their commercial flag. Yet a learned writer has spoken of '*de facto* States' as 'a phenomenon of this illogical twentieth century' and as a 'bastard institution' of recent times (Baty in *A.J.* vol. XXX (1936), p. 378).

2 *Commentaries upon International Law* (3rd ed. 1879–88), vol. II, p. 23. Wiesse, op. cit. p. 237, sees the distinguishing feature of *de facto* recognition in the circumstance that it does not imply the affirmation of the legitimacy of the new government from the point of view of the constitutional law of the State concerned. Recognition, he says, means merely that the government is the actual repository of authority and that it possesses the means to make it effective.

3 For some instances see Moore, vol. I, pp. 142, 148, 156. And see above, p. 125.

which is the Government *de facto* is equally so *de jure*.'[1] Pending such recognition it was the general practice to maintain unofficial relations, for the protection of nationals and otherwise. But these did not amount to and were not intended as recognition. It was only in the first and second decades of the twentieth century that there took place the adoption, especially by the United States, of the practice of *de facto* recognition conceived as formal though provisional recognition of an authority actually in power but not considered to fulfil all conditions of recognition because of doubts as to its permanency or for other reasons. In the case of Panama the United States formally granted recognition *de facto* on 6 November 1903, within three days of the Panamanian declaration of independence. Full recognition was granted a week later.[2] Probably the circumstances surrounding this event preclude it from being regarded as an instructive precedent. This cannot be said of the formal recognition of the revolutionary Government of General Carranza by the United States and other States on 19 October 1915. On that day the United States, acting in concert with a number of American Republics, 'extended recognition to the *de facto* Government of Mexico' of which General Carranza was the Chief Executive.[3] The recognition was preceded by elaborate and exhaustive investigation and by consultation between the United States, Brazil, Chile, Argentina, Bolivia, Uruguay and Guatemala. The representatives of those Governments, acting in conference, found that 'the Carrancista party is the only party possessing the essentials for recognition as the *de facto* government of Mexico'.[4] In December 1915, Great Britain, after consultation with the United States, recognized the Mexican Government *de facto*[5]—a step which, in that period, never reached the stage of recognition *de jure*.[6] The *de facto* recognition thus granted was accompanied by an intimation that the United States was willing to receive and to accredit diplomatic representatives. It was not until two years later that full *de jure* recognition was granted.[7]

The events which accompanied the rise of a number of new States after the First World War and the uncertainty as to their future position and territorial extent gave a new impetus to the practice of recognition *de*

1 Moore, vol. I, p. 137. 2 Ibid. vol. V, p. 55. 3 *U.S. For. Rel.* 1915, p. 771.

4 Hackworth, vol. I, p. 260. For an account of the circumstances preceding the recognition see Finch in *A.J.* vol. X (1916), pp. 357–67. See also *Annual Register*, 1915, p. 347. In *Oetjen* v. *Central Leather Company* the Supreme Court took 'judicial note of the fact that...the Government of the United States recognized the Government of Carranza as the *de facto* government of the Republic of Mexico on 19 October 1915, and as the *de jure* government on 31 August 1917' ((1918) 246 U.S. 301).

5 See statements in the House of Commons on 2 and 8 November 1915, *H.C. Debates*, vol. LXXV, cols. 482 and 1042.

6 See below, p. 345. 7 *U.S. For. Rel.* 1917, pp. 938, 943.

facto. The governments of the new States which established themselves within the territories of the Austro-Hungarian Monarchy and of Russia were in the first instance recognized *de facto*. The majority of them—Poland, Czechoslovakia, and the Baltic States—were subsequently recognized *de jure*. With regard to others—Armenia, Georgia, and Azerbaijan[1]—recognition *de facto* never matured into recognition *de jure* for the reason that the inhabitants of those territories did not succeed in establishing themselves as independent States.[2] The provisional character of recognition *de facto* is shown by a survey of the British instruments of *de facto* recognition in that period. In the case of *The Gagara* the British Government informed the Court that it had 'for the time being provisionally, and with all necessary reservations as to the future, recognized the Esthonian National Council as a *de facto* independent body, and accordingly has received a certain gentleman as the informal representative of the provisional Government'. It was added that 'the state of affairs is of necessity provisional and transitory'.[3] With regard to Latvia the British

1 In January 1920 the Supreme Council of the Allied Powers decided that the Governments of those States should be recognized as *de facto* Governments on condition that that step in no way prejudged the question of their eventual frontiers (*U.S. For. Rel.* 1920 (III), pp. 775–8).

2 In a communication of the United States Department of State it was stated, in January 1934, that 'the recognition which the United States accorded in 1920 to the "*de facto* Government of the Armenian Republic" is no longer effective since the Armenian Republic has ceased to exist as an independent State' (Hackworth, vol. I, p. 222). In the unratified Treaty of Peace of Sèvres Turkey recognized Armenia *de jure* (Martens, *N.R.G.* 3rd ser. vol. XX, p. 664).

3 [1919] P. 95. The recognition *de facto* was expressed in the following letter to the Esthonian representatives of 3 May 1918:

'I have the honour to acknowledge the receipt of your letter enclosing a memorandum on the political situation of Esthonia, and asking for recognition from His Majesty's Government.

'It gave me much pleasure to receive your recent visit, and I take this opportunity of assuring you that His Majesty's Government greet with sympathy the aspirations of the Esthonian people and are glad to reaffirm their readiness to grant provisional recognition to the Esthonian National Council as a *de facto* independent body, until the peace conference takes place, when the future status of Esthonia ought to be settled so far as possible in accordance with the wishes of the population. It would obviously be impossible for His Majesty's Government at the present time to guarantee to Esthonia the right to participate at the peace conference, but at any such conference His Majesty's Government will do their utmost to secure that the above principle is applied in Esthonia.

'In the meantime His Majesty's Government will be glad to receive Professor Antonius Piip as the informal diplomatic representative of the Esthonian provisional government' (*U.S. For. Rel.* 1918, *Russia*, vol. II, p. 829). At the same time Esthonia was informed of the French decision 'à reconnaître provisoirement le Conseil national Esthonien comme une organisation indépendante de fait jusqu'à ce que la Conférence de la Paix permette d'établir définitivement le statut futur de l'Esthonie, conformément au vœu de la population' (see De Visscher in *R.I.* 3rd ser. vol. III (1922), p. 152).

Government announced on 11 November 1918, that 'His Majesty's Government has expressed its readiness to grant provisional recognition to the Lettish National Council as a *de facto* government until such time as the Peace Conference comes to a decision in regard to the future of Lettland. In the meantime His Majesty's Government has agreed to receive Mr Meierovics as the informal diplomatic representative in Great Britain of the Lettish Provisional Government'.[1] On 24 September 1919 an announcement was made of the provisional recognition by the British Government of the Lithuanian Government as a *de facto* independent body.

In these and similar cases the expedient of *de facto* recognition was adopted owing to the uncertainty of the situation pending the absence of a definite settlement. Most of the governments in question were effective, for the time being, in their territories. But there was, in the circumstances, no guarantee of the permanence of their rule. Russia, the parent State, lay shattered in the throes of revolutionary convulsion. It was thought that she was only temporarily incapable of resisting by force the creation of the new States, and that there was no legal basis for definitely recognizing the new States as independent of their mother State at a time when the legal capacity of the latter was suspended. It appears, in particular, from contemporaneous pronouncements of the authorities of the United States that the revival of a Federalist Russia, with her territory largely unimpaired, was considered to be a distinct possibility.[2] Recognition *de facto* afforded a convenient solution of the difficulty. A measure of recognition as a *de facto* government was also granted by the United States, in the concluding stages of the First World War, to the Czechoslovak National Council.[3]

1 The French formula of recognition was on the same lines: '...le gouvernement français reconnaissait provisoirement l'existence de fait de l'Etat indépendant de Latvie, en attendant que les Puissances alliées eussent pu résoudre, de concert, la question de droit' (Lagarde, *La reconnaissance du gouvernement des Soviets* (1924), p. 20, n. 1).

2 See, for a review of the various acts of recognition of these countries by the United States, Hackworth, vol. I, § 37; *U.S. For. Rel.* 1918, *Russia*, vol. II, pp. 841, 851; 1920 (III), p. 463. See also, as to Latvia, Laserson in *A.J.* vol. XXXVII (1943), pp. 233–47. As to Esthonia, see Heumann, *Aspects juridiques de l'indépendance estonienne* (1938). As to Finland see Hackworth, vol. I, § 41, and Graham, *Diplomatic Recognition of Border States*, Part I: *Finland* (1936).

3 But only a measure. It appears that on 3 September 1918, the United States accorded recognition to the Czechoslovak National Council as a '*de facto* belligerent government clothed with proper authority to direct the military and political affairs of the Czechoslovaks' (Hackworth, vol. I, p. 206). It is doubtful whether this amounted to recognition as a *de facto* government in the accepted sense. As late as 14 February 1919, the American Secretary of State doubted whether 'any further act of recognition of the Czechoslovak Republic' was desirable at that time in view of the fact that the frontiers of that State had not yet been definitely determined (ibid. p. 208). In general, it is of interest to note that although, with regard to the Czechoslovak and

The manner of the recognition of the Government of Soviet Russia in 1920 and in subsequent years provides a further illustration of the wide adoption of the expedient of *de facto* recognition. A number of States which recognized the Soviet Government did so in the first instance by way of *de facto* recognition in a series of provisional agreements.[1] In some of those agreements the *de facto* character of the recognition was emphasized by being expressly distinguished from *de jure* recognition.[2] In some cases the parties attached practical consequences to the circumstance that only *de facto* recognition had been given. Thus Article II of the Danish-Russian Preliminary Agreement of 23 April 1923 provided that, except in exchange for corresponding compensation, Denmark shall not be entitled to claim the special privileges granted by Russia to States which had recognized or may recognize her *de jure*.[3]

Polish representative bodies in the course of the First World War, the term 'recognition' was used in various connotations, they were not recognized either by Great Britain or by France as governments, either *de facto* or *de jure*. See above, p. 164. The limited recognition given by the United States to the Czechoslovak forces as a co-belligerent army and to the Czechoslovak Council as a government directing that army cannot, within its limited scope, be regarded as an improper exercise of the power of recognition. For while the effectiveness of that authority, exercising responsible control over organized military forces, did not extend to its national territory, it was not, within its limited sphere, a pure pretension. For this reason the recognition given to the Czechoslovak National Council in 1918 may be put on a higher plane than that of a 'form of belligerent activity' as suggested by Hyde, vol. I, § 40. See also Hobza in *R.G.* vol. XXIX (1922), pp. 387, 388, and Buza in *Z.V.* vol. XIII (1924), pp. 114, 155. For the texts of the successive acts of recognition of the Czechoslovak and Polish authorities in 1918 see Hackworth, vol. I, §§ 39, 44; *U.S. For. Rel.* 1918, Suppl. I, vol. I, pp. 813–51, 878–81; Smith, vol. I, pp. 234–7.

1 These will be found in *A.J.* vol. XXVIII (1934), p. 97. See also Appendix XXIV in Taracouzio, *The Soviet Union and International Law* (1935); and see ibid. pp. 173–5. And see Toynbee, *Survey of International Affairs*, 1924, pp. 228–62.

2 In Article I of the Provisional Treaty of Commerce, of 5 June 1922, between Czechoslovakia and Russia the parties stated expressly that the Treaty did not prejudice the question of recognition *de jure* (Martens, *N.R.G.* 3rd ser. vol. XVIII, p. 643).

3 Martens, *N.R.G.* 3rd ser. vol. XIV, p. 415. Similar provisions appeared in Articles IV, VII, VIII and IX of the Agreement. In June 1924 Denmark informed the Russian Government that it was extending recognition *de jure* and claimed simultaneously the concession of most-favoured-nation treatment in accordance with Article II of the Agreement of 1924. In reply the Russian Government stated that it felt compelled to limit the most-favoured-nation treatment to States which had recognized the Union *de jure* on or before 14 February 1924—a somewhat unilateral interpretation. For the exchange of correspondence see Martens, *N.R.G.* 3rd ser. vol. XXIV, pp. 868–71. When, on 15 December 1925, Norway recognized the Russian Government *de jure*, by means of a comprehensive Treaty of Commerce and Navigation, the Treaty provided, in Article 32, that, subject to comprehensive exceptions, the stipulations of the Treaty would not apply to rights and privileges accorded to States which had recognized the Russian Government *de jure* before 15 February 1924 (Martens, *N.R.G.* 3rd ser. vol. XXVI, p. 472).

In the course of the international crisis brought about by the invasion and annexation of Abyssinia by Italy in the years 1935 and 1936, recognition *de facto* once more played a prominent part. The Italian rule over Abyssinia was recognized by a number of States, in the first instance, *de facto* only; recognition *de jure* followed at a later date.[1] The recourse to recognition *de facto* was, in this case, the result not of any uncertainty as to the effectiveness or even of the permanence of the conquest. It was due to the belief that the new situation was brought about by means contrary to international law and that it did not, therefore, in itself afford an adequate basis for acquisition, *de jure*, of a legal title.

Finally, in the grave international situation which arose out of the Spanish Civil War in the years 1936–9 recognition *de facto* once more played a prominent part. Thus the revolutionary (Nationalist) Government of Spain under General Franco was originally recognized by Great Britain as a government (or 'insurgent government'[2] or 'nationalist government'[3]) exercising '*de facto* administrative control over the larger portion of Spain'.[4] After the decision had to all appearances been reached in the civil war, the revolutionary Government was recognized *de jure*.

§ 97. *The Meaning of the Distinction between* de jure *and* de facto *Recognition*. It has been shown that *de facto* recognition has been repeatedly resorted to in difficult international situations and that, whatever may be its merits, it must now be regarded as firmly established in international practice. This being so, what is the meaning of *de facto* recognition as distinguished from *de jure*? In the first instance it ought to be clearly understood that the distinction between *de jure* and *de facto* recognition is altogether unrelated to the question of the legality, from the point of view of internal constitutional law, of the new State or government. When

1 In particular by Great Britain and France. Since December 1936 Great Britain recognized the Italian Government as the Government *de facto* of the parts of Abyssinia under its control. See below, pp. 418, 432. For a series of statements of the British Government on the subject see *Parl. Debates*, House of Commons, 17 March 1938, vol. CCCXXXIII, cols. 617–18, and 11 May 1938, vol. CCCXXXV, cols. 1608–9. See also Rousseau, *Le conflit italo-ethiopien devant le droit international* (1938), pp. 237–51. In January 1938, the Queen of Holland, while drawing attention to the necessity of taking into account the fact of military occupation of Abyssinia, assured the Emperor Haile Selassie that 'Her Government had no intention of proceeding to recognition *de jure*' (*Documents on International Affairs*, 1938, vol. I, p. 252).

2 As stated in the certificate of the Foreign Office in *Banco de Bilbao* v. *Rey*, [1938] 2 K.B. 176. See below, p. 365.

3 As stated in *Compañia Naviera Sota y Azner* v. *Ramón de la Sota*, below, p. 365.

4 *The Arantzazu Mendi*, [1938] P. 233; [1939] P. 37; [1939] A.C. 256. See above, p. 279.

therefore a State or government is recognized as being *de facto* or *de jure*, the distinction refers not to any conformity with the internal law of the State but to the requirements of international law. Some writers define a *de jure* government as one which has come into power in conformity with the constitution of the State;[1] while a *de facto* government is, according to that definition, one which has come into power in disregard of the constitutional provisions but which effectively exercises power over the entire territory of the State. That definition may be useful for some purposes, but it is not easy to see what is its relevance for the purpose of recognition in international law. Does it mean that only the *first* effective revolutionary government is a *de facto* government and that its successors, which come into power in pursuance of the constitution adopted under the aegis of the new constitutional regime, are *de jure* governments? This would reduce the definition to a mere technicality. If, on the other hand, we extend the requirement of legitimacy of origin not only to the government originally responsible for the breach of the constitution, but also to its successors, then clearly no government can properly be described as being *de jure*. Each of them is based on a constitution which, in a more or less distant past, owes its origin to a revolution. In 1921 the British Government recognized the Soviet Government as the *de facto* Government of Russia. In 1924 it formally recognized that Government as the *de jure* Government of Russia. What happened in the intervening period to make possible a change in the situation? The origin of the Soviet Government was as unconstitutional in 1924 as it was in 1921. Neither could the change in the character of the recognition be explained by the disappearance of any doubts as to the stability of the new Government. The position of the Soviet Government was no more precarious in 1921 than it was in 1924. The origin of the revolutionary Government of General Franco in Spain was no more legitimate in 1939, when it was recognized *de jure*, than it was in 1937, when it was merely recognized *de facto*.

The unhelpfulness of the attempt to base the distinction between *de jure* and *de facto* recognition on considerations of the municipal law of the State concerned is even more apparent in the case of recognition of new States or of annexation of old States as in the case of Abyssinia. The recognition *de jure* of the Italian annexation of Abyssinia in 1938 had, when contrasted

1 For a clear expression, from this point of view, of the opinion that the characterization of a government as *de jure* or *de facto* is a matter solely for the constitutional law of the State concerned, see the Opinion of the French-Mexican Mixed Claims Commission in *Georges Pinson Claim* (*Annual Digest*, 1927–8, Case no. 136 (at p. 204)). See also the award of President Taft in *Great Britain* v. *Costa Rica* (ibid. 1923–4, Case no. 15 (at p. 37)).

with the recognition *de facto* which preceded it, no meaning if related to the municipal law of either Italy or Abyssinia. These considerations show that unless we direct our attention to a province other than the municipal law of the State in question we are not likely to benefit by the accepted explanations of *de facto* recognition such, for instance, as that given by Mountague Bernard, adopted by Wheaton,[1] and frequently relied upon in judicial decisions:[2] 'A *de jure* government is one which, in the opinion of the person using the phrase, *ought to possess the powers of sovereignty*, though at the time it may be deprived of them. A *de facto* government is one which is really in possession of them, although the possession may be wrongful or precarious.' What is meant by saying that a government is *de jure* if it 'ought to possess the powers of sovereignty'? Ought it to possess them as a matter of municipal or of international law? It has been shown that only the latter alternative supplies a satisfactory explanation of the distinction between *de jure* and *de facto* recognition. Recognition *de facto* takes place when, in the opinion of the recognizing State, notwithstanding the presence of the principal condition of recognition, namely, that of effectiveness, there are absent other conditions of recognition which, in the opinion of the State in question, are required by international law. The result is—and this is the essential feature of *de facto* recognition—that for the time being recognition thus granted must be regarded as provisional and liable to withdrawal in case the prospect of those conditions being fulfilled should finally disappear. It is in this sense that *de facto* recognition must be regarded as revocable—'revocable' meaning not 'revocable at will' but on account of supervening or continued absence of the conditions of recognition as laid down by international law.

The recognition *de facto* of the Soviet Government in 1921 provides a good example of this aspect of recognition. The effectiveness of that Government was not in question. Popular approval was, at that time, ceasing to be a test of recognition possessing any degree of reality. When Great Britain concluded on 16 March 1921 a Trade Agreement with Soviet Russia, the British Government treated it as an agreement 'recognizing the Soviet Government as the *de facto* Government of Russia'.[3] The British Prime Minister stated that 'They [the Soviet Government] have as complete control over that vast territory as any Government could possibly have under present conditions, and therefore they have to

1 *International Law* (5th English ed. 1916), p. 36.

2 See, for example, *Luther* v. *Sagor*, [1921] 3 K.B. 532, at p. 543.

3 The Prime Minister in the House of Commons on 22 March 1921 (*H.C. Debates*, vol. CXXXIX, col. 2506).

be recognized as the *de facto* Government of that Empire.'[1] But recognition *de jure* was withheld and was not granted until 1 February 1924. The reason, generally adduced, for the refusal of *de jure* recognition was the unwillingness of the Soviet Government to give assurances as to the fulfilment of its international obligations with regard to the liabilities of its predecessors and its own conduct in such matters as confiscation of foreign property and revolutionary propaganda abroad.[2]

Effectiveness—either in its literal sense or as evidenced by an adequate expression of popular consent[3]—of power within the territory of the State is an essential and the principal condition of recognition both of States and of governments. However, in practice other conditions have often been regarded as essential. Some of these, such as a reasonable prospect of permanency and stability (in the case of new governments) or the final and apparently irrevocable defeat of the pretensions of the parent State (in the case of the rise of new States), are generally admitted.[4] Others, such as the free acceptance of the new regime by the majority of the population, or the ability or willingness to fulfil international obligations, although more controversial and, occasionally, less capable of supplying a working test of recognition, have nevertheless found a place in the practice of States.[5] They have often been acted upon not as a matter of political bargaining and convenience, but as representing, in the view of recognizing States, proper conditions of recognition as laid down by international law. The government of an established State or of a new State may for the time being be in full exercise of effective power within its territory without, however,

1 Ibid.

2 See above, p. 110. Sir Frederick Pollock, in a valuable contribution—in *The Times* newspaper, 4 February 1924—to the subject, dealt squarely with some of the difficulties inherent in the question. He defined as a government *de jure* one which either derives its power by succession under the constitution or custom of the land (a definition which is clearly provisional inasmuch as few governments, if any, derive their legal power in an unbroken chain of continuity from the original constitution) or one 'which had not a legal origin, but has acquired the consent of the governed by express ratification, such as, in our time, a popular vote, or by general acquiescence coupled with the absence of any effective adverse claim'. The latter possibility was, apparently, intended to cover the case of the recognition *de jure* of Soviet Russia in 1924, but it is doubtful whether the explanation really covered the case at issue. For the degree of general acquiescence in the Soviet regime was probably not higher in 1924 than in 1921 when merely recognition *de facto* had been granted. General acquiescence is a good reason for granting *de facto* recognition; it does not explain *de jure* recognition. The latter has a meaning only as a term of international law, namely, as a declaration that in the view of the recognizing State there are present all the conditions of recognition as required by international law.

3 See above, pp. 115 et seq.

4 See above, pp. 8, 9, 88, 158.

5 See above, pp. 109 et seq., 115 et seq.

fulfilling all or some of the other conditions. It may be maintained that so long as those other conditions have not been complied with there can be no recognition at all, and that full recognition or complete refusal of recognition are the only alternatives. But the necessities of international intercourse do not favour any such rigid dichotomy. They demand that as soon as the most important condition is fulfilled—namely, that of effectiveness—its consequences should be admitted by an appropriate act of recognition. This is the purpose of *de facto* recognition. It is a declaration that the body claiming to be the government of an established or a new State actually wields effective authority without, however, satisfying other conditions of full, *de jure*, recognition. Should these remaining conditions be forthcoming, full recognition *de jure* will become a matter of course; should they remain permanently absent, recognition will lapse automatically or will be finally and expressly withdrawn.[1]

To explain the meaning of *de facto* recognition as being due to the absence of requisite conditions of recognition other than effectiveness is not necessarily to maintain, at least with regard to recognition of States and governments, that it is a sound and unavoidable expedient. The principal and probably the only essential condition of recognition of States and governments is effectiveness of power within the State and of actual independence of other States. Other conditions are irrelevant to the true

1 Liability to withdrawal seems to have been regarded by the Court as the essential feature of the *de facto* recognition which Great Britain had extended to Esthonia: 'I read the letters of the Foreign Office as being statements which do recognize, and recognize to the full, the sovereignty of Esthonia; but with the limitation that under the exceptional conditions due to the setting up of the Peace Conference no undertaking could be given to continue the recognition if conditions altered' (*The Gagara*, [1919] P. 95 at p. 103). Strupp, in *Theorie und Praxis des Völkerrechts* (1925), p. 19, and in *Recueil des Cours*, vol. XLVII (1934) (i), p. 451, considers limitation of international capacity to be an essential feature of recognition *de facto*. So also does Fedozzi, *Trattato di diritto internazionale* (2nd ed. 1933), p. 194. But see Spiropoulos, *Théorie générale du droit international* (1930), p. 137. Probably the limitations of the international rights of the State or government which has been recognized *de facto* are one of the consequences of the limited nature of such recognition; they are not in themselves the *differentia specifica* distinguishing *de facto* and *de jure* recognition. This seems to be the view of Strupp in *Recueil des Cours*, vol. XLVII (1934) (i), p. 449, and Liszt, *Völkerrecht* (12th ed. by Fleischmann, 1925), p. 9. See, for a discussion of this question, Scalfati, pp. 239–52. See also Erich in *Recueil des Cours*, vol. XIII (1926) (iii), p. 486; Kunz, pp. 50–3, 132–4. Some, like Fauchille, p. 325, regard recognition *de facto* as synonymous with tacit recognition. Actually, tacit (or implied) recognition may be either *de jure* or *de facto*. There are interesting observations by Chief Justice Chase in *Thorington* v. *Smith* ((1868) 8 Wallace, 1, 8–10; Moore, vol. 1, p. 41) and in *Williams* v. *Bruffy* ((1877) 96 U.S. 176, 185–6) on the meaning of a *de facto* government, but these, although often quoted in this connection, are not germane to the issue of *de facto* recognition.

purpose and nature of recognition. This means that, on sound principle, an effective government is entitled to recognition not only *de facto* but also *de jure*—'effectiveness' in this connection meaning either effectiveness of power pure and simple regardless of any adequately expressed acquiescence of the population or, perhaps more accurately, effectiveness based on popular consent which alone, as a rule, provides evidence of permanence. However, that principle of recognition has not yet become fully part of accepted practice and to that extent *de facto* recognition seems to be a necessary expedient, especially in cases when effectiveness is not accompanied by a reasonably assured prospect of stability. On the other hand, there would seem to be full scope for *de facto* recognition in situations where conditions other than effectiveness of power are a legitimate consideration. This applies in particular to recognition of a new international title which has its origin in an international wrong, as was the case of the Italian annexation of Abyssinia in 1936. In such cases *de facto* recognition, which takes into account the actuality of power while expressly refusing to admit its legality in the field of international law, is a proper device for combining disapproval of illegal action with the requirements of international intercourse. But when preceded by the acceptance of an obligation of non-recognition, it is a legitimate device only so long as we bear in mind that the difference between *de jure* and *de facto* recognition is one of substance and so long as *de facto* recognition is not used for the purpose of avoiding any obligation of non-recognition that may have been undertaken.[1]

§ 98. *Legal Effects of* de facto *Recognition as distinguished from* de jure *Recognition*. It is occasionally maintained that the difference between *de facto* and *de jure* recognition is purely political, which is probably intended to mean that for the purposes of municipal and international law there is no difference between *de jure* and *de facto* recognition.[2] Having regard to the function which, as shown above, *de facto* recognition fulfils in the present stage of international organization, that view cannot easily be accepted. Neither is it a view which finds support in judicial practice. Undoubtedly, in the decisions of English and American courts recognition *de facto* has been treated for some purposes as having the same legal consequences as recognition *de jure*. Thus it is now an established rule that States and governments recognized *de facto* enjoy full jurisdictional im-

1 See below, p. 433.

2 See, for example, Brierly, *The Law of Nations* (2nd ed. 1936), p. 110—a view which has been modified in the third edition (1942), pp. 107, 109; McNair, *Legal Effects of War* (2nd ed. 1944), p. 353, who suggests that the 'distinction is mainly, if not entirely, political'. See also above, p. 340, n. 1.

munities[1]—a rule which commends itself for its soundness seeing that in the present state of opinion on the subject the assumption of jurisdiction over a foreign State or government is incompatible with normal international intercourse (the extent of which is essentially the same in both kinds of recognition) and as such is calculated to cause international friction. For this reason courts in the United States have, perhaps somewhat illogically, extended such immunity, in some respects, to governments which have not been recognized at all.[2] It has also been held repeatedly that there is no distinction between *de jure* and *de facto* recognition for the purpose of acknowledging the validity of the internal acts, legislative and others, of the recognized authority—a principle clearly following from the admitted effective existence of the State or government in question.[3] Moreover, in an authoritative case English courts have conceded jurisdictional immunity to a *de facto* government against the *de jure* government of the same State—a decision which, it is submitted, is open to question.[4] But otherwise courts have shown no disposition to assimilate generally *de jure* and *de facto* recognition—even in cases in which, in the issue directly before the court, the distinction was ignored.

Thus in *Luther* v. *Sagor*—a case which frequently, though inaccurately, has been referred to as an authority for the view that there are no legal consequences attaching to the distinction between *de jure* and *de facto* recognition—an attempt was made, on the part of the respondents, to draw a distinction between *de jure* and *de facto* recognition in respect of retroactivity of recognition. It was maintained on behalf of the respondents that only *de jure* recognition could have a retroactive effect. The Court rejected that view. But neither Bankes L.J. nor Warrington L.J., who dealt with this point, committed themselves to the opinion that there was no distinction at all between *de facto* and *de jure* recognition. The former said: 'For some purposes no doubt a distinction can be drawn between the effect of the recognition by a sovereign State of the one form of government or of the other, but for the present purpose in my opinion no distinction can be drawn.'[5] Similarly, Warrington L.J. was of the opinion

1 *The Gagara*, [1919] P. 95.

2 *Wulfsohn* v. *Russian Socialist Federated Soviet Republic*, 234 N.Y. 372, and other cases cited above, p. 149.

3 *Luther* v. *Sagor*, [1921] 3 K.B. 532. See above, p. 284. In *Oetjen* v. *Central Leather Company*—(1918) 246 U.S. 302—the language of the Supreme Court seems to have confined the operation of the principle of retroactivity to governments recognized *de jure*, but it is probable that that apparent limitation was not intentional.

4 *The Arantzazu Mendi* (pp. 290 et seq. above).

5 [1921] 3 K.B. 532, at p. 543.

that 'there is no difference for the present purpose between a government recognized as such *de jure* and one recognized *de facto*'.[1]

That there exists a substantial difference between the two kinds of recognition is shown by the decision in the case of *Haile Selassie* v. *Cable and Wireless, Limited* (no. 2).[2] In this case, at a time when Great Britain had recognized the Government of Italy as the *de facto* Government of Ethiopia, Italy claimed to be the successor to the rights of the Emperor of Ethiopia and as such entitled to certain sums owed to the latter by the defendant Company. An attempt was made to rely on the decision in *Luther* v. *Sagor* as an authority for the view that as there is, in law, no distinction between *de jure* and *de facto* recognition, the accepted rules of State succession operated with the effect of depriving the Emperor of Ethiopia of his title and of vesting it in Italy. The Court rejected that view. It held that the decision in *Luther* v. *Sagor* and similar cases had reference only to the validity of the internal acts of the recognized authority and that it had no bearing on the question of State succession. As the Emperor of Ethiopia continued to be recognized as the *de jure* sovereign of Ethiopia, he was entitled to judgment.[3] It is a legitimate inference from the principle acted upon in this case, as well, generally, as from the practice of States, that the government which is recognized *de jure* is entitled, as against the *de facto* government, to continued title in and control of the property of the State situated abroad such as legation buildings, archives, and so on.

A further difference between the two kinds of recognition is that, unlike

1 Ibid. p. 551. In *Republic of Peru* v. *Peruvian Guano Company*, (1887) L.R. 36 Ch.D. 489, and, to a lesser extent, in *Republic of Peru* v. *Dreyfus Brothers and Co.* (1888) L.R. 38 Ch.D. 348, the parties relied on the argument that as certain contracts were made by a *de facto* government of Peru, which came to power by way of revolution, it was competent for its successor, which they described as the *de jure* government, to repudiate the contracts. The question of any distinction between *de facto* and *de jure* recognition was not raised in either case. It was admitted that the *de facto* government in question 'was duly [apparently as the *de jure* government] recognized by the Queen', and the Court proceeded on that assumption. It declined to investigate the title of the government thus recognized.

2 [1939] Ch. 182. That decision was overruled by the Court of Appeal on the ground that in the meantime the Italian Government had been recognized as the *de jure* Government of Ethiopia ([1939] Ch. 182, 195).

3 For the converse suggestion, that recognition *de jure* may also be the starting point for the assumption of the obligations of its predecessors by the recognized government, see the communication of the Russian Delegation to the British Prime Minister at the Genoa Conference of 1922: 'The Russian Delegation wish also to make it clear, although it seems to be self-evident, that the Russian Government could not admit liability for the debts of its predecessors until it has been formally recognized *de jure* by the Powers concerned' (as quoted by Sack in *Diplomatic Claims against the Soviets* (1918–1938). New York University School of Law. *Contemporary Law Pamphlets*, Series 1, no. 7 (1938), p. 70, n. 87).

de jure recognition, mere *de facto* recognition does not, according to the British practice, necessarily carry with it full and normal diplomatic intercourse, although this may be conceded in individual cases.[1] In reply to a question addressed to it in the course of the proceedings in *Fenton Textile Association* v. *Krassin* the Foreign Office stated: 'It is not the practice of the Sovereign to receive the representative of States which have not been recognized *de jure*, and, further, quite apart from the question of M. Krassin's position, no representative of the Soviet Government would be received by His Majesty's Government because the Soviet Government has not been recognized *de jure* as a State [*sic*].'[2] It also appears, although not conclusively,[3] from the same case that the representatives of a government which is recognized *de facto* only are not entitled to full diplomatic immunities. The defendant in the present case was a representative of the Soviet Government whose functions and immunities were defined in the Trade Agreement of 16 March 1921 between Great Britain and Russia. That Agreement was subsequently interpreted by the Foreign Office as connoting recognition *de facto*.[4] The Court held that the status of M. Krassin was not such as to confer upon him immunity from civil process; his immunity, as defined by the Agreement, was limited to exemption from arrest and search.[5] The British Government had previously made the position clear to some extent. Subsequent to the recognition *de facto* of the Soviet Government it stated, in an answer to a question in the House of Commons, that the Soviet official agents in Great Britain would not be recognized as diplomatic representatives.[6] When Great Britain recognized in 1915 the Carranza administration as the *de facto* Government of Mexico she did not resume diplomatic relations with it. In fact, she expressly

1 Thus it was stated, on 25 October 1944, in reply to a question in the House of Commons, that the representative in London of the French Provisional Government would be entitled to the same privileges, immunities and precedence as other heads of mission of corresponding rank after he had presented his Letters of Credence to the King as French Ambassador (*H.C. Debates*, vol. CCCCIV, col. 143).

2 (1922) 38 T.L.R. 260.

3 See below, n. 5.

4 See *Luther* v. *Sagor*, ubi supra.

5 The language used by both Scrutton and Acton L.JJ. suggests that the question might have been open to doubt if the immunities of M. Krassin had not been defined in the Trade Agreement but had to be deduced from general international law. As Atkin L.J. (as he then was) said: '...it appears to me that even if the official agents when received in this country would, in the absence of agreement, have been entitled to full immunity, yet if the respective Governments by whom and to whom respectively they are sent choose to agree as to the precise immunity to be given them, such an agreement must prevail' (ubi supra, at p. 262). However, it is not customary for governments recognized *de jure* to stipulate the extent of the immunities of their representatives.

6 *H.C. Debates*, vol. CXXXIX, col. 2198.

declined—on account of the attitude of the Mexican Government towards British subjects and their property—'to resume diplomatic relations with the Mexican Government and accord it the recognition implied by such a resumption'.[1]

When in June 1924 Denmark informed the Russian Government of her decision to recognize 'the Union Government *de jure*', she did it by proposing that 'the position of the official representatives to be so modified in accordance with the general principles of the law of nations as the establishment of normal diplomatic relations between the two countries entails'.[2] On the other hand, when in 1915 the United States recognized the *de facto* Carranza Government, that act was accompanied by an intimation of willingness to resume formal diplomatic relations.[3]

It would also appear that decisive importance attaches to *de jure* recognition, as distinguished from *de facto* recognition, with regard to transfer of property of the State concerned. Thus, although the Soviet Government was recognized by Great Britain *de facto* in 1921, it was not until *de jure* recognition had been granted in 1924 that the Soviet Government claimed, successfully, the archives and other property belonging to its predecessor.[4]

It will thus be seen that in some respects the legal effects of *de facto* recognition are indistinguishable from those of *de jure* recognition inasmuch as the former constitutes the acknowledgment of the effective authority of the government concerned within the territory. In particular, the result of such acknowledgment is the recognition of the internal validity of the acts of the authority recognized *de facto* and the concession to it *de facto* of jurisdictional immunities in the courts of the recognizing State. On the other hand, it follows from the provisional character of *de facto* recognition that the *de jure* authority continues to represent the State in the matter of State succession and otherwise. Secondly, unlike recognition *de jure*,

1 See statement in the House of Commons on 13 May 1919 (*H.C. Debates*, vol. CXV, col. 1472). See also ibid. vol. CXIX, col. 348, as well as the statements of 24 and 25 May 1916, ibid. vol. LXXXII, cols. 2073, 2306. In August 1919 the British agent who was in charge of the British archives in Mexico was ordered by the Carranza Government to leave (*The Times* newspaper, 18 August 1919).

2 Martens, *N.R.G.* 3rd ser. vol. XXIV, p. 868. This does not necessarily mean that the absence of normal diplomatic relations is the only consequence of withholding recognition *de jure*.

3 See above, p. 332. See also Hackworth, vol. I, p. 260, and *U.S. For. Rel.* 1917, pp. 910–12, 915, to the effect that in 1917 the Mexican representative to the United States was formally received as the ambassador of the *de facto* Government of Mexico.

4 *Union of Soviet Socialist Republics* v. *Onou* (*Annual Digest*, 1925–6, Case no. 74); *Union of Soviet Socialist Republics* v. *Belaiew* (ibid. Case no. 123). See also the answers in the House of Commons on 12 and 14 May 1924 (*H.C. Debates*, vol. CLXXIII, cols. 878, 1312).

recognition *de facto* does not necessarily result either in resumption of full diplomatic intercourse or in conferment of diplomatic immunities upon the representatives of the authority recognized *de facto*. Finally, as *de facto* recognition is in its essence provisional and its transformation into recognition *de jure* conditional upon the fulfilment of the absent requirements of recognition, it follows that it may be withdrawn for reasons additional to those warranting the withdrawal of recognition *de jure*. In view of this, it cannot correctly be maintained that the distinction between *de facto* and *de jure* recognition is of a purely political nature.[1]

§ 99. *Implied Recognition,* de facto *Recognition, and* de facto *Intercourse.* *De facto* recognition is an act as deliberate and explicit as *de jure* recognition. Because of the nature of the situations which give rise to it, it is occasionally of a more formal character than recognition *de jure*. Accordingly, there is no warrant for implying *de facto* recognition more readily than *de jure* recognition. In other words, it is not permissible to confuse implied recognition with *de facto* recognition—although this is occasionally done by writers[2] and although the Resolutions of the Institute of International Law of 1936 concerning the recognition of States and Governments seem to a large extent to support that view.[3] Thus, according to the latter, recognition *de facto* of a new government is manifested, *inter alia*, 'by the maintenance of relations with the new government for the purposes of current affairs' (Article 14 (3)). Actually, practice abounds in instances of intercourse between States coupled with express denial of recognition either *de facto* or *de jure*.[4]

1 When in December 1920 Esthonia and Latvia were refused admission to the League of Nations, one of the main reasons of the decision of the Assembly was the circumstance that at that time those States were recognized *de facto* only.

2 See Fauchille, no. 206.

3 See *A.J.* vol. XXX (1936), Suppl. pp. 186, 187. See also Rolin in *Annuaire*, vol. XXXVIII (1934), p. 354.

4 See below, pp. 369 et seq. See also, as to Great Britain, the instructions issued in 1820 to the British Minister at Lisbon to the effect that though there was no intention to accredit him to the revolutionary authorities in the capital, this need not interfere with his informal residence there for the purpose of transacting ordinary intercourse between the two countries (Smith, vol. I, p. 172). And see the statement by Sir John Simon, on 31 January 1934, to the effect that British consular representatives continued to be stationed in some of the principal cities of Manchuria, that they maintained such relations with the appropriate local authorities as appeared to be necessitated by British interests, and that no question of recognition was involved in those relations (*H.C. Debates*, vol. CCLXXXV, col. 336). With regard to Mexico it was stated in the House of Commons on 13 May 1919: 'His Majesty's Government are not disposed, in view of the attitude of the Mexican Government, to accord recognition, implied by the resumption of diplomatic relations, but they have never ceased to make informal

This being so, *de facto* recognition, express or implied, must be clearly distinguished from various forms of intercourse conducted either through special agents or by persons previously accredited in a diplomatic capacity to recognized constitutional authorities. *De facto* intercourse is not *de facto* recognition, and it is only because of the exaggerations of the notion of implied recognition that there has been a tendency to identify intercourse with *de facto* recognition.

§ 100. De facto *Recognition and the Obligation of Non-Recognition.* The circumstance that recognition *de facto* is, as a rule, a formal act and that international practice shows constant examples of actual intercourse in a variety of matters would seem to supply an answer to the question whether *de facto* recognition is compatible with any assumed obligation of non-recognition. The Advisory Committee set up by the Assembly of the League of Nations in connection with the non-recognition of Manchukuo was of the view that recognition *de facto* would not be compatible with the obligation of non-recognition.[1] On the other hand, in his statement to the Council of the League of Nations on 12 May 1938, the Emperor Haile Selassie insisted that recognition *de jure*—but not, it seems, recognition *de facto*—of the Italian conquest of Abyssinia was contrary to the obligations

representations with regard to the treatment of British interests' (*H.C. Debates*, vol. cxv, col. 1472).

In 1931 we find the United States State Department instructing the authorities of the Panama Canal that there was no objection to recognizing the signatures of the authorities of the new revolutionary government 'provided it is made clear that this does not imply recognition of the authorities as the *de facto* Government' (Hackworth, vol. I, p. 341). Explicit reservations to the effect that intercourse is not intended as recognition constitute a frequent feature of the practice of the United States (ibid. pp. 329, 330, 331). In 1920 the United States Chargé d'Affaires in Mexico was instructed to conduct any necessary negotiations with the new authority in such a way as 'not to permit any imputation that the present regime has been even *de facto* recognized by the Government of the United States' (ibid. p. 261). In December 1920 the United States were willing to accord merely *de facto* recognition to the new Government of Bolivia after proper elections had taken place and after the Bolivian Congress thus chosen had elected a Provisional President. It was only after further evidence of stability that the United States decided to grant recognition 'not as the *de facto* Government, but as the constitutional Government of that Republic' (ibid. p. 225). In 1924 the United States Department of State instructed the consular officer at Vera Cruz in Mexico to refer to the Huerta administration not as a '*de facto* government' but as '*de facto* authorities' (ibid. p. 128). In 1867, at a time when Germany refused to recognize the Juarez Government in Mexico, Bismarck requested the German Minister in Mexico to instruct the commander of a German warship sent to protect German interests there to render the customary salute to the Mexico flag. He insisted on the necessity of avoiding any neglect of 'international courtesy which is not dependent upon the diplomatic recognition of the Government' (*Fontes Juris Gentium, Digest of the Diplomatic Correspondence of the European States*, 1856–71, p. 176).

1 *Off.J.* 1932, Special Supplement, no. 113, p. 11.

of the Covenant.[1] This, moreover, was the interpretation which Great Britain and other States put upon their obligation of non-recognition. Thus Great Britain, while professing to adhere to the obligation of non-recognition, recognized *de facto* the Italian occupation o of Abyssinia.[2] Other States acted in the same way[3]—a line of conduct which was not challenged as being contrary to the assumed obligation of non-recognition.

Regardless of the part which the principle of non-recognition may be called upon to play in the future, the question of its relation to *de facto* recognition is one of intrinsic interest and merits consideration.[4] On the one hand, it would appear that as the practice of States admits of a measure of intercourse unaccompanied by recognition either *de jure* or *de facto*, the latter, no less than the former, is a gratuitous relaxation of the obligation of recognition. However, it is clear that the amount of intercourse which is possible in the absence of recognition is limited; it is largely of a remedial character. Moreover, in the absence of recognition, *de facto* or *de jure*, courts are not normally in a position to treat as valid the legislative and administrative acts within the territory in question—a result which may be productive of much inconvenience and injustice. The attitude of non-recognition cannot, in the nature of things and without giving rise to international complications over a prolonged period, be an instrument of effective pressure in the economic and cognate fields. Its purpose is an expression both of moral disapproval and, in law, of reservation of freedom of action in relation to a change brought about by means contrary to international law and expressly declared to be illegal. An attitude of this kind may be compatible with *de facto* recognition. The provisional character of the latter emphasizes the absence of any obligation to continue the recognition. It stresses the irregularity and the illegality of the new situation. As such it may be deemed to be compatible with the limited purpose of the necessarily imperfect sanction of non-recognition.[5]

1 *Off.J.* 1938, pp. 336–47.

2 On 16 December 1936, the Secretary of State for Foreign Affairs informed the House of Commons that the British Government had no intention of recognizing *de jure* the annexation of Abyssinia. In a certificate issued by the Foreign Office in connection with the proceedings in *Bank of Ethiopia* v. *National Bank of Egypt and Liguori*, ([1937] Ch. 513) it was stated that by the middle of December 1936 His Majesty's Government had recognized the Italian Government as being in fact the government of the area of Abyssinia then under Italian control. See below, p. 418.

3 See above, p. 336. See also Rousseau, *Le conflit italo-ethiopien devant le droit international* (1938), pp. 237–51.

4 See below, pp. 431–4.

5 This seems also to be the view of Professor Scelle, who considers recognition *de facto* in this connection to go no farther than the admission of a 'competence which is limited, precarious, devoid of any guarantee, exposed to all vicissitudes of enforced

II. WITHDRAWAL OF RECOGNITION

§ 101. *Withdrawal of Recognition in General. De facto* recognition, it has been shown, is provisional in its nature and is, therefore, liable to be withdrawn as soon as it becomes clear that there is no prospect of the requisite conditions of recognition being fulfilled. Does this mean that *de jure* recognition cannot be withdrawn? This is the view held by many. Even those who regard recognition as being in the nature of a contractual bargain or voluntary grant are emphatic that once recognition has been given it is binding on the recognizing State by virtue of the rule *pacta sunt servanda* or otherwise.[1] The very idea that the legal personality of a State or the representative capacity of its government should be dependent on the continued good will of other States is deemed to be derogatory to the independence and the dignity of the State and inimical to the stability of international relations. Yet withdrawal of recognition is a frequent—and inevitable—feature of the practice of States. In principle there would seem to be no reason why recognition should not be liable to withdrawal so long as that act, like that of granting recognition, is conceived not as an arbitrary act of policy but as one of application of international law, namely, as a declaration that the objective requirements of recognition have ceased to exist.[2]

Recognition—whether of States, governments or belligerency—is a declaration that there exist the requirements of international law, as ascertained *bona fide* by the recognizing State, with regard to the particular category of status. Recognition is not a contract or grant. It is a declaration of capacity as determined by objective facts. These facts are not necessarily

change, and which cannot be regularized except by the intervention of the League of Nations or of prescription *longi temporis* of indeterminate duration' (*Friedenswarte*, 1937, no. 2, p. 67). And see below, pp. 429, 430.

1 See, e.g. Kunz, p. 99.

2 Up to a point, these alternatives are put with some clarity by Fauchille (in no. 213). He agrees that the answer to the question of revocability of recognition depends on the character attributed to the act of recognition. If, he says, recognition consists in the declaration of the existence of certain conditions of fact, it cannot, so long as these conditions are present, be withdrawn. If, on the other hand, it is a discretionary and voluntary act, a view which he prefers, then it can be withdrawn at will in accordance with political considerations. He adds, by way of illustration, that as the capacity to fulfil the obligations of a civilized State is an original condition of recognition, it may be withdrawn if a State has shown that it is incapable of conducting itself in a civilized manner. The illustration is, of course, inconsistent with the view that withdrawal of recognition is a purely discretionary act. For it assumes the existence of an objective, though highly controversial and elastic, test of recognition.

enduring. A State may lose its independence or the necessary degree of cohesion as an organized community;[1] a government may cease to wield effective authority; a recognized belligerent may be utterly defeated. In all these cases the basis of recognition disappears, and outside States are entitled and bound to take cognizance of that fact. Undoubtedly, the decision, pertaining as it does to the principal manifestations of existence of States and governments, is one of obvious delicacy and responsibility. It must be exercised with a circumspection and restraint even more pronounced than the positive act of granting recognition. It cannot properly be used as an instrument of political pressure or disapproval.[2] But that does not mean that the decision need not be taken or that it is not constantly taken.

§ 102. *Withdrawal of Recognition of States.* Withdrawal of recognition from a State is often obscured by the fact that, having regard to the

1 This clearly remote contingency was made the starting point of some special pleading in connection with the suggestion that in 1931 and in the subsequent years Japan was entitled to withdraw her recognition of China as a State on the ground that because of internal disorders she had ceased to be an independent State. For the assertion that prolonged civil war or 'anarchy' affect the continued existence of a State see Baty in *A.J.* vol. XXVIII (1934), pp. 444–55. See also Smith, vol. I, pp. 18–30. In the course of the Manchurian dispute between China and Japan in 1932 the latter maintained that as the result of prolonged disorders within her border, China ceased to be an 'organized people' within the meaning of the Covenant (*Off.J.* 1932, pp. 383, 384).

2 It was suggested in 1920 by Pillet that after the First World War the Allied and Associated Powers ought to have withdrawn from the German Empire the benefits of international recognition, on the ground that it was incapable of fulfilling the obligations of a civilized State, and that they ought to have negotiated the treaty of peace with the representatives of the individual member States of Germany (*Le traité de Versailles* (1920), p. 28). For a similar suggestion with regard to National-Socialist Germany see Schwarzenberger, *International Law and Totalitarian Lawlessness* (1943), pp. 107–10.

In October 1918 France withdrew the recognition granted in January of that year to the provisional Government of the Finnish Republic. It is not clear whether this was a case of withdrawal of recognition from a State or from a particular government. Probably the latter was the case. See the declaration made by the French Legation in Stockholm on 1 June 1918, that France 'will not recognize in Finland any regime which may be established in an illegal way' (*U.S. For. Rel.* 1918, *Russia*, vol. II, p. 791). The reason given for the withdrawal of recognition was that the new Finnish State proclaimed in December 1917 was intended as an independent Finnish Republic and that in October of that year, in defiance of the expressed wish of the people, Finland adopted a monarchical form of government and invited a German Prince to become King (see Fauchille, nos. 167 (4), 213). See also Graham, op. cit. pp. 160–1. It is probable that the incident, far from constituting an instructive illustration of the power to withdraw recognition, was in the nature of an exceptional political measure in time of war.

circumstances, it does not take place through an express declaration announcing the withdrawal but through the act of recognition, express or implied, of the new authority. In the case of extinction of a State through annexation, the government of the conquered State is as a rule reduced to a handful of persons in exile, and it may be both invidious and unnecessary to address to them an express declaration of withdrawal of recognition. On such occasions withdrawal of recognition has at times been effected by an intimation to the diplomatic representatives of the defunct State that their mission must be regarded as terminated and that they will not henceforth continue to be recognized as representing the State in question.[1] But, generally speaking, it is the recognition of the new authority which operates as withdrawal of recognition from the defunct State. Probably[2] there is no case on record in which recognition has been withdrawn from a State without a corresponding measure of recognition being granted to its successor. There are good reasons why this should be so. When a State is deprived of its independence and of its territory, these do not vanish into a legal vacuum. They are acquired by another State or by a number of States which have arisen on what was formerly its territory. When Great Britain withdrew in 1938 her recognition of Abyssinia, this step took the

1 See, for example, the British communication, in 1861, to the Chargé d'Affaires of Naples that he could no longer be accredited as a representative of the King of the Two Sicilies. This was after Great Britain had recognized the Kingdom of Italy, which had annexed the Neapolitan territories (Satow, *A Guide to Diplomatic Practice* (3rd ed. 1932), p. 113). On the other hand, in recognizing in 1861 the new Kingdom of Italy the French Government stated that while acting in conformity with the facts of the situation it must reserve 'la liberté d'appréciation vis-à-vis des éventualités qui pourraient modifier cet état de fait' (*Archives diplomatiques*, 1861, vol. IV, p. 361). As to the withdrawal of recognition from Montenegro, see the letter of the Acting Secretary of State of the United States, of 21 January 1921, to the Montenegrin Consul-General in charge of the Legation informing him that 'in view of the present status of Montenegro, this Government no longer considers it necessary to accord recognition to her diplomatic and Consular officers' and that the Letters Patent recognizing him as Honorary Consul of Montenegro were thereby revoked (*U.S. For. Rel.* 1921 (II), p. 946). See ibid. pp. 947–9, for the protest of the Prime Minister and Minister for Foreign Affairs of Montenegro sent on 15 April 1921 from Rome to the Secretary of State declaring that 'no fact, either juridical or international, exists, on the strength of which the Government of the United States could break off diplomatic relations with the Kingdom of Montenegro'. Previously, France had informed Yugoslavia that she had decided to recall the French diplomatic and consular representatives in the former Kingdom of Montenegro and to withdraw recognition from the representatives of ex-King Nicolas in France. See also *In re Savini and Others*, decided in 1927 by the Court of Appeal of Rome, where the Court held that the State of Montenegro ceased to exist, so far as Italy was concerned, when the Italian diplomatic representation in Montenegro was abolished in 1921 (*Annual Digest*, 1927–8, Case no. 106). In March 1921 Great Britain cancelled the exequaturs of Montenegrin consuls.

2 See above, p. 350, n. 1, as to Japan and China.

form of the *de jure* recognition of the Italian annexation of the Ethiopian Empire.[1]

§ 103. *Withdrawal of Recognition of Governments.* The position is to a large extent identical with regard to recognition of governments. Withdrawal of recognition from a group of persons hitherto representing the State and the subsequent or simultaneous grant of recognition to a new government which has been successful in displacing its predecessor, are constant occurrences. Such withdrawal is as a rule implied in the unequivocal recognition of the new regime. Occasionally recognition of the new government and its withdrawal from the former government take the form of two separate acts. Thus on 16 November 1933 there took place an exchange of Notes between the United States and the Union of Soviet Socialist Republics the object of which was, in effect, to put on record the recognition of the Soviet Government by the United States. On the same day an announcement was made that the latter 'ceased to recognize' M. Ughet, the Financial Attaché to the Russian Embassy appointed by the Russian Provisional Government of 1917, who had been entrusted with the custody of the property of the Russian State.[2] But circumstances may render necessary express withdrawal of recognition combined with the recognition of the new authority. This was the case, in July 1945, in connection with the recognition by Great Britain, the United States and other States, of the Polish Provisional Government established in Polish territory. Thus the Report of the Potsdam Conference, of 2 August 1945, stated that 'the establishment by the British and United States Government of diplomatic relations with the Polish Provisional

1 Withdrawal of recognition cannot be implied from a mere *de facto* recognition of the new authority or, still less, from acts falling short even of *de facto* recognition. When in 1939 Great Britain (as well as other States) closed their legations in Prague and applied for exequaturs for consuls in Bohemia and Slovakia, these steps, although described by the British Government as a *de facto* recognition of the position in these parts of Czechoslovakia did not amount to a withdrawal of recognition from the Czechoslovak State. The same applies to similar steps taken in 1938 with respect to the annexation of Austria by Germany. See below, pp. 399, 400. Similarly, no withdrawal of recognition was implicit in the act of closing the British Legation in Addis Abbaba in December 1936. It was stated by the British Government on 21 December 1936 that that act did not constitute a recognition *de jure* of the Italian annexation of Abyssinia.

2 Department of State Publication No. 528 (Eastern European Series No. 1). On the same day the State Department informed M. Ughet that in view of the recognition of the Soviet Government by the United States the latter ceased to recognize him as Russian Financial Attaché (*A.J.* vol. XXVIII (1934) Suppl. p. 13). Various Russian consuls appointed by the Czarist Government were informed that the exequaturs issued to them were revoked and their status as Russian consuls considered terminated (ibid. pp. 13, 14).

Government has resulted in the withdrawal of their recognition from the former Polish Government in London which no longer exists'.[1] Machinery was set up in Great Britain for liquidating the affairs of the former Polish Government.[2] In some instances the withdrawal of recognition has not been accompanied by the recognition of a rival authority. Thus in 1856 the United States withdrew the recognition of the revolutionary Walker Government in Nicaragua after they had recognized it several months before. The reason given was that the authority of that Government was seriously contested in Nicaragua.[3] Instances of withdrawal of recognition

1 Notwithstanding the political implications of the decision taken at the Crimea Conference by Great Britain, the United States and Russia (see the Report of Conference, Cmd. 6598 (1945), para. vi, Poland) to recognize the Polish Provisional Government in Poland and to withdraw recognition from the Polish Government in London, the decision—and its execution—cannot be deemed to be inconsistent with a proper exercise of the function of recognition. It was clear that, in the long run, the claim of the latter to continued recognition—a claim based not on the circumstance of effectiveness of power but on legal continuity in relation to the Polish Government and State as they existed in 1939—was bound, in accordance with the legal principles of recognition of governments, to yield to the claim of the authority wielding effective power in Polish territory provided that such power was exercised by a government independent of the control of any other State and supported by a freely expressed vote of the population. The latter condition was stipulated by the Potsdam decision (see above, p. 173).

2 In Great Britain an Interim Treasury Committee was established for the purpose. For an account of its activities see the statement of the House of Commons on 2 August 1945.

3 See Moore, vol. I, p. 143. Recognition was in fact twice withdrawn within a short space of time. The first withdrawal was explained on the ground that the recognition granted by the United States Minister in Nicaragua was unauthorized by the home Government and unwarranted by the circumstances of the situation. In his instructions of 7 December 1855 to the Minister, the Secretary of State said: 'Considering the means by which the power that now predominates in that State was obtained, and the manner in which it is exercised, it can have no just pretension to be regarded as even a *de facto* Government. You will therefore on the receipt of this despatch at once cease to have any communication with the present assumed rulers of that country' (Manning, *Diplomatic Correspondence of the United States, Inter-American Affairs, 1831–1860, Central America*, vol. IV (1934), pp. 77–8). Eight months later the United States, considering that the Government showed signs of stability and that the population was acquiescent, recognized the Rivas-Walker Government. But the recognition thus granted was soon withdrawn after General Rivas was displaced and Walker, a citizen of the United States, assumed the Presidency. For an account and interpretation of these events see the letter of Dana, the United States Minister Resident in Bolivia, to the Foreign Minister of that country, printed in Manning, ibid. *Bolivia, Brazil*, vol. II (1932), pp. 53–4. The withdrawal in 1862 of the recognition by the United States of the Paez Government in Venezuela was an instance of disavowal and annulment of the recognition granted by the United States Minister without the authority of his Government (Moore, vol. I, p. 149). See also the instructions issued in July 1883 by the United States Secretary of State to the Minister in Peru to the effect that although it was not the intention of the United States hastily to withdraw or to transfer the recognition conceded to the Calderon Government, that step would

of a government, unaccompanied by a recognition of the new authority, are, and ought to remain, rare. Undoubtedly, a government which has ceased to be effective has no claim to recognition. However, so long as the party or parties which challenge its authority have not asserted themselves to the point of being themselves entitled to recognition, the established government, however weakened, is entitled to continued recognition. Effectiveness is presumed to exist so long as the lawful government has not been definitely displaced by a rival authority. Adherence to this principle is not likely to cause undue inconvenience seeing that there is no objection to regular communication with the insurgent authorities and that the fact of non-recognition does not prevent outside States from insisting on or exacting the fulfilment of generally recognized rules of international law.

The action taken by Great Britain in 1860 against the Miramón Government in Mexico exhibits some features of withdrawal of recognition unaccompanied by the simultaneous recognition of a new government. This took place after the British mediation with both parties to the civil war had been rejected. However, the incident is one not of withdrawal of recognition but of severance of diplomatic relations on account both of continuing disorders in the country and of criminal acts committed by the agents of the government in power against their opponents and against British subjects.[1] In fact what is in this connection often referred to as withdrawal of recognition amounts to and is intended merely as severance of diplomatic relations—a step which frequently takes place as a sign of disapproval of an unfriendly or an illegal act. While the withdrawal of recognition as a measure of disapproval of the conduct, however illegal, of a State or government is incompatible with the purpose of recognition, severance of diplomatic relations may be and has often been resorted to for that purpose. Thus, within three years of the recognition *de jure* of the Soviet Government in 1924, the British Government severed diplomatic relations with Russia on the ground that her Government was responsible for fomenting revolutionary propaganda in Great Britain. But there was

be taken if it were clearly shown that the rival revolutionary Government of General Iglesias was supported by the overwhelming majority of the nation (Moore, vol. I, p. 158). As to the withdrawal of recognition from the Russian diplomatic and consular representations in China in 1920 see *U.S. For. Rel.* 1920 (I), p. 765.

1 The relevant part of the British Note—reprinted in Manning, *Diplomatic Correspondence of the United States, Inter-American Affairs, 1831–1860, Mexico*, vol. IX (1937) p. 1211—ran as follows: 'The Undersigned has been instructed to break off relations with the Government of His Excellency General Miramón and to retire from Mexico: nor can His Majesty's Government consent to reopen relations with Mexico as a civilized power, until they see established either a Government possessed of some well founded prospect of stability, or a provisional arrangement likely to ensure such a result.'

no tendency, either on the part of the Government or of courts,[1] to consider the severance of diplomatic relations as tantamount to withdrawal of recognition. The British Government announced that that step was not intended to interfere with the ordinary course of legitimate Anglo-Russian trade and that no obstacles would be placed in the way of such trade.[2] Severance of diplomatic relations often takes place as a preliminary to a declaration of war and does not imply in any way withdrawal of recognition of the government affected.[3]

§ 104. *Withdrawal of Recognition of Belligerency.* Recognition of belligerency naturally comes to an end, whether the withdrawal of it takes place through a formal act or otherwise, when, with the defeat of one of the parties to the conflict, there disappears the principal condition of recognition of belligerency, namely, the existence of a state of hostilities on a wide scale. The action of the British Government at the close of the civil war in the United States provides, from this point of view, an instructive example of withdrawal of recognition.[4] However, actual termination

1 In *Princess Paley Olga* v. *Weisz*, decided in 1929 at a time when the diplomatic relations between the two countries were still severed, it was held, in effect, that the consequences of recognition, as laid down in *Luther* v. *Sagor* and other cases with regard to the validity of the internal acts of the recognized authority, continued to operate notwithstanding the severance of diplomatic relations ([1929] 1 K.B. 728). There is occasionally a tendency to speak of 'severance of diplomatic relations' when what is meant is simply the absence of recognition. See, for example, Harvard Research, *The Law of Treaties* (1935), p. 1055. See also Hackworth, vol. I, pp. 280–1, for an account, under the heading 'Recognition of New Governments', of the severance of diplomatic relations with Venezuela in connection with outstanding differences arising out of injuries to American interests.

2 See *Survey of International Affairs*, 1927, p. 272. As to the severance of diplomatic relations between Uruguay and Soviet Russia and the contention of the latter that the severance of relations was incompatible with membership of the League see *Off.J.* 1936, p. 92. When in 1936 the Iranian Government withdrew its diplomatic representative from the United States as a measure of disapproval of an alleged insult to the person of the ruler of Iran, it explained that that measure in no way affected the status of the American Legation in Teheran and that the Iranian Government would continue to conduct business with it (Hackworth, vol. IV, p. 459). In 1938 Mexico severed diplomatic relations with Great Britain because of the alleged sharpness of the British protest against seizures of British property (Cmd. 5758 (1938)). See also *H.C. Debates*, vol. CCCXXXVIII, col. 2690 and vol. CCCXL, col. 186; *The Times* newspaper, 16 May 1938.

3 See, for example, the severance of diplomatic relations between the United States and Germany on 3 February 1917 (*U.S. For. Rel.* 1917 Suppl. 1, pp. 106, 108) and between the United States and Austria-Hungary on 9 April 1917 (ibid. p. 594).

4 See the *London Gazette* of 6 June 1866 for a letter from Earl Russell to the Admiralty and other Departments dated 2 June 1865, announcing that 'Her Majesty's Government were of opinion that Neutral Nations could not but consider the Civil War in America at an end'. In an Opinion of the Law Officers of 24 November 1868 (F.O. 83/2225), 2 June 1868 was given as the date on which in the view of the

of hostilities is not the only reason for withdrawing recognition of belligerency. This may happen owing to the disappearance of conditions of recognition other than the existence of an actual state of hostilities, as, for instance, would be the case if the parties to the struggle ceased to conduct themselves in accordance with the rules of warfare.

§ 105. *Withdrawal of Recognition of Annexation.* In a communication sent in November 1940 by the British Secretary of State for the Colonies to the High Commissioner for Palestine, in connection with an action pending there, it was stated that the '*de jure* recognition by His Majesty's Government of the Italian conquest of Ethiopia had been withdrawn'.[1] In view of this the Supreme Court of Palestine held, on the authority of *Haile Selassie* v. *Cable and Wireless, Limited,*[2] that 'the title of the Italian Government to the property in question can no longer be recognized'. It does not appear that any other announcement of the withdrawal of recognition was made to the world at large. On 5 February 1941, the Foreign Secretary announced in the House of Commons that 'His Majesty's Government would welcome the re-appearance of an independent Ethiopian State, and recognize the claim of the Emperor Haile Selassie to the throne'.[3] It would thus seem that the withdrawal of *de jure* recognition of the Italian conquest was independent either of the circumstance of any cessation of effective Italian rule over Abyssinia—this did not happen until later in the war—or of any simultaneous recognition of Abyssinian sovereignty. The legal explanation of that measure was probably the fact that the object of the recognition *de jure* as given in 1938, namely, the achievement of a general settlement aiming at the pacification of Europe and of the world, was destroyed by the action of Italy in 1940 in declaring war upon Great Britain and France. In so far as the recognition of new titles has, in contradistinction to other forms of recognition, the character of a contractual arrangement, the British action cannot be regarded as arbitrary. But there may be objections to treating in this way what is in essence an executed territorial arrangement.

British Government the belligerent character of the so-called Confederate States had ceased. See, on the other hand, the Opinion of the Law Officers of 29 April 1869 (F.O. 83/2299) advising that it was not necessary for Her Majesty to revoke formally her Order in Council of 14 May 1868, enjoining neutrality on all British subjects in Japan: 'That order only applied to British subjects abetting either of the contending parties during the hostilities then existing between the Mikado and other belligerents within the Japanese Dominions, and as such hostilities have come to an end Her Majesty's Order in Council ceases to be operative for want of parties, to whom it would be applicable.'

1 *Azazh Kebbeda Tesema* v. *Italian Government* (*Annual Digest*, 1938–40, Case no. 36).

2 See above, p. 343.

3 *H.C. Debates*, vol. CCCLXVIII, col. 804.

§ 106. *Liability to Withdrawal and the Distinction between* de jure *and* de facto *Recognition.* It has been submitted that the principal distinguishing feature of *de facto* recognition as compared with *de jure* recognition is that it is provisional and subject to withdrawal if the conditions of recognition, as laid down by international law, cease to exist or if the conditions still to be fulfilled at the time of recognition fail to materialize. However, if, as is believed to be the case, recognition *de jure* is in principle subject to withdrawal for the same reasons, how can it be maintained that liability to withdrawal is the principal distinguishing feature of *de facto* recognition? The answer is that, in a substantial sense, the distinction is one of degree. In the case of *de facto* recognition the liability to withdrawal is prominently in the mind of the State giving or receiving recognition. That liability to withdrawal is contemplated by reference to a given set of circumstances with regard to which withdrawal of recognition follows in the ordinary course, whether there exists an alternative recipient of recognition or not. On the other hand, recognition *de jure* can properly be withdrawn only if at the same time it is granted to another authority which combines more effectively the requisite conditions of statehood or of governmental capacity. The result is that recognition *de jure*, at the time when it is given, partakes of a finality which can be destroyed only in exceptional cases and subject to exacting proof. It is that finality which explains the different treatment, by courts and otherwise, of *de jure* and *de facto* recognition.

The problem of withdrawal of recognition raises, in a manner even more pronounced than that of grant of recognition, the question of collectivization of the process of recognition. The rise of international personality, the acknowledgment of the representative capacity of persons claiming to be the government of a State, and the grant of belligerent rights are acts of primary importance in the life of States, and it has been suggested elsewhere that only the collectivization of the process of recognition can be regarded as commensurate with its significance.[1] Even more cogent considerations urge the necessity of applying such collective procedure to the withdrawal of recognition.

III. CONDITIONAL RECOGNITION

§ 107. *Liability to Withdrawal on account of Non-Fulfilment of Conditions of Recognition.* Recognition, it has been shown, can be withdrawn on account of the supervening disappearance of conditions of recognition as

1 See, with regard to recognition of States, pp. 67–70 above and with regard to recognition of governments, pp. 165–9 above.

laid down by international law. In that sense all recognition is conditional and there would appear to be no objection to referring specifically in the act of recognition to such conditions. Thus, for instance, when Great Britain recognized *de jure* the Czechoslovak Government in July 1941, it was stated that 'the present Czechoslovak Government will, after the war, at once submit to the regulations of a democratic Czechoslovak constitution'.[1] However, conditional recognition as generally understood means recognition the grant or continuation of which is made dependent upon the fulfilment of stipulations other than the normal requirements of statehood, of governmental capacity, or of belligerency. Recognition has occasionally, though not frequently, been granted subject to the new State or government undertaking an obligation such as the concession of most-favoured-nation treatment or of other commercial advantages,[2] settlement of outstanding claims,[3] abstention from and suppression of trade in slaves,[4] respect of private property,[5] proper treatment of minorities,[6] or some line of conduct with regard to a specific situation.[7] It is usual, when such

1 For an Exchange of Notes, bearing on the subject, between Great Britain and Czechoslovakia of 5 August 1942, see *Treaty Series*, no. 3 (1942). See also Táborský, *The Czechoslovak Cause* (1944), p. 98.

2 As in the case of the recognition of Albania by the United States in 1922 (see Hackworth, vol. I, p. 192). See also *U.S. For. Rel.* 1922 (I), p. 594. And see above p. 33.

3 See, for instance, the various assurances insisted upon by the United States in 1913 with regard to the recognition of the Mexican Provisional Government (Hackworth, vol. I, p. 258); or ibid. pp. 261 et seq. with regard to the Obregón Government in 1923. And see above, pp. 109–14.

4 See Canning's despatch of 15 February 1823, as to the denunciation of the slave trade by Brazil (printed in Webster, *Britain and the Independence of Latin America, 1812–1830*, vol. I (1938), p. 221). See above, p. 36.

5 See above (n. 3) and Hackworth, vol. I, p. 228, in connection with the recognition of the Bolivian Government by the United States in 1937.

6 See below, p. 362.

7 Such as the provisions relating to the permanent neutrality imposed upon Belgium by the Treaty of 15 November 1831, or the provisions of the General Act of the Congo Conference of 1885 concerning freedom of commerce. The relevant Article of the Treaty of 1831 provided as follows: 'La Belgique, dans les limites indiquées aux articles 1, 2 et 4, formera un État indépendant et perpétuellement neutre. Elle sera tenue d'observer cette même neutralité envers tous les autres États.' Article 1 of the Congo General Act of 26 February 1885 provided, *inter alia*, that the trade of all nations shall enjoy complete freedom in all the regions forming the basin of the Congo and its outlets. In 1829 and 1830 Great Britain offered to recognize the Government of Dom Miguel in Portugal provided that an amnesty were granted to the former supporters of Queen Maria. The British Government attached importance to stating that that request was not in the nature of a condition of recognition, but that it 'was to be considered merely in the light of friendly advice' (Smith, vol. I, pp. 176, 178). He suggests that 'in substance, if not in form, the proposal was equivalent to an absolute condition'—which probably does not mean a condition in the accepted legal sense.

obligations are imposed or entered into as a concomitant of recognition, to speak of conditional recognition. Such terminology, in these and similar cases,[1] is not in keeping with the use of the term 'condition' in its ordinary legal connotation.

The so-called conditions, in the instances enumerated above, resemble very little, if at all, any type of conditions accompanying contracts in private law. In practice they have not been intended or treated as conditions in the sense of a vital part of the contract which is discharged by a breach of the condition. Neither have they been treated as an event which, until it materializes, suspends the operation of the contract. As a rule they have formed part of the arrangements accompanying the act of recognition whenever circumstances have rendered such arrangements necessary. They are often necessary in view of the fact that recognition is frequently preceded by a prolonged period of absence or suspension of intercourse with a resulting accumulation of matters requiring a settlement or clarification. When the Soviet Government was recognized in 1933 by the

1 It is inaccurate to attach literal significance to the expression 'conditions' occasionally used in this connection. Thus, for instance, when Germany recognized in 1909 the independence of Bulgaria she referred in her declaration of recognition to the fact of the previous recognition of Bulgaria by Turkey and to the arrangement reached with regard to the Oriental Railway. 'Étant donné ces conditions', the declaration proceeded, 'le Gouvernement Impérial d'Allemagne...est heureux de pouvoir reconnaître de son côté le Royaume indépendant de Bulgarie' (Martens, *N.R.T.* 3rd ser. vol. II, p. 666). This clearly was not a case of conditional recognition. The same applies to the expression 'reservations' used in connection with recognition. See, for instance, the statement in the Report of the Committee of Jurists appointed by the Council of the League of Nations in connection with the question of the Aaland Islands to the effect that 'the recognition of any State must always be subject to the reservation that the State recognized will respect the obligations imposed upon it either by general International Law or by definite international settlements relating to its territory' (*Official Journal*, Special Supplement, no. 3 (1920), p. 18). When in March 1922 Great Britain terminated the protectorate over Egypt and recognized her independence she did so subject to certain reservations, but these were not conditions of recognition making legally possible its withdrawal. When in subsequent years, prior to the Treaty of 1936, difficulties arose between Great Britain and Egypt with regard to some of the reserved points, as, for example, the status of the Sudan, there was no suggestion on the part of Great Britain that the recognition might be withdrawn.

When in May 1920 Great Britain recognized Danish sovereignty over Greenland she did so subject to the condition that 'in the event of Denmark wishing to dispose of the territory she will grant the British Empire the right of pre-emption'. The United States thereupon informed Great Britain that they were not disposed to recognize the existence in a third government of the right of pre-emption and reserved their attitude in case a specific proposal for such a transfer should be made in the future (*U.S. For. Rel.* 1922 (II), pp. 1, 2). Subsequently, Great Britain modified her attitude. She reserved the right to be consulted should Denmark at any time contemplate the alienation of the territory (note of May 20, 1920, printed in *P.C.I.J.* Series C, no. 62, 26th Session, 1933, p. 48).

United States it gave, on the basis of reciprocity, certain undertakings and explanations of its future policy with regard to religious freedom and the protection of economic rights of American citizens in Soviet Russia; it also agreed to assign to the United States amounts due from American citizens to Soviet Russia as the successor of former governments of Russia. These and similar undertakings and assurances have occasionally—and inaccurately—been described as constituting conditional recognition.[1] At times such 'conditions' have been in the nature of a partial consideration, either in the interest of the recognizing State or in the general interest, for the act of recognition. To say that is to bring into relief the inappropriateness of so-called conditional recognition and its inconsistency with the true purpose of recognition which is the ascertainment and declaration of the existence of certain factual requirements of statehood, of governmental capacity and of belligerency.[2] Such extraneous conditions are irrelevant to these factual requirements—although in some cases a certain amount of ingenuity may succeed in bringing these stipulations within the orbit of an objective requirement of recognition. Thus it may be said, with regard to recognition of governments, that the insistence on a specific demand such as the settlement of outstanding claims or undertakings in the matter of treatment of the nationals of the recognizing State is no more than the application of the principle that willingness to fulfil international obligations is a valid requirement of recognition.

However that may be, the imposition of conditions in consideration of recognition is an exceptional occurrence.[3] The very rarity of such stipulations testifies to the fact that the practice of States does not treat recognition as a contract or bargain affording a legitimate occasion for extracting promises and gaining advantages.[4] The impropriety of such attempts has

1 It was with reference to these various arrangements and undertakings that the Supreme Court said in *United States* v. *Pink* (315 U.S. 203, 229): 'Recognition is not always absolute; it is sometimes conditional.'

2 On the other hand, conditional recognition seems to be consistent with the conception of recognition as an act of unfettered political discretion. See, for example, Scalfati, p. 266.

3 Hackworth summarizes the practice of the United States since 1906 by saying that 'The United States has not, strictly speaking, accorded conditional recognition to any State' in that period (Hackworth, vol. 1, p. 192). He describes—correctly, it is believed—the 'two or three' apparent exceptions to that practice as being instances of assurances required coincidentally with recognition (ibid). Neither are there any instances of conditional recognition by the United States before 1906. (See Moore, vol. 1, § 27.)

4 The recognition of Lithuania by the decision of the Conference of Ambassadors of 13 July 1922 is an example of conditional recognition. The decision was in the following terms:

'Les soussignés, représentants de la France, de la Grande Bretagne, de l'Italie et du

occasionally brought forth protests by the government affected[1] and has been criticized by statesmen of authority, as was the case in connection with the recognition of Finland in 1919. When the Council of Foreign Ministers at the Peace Conference in 1919 discussed the question of the recognition of that country, the Japanese representative suggested that

Japon à la Conférence des Ambassadeurs et dûment mandatés à cet effet, ont l'honneur de faire savoir que les Gouvernements susdits ont décidé de reconnaître *de jure* le Gouvernement lithuanien, à la condition que celui-ci s'engage à agréer purement et simplement et à observer les dispositions du Traité de Versailles en tant qu'elles concernent le régime de navigation sur le Niemen et, par les présentes, déclarent reconnaître *de jure* le dit Gouvernement sous les conditions susénoncées.

'La présente reconnaissance prendra date et effet du jour de l'accusé de réception contenant l'engagement ci-dessus visé....'

The Lithuanian answer of 4 August 1922 was couched in a somewhat roundabout manner. The assurance was given that the Lithuanian Government, which had signed the Convention and Statute of Barcelona, would observe the arrangements of the Treaty of Versailles in so far as they relate to the Niemen. However, the reply stated that as the above arrangements of the Treaty of Versailles were applicable only in times of peace, the Lithuanian Government was prepared to conform with them as soon as Poland who, notwithstanding her engagements towards Lithuania, was holding parts of Lithuanian territory, shall have permitted Lithuania to establish amicable relations with her and to open the Niemen to free navigation. The Conference of Ambassadors considered that this was not an unconditional acceptance of the recognition. For a time it was intended to send a communication that in view of the Lithuanian reply the recognition could not be regarded as effective. But on 13 October a modified note was sent stating simply that the Lithuanian reply could not be regarded as an 'acceptation pure et simple des conditions de 13 Juillet'. An opportunity was given to Lithuania to give a more satisfactory answer by way of an explanation 'quelle portée le Gouvernement lithuanien attribue aux réserves qu'il a formulées'. Lithuania replied on 18 November 1922. The gist of her answer was that as the stipulation in question assumed the existence of a state of peace between the contracting parties and as there existed between Poland and Lithuania a condition approaching that of war, 'l'état actuel des relations entre le Lithouanie et la Pologne ne saurait être considéré par le Conférence des Ambassadeurs comme l'état de paix permettant l'application des conventions collectives sur le régime des fleuves internationaux'. On 20 December 1922, the Conference of Ambassadors decided to recognize Lithuania *de jure* on the understanding that in so doing it did not express any opinion whether or not such a state of war existed between Lithuania and Poland, whether such a state of war would justify the postponement of the internationalization of the Niemen, or what were the rights and wrongs of Lithuania in her dispute with Poland.

1 When in 1921 the United States made the recognition of the Obregón Government conditional upon the previous conclusion of a treaty embodying certain principles insisted upon by the United States, Mexico objected on the ground that 'the Mexican Republic being a state whose existence and complete sovereignty have not been questioned for a hundred years, its governments have the right to be recognized by the governments of other countries, in accordance with established usage, without other condition than their legality [*sic*] and their capacity to fulfil the international duties and obligations of Mexico'. The admissibility of conditional recognition as suggested by Moore (vol. I, p. 73) was asserted to be limited to recognition of States (*U.S. For. Rel.* 1921 (II), p. 410 (4 June 1921)).

recognition should be made dependent upon compliance with certain conditions connected with the military situation in the Baltic, especially in relation to Soviet Russia. Both the British and the American representative objected to that proposal. Mr Lansing insisted that '...a nation was entitled to recognition of her independence, and her government was equally entitled to recognition as a *de facto* or *de jure* government, as a matter of right, and it was not justifiable to put conditions on such a recognition simply to serve some political purpose'.[1]

In the exceptional cases in which a stipulation approaching a condition has been linked with recognition there has been no tendency to assert that it can be withdrawn on the ground that the condition has not been complied with. This view has been expressed in particular with regard to what is perhaps the only important example of conditional recognition, namely, the stipulations of Article 34 of the Treaty of Berlin of 1878 with regard to the treatment of religious minorities in Bulgaria, Serbia, Montenegro and Roumania. On that occasion the language used seems to suggest a condition in the ordinary sense of the term.[2] There has been general agreement that, notwithstanding the terms used, the stipulations in question did not constitute a condition in the strict meaning of the term but a direction known in Roman law as *modus*,[3] and that its effect was merely to confer a

1 Graham, *The Diplomatic Recognition of Border States*, Part I: *Finland* (1936), p. 142. Lord Hardinge, who raised the question of the amnesty for the Red Finns who had been fighting as the allies of Great Britain, agreed that a formal stipulation on this question could not be introduced in the document recognizing the independence of Finland. He believed that it would be proper to inform the Finnish Government that the Allies in recognizing the independence of Finland hoped that the Finnish Government would act in a liberal and generous spirit towards the Red Finns (ibid. p. 140). On 5 May 1919, the Foreign Ministers of the United States, Great Britain, France and Japan agreed that the Governments of the United States of America and Great Britain would forthwith severally recognize the independence of Finland and its *de facto* government and that the 'Finnish Government be urged to treat the Red Finns who had fought with the Allies in a liberal and generous spirit by the grant of an amnesty' (*U.S. For. Rel.* 1919 (II), p. 214).

2 As may be seen from the following passage in the protocol of one of the meetings of the Conference: 'Le Prince de Bismarck, après avoir constaté les résultats du vote, déclare que le Congrès admet l'indépendance de la Servie, mais sous la condition que la liberté religieuse sera reconnue dans la Principauté. Son Altesse Sérénissime ajoute que la commission de rédaction, en formulant cette décision, devra constater la connexité établie par le Congrès entre la proclamation de l'indépendance serbe et la reconnaissance de liberté religieuse' (*B.F.S.P.* vol. LXIX, p. 959; *Archives diplomatiques*, 1882–1883, vol. II, p. 147).

3 See, in particular, Rivier, *Principes du droit des gens*, vol. I (1896), p. 61; Mérignhac, *Traité de droit public international*, vol. I (1905), p. 325; Nys, *Le droit international* (2nd ed. 1912), vol. I, pp. 76–8; and Politis in *Mélanges Antoine Pillet*, vol. I (1929), p. 185. See also Goebel, *The Recognition Policy of the United States* (1915), p. 65.

right of intervention as distinguished from the right to withdraw recognition.[1]

It thus appears that the term 'condition' has been used in relation to recognition in, at least, three senses:

(1) It has been resorted to by reference to the existence of requirements, as laid down by international law, of independent statehood, of governmental capacity and of the qualifications of belligerency in a civil war. Thus, for instance, it is correctly asserted that an authority, in order to be entitled to recognition as a government, must fulfil certain objective conditions, in particular that it must enjoy the habitual obedience, properly expressed, of the population of the country. This is not a 'condition' in the accepted legal connotation.

(2) It has been employed in connection with the reservation, made concurrently with recognition, of certain disputed rights claimed by the recognizing State. This, again, is not a 'condition' in the accepted sense of the word.

(3) It has been adopted to describe promises given and obligations undertaken by the recognized State in connection with and, occasionally,

1 A gift *sub modo* was an absolute gift with a direction as to how it was to be applied. It has been suggested by Anzilotti (*Corso* (3rd ed. 1927), p. 160) that Article 34 of the Treaty of Berlin constituted an agreement between the Great Powers obliging them to recognize the new States on condition that they introduced legislation concerning equality of treatment, and that the obligations of the new States in this matter were grounded not in the Treaty of Berlin but in their subsequent acceptance of the recognition.

In the various Minorities Treaties concluded in 1919 the Preamble linked the question of recognition with that of the acceptance of the provisions concerning the treatment of minorities. In replying to the Polish objections to the proposed minorities treaty M. Clemenceau said: 'This Treaty does not constitute any fresh departure. It has for long been the established procedure of the public law of Europe that when a State is created, or even when large accessions of territory are made to an established State, the joint and formal recognition of the Great Powers should be accompanied by the requirement that such States should, in the form of a binding international Convention, undertake to comply with certain principles of Government' (as quoted in Macartney, *National States and National Minorities* (1934), p. 238). It would not be accurate to regard that requirement as a 'condition' of recognition. A time may arrive when the proper treatment of minorities and of the individual in general will be regarded as an essential function of statehood as conceived by international law with the result that conditions of the kind adopted in the Berlin Treaty of 1878 will be in the same category as continued independence or effectiveness of governmental power. See the Report of the Mandates Commission to the Council of the League of Nations of 27 June 1931, in which the provision of guarantees concerning the treatment of minorities is suggested as one of the conditions of emancipation of a community from the status of a mandate to that of an independent State (*Minutes*, vol. XX, pp. 228–9). And see Ritsher, *Criteria of Capacity for Independence* (1934).

as an inducement to, recognition in the interest either of the recognizing State or in pursuance of a more general interest. The practice of States shows no instances of such stipulations being treated as giving the right, in case of non-fulfilment, to withdraw recognition. There is accordingly no warrant for regarding them as conditions in the accepted legal sense of the word. However, even when treated as ordinary obligations unrelated to the continued validity of recognition, they are objectionable as being contrary to the true function of recognition. Their main redeeming feature is the rarity of their occurrence.

Appendix to Chapter XIX

NOTE ON COMMUNICATIONS OF THE EXECUTIVE DEPARTMENT IN RELATION TO DE FACTO RECOGNITION

A NUMBER of cases which arose before English courts in connection with the Spanish Civil War of 1936–9 raised the question of the form of communications from the Foreign Office produced before the court and of their interpretation in so far as they relate to *de facto* recognition. Thus in *The Arantzazu Mendi* the crucial passage of the statement received from the Foreign Office was that 'His Majesty's Government recognizes the Nationalist Government as a government which at present exercises *de facto* administrative control over the larger portion of Spain'.[1] In contrast with similar cases, such as *Luther* v. *Sagor*[2] or *Bank of Ethiopia* v. *National Bank of Egypt and Liguori*,[3] there was, in *The Arantzazu Mendi*, no formal reference to the recognition of a *de facto* government. In *Banco de Bilbao* v. *Rey*,[4] the Court was informed that 'His Majesty's Government in the United Kingdom recognize the Government of General Franco as an insurgent government which at present exercises *de facto* effective administrative control over a considerable portion of Spain'. In addition to the absence of a formal reference to the recognition of a *de facto* government, the unusual wording of the reply raised the question, which does not seem to have been considered by the Court of Appeal, whether and how far the recognition as a government was qualified by the word 'insurgent'. Diplomatic practice shows no instance of an express recognition of an 'insurgent government'. In the certificate issued on 8 March 1938, with reference to *Compañia Naviera Sota y Azner* v. *Ramón de la Sota* (an unreported case which was heard for several weeks before Mr Justice Crossman and settled by agreement), it was stated that 'His Majesty's Government in the United Kingdom recognizes the Government of General Franco as a *nationalist* Government which at present exercises *de facto* effective control over a considerable portion of Spain'. The expression 'nationalist Government' is not a term which has any recognized meaning in international law or, for that matter, in political science. Probably in each of these three cases, where different language was used to describe the same state of affairs, the emphasis was not on the nature of the government in question, but on the circumstance that it wielded effective power.

Such unorthodox terminology, when coupled with a rigid adherence to the technical distinction between *de jure* and *de facto* recognition and with a complicated statement as to the degree of recognition accorded to the rival governments, may

1 See above, p. 280. 2 See above, p. 342.

3 [1937] Ch. 513: 'His Majesty's Government...now regard the Italian Government as the Government *de facto* of the parts of Ethiopia which they control.'

4 [1938] 2 K.B. 176; [1938] 2 All E.R. 253.

easily become a source of difficulty for the court. Yet it is a debatable question whether a reply thus framed affords legitimate ground for criticism. The purpose of the communication from the Secretary of State is to inform the court of certain facts relevant to the case. But if the facts are complicated and unprecedented, his statement cannot be an example of lucidity. On the other hand, as the foreign relations of the Crown ought to be conducted within the framework of international law, it is arguable that the statements of the responsible Minister of the Crown should be couched in terms which have an accepted meaning in international usage. They are, in the matter of recognition, statements as to legal status, and if they are to be at all useful they ought to be expressed in legal terms descriptive of status. This, it may be rightly objected, is a counsel of perfection when the situation is unprecedented and when circumstances demand a departure from established forms. However, even in such cases it is desirable to frame the statement so as to make it approximate so far as possible to accepted terminology. It is submitted that such ambiguity as necessarily remains must, as in the corresponding case of statutes, be approached by the court with the help of the rule of interpretation which assumes that the intention of the government is to abide by the rules of international law and the international obligations of this country.[1]

Finally, the problem arises as to the position created by the refusal of the Secretary of State to give a direct answer to the question put to him. As pointed out by Roche J. in *Luther* v. *Sagor*,[2] 'the proper source of information as to a foreign power, its status and sovereignty, is the Sovereign of this country through the Government'. But what is the position if the Secretary of State, while ready to supply much useful information as to the degree of recognition accorded by His Majesty's Government, declares that the question of the status of the foreign authority is not a question of fact but a question of law to be determined by the court in the light of the information given? This is what actually happened in *Banco de Bilbao* v. *Rey* and in *The Arantzazu Mendi*, where the closing passage in the reply of the Foreign Office was as follows: 'The question whether the Nationalist Government is to be regarded as that of a foreign sovereign State appears to be a question of law to be answered in the light of the preceding statements and having regard to the particular issue with respect to which the question is raised.'[3]

It is difficult to be positive in the criticism of the passage just quoted. Whether a community possesses a sufficient degree of independence so as to acquire the status of a sovereign community in international law is a mixed question of fact and law as distinguished from the question of the *consequences* resulting from its sovereign status, if any, which is a pure question of law. But in so far as it is a question of law, the practice has been to leave the determination of that matter to the Crown—just

1 See above, p. 290.

2 [1921] 1 K.B. 456.

3 See above, pp. 280–2. See also *White, Child & Beney, Ltd.* v. *Simmons*, (1922) 38 T.L.R. 367; 38 T.L.R. 616, for an example of a refusal of the Foreign Office to supply information on a question of fact, namely, the date to which the recognition of the Government of Soviet Russia should be deemed to be retrospective. And see below, p. 368.

as courts have been content to rely on the statement of the Crown as to whether certain facts constitute in law a state of war between this country and a foreign State. In matters of status that question of law—or of fact and law—has as a rule been reduced to the question whether the Government has granted the necessary degree of recognition to the foreign community. But the Secretary of State is under no legal obligation to answer the question put to him. As Lord Sumner said in *Duff Development Company* v. *The Government of Kelantan*, it is conceivable that the Crown may refuse to answer the enquiry, 'as in changing and difficult times policy might require it to do'.[1] The Secretary of State did so in fact decline an answer in *Banco de Bilbao* v. *Rey* and in *The Arantzazu Mendi*. It may be a matter of dispute whether the reason given (namely, that the crucial question was one of law) will commend itself to everyone. But seeing that the Secretary of State did refuse to give an answer, the further question arises whether the court in giving its own reply may, in case of doubt, have recourse to sources of evidence other than the facts enumerated in the letter from the Foreign Office, for instance, the statements made by Ministers in both Houses of Parliament. The accurate answer is probably that while the court must not disregard the information received from the Crown, in cases in which that information is insufficient or obscure it may properly be supplemented from other sources. To quote Lord Sumner once more: 'The Court might be entitled to accept secondary evidence in default of the best.'[2] The principle of the conclusiveness of the statements of the Crown can apply only so long as these statements are intended to be conclusive in the sense that they are meant to supply a full answer to the enquiry put by the court or by the parties. But when there is no such intention, the statement, while conclusive of the facts which it recites, is not exclusive of other sources of evidence. Otherwise there is a danger that a 'temporary if not temporizing'[3] answer may be made a starting point for a purely logical interpretation in disregard of wider considerations of international law.

The communication of the Foreign Office is a weighty piece of evidence emanating from an important Department of the Government. But it does not invariably claim and is probably not entitled to any attributes of finality with regard to questions of law arising from it. Its composition may be faulty. It may be shrouded in obscurity, accidental or deliberate.[4] There is no reason why, in such

1 [1924] A.C. 797, 824.

2 Ibid. In *Mighell* v. *Sultan of Johore*, [1894] 1 Q.B.D. 149, Lord Esher M.R. disapproved of the course taken by Sir Robert Phillimore in *The Charkieh* (4 Adm. and Eccl. 59) in so far as he resorted to sources other than the communication of the Foreign Office. However, in that case the answer of the Foreign Office purported to be exhaustive. See also *White, Child & Beney, Ltd.* v. *Simmons*, supra.

3 *Per* Lord Sumner, [1924] A.C. 797, 824.

4 See, for example, the communication of the Foreign Office in *Kawasaki Kisen Kabushiki Kaisha of Kobe* v. *Bantham S.S. Co. Ltd.* [1938] 3 All E.R. 80; [1939] 2 K.B. 544, where the Court had to interpret a clause in a charter-party authorizing its cancellation 'if war breaks out involving Japan'. In reply to the question whether the hostilities then in progress between China and Japan amounted to war, the reply of the

cases, the court should reduce its status to that of a passive and perplexed recipient of ambiguous information. The case of *de facto* recognition—in itself a notion of considerable elasticity—calls for the exercise of those qualities of judicial independence in matters of interpretation which are best calculated to ensure an enlightened application of the law. Moreover, in so far as the determination of questions of law is one which falls more properly within the province of courts,[1] the disinclination of the Executive Department to embark upon an authoritative elucidation of such questions is not a legitimate subject of criticism—provided always that courts interpret their task not in the light of political realism aiming at avoiding embarrassment to the Executive or of smoothing the path of its foreign policy, but by reference to principles of international law and of the international obligations of the country.[2]

Foreign Office was that 'the current situation in China is indeterminate and anomalous and His Majesty's Government are not at present prepared to say that in their view a state of war exists'. But it was intimated in the communication that 'the attitude of His Majesty's Government may not necessarily be conclusive on the question whether a state of war exists within the meaning of the term "war" as used in particular documents or statutes'.

1 In this respect the system adopted by English courts—where the principle of conclusiveness of the statements of the Executive is to a large extent a rule of evidence (see Bankes L.J. in *The Gagara*, [1909] P. 96)—seems to be preferable to that acted upon by the courts of the United States which accept as conclusive the substantive ruling of the Executive on the question whether a claim to immunity is well founded. See, for example, *Ex parte Republic of Peru*, (1943) 318 U.S. 578, where it was held that the Court is bound by the 'recognition and allowance of the claim [to immunity] by the State Department and certification of its action presented to the court by the Attorney-General'. See also, to the same effect, *The Ucayali*, (1943) 318 U.S. 578 (*Annual Digest*, 1941–2, Case no. 53); *Banco de España* v. *Federal Reserve Bank of New York* (ibid. 1938–40, Case no. 6); *Miller* v. *Ferrocarril del Pacifico de Nicaragua* (ibid. 1941–2, Case no. 51); *Republic of Mexico* v. *Hoffmann* (a decision of the Supreme Court) (*A.J.* vol. XXXIX (1945), p. 585). For some qualifications see *Sullivan* v. *State of Sao Paulo* (*Annual Digest*, 1941–2, Case no. 50). And see the writer's note on the American practice in Oppenheim, vol. I (6th ed. 1946), § 357*a* and Jessup in *A.J.* vol. XL (1946), pp. 168–72.

2 See above, pp. 279–94, as to *The Arantzazu Mendi*.

Chapter XX

IMPLIED RECOGNITION

§ 108. *Presumption of Recognition.* The question of implied recognition resolves itself into an enquiry as to the kind and type of conduct which, in the absence of clear indications to the contrary, the law will interpret as amounting to recognition. How far does the conclusion of a treaty with a hitherto unrecognized government or State, or the appointment of a diplomatic or consular agent to such government or State, or participation in a conference attended by it, amount conclusively to recognition of statehood or of governmental capacity? How far does the use of a mode of address or repeated or sporadic acts of intercourse have that effect? How far does passive acquiescence in the exercise of all or some belligerent rights, especially when coupled with a substantial measure of official intercourse with the insurgents, constitute implied recognition of belligerency? The frequency with which these questions arise shows that they are not of a merely theoretical nature.

There are many occasions on which the law, municipal or international, finds it necessary, in the interests of good faith and fair dealing, to imply intention from conduct either active or passive. But to imply an intention to consent or to promise is not to make the actual existence of such intention legally irrelevant. There is, as a rule, no conduct, however conclusive in ordinary circumstances, the normal legal consequences of which cannot be averted or interpreted by a clear manifestation of a contrary intention. Two examples in the law of contract will illustrate the position. As a rule the law requires an express offer and acceptance as a condition of a contract. On occasions, however, the law will infer from the conduct of the parties the intention to conclude a binding agreement. If I permit a person to do work for me in circumstances in which he may reasonably infer that I did not intend him to give his services for nothing, I shall be deemed to have entered into a contract and, in consequence, be held liable to pay for the work done. But no such results will arise if I clearly manifest my intention not to enter into a contract. Or the law may imply a condition in the contract. Thus, according to Section 14 (1) of the English Sale of Goods Act of 1893, where the buyer makes known to the seller the particular purpose for which the goods are required so as to show that the buyer relies on the seller's skill or judgment and where the goods are of a description which it is in the course of the seller's business to supply, there is an implied condition that the goods shall be reasonably fit for such purpose. But a clear caveat on the part of the seller will do away with that presumption of the law.

These examples explain the reasons for the determination of the law to imply intention in the interests of the security of transactions and of good faith. A substantial part of the law of estoppel belongs to the same category. However, in all these cases there is nothing artificial or purely technical in the intervention of the law. It does not spring a surprise upon an unwilling party. In particular, it does not compel him to abide by consequences which he clearly wished to avoid, which the other party knew he did not intend, and which it is not in the interest of security of transactions to presume. In Roman law, though the implied warranty of livestock dealers for serious defects was of a penal character, it was possible to contract out of it. The same considerations must apply to international law. They must apply here for the special reason that rigid presumptions and formal inferences cannot be admitted without exacting proof in a system of law in which freedom of action and the absence of imposed obligations still form one of the basic features of the law.

There are few branches of international law in which the adoption of a presumption can have more serious legal consequences than in the matter of recognition. Recognition, properly conceived, is a duty whose fulfilment must not be withheld when the required conditions are present. When granted, it is the starting point of rights of statehood, of governmental capacity, of belligerency. These rights are inoperative so long as, in the exercise of a necessarily wide discretion, a State has declined to grant it. To say that, in matters of such import, the results of recognition follow upon certain actions of States, regardless of their intention or even regardless of an intimation to the contrary, is to lay down a rule of the utmost gravity. Nothing short of a compelling legal principle or of an acknowledged and unequivocal practice of States can be sufficient for the admission of any such rule as a rule of international law. As often happens, the doctrine of implied recognition has been more conspicuous in the writings of authors than in the practice of States. In the literature of international law it has often appeared under the more innocuous name of modes of recognition. It is true that recognition may be granted in a manner other than an express and formal declaration to that effect. In this sense we are justified in referring to various modes of recognition. But it is permissible to speak of modes of recognition only so long as we keep in mind the fact that we are entitled to treat a particular act as amounting to recognition only when there is no doubt as to the intention to recognize. Otherwise, and this is what happens with perplexing regularity, we run the danger of introducing the vagaries of implied recognition through the backdoor of modes of recognition. Recognition is primarily and essentially a matter of intention. Intention cannot be replaced by questionable inferences from conduct. Such inferences are particularly inappropriate when the general attitude of the State in question points to its continued determination to deny recognition.

The best method of approaching the subject is to survey the various so-called modes of recognition—or, what is largely the same, the various forms of implied recognition—and to examine how far they amount to recognition in each particular case.

§ 109. *The Conclusion of Treaties.* The conclusion of a treaty,[1] and even the appointment of agents charged with the task of negotiating and concluding a treaty,[2] have often been described in general terms as evidence of recognition of a State or of a government. Such statements are probably too wide. They must be considered separately in relation to bilateral and multilateral treaties.

(*a*) *Multilateral Treaties.* On the face of it there would appear to be no difference, for the purpose of recognition, between the conclusion of a multilateral and of a bilateral treaty. In both, logic would seem to demand that a State cannot become a party to a treaty with a State or government which it does not recognize—that is to say, whose existence it denies—and that therefore the conclusion of a treaty amounts to recognition. Occasional pronouncements by governments substantiate that opinion.[3] However, the logic of that view is too rigid to be acceptable. The purpose of a multilateral treaty is not frustrated nor are its clauses necessarily rendered meaningless if its operation does not extend mutually to all parties to the treaty. If State *A* refuses to recognize State *B* and to have effective treaty relations with it, that is no reason why both these States should not, in the same treaty, enter into relations with other States. The cumbersome alternative would be to conclude two sets of multilateral treaties—one with State *A*, the other with State *B*, as a party. Moreover, when the number of States (or governments) to which recognition is refused is considerable, the number of the required multilateral conventions would grow in proportion.

In fact it may be doubted whether mere considerations of logic render absurd participation in a general treaty combined with non-recognition of

1 See Kunz, p. 48; Oppenheim, *International Law*, vol. I (4th ed. 1928), pp. 145, 146; Scalfati, pp. 254, 255 (with numerous other references).

2 See Moore, vol. I, p. 90, on the recognition of Ecuador by the United States in 1838 and of Paraguay in 1852 (p. 91).

3 See below, p. 378.

one or more of the parties to it. There is no compelling reason why there should be a full contractual relation between each contracting party and all other signatories to the treaty. There is no such relation when the operation of some provisions of the treaty or the treaty as a whole are excluded as the result of reservations extending to all or some of the contracting parties—as was the case, for instance, when, in signing the Optional Clause of Article 36 of the Statute of the Permanent Court of International Justice, Great Britain excepted from its operation disputes with the members of the British Commonwealth of Nations. The result of that reservation was the same as if Great Britain had declared that she did not recognize the Dominions or their governments and therefore refused to apply as between herself and them the provisions of the multilateral treaty as constituted by the Optional Clause. When in consequence of war the operation of a multilateral treaty is suspended or altogether eliminated as between the belligerents, it still remains effective as amongst the other parties. The list of signatories appearing in the Preamble can conveniently be conceived of as a framework; it is not an essential part of the treaty. When therefore a State agrees to become a party to a multilateral treaty, one or more of the parties to which it does not recognize, the treaty remains inoperative as between the parties in question but probably comes into effect as between them as soon as recognition is granted.[1] This solution is preferable to the alternative of either refraining from participation in the conclusion of multilateral treaties or being driven into granting recognition.

On occasions, doubts arising under this head have been resolved in advance by the addition of an express rider to the effect that participation in the treaty does not amount to recognition. This course has often, but not invariably, been adopted by the United States.[2] In

1 The position is analogous to that of the interruption of the operation of a treaty as the result of refusal to recognize the government of a State with which the treaty had been previously concluded. Thus, for instance, a Dutch Court held in 1931 (*Shipoff* v. *Elte Ltd.* (*Annual Digest*, 1931–2, Case no. 17)) that although the Convention on Civil Procedure of 17 July 1905 remained in force as between Holland and Russia, it was not operative on account of the Dutch refusal to recognize the Soviet Government. But see ibid. Case no. 16, for a different decision of another Dutch Court.

2 When signing the International Sanitary Convention of 21 June 1926, the United States made the following declaration: 'The Plenipotentiaries of the United States of America formally declare that their signing of the International Sanitary Convention of this date is not to be construed to mean that the United States of America recognizes a regime or entity acting as Government of a signatory or adhering Power when that regime or entity is not recognized by the United States as the Government of that Power. They further declare that the participation of the United States of America in the International Sanitary Convention of this date does not involve any contractual obligation on the part of the United States to a signatory or adhering Power represented by a regime or entity which the United States does not recognize as representing

fact, the somewhat hesitating practice of the United States is an instructive example of the fascination exercised by the theory of implied

the Government of that Power, *until it is represented by a Government recognized by the United States*' (Hudson, *International Legislation*, vol. III (1931), p. 1975). The passage reproduced in italics confirms the possibility of the construction put forward above according to which the absence of recognition results merely in the postponement of the operation of the treaty. It is significant that the United States was the only State which made a declaration of this nature although a number of other contracting parties were in a similar position. When signing, on 13 July 1931, the Convention for Limiting the Manufacture and Regulating the Distribution of Narcotic Drugs, the United States made an identical declaration (*League of Nations, Treaty Series*, vol. CXXXIX, p. 336). It is of interest to note the reply which Salvador made to that declaration: 'The Republic of Salvador states that it disagrees with the reservations embodied in Nos. 5 and 6 of the declarations made by the plenipotentiaries of the United States of America regarding governments not recognized by the Government of that country; in its opinion, those reservations constitute an infringement of the national sovereignty of Salvador, whose present Government, though not as yet recognized by the United States Government, has been recognized by the majority of the civilized countries of the world.... As it respects the internal regimes of other nations, the Republic of Salvador considers that the Convention in question, being of a strictly hygienic and humanitarian character, does not offer a suitable occasion to formulate such political reservations as have called forth this comment' (ibid. p. 343).

When the Straits Convention of 24 July 1923 was signed at Lausanne, elaborate precautions were taken in order to prevent the possibility of the signature of the Convention being interpreted as recognition *de jure*. Thus while the full powers of 'the Russian plenipotentiaries were described to have been issued on behalf of the Federated Soviet Republic of Russia, the Ukraine and Georgia', the Convention was signed simply on behalf of Russia (Hudson, op. cit. vol. II (1931), p. 1028).

Reservations similar to that made when signing the International Sanitary Convention were made by the United States on other occasions, such as the Convention for the Safety of Life at Sea of 1922 and the Narcotic Drugs Convention of 1931. It made no such reservation on other occasions such as the signing of the Convention on the Regime of the Straits of 1923; the Convention on the Suppression of Counterfeiting Currency of 1929; the Postal Conventions of 1924 and 1929; the Telecommunications Convention of 1932; the International Air Sanitary Convention of 1932.

See also, as to the Universal Postal Convention of 28 August 1924, Hudson in *A.J.* vol. XXIII (1929), p. 130; and see ibid. p. 132, as to the General Treaty for the Renunciation of War of 27 August 1928, which was ratified by the United States without any reservations relating to recognition. For a detailed explanation of the attitude of the State Department in this connection with regard to any future adherence by Soviet Russia see Hackworth, vol. I, p. 353.

In 1924 the Government of the United States raised no objection to Soviet Russia being invited to adhere to the Spitsbergen treaty 'through the medium of the regime now functioning therein, which has not been recognized by the United States... provided it were clearly understood that the absence of such an objection should not be construed by any party to the Treaty or by the regime functioning in Russia as constituting the recognition of that regime by the Government of the United States' (*U.S. For. Rel.* 1924 (I), p. 5).

On 11 June 1903, Great Britain broke off diplomatic relations with Serbia following upon the murder of the Serbian King and Queen. On 10 July 1903, Great Britain and Serbia became parties to a *Règlement* annexed to the Telegraphic Convention of St Petersburg of 22 July 1875.

recognition.[1] The reservation of non-recognition is appended in some multilateral treaties and omitted in others—which latter course represents the more recent practice. Occasionally a distinction is made between the joint signature of a multilateral treaty (said to require a reservation expressly repudiating the intention to recognize) and adherence to it on the part of the unrecognized State (which, it has been rightly said, cannot be given the easy option of obtaining recognition, thrust upon the unwilling State, by the act of adhesion). On other occasions the State Department has tended to distinguish between treaties requiring contact, exchange of information and co-operation between signatories and, therefore, believed to imply recognition, and treaties where no such contact is required—a reason the inadequacy of which is illustrated by the fact that international practice constantly shows instances of administrative contact between governments notwithstanding the absence of recognition.[2]

The legal position with respect to multilateral treaties may be correctly summarized to the effect that neither signature nor adherence on the part either of the non-recognizing or the unrecognized State result by themselves in bringing about recognition. Any reservations disclaiming the intention to recognize must be regarded as appended *ex abundante cautela*. They do not amount to an indirect admission of the doctrine of implied recognition in this respect.[3]

1 For a survey of that practice, see Hackworth, vol. I, pp. 347–55.

2 See below, pp. 388–90.

3 When the International Telegraphic Conference was signed at Paris on 17 May 1865, the President of the Conference declared that as the object of the Convention was to regulate the telegraphic services, its signature could not prejudice, from the political point of view, the existing relations between the parties. The declaration, which followed the lines of a similar formal statement made in 1863 in connection with the signature of the Scheld Convention, was the result of a prolonged exchange of views. On the latter occasion, the original intention was to present on behalf of Austria the following declaration: 'Le Représentant de l'Autriche, au moment de signer au nom de son Gouvernement le Traité collectif avec le Représentant du Roi d'Italie, déclare qu'il doit le faire sous toutes réserves et sans préjudicier en rien l'attitude de l'Autriche vis-à-vis de ce Souverain, qu'elle ne reconnaît que comme Roi de Sardaigne.' Italy objected to the proposed declaration. Eventually, the following agreed statement was made by the President of the Conference: 'La Convention ayant un caractère exclusivement économique et commercial, doit avoir pour effet de faciliter les rapports mutuels des États contractants sans rien préjuger, au point de vue politique, à l'attitude réciproque des Gouvernements respectifs entre eux.' See *Fontes Juris Gentium, Digest of the Diplomatic Correspondence of the European States*, 1856–71, vol. I (1932), pp. 156–8. On the refusal of the British Government in 1921 to meet delegates of the De Valera party as representatives of an independent and sovereign State on the ground that acquiescence in such a conference might imply recognition of the independence of Ireland see *Irish Free State and Others* v. *Guaranty State Deposit Company* (in Dickinson, *Cases and other Readings on the Law of Nations* (1929), pp. 929, 930).

(*b*) *Bilateral Treaties*. In the case of bilateral treaties the presumption of recognition appears to be cogent to the point of being conclusive. While a multilateral treaty may be fully operative as between governments which recognize one another although it is in abeyance as between others, no such situation is possible in a bilateral treaty. Yet even in such cases there is no absolutely compelling reason to assume that a contractual relation is tantamount to recognition. There are intermediate stages between full recognition and the total absence of contractual relations. The very absence of normal relations which follows from the refusal of recognition may necessitate temporary arrangements and agreements. In fact, so long as we retain in mind the essential nature and purpose of recognition, there is nothing necessarily illogical in the conclusion of an agreement with an unrecognized State or government. Recognition as a State implies that in the opinion of the recognizing State the nascent community possesses the requirements of statehood and is therefore a normal subject of international rights and duties. Recognition as a government implies that the recognized government possesses the necessary qualifications to represent the State in question. In both cases, the result of recognition is the conferment of a status, which means a variety of rights and obligations flowing from statehood or governmental capacity. However, independent of any general recognition, a community claiming to be a State or an authority claiming to be a government may enjoy rights—including the faculty to enter into engagements—to the extent to which they are conceded by other States. It is merely the current view that only fully recognized States can be subjects of international rights and duties which prompts the contrary opinion. The existing State or States, by concluding an arrangement with the community or authority in question, admit, *pro tanto*, its contractual capacity in the domain of the treaty-making power while refusing recognition for any other purpose.[1]

1 When Dr Baty refers (in *A.J.* vol. XXX (1936), p. 380) to 'the heretical doctrine that acts of recognition can be contradicted by words', he is probably begging the question. Recognition is a matter of intention of governments rather than of inference by writers. There is nothing 'absurd' (ibid. p. 379) in the fact that conclusion of a treaty is accompanied by a denial of 'complete statehood'. The difficulty lies in the suggestion that short of recognition of complete statehood no legal relationship is possible at all. For a cogent refutation of any such suggestion see Hudson, 'Recognition and Multilateral Treaties' in *A.J.* vol. XXIII (1929), p. 128, and Jaffe, *Judicial Aspects of Foreign Relations* (1933), pp. 113–18.

In 1865 Bismarck attempted to avoid any implication of recognition of Italy which might be deduced from the conclusion of a treaty. He proposed, instead, the signature of a protocol embodying a *modus vivendi*—a proposal which was not accepted. Italy insisted throughout on the conclusion and ratification of a formal treaty of commerce intended, *inter alia*, as a means of full recognition. Prussia and the *Zollverein* eventually

For these reasons it is doubtful whether the conclusion of even a bilateral treaty necessarily implies recognition. On 23 March 1935, the Governments of Manchukuo and the Union of Soviet Socialist Republics concluded an Agreement for the cession to Manchukuo of the rights of Russia concerning the North Manchurian Railway (Chinese Eastern Railway). To that Agreement there was annexed a detailed Protocol providing for the purchase of goods by Soviet Russia from Manchukuo and Japan in lieu of payment for the railway.[1] The Agreement and Protocol were intended to cope with a situation likely to cause friction between Soviet Russia and Japan, but it would be inaccurate to maintain that, beyond the admission of the existence of a government claiming to represent an independent State, any other recognition was intended or given. In fact the Agreement was concluded in Tokyo and the principal Russian signatory was the Russian diplomatic representative accredited to the Japanese Government. No Russian diplomatic representative was at that time accredited to the body styling itself the Government of Manchukuo. Between 1918 and 1920, at a time when neither *de jure* nor *de facto* recognition had been granted, Soviet Russia concluded a number of agreements with various States with regard to repatriation of prisoners of war and other matters. Thus on 12 February 1920 an Agreement was concluded at Copenhagen between 'His Majesty's Government and the Soviet Government of Russia' for the exchange of prisoners of war. On 7 September 1920 the British Foreign Office forwarded the text of the Agreement to the Secretariat of the League of Nations for registration in accordance with Article 18 of the Covenant.[2] On 20 November 1920 the Foreign Office, in connection with the proceedings in *Luther* v. *Sagor*, stated that 'His Majesty's Government have never officially recognized the Soviet Government in any way'.[3] It was only at a later date, on 20 April 1921, after the conclusion of the Trade Agreement of 16 March 1921, that the Foreign Office was in the position to inform the parties that 'His Majesty's Government recognize the Soviet Government as the *de facto* Government of Russia'.[4] Similar agreements were concluded between Soviet Russia and other States at a time when they

complied with the Italian wishes. Moreover, in the Final Protocol signed simultaneously with the Treaty of Commerce between Italy and the *Zollverein* on 31 December 1865, it was expressly stated that the exchange of ratifications would imply the recognition of the kingdom of Italy by those members of the *Zollverein* who had so far no regular relations with Italy. For various extracts from the correspondence on the subject see *Fontes Juris Gentium, Digest of the Diplomatic Correspondence of the European States*, 1856–71, vol. 1, pp. 147–9.

1 For the text of both see *A.J.* vol. xxx (1936), Suppl. pp. 85 and 97 respectively.

2 *League of Nations, Treaty Series*, vol. 1, p. 264.

3 [1921] 1 K.B. 456.

4 *Luther* v. *Sagor*, [1921] 3 K.B. 536.

denied the former both *de facto* and *de jure* recognition. Some of these agreements went beyond providing for the repatriation of prisoners of war.[1] Thus in the Agreement with Hungary, signed on 28 July 1920, the Contracting Parties agreed 'not to take any military action against each other...in a civil war, and not to assist the enemies of the other either directly or indirectly'.[2]

If the reason for denying recognition were simply—as perhaps ought to be the case—that the government or the State to which recognition is denied does not exist in fact or in law, then it might be easier to accept the view that any contact which is logically impossible without assuming the existence of the government or State in question amounts to recognition. But recognition is often denied for other reasons. The refusal of recognition has occasionally been coupled with the admission that the State or government to which recognition is refused does in fact exist. Of this the statement of the Department of State in the case of *Salimoff & Co.* v. *Standard Oil Company*[3] is an instructive example. If recognition is refused for reasons other than the non-existence of the unrecognized State or government, then it is difficult to see how contact with it for limited purposes, including the conclusion of agreements, necessarily implies recognition.

If the conclusion of a treaty were tantamount to recognition, it would follow that the appointment of agents or plenipotentiaries for that purpose has the same effect. For by appointing them the State in question would signify that it regards the other party as capable of concluding a treaty regardless of whether the negotiations actually lead to its conclusion. Yet the appointment of agents entrusted with the negotiation of an agreement is not sufficient evidence of the intention to recognize. In 1920 Great Britain received M. Krassin, of Soviet Russia, for the purpose of negotiating a trade agreement, but, as mentioned above, the British Foreign Office declined to admit that recognition *de facto* or *de jure* had taken place. It stated that the British Government had merely 'assented to the claim that that which Monsieur Krassin represents in this country is a State Government of Russia'.[4] The practice of the United States uniformly confirms the view that though, in general, the conclusion of a treaty implies recognition,

1 See for an enumeration and discussion of some of these treaties Jaffe, *Judicial Aspects of Foreign Relations* (1933), pp. 114, 115 and Taracouzio, *The Soviet Union and International Law* (1935), pp. 255, 256.

2 Taracouzio, ibid. p. 255.

3 (1933), 262 N.Y.S. 693; 262 N.Y. 220. See above, p. 148.

4 As stated in the communication of the Foreign Office in *Luther* v. *Sagor*, [1921] 1 K.B. 456.

the appointment of agents for that purpose does not have that effect.[1] In a sense it may be accurately argued that, far from recognition being legitimately implied from the treaty, it is recognition which confers upon the agreement the character of a treaty. This apparently was the view of the Canadian Government in connection with the complaint put forward in 1923 by the Iroquois Indians. The latter contended that they were a State within the meaning of Article 17 of the Covenant of the League of Nations and relied for that purpose on their implied recognition resulting from the conclusion of various 'treaties'. The Canadian view was that 'naturally and obviously it was not the intention in this or preceding "treaties" to recognize or to infer the existence of any independent or sovereign status of the Indians concerned'.[2]

On the other hand it is clear that the conclusion of a bilateral treaty is a proper mode of recognition in all cases in which there is no reasonable doubt as to the intention of the parties on the subject. This would apply in particular to such treaties as a comprehensive treaty of commerce and navigation or a treaty of alliance. Occasions may arise when for political reasons a State may choose to grant recognition by means of concluding a treaty of this character in circumstances which leave no doubt as to its intention to grant recognition. This will be the case whenever express recognition is deemed to be inexpedient as likely to offend the suscepti-

1 See, as to intercourse with unrecognized governments, Houghton in *Indiana Law Review*, vol. IV (1928–9), p. 519, and in *Minnesota Law Review*, vol. XIII (1928–9), p. 216. In 1921 the United States insisted on negotiating and signing a Convention with Mexico before they recognized its Government (*U.S. For. Rel.* 1921 (II), pp. 412 et seq., 418 et seq.): 'In entering into this treaty with you recognition would be effected, ipso facto', wrote President Harding to General Obregón on 21 July 1921 (ibid. p. 421). In 1922 the Mexican Government of General Obregón, at that time unrecognized by the United States, was willing to regard the signature of a claims convention with the United States as implying recognition (see ibid. pp. 639, 674).

For an example of protracted negotiations with the unrecognized Government of Mexico in 1921 and 1922 for the conclusion of a Treaty of Amity and Commerce and other conventions see ibid. pp. 397, 508, 511, and ibid. 1922 (II), pp. 639 et seq. Secretary of State Hughes wrote at that time to the Chargé d'Affaires in Mexico:

'The question of recognition is a subordinate one, but there will be no difficulty as to this, for if General Obregón is ready to negotiate a proper treaty it is drawn so as to be negotiated with him and the making of the treaty in proper form will accomplish the recognition of the Government that makes it. In short, when it appears that there is a government in Mexico willing to bind itself to the discharge of primary international obligations concurrently with that act its recognition will take place' (ibid. 1921 (II), p. 407).

2 *Official Journal*, 1924, p. 836. See also above, p. 49. For the allegation, rejected by the Court, that by entering into certain agreements with Eire scheduled to the Eire (Confirmation of Agreements) Act, 1938, Great Britain recognized the full separation of the Irish Free State from the British Empire see *Murray* v. *Parkes*, (1942) 58 T.L.R. 231.

bilities of the parent or other States. These were the reasons which in 1825 prompted Canning to insist on this mode of recognition with regard to the Latin-American Republics. The relevant part of his despatch merits quotation. He said:

'My opinion and my language have always been that the signature of a treaty by a Plenipotentiary of His Majesty with the Plenipotentiary of a New State, which last mentioned Plenipotentiary is designated in the Preamble to such treaty *as* the Plenipotentiary of that New State, described by its proper style (whether monarchy or republic), was in itself an effective and valid recognition of that State by His Majesty, and as valid as if the word "His Majesty recognizes" were *totidem litteris* introduced into it. I also thought, and continue to think, this mode of recognition better calculated for the advantage and dignity of the State to be recognized than any form of words distinctly expressing Recognition; more for its dignity, because the assumed independence is therein admitted, not created; and more for its advantage, because as nothing is so desirable for the New State as that other Governments should follow our example in acknowledging them, nothing can contribute to that end so much as the removing of any stumbling block out of the way of that acknowledgment. Any person must have attended very little to the present state of opinions in Europe who does not believe that there are Governments which might make a commercial treaty with a New State in the simplest form of words which yet would be staggered at a Preamble of formal Recognition.'[1]

It has not always been easy to adhere to the policy of avoiding express recognition. The importance which a new State attached to express as distinguished from implied recognition by treaty may be seen from the report to Canning sent by the British plenipotentiaries who were instructed to negotiate a treaty with Mexico. The Mexican plenipotentiaries were reported to have expressed the view that implied recognition was 'not sufficient for the people who, just emerging from a long and arduous struggle for liberty, required a clear and positive declaration to that effect'. In emphatic terms they expressed preference for formal recognition 'even though purchased by extensive concessions, than an acknowledgment *de facto*, however liberally offered, provided it was necessary...to reflect upon it in order to discover that it was really an acknowledgment at all'.[2] The Mexican delegates proposed to offer special commercial privileges in exchange for express recognition.

1 George Canning to Sir Charles Stuart, 1 December 1825, printed in Webster, *Britain and the Independence of Latin America*, 1812–1830, vol. I (1938), p. 291. However, Sir Charles was instructed to agree to express recognition in case Brazil should insist upon it.

2 Mr Morier and Mr Ward to Mr Canning, 10 April 1825 (Webster, op. cit. p. 469).

§ 110. *Participation in Conferences.* Participation in a conference attended by the unrecognized State or government does not amount to recognition of that State or government. Notwithstanding occasional hesitation, this is a view constantly acted upon by governments.[1] Its cogency is obvious. As a matter of principle, if the signature of or adherence to a multilateral treaty to which an unrecognized State is a party does not amount to recognition, it is difficult to see how participation in a conference, which normally leads to such treaties, can amount to recognition. As a matter of convenience, there would seem to exist the strongest objection to a rule which would make it impossible for a State to participate in a conference attended by one or more unrecognized governments or which would mar the atmosphere of the conference by precautionary declarations. Undoubtedly, official and solemn admission to an international conference may be a convenient way of granting recognition, but there must be persuasive evidence of intention to grant recognition in that way. Thus, for instance, it has been suggested that the formal admission of Poland's plenipotentiaries to the Peace Conference on 18 January 1919 amounted to recognition.[2] Actually, Poland was recognized by individual and express declarations.[3]

The view of the Advisory Committee of the Assembly of the League of Nations set up in connection with the non-recognition of Manchukuo was that participation in multilateral treaties, both closed conventions and those open to future adhesion, does not imply recognition. But the Committee was of the opinion that it was in the spirit of the policy or of the obligation of non-recognition to discourage the participation of the unrecognized State.[4]

1 In its instruction to the American Delegation sent in 1925 to the Conference on the Supervision of the International Trade in Arms and Ammunition the Department of State expressed the view in emphatic terms that the bare participation of the United States through an American Delegation in a conference attended by the delegates of the Soviet Government, which at that time was not recognized by the United States, 'would signify nothing' (Hackworth, vol. I, p. 348). This was also the view of the Department on the occasion of the Bolivar Congress in 1926, at which time the Nicaraguan and Ecuadoran Governments were not recognized by the United States (ibid. p. 346). In 1924, at a time when the United States did not recognize the Chilean Government, they took part in the Fourth Pan-American Congress convened at Santiago, Chile. It was not considered that such participation could properly be construed as recognition. The United States Delegation was instructed formally to make that clear in case an attempt should be made to construe the participation of the United States in that sense.

2 See Temperley, *A History of the Peace Conference of Paris*, vol. V (1920–4), p. 158.

3 See below, p. 381.

4 *Off.J.* Special Supplement, no. 113, pp. 11, 12.

§ 111. *Accrediting and Receiving of Diplomatic Representatives.* The formal appointment or reception of diplomatic representatives is properly regarded both as a mode of and as an irrebuttable presumption of recognition. Persons clearly and solemnly endowed with diplomatic character represent the State in all its aspects. Diplomatic intercourse is a sign of normal relations, and the solemnity and formality with which it is inaugurated leave no doubt as to the intention of recognition pure and simple. Practice shows numerous examples of adoption of this method of recognition.[1]

1 Thus, for instance, the British recognition of Poland in 1919 was in the form of the following communication addressed by the head of the British Mission in Warsaw to the Polish Government:

British Mission, Warsaw,
26 February 1919

'Sir,

With reference to my Note of February 25th, I have been instructed to inform your Excellency that, as soon as practical arrangements are possible, His Majesty's Government will be most happy to enter into formal diplomatic relations with the Government of Poland....'

Previously, on 23 February 1919, the following telegram had been sent from London to Sir E. Howard, the British representative at Warsaw:

'His Majesty's Government have decided to recognize Poland as an independent Sovereign State.

'Please inform General Pilsudski of this decision and offer him the congratulations of His Majesty's Government on the occasion.

'You should at the same time inform M. Paderewski that his Government are henceforth recognized by His Majesty's Government as the official Polish Government with whom they will be happy to enter into formal diplomatic relations as soon as practical arrangements permit. Mr Balfour telegraphed to London on February 22, 1919, that it was decided at yesterday's meeting [of the Peace Conference] to recognize the Polish Government....'

The following was regarded as the full recognition of the Provisional Polish Government by the United States on 22 January 1919:

'The President of the United States of America directs me to extend to you as Prime Minister and Secretary for Foreign Affairs of the Provisional Polish Government his sincere wishes for your success in the high office which you have assumed and his earnest hope that the Government of which you are a part will bring prosperity to the Republic of Poland.

'It is my privilege to extend to you at this time my personal greetings and officially to assure you that it will be a source of gratification to enter into official relations with you at the earliest opportunity.' Telegram from the American Peace Mission in Paris to M. Paderewski (*U.S. For. Rel.* 1919 (II), p. 741).

In connection with the recognition of the French Government in 1870 it was assumed by the British Government that the recognition would take the form of 'the issue of regular credentials on behalf of the British Ambassador in France to the actual head of the Government' of France (Lord Granville to Lord Lyons, *B.F.S.P.* vol. LXI, p. 995). When in April 1939 the United States informed the Spanish Government that it intended to appoint an ambassador to Spain and asked for an *agrément* for the person named, the Spanish Government asked for an explicit confirmation that that step signified full recognition of the Spanish Government as the sole and legitimate Government of Spain. That assurance was formally given. See Hackworth, vol. I, p. 297.

On the other hand, the retention of diplomatic representatives for the purpose of communicating with a government established as the result of a revolution does not imply its recognition. In 1870 the British Government instructed the Ambassador in Paris to enter into communication with the 'Gouvernement de la Défense Nationale' for the purpose of protecting British interests, but without recognizing the new government. It has been for a long time the practice of the British Foreign Office in cases of revolutionary changes to instruct the diplomatic representatives to remain at their posts and to maintain the necessary contacts without, however, recognizing officially the new government.[1] The same applies to the practice of the United States[2] and of

1 In connection with the Chilean revolution in 1891 the British Minister was instructed as follows: 'You are authorized to recognize the new Government provisionally, and to enter into unofficial relations with it as soon as its formation has been duly announced to you' (*State Papers*, vol. xcv (1892), p. 229). The Under-Secretary of State addressed a letter to the newly appointed Chilean Minister informing him that 'according to the usage observed by this country in such cases, formal and full recognition with the establishment of official relations would follow as soon as a President has been constitutionally elected and installed' (ibid. p. 235).

When in 1889 a revolution broke out in Brazil the British Minister was instructed in the following terms: 'You should for the present maintain friendly relations unofficially with the new Government, and *when it is legally established* you should refer to me for further instructions as to its official recognition by Her Majesty's Government.' On 2 October he was authorized to inform the Brazilian Government that 'as the recent elections for the constituent assembly showed the acquiescence of the mass of the population in the new form of government, Her Majesty's Government were ready to recognize the flag of the Republic, and that as soon as a President of the Republic had been formally and constitutionally installed Mr Wyndham [the Minister] would be accredited to him in due form' (F.O. Brazil, 1889).

2 The instructions sent in 1879 by Secretary Evans to the United States representative in Venezuela were based on the same view: 'The American Minister was...to "maintain a considerate and conciliatory attitude" in his "unofficial relations with the new government" and to "co-operate in all proper ways (short of formal recognition until so instructed)"....The actual formula of recognition is unmistakable and, short of that evident step, the diplomatic fiction of "officious" intercourse, or "unofficial" action is elastic enough to admit of continuing ordinary intercourse' (Moore, vol. I, pp. 150, 151). And see generally ibid. pp. 235–41, on acts falling short of recognition of governments. Moore—correctly, it is believed—summarizes the existing practice as follows: '...the sending of a new minister or the retention of an old one, while it implies continued recognition of the state, does not constitute a recognition of the new government, so long as there is no formal presentation of credentials and communications bear only an unofficial character' (ibid. p. 235).

In 1913 and in the subsequent years, although the United States refused to recognize the Huerta Governments, they nevertheless maintained a diplomatic mission in Mexico City which transacted business with those in *de facto* control of the capital. The Notes sent by the Minister to the unrecognized authorities were marked 'Personal—Unofficial', but the relations with the unrecognized Government were otherwise in many ways hardly distinguishable from ordinary diplomatic intercourse. See Houghton in *Temple Law Quarterly*, vol. v (1930–1), pp. 340–67 and *George W.*

France.[1] Moreover, there is authority for the view that the sending of diplomatic representatives, unaccompanied by official and formal presentation of credentials, does not amount to an implied recognition of a government. Such persons are merely agents, the sending or reception of whom, far from amounting to recognition, is the frequent concomitant of its refusal.[2]

§ 112. *Appointment and Reception of Consuls.* (*a*) *Appointment and Reception without Request for or Issue of Exequatur.* These do not carry any implication of recognition. This applies not only to the retention of consuls in countries with unrecognized governments, but also to the renewal of consular personnel and the sending of consuls, without a request for or issue of an exequatur, when none had been previously sent.[3] The function

Hopkins case decided on 31 March 1926, by the United States Mexican General Claims Commission (*Opinions of Commissioners*, 1929, pp. 45, 46).

On the other hand, the practice of the United States agrees with that of other States inasmuch as formal recognition of diplomatic representatives or the issue or renewal of letters of credence is held to imply recognition. Thus various French revolutionary governments were recognized by the United States through this method: in 1793 by the reception of M. Genet as Minister (Moore, vol. I, p. 121); in 1804 by the issue of new credentials to the American Minister in Paris (ibid. p. 122); in 1848, in the same way (ibid. p. 124); so also in 1852 (ibid. p. 126). And see ibid. pp. 139, 147, 148, 154, for other examples.

The Fifth Committee of the First Assembly of the League of Nations expressed the view, in connection with the Ukrainian demand for admission, that the appointment of representatives with a government implied recognition *de facto* of that government (*Records of the First Assembly, Plenary Meetings*, p. 666). On the other hand, the same Commission apparently held that the circumstance that a *de facto* government receives and sends unofficial agents and that it enters into negotiations with other States does not necessarily imply its recognition *de facto* by those States (ibid. pp. 669, 670). In connection with the admission of the Dominican Republic, the Sixth Committee of the Fifth Assembly answered the question whether the Dominican Republic was recognized *de jure* or *de facto* by finding that the majority of European and American States had diplomatic or consular representatives there (*Records of the Fifth Assembly, Sixth Committee*, Special Supplement, no. 29, p. 24).

1 See, for example, the instructions given in 1873 to the French diplomatic representative at Madrid (*Documents diplomatiques français*, vol. I, i, p. 201).

2 See below, pp. 388–90.

3 In *Taylor* v. *Barclay*, (1828) 2 Sim. 214, it was contended on the part of the plaintiff that the appointment of consuls to the Latin-American countries as well as a meeting between the officers of the King and the officials of Guatemala at a Congress at Panama implied the recognition of Panama. The Foreign Office, fortified by an Opinion of the Law Officers, gave a negative reply to the question whether recognition had been granted. See Bushe-Fox in *B.Y.* vol. XII (1931), pp. 71, 72. The British, and some American, practice on the subject are surveyed in a memorandum prepared in 1873 by Mr Hertslet, Librarian of the Foreign Office, and printed in Smith, vol. I, pp. 251–7. For the more recent practice of the United States see Moore, vol. I, § 72, and vol. V, § 698; Hackworth, vol. IV, pp. 688 et seq. See also *Harvard Research in International Law* (*Consuls* (1932), Article 6, pp. 238–41). And see Bonham, *The British Consuls in the Confederacy* (1911), and Moore, vol. I, p. 207, on the maintenance,

and the status of consuls thus sent and received are, in practice, indistinguishable from those furnished with an exequatur. Acquiescence in activities of consuls sent by unrecognized regimes as well as the toleration by the latter of consuls sent to them by non-recognizing States are a persistent feature of international practice.[1]

(*b*) *Request for an Exequatur.* Governmental practice seems to be divided on the question as to whether the request for an exequatur implies recognition. The United States have repeatedly requested exequaturs in circumstances in which there was a clear absence of any intention to grant recognition. Moore summarizes the practice of the United States in the matter by saying that 'the act of soliciting and receiving from the govern-

for a time, by Great Britain of consuls in the Confederacy notwithstanding the absence of recognition. And see below, p. 388. After the establishment of the new Kingdom of Italy under Victor Emmanuel Spain refused to recognize it. She continued, with respect to the Kingdom of the Two Sicilies, to recognize the authority of King Francis II whose consular agents continued to exercise their functions in the Spanish ports. Vessels arriving from the ports of the Kingdom of Naples were given option to transact business with the consuls either of King Francis II or of King Victor Emmanuel. It was made clear that this in no way implied the recognition of the Kingdom of Italy (*Archives diplomatiques*, 1862, vol. I, p. 435). Spain adopted a similar course with regard to vessels coming from the Confederate States (*Parl. Papers*, 1862, vol. LXII, p. 238).

1 The Advisory Committee of the Assembly of the League of Nations set up in connection with the non-recognition of Manchukuo did not consider the replacing of consuls to imply the recognition of Manchukuo. The reason adduced was that those agents were appointed for the purpose of keeping their Governments informed and of protecting their nationals (*Official Journal*, Special Supplement, no. 113, p. 13). But the Committee thought it to be in conformity with the recommendation of the Assembly that the consuls, in their contact with the Manchukuo authorities, should not, so far as possible, do anything which might be interpreted 'expressly or by implication' that they regard the authorities established in Manchuria as being the proper government of the country. For numerous examples of continuation of consular activities notwithstanding the absence of recognition see Hackworth, vol. IV, pp. 684–99. In the course of the Spanish Civil War between 1936 and 1938, while the United States declined to recognize passports issued by agents of General Franco, whose Government they did not recognize, it was pointed out to General Franco's representative that in practice persons bearing such documents were granted visas without being required to present any other papers. See, for the Instructions of the Department of State on the matter in May 1938, Hackworth, vol. IV, p. 698. Similarly, no restrictions were imposed on the issue of necessary papers by Franco agents to enable vessels to proceed to ports in Spain under their control. In 1926 no objection was raised to the payment of fees to the agent of the unrecognized Nicaraguan Government for ships clearing to ports under its control (ibid. p. 695). In 1922, at a time when the United States refused to recognize the Government in power in Guatemala, the United States authorities transacted business with a person appointed as Consul-General of Guatemala in New York, but the United States Chargé d'Affaires in Guatemala was instructed to make it clear to the authorities concerned that 'such action does not constitute recognition but is taken simply to avoid inconvenience and loss to commercial interests' (*U.S. For. Rel.* 1922 (II), p. 459).

ment of a certain country an exequatur for a consular officer at a particular place, is not a conclusive recognition of such country's sovereignty over the place in question'.[1] He quotes a number of examples indicative of that view.[2] However, the practice of the United States in the matter has not been uniform. When in 1818 Brazil, at that time not recognized as a State, requested the United States to receive a Brazilian consul on the ground, *inter alia*, that a consul of the United States functioned in Brazil, the answer was that while the continued residence at Buenos Ayres of the American consul, appointed before the revolution, 'implied no recognition of any particular Government', the issue of an exequatur to a Brazilian consul would imply recognition.[3]

In 1911, notwithstanding its refusal to recognize the annexation of the Congo by Belgium, the United States applied for and received from the Belgian Foreign Office the recognition of an American 'Vice and Deputy Consul General' in the Congo.[4] When in 1924 the United States refused to recognize the Chilean Government, they agreed to accept exequaturs issued by the Chilean Government provided it were understood that such acceptance did not involve recognition. The Department of State was apparently of the view that formal and unconditional acceptance of the exequatur would have the effect of recognition,[5] a view not necessarily based on former practice.

After the purported assumption by Germany of a protectorate over Czechoslovakia in 1939, Germany, possibly in order to obtain recognition by the backdoor of implied recognition resulting from an application for a consular exequatur, informed various governments that consulates in Prague required an exequatur from Germany and that they would have to discontinue their consular functions unless an exequatur was applied for within six weeks. The United States thereupon applied for an exequatur, but the Embassy in Berlin was instructed to inform the German Foreign Office orally that this step would not involve a change in the attitude of the United States as to the status of Czechoslovakia. Thereupon the German Government refused to comply with the application on the ground that

1 Vol. v, p. 13.

2 Such as obtaining exequaturs from Nicaragua for a consul at Corn Island; from the Hovas Government for a consul at Madagascar; and from Great Britain for a consul at Belize.

3 *B.F.S.P.* vol. VIII, p. 1062.

4 In its instructions to the American Minister the Department of State said: 'In instructing you to apply to the Belgian Foreign Office for the recognition of Mr Broy the Department was simply carrying out the rule and custom of asking consular recognition by the *de facto* authorities, it not being a question of *de jure* determination.' Hackworth, vol. IV, p. 684.

5 Ibid. p. 688.

'when one government addresses to another government a request that such an exequatur be granted, it must recognize that the other government is entitled to sovereignty over the area in question' and that 'it is an evident self-contradiction to ask a government to perform an act in the exercise of its sovereignty and at the same time to contest the right of that government to exercise such sovereignty'.[1] The United States maintained its attitude, but the consulate was not closed.

On the other hand, some, though not all, British official pronouncements seem to indicate that a request for an exequatur is tantamount to recognition. In the course of the Mosul Boundary Dispute between Great Britain and Turkey, in reply to the Turkish contention that she had declined to recognize the mandatory system, the British representative on the Council of the League submitted that by applying for and succeeding in obtaining exequaturs for Turkish consuls at Beirut, Aleppo and Jerusalem, Turkey had recognized these mandates.[2] In 1931 the British representative before the Mandates Commission stated that 'foreign states had been informed that their request for King Faisal's exequatur would imply *de jure* recognition'.[3] In 1937, in connection with the Spanish Civil War, the language used was less emphatic. When explaining, on 8 November 1937, the reasons for the mutual appointment of agents by Great Britain and the insurgent authorities in Spain, the Foreign Secretary pointed out that while it would have been possible to meet the existing difficulties by the transfer of consular offices to insurgent territory, that course was not adopted because 'the appointment of new Consuls with commissions from His Majesty the King and the grant to them of an exequatur by the authorities at Salamanca would have implied *a measure*[4] of recognition of these authorities'.[5] In May 1939 Great Britain, in consequence of the German announcement that the exequaturs granted by the former Czechoslovak Government would no longer be recognized, applied for a new exequatur for the British consul in Prague. However, in the statement before the House of Commons the Government did not go beyond the admission that the application for a new exequatur implied a *de facto* recognition of the existing position in Bohemia and Moravia.[6] Similarly, it was stated in the House of Commons on 15 May 1939 that the request to the Slovak Government for an exequatur for the British Consul in Bratislava amounted to *de facto* recognition.[7]

1 Hackworth, vol. IV, p. 689.
2 *Official Journal*, 1925, p. 1334.
3 Permanent Mandates Commission, *Minutes*, vol. XX, p. 133.
4 *H.C. Debates*, vol. CCCXXVIII, col. 1386.
5 Italics added by the writer.
6 *H.C. Debates*, vol. CCCXLVIII, col. 1786.
7 Ibid. vol. CCCXLVII, cols. 961, 962.

There is no compelling reason of logic why a request for a consular exequatur should signify general recognition, i.e. an admission other than that the requested authority is in power in the territory in question and that it is in a position to ensure the conditions necessary for the normal performance of consular functions. If, for the sake of prestige or for other reasons, that authority attaches importance to the formal request for an exequatur,[1] the non-recognizing State may comply with that wish without committing itself to the wider consequences of general recognition. The importance and the character of the exequatur and of the consular function in general would not seem to make it a proper or natural instrument of recognition. However, in view of the preponderance of opinion that a request for an exequatur implies recognition, a government making that request and wishing to avoid any such implication will be acting wisely in entering a caveat calculated to prevent that effect.

(*c*) *The Issue of an Exequatur.* The same considerations would seem to apply to the question whether the issuing of an exequatur to the consuls of a hitherto unrecognized State or government amounts to recognition. However, such scant practice and expression of opinion as exist in the matter clearly favour the implication of recognition.[2]

1 For an example of a more dignified attitude, subsequently abandoned, in refusing to treat the request of an exequatur as implied recognition see the statement made on behalf of the President of the American Confederacy in 1863 in a communication to its representative in London: 'The President has hitherto steadily resisted all influences which have been exerted to induce him to exact of foreign Consuls that they should ask for an exequatur from this Government as a condition of the continued exercise of their functions. It was not deemed compatible with the dignity of the Government to extort, by enforcing the withdrawal of national protection from neutral residents, such inferential recognition of its independence as might be supposed to be implied in the request for an exequatur. The Consuls of foreign nations, therefore, established within the Confederacy, who were in possession of an exequatur issued by the Government of the United States prior to the formation of the Confederacy, have been maintained and respected in the exercise of their legitimate functions, and the same protection and respect will be accorded to them in future, so long as they confine themselves to the sphere of their duties, and seek neither to evade nor defy the legitimate authority of this Government within its own jurisdiction.' *Parl. Papers*, 1864, vol. LXII, *North America*, no. 13, *Correspondence respecting the removal of British Consuls from the so styled Confederate States of America.*

2 That the grant of an exequatur implies recognition was apparently the view of the United States in 1819 when they refused the request of the United Provinces of South America for the grant of an exequatur to their consul: '...the exequatur for a consul can obviously not be granted without recognizing the authority from whom his appointment proceeds as sovereign' (Moore, vol. I, p. 79). While Manchukuo granted exequaturs to consuls sent by Russia, it was reported that the latter permitted Manchukuan consuls to function within her territories (*Manchukuo Year Book*, 1934, p. 154). The distinction is significant.

§ 113. *The Appointment of Agents.* The appointment of agents or missions not endowed with diplomatic character does not constitute recognition. On the contrary, the very reason for their appointment is the unwillingness or inability to grant recognition and to maintain ordinary diplomatic relations. In 1919 Great Britain sent agents to and received agents from the Provisional Government of Northern Russia with which she and the Allied Powers were co-operating. But the Foreign Office, in reply to an enquiry from the Court, stated that that Government 'has not been formally recognized either by His Majesty's Government or by the Allied Powers as the Government of a sovereign independent State'. The Court thereupon decided that the Government in question was not entitled to the ordinary jurisdictional immunities enjoyed by governments of independent States.[1] In the course of the discussions arising out of the *Trent* case—in which two political agents sent to Great Britain and France in 1861 by the Confederate States were forcibly removed from a British ship by a Federal cruiser—Great Britain based her case largely on the right of receiving agents from the Confederacy. The latter, although recognized as belligerents, had not received recognition as a government either *de facto* or *de jure*. In reply to the remonstrances of the United States Earl Russell insisted on the right of neutral States to receive from unrecognized governments special agents, enjoying no representative character and no diplomatic honours, but otherwise entitled to the 'immunities of ministers'. In another Note he emphatically asserted the right to enter into communication with a *de facto* government in order to provide for the temporary security of the persons and property of British subjects, but he insisted that such intercourse did not imply recognition of the Confederates as an independent State.[2] The United States, it is true, did not agree with that

1 *The Annette*; *The Dora*, [1919] P. 105.

2 In a series of despatches in connection with the maintenance of British agents in the Confederacy during the American Civil War, see, for example, the communications of Earl Russell to Mr Adams on 26 February 1861 (*Parl. Papers*, 1862, vol. LXII, p. 575, no. 24, p. 25) and of 4 December 1861 (ibid.). In the first of these communications Earl Russell said: '...as to a question of international law, H.M.'s Government hold it to be an undoubted principle of international law, that when the persons or property of the subjects or citizens of a State are injured by a *de facto* Government, the State so aggrieved has a right to claim from the *de facto* Government redress and reparation; and also that, in cases of apprehended loss or injury to their subjects, States may lawfully enter into communication with *de facto* Governments to provide for the temporary security of the persons and property of their subjects....It may be necessary in future, for the protection of the interests of H.M.'s subjects in the vast extent of country which resists the authority of the United States, to have further communication, both with the Central Authority at Richmond, and with the Governors of the separate States; and in such cases such communications will continue to be made, but such communications will not imply any acknowledgement of the Confederates as an independent State.'

view, but their past—and subsequent—record in this matter fully supported the British contention. Already in 1792 Jefferson, writing as Secretary of State to the American Minister in Paris, pointed out that with a mere *de facto* government which could not yet be recognized by the United States because, apparently, it was not 'formed by the will of the nation, substantially declared', some kind of business could be transacted without implying recognition, such as 'reforming the unfriendly restrictions on our commerce and navigation'.[1] In 1810, long before they recognized the independence or belligerency of the rebellious South American provinces, the United States sent an agent to Buenos Ayres charged with the mission 'to explain the mutual advantages of commerce with the United States, to promote liberal and *stable* regulations, and to transmit seasonable information on the subject'. He was furnished with a 'credential letter'.[2] In 1849 the United States sent a special agent to Hungary, which had risen in revolt against Austria, for the purpose, among others, of communicating with the rebel authorities.[3] Secretary Seward himself—who protested vigorously against the reception by Great Britain of the agents of the Confederacy—insisted in his instructions of 9 March 1863 to the United States representative in Venezuela, that the United States had 'under the law of nations and by treaty, a clear right to have its properly appointed agents residing in Venezuela...without a previous recognition of the existing authorities....'[4] In their relations with the numerous unrecognized governments in Latin-America the United States have widely followed the practice of appointing agents, commercial and other.[5]

When, following upon the Venizelos revolution in December 1916, the Greek Minister in London and the Greek Consul-General in London sent their resignations to the Athens Government, they were after a short delay

1 Moore, vol. I, p. 120.

2 Ibid. pp. 214, 215.

3 Ibid. pp. 220–4.

4 Ibid. pp. 235, 236.

5 See Houghton in *Temple Law Quarterly*, vol. v (1930–1), pp. 349–67, on the practice of the United States with regard to communication with unrecognized governments. And see in particular Wriston, *Executive Agents in American Foreign Relations* (1929). It was stated in 1924 by the State Department that the legalization of documents issued by the officials of the non-recognized Government in Chile in no way constituted recognitions of the new government. It was suggested that the authentication of the documents thus issued should be accompanied by an indication that 'the officials in question are the *de facto* authorities now functioning in Chile'. The Secretary of State said: 'It is the policy of the United States either to recognize or not to recognize a new government as such....Until circumstances impel it to recognize a regime as the government of a country, the dealings with that regime are to be deemed merely dealings with the authorities actually in control and as having no other significance' (*U.S. For. Rel.* 1924 (I), p. 360).

recognized, respectively, as representative in London of the Provisional (Venizelos) Government and as Consul-General of that Government. But the former did not apply for recognition as envoy extraordinary and minister plenipotentiary, and was recognized only as 'the diplomatic agent in London of the provisional government at Salonica'. He did not present letters of credence to the King. No exequaturs were issued to the consular officers serving under him.

In the course of the Spanish Civil War the Foreign Secretary announced in the House of Commons, on 8 November 1937, that in order to protect British commercial, industrial and financial interests in the part of Spain under the control of the insurgents it was decided to appoint an agent charged with the protection of those interests throughout the area as well as a number of sub-agents stationed at a limited number of places. The appointment of the agent and sub-agents was to be reciprocal. He stated that 'the reception of such an agent in London will not in any way constitute recognition by His Majesty's Government of the authorities of the territories under the control of General Franco', and that 'neither party will accord or expect to receive diplomatic status for their agents'.[1] It was mutually agreed that the agents and sub-agents should exercise, in the same way as consular representatives, all the normal functions of consuls in relation to matters of commerce and navigation. Subsequent to the appointment of the British and Spanish agents, the Government informed the House of Commons on 4 April 1938 that as it was 'felt desirable to secure for the British Agent and his staff certain privileges of a kind which are commonly enjoyed by diplomatic officials in order to facilitate the discharge of their duties', 'it was found necessary to concede corresponding privileges...to General Franco's Agent and his staff'.[2] But the Government made it clear that such concessions involved no admission that the recipients possessed diplomatic status and that the designation, used in a Foreign Office communication, 'Spanish Nationalist Government' did not involve recognition of General Franco's administration.[3]

1 *H.C. Debates*, vol. CCCXXVIII, col. 1386. The Foreign Secretary was emphatic that the exchange of agents did 'not constitute recognition, official or unofficial. ...No recognition whatever' (ibid. col. 1510). Previously, the Prime Minister, in answer to a question whether the appointment of the agents would not in effect mean a *de facto* recognition of the insurgent government, stated that he was advised that the appointment could not make any difference in the existing situation: 4 November 1937 (ibid. col. 1126). And see ibid. vol. CCCXXIX, col. 834, for a similar statement by the Foreign Secretary. See also Briggs in *A.J.* vol. XXXIV (1940), pp. 47–57.

2 *H.C. Debates*, vol. CCCXXXIV, col. 4.

3 Ibid. See also above, p. 281.

§ 114. *Fact and Mode of Address.* Once we are determined to view recognition as a deliberate and formal act referring comprehensively to international personality or governmental or belligerent capacity as a whole, it is not difficult to avoid the mistake of attributing the effect of recognition to various kinds of address and contact or communication with the foreign authority. It has been shown that no such automatic effect can be attributed to the conclusion of multilateral treaties, to the retention of diplomatic representatives, and to the appointment of consuls and agents. But there has been a pronounced tendency to imply recognition or to anticipate the dangers of such implication, and international practice abounds in examples of precautions—on occasions ingenious to the point of being diverting—taken by governments in order to prevent any such interpretation of their actions.[1] Governments emphasize repeatedly that recognition is a question of intention, not of inference. At the same time

1 For a collection of some interesting examples see Hackworth, vol. 1, pp. 343 et seq. The following other examples taken from the recent practice of the United States may be mentioned as an illustration: On 20 November 1920, the United States Chargé d'Affaires in Mexico was advised 'that although you are not authorized to be present officially at Obregon inauguration, you will be pleased to attend in private capacity' (*U.S. For. Rel.* 1920 (III), p. 197).

When the King of Greece, who at that time was not recognized by the United States, sent a telegram to the President of the United States informing him of the death of his father, no reply was sent by the President but the United States Chargé d'Affaires at Athens was directed 'to say informally to the Minister for Foreign Affairs that the President has received a telegraphic communication from the King announcing the death of his father, and to express suitably, under the circumstances, the condolences of the President' (ibid. 1922 (II), p. 414).

On 29 February 1912, the House of Representatives and the Senate of the United States adopted a Joint Resolution congratulating the people of China on the assumption of responsibilities of self-government. While publicity was given to that Resolution, the United States Minister in China was instructed to take care that this action should 'not be confused with recognition, which is a prerogative of the Executive and as to which it is the present intention of the President and the Department to proceed in harmony with the other Powers' (ibid. 1912, p. 71). When, on 4 April 1912, the American Minister in China was asked by the Minister for Foreign Affairs to visa certain certificates issued by the Provisional Government, he enquired from the home authorities whether such action would involve recognition of the administration. The answer was in the negative. Such action, he was told, 'would be in harmony with our *de facto* relations with the present administration' (ibid. p. 77).

When in March 1922 Great Britain terminated the Protectorate over Egypt and declared her independence, the diplomatic agents in Egypt were officially notified that all matters affecting their respective States should henceforth be taken up with the Egyptian Minister of Foreign Affairs. In reply to the enquiry by the United States Agent and Consul-General at Cairo whether communications addressed to the Foreign Minister would be regarded as recognition of the independence of Egypt, the Secretary of State issued an instruction to the effect that such intercourse as was essential should be informal so as to avoid the giving of the impression of recognition (ibid. 1922 (II), p. 104).

they exhort their representatives to exhibit meticulous caution lest their action be construed as implied recognition.[1]

Similarly, it may seem pedantic to attach the consequences of recognition to mere mode of address. Yet this has been done on occasions. Thus it is often thought that to address the head of a State by the title through which he claims sovereignty over territory is necessarily tantamount to a recognition of the title thus claimed. In the years 1937 and 1938 a number of States found it incumbent upon them to refrain from entertaining diplomatic relations with Italy on the ground that to accredit an envoy to 'the King of Italy and Emperor of Abyssinia' would be tantamount to recognizing *de jure* the conquest of Abyssinia. The implication was not unavoidable. There would have been no inconsistency in holding that the title of the King of Italy was primarily a matter of Italian municipal law, and that so long as there was no clear expression of intention to depart from the attitude of non-recognition, the accrediting of diplomatic representatives to the King of Italy and Emperor of Abyssinia was merely a recognition of a *de facto* situation. This was, in fact, the attitude taken up by some States.[2]

Neither does the conclusion of a treaty in which the head of the State is described in a specific manner necessarily signify the recognition of the title thus claimed. When, on 8 May 1937, the Montreux Convention concerning the abolition of the capitulations in Egypt was signed by the Italian delegates in the name of 'His Majesty the King of Italy, Emperor of Ethiopia', the general view was that the signature of the Treaty by other delegates did not in any way involve the recognition of any Italian title over Ethiopia since the responsibility for the description of its 'Head of State' in the preamble of the Convention rested with the Italian delegation.[3] A less technical reason would have been equally persuasive.

1 The United States Secretary of State wrote to the Chargé d'Affaires in Mexico on 25 May 1920: 'You should...be cautious in any necessary dealings with the parties now in possession, not to permit any imputation that the present regime has been even *de facto* recognized by the Government of the United States. Recognition cannot be accomplished by inference merely but by the full and formal entrance into international relations through the public action of the respective executives of the two countries' (*U.S. For. Rel.* 1920 (III), p. 167).

2 See, for example, the announcement made by the Irish Free State on 14 December 1937 that an Irish diplomatic representative would be accredited to the King-Emperor. See *The Irish Press* of 15 December 1937, for Mr De Valera's statement.

3 For the statement of this principle by M. Politis, President of the General Committee of the Conference, see *Actes de la Conférence des Capitulations*, pp. 129, 137.

An incident in a lighter vein arising out of the refusal of most members of the League of Nations to recognize the Italian conquest of Abyssinia may be mentioned. At a State banquet held early in 1937 in Vienna, the Austrian Chancellor, apparently without having given due notice to those likely to be interested, gave the toast of 'the King of Italy and Emperor of Ethiopia'. It was subsequently reported that, by a

It has been noted above that, whenever they deem it necessary, governments do not decline to have communications with those whom they refuse to recognize. Neither, as a rule, are such attempts at communication rejected by the unrecognized authority. The latter is, of course, under no obligation to listen to a communication emanating from that source. On 2 December 1929, the Government of the United States, which at that time refused to recognize the Government of Soviet Russia, addressed identical notes to the latter and China reminding them, in view of the conflict in which they were engaged at that time, of their obligations under the General Treaty for the Renunciation of War. The Soviet Government in its reply expressed astonishment that the Government of the United States, which refused to entertain normal relations with the Soviet Government, found it possible to address to that Government its views and advice.[1] No such objection was raised when, on 16 May 1933, the President of the United States addressed the Soviet Government, alongside fifty-three other governments, in connection with the Disarmament Conference.[2]

It is clear that intervention with the unrecognized authority, like lodging of protests and other measures of protection of nationals, does not

convenient coincidence, the glasses of the British and French Ministers happened to be empty at the crucial moment so that the drinking of the toast of 'Emperor of Abyssinia' proved, so far as they were concerned, a physical impossibility.

It was reported in the *New York Times* of 17 September 1941, that when the President of the United States accepted from the High Commissioner of French Equatorial Africa the gift of a gorilla, 'the largest and most ferocious' ever sent out of Africa, the question was raised whether the acceptance of the gift signified an implied recognition of the Free French movement.

In 1861 Prussia had not recognized the Kingdom of Italy. Italy being desirous of sending an ambassador to attend the coronation of King William I of Prussia, General de la Rocca was appointed ambassador of King Victor Emmanuel, without reference to the country of which he was king (Satow, *A Guide to Diplomatic Practice* (3rd ed. 1932), p. 113).

When in November 1943 the Spanish Foreign Minister sent a message of congratulation to one Laurel, appointed President of the Philippines by the Japanese authorities then in occupation of that territory, the United States were inclined to take a serious view of what on the face of it appeared as recognition of the independence of the Philippines. The United States subsequently accepted the explanation of the incident as being no more than a message of sympathy for the Philippine people at large.

1 *Documents on International Affairs*, 1929, pp. 277 and 280.

The Polish-Lithuanian dispute concerning Vilna was throughout rendered more intractable as the result of the Lithuanian view, frequently expressed, that the re-establishment of communications between the two States would imply recognition of the sovereignty of Poland over the disputed territory. See *Off.J.* 1928, p. 1478; 1929, p. 144; 1931, p. 480. The same consideration played a part in the controversy concerning Memel (ibid. 1924, pp. 131, 143).

2 In an interview to the Press, the President is reported to have declared: 'As at previous world gatherings the American delegates will have the ordinary relations and communications with the Russian delegates which they maintain with delegates from other countries' (as reported in Jaffe, *Judicial Aspects of Foreign Relations* (1933), p. 118).

in any way imply recognition. The very reason for the retention of diplomatic and consular representatives in countries with unrecognized regimes, as well as the sending of agents to them, is to protect nationals. The practice of States abounds in instances of express insistence on the right to protect the interests of nationals within the territory of unrecognized regimes without any implication of recognition.[1] This applies in particular to unrecognized governments. The duty to treat aliens in accordance with international law is a duty of the State irrespective as to who holds power at any given moment.[2]

The ingenuity of special pleading intent upon implying recognition is shown by the argument put forward in *The Annette*,[3] a case in which the so-called Provisional Government of Northern Russia claimed that, being a recognized government, it was entitled to jurisdictional immunities. The Court had before it a statement of the Foreign Office informing it that the Provisional Government 'has not been formally recognized by His Majesty's Government'. The Court was asked to infer from that statement that the Provisional Government had been 'informally recognized'. This the Court was not prepared to do.

Finally, reference may be made to the assertion that surrender of criminals or request for their surrender implies recognition.[4] Neither principle[5] nor practice[6] substantiate that view. If, as has been shown, a certain amount of

1 See Hackworth, vol. I, pp. 360–3, for instances of communications to Mexican insurgents in 1912 and to Spanish insurgents in 1936. Professor Podesta Costa, in a careful study of the subject, rejects the implication of recognition said to result from various forms of 'relations officieuses'. He says, in particular: 'Les démarches officieuses effectuées par l'intermédiaire des représentants diplomatiques qui étaient accredités devant le gouvernement déposé, ou par des envoyés devant le nouveau gouvernement, ou par des agents speciaux reçus de lui ne signifient pas la reconnaissance du gouvernement *de facto*, même si elles sont répétées au point de prendre l'aspect de relations continues' (*R.G.* vol. XXIX (1922), p. 458).

2 But even in this respect the doctrine of implied recognition dies hard. Thus when in March 1944 the United States refused to recognize General Farrell's Government in Argentina, it was reported that this was the reason why the United States were unable to take action in respect of restrictions imposed by that Government upon the citizens of the United States (see *The Times* newspaper, 20 March, 1944).

3 *The Annette*; *The Dora*, [1919] P. 105.

4 See, for example, Holtzendorff, *Handbuch des Völkerrechts*, vol. I (1885), § 8.

5 See Hall, *International Law* (4th ed. 1895), p. 93, who points out that it is not clear 'why the surrender of an ordinary criminal to a *de facto* Government, in the possession of regular courts, need more necessarily constitute recognition than does recognition of belligerency'.

6 See Memorandum of 22 July 1920, by the Solicitor for the Department of State: 'It is established by sound authority that, in international practice, the surrender of criminals to *de facto* authorities does not indicate expressly or by implication political recognition. The recovery of fugitive criminals merely affects the practical course of the administration of justice' (Hackworth, vol. IV, p. 37).

contact is not inconsistent with non-recognition, it is difficult to see how contact in a matter as elementary as suppression of crime could have the effect of bringing about recognition.

§ 115. *Implied Recognition and the Policy or Obligation of Non-Recognition.* Some of the questions discussed above show the connection between the doctrine of implied recognition and the principle of non-recognition as enunciated in 1932 by the United States and the Council of the League of Nations subsequent to the invasion of Manchuria.[1] That principle pursues two independent objects. The first is to preserve the existing legal position and to prevent the operation of prescription. The second is to express moral disapproval manifested in the continued denial of legal title regardless of the apparent success achieved by the conduct, stigmatized as unlawful, as well as to exercise pressure upon the wrongdoer in consequence of such disadvantages as normally follow from the absence of recognition. That second purpose may, without affecting the first, be modified in practice, having regard to the necessities of commercial and other intercourse. Such modifications may materially impair the effectiveness of the weapon of non-recognition as an instrument of direct pressure, but its indirect value in the system of international jurisprudence and morality may still remain substantial and beneficent. This is one of the reasons why the exaggerations of the doctrine of implied recognition must be carefully scrutinized in relation to the principle of non-recognition. If we fall a prey to the tendency to interpret various kinds of conduct as implied recognition, we may often be led to assume, without good cause, that the principle of non-recognition has been abandoned in a particular case. Conversely, if the doctrine of implied recognition is confined within its proper sphere, States may be in a position, without necessarily becoming disloyal to the general obligation of non-recognition, to adapt their conduct to the requirements of international intercourse and to the protection of their interests and those of their nationals.

Any general attitude of non-recognition, i.e. the proclaimed assumption of the policy or obligation of non-recognition, has a direct bearing on the operation of the doctrine of implied recognition. It reduces the operation of that doctrine even below the modest limits which can otherwise be assigned to it. This means that particularly exacting evidence of recognition is required in the case of States which have declared themselves to be pursuing a policy of non-recognition or, even more so, as being bound by

1 The subject is here discussed in some detail irrespective of the future development of the doctrine of non-recognition. See below, p. 435.

an obligation of non-recognition. There is room for the view that in such circumstances nothing short of an explicit and unequivocal act of recognition will have the result of recognition.[1] Whatever other effects the doctrine of non-recognition may have, this much may be expected of it, that it has at least the effect of ruling out implied recognition. In the circumstances, any caveat which might otherwise be necessary is redundant.

These incidental results of the proclaimed attitude of non-recognition have not always been appreciated, as may be seen from some of the ingenious precautions recommended by the Advisory Committee of the Assembly of the League of Nations set up in connection with the non-recognition of Manchukuo. In January 1934 the General Post Office in London received from 'The Department of Communications of Manchukuo' a request to be furnished with statistics in accordance with the provisions of the Postal Union Convention with a view to the liquidation of the transit payments due in respect of mails sent through Manchuria. The British Government thereupon requested the Secretary-General of the League of Nations to put the matter before the relevant Sub-Committee in order to obtain a ruling as to the extent to which *de facto* relations may be permitted between foreign postal administrations and the Manchurian postal authorities, without involving, by implication or otherwise, recognition of the existing regime in Manchuria.[2] The enquiry was answered in May 1934 with an elaboration of detail showing both the attraction of the doctrine of implied recognition and the meticulous care taken to meet its dangers in circumstances in which reliance upon the general attitude of non-recognition would have been sufficient. While the Committee considered that administrative postal relations with the Manchukuo authorities were permissible, it added: 'Lest these technical relations lead to confusion, it is recommended that, should the postal administrations of States Members of the League address correspondence to the postal administration of "Manchukuo", such communications should contain once for all an explicit statement that they are only to be regarded as communications between one administration and another, for the sole

1 It was reported in October 1945 that when Mr Justice Jackson, Chief Prosecuting Counsel of the United States, signed the indictment of the major war criminals in pursuance of the Agreement of 8 August 1945 (Cmd. 6668), he made a statement to the effect that the signature of the indictment on the part of the United States did not imply the recognition of the annexation by Russia of Latvia, Lithuania and Esthonia (which territories figured conspicuously in the part of the indictment for which Russia was responsible in the first instance). In view of the well-known attitude of the United States in the matter of non-recognition of the annexation of these countries the contingency of implied recognition must be deemed to have been remote.

2 *Off.J.* 1934, p. 429.

purpose of ensuring the proper conduct of technical services, and not as communications between one government and another, and that they do not imply that the Universal Postal Convention is applicable.'[1] It would have been open to the Advisory Committee to state that as recognition was a matter of intention and that as Members of the League had clearly manifested their determination to refuse recognition to Manchukuo, the British, and any other, postal administration may properly maintain with the postal authorities of Manchukuo such relations as may be deemed indispensably necessary for the matter covered by the enquiry and that no such action could accurately be construed as recognition.[2]

The ingenuity with which the Advisory Committee of the Assembly approached other situations in this connection is instructive. The Committee was emphatic that the non-recognizing governments could not regard as a passport a document issued by authorities dependent upon the 'Manchukuo Government' and could not therefore allow their consuls to visa such documents. But the Committee saw no reason why an inhabitant of Manchukuo desirous of leaving the country should not be able to receive an identity document from the consul of the country which he wished to visit, nor why, in issuing that document, the consul should not, for the purpose of establishing the identity of the person in question, utilize documents issued by the Manchukuo authorities and called by them passports, *laisser passer*, etc.[3]

The question of the recognition by Great Britain and the United States of the annexation of Austria by Germany in 1938 supplies another instructive illustration of the subject under discussion. As mentioned, the United States announced in 1932 its policy of non-recognition, *inter alia*, of territorial arrangements accomplished by force. Great Britain, alongside of other members of the League, declared herself in March 1932 to be

1 Ibid. p. 430.

2 In the same month the Chinese Government suggested in an elaborate memorandum that the export of opium or other dangerous drugs to Manchuria be stopped and be replaced by a modified system of control by import certificates issued by consular representatives in Manchuria. One of the reasons for the proposal was 'the added advantage of being free from any implication prejudicial to the principle of non-recognition of the present regime in Manchuria' (ibid. p. 432). This proposal was put forward notwithstanding the fact that the Advisory Committee had previously made an elaborate recommendation calculated to rule out any implication of recognition. It had recommended, on 7 June 1933, that while a copy of the export authorization should accompany any consignments sent to Manchukuo for purposes not contrary to the Opium Convention, 'Governments should refrain from forwarding a second copy of the export authorization to "Manchukuo", since such action might be interpreted as a *de facto* recognition of "Manchukuo"' (ibid. Special Supplement, no. 113, p. 12).

3 Ibid. p. 13.

bound by a similar and, having regard to the provisions of the Covenant, wider obligation. In March 1938 Germany accomplished what was in fact a forcible annexation of Austria. On 19 March 1938 the United States Secretary of State, after having previously denounced the German action as being one of forcible intervention in violation of treaty obligations, issued a statement accepting as a 'fact' the disappearance of Austria as an independent State. On 6 April the United States Ambassador in Berlin informed the German Government that, in view of the notification received from the Austrian Minister at Washington that Austria 'had ceased to exist as an independent nation and had been incorporated in the German Reich', it was 'under the necessity for all practical purposes of accepting what he says as a fact'. The Government of the United States also informed Germany that it 'finds itself under the necessity as a practical measure' of closing its Legation at Vienna and of establishing a Consulate-General in its place.[1] Did these statements and actions amount to a recognition of the annexation of Austria? Such is the fascination of the doctrine of implied recognition that even writers who were critical of the action taken interpreted it as constituting both *de facto* and *de jure* recognition.[2] One court in the United States went to the length of stating that 'this change has occurred in a manner acceptable to our notions of international law' and that 'the *Anschluss* has in no wise been disavowed by the Department of State'.[3] But this has not been the attitude of other courts.[4] The view of the State Department as to the legal significance of its action was made known on a much later occasion, namely, on 29 July 1942. The Secretary of State referred to the prevalent confusion as to the status of Austria and said: 'It is probable that such confusion, if it exists, has arisen from administrative steps which may have been taken by this Government in pursuance of its own laws designed to afford adequate protection to this country's interests in dealing with the situation presented by the imposition of military control over Austria, and residents of Austria, by Germany.

1 *Documents on International Affairs*, 1938, vol. II, p. 96.

2 See Garner in *A.J.* vol. XXXII (1938), p. 423.

3 *Land Oberoesterreich* v. *Gude*, (1940) 109 F. (2*d*) 635 (*Annual Digest*, 1938–40, Case no. 34 (a case involving the question whether the Province of Upper Austria had capacity to sue)).

4 See *Johnson* v. *Briggs*, (1939) 12 N.Y.S. (2*d*) 60 (*Annual Digest*, 1938–40, Case no. 33). In *United States ex rel. Zdunic* v. *Uhl*, (1942) 46 F. Supp. 688; 47 F. Supp. 520, the Court found it unnecessary to decide whether after April 1938 Austria was *de jure* or *de facto* a German State so far as the United States was concerned: 'Our nation had taken cognizance of that fact, at least *de facto*, so that its affairs and its [*sic*] affairs of its nationals might not be prejudiced, and under necessity, as a practical measure, had closed its Legation at Vienna, established a Consulate-General, and had requested of Germany approval of a provisional consular status.' And see below, p. 400, n. 2.

This Government very clearly made known its opinion as to the manner in which the seizure of Austria took place and on the relation of that seizure to this Government's well-known policy toward the taking of territory by force. This Government has never taken the position that Austria was legally absorbed into the German Reich.'[1]

It is clear that quite apart from any subsequent explanatory declaration of the State Department, the action of the United States in 1938 could not accurately be interpreted in any sense as recognition *de jure* of the annexation of Austria. Neither could it properly be interpreted as recognition *de facto* for purposes other than the recognition of the validity in Austria of the acts of the authority in power and for such purposes as were necessary to protect the interests of the United States and its nationals. It consisted of measures described at the time as dictated by the practical exigencies of the moment and limited in their scope. Caution in implying recognition is a sound maxim. Double caution is imperative in relation to actions which must be viewed against the general background of a policy or of an obligation of non-recognition.

The same considerations apply, in some respects with greater cogency, to any implied recognition by Great Britain of the annexation of Austria by Germany. The main pronouncements by Great Britain on this matter were made on two occasions. On 16 March 1938 Lord Halifax, Secretary of State for Foreign Affairs, stated before the House of Lords that 'The Government...are bound to recognize that the Austrian State has been abolished as a national entity and is in process of being completely absorbed into the German Reich.'[2] He added that 'they do so without waiting for the plebiscite, the result of which, in view of the circumstances in which it is going to be held, is a foregone conclusion'. In a preceding passage he referred to the Austrian independence which 'in complete disregard of treaty provisions, has disappeared overnight'. On 2 April 1938 the British Ambassador handed to the German Government two Notes. The crucial passage of the first was that the British Government 'have decided to withdraw their Legation in Vienna and to replace it by a Consulate-General'. An exequatur was requested for the Consul-General. In the second Note the German Government were informed that the British Government 'must, as a matter of course, reserve their standpoint on those questions relating to treaties and other matters which arise from the

1 As quoted in *United States ex rel. Zdunic* v. *Uhl*, supra. See also *United States ex rel. Schwarzkopf* v. *Uhl*, (1943) 137 F. (2*d*) 898, and *United States ex rel. D'Esquiva* v. *Uhl*, ibid. 903, where the Court considered that the evidence as to the recognition of the annexation was controversial.

2 *H.C. Debates*, vol. CVIII, col. 180.

fact that Austria has ceased to exist as an independent State'.[1] On no occasion was there any express recognition of the annexation. In reply to a series of questions in the House of Commons as to whether recognition had been given to the annexation, the Government, in studiously evading a direct answer, referred to the statement, already quoted, made by the Foreign Secretary in the House of Lords.[2] It is clear that no *de jure* recognition of the annexation took place. On the other hand, the express language used on the relevant occasions by the British Government was tantamount to a *de facto* recognition of German control over Austria. The legal effects of such recognition, though considerable, were of limited scope and confined largely to a recognition of the internal validity of the measures of the authority actually in power.[3]

§ 116. *Admission to the General International Organization and Implied Recognition.* The question of the effect, in the matter of recognition, of the admission to a general political international organization of a State which is not recognized or whose government is not recognized by some members

1 *Documents on International Affairs*, 1938, vol. II, p. 96. See also the announcement on 5 April 1938, by the Under-Secretary of State for Foreign Affairs in the House of Commons, on the closing of the Vienna Legation (*H.C. Debates*, vol. CCCXXXIV, p. 194).

2 In the negotiations with Germany which ensued in the matter of the Austrian loans the British Government did not deem it necessary to observe the caution which the Government of the United States followed in order to avoid the appearance of general recognition. The Note addressed by the United States on 6 April 1938 to Germany on this subject began as follows: 'In view of the announcement made to the Government of the United States by the Austrian Minister on 17 March 1938, my Government is under the necessity for all practical purposes of accepting what he says as a fact and accordingly consideration is being given to the adjustments in its own practices and procedure in various regards which will be necessitated by the change of status of Austria' (*Documents on International Affairs*, 1938, vol. II, p. 98). When in December 1936 the British Government decided to close the legation at Addis-Abbaba and to replace it by a consulate, it was officially explained that that step did not involve recognition *de jure* of the annexation of Abyssinia. See Rousseau, *Le conflit italo-éthiopien devant le droit international* (1938), pp. 241, 242.

3 On 30 October 1943, in a Declaration on Austria issued in Moscow, the Governments of Great Britain, Russia and the United States stated that 'they regard the annexation imposed upon Austria by Germany on 15 March 1938 as null and void' (*A.J.* vol. XXXVIII (1944), Suppl. p. 7). The Declaration, however important, is probably not germane to the subject discussed above. The wording of the Declaration is not necessarily inconsistent with any previous recognition of the annexation of Austria by the three States in question. It may mean that *henceforth* they will treat the annexation as null and void. But see the decision of Morton J. in *In the Matter of Application for patents by A.B.* before the Patents Appeal Tribunal (*Reports of Patent, Design and Trade Mark Cases*, 1944, vol. LXI, p. 89), laying down that a person who, immediately before 11 March 1938, was a person of Austrian nationality, and who had not since that date voluntarily changed his nationality, was entitled to describe himself as of Austrian nationality on an application for a passport. Morton J., after quoting a

of the organization furnishes another example of the problem of implied recognition. It is a question which must confront any international political organization of States whose membership is not compulsory for all States and in which States obtain membership by way of an express act of admission. It is convenient to consider the matter separately by reference: (*a*) to the past, but instructive, experience of the League of Nations, and (*b*) to the United Nations.

(*a*) *The League of Nations.* Those who considered admission tantamount to recognition by all members of the League held that any other result would be unsound having regard to the obligation of guarantee of Article 10 of the Covenant,[1] or the duty of members of the League to maintain close relations with one another,[2] or to the general legal principle that admission to partnership of a new member, decided upon by the majority, binds the dissenting minority.[3] Actual practice did not substantiate these postulated implications of admission. On a number of occasions members of the League, like Switzerland and Belgium in the case of Soviet Russia,[4] expressly asserted the right to continue their refusal of recognition. Their right to do so was not challenged by other members of the League. Neither were there decisive reasons of principle in favour of the view that by signing the Covenant States deprived themselves of freedom of action

statement by the Foreign Secretary made in the House of Commons on 9 September 1942, interpreted that statement as meaning that 'the Foreign Secretary appears to regard Austria as being in existence as a country when this country drew the sword at the beginning of September 1939'. See, on the legality of the annexation of Austria, Herbert Wright in *A.J.* vol. XXXVIII (1944), pp. 620–35. See also Kelsen, ibid. pp. 689–91 and Garner, ibid. vol. XXXII (1938), p. 422.

1 Thus the Commercial Tribunal of Luxemburg, in a judgment given on 2 March 1935, held that for that particular reason the admission of Soviet Russia into the League implied the recognition by Luxemburg of the Government of that country (*Union of Soviet Socialist Republics* v. *Luxemburg and Saar Company* (*Annual Digest*, 1935–7, Case no. 33); *Sirey*, vol. IV (1936), p. 26). See also Scelle in *R.G.* vol. XXVII (1921), pp. 122–38; Fauchille, pp. 334, 335; Anzilotti, *Corso* (3rd ed. 1927), p. 172. When Colombia became a member of the League of Nations on 20 July 1920 she announced that her acceptance of Article 10 of the Covenant did not imply recognition of the independence of Panama (*U.S. For. Rel.* 1920 (I), p. 825).

2 Schücking-Wehberg, *Die Satzung des Völkerbundes* (2nd ed. 1924), p. 268; Verdross, *Strupp's Wörterbuch*, vol. I, pp. 51, 52 (who for this reason limit that effect of admission to the period of mutual membership in the League).

3 McNair in Oppenheim's *International Law* (4th ed. 1928), vol. I, § 72, n. 3. See also ibid. and Scalfati, pp. 278–82, for a detailed bibliography.

4 See Makarov in *Z.ö.V.* vol. V (1935), pp. 58, 59. In the course of the discussions preceding the admission of Soviet Russia into the League there was no tendency, even on the part of the States opposing the admission, to assert categorically that admission would imply the recognition of its Government by all members of the League. The representative of Portugal merely asked questions: 'Are we to have

in the matter of recognition. Membership of the League undoubtedly presupposed a certain measure of intercourse, but it was not necessary for such intercourse to be either direct or general. There were numerous cases of members of the League severing diplomatic relations with one another.[1]

Undoubtedly, membership of the League, combined with the continued refusal to recognize an admitted member, was in the nature of an anomaly. However, it was not an anomaly that could be removed by the enlargement of the obligations of the Covenant through the importation of the doctrine of implied recognition. There might have been some justification for such an assumption in the case of members of the League who voted for admission; *they* might have found it difficult to continue in their refusal to grant recognition after having voted for admission. But even they were entitled to resist the attempt to establish an irrefutable presumption in the matter. They could urge that full statehood, such as would make recognition an obvious duty, was not predicated by Article 1, paragraph 2, of the Covenant; and they could argue that they deemed membership of the State in question desirable and possible notwithstanding the absence of the normal relationship following upon recognition.[2] The argument may not have been entirely convincing, but so long as the States in question declared their position clearly in advance, they were in strict law entitled to disregard any consequences of implied recognition. The real difficulty with which States adopting that position had to contend was that the vote—especially their own vote—in favour of admission was strong evidence that the government of the State admitted possessed such qualifications of independence and stability as in international law entitled it to recognition.

(*b*) *The United Nations.* The experience of the League of Nations suggests that a clarification of the law in this matter can be achieved not through reliance upon the precarious doctrine of implied recognition, but

recognition in Geneva and non-recognition elsewhere?... Will not the admission of the Soviet Union into the League logically and necessarily involve the *de jure* recognition of the Soviet Government by the various States?' The Swiss representative pointed out that an affirmative vote of Switzerland 'would in fact, if not necessarily in law, lead to the resumption of regular diplomatic relations'. *Records of the Fourteenth Assembly, Sixth Committee*, Special Supplement, no. 130, p. 18. After Lithuania had been admitted to the League in 1921 Great Britain informed Belgium, in reply to an enquiry, that 'His Majesty's Government are not disposed to accord to Lithuania *de jure* recognition until the situation arising from the dispute about the possession of Vilna becomes clearer'.

1 See Oppenheim, loc. cit. for some examples.

2 See, for example, Romano, *Corso di diritto internazionale* (2nd ed. 1929), p. 101.

by the express adoption of a rule laying down that admission by a requisite majority of the members of the organization is sufficient proof of the existence of the requirements of statehood or of governmental capacity and, for that reason, involves the obligation of and the right to recognition. This in itself would constitute a weighty step in the direction of the rational solution of the problem of recognition in general, namely, its collectivization by joint action of the organized international community. The provisions of the Charter of the United Nations in the matter of admission of new members are such as to render feasible the adoption of a rule as here suggested. As the concurrence of all the permanent members of the Security Council and of two-thirds of the General Assembly is required for the admission of a new member,[1] it would appear that a majority thus constituted ought to be treated as sufficient proof that the new State or government possesses the necessary qualifications entitling it to recognition.

§ 117. *Implied Recognition of Belligerency.* Like other aspects of recognition, so also recognition of belligerency is an act fraught with far-reaching consequences both for the recognized authority and for the recognizing State. For the latter it involves the surrender of important maritime rights and the assumption of the obligations of neutrality. It requires all the caution necessary to avoid the reproach of premature recognition. Accordingly, as in other kinds of recognition, nothing short of a deliberate intention to that effect can properly be interpreted as recognition of belligerency. It is not enough that official contact, however regular, is maintained with the rebellious community. For such contact is compatible with the treatment of the rebels as insurgents only. As shown above, official contact, through agents, consuls, and even diplomatic representatives previously appointed, can be maintained with governments from which recognition is withheld. The same applies to insurgents.[2]

Neither is there any valid reason for assuming recognition of belligerency on the ground that a State has voluntarily imposed upon itself and its

1 See Articles 18 (2) and 27 (3). Neither, it will be noted, does the Charter of the United Nations contain any provision for a regular procedure for deciding on the question of recognition of new revolutionary governments of existing members of the Organization.

2 There is no legal objection to maintaining normal channels of communication with an authority which has established itself in a considerable part of the territory of the country concerned and whose measures in the commercial and other fields affect the interests of foreign States. It is impracticable to disregard the fact that there are two effective authorities in the country torn asunder by a civil struggle. This being so, there was no reason to assume that the British and other Governments, by agreeing in the course of the Spanish Civil War of 1936–8 (see above, p. 390) to the appointment

subjects some of the restraints of neutrality. Thus the Government and the courts of the United States have repeatedly held that the application of the Neutrality Act is not dependent upon the recognition of belligerency and that it is fully compatible with a mere condition of insurgency. The British Government and British courts have adopted the same view with regard to the Foreign Enlistment Act. Even a formal declaration by a government calling upon its subjects to observe neutral conduct does not constitute implied recognition of belligerency. During the Cuban insurrection in 1895 the President of the United States issued a proclamation in which he enjoined the observance of the United States Neutrality Act and which in many respects was hardly distinguishable from a proclamation of neutrality.[1] But the United States emphatically refused to grant recognition of belligerency. During the Spanish Civil War of 1936–9 Great Britain declared the Foreign Enlistment Act to be applicable. She adopted legislation in the matter of export and transport of munitions going beyond the requirements of the Act and of accepted duties of neutrality. At the same time, together with other States, she repeatedly refused to recognize a state of belligerency. It is true that there is no express formula for recognizing belligerency, but practice shows that when governments intend to grant belligerent rights they leave no doubts as to their intention. During the struggle of the Latin-American Republics for independence Great Britain and the United States declared repeatedly that they were treating both the mother country and the rebellious provinces as equal parties to the war. A formal proclamation of neutrality is clearly the best method of giving expression to the intention to grant belligerent rights. That was the procedure adopted by Great Britain and other States during the American Civil War. But although a proclamation of neutrality is not the only way of recognizing belligerency there must be a clearly expressed intention to that effect. It cannot lightly be inferred from conduct which, as we have seen, may in some matters be indistinguishable from recognition of belligerency while differing from it fundamentally. It is certainly not permissible to thrust it upon a State which expressly disclaims any such intention. From the fact that a formal declaration of neutrality is not necessary for recognition of belligerency we are not entitled to draw the facile conclusion that we are at liberty to interpret as such any particular line of conduct from which, in our view, there follows 'in law

of agents to and from the insurgent authority, were taking a step which they expressly disclaimed to take, namely, the recognition of the insurgents as belligerents. It is neither necessary nor permissible to identify the regularized maintenance of intercourse with the significant process of recognition.

1 Moore, vol. VII, p. 1081. And see above, p. 271.

and logic'[1] the admission of full belligerent rights. It may be argued that a State is not free to act in a way fully consistent with recognition of belligerency and yet maintain that its action does not amount to recognition. To put forward that argument is to beg the question as to the meaning of recognition of belligerency and to disregard the fact that the essence of it is the intention to concede fully and comprehensively the exercise of belligerent rights as distinguished from acquiescence in the exercise of certain rights—such as is present in mere recognition of insurgency—or from the maintenance of regularized intercourse.

§ 118. *Conclusions.* It is convenient to summarize briefly the conclusions of this chapter. There is no implied recognition in the fact of a State becoming a party or continuing as a party to a multilateral treaty to which an unrecognized State is or becomes a party. Neither does that effect attach to participation in an international conference attended by an unrecognized State or government; to retention and continued maintenance (as distinguished from appointment), for an interim period, of diplomatic representatives; to retention, replacing, sending and reception of consuls and, possibly, though this is controversial, to a request for and acceptance of an exequatur for them (as distinguished, probably, from the issue of an exequatur); to the sending of agents and representatives not possessing diplomatic character; to the fact, form and manner of communication with and address of foreign authorities, especially in connection with the protection of nationals; to request for and grant of extradition; to the maintenance of contact with the insurgents in a civil war; to admission to an international organization such as the United Nations. Such controversial evidential value as may otherwise attach to any of these acts is further reduced, if not altogether eliminated, by the proclaimed assumption of a policy or of an obligation of non-recognition. A State committed to such policy or obligation is bound to choose an express and unequivocal mode of recognition if it wishes to depart from its general policy as publicly announced. The only legitimate occasions for implying

1 Smith in *B.Y.* vol. XVIII (1937), p. 29. It is therefore doubtful whether 'belligerent recognition is a matter of conduct, not of words' (ibid. p. 28). Recognition of belligerency—like any other recognition—is a matter of intention. In *Great Britain and the Law of Nations*, vol. I (1932), p. 79, the same writer deprecates the tendency to imply recognition from intercourse with unrecognized authorities. See also O'Rourke in *A.J.* vol. XXXI (1937), p. 408. In *The Ambrose Light*, which is an isolated case in the matter of recognition of belligerency by implication, the Court held that a note sent by the American Secretary of State amounted to 'recognition by implication of a "state of war" and of belligerent rights, sufficient to prevent subsequent condemnation of rebel vessels as piratical' (25 Fed. 408). See, on the other hand, *The Conserva*, (1899) 38 Fed. 431, 437.

recognition are: (1) the conclusion of a bilateral treaty which regulates comprehensively the relations between the two States (and which must be distinguished from temporary arrangements and agreements for limited purposes); (2) the formal initiation of diplomatic relations and, probably, the issue of consular exequatur; and (3), in the case of belligerency, a proclamation of neutrality or some such unequivocal act.

These conclusions are, on the face of it, of a negative character with regard both to the doctrine of implied recognition as a whole and to its particular manifestations. It is not believed that, in view of this negative result, a discussion of this subject ought to have been avoided. The proper understanding of recognition as an institution of international law has suffered, in an equal degree, from two causes. The first, and by far the more important, has been the conception of recognition as an unfettered act of national policy divorced from any element of legal duty to the community claiming recognition or to the international community at large—an aspect of the subject of recognition which is outside the purview of this chapter. The second and, by comparison, minor cause have been the exaggerations and the artificialities of the doctrine of implied recognition. That doctrine, often supported by no mean authority,[1] has here been exposed to criticism. It has been shown, in the first instance, that there can be no question of implied recognition so long as the State whose action is so interpreted manifests a contrary intention. It is permissible to infer implied recognition from a line of conduct only when there is clear evidence that such effect was intended by the State in question.[2] Whenever the law implies a condition of things or a legal result it does so as a rule for the reason that the other party or parties have been led or are

1 See, for instance, Moore, vol. I, p. 73, who says: 'Recognition is not necessarily express; it may be implied, as when a State enters into negotiations with the new State, sends it diplomatic agents, receives agents officially, gives exequaturs to its consuls, forms with it conventional relations.' Article 9 of the Resolutions on the Recognition of New States and New Governments adopted in 1936 by the Institute of International Law provides that recognition *de facto* of new States 'results either from an express declaration or from an act implying this intention, such as an agreement or *modus vivendi* having a limited purpose or a provisional character' (as translated in *A.J.* vol. XXX (1936), Suppl. p. 186). According to Article 14 of the Resolutions 'Recognition *de facto* of a new government is manifested: (1) either by an express declaration, (2) by the signing of agreements having a limited purpose or a provisional character, (3) or by the maintenance of relations with the new government for the purposes of current affairs' (ibid. p. 187). Most of these instances of implied recognition have here been shown to be inconclusive.

2 Professor Briggs, in a useful survey of authorities, urges reliance on the intention of governments as distinguished from implied recognition. This is so because, in his view, the granting or withholding of recognition is a matter of policy (*A.J.* vol. XXXIV (1940), p. 57). Probably the same result follows, even more cogently, from the view that recognition is a matter of law.

likely to be led to rely on some defined manifestations of will. Even in those cases in which municipal law attaches consequences to acts of parties regardless of their intention, it does so, as a rule, only when there is no express declaration to the contrary. There is no good reason why a greater rigidity should prevail in what has been called the rougher jurisprudence of States. Recognition—of States, of governments, of belligerency—is a matter of primary significance in the life of States. It is an important occasion calling for formal and deliberate declarations of will. It is undesirable that its significance should be obscured by a spurious importation of the refinements of implied recognition. This is so irrespective of whether there has been any general manifestation of an intention not to grant recognition. Recognition must be express and unequivocal. It has been the main purpose of the present chapter to attempt to show that this view is in accordance both with principle and with the practice of governments.

Undoubtedly, it is a sound precept of law that a State—like any other person—should not be allowed to cause confusion and to disappoint legitimate expectations by blowing hot and cold at the same time—by acting in a manner implying recognition and by denying any intention to that effect. However, to enounce that maxim is merely to state the issue. For the question is: what is the manner of conduct which may legitimately be held to imply recognition? It has been shown that, in practice, such conduct has been held to be confined within a narrow compass. The legal significance of recognition is too far-reaching to permit it to become a prey of ingenious deductions and an object of uncertainty and controversy. States must in this matter retain freedom to act without having to discover that, without willing it and even while denying it,[1] they have committed themselves to recognition. Clearly, occasions may arise when some formula other than the express words of recognition may be helpful.[2] The establishment of diplomatic relations and the conclusion of a bilateral treaty of a comprehensive character may properly be used for that purpose. Apart from these, it is improper that a legal act of profound significance

1 During the Spanish Civil War of 1936–8 the British Government—alongside of other governments—deliberately and consistently refused to grant recognition of belligerency. But writers expended much ingenuity in an attempt to prove that such recognition had in fact been granted by implication.

2 See above, p. 378. In the exchange of communications between the United States and Soviet Russia in November 1933, the two Governments informed one another of their decision to establish normal diplomatic relations, to exchange ambassadors, and to co-operate for their mutual benefit and for the preservation of the peace of the world (*A.J.* vol. XXVIII (1934), Special Supplement, p. 2). There was an advantage in not referring *expressis verbis* to recognition, the grant of which had been repeatedly refused in uncompromising and solemn language.

should be exposed to the vagaries and abuse of inference. It is possible—as it is certainly desirable—that the function of recognition may in the future be freed from the vicissitudes of individual action of States and that collective recognition in all its aspects may become a rule of international law and organization. Pending that consummation it is imperative that the science of international law should free the doctrine of recognition from the exaggerations of the notion of implied recognition which find no support in the practice of States and which are inimical to that minimum of intercourse which is often unavoidable even in the absence of recognition.

Chapter XXI

THE PRINCIPLE OF NON-RECOGNITION

§ 119. *Facts as a Source of Legal Rights.* International law acknowledges as a source of rights and obligations such facts and situations as are not the result of acts which it prohibits and stigmatizes as unlawful. Thus, for instance, secession from an existing State, although constituting a breach of the law of the State concerned, is not contrary to international law. Accordingly, the realization of the requirements of fact identical with conditions of statehood as laid down by international law gives rise, respectively, to the right to recognition as a State and to the duty of recognition on the part of the existing States.[1] Although rebellion is treason in the eyes of municipal law, it results—when followed by the establishment of an effective government wielding power over the entirety of national territory with a reasonable prospect of permanency and with the consent or the acquiescence of the people—in a duty of other States to recognize the change and to treat the new government as representing the State in the international sphere.[2] For the same reason, even prior to and independently of the success of the revolutionary movement, once a rebellion has assumed dimensions of widespread hostilities in the form of a civil war as understood by international law, there arises the duty to admit the consequences of the situation thus created and to recognize a state of belligerency with all the rights appertaining thereto.[3]

These forms of recognition have been most conspicuous in international practice. But the same principle applies to any other situation created in a manner not inconsistent with international law. Thus, for instance, effective occupation of *terra nullius* in conformity with the rules of international law relating to acquisition of territory gives rise to a valid title and to a corresponding duty, on the part of other States, to recognize its international validity.[4] This correspondence of the lawful acquisition of title and of the duty of States to treat it as such is a proposition so obvious that it appears to be tautologous. For a lawful acquisition would be meaningless unless it were accompanied by the right to have it acknowledged and respected. It is by reason of their obviousness that the aspects of recognition other than those connected with statehood, governmental

1 See above, pp. 6, 78.

2 See above, pp. 87, 88.

3 See above, pp. 228–38.

4 See below, p. 411.

capacity and belligerency, have not been prominent in the literature of international law and in the practice of States.

It follows from the same principle that facts, however undisputed, which are the result of conduct violative of international law cannot claim the same right to be incorporated automatically as part of the law of nations. They do not impose upon other States the duty of recognition. These may, if they so wish and if, in exceptional circumstances, they deem it compatible with the maintenance of the authority of international law, recognize them as creating internationally valid rights as against themselves. If they do so, it is a concession on their part which they are under no duty to grant. On the other hand, they may announce their intention to treat in the future such unlawful acts as devoid of any validity in international law. They may go further and obligate themselves in a mutually binding instrument not to validate as part of international law the consequences of an unlawful act. Such a duty of non-recognition may follow indirectly from obligations of a different character previously undertaken. This distinction between acts consistent with and those contrary to international law enables us to understand the principle of non-recognition in terms of the general doctrine of recognition conceived as an act of application of international law.

§ 120. *Recognition of New International Rights as a Condition of their Validity.* It has been submitted that when the lawfulness of the acts giving rise to a new legal title or situation is clear and undisputed, the question of recognition or non-recognition does not arise. For this reason recognition is, as a rule, dispensed with in the normal course of international practice. In this sense it is true to say—and the practice of States shows that this is the case—that recognition is not a condition of acquisition of new territorial or other titles. In connection with the doctrine of the balance of power recognition of colonial acquisitions has on occasions been sought and given, but, like the principle of the balance of power itself, it has been of political and not legal significance. The Berlin Conference of 1885 established, as between the contracting parties,[1] the duty of notification, but its purpose was not germane to the question of recognition. Its object was to prevent competing colonial claims and to regularize this mode of acquisition of territory by stipulating for a certain amount of publicity.[2]

1 See the Award in the *Island of Palmas Arbitration* (*Annual Digest*, 1927–8, Case no. 71).

2 See Lindley, *The Acquisition and Government of Backward Territory in International Law* (1926), p. 300. In 1912 Italy obtained the express recognition by a number of States of her annexation of Tripoli and Cyrenaica. But she did not regard such recognition as being legally essential. When in September 1912 she approached the

However, from the fact that recognition is normally not necessary for the valid acquisition of new titles we are hardly justified in drawing the conclusion that it is never necessary and always irrelevant. Recognition is unnecessary and irrelevant only when the lawfulness of the act giving rise to the pretended title is clear and undisputed—'lawfulness' meaning its conformity either with general international law or with particular legal rights of other States. But recognition of a new title acquires definite significance as soon as the legality of the act or the existence of the legal title on which the act is based becomes a matter of doubt or dispute. When this happens, recognition removes the uncertainty by acknowledging the conformity of the title in question with international law. In such cases recognition cannot naturally be regarded as the mere fulfilment of a legal duty. It is a combination of waiver of a competing claim and of an undertaking not to challenge the title in question in the future. For this reason recognition of this type often contains qualifications expressly limiting its scope. Thus when Great Britain recognized in November 1930 Norwegian sovereignty over Jan Mayen Island, the British Government stated that as it had no information concerning the reasons for the Norwegian decree extending Norwegian sovereignty to the island in question, the recognition was given 'independently of and with all due reserves in regard to the actual grounds on which the annexation may have been based'.[1] When in August 1930 Norway informed the Canadian Government that she recognized the sovereignty of his Britannic Majesty over the Otto Sverdrup Islands, she expressly stated that the recognition in no way implied consent to the so-called 'sector principle'.[2] The function of recognition in removing doubts as to the existence of title appears clearly from the recognition by various Powers of Danish sovereignty over Eastern Greenland and the persistent Danish attempts, as surveyed in the relevant Judgment of the Permanent Court of International Justice,[3] to

United States with a request for recognition, the United States Government replied that it was not its custom 'to proceed in that manner, especially with regard to European affairs; that when the United States took over the Philippine Islands and Porto Rico, foreign governments were not asked for their acquiescence nor for their recognition, and none was given'. It was pointed out that the United States was fully aware of what had taken place and while it had no objection at all to the attitude of Italy, an express form of recognition could not be expected (*U.S. For. Rel.* 1913, p. 609). Implied recognition was granted by the fact that the appropriate United States diplomatic and consular representatives were instructed to conform to the legal situation established in Libya in connection with the abolition of extraterritorial rights. It will be noted that, at that time, the Italian declaration of war on Turkey was not in violation of international law.

1 *Treaty Series*, no. 14 (1931), Cmd. 3192.

2 *Treaty Series*, no. 25 (1931), Cmd. 3815.

3 *P.C.I.J.* Series A/B, no. 53.

secure such recognition from as many States as possible. In cases of this description recognition amounts to an acknowledgment that the title in question is in conformity with international law both in general and in so far as the legal interests of the recognizing State are concerned.[1] The same applies to cases in which recognition is given under conditions safeguarding the rights of the recognizing State. When the United States recognized in April 1919 the British protectorate over Egypt subject to the maintenance of American capitulatory and similar rights,[2] the insistence on that condition merely signified that without it the new regime would not be in conformity, in the view of the United States, with particular international law as applying to the rights of the United States.

The position is altogether different when the facts giving rise to the pretended new title are in violation of international law. In such cases recognition fulfils a function altogether distinct from other aspects of recognition. It is no longer an act of administration of international law; it is a political function. While not intended to do away with the moral or legal opprobrium attaching to the original illegality, it validates its consequences. It is against recognition of this nature that the policy or the obligation of non-recognition is directed. The illegal act in question may be in violation of the individual right of another State. In that case recognition is in the nature of a waiver of a right affected by the attempted or consummated acquisition of the new title. Translated into simple language, the act of recognition in such cases amounts to saying: 'Your pretended new title was in derogation of our legal rights. As such it was contrary to international law. We, therefore, refused to treat it as valid and as establishing any legal right against us. We refused to recognize it. This we were perfectly entitled to do. But now we waive our rights. Your new title is, accordingly, no longer contrary to an internationally protected right of ours. It is no longer contrary to international law. We recognize it.' When the acts in question are in breach of general international law, such recognition, as we shall see, assumes the character of a quasi-legislative measure in the general interest of international society and of international peace.[3]

§ 121. *The Meaning of Non-Recognition.* From the fact that recognition is not necessary for the validity of an otherwise legally unimpeachable title,

1 See in this connection the Advisory Opinion of the Permanent Court in the case of the *Tunis and Morocco Nationality Decrees* laying down that the extent of the powers of a protecting State in the territory of a protected State depends, *inter alia*, 'upon the conditions under which the Protectorate has been recognized by third Powers as against whom there is an intention to rely on the provisions of these Treaties' (*P.C.I.J.* Series B, no. 4, p. 27).

2 *U.S. For. Rel.* 1919 (II), p. 203. And see above, p. 35.

3 See below, p. 429.

the conclusion cannot properly be drawn that *every* pretended acquisition of title is valid—and, therefore, in no need of recognition. The inaccuracy of any such conclusion follows clearly from the examination of the legal nature of non-recognition of new titles or situations as distinguished from non-recognition of new States or governments. Refusal of recognition of the former is, upon analysis, a declaration that the particular attempt to create the new title or situation is contrary to international law or, what is often the same, to the acquired rights of the non-recognizing State; that, accordingly, it is not a source of legal right; that it is a nullity; and that it is proposed to treat it as such in the future. The object of the policy or the obligation of non-recognition is not to render illegal an otherwise lawful and valid act; its object is to prevent the validation of what is a legal nullity.

The above analysis of the meaning of non-recognition is based on two assumptions, both of which have been questioned. The first is that illegal acts cannot produce legal results beneficial to the wrongdoer. The objection to this proposition is discussed in a subsequent section.[1] The second assumption, which has been exposed to vigorous criticism, is that it is competent for one State to pronounce judgment on the legality of the acts of another and to determine the validity of a new title acquired by such acts.[2] It is difficult to admit the force of this criticism. Undoubtedly, the position would be more satisfactory if an international court were endowed, as a matter of course, with obligatory jurisdiction to decide questions relating to the legality of the conduct of States. But as no such obligatory jurisdiction is normally vested in any international tribunal, States themselves are both entitled and constrained to pass judgment upon the legality of the actions of other States; the inescapable alternative would be for them to treat such acts invariably as valid and as establishing legal rights. The anomalous fact that international tribunals do not, in principle, possess compulsory jurisdiction need not result in an absurdity consisting in a duty of States to refrain from questioning the legality of actions of other States in any circumstances—unless, of course, we attach importance to the suggestion that as every State is in the habit of committing illegalities at some time or another it ill behoves it to assert an illegality in the conduct of other States.[3]

1 See below, p. 421.

2 This particular criticism has been repeatedly voiced by Sir John Fischer Williams: see *Hague Recueil*, vol. XLIV (1933) (ii), pp. 282 et seq.; *Harvard Law Review*, vol. XLVII (1933–4), pp. 787 et seq.

3 '...nations are but aggregations of human beings, who may not relish daily reminders of their shortcomings by others whom they may not deem above reproach' (Moore in *Harvard Law Review*, vol. L (1937), p. 436). See also, to the same effect, Borchard and Morrison in *Legal Problems in the Far Eastern Conflict* (ed. by Quincy Wright, 1941), pp. 157–78.

§ 122. *Announcement of Non-Recognition or of the Policy of Non-Recognition.* The refusal to recognize titles, treaties and situations on the ground that they are inconsistent with the rights of the State refusing recognition is a frequent feature of international practice. In the bulky volumes of J. J. Moser's *Versuche* and *Beyträge*, published in 1777 and 1778, respectively,[1] as well as in his more theoretical treatise (a somewhat pretentious term when applied to a chronicler of international events of Moser's type) published in 1763,[2] the student will find lengthy accounts and discussions of refusal of recognition in the seventeenth and eighteenth centuries. One of the earliest monographs concerning recognition arose out of a case of denial of recognition to an elected monarch.[3] The diplomatic history of the nineteenth and twentieth centuries supplies numerous examples of refusal of recognition on the ground of the inconsistency of the new title with existing obligations.

When in 1890 Great Britain and Germany concluded a treaty regulating, *inter alia*, the British protectorate over Zanzibar, France refused to recognize it on the ground that the arrangement was contrary to the Treaty of 1862 between France and Great Britain.[4] The continued refusal of France, prior to the Anglo-French Treaty of 1904, to recognize the British occupation of Egypt constituted a conspicuous feature of the international situation at that time.[5] In 1908 Great Britain refused to recognize the acquisition of the Congo by Belgium so long as the provisions of existing treaties relating to the treatment of natives had not been complied with.[6] When Bosnia and Herzegovina were annexed in the same year, Sir Edward Grey caused Austria-Hungary to be informed that Great Britain could not 'approve of an open violation of the Treaty of Berlin, nor recognize an alteration of it when the other Powers, and especially in this case Turkey,

1 In the second book of Part I of his *Versuch des neuesten europäischen Völckerrechts in Fridens- und Kriegs-Zeiten* (1777), in the section on the Sovereign Persons and Families, there are frequent references to recognition and refusal of new titles, etc. in Hereditary and Electoral Kingdoms. These cases are again referred to and discussed in *Beyträge zu dem neuesten europäischen Völckerrecht in Fridens-Zeiten* (1778), Part I: *Thronfolge in denen Erbreichen* (pp. 81–267), *Thronfolge in denen Wahlreichen* (pp. 268–76), and *Erkennung einer Titulatur* (pp. 387–90).

2 *Grundsätze des jetzt üblichen Europäischen Völcker-Rechts in Fridens-Zeiten* (1763), where he discusses recognition, guarantee and non-recognition of succession to the throne (chapter v), of new titles (*neue Würde*) acquired by force or treaties (chapter VII) or of revolution (chapter VIII).

3 See L. G. Mogen, *De eo, quo circa Imperantem agnoscendum est gentium; occasione denegatae agnitionis Aug. Imp. Francisi legitime electi e Rege Galliae ejusque Fœderatis* (1748).

4 For an account of the controversy see Fischer Williams in *Hague Recueil*, vol. XLIV (1933) (ii), p. 276.

5 See Gooch, *Before the War. Studies in Diplomacy*, vol. I (1936), pp. 43–4.

6 Cmd. 6606 (1913), p. 22.

have not been consulted'.[1] He used similar language with regard to the Bulgarian proclamation of independence in contravention of the Treaty of 1878.[2] When in May 1915 Japan presented to China an ultimatum, subsequently accepted by that country, the United States communicated to China and Japan identical notes which ran as follows:

'In view of the circumstances of the negotiations which have taken place and which are now pending between the Government of China and the Government of Japan and the agreements which have been reached as a result thereof, the Government of the United States has the honor to notify the Government of ... that it cannot recognize any agreement or undertaking which has been entered into or which may be entered into between the Governments of China and Japan impairing the treaty rights of the United States and its citizens in China, the political or territorial integrity of the Republic of China, or the international policy relative to China commonly known as the Open Door Policy.'[3]

The British announcements of non-recognition in 1908 and the United States declaration in 1915 show the development of the principle of non-recognition in two directions. In the first instance, they signify the determination to refuse recognition not only on account of a violation of the particular rights of the State concerned, but also because of a violation of a general rule of international law as embodied in a treaty or in fundamental principles of international law relating to the respect of the independence of States. Secondly, some of the declarations in question, such as that of the United States in 1915, had reference not to any specific title claimed to have been acquired but, more generally, to possible future situations arising out of a violation of certain treaties and principles. For an individual act of non-recognition there was thus substituted a policy of non-recognition of a more general scope. This was the feature of the declaration of non-recognition issued by the United States on 7 January 1932, in the note addressed by the Secretary of State, Mr Stimson, to China and Japan. The declaration followed closely the Note of 13 May 1915, with the important addition that the United States 'does not intend to recognize any situation, treaty, or agreement which may be brought about by means contrary to the covenants and obligations of the Pact of

1 Printed in Gooch and Temperley, *British Documents on the Origins of the War, 1898–1914*, vol. V (1928), p. 390.

2 Ibid. p. 398 (in a telegram sent to the British Agent and Consul-General in Sophia). See also Lord Rosebery's despatch on 13 July 1886 to the British Ambassador at St Petersburgh concerning the abrogation by Russia of Article 59 of the Treaty of Berlin (as cited by McNair, *The Law of Treaties* (1938), p. 357).

3 *U.S. For. Rel.* 1915, p. 146; McMurray, *Treaties and Agreements with and concerning China*, vol. II (1921), p. 1236. For a similar declaration made by China in 1917 after the publication of the Lansing-Ishii Agreement see *U.S. For. Rel.* 1917, p. 270.

Paris of 27 August 1928, to which treaty both China and Japan, as well as the United States, are parties'.[1] The Note showed the principle of non-recognition as not limited either to any particular title or to the exclusive defence of the interests of the non-recognizing State. Whatever may have been the political reasons for thus instilling renewed vigour into the principle of non-recognition—it is not permissible to dismiss summarily the evidence suggesting that it was resorted to as a convenient substitute for postponing a more tangible contribution towards enforcing international law[2]—it was clear that non-recognition was being transformed into an instrument of general application.

§ 123. *Acceptance of the Obligation of Non-Recognition.* However important the announcements and declarations of an intention or of a policy of non-recognition may have been, they left to the State in question full freedom of action in the future. They did not imply an *obligation* of non-recognition. The announcement of the United States of 7 January 1932 was not intended as implying any such obligation.[3] This fact, as well as general considerations of international law, militate against the suggestion that that announcement was declaratory of an international duty which

1 *A.J.* vol. XXVI (1932), p. 342. It appears that the United States Government sought some measure of co-operation with other States in this connection. On 5 January 1932 the British Ambassador to the United States was informed that the United States Government intended to address to both China and Japan a note on the lines of their note sent in 1915. The British Government did not associate itself with the démarche—probably on the ground that it did not wish to take action independently of the League. The other signatories of the Nine Power Treaty (whom the United States approached) adopted a similar attitude.

2 See below, p. 434.

3 On 12 March 1932 the United States Minister at Berne, after having been apprised of the terms of the Resolution of the Council, addressed to the Secretary-General of the League a communication as follows: 'My Government is especially gratified that the nations of the world are united on a policy not to recognize the validity of results attained in violation of the treaties in question. This is a distinct contribution to international law and offers a constructive basis for peace.' On 25 February 1933, the United States Minister wrote with regard to the recommendations of the Assembly concerning the non-recognition of Manchukuo that in their affirmation of the principle of non-recognition and their attitude in regard thereto, the League and the United States were on common ground. But, it was added: 'As it is necessary that the American Government exercise independence of judgment with regard to proposals which may be made and/or action which the Advisory Committee may recommend, it would seem that appointment by it of a representative to function as a member of the committee would not be feasible.' After the Resolution of the Assembly of 11 March 1932 (see below, p. 417), which apparently imposed upon Great Britain and other members of the League a substantial measure of obligation, the impression seems to have prevailed in Great Britain that the United States attached decisive importance to treating the question of non-recognition as one of policy rather than of obligation and to reserving their freedom of action in the matter.

followed, *inter alia*, from the General Treaty for the Renunciation of War to which the United States, Japan and China were parties. This suggestion explains, for instance, the Resolution of the International Law Association of 1934 which laid down, by way of a legal interpretation of the Treaty, that it was the duty of its signatories not to recognize *de jure* any territorial or other advantages acquired *de facto* by means of a violation of the Treaty.[1] It is not believed that the duty goes beyond a moral obligation. A State signing a treaty does not automatically undertake a legal obligation to contribute to its enforcement by a refusal of recognition or otherwise.

A definite step towards transforming the policy of non-recognition into an obligation of non-recognition was made by the Council and the Assembly of the League of Nations in connection with the invasion of Manchuria by Japan. On 16 February 1932 the members of the Council, other than China and Japan, addressed a note to Japan drawing her attention to the terms of Article 10 of the Covenant from which it appeared 'to them to follow that no infringement of the territorial integrity and no change in the political independence of any member of the League brought about in disregard of this article ought to be recognized as valid and effectual by the members of the League of Nations'.[2] On 11 March 1932 the Assembly of the League adopted a Resolution in which it declared 'that it is incumbent upon the members of the League of Nations not to recognize any situation, treaty, or agreement which may be brought about by means contrary to the Covenant of the League of Nations or to the Pact of Paris'.[3]

It appears from the wording of the pronouncement of the Council and the Resolution of the Assembly that non-recognition was considered to be a legal obligation binding upon the members of the League by virtue of the Covenant. In fact, the refusal to recognize a conquest accomplished in violation of the Covenant would seem to have constituted the very minimum of the obligation to respect and to preserve the territorial integrity and political independence of other members of the League.[4] The

1 For the text of the Resolution see *Transactions of the Grotius Society*, vol. XX (1935), p. 205.

2 *Official Journal*, 1932, p. 383.

3 Ibid. Special Supplement, no. 100, p. 8.

4 This being so, it is unnecessary to pursue the controversy as to whether the Resolution of the Assembly, in addition to being declaratory of existing obligations, was in itself a source of obligation. The question of legal nature of that Resolution has been a controversial one. On the one hand, there seems to be no reason why, as a rule, a Resolution of the Assembly or the Council should not have been binding upon the States assenting to it. A ratified treaty is not the only means of undertaking international obligations. At least in one case—in the Advisory Opinion concerning the *Lithuanian Railway Traffic*—the Permanent Court of International Justice treated a

British Government, it appears, acted on the view that in the matter of recognition of the conquest of Abyssinia it was bound by an obligation of non-recognition, and in May 1938 it took steps to obtain a measure of release from that obligation. This punctilious attitude is of greater significance than the further question whether, in view of the rule of unanimity, such release could be validly given except by a unanimous decision of the Assembly or of the Council.[1]

While it is controversial whether the pronouncements of the League of Nations in 1932 amounted to laying down an obligation—declaratory or

Resolution of the Council assented to by the two parties to the dispute as an engagement binding upon them (Series A/B, no. 42). On the other hand, it may be argued that if resolutions interpreting the Covenant were binding on the States voting for them, the procedure might in certain circumstances amount to amending the Covenant in a way different from that prescribed in Article 26. A more persuasive, although not necessarily decisive, argument is that in actual practice interpretative resolutions like that of 1921 relating to Article 16 were not regarded as formally binding. It will also be noted that the Resolution of the Assembly of 4 July 1936, in the matter of Abyssinia, studiously avoided any express reference to the Assembly Resolution of March 1932. That Resolution merely reaffirmed the firm attachment 'to the principles of the Covenant, which we also expressed in other diplomatic instruments such as the declaration of the American States dated the 3rd August, 1932, excluding the settlement of territorial questions by force' (as to the latter see below, p. 419, n. 1). On the other hand, in its Resolution of 18 March 1933 concerning the Letitia dispute between Colombia and Venezuela the Council recalled the Resolution of 11 March 1932. For the Report embodying that Resolution see *Official Journal*, 1933, pp. 598–609.

1 At the meeting of the Council of the League in May 1938 the British representative expressed the opinion that the question of recognition of the position of Italy in Abyssinia was one for each member of the League 'to decide for itself in the light of its own situation and its own obligations' (*Official Journal*, 1938, p. 335). No formal decision was taken by the Council and there was no opposition to the President's statement at the end of the discussion that the great majority of its members concurred in the British view (ibid. p. 346). Previously, on 13 April 1938, the Prime Minister of Great Britain stated in the House of Commons that His Majesty's Government 'have in no way changed their view of the importance of the principles enunciated in the Assembly Resolutions...but in their application to any case His Majesty's Government must be entitled to take into account the attitude of other Members of the League and the facts of the international situation' (*H.C. Debates*, vol. CCCXXXIV, col. 1099). At the time when Great Britain requested that the matter be put before the Council five Members of the Council had already recognized *de jure* the annexation of Abyssinia.

As to the non-recognition of the annexation of Austria by Germany in 1938 see above, pp. 398, 399. As to the non-recognition of the establishment of the German Protectorate over Czechoslovakia see above, p. 385. Neither did there take place any automatic recognition of the changed status of Albania as the result of the invasion of that country by Italy in April 1939. On 1 May 1939, when a question was asked whether the new British Ambassador would be accredited to the King of Italy in his capacity as King of Albania, the Prime Minister announced in the House of Commons that the credentials of the new Ambassador signed on 28 March were addressed to 'H.M. the King of Italy, Emperor of Ethiopia' and that the Italian authorities expressed their willingness to accept these credentials (*H.C. Debates*, vol. CCCXLVI, col. 1484).

constitutive—of non-recognition, a clear duty to that effect was undertaken in Article 2 of the Anti-War Treaty of Non-Aggression and Conciliation of 10 October 1933 (often referred to as the Saavedra Lamas Treaty) concluded between a number of American States, including the United States. In that Article the contracting parties declared that 'they will not recognize any territorial arrangement which is not obtained through pacific means, nor the validity of the occupation or acquisition of territories that may be brought about by force of arms'.[1] In Article 11 of the Convention on Rights and Duties of States signed at Montevideo on 26 December 1933, it was laid down that 'the contracting States definitely establish as the rule of their conduct the precise obligation not to recognize territorial acquisitions or special advantages which have been obtained by force whether this consists in the employment of arms, in threatening diplomatic representations, or in any other effective coercive measure'.[2] That pledge was reiterated at the Eighth International Conference of American States in 1938 and declared to be an obligation 'which cannot be avoided either unilaterally or collectively'.[3]

These collective obligations of non-recognition of consequences of acts contrary to international law constitute a new feature of international practice. They differ essentially from such obligations as those accepted in the declaration of the signatories of the Holy Alliance at Troppau on 13 November 1820,[4] or by the Central American States in 1907 and 1923[5] as

1 Hudson, *International Legislation*, vol. VI (1937), p. 450. This provision was recited in the Pan-American Convention of December 1936 concluded in order 'to coördinate, extend and assure the fulfilment of existing agreements' between the American States (*A.J.* vol. XXXI (1937), Suppl. p. 59). Previously, on 3 August 1932, nineteen American States sent identical notes to Bolivia and Paraguay in connection with the Chaco dispute announcing their intention to apply to that dispute the principle of non-recognition enunciated earlier in the year by Mr Stimson (Toynbee, *Survey of International Affairs*, 1933, p. 407).

2 Hudson, loc. cit. vol. VI, p. 623.

3 *International Conferences of American States, First Supplement*, 1933–1940 (1940), p. 255.

4 Article 2 of the Declaration read as follows: 'The Allied Powers not only formally declare the above to be their unalterable policy, but, faithful to the principles which they have proclaimed concerning the authority of legitimate governments, they further agree to refuse to recognize any changes brought about by other than legal means' (as quoted by Cresson, *The Holy Alliance* (1922), p. 99, n. 2). The basis of the doctrine of non-recognition is the illegality from the point of view of international law of the acts giving rise to the situation in question. For this reason it is probably inaccurate to regard, as does Bilfinger in *Hague Recueil*, vol. LXIII (1938) (i), p. 219, the modern doctrine of non-recognition as based on the same principle as that which marked the pronouncement of the Holy Alliance at the Congress of Laibach of 1821, which laid down that the allied sovereigns will regard as legally void any changes effected by revolt or overt force. Internal revolutionary changes are not contrary to international law.

5 See above, p. 129.

to non-recognition of changes resulting from a revolution. The obligations of non-recognition as expressed in the Resolution of the Assembly and in the American Treaties of 1933 and 1938 can, as a rule, have no bearing on the question of recognition of States or governments. A State cannot come into existence contrary to a treaty; there is no rule of international law prohibiting secession from the parent State. If, to give a concrete example, Manchuria had voluntarily seceded from China in 1932 and formed a new State, there would have been no question of non-recognition as intended by these instruments. The proper legal basis of non-recognition of Manchukuo as a State in the years after 1932 was probably the fact that it was not a State inasmuch as, in view of its relations with Japan, it lacked actual independence.[1] In so far as the doctrine of non-recognition applied in that case it was an announcement of the intention or the acceptance of the obligation of non-recognition of any future situation amounting either to a formal incorporation of Manchuria as part of Japan or to a relationship involving the actual overlordship of Japan.

§ 124. *The Jurisprudential Basis of the Principle of Non-Recognition.* Neither the announcement of non-recognition by the United States in January 1932, nor the Resolution of the Assembly of the League of Nations of March of that year, nor the American Treaties of 1933 and 1938 were intended to have or could have the effect of invalidating any act, or the results thereof, which but for the declaration of non-recognition would have been legally valid. Their effect and, probably, their intention were of a different nature. They constitute, as in the case of the United States, either a unilateral announcement or, as in the other cases, the assumption of an obligation or the declaration of an already existing duty not to contribute by a positive act to rendering valid the results of an act which is in itself devoid of legal force. This construction of non-recognition is based on the view that acts contrary to international law are invalid and cannot become a source of legal rights for the wrongdoer. That view applies to international law one of 'the general principles of law recognized by civilized nations'.[2] The principle *ex injuria jus non oritur* is one of the fundamental maxims of jurisprudence. An illegality cannot, as a rule, become a source of legal right to the wrongdoer. This does not mean that it cannot produce any legal results at all. For it gives rise to a legal liability of the lawbreaker; it may become, in the interests of intercourse and general security, a source of rights for third persons acting in good faith; it may,

1 See above, p. 47.
2 Article 38 (3) of the Statute of the International Court of Justice.

temporarily and provisionally, confer upon the wrongdoer a measure of protection of his possession; it may, if the rigid conditions of lapse of time and of other requirements have been complied with, crystallize into a legal right as the result of the operation of prescription. But to admit that, apart from well-defined exceptions, an unlawful act, or its immediate consequences, may become *suo vigore* a source of legal right for the wrongdoer is to introduce into the legal system a contradiction which cannot be solved except by a denial of its legal character.[1] International law does not and cannot form an exception to that imperative alternative.

§ 125. *The Maxim* ex injuria jus non oritur *in International Law.* For reasons connected with the substantive and procedural weakness of international law the operation of the principle *ex injuria jus non oritur* is, in the sphere of international relations, exposed to considerable strain and to wide exceptions. On the other hand, the absence of more direct means of enforcement tends to endow the principle of nullity of illegal acts with particular importance in the international sphere. It is of interest to note the way in which the Permanent Court of International Justice has given expression, on a number of occasions, to the principle that no rights can be derived from an illegality. Thus in the *Free Zones* dispute between Switzerland and France the Court pointed out in its Order of 6 December 1930

1 By an interesting coincidence, in May 1938, on the day of the opening of the meeting of the Council of the League of Nations whose main business was to endow with a semblance of legality the impending recognition by the principal Powers of the League of a situation brought about in violation of international law, namely, the annexation of Abyssinia, the House of Lords gave, *per* Lord Atkin, a decision which was based on the following passage from another judgment: 'It is clear that the law is that no person can obtain or enforce any rights resulting to him from his own crime; neither can his representative claiming under him obtain or enforce any such rights. The human mind revolts at the very idea that any other doctrine could be possible in our system of jurisprudence.' *In the Estate of Cora Crippen* (27 T.L.R. 258; [1911] P. 108), cited in *Beresford* v. *Royal Insurance Company, Ltd.* (1938) 54 T.L.R. 789. See also, decided in the same year, *Geo. Legge and Sons* v. *Wenlock Corporation*, [1938] A.C. 204, in which it was held that the 'pollution of a natural stream in contravention of statute cannot make it in law a "sewer"'. *Per* Lord Maugham: 'there is no case... in which repeated violation of the express terms of a modern statute passed in the public interest has been held to confer rights on the wrongdoer' (at p. 222). And see *R.* v. *Lynch*, [1903] 1 K.B. 444, to the effect that no rights can be derived from an act which is in itself an act of treason. As to Roman Law, see D. 47 . 2 . 12 . 1: 'sed nemo de improbitate sua consequitur actionem'; D. 47 . 2 . 14 . 3: 'sed non debet ex dolo suo furti quaerere actionem'; D. 24 . 1 . 3 . 1: 'sed fas non est eas donationes ratas esse ne melior sit conditio eorum qui deliquerunt'; D. 50 . 17 . 134 . 1: 'Nemo ex suo delicto meliorem suam conditionem facere potest'; less explicitly, in D. 4 . 3 . 1 pr.; D. 10 . 4 . 3 . 11; and, in the view of the late Professor Buckland, to whom I am indebted for these references, no doubt elsewhere.

that France could not invoke against Switzerland any changes resulting from the unilateral transfer, which the Court held to be illegal, of the French customs line.[1] In the Advisory Opinion of 3 March 1928, the Court held that Poland was not entitled to invoke the fact that, contrary to her international obligations, she had failed to incorporate the relevant treaty into Polish municipal law.[2] In the Judgment of 26 July 1927 in the *Case concerning the Factory at Chorzów*, the Court disposed of one aspect of the Polish objection to its jurisdiction by stating that it is 'a principle generally accepted in the jurisprudence of international arbitration, as well as by municipal courts, that one Party cannot avail himself of the fact that the other has not fulfilled some obligation or has not had recourse to some means of redress, if the former Party has, by some illegal act, prevented the latter from fulfilling the obligation in question, or from having recourse to the tribunal which would have been open to him'.[3] In refusing, in August 1932, the Norwegian request for interim measures of protection against certain acts of Denmark with regard to the *South-Eastern Territory of Greenland*, the Court drew attention to the fact that the acts in question could not in any event, or to any degree, affect the sovereign rights of Norway over the territory in question if such rights were otherwise valid.[4] In the final Judgment in the principal case, given on 5 April 1933,[5] the Court held that the Norwegian declaration of occupation and other measures taken by Norway in that connection constituted a violation of the existing legal situation and were accordingly '*illégales et non valables*' ('unlawful and invalid'). This finding, given by a practically unanimous Court, is the more significant if we recall that, as may be inferred from the Dissenting Opinion of Judge Anzilotti, the Court probably had the opportunity to consider fully this aspect of the question. In his Dissenting Opinion Judge Anzilotti maintained that 'the Court could not have declared the occupation invalid, if the term "invalid" signifies "null and void"'.[6]

In one important respect international law has disregarded the vitiating influence of illegality upon the creation of rights: war undertaken in violation of a particular obligation or of a general obligation not to resort

1 *P.C.I.J.* Series A, no. 24.

2 Ibid. Series B, no. 15, pp. 26, 27 (*Jurisdiction of the Courts of Danzig*).

3 Ibid. Series A, no. 9, p. 31.

4 Ibid. Series A/B, no. 48, p. 285.

5 Ibid. no. 53, p. 75 (*Legal Status of Eastern Greenland*).

6 Ibid. p. 95. The Judgment of 24 June 1932, concerning the *Interpretation of the Statute of the Memel Territory* (Series A/B, no. 47) and affirming the validity in *municipal law* of a measure declared to be contrary to an international obligation, does not in fact deny the general principle of the invalidity of acts contrary to international law.

to war—in classical terminology, an 'unjust' war—nevertheless brings into being the operation of the law of war as between both belligerents. The belligerent who has unlawfully resorted to war acquires the right to be treated in accordance with the rules of warfare. This exception, dictated by reasons of humanity and by the absence of an impartial organ to determine the justice of the war and the fact of aggression, goes back to Grotius.[1] However, Grotius did not extend that exception to cover the obligations of neutrality. In the field of neutral duties he had no hesitation in drawing decisive consequences from the distinction between just and unjust wars;[2] no right to impartial treatment accrued to the State waging an unjust war. That denial of a right based on an illegality became unworkable in the nineteenth century when all war became legal. But the authority of the Grotian doctrine was restored, to a large extent, when, with the Covenant of the League of Nations and the General Treaty for the Renunciation of War, war ceased to be an unrestricted legal prerogative of States. During the Second World War the United States, for a time the principal neutral, in discriminating against the aggressor States and relying on the latter instrument, expressly repudiated the view that the right to impartial treatment accrued from illegal recourse to war.[3] Previously, in 1938, the United States rejected the claim of Japan to be entitled, in the course of her unlawful invasion of China, to rights ordinarily enjoyed by belligerents against neutral subjects.[4]

1 *De jure belli ac pacis*, Book III, 4. 4.

2 This is a theme which dominates not only chapter XVII in Book III ('On those who are of neither side in War'), the burden of which is the paramount duty of the neutral to do nothing which impedes the State waging a just war and which assists its opponent (III, 17. 3). It is a principle which is frequently given expression in other parts of his work. See, for example, II, 2. 10 (a State waging a just war may take possession of a place situated in a country free from hostilities), or II, 2. 13 (in connection with the right of passage).

3 See the writer's account and discussion of the modifications of neutrality in the Second World War in Oppenheim, *International Law*, vol. II (6th revised edition, 1944), § 292 *Aa*.

4 On 25 February 1938 the Government of the United States announced that American citizens in China were under 'no obligation whatsoever to take precautionary measures' against injury by the parties to the conflict, and that 'if American nationals or property are injured in consequence of the operations of Japanese armed forces, the United States would be compelled to attribute' to Japan 'responsibility for the damage'. (See Lauterpacht in *Legal Problems in the Far Eastern Conflict*, ed. by Quincy Wright, 1941, p. 155.) It is an established principle of international law that neutral States are not entitled to compensation for losses arising to them as the result of legitimate acts and measures of war, international or civil. This rule is based on the principle that civil war, i.e. rebellion against the constituted authority, is not prohibited by international law and that, in the absence of express obligations to the contrary, war is not an illegal act. On the other hand, when the war is illegal in the sense that it is

There are other questions of minor compass, in the field both of the law of war and of the law of peace, in which the problem of the application of the rule *ex injuria jus non oritur* has arisen. One of them is the question of the effect of requisitions in occupied territory undertaken in violation of international law. If the occupying authorities purport to effect a requisition in disregard of the laws of war, for instance, by omitting to pay for articles taken away, do they acquire property in such articles? Does the fact of seizing the property confer a right upon the State which has acted unlawfully in disregard of the Hague Convention? International and municipal tribunals have, on the whole, given a negative answer to this question.[1] It is clear that if the occupant acquires no right in the property in question, he is unable to pass such title to it as international law would recognize. From this point of view the warning issued in 1943 to neutrals by those of the United Nations whose territories were occupied by the enemy was not a mere political declaration devoid of a legal basis.[2]

On the other hand, municipal courts have not uniformly acted on the principle that it is not proper for them to exercise jurisdiction when such jurisdiction can only be exercised as the result of a wrongful act, namely,

undertaken in violation of existing obligations or when the hostilities do not amount either to civil or to international war in its ordinary meaning or to a use of force short of war in accordance with international law, then the question arises whether the parties to the conflict or the party waging hostilities contrary to its international obligations is entitled to rely on the rule outlined above. The basis of the announcement of the United States of 25 February 1938 was apparently the view: (*a*) that the hostilities in China, being neither a war in the meaning attached to it by international law nor a civil war, did not confer upon Japan the rights otherwise enjoyed by belligerents in respect of the persons and property of aliens; (*b*) that the action of Japan having been declared illegal, it could not, also in this respect, produce legal consequences affecting States which have, by declaring the policy of non-recognition, declined to treat such illegal action as a source of possible rights against them. See Woolsey in *A.J.* vol. XXXII (1938), pp. 314–20. See also the statement by the British Government in the House of Commons on 18 February 1932, *H.C. Debates*, vol. CCLXI, col. 1831, and, for comment thereon, Wright in *A.J.* vol. XXVI (1932), pp. 586–90.

1 See, for example, *Gros Roman et Cie* v. *German State*, decided in 1924 by the Franco-German Mixed Arbitral Tribunal (*Annual Digest*, 1923–4, Case no. 245); *Zurstrassen* v. *Germany*, decided in 1924 by the Germano-Belgian Mixed Arbitral Tribunal (ibid. n. 3 to Case no. 244). The apparently contrary decision in *Ralli Brothers* v. *German Government* (ibid. Case no. 244) is concerned with a different question. See also *Laurent* v. *Le Jeune*, a decision of the Belgian Court of Cassation, to the effect that an unlawful requisition was no more capable of transferring property than theft (ibid. 1919–22, Case no. 343). And see Oppenheim, *International Law*, vol. II (6th revised edition, 1944), p. 318, n. 5, for other cases.

2 Misc. No. 1 (1943), Cmd. 6418. In the declaration in question the governments concerned reserved their right to declare invalid transfers of property and interests situated in territories under enemy occupation.

when the accused—or a vessel—has been seized in contravention of international law.[1]

However, the main practical application of the principle *ex injuria jus non oritur* has lain in the non-recognition of conquest and other territorial changes accomplished by recourse to force contrary to such instruments as the Covenant of the League of Nations and the General Treaty for the Renunciation of War.[2]

1 In *Cook* v. *United States*—(1933) 288 U.S. 102—the Supreme Court of the United States refused to exercise jurisdiction following upon a seizure which it held to be contrary to international law. See, for comment thereon, Dickinson in *A.J.* vol. XXVIII (1934), pp. 231–45, and *Harvard Research, Jurisdiction with respect to Crime* (1935), p. 625. In a previous case—*United States* v. *Ferris* (*Annual Digest*, 1927–8, Case no. 127)—where members of the crew of a foreign ship seized 270 miles off the west coast of the United States were indicted for conspiracy to violate the Prohibition and Tariffs Acts, the United States District Court with equal emphasis declined jurisdiction. The Court said: '...As the instant seizure was far outside the limit [established by treaty] it is sheer aggression and trespass...contrary to the treaty, not to be sanctioned by any court, and cannot be the basis of any proceeding adverse to the defendants.' Both cases illustrate the principle that a wrongful act cannot be a source of jurisdictional rights. However, at the same time courts in the United States occasionally still follow the important case of *Ker* v. *Illinois* (119 U.S. 436) in which jurisdiction was assumed notwithstanding the wrongfulness of the apprehension. See, for example, *United States* v. *Insull et al.* decided by the United States District Court, N. D. Illinois, E.D. in 1934 (*Annual Digest*, 1933–4, Case no. 75). The defendant contended that he had been unlawfully brought into the jurisdiction in violation of his rights under the law of the United States and under international law. The Court rejected that contention. It said: 'It is plain, by weight of authority, that one charged with crime, and in the custody of the proper officers in the jurisdiction wherein the indictment against him is pending, cannot escape prosecution under the indictment by showing some irregularity, or even an unlawful kidnapping by officers of the government, which results in placing him within the jurisdiction of the court where the indictment against him is pending.' See also, to the same effect, *Ex parte Campbell*, decided in 1932 by the United States District Court, Southern District of Texas (1 F. Supp. 899), and *Ex parte Lopez* (*Annual Digest*, 1933–4, Case no. 76). Adherence to the stricter rule denying jurisdiction would not in such cases necessarily result in the impunity of the offender. There is often the available alternative of returning the accused to the jurisdiction in which he was improperly seized and of instituting extradition proceedings. This is one of the reasons why the award of the Permanent Court of Arbitration in the *Savarkar* case is open to criticism (see Lauterpacht, *The Function of Law in the International Community* (1934), pp. 88–9). But see *In re Jolis* (a French decision) (*Annual Digest*, 1933–4, Case no. 77). And see, for an emphatic criticism of the practice of assuming jurisdiction in violation of international law, *Harvard Research, Jurisdiction with respect to Crime*, (1935), pp. 623–32. With regard to so-called 'claim of territory' in time of war, in cases where a seizure has taken place in neutral territorial waters, English and American (but few other) courts follow the practice of releasing the prize only at the instance of the neutral State in question and not of the owners of the seized ship (*The Bangor*, [1920] A.C. 1034, 1037; *The Purissima Conception*, (1805) 6 C. Rob. 45, 47).

2 See above, pp. 416–19. See also McMahon, *Conquest and Modern International Law* (1940), pp. 150–80.

§ 126. *Invalidity of Titles based on Treaties inconsistent with Former Treaty Obligations.* The operation of the principle rendering invalid the results of an unlawful act shows itself with particular emphasis in the wider sphere of treaties inconsistent with the international obligations of the contracting parties. It is unlawful for a State to act or to agree to act in violation of the international rights of another State. This rule necessarily applies to the conclusion of a treaty the performance of which would interfere adversely with the existing contractual rights of another State. A treaty which to the knowledge of both contracting parties is contrary to pre-existing treaty obligations binding upon one or both of them is, in general, illegal, invalid and unenforceable. The doctrine of non-recognition does not invalidate the treaty in question; the latter is invalid *ipso facto*, by reason of the circumstances of its creation.[1] The example of illegality resulting from treaties conflicting with general or particular international law is of special importance seeing that general instruments such as the General Treaty for the Renunciation of War of 1928 or the Charter of the United Nations have affected with illegality acts which international law has hitherto left to the unlimited discretion of States. Thus a treaty imposed by the victor upon the vanquished as a consequence of a war undertaken by the former is devoid of legal force in all cases in which he had resorted to war contrary to his obligations under the Charter of the United Nations or the General Treaty for the Renunciation of War. It is void on the ground that the established rule disregarding the vitiating effect of duress does not apply to treaties concluded under compulsion and following upon wars undertaken by the victor in breach of these general international enactments. It is, moreover, invalid on the independent ground of being the result of a violation of the provisions of former treaties prohibiting or limiting recourse to war.

§ 127. Ex factis jus oritur. The fundamental principle *ex injuria jus non oritur* is unaffected by the far-reaching qualification expressed in the rival maxim *ex factis jus oritur*. Law is a product of social reality. It cannot lag

1 For a detailed discussion of the question of the validity of treaties inconsistent with previous treaty obligations and for judicial and other authority in support of the view put forward in the text see the author's article in *B.Y.* vol. XVII (1936), pp. 60–5. See also for a discussion of the same question with regard to contracts in municipal law his article entitled 'Contracts to break a Contract' in *Law Quarterly Review*, vol. LII (1936), pp. 494–529. And see the writer's note on the Opinions of Judges Van Eysinga and Schücking in the *Oscar Chinn* case (*B.Y.* vol. XVI (1935), p. 164). But see Sir John Fischer Williams in *Hague Recueil*, vol. XLIV (1933) (ii), pp. 281 et seq. and in *Transactions of the Grotius Society*, vol. XVIII (1935), pp. 120–3. See also for references to British practice McNair, *The Law of Treaties* (1938), pp. 116–24.

for long behind facts. This antinomy of law and fact is an abiding problem of jurisprudence. On the one hand, the validity of the law is not dependent upon its actual observance in any given set of circumstances, just as the validity of grammar is not dependent upon our compliance with its rules in any given case. They are what has been called 'normative rules'. Law, once established, tells us what, under the pain of compulsion, is the right conduct; it is not a generalization of actual behaviour; its validity is not affected by wrongful acts. On the other hand, while law, so long as it is valid, is unaffected by a violation of its rules, its continuous breach, when allowed to remain triumphant, ultimately affects the validity of the law. As the sociological basis of the legal system as a whole is ultimately determined by the social realities of consent and power, so also the validity of its individual rules cannot in the long run be divorced from that foundation. Law conceived as an enforceable rule of conduct is to a large extent determined by what we judge to be socially feasible and practicable. Continued acquiescence in or toleration of illegality is a powerful element in the formation of such judgment.

However, although accumulation of illegal conduct, when tolerated or left unpunished by the society, may have the consequence of changing the law and of sanctioning rights originating in illegality, no such result can be attributed to single acts of lawlessness, however successful. International law, being a weak law, is fully exposed to the impact of the phenomenon to which jurists have referred as the 'law-creating influence of facts'. But unless law is to become a convenient code for malefactors, it must steer a middle course between the law-creating influence of facts and the principle, which is the essence of law, that its validity is impervious to individual acts of lawlessness. Law is a body of rules operating under the aegis of a system of force actually operative in society. This does not mean that all breaches of the law, if successful, become part of the legal order. A balance must be achieved somewhere. It cannot be found in the immediate validation of the illegal act; it must be sought in considerations of a general nature which would justify the legislator in incorporating the result of the illegality as part of the law. In the absence of such incorporation, a provisional balance may be found, in the international sphere, in *de facto* recognition combining the necessities of international intercourse with the maintenance of an essential legal principle.[1]

§ 128. *The Validation of Illegality: (1) By Prescription.* If the maxim *ex injuria jus non oritur* is a fundamental principle of international law no less

1 See below, pp. 431–3.

than of municipal law, then the further question arises whether the results of the illegal act can ever become part of international law. In other words, how much substance is there in the view that the principle of non-recognition is justly open to the reproach of immutability and rigidity? Can the effects of the illegal act ever be freed of the stigma of their origin? This, it is believed, may be done in three ways.

The first is the operation of the rule of prescription. The limits and conditions of acquisitive prescription in international law are not above controversy. Although its requirements are not as stringent as in the municipal sphere, the patent illegality of the purported acquisition, combined with continued protests on the part of the dispossessed State, are sufficient to rule out the legalization, in that manner, of the original illegality. Moreover, assuming that the principle of prescription is applicable in any given case, it must comply at least with the requirement of the lapse of a substantial period of time. To invoke the institution of prescription in municipal law as a reason for the immediate recognition or validity of internationally unlawful acts is to use the term 'prescription' in a sense unknown to any system of law.[1] In the course of the discussions concerning the recognition of the state of affairs established by the Japanese invasion of Manchuria and of the Italian annexation of Abyssinia the principle of non-recognition was criticized by some on the ground that all systems of law admit the operation of prescription. Seeing that this particular criticism was voiced in the years immediately following the illegal acts in question, the reference to prescription must be regarded as having been used in a popular rather than a legal sense.[2]

(2) *By Consent of the Injured Party.* Can the defect of illegality be waived and the title thus validated as the result of the consent of the State whose interests are primarily affected? It would seem that such consent might, as a rule, cure the original invalidity only when the right violated is grounded in a bilateral treaty or a customary rule operating exclusively for the benefit of the injured State. On the other hand, in case of a violation of a multilateral treaty laying down rules of conduct, the observance of which is in the interest of all the contracting parties, it is difficult to see how waiver on the part of one of them—assuming that such waiver is juridically possible in the circumstances, e.g. in case of duress—can free the original

1 Also, it may be argued that, even when admissible, prescription does not in law amount to a validation of the unlawful title. It is an original acquisition of a new title.

2 Thus we find a distinguished American jurist saying in 1937: 'All systems of law recognize, by the doctrine of prescription and otherwise, that the recognition of accomplished facts plays, as a principle of certainty in peace, a large part in human affairs' (Moore in *Harvard Law Review*, vol. L (1937), p. 436).

act of its unlawfulness and its results of the taint of invalidity. If the invalidity be due, for instance, to a breach of the General Treaty for the Renunciation of War, the consent of the defeated State alone can hardly influence the legal situation.

(3) *By Recognition.* There remains the possibility of curing the invalidity of the results of the unlawful conduct by recognition on the part of States proceeding, as it were, as organs of the international community, i.e. when acting in pursuance of the general interest and not with a view to promoting their private advantage. They may do it individually or collectively, although in the former case the presumption of the general good is less cogent. They may, by what may be called a quasi-legislative act, give legal force to a situation which is in the eyes of the law a mere nullity. The term 'quasi-legislative' is here used because, while there is in the international sphere no legislation in the strict meaning of the term, there are cases in which, because of the absence of a legislature proper, a State or a number of States must fulfil the functions ordinarily reserved to legislation. This means that there may arise situations in which the assumption of legislative powers of this nature, if exercised in good faith and in the interest of general international welfare, is a course preferable to the perpetuation of an anomaly. There is nothing obnoxious to legal principle in the idea of legalizing in this way the results of wrongful conduct. Such legislation consists, upon analysis, in the waiver by each of the recognizing States of its right, grounded in customary international law or in a treaty, to treat the new title as invalid.

Professor Scelle has expressed the view that recognition *de jure* constitutes in such cases 'a logical absurdity seeing that it is impossible to give juridical consecration to a situation which is contrary to law'.[1] It is difficult to see the force of that objection. There is no question here of legalizing the illegal act; the question is one of disregarding the effects of the illegality. The results of an illegal act are a legal nullity; they are legally non-existent. The wrongdoer acquires no right under it. But there is no logical objection to the community acquiescing, through collective or individual acts of its members acting in the general interest, in the assertion of a right which did not previously exist. To rule out that possibility altogether would mean to postulate for the law a degree of rigidity which may not be compatible with international peace and progress. Occasions may arise when the continuation of the policy or the obligation of non-recognition may not be conducive to the general good. When that

1 Preface to Rousseau, *Le conflit italo-éthiopien devant le droit international* (1938), p. x.

happens, non-recognition may be adjusted to the requirements of peace and stability. It may merge in a general international settlement, as distinguished from individual acts of recognition resulting from opportunism, from a complacent claim to a sense of realities, or from less worthy motives of direct political or commercial advantages. There is a difference between this manner of recognition on general grounds and the almost automatic incorporation of any successful breach of international law as part of the law of nations on the ground that the law must follow the facts. Law follows facts which are not unlawful. When they are unlawful, and in particular when their illegality consists in acts of aggression against the very life of other members of the community in deliberate disregard of fundamental legal obligations of conduct, a heavy and most responsible burden of proof falls upon those embarking upon the legalization of the effects of illegality. Recognition of the effects of illegality may be a wise weapon of international policy or a bitter pill of unavoidable political necessity. Its merits in any particular case are not a matter for legal judgment so long as it is clear that in the opinion of those taking the decision non-recognition of the fruits of lawlessness is and remains an essential principle of law.[1]

§ 129. *The Significance of the Principle of Non-Recognition in International Law*. The principle of non-recognition fulfils in the present stage of international organization an important function in the maintenance of the authority of the law. From the jurisprudential point of view the acceptance of the policy or of the obligation of non-recognition amounts to a vindication of the legal character of international law as against the 'law-creating effect of facts'. In a society in which the enforcement of the law is precarious, there is a natural tendency to regard successful breaches of the law as a source of legal right. Non-recognition obviates that danger to a

1 The decision of Great Britain and of other countries to recognize, in 1938, the annexation of Abyssinia by Italy (see above, p. 336) must be judged by considerations of this nature. In so far as in the intention of its authors the recognition was contemplated as the first and indispensable condition of pacification of Europe and of the world, it is arguable that such recognition could be regarded as having been conceded in the general interest. It was an act of international policy which, although open to criticism by reference to its political wisdom and to its readiness to assume the probability of a radical change in the future conduct of the State responsible for the original illegality, could be questioned on legal grounds only on account of any disregard of the obligation of non-recognition binding upon members of the League. While the Council of the League seems to have granted to the members of the League a measure of release from that obligation—see above, p. 418—it is controversial to what extent it was legally competent to grant such release. And see above, p. 356, on the withdrawal by Great Britain of her recognition of the conquest of Abyssinia on the ground of the failure of Italy to live up to the basic assumption of the recognition granted in 1938.

large extent. It is the minimum of resistance which an insufficiently organized but law-abiding community offers to illegality; it is a continuous challenge to a legal wrong. In a sense, the effectiveness of non-recognition grows with the passage of years. For it brings into relief the contrast between the consolidating power of the successful defiance of the law and its status as a mere legal nullity. As such it adds substantial emphasis to the legal character of international law. It shows the vital difference between a law worthy of the name and a law concealing behind its misleading designation the unfettered rule of violence. The significance of non-recognition, from this point of view, is demonstrated indirectly by the importance usually attached to it by the State whose wrongful conduct has occasioned the necessity for non-recognition. As a matter of tangible economic advantage, recognition *de jure* means little to the law-breaking State. So far as the courts of the recognizing State are concerned, it probably goes no further than to give to the conqueror title to the property of the State which he has destroyed and to deprive the latter or its representatives of the jurisdictional immunities enjoyed hitherto.[1] Its operation, from the point of view of its legal effects, is symbolic rather than directly effective. As recognition *de jure* terminates the diplomatic relations with the conquered State, it formally marks the legal demise of the victim. As such it may act as a discouragement to any surviving hopes of resistance. But this is an advantage hardly comparable with the success already accomplished by the wrongdoer. The importance which he attaches to recognition is to a large extent due to the fact that it signifies the cessation of the embarrassing and disturbing atmosphere of moral censure implied in the maintenance of the attitude of legal condemnation. These are the reasons which prompt the law-breaker to seek recognition by that very law which he has defied. They show, from a different angle, the significance of non-recognition in the system of international law.

§ 130. *The Principle of Non-Recognition and the Necessities of International Intercourse.* Assuming that non-recognition is a weighty factor in the maintenance of the authority of international law, the further question arises whether it is necessarily an instrument of such rigidity as to constitute a serious impediment in the way of international intercourse. If it could be shown that adherence to the principle of non-recognition unavoidably results in ignoring altogether the existence of the power which actually exercises control and in avoiding anything which may bring the non-recognizing State in contact with the effective authority, then there might

1 See above, pp. 336–41.

be room for the suggestion that the price paid for the symbolic upholding of a principle is unduly high. However, in normal circumstances there is nothing in the attitude of non-recognition which necessarily constitutes an obstacle in the way of a measure of intercourse—so long as the State against which it is directed does not insist on full and formal recognition of the results of the illegal act. *Ad hoc* agreements—bilateral and certainly multilateral—may be concluded with the unrecognized State or government or in respect of territory claimed by virtue of an unrecognized title—without it being necessary (or permissible) to strain such conduct into implied recognition.[1] In the case of conquest, recognition of the *de facto* authority of the annexing State provides a sufficient basis for ordinary commercial intercourse and for the recognition of the legislative, administrative and judicial acts of the annexing State within the territory under its sway. Thus British—and other—courts have repeatedly held that there is for the latter purpose no distinction between *de facto* and *de jure* recognition. They so held, in particular, after Great Britain had recognized in 1936 the *de facto* authority of Italy over Abyssinia while refusing to recognize the *de jure* sovereignty of Italy.[2]

1 See above, pp. 371–9.

2 *Bank of Ethiopia* v. *National Bank of Egypt*, [1937] Ch. 513. The relevant part of the Foreign Office certificate was as follows:

'(*a*) His Majesty's Government in the United Kingdom have not recognized the Italian annexation of Ethiopia *de jure* but they now regard the Italian Government as the Government *de facto* of the parts of Ethiopia which they control.

'(*b*) While detailed information is hard to obtain, such information as His Majesty's Government possess tends to show that the Italian Government control the whole of Ethiopia with the exception of certain areas in the South and South West of the country.'

And see above, pp. 341–6. The position is different where non-recognition is accompanied by the refusal to grant either *de facto* or *de jure* recognition. Thus, in connection with the non-recognition by the United States of the incorporation into Soviet Russia of Latvia, Lithuania and Esthonia in 1940, American courts declined to issue letters rogatory to a Russian court for taking depositions of residents of Esthonia (*The Kotkas* (*Annual Digest*, 1941–2, Case no. 15); *The Signe* (ibid. Cases nos. 16 and 19)), or to admit that the unrecognized Lithuanian Soviet Socialist Republic has a right to sue (*The Denny* (ibid. Case no. 18)). For comment on these cases see Briggs in *A.J.* vol. XXXVII (1943), pp. 585–96. Similarly in 1943 the New York Supreme Court, Queens County, held that, in view of the non-recognition of the absorption of Esthonia by Russia, the Acting Esthonian Consul-General was competent, by virtue of the Treaty between Esthonia and the United States, to appear before courts on behalf of Esthonian nationals (*Buxhoeveden* v. *Esthonian State Bank*, 41 N.Y.S. (2*d*), 752; 181 Misc. 155). See also to the same effect, with regard to Latvia, *In re Graud's Estate*, (1943) 41 N.Y.S. (2*d*), 263; 45 N.Y.S. (2*d*), 318. And see *The Maret*, (1944) F. (2*d*) 431. In *The Ramava* the High Court of Eire held that, in view of the non-recognition by Eire of the incorporation of the Baltic Republics into Soviet Russia, no effect could be given to the nationalization decrees issued by the Soviet authorities in those countries (*Annual Digest*, 1941–2, Case no. 20).

Such *de facto* recognition may be open to criticism on the ground that a State may, by means of a technical device, ignore its obligations in the matter of non-recognition. However, that criticism cannot be regarded as fully justified. Apart from the circumstance that courts acknowledge some juridical consequences attaching to the continued *de jure* recognition of the dispossessed authority, the decisive consideration is that the value of non-recognition does not depend primarily upon the degree of immediate hardship and inconvenience which it entails upon the law-breaker. Non-recognition is not a sanction in the nature of punishment aiming at bending the will of the wrongdoer by the overwhelming pressure of its immediate effects. Its principal function must, more accurately, be conceived as a somewhat symbolic instrument for upholding the challenged authority of international law. That function it can perform without insisting on a rigid disregard of the realities of the situation. For that very reason *de jure* recognition is not, as a rule, an urgent practical necessity from the point of view of international intercourse.[1]

While therefore *de facto* recognition is open to criticism inasmuch as it renders non-recognition largely unreal by reducing to a bare minimum the element of direct pressure inherent in non-recognition conceived as a sanction, it has the advantage of diminishing the urgency of *de jure* recognition. This was not sufficiently realized when the League of Nations first gave expression in 1932 to the obligation of non-recognition. In the final recommendations of the Report of the Assembly of 24 February 1933, it was laid down that the Members of the League would continue not to recognize the new regime either *de jure* or *de facto*. The Advisory Committee of the League set up for co-ordinating the action of its Members in the matter of non-recognition made recommendations which went a long way in the direction of *de facto* recognition. While suggesting a series of measures such as the prevention of the accession of Manchukuo to international conventions and the refusal to admit official quotations in Manchukuan currency, the recommendations did not oppose the replace-

1 From this point of view it may not be easy to follow the rigid alternative suggested by the British Secretary for Foreign Affairs at the meeting of the Council of the League of Nations in May 1938. He said: 'It is the considered opinion of His Majesty's Government that, for practical purposes, Italian control over virtually the whole of Ethiopia has become an established fact, and that sooner or later, unless we are prepared by force to alter it, or unless for ever we are to live in an unreal world, that fact, whatever be our judgment on it, will have to be acknowledged' (*Official Journal*, 1938, p. 335). See also Rousseau, *Le conflit italo-éthiopien devant le droit international* (1938), pp. 274–5, who considers non-recognition to be no more than a fiction once it has become clear that there is no intention to use force for the reestablishment of the law.

ment of consuls, the issue of travelling documents by the consuls of the sending State and, at a later stage, technical agreements between the postal administrations of Members of the League and that of Manchukuo.[1]

§ 131. *The Principle of Non-Recognition and the Maintenance of International Law.* The principle of non-recognition has met with criticism from apparently opposed quarters. Inasmuch as it implies a measure of sanction for and repression of breaches of international law, it has been assailed by those who believe that real progress in international affairs lies in the abandonment of any effort of collective enforcement of international law.[2] This view need not be discussed here—except to the extent of noting that being a sanction is not the only, and perhaps not the main, function of the principle of non-recognition. On the other hand, that principle has been exposed to criticism by those who have seen in it a wordy and ineffectual device for avoiding the fulfilment of the obligation to enforce the law of nations.[3] It has also been maintained that in so far as the principle of non-

1 For the recommendations of the Committee of 7 June 1933 and 16 May 1934 see, respectively, *Official Journal*, Special Supplement no. 113, p. 11, and ibid. 1934, p. 430. And see above, p. 396. On some questions connected with the non-recognition of Manchukuo see Willoughby, *The Sino-Japanese Controversy and the League of Nations* (1935), pp. 516–35; Chailley in *R.I.* vol. XIII (1934), pp. 151–74; Cavaré in *R.G.* vol. XLII (1935), pp. 5–99. For a discussion of the consequences of a complete refusal of recognition see McNair in *B.Y.* vol. XIV (1933), pp. 72–4, and Fischer Williams in *Hague Recueil*, vol. XLIV (1933) (ii), pp. 294 et seq. See also, in this connection, on non-recognition generally Wright in *A.J.* vol. XXVI (1932), pp. 342–8, vol. XXVII (1933), pp. 509–16, and vol. XXXII (1938), pp. 526–35; Middlebush in *Proceedings of the American Society of International Law*, 1933, pp. 40–55; Hill, *Recent Policies of Non-Recognition, International Conciliation*, no. 293 (October 1933); Garner in *A.J.* vol. XXX (1936), pp. 679–88. And see Sharp, *Duties of Non-Recognition in Practice*, 1775–1934 (Geneva Special Studies, 1934).

2 Thus Mr Moore, a former Judge of the Permanent Court of International Justice, has criticized it in the following scathing terms: 'Its chief weakness lies in the fact that those who employ it often must content themselves with futile words or must fight, while the adoption of the latter alternative would necessarily be a confession of failure. All systems of law recognize, by the doctrine of prescription and otherwise, that the recognition of accomplished facts plays, as a principle of certainty and peace, a large part in human affairs; and nations are but aggregations of human beings, who may not relish daily reminders of their shortcomings by others whom they may not deem above reproach, or wholly disinterested or unprejudiced' (*Harvard Law Review*, vol. L (1937), p. 436); and see above, p. 413. For comment on this criticism see also Wild, *Sanctions and Treaty Enforcement* (1934), pp. 160–79; Sir John Fischer Williams, referred to above, p. 426, n. 1.; and Borchard and Morrison in *Legal Problems in the Far Eastern Conflict* (ed. by Quincy Wright, 1941), pp. 157–78.

3 There is support for the belief that in some quarters in the United States the principle of non-recognition was resorted to during the Manchurian conflict in 1931 with the view to finding a convenient substitute for active participation in the maintenance of international law (see Wallace in *American Political Science Review*, vol. XXXIX (1945), pp. 101–16).

recognition postulates the necessity of recognition for the acquisition of title, it is not supported by international practice; that, in so far as it asserts the general invalidity of treaties and situations contrary to international law, it cannot be admitted as a sound legal doctrine; and that the principle of non-recognition is inadmissible in so far as it usurps for one State or group of States the right to invalidate international acts. These criticisms have been discussed above.[1]

There is undoubtedly some force in the view that the authority of international law may be impaired in consequence of the principle of non-recognition inasmuch as it may be used as an instrument for avoiding substantial obligations of actively enforcing the law. However, in some cases, as in the General Treaty for the Renunciation of War, such obligations are non-existent; in the Covenant of the League they were less rigid and comprehensive than was commonly assumed; in the Charter of the United Nations their implementation is subject to the exacting requirement of unanimity among the permanent members of the Security Council.[2] With regard to all these instruments, non-recognition is an addition to the forces making for the reality of international law. Even when there exists a duty to vindicate the law of nations by means more substantial than a verbal declaration of non-recognition, such advantages as that declaration possesses are preferable to total inaction. The attitude of non-recognition shows that the law, though temporarily shorn of its strength, is potentially a powerful factor so long as there is predominant the sentiment of its ultimate authority. Law is not necessarily disintegrated by impotence; but it is destroyed by unqualified submission to the lawlessness of force. Non-recognition prevents that contingency. For this reason, so long as there is no assurance that international law will be enforced invariably and effectively by ordinary processes, non-recognition is a legal principle of value.

1 See pp. 410–13, 431–3.

2 For this reason there must be envisaged the possibility that no effective collective redress may be available against what one or more members of the Organization of the United Nations consider to be an illegality. In such cases, probably in addition to other measures, non-recognition may be lawfully and properly resorted to by the individual members of the Organization. It is not without significance that, in a case decided by an English court in 1946, the British Foreign Office informed the Court that 'His Majesty's Government recognise the Government of the Estonian Soviet Socialist Republic to be the *de facto* Government of Estonia, but do not recognise it as the *de jure* Government of Estonia' and that 'His Majesty's Government recognise that Estonia has *de facto* entered the Union of Soviet Socialist Republics, but have not recognised this *de jure*' (*Tallinna Laevauhisus and Others* v. *Tallinna Shipping Company and Esthonian State Shipping Line*, (1946) 79 *Lloyd's List Law Reports*, p. 245). The incorporation of Esthonia in the U.S.S.R. took place in 1940.

Index

For EU product safety concerns, contact us at Calle de José Abascal, 56–1°, 28003 Madrid, Spain or eugpsr@cambridge.org.

www.ingramcontent.com/pod-product-compliance
Lightning Source LLC
Chambersburg PA
CBHW020952010626
45994CB00003B/6
9781107609433